Cambodia After the Khmer Rouge
Inside the Politics of Nation Building

Evan Gottesman

Yale University Press

New Haven & London

The map of Cambodia is adapted from map no. 3860 rev. 1, August 1995, produced
by the Cartographic Section of the United Nations Department of Public
Information. The photographs reproduced in the gallery are all from SPK,
the official Cambodian news agency.

Set in Adobe Garamond and Stone Sans by The Composing Room of Michigan, Inc.
Printed in the United States of America by Sheridan Books.

The Library of Congress has cataloged the hardcover edition as follows:

Gottesman, Evan R.
    Cambodia after the Khmer Rouge : inside the politics of nation
building / Evan R. Gottesman.
        p.   cm.
Includes bibliographical references and index.
    ISBN 0-300-08957-0 (cloth : alk. paper)
    1. Cambodia—Politics and government—1979– 2. Cambodia—Politics and
government—1975–1979. I. Title.
    DS554.8 .G68   2002
    959.604′2—dc21

                                                        2002005653

A catalogue record for this book is available from the British Library. The paper
in this book meets the guidelines for permanence and durability of the Committee
on Production Guidelines for Book Longevity of the Council on Library Resources.

ISBN 0-300-10513-4 (pbk. : alk. paper)

10 9 8 7 6 5 4 3 2

To my parents
Max and Kay Gottesman

Cambodia is like a play with too few actors, all of whom have
to play several roles.
—*Om Radsady, former member of parliament, Kingdom of Cambodia*
In Memoriam, 1952–2003

Contents

Preface

Democratic Kampuchea, the regime established by the Khmer Rouge in 1975, has come as close as any in history to achieving universal condemnation. There are, of course, academic, political, and legal debates over the nature of its rule and the culpability of its leaders. But for Cambodians, the verdict is already clear. The Khmer Rouge experiment—the dismantling of Cambodia's political, economic, social, religious, and cultural institutions—failed miserably. Whatever Pol Pot and his comrades were trying to accomplish, the tens of thousands of executions and more than one million deaths by starvation and disease that resulted from their policies remain inexcusable.

Yet Cambodians continue to disagree on the political meaning of January 7, 1979, the day the Vietnamese army entered Cambodia and overthrew the Khmer Rouge. Was Cambodia liberated that day or was it invaded? Were the Vietnamese there to protect Cambodians from the Khmer Rouge or to occupy and exploit their country? More than two decades later, these questions still invite bitter debate and even, as recent news reports have described, occasional violence:

Students from an anti-Vietnamese student organization and a pro-government group clashed in front of the Cambodian parliament on Monday on the 23rd anniversary of the overthrow of the Khmer Rouge. . . .

Three or four students from the anti-Vietnamese group were beaten, but no one was seriously wounded in the scuffle that erupted over the group's protest of the government's celebrations of "Victory Day over Genocide," students said. "The Vietnamese claimed that on January 7, 1979, they came to liberate Cambodia," said Phang Vanak, one of the students who was beaten during the clash. "Really they came here to kill people and take our property." (Deutsche Presse-Agentur, Jan. 7, 2002)

Demonstrations such as these are part of the Cambodian political scene. Since much of the current leadership was installed by the Vietnamese in 1979, supporters of the government are inclined to celebrate Cambodia's liberation from the Khmer Rouge and to hail the country's achievements in the years that followed. The opposition, on the other hand, tends to emphasize the oppressive nature of the communist regime established by the Vietnamese and their Cambodian "puppets." The stridency with which both sides hold to their interpretations of history is thus political. It is perpetuated, however, by what has been an extremely murky, inconclusive historical record.

In the early months of 1979, Cambodia barely existed as a nation. Millions of ragged, malnourished Cambodians wandered around a bewildering void, a fragmented landscape of violence, grief, anger, and uncertainty. As for Cambodia's new leaders, put to work in an empty capital overgrown with weeds, they kept calling what they were doing a "revolution." But there was nothing to overturn, just an emptiness to fill.

This is a story about the emergence of a country and about personal and political choices. Released from the tyranny imposed on them by the Khmer Rouge, Cambodians looked at an agonizing set of options. Should they flee abroad or return to the towns and villages from which they had been evacuated? Should they remain loyal to the new regime and its Vietnamese patrons or associate themselves with opposition forces? Should they plant rice in the countryside or trade on the black market?

Cambodian and Vietnamese officials, handed a blank slate of a country, were faced with other, extraordinary decisions. There were no institutions of any kind—no bureaucracy, no army or police, no schools or hospitals, no state or private commercial networks, no religious hierarchies, no legal system. More confounding still was that the new regime, installed by a foreign power, had no popular support other than as an alternative to the Khmer Rouge. Fundamental questions arose faster than they could possibly be deliberated. How ideological can a postcommunist communist regime be? Who are its constituents? Who are its enemies? What institutions does an empty country need, and what are its priorities? How much economic, cultural, and political freedom is too much? How does a country establish a national identity when it is being occupied?

I came to the story late, in May 1994, a year after a United Nations–sponsored election. With the promulgation of a new constitution that promised democracy and a free market, international organizations sent dozens of lawyers such as myself to promote the rule of law, economic stability, and human rights. Government ministers and members of parliament made time to meet me and to patiently explain what they saw to be the gaps in Cambodia's legal system. There was plenty of work to do: sample laws from other countries to collect and synthesize, Cambodian precedents to consider, translations to undertake, and meetings to arrange. I was grateful to my colleagues at the American Bar Association and the Asia Foundation for all their assistance and to the Cambodian officials who actually listened. But what I discovered, not unexpectedly, was that the courts, the police, the legislature, and the ministries responded to political and economic pressures put in place long before my arrival. Sometimes it was easy to put a face to intransigence, to identify some minister whose interests did not include law reform; often it was not.

This book began modestly, in late 1996, as a history of law in the Cambodian context, an attempt to more fully understand and then to document the challenges I had faced over the preceding two and a half years. What really interested me, though, was the history of the period between the overthrow of the Khmer Rouge and the arrival of the United Nations. These were the years during which most of the country's leaders first came to power. If I was ever to understand their motives for promoting or resisting reform, it was necessary, I felt, to consider their political careers and the positions they staked out along the way. It was also during this period that the country's current political institutions were created and that certain practices of governance—including the corruption and lawlessness that we foreigners were proposing to change—became entrenched. Finally, I was simply fascinated by what I imagined that history to be—the initial chaos and the incremental establishment of order, the competing forces that rushed in to fill the vacuum, the leaders who rose and fell and the choices they made. My problem was that the Marxist-Leninist regime that governed Cambodia after the Khmer Rouge was closed and secretive. The public documents of the People's Republic of Kampuchea (PRK)—

which was renamed the State of Cambodia (SOC) in 1989—revealed little, and officials, when they were willing to talk to me and when they remembered names and dates, rarely painted a complete picture. Reluctantly, I was prepared to describe the whole period in one rather superficial introductory chapter of my book.

Then, in my wanderings through Cambodian government buildings, I came across thousands of documents from the PRK and SOC: internal reports, secret telegrams, draft laws and regulations, and, most important, hundreds of minutes of meetings of high-level Communist Party and state institutions. Unsorted, uncatalogued, and left to gather dust, they were the product of a bureaucracy that was adept at recording its own activity but extremely disorganized. Most of the documents contained the recitations of official policy, communist jargon inflated with the kind of gung-ho optimism and affirmations of solidarity with which struggling revolutions reassure themselves. Included in the propaganda, however, were candid descriptions of the country's problems, as well as harsh and sometimes contradictory accusations of who was to blame.

Of greatest interest to me were the minutes of meetings, which, I quickly discovered, revealed the views and personalities of individual Cambodian leaders and their Vietnamese advisors. Secretaries assigned to take notes likely paraphrased, summarized, or simply misunderstood the participants. But they had little reason to invent. The purpose of the minutes was to allow leaders to record their own deliberations and to review the positions taken by their subordinates. Secretaries were expected to provide an accurate account of events.

Many of the highest-level Party documents, in particular Politburo documents, are still inaccessible. According to one Party official, Vietnamese authorities took many Cambodian Communist Party documents to Vietnam in 1989, when they withdrew from the country. What remained were documents either produced by the state apparatus or distributed by the Party to state offices. Much of the Party's decision-making process is nevertheless apparent from the documents that are available. In the early years, when the distinction between Party and state was less clear, the minutes of many high-level Party meetings found their way into stacks of state documents. Later, the substance of internal Party debates appears in the minutes of meetings of state institutions, since the top Party leaders were willing to express their views in state as well as Party settings.

Drawn in by the wide range of political, economic, and cultural issues that the Cambodian leadership debated in these meetings, I changed the focus of the book from law in the post-U.N. period to a history of the PRK and the SOC. In doing so, however, I learned an important lesson about law reform in Cambodia. As it turned out, most of the arguments that I and other foreigners had been making, especially about human rights, had been the subject of extensive internal debate for years. I found this revelation reassuring because it confirmed that human rights was not a foreign concept. It was also depressing. Cambodia's top leaders were clearly familiar with the concepts of human rights and the rule of law. Having thought through their political and legal options and having already made what they felt were informed policy choices, they were unlikely to alter the way they governed the country merely in response to Western advisors.

In recounting the history of the PRK–SOC period, I confronted three imposing themes: the legacy of the Khmer Rouge, the Vietnamese occupation, and the geopolitics of the 1980s. The first defines many popular perceptions of Cambodia. Many Westerners who know little about Cambodia have heard of the Khmer Rouge, Pol Pot, and the "killing fields." More recently, negotiations between Cambodian leaders and the United Nations over whether to conduct trials for Khmer Rouge leaders have prompted journalists, scholars, politicians, and activists to wonder how ordinary Cambodians feel about historic wrongs, impunity, and justice. In examining the period after Democratic Kampuchea, I have asked a slightly different set of questions. How has the legacy of the Khmer Rouge shaped the country, its people, and the political and economic institutions that govern the lives of Cambodians? In the first year of the PRK, former Khmer Rouge officials and soldiers assumed positions of authority throughout the new regime. How did this happen, and what has come of this arrangement? The Khmer Rouge attempted to destroy Cambodia's intellectual class. How does a country function without educated people, and what role is there for the few who remain? And, finally, the Khmer Rouge prohibited commercial, religious, and cultural practices familiar to Cambodians for hundreds of years. How did Cambodians set about retrieving their history, and how did the PRK-SOC regime seek to control the process?

As the sometimes violent disagreements over the annual January 7 holiday demonstrate, the Vietnamese occupation of the 1980s remains a deeply divisive issue among Cambodians. Critics of the Vietnamese have portrayed them as historical enemies bent on colonizing and ultimately absorbing Cambodia. Hanoi's defenders accuse the critics, accurately in many instances, of racism. They also frequently ignore anecdotal evidence of economic exploitation and political domination. By examining documentary sources, I have sought to confirm, debunk, or provide detail to these allegations and to contribute to a common, less polarizing understanding of this history.

From 1979 to 1991, the period covered in this book, Cambodia was a divided nation caught in the middle of a geopolitical standoff. The regime in Phnom Penh survived by virtue of the Vietnamese occupation and the political and economic support of the Soviet Union and the Eastern Bloc. Meanwhile, along the Thai-Cambodian border, some three hundred thousand Cambodians lived in refugee camps controlled by resistance factions that included exiled royalists, republicans, and the Khmer Rouge. Bound together only by their opposition to the Vietnamese occupation, these groups received the support of China, the West (including the United States), and the noncommunist countries of Southeast Asia. The PRK, denied a seat at the United Nations and deprived of Western economic aid, was caught up in one of the most complex conflicts of the Cold War. As a result, much of what was said and written about Cambodia during the 1980s described the country in terms of its role in this larger struggle. When scholars and journalists spoke of events inside Cambodia or when Cambodian refugees recounted their experiences, partisans were quick to politicize their accounts. The successes and failures of the regime, its human rights record, and the nature of the Vietnamese occupation carried global implications, legitimizing or delegitimizing the regime, justifying or undermining the resistance.

I have chosen not to pass judgment on whether the PRK and the SOC should have occupied Cambodia's U.N. seat, whether Western and Chinese support for the resistance was appropriate, or whether Vietnam and the PRK-SOC deserved the economic sanctions imposed on them by the West. The international debates over the Cambodia conflict are well documented, and I am grateful to the authors of books and chronologies that describe the diplomatic history and that provide context for the domestic politics and internal developments that are the subject of this book. My one regret, however, is that by focusing on life inside Cambodia, I have neglected to address the plight of the refugees. The forces that controlled how they lived and how they died are as much Cambodian history as are internal events. To the refugees, I can say only that I decided to write one story at a time, to start by shining light on the darkest side of the conflict.

Wherever the sources have permitted, I have aspired not just to describe events in Cambodia but to reconstruct a national debate over the direction of the country. Not all Cambodians had an equal voice, of course. Ordinary citizens risked arrest and imprisonment for questioning the regime's ideology or its policies. Yet by refusing to follow a particular course set out by their leaders, they could ensure its failure. The eventual collapse of the PRK's agricultural collectives, for example, resulted more from the choices made by Cambodian peasants than from Party initiatives.

For the individual Cambodians whose lives and careers I have followed— former Khmer Rouge cadres who defected to the new regime, educated communists returning from a quarter-century of exile in Vietnam, and the few intellectuals who survived the Khmer Rouge and remained in Cambodia in the 1980s—the political environment was only slightly less oppressive. Yet within the constraints of a communist system and the Vietnamese occupation, they expressed different visions of how the country should be governed. There were theoretical debates and personal feuds. Often the perspectives of various Cambodian leaders seemed predetermined by their political or educational backgrounds. But just as frequently, the leaders were motivated by an awareness of the country's shifting political terrain, naked opportunism, or simply the mysteries of personality. People change, for better or worse, never more so than in times of turmoil and transition. A former Khmer Rouge cadre promotes human rights. A banker embraces communism. A Vietnamese-trained revolutionary defies his mentors.

Too frequently, opaque regimes are assumed to be monolithic. Absent evidence of internal deliberations, we are unable to attach individual responsibility to state action. We are also deprived of historical theater. Fortunately, in this case, the documentary sources have given us a cast of characters, a relatively small number of Cambodians who have remained in power despite the departure of the Vietnamese, the end of the Cold War, the abandonment of communism, and the arrival of peace. For them, Cambodian politics has required constant adaptation—an ability to accommodate new patrons, accumulate power in the absence of established political institutions, and adjust to a shifting ideological landscape.

Acknowledgments

I would like to thank the John D. and Catherine T. MacArthur Foundation, whose grant for research and writing helped me start this book, and Yale University Press, whose efforts saw it to print. I am particularly grateful to my editors, Otto Bohlmann, John Kulka, and Mary Pasti, for their expertise, hard work, and patience.

The individuals who have provided assistance and support are too numerous to name, so a partial list will have to do. David Chandler generously read multiple drafts and provided guidance both substantive and stylistic. Stephen Heder, Brad Adams, and David Ashley also reviewed drafts and provided detailed comments. Many, many others read sections of the book and offered valuable input, sent me materials, responded to my inquiries, helped set up interviews, or provided support of other kinds. They include Rich Arant (who also helped translate documents from the Khmer), Bama Athreya, Bui Tin, Lili Cole, Penny Edwards, David W. P. Elliott, Christopher Goscha, Jeff Kaplan, Bob Lang, Le Duc Minh, Stephen Murdoch, Phuong-Khanh Nguyen, Sim Sorya, Chivy Sok, Lewis Stern, Demelza Stubbings, Sum Sok Ry, and Yogi Thami. This book would have been impossible to write without their help. Any remaining errors or omissions are, of course, entirely my own.

I wish to thank the staffs of the Cambodian National Archives and other Cambodian governmental and nongovernmental institutions who assisted me in my research and everyone who submitted to an interview. The two organizations for which I worked, the American Bar Association Cambodia Law and Democracy Project and the Asia Foundation, were extremely supportive, not only during my term of employment but afterwards, when I was conducting research for this book. I am forever indebted to the staffs of these organizations—the guards, drivers, translators, and administrators who, throughout the three years I lived in Cambodia, consistently went out of their way to help me. There are also many Cambodians whose willingness to discuss their own experiences provided me with a better and more personal understanding of the country. I am particularly grateful to Meng, my friend and Khmer teacher, who inspired me to explore Cambodian history and gave me the language skills with which to do so.

A special thanks goes to Jeannie Brusky, who supported me in many ways. And, finally, it is with great affection that I acknowledge my wonderful family. In addition to my parents, to whom this book is dedicated, I am grateful to my brother Brian, my grandmother Gertrude, aunts Jean and Janice, Betsy, Zachary, Megan, Bob, Nijole, and all my aunts, uncles, cousins, stepbrothers, and in-laws. Their patience, faith, and good humor got me through this. So, too, did the loving memory of my grandmother Helen.

Note on Transliteration

Throughout this book, transliterations of Khmer names and words are based on the standard Franco-Khmer transcription system developed by Franklin E. Huffman in 1983, though absent diacritics. The other exception applies to Khmer names whose spellings have been altered from the direct transliteration by journalists, historians, and the Khmers themselves. Thus, I refer to Hun Saen as Hun Sen, as it is commonly written.

Cast of Characters

Bou Thang: A Vietnam-trained revolutionary from Cambodia's northeast and a member of the Tapuon minority, Bou Thang returned to Cambodia in the early 1970s and joined the Khmer Rouge military before fleeing back to Vietnam in 1974. Under the People's Republic of Kampuchea (PRK), he served as the chair of the Party's Central Propaganda Committee, a member of the Politburo, deputy prime minister (from 1982 to 1992), and minister of defense (from 1982 to 1986). Bou Thang's influence receded in the late 1980s with the rise of the former Khmer Rouge Eastern Zone cadres and the increasing irrelevance of communist ideology. He remains a member of the Politburo and currently serves in the National Assembly.

Chan Si: Trained in Hanoi, Chan Si returned to Cambodia in 1979 as chief of the Political Department of the army and a member of the Politburo. In 1981 he became minister of defense, replacing Pen Sovan. Chan Si served as prime minister from December 1981, after the arrest of Sovan, until his death in late 1984.

Chan Ven: A teacher, Chan Ven lived under the Khmer Rouge until 1978, when he took refuge in Vietnam. As a founding member of the Kampuchean United Front for National Salvation, minister of education, and mayor of Phnom Penh, he served as a symbol of the PRK's appeal to Cambodian intellectuals. Suspected of ideological nonconformity, Chan Ven was removed from his government positions and appointed secretary-general of the largely powerless Council of State. He is currently deputy secretary-general of the National Assembly.

CHEA SIM: A former Khmer Rouge Eastern Zone district chief, Chea Sim fled Pol Pot's purges in 1978 and went to Vietnam. As a member of the Politburo and as minister of the interior, he helped the Vietnamese co-opt former Khmer Rouge cadres while also developing a personal patronage network in the provinces and in the security apparatus. After his influence had begun to concern the Vietnamese, Chea Sim left the Ministry of the Interior in 1981 and took the ceremonial role of president of the National Assembly. Working mostly behind the scenes, Chea Sim continued to promote family members and other loyalists and became one of the two most powerful men in Cambodia, along with Hun Sen. He is currently chair of the Cambodian People's Party, a member of the Politburo, and president of the Senate.

CHEA SOTH: A Hanoi-trained revolutionary, Chea Soth served as the PRK's first ambassador to Vietnam and as a member of the Politburo. As deputy prime minister and minister of planning, Soth oversaw Cambodia's centrally planned economy and its economic relationship with Vietnam. In 1986, as Hun Sen was promoting a less ideological set of leaders, he lost the planning portfolio but stayed in the Council of Ministers, where he had little independent power. Chea Soth remains a member of the Politburo and is currently serving in the National Assembly.

HENG SAMRIN: A former military officer in the Khmer Rouge Eastern Zone, Heng Samrin fled Pol Pot's purges in 1978 and went to Vietnam. Selected by Vietnamese authorities as president of the first government (the Kampuchean People's Revolutionary Council, or KPRC) and head of state, his name became synonymous with the regime itself. At the end of 1981, the ideologically rigid Samrin replaced the ousted Pen Sovan as secretary-general of the Party. Less adept at patronage politics than Hun Sen or Chea Sim, Heng Samrin never accumulated much personal power. In 1991 he was replaced as secretary-general by Chea Sim. Heng Samrin remains a member of the Politburo and currently serves as vice president of the National Assembly.

HUN SEN: A former military officer in the Khmer Rouge Eastern Zone, Hun Sen was among the first to flee to Vietnam, in 1977. Two years later, at the age of twenty-six, he became minister of foreign affairs and a member of the

Politburo. On the strength of ambition, shrewd bureaucratic skills, and loyalty to Vietnamese authorities, Hun Sen rose quickly, to deputy prime minister in 1981 and prime minister in 1985. Nonideological, Hun Sen pursued pragmatic economic policies and promoted technocrats with noncommunist backgrounds, developing a patronage network at the Council of Ministers. By virtue of his role in the peace negotiations and his ability, at a later date, to develop a provincial patronage network of his own, Hun Sen eventually became one of the two most powerful men in Cambodia, along with Chea Sim. Hun Sen is currently the prime minister of Cambodia and a member of the Politburo.

KAEV CHENDA: A Vietnam-trained revolutionary, Kaev Chenda served the PRK in many capacities. As minister of propaganda and information, he presided over the trial of Khmer Rouge leaders Pol Pot and Ieng Sary in absentia in 1979. He also served as minister of industry, in which position he was reportedly linked to a corruption scandal. After being recalled to Hanoi for "education," Chenda returned as mayor of Phnom Penh, where he exhibited a level of independence and a tolerance of market economics that annoyed the more ideological members of the leadership. Chenda was removed from power in late 1984 or early 1985 and died in 1989.

NHEUM VANDA: A former militia chief in the Khmer Rouge Eastern Zone, Nheum Vanda fled to Vietnam in 1978. Under the PRK, he rose through the ministries of economics and planning. In the mid-1980s, as deputy minister of defense and deputy minister of planning, he took charge of K5, a border defense program that involved the conscription of tens of thousands of Cambodian civilians and that evolved into a vast military-economic network. A practitioner of patronage economics, Vanda found favor with Cambodia's increasingly nonideological leadership, particularly Hun Sen, who granted him control over the Thai-Cambodian border crossing. He is currently a member of the National Assembly.

PEN SOVAN: The most important of the Vietnamese-trained revolutionaries, Pen Sovan served as secretary-general of the Party, vice president of the KPRC, minister of defense, and, in 1981, prime minister. In these capacities, Sovan promoted noncommunists over former Khmer Rouge cadres. His independent attitude as well as specific actions—including his complaints about Vietnamese immigration and pursuit of economic ties with third countries—prompted Vietnamese authorities to arrest and depose him in December 1981. He spent the rest of the decade detained in Hanoi. Pen Sovan returned to Cambodia in 1991 and ran unsuccessfully for office in 1998.

ROS SAMAY: The Vietnam-trained cousin of Pen Sovan, Ros Samay exhibited a similar propensity to act independently. As minister of economics in 1979, he was more permissive of Western humanitarian organizations than were the rest of the leadership. Later, as secretary-general of the Constitutional Drafting Council, he pushed through a draft constitution that had not been authorized by Vietnamese officials. After being forced by Vietnamese advisors to amend the draft, Samay was rumored to be planning to defect and was quietly arrested. After spending the 1980s in detention in Hanoi, Ros Samay returned to Cambodia in the early 1990s and is currently undersecretary of state for post and telecommunications.

SAY PHOUTHANG: A Vietnam-trained revolutionary, Say Phouthang returned, in 1970, to his native Koh Kong province in southwest Cambodia. There he joined the Khmer Rouge military and, in 1973, rebelled against Pol Pot. Phouthang, who is ethnic Thai, spent most of the Khmer Rouge period in Thailand or along the border. Brought back to Phnom Penh by Vietnamese agents in the spring of 1979, he served as a member of the Politburo and as chair of the Central Organization Committee of the Party. Following the arrest of Pen Sovan in December 1981, Say Phouthang was perhaps the most powerful Cambodian leader. His influence began to recede in 1985, when he was moved to the Party Inspection Committee. With the ascendance of Hun Sen and Chea Sim, Say Phouthang became less important and, faced with declining health, began spending more time in Thailand. He currently holds no official position, other than his seat on the Politburo.

SIN SONG: A former Khmer Rouge Eastern Zone cadre, Sin Song fled to Vietnam in 1977. As deputy minister of the interior, he defended the interests of the police against Uk Bunchheuan's Ministry of Justice. Temporarily exiled to the powerless Ministry of Inspection, he returned as minister of the interior in 1988. Working closely with Chea Sim, Sin Song presided over the expansion of the security apparatus during and immediately after the withdrawal of the Vietnamese army. He died of cancer in March 2001.

TANG SAREUM: One of the few Vietnam-trained revolutionaries to have remained in Cambodia after 1975, Tang Sareum fled to Vietnam in 1978 with the Eastern Zone cadres. As minister of commerce, Sareum jostled for power with Minister of Economics Ros Samay, eventually taking control of an antagonistic relationship with Western donors. Later he fought to protect the interests of the PRK's faltering state commercial sector, bitterly opposing the quasi-private trading tolerated by Phnom Penh Mayor Kaev Chenda. Tang Sareum gradually lost power to more technocratic economic administrators. He currently holds no official position.

THUN SARAY: An economist who survived the Khmer Rouge regime, Thun Saray participated in the 1979 trial of Pol Pot and Ieng Sary but remained doggedly independent of the PRK. A founder, along with Vandy Ka-on, of the Institute of Sociology, Saray took over the institute after Ka-on left Cambodia in 1989. The following year, Saray was arrested for his association with an effort to form an opposition party. He was imprisoned for a year and a half. Thun Saray currently runs ADHOC, a nongovernmental human rights organization in Cambodia.

UK BUNCHHEUAN: A former Khmer Rouge Eastern Zone cadre, Uk Bunchheuan fled to Vietnam in 1978. More suspicious than many of his comrades of Vietnamese authorities, he received a political education in Vietnam up until 1980, when he returned to Cambodia to take over the drafting of the constitution from Ros Samay and to serve as minister of justice. In the former role, he presided over the removal of civil liberties from the draft. As minister of justice, however, he protected noncommunist jurists, defended the interests of a weak court system against the police, and became an advocate, relatively speaking, for the rule of law and human rights. Uk Bunchheuan is currently chair of the Legislation Commission of the Senate.

UNG PHAN: A former military officer of the Khmer Rouge Eastern Zone, Ung Phan fled with Hun Sen to Vietnam in 1977. Appointed minister in charge of the Council of Ministers, Phan promoted pragmatic economic policies while helping Hun Sen develop a patronage system within an expanding and increasingly technocratic bureaucracy. His dissatisfaction with Vietnamese domination contributed to his general unhappiness with the regime. While serving as minister of communications in the late 1980s, he attempted to form an opposition party. Arrested in May 1990, Ung Phan spent a year and a half in prison. He currently holds no official position.

VANDY KA-ON: A French-trained sociologist who survived the Khmer Rouge regime, Vandy Ka-on became a symbol of the PRK's inclusion of noncommunist intellectuals in the government. As a member of the Council of State and as chair of the National Assembly's Legislation Commission, he was sometimes critical of corruption and human rights abuses. Granted permission to establish the Institute of Sociology, he and Thun Saray distributed a publication that cautiously skirted the boundaries of acceptable public discourse. He gradually became more outspoken, fleeing Cambodia for France in 1989 under a cloud of political suspicion and alleged financial entanglements.

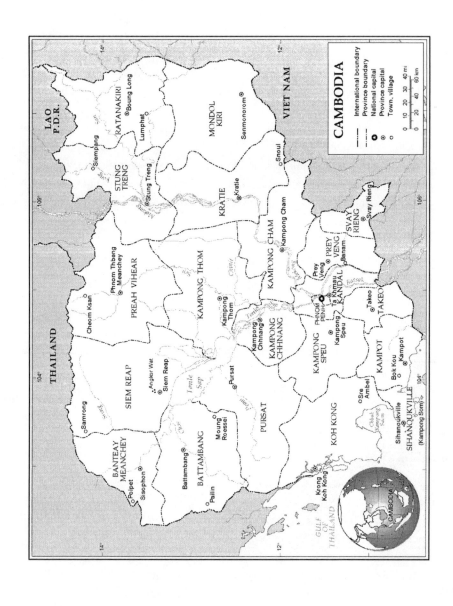

Part One **Beginnings**

Chapter 1 Liberation

In February 1979, around the time of his forty-sixth birthday, a small, unassuming peasant named Heng Chi recalled that he had once been a judge. It was a distant memory, clouded by exhaustion and hunger, constant fear, and the half-dead state of mindless slavery. In a sense, it had already been forgotten. "All that time, I pretended that I had been a construction worker," Heng Chi explains. "I told my children to forget their own names." Assigned by the Khmer Rouge to an anonymous and isolated patch of rice fields known as Cooperative 15, he and his family kept their background secret for three years and ten months.[1]

Heng Chi's life vanished on April 17, 1975, the day Khmer Rouge soldiers marched him out of Phnom Penh, along with his wife, their three children, and hundreds of thousands of other confused and terrified Cambodians. For days he and his family walked amid this stream of people, watching what happened around them until a clear picture emerged. As Cambodians were discovering, the revolution intended to eliminate all remnants of the country's political, economic, and cultural life. Judges, teachers, bankers, soldiers, and politicians were subject to execution. In the fury of the moment, only a lucky few real-ized what was happening before it was too late. Heng Chi was lucky—lucky enough to successfully erase his own identity and invent a new name and a new past. He was prepared—for the rest of his life, for all he knew—to work as a peasant in the rice fields.

Battambang, the northwestern province where Heng Chi and his family had been sent, was one of the last areas of the country to be reached by the Vietnamese forces that swept into Cambodia at the end of December 1978. Planning their retreat to the Thai border, Khmer Rouge soldiers and cadres throughout the province attempted to take as many Cambodian civilians with them as possible. The civilians, in response, seized whatever opportunities the invasion offered to flee. In the confusion, Heng Chi and his wife were separated from their children.

Grief-stricken, weak, and malnourished, they could barely move. Heng Chi's wife was so sick that she could travel no more than a kilometer a day, but there was fighting nearby, and they had no choice but to flee. Days later, they arrived at the first crossroads, a former middle school in neighboring Siem Reap province. Vietnamese soldiers periodically drove by on their way to and from the front. For twenty days Heng Chi and his wife asked for rides to the provin-cial capital. At night they slept in a field near the school.

It was already March by the time they reached Siem Reap's provincial capital. The town, evacuated by the Khmer Rouge in 1975, now served as a base for the Vietnamese army and a few Cambodians selected by the Vietnamese as provin-cial officials. Prevented from entering, former residents squatted on the out-skirts of the town, where they searched for rice left behind by the Khmer Rouge and sold recently unearthed gold and family jewels for food. Not for several more weeks did Heng Chi and his wife find another set of Vietnamese soldiers to drive them south in the direction of Phnom Penh.

With Phnom Penh also off-limits, they headed to the town of Takmau in Kandal province, just outside the capital. There Heng Chi finally spotted a family member, a cousin, who offered to bring the couple back to his village, where they could settle. For the next year he worked in the rice fields, oblivious to the new regime and its plans. "All I knew was that I'd lost my children," he says.

In March 1980, Heng Chi returned to Phnom Penh to seek medical care for his wife and to find a state job. One of only eight jurists to survive the revolu-tion, he soon found work at the Ministry of Justice. His initial experiences were not encouraging. Serving under a former Khmer Rouge official whose past had earned him a reputation for cruelty, Heng Chi was assigned to explain to a new and largely uneducated corps of state officials the provisions of a communist constitution drafted, in large part, by Vietnamese advisors. Not surprisingly, he remained suspicious of the new regime. Life, at that moment, was defined by small favors—an allocation of rice, a house, physical security—and by despair, conflicting emotions that only deepened when, one day in June, one of Heng Chi's children arrived in Phnom Penh with news of the others' deaths.

The invitation to return to the civil service was, for Heng Chi, as it was for many other educated Cambodians, a sign of relative normalcy. *Chaul steung tam bat, chaul srok tam brates,* say the Khmer. "Enter a stream; follow its turns. Enter a land; follow the [laws and customs of the] country." As Heng Chi had feared, the ideology to which he was now expected to adhere was not that of the prerevolutionary era. But, in contrast to the Khmer Rouge—whose revolution had been geared to destroying the educated—the new leadership issued a reassuringly familiar promise: support the regime and you shall be rewarded. Cambodia's second revolution, installed by Vietnamese communists, had brought with it a resumption of the traditional arrangement between ruler and technocrats, a relationship of adaptation, co-optation, and perhaps some subtle influence by the technocrats over the direction of the country. The new regime demanded acquiescence to Vietnamese occupation and to communist policies. In return, Heng Chi was offered the chance to teach the minister of justice, the former Khmer Rouge official, the meaning of law.

Many educated Cambodians refused to make these compromises. One young man who would soon choose a different path was Thun Saray. Just a few months short of a degree in economics when the Khmer Rouge took Phnom Penh, Saray was unable to hide his education and was sent, along with his brother and his wife, to an "education camp" in the eastern province of Kampong Cham. There he spent ten months engaged in menial labor under the intense supervision of the Khmer Rouge. All students were suspect, and those among them deemed to be the "enemy" were killed. Saray, however, offered no indication of disloyalty, and the Khmer Rouge found no evidence against him. Ordered to construct a dirt road, he worked quietly. "The pen of the revolution is the hoe," the Khmer Rouge cadres reminded him. Meanwhile, his wife, who had been released earlier, gave birth. Their daughter was born in a chicken coop without walls and without a roof, "in nature," Saray recalls, "like an animal."[2]

When he was released, Saray was sent to a cooperative three kilometers from his wife and infant daughter. His wife begged the village chief to let her see her husband, giving him her remaining possessions until he relented. Saray's reunion with his wife was a stroke of luck; just a few days later, they were marched north out of Kampong Cham to Kratie province, where they remained for the rest of the Khmer Rouge period. By Saray's reckoning, the trip to Kratie saved their lives. Although his status as a student (as opposed to a member of the civil service) had initially meant the difference between detention and execution, the Khmer Rouge soon launched a furious purge in Kampong Cham in which thousands of Cambodians were killed with little regard to such distinctions.

The fall of Kratie to the Vietnamese army provided Thun Saray and his family the opportunity to leave their cooperative and head for the provincial capital. After a few days' rest, they attempted to return to Phnom Penh but were prevented from entering the city by Vietnamese soldiers. Saray then took the family to Kandal province, where he soon found work at a small district office. For the next three to four months he helped the new regime "educate" local Cambodians on the atrocities of the Khmer Rouge in exchange for a salary of rice. It was also at the district office that Saray first met Vandy Ka-on, a thirty-six-year-old French-trained sociologist who had survived the Khmer Rouge by feigning mental incapacity. Ka-on was just as suspicious of the new regime as Saray and had not identified himself. It was difficult, however, to remain anonymous. To gain the support of the population, the Vietnamese had permitted a number of prerevolutionary officials to become village chiefs, one of whom, a former army colonel, recognized Vandy Ka-on and set him to work.[3]

In May 1979, Vietnamese and Cambodian officials contacted Ka-on and asked him to participate in a trial for Khmer Rouge leaders Pol Pot and Ieng Sary. Ka-on invited Saray to join him, and despite the misgivings they shared about Cambodia's new leadership, they joined in the one project in which their interests and those of the regime coincided. As surviving intellectuals, Ka-on and Saray understood that they were helping to legitimize a political show trial, and yet they applied themselves to their assignment: drafting what was called the "Investigative Report on the Pol Pot–Ieng Sary Clique's Crimes Against the Phnom Penh Population." Saray interviewed other survivors, collected Khmer Rouge documents, and, three months later, when the tribunal convened, testified. It wasn't much of a trial, he says now, "not in terms of fair procedure." In his own testimony, moreover, Saray was required to parrot the new regime's political line, referring to the prerevolutionary "imperialist, feudal, and bourgeois regimes," to the Khmer Rouge's "long struggle against the American imperialist aggressors," and to the "traitors who sold out our country to the Chinese imperialists."[4] Despite these pressures, Saray, who lost his father, a brother, and all his sister's children to the Khmer Rouge, does not regret his role. "The important thing was to prosecute them," he explains. "They killed so many people."

The trial was Thun Saray's last concession to the new regime. Like tens of thousands of other Cambodians, Saray's two younger brothers responded to the Vietnamese occupation, the imposition of communism, and the threat of conscription by fleeing to the Thai-Cambodian border. Tempted to follow, Saray was ultimately dissuaded by a friend who had made part of the journey and had returned with stories of soldiers and border guards and of bandits willing to cut open a traveler in search of swallowed diamonds. "I'd survived the Khmer Rouge. The most important thing was my life," he recalls. "I had a wife and a child." Living for years outside the umbrella of state employment, the family survived on his wife's meager earnings in the illicit private market.

Meanwhile, Saray worked at a quasi-independent research institution, the Institute of Sociology, which he helped establish with Vandy Ka-on and which was tolerated by the leadership only because Ka-on had accepted a series of high-profile, powerless positions. While under scrutiny by Cambodian and Vietnamese officials, Thun Saray and Vandy Ka-on professed their loyalty to the new regime at the same time as they wrote articles and distributed publications that gingerly tested the boundaries of acceptable discourse.[5]

THE NEW LEADERSHIP

On the morning of December 2, 1978, in a small clearing inside a rubber plantation just east of the township of Snoul in Kratie province and just over the border from Vietnam, the future leaders of Cambodia emerged. Calling themselves the Kampuchean United Front for National Salvation (KUFNS, or the Front), they assembled before several hundred Cambodian refugees who had fled to Vietnam and who had now been trucked into Cambodian territory for the occasion. With what official accounts later described as "boundless enthusiasm," the Cambodians watched as a short, balding, inconspicuous-looking man stepped forward and began to speak. "Dear and respected compatriots, dear cadres and combatants, dear compatriots abroad. Throughout the long period when Kampuchea was under the yoke of colonialism, imperialism, and feudalism . . ."[6]

The speaker, Heng Samrin, had only recently defected from the Khmer Rouge. Described in the Front's official pronouncements as a "former member of the Executive Committee of the Communist Party of Kampuchea for the

Eastern Zone, former political commissar, and commander of the 4th Division," the newly selected president of the KUFNS had nothing but praise for the Khmer Rouge revolution. "Our people won the glorious victory of April 17, 1975, totally liberating our country, opening for the Kampuchean people a new era, the era of independence, freedom, and socialism."

Cambodia's troubles, he continued, began "a few days after liberation," when "the reactionary Pol Pot–Ieng Sary gang and their families" launched their destruction of Cambodia. Samrin ticked off the gang's crimes: the "razing of towns," the severing of the "sacred sentiments of people" toward family and neighbors, the "abolition of money and markets," "forcible cooperativization," and "camouflaged concentration camps." "Everywhere," he concluded, "our people have witnessed massacres, more atrocious, more barbarous, than those committed in the Middle Ages or perpetrated by the Hitlerite fascists." "Worst of all," he said, were the purges in the Khmer Rouge Eastern Zone, from which he himself had fled and which had claimed the lives not only of civilians but also of Samrin's revolutionary compatriots. "How many cadres, Party members, authentic revolutionaries and patriots, and cadres and combatants in the armed forces who had contributed to the liberation of the country and proved absolute loyalty to the motherland have been killed en masse at all levels and in all places for the sole reason that they did not approve of the reactionary and barbarous policy of the Pol Pot–Ieng Sary gang."

Heng Samrin had two messages to deliver, one to Cambodian civilians and one to Khmer Rouge cadres. To ordinary Cambodians, those forced "to live in misery as slaves," he promised inclusion and tolerance. The Front, he said, "unites all nationalities in the country and rallies all patriotic forces regardless of political and religious tendencies—workers, peasants, petty bourgeois, intellectuals, Buddhist monks and nuns." After the overthrow of Democratic Kampuchea, Cambodia would be a very different place. "All Kampucheans have the right to return to their old native land, and to build their family life in happiness. All Kampucheans have freedom of residence, the right to stand for election and to vote, freedom of thought, association, and religion, and the right to work, recreation, and education." The Front, continued Samrin, planned: "To abolish the compulsory 'work-and-eat-together' system. . . . To put an end to the Pol Pot–Ieng Sary policy of seizing the people's rice and other property. . . . To establish banks, issue currency, restore and develop the circulation of goods. To broaden home trade and increase economic relations with all foreign countries on an equal footing and with mutual benefits."

Samrin's speech was also intended to reassure those Khmer Rouge cadres "still in the ranks of the ruling clique." "Die-hard reactionary chieftains who have committed bloody crimes against the people" would be punished. No one else needed to be afraid. The Front intended "to warmly welcome, and create favorable conditions for, officers and soldiers, as well as public servants, in the administration of the reactionary regime to rally with the people and fight back against the Pol Pot–Ieng Sary gang to save the motherland and their own families. . . . To practice leniency toward those who sincerely repent. To give appropriate rewards to those who had performed feats of arms in service of the revolution."

The man most responsible for the Front's lenient policies toward the former Khmer Rouge cadres was standing nearby. Chea Sim, forty-six, was two years older than Samrin. Thickset, with dense, closely cropped hair, Sim appeared to be one of the few Cambodians not suffering from malnutrition. Identified as the "former secretary of the Party Committee for Region 20 [and] former member of the Kampuchean People's Representative Assembly," Chea Sim had defected from the Khmer Rouge's Eastern Zone around the same time as Heng Samrin. He was now vice president of the Front.

A third Eastern Zone cadre, a scrawny, angular soldier whose flight to Vietnam had preceded those of Heng Samrin and Chea Sim by more than a year, was also in attendance. With an ill-fitting glass eye and thick black glasses correcting what remained of his vision, he stared out at the proceedings. Hun Sen was twenty-six years old.

Although few people in Cambodia or overseas had ever heard of these three men, an elderly Vietnamese man in attendance would have been instantly recognizable if the Front had bothered to announce his presence. Le Duc Tho, a founding member of the Indochinese Communist Party, was most famous for negotiating the 1973 cease-fire with the United States and for having been awarded, along with Henry Kissinger, the Nobel Peace Prize, an honor he turned down. Tho was also a powerful Politburo member whose political machinations had earned him a reputation as a kingmaker within Hanoi's political circles. His most important contribution to the Indochinese communist movement, however, began in 1950, when Ho Chi Minh sent him south into the Mekong Delta. In addition to designing Hanoi's southern strategy throughout the two Indochina wars, against France and against the United States, Tho assumed responsibility for Vietnamese assistance to the Cambodian revolution, establishing a special Politburo office for Cambodian affairs.[7]

Heng Samrin was still speaking. "The Pol Pot–Ieng Sary gang," he was say-ing, "had provoked a border conflict with Vietnam, thus turning friend into foe."

To Le Duc Tho, the collapse of the once fraternal Cambodian-Vietnamese relationship had meant the resumption of a familiar task: identifying, guiding, and promoting pro-Vietnamese Cambodian revolutionaries. Having spent the previous year and a half with this particular set of defectors, he must have been proud of their apparent loyalty. For Tho, the revolutionary midwife, the man who had been in Bac Bo in 1941 for the formation of the Viet Minh and in Hanoi in 1945 for the creation of the provisional government and who had par-ticipated in the 1960 formation of the South Vietnamese National Liberation Front, not to mention the historic 1950 congress at which the first Cambodian communists had announced their United Issarak Front, the morning's cere-monies were only the latest in a series of political births.[8]

Heng Samrin was finishing his speech. "The time of the revolution has come!

"Cadres and combatants, unite and march forward heroically!

"Struggle resolutely to overthrow the reactionary Pol Pot–Ieng Sary gang!

"Our people will surely achieve a peaceful, independent, democratic, neu-tral, and nonaligned Kampuchea, which will advance to socialism. The Kam-puchea revolution will win!" According to various accounts, Heng Samrin then walked over to Le Duc Tho, shook his hand, and thanked him. Official reports, broadcast the following day from a radio station in Ho Chi Minh City, pre-sented a more theatrical finale. "The meeting," boomed the Voice of the Kam-puchean People, "wound up with folk songs and dances full of combative and revolutionary spirit."[9]

INVASION

On Christmas Day, 1978, the People's Army of Vietnam sent 150,000 heavily armed troops into Kratie. A week later, the Vietnamese invaded from Laos, tak-ing the northern province of Steung Treng and pinching off the northeast from the Khmer Rouge's central authority. The heaviest fighting, however, took place in the southeast, where the Vietnamese prepared for the invasion with re-lentless bombing runs over areas with large numbers of Khmer Rouge soldiers. Despite Vietnamese tanks, heavy artillery, and thousands more troops, the fighting on the ground was fierce. Not until January 4 did Vietnam control the seven Cambodian provinces east of the Mekong. Two days later, Vietnamese soldiers finally crossed the river, forcing the Khmer Rouge leadership to flee Phnom Penh and head west toward Thailand.[10]

Vietnamese soldiers entered the Cambodian capital on the morning of January 7, their jeeps roaring down the city's deserted avenues. At noon, radio broadcasts announced that the Front had liberated Phnom Penh. By evening hundreds of Cambodian soldiers—Khmers who had fled the Khmer Rouge and taken refuge in southern Vietnam—arrived. Housed in Phnom Penh's airport, they joined Vietnamese troops in scouting the empty streets and buildings for lingering Khmer Rouge soldiers, engaging the few they found in rounds of gunfire.

Over the next few days, pronouncements poured forth on behalf of the Cambodian leadership. On January 8 an ostensibly Cambodian news agency announced the composition of a Cambodian government, the Kampuchean People's Revolutionary Council (KPRC), to be headed by Heng Samrin. On January 10 the KPRC officially declared the establishment of a new regime, the People's Republic of Kampuchea, or PRK.[11]

When it was considered safe, Samrin, Chea Sim, Hun Sen, and the rest of leadership boarded Vietnamese jeeps and entered Phnom Penh, a city none of them had seen for more than a decade. The scene was bleak. As the Cambodians inspected their capital, block after block passed by without a sign of life. In some places, there were indications of sudden flight: laundry left hanging out to dry, food left behind. But in most places, the years of neglect were obvious. In houses, apartment blocks, and markets, people had seemingly been replaced by encroaching vegetation. Banana, coconut, and papaya trees grew from the sidewalks. Pigs and chickens roamed the city. Snakes slid through the high grass. And rats found their way from house to house, hiding among the toppled furniture and family photo albums of Phnom Penh's missing residents. Meanwhile, the remnants of the city's former life lay upended in stacks of televisions and phones, kitchen utensils, clothes, and books. Cars were assembled to rust. In the schools, equipment had been systematically ruined; the test tubes and microscopes of the medical school lay shattered on the floor. Anywhere that culture, education, or wealth had thrived, these bizarre refuse heaps were all that remained, testaments to both political and literal upheaval.[12]

Chapter 2 Turning Waters:
The Patterns and Myths
of Cambodian History

Cambodia's rivers tell many stories. The Mekong, the longest river in Southeast Asia, originates in the Himalayas and passes through China, Thailand, and Laos before entering Cambodia and heading toward the delta of southern Vietnam. A route for trade and immigration, it links Cambodia to the rest of the region geographically, politically, and economically. The Tonle Sap, by contrast, is a purely Cambodian river that flows from a lake of the same name in the center of the country south to Phnom Penh, where, a mere 110 kilometers from its source, it joins the Mekong.

Separately, each river represents a way to look at Cambodia—as a country swept along by regional and global trends or as a unique nation proceeding according to its own traditions. Small and vulnerable, Cambodia has been colonized, overwhelmed by foreign ideologies, torn apart by international conflict, and occupied by other countries. Faced with these incursions, Cambodians have attempted to define an uncontaminated national identity. One version of history thus inspires the other. In riparian terms, the mightier the flow of the international Mekong, the more the Tonle Sap stands as a symbol of Cambodian purity.

Remarkably, this relationship is borne out by reality. For six months every year the Tonle Sap flows south from the lake to its juncture with the Mekong. Then, toward the end of the monsoon rains, the Mekong swells, overwhelming its smaller sister. Over the course of several weeks, the waters of the Tonle Sap begin to churn and then, gradually, reverse course. The river then heads upstream, and the lake expands, flooding the shrubs and trees that skirt its shores and nourishing the fish that teem in its waters. In Phnom Penh, Cambodians celebrate this miracle by observing the Water Festival. There are boat races, family outings, and prayers. Although many holidays are intended as a reaffirmation of nationhood, something about the Water Festival is perhaps especially reassuring. After all, a Cambodian river has been returned to its source.

Like other communist movements, the Khmer Rouge had intended their victory to be linear, continuous, and permanent. Cambodia, they assumed, was on a direct course toward a glorious horizon the price of which was an absolute repudiation of the past. Under Democratic Kampuchea, Cambodians were prohibited from practicing religion, singing traditional songs, or exhibiting any political or ethnic diversity. They were starved, beaten, and sometimes executed merely for mentioning the lives they had lived prior to the revolution. To be sure, the regime had its own notions of nationalism, defined in particular by hatred of Vietnam. At the same time, however, it denied its citizens a celebration of their own cultural heritage. From Pol Pot down to village chiefs, the Khmer Rouge were committed to a constant, vigilant struggle against history. The Water Festival, like other traditional Cambodian holidays, was not observed. It was as if the Tonle Sap were to flow perpetually downstream.

After the overthrow of Democratic Kampuchea, the next regime, the People's Republic of Kampuchea (PRK), disseminated a different variation on Cambodian communist ideology: Indochinese solidarity. To differentiate itself from the Khmer Rouge, the PRK promised that religion, culture, ethnic identity, and economic freedoms would be tolerated, so long as they did not offend Marxism-Leninism or pose a threat to the state, the ruling Party, or the Vietnamese. As the PRK's leadership discovered, however, most Cambodians were not satisfied with a partial (and heavily politicized) cultural revival. Years of lost nationhood had left them homesick in their own land, and they were ready to reverse the flow of history. A mythologized source, a kind of prewar, prerevolutionary, pre-occupation national starting point, beckoned.

MEMORIES OF EMPIRE AND OCCUPATION

Angkor Wat, the five-towered archeological wonder that has adorned almost every Cambodian flag, has come to represent a glorious national heritage. The Angkor empire at its zenith in the twelfth century controlled much of Southeast Asia. To the west and north, it extended over what is now Thailand and parts of Burma and Laos. To the east, for about a century, it also controlled the Mekong Delta.

From a historical perspective, Angkor's value as a symbol of Cambodian and Khmer nationalism is tenuous. The empire was polyglot (Angkor Wat's temples are adorned with Sanskrit and Pali) and multiethnic. Most Khmers had not even heard of Angkor before French colonial archeologists began publicizing and interpreting their findings. Still, as a mythologized past for modern Cambodia, the Angkor empire has found much use, particularly in light of subsequent historical events. The empire's western lands were absorbed by the Siamese, into what is now Thailand. Meanwhile, to the east, the Le and Nguyen dynasties of what is now Vietnam gradually colonized and then took control of the Mekong Delta. Because the Angkor empire once held this territory and because there are ethnic Khmers in southern Vietnam, many Cambodians refer to this land as Kampuchea Krom, or "Lower Cambodia."[1]

In times of internal conflict, the successors to the Angkor empire often allied themselves with Siam or with the Vietnamese dynasties. In the early nineteenth century one such arrangement, between King Chan and the Nguyen dynasty, contributed to a brief but memorable period during which a Khmer puppet princess occupied the throne and Vietnamese officials attempted to govern Cambodia. Although Nguyen documents from the time suggest mostly frustration with the Khmers, the history of this period is frequently recounted in Cambodia as a cautionary tale of cultural subjugation. As it is told, Nguyen officials promoted the Vietnamese and Chinese languages along with the precepts of traditional Vietnamese Confucianism, desecrated Buddhist pagodas, and forced Cambodian officials to dress as Vietnamese mandarins. Cambodia itself was divided into provinces connected to the Nguyen administration, and its people were subject to Vietnamese taxes. Cambodians were drafted into labor projects designed to improve canals and drainage in the Mekong Delta, even as Vietnamese farmers, responsible only to the laws and authorities of Vietnam, settled in Cambodia.

Whether these indignities were systematic or anecdotal, and whether or not the Nguyen were capable of administering Cambodia, much less imposing a foreign culture on the Khmers, the entire occupation lasted only nine years. Nonetheless, Cambodians frequently invoke this period to justify their fear of Vietnamese expansion and their opposition to ethnic Vietnamese on Cambodian soil. In the 1980s, during the Vietnamese occupation, comparisons with the 1830s were inevitable and, at times, apt. Many Cambodians, however, also cited these parallels as proof of a historical, racial predisposition to colonization. As a result of such suspicions, even the Khmer word used to identify Vietnamese ethnicity—*yuon*—has become derogatory and synonymous with exploitation.[2]

CAMBODIA UNDER THE FRENCH

Cambodia was under the joint protection of Vietnam and Siam in the 1860s when the French decided to establish a protectorate. Initially intending to treat Cambodia as a buffer between Siam and its more valuable colony of Cochin China (southern Vietnam), France eventually took full control over its administration, its financial and legal systems, and its commercial affairs. Perceiving the Cambodians as lazy and simple, as "noble savages" with a great but lost civilization, the French brought in Vietnamese bureaucrats to staff the civil service in Phnom Penh and Vietnamese workers to tap the rubber plantations of eastern Cambodia. They also allowed large numbers of Vietnamese farmers and fishermen to settle in Cambodia.

French colonial authorities, while building roads, cities, and schools, did little to modernize the Cambodian economy. Instead, they built large plantations for the production of rubber and other agricultural commodities, which they exported. For the vast majority of Cambodians, life did not improve significantly. Although they were not deprived of their land, they were heavily taxed. The confiscation of large percentages of rice harvests also created a level of rural indebtedness not previously known in Cambodia, which, in turn, forced Khmer peasants into a state of increased dependence on Chinese moneylenders.

The first indications of a nationalist movement appeared among Cambodia's small Francophone urban elite and its Theravada Buddhist clergy. In 1936 a French-educated Khmer from southern Vietnam, Son Ngoc Thanh, began publishing a subtly anticolonial newspaper out of the Phnom Penh–based Buddhist Institute. Six years later, with Japanese soldiers quietly coexisting with the Vichy France administration, Thanh organized Cambodia's first anticolonial demonstration. Unnerved by the sudden appearance of some seven hundred monks and civilians, the French promptly cracked down, sending the leaders fleeing in opposite directions. Some traveled east, joining up with the Vietnamese-dominated Indochinese Communist Party (ICP). Among these first Cambodian communists was a monk whose nom de guerre, Son Ngoc Minh, was intended to invoke both the better-known Son Ngoc Thanh and Minh's Vietnamese mentor, Ho Chi Minh. Most of the Cambodian anticolonialists, including Son Ngoc Thanh, fled to western Cambodia, which, at the time, was occupied by Thailand. It was the Thais, therefore, who provided safe haven for Cambodia's first armed resistance, the Khmer Issarak.

The Japanese decision, in March 1945, to disarm and dissolve the French administration offered, for Cambodians, a glimpse of independence and, for Norodom Sihanouk, the twenty-two-year-old Cambodian king, a brief taste of power. Five months later, with the defeat of the Japanese, the French resumed power, only to find that the expectations of their subjects had changed. Throughout the late 1940s and early 1950s educated Cambodians pursued anticolonial ends through a newly formed Democratic Party, winning elections and prompting waves of arrests by the French. Sihanouk, meanwhile, was positioning himself as the central figure in Cambodian politics.

Some of the most important events in Cambodian history were occurring elsewhere, in Thailand, in Vietnam, and in France. Thailand's loss of western Cambodia (as a result of a treaty with France) and a coup that overthrew an anticolonial Thai government effectively denied the Khmer Issarak their sanctuary and forced them either to return to French-controlled Cambodia or to join the Viet Minh communists. The focus of the anticolonial movement thus shifted east, where the Vietnamese, focused on their own war with France, had decided to transform the ICP into the Vietnamese Workers Party (VWP) and to encourage the Cambodian communists to pursue their own revolutionary movement. In April 1950 the Cambodians thus convened the First National Congress of Khmer Resistance, creating a communist-dominated United Issarak Front under the leadership of Son Ngoc Minh and the guidance of Le Duc Tho. The following year the Vietnamese delivered the statutes and draft platform for the first Cambodian communist party, the Khmer People's Revolutionary Party (KPRP). The Party remained under Hanoi's control. A Viet Minh document from November 1951 stated: "The Vietnamese Party reserves the right to supervise the activities of its brother parties in Cambodia and Laos. . . . Later, however, if conditions permit, the three revolutionary Parties of Vietnam, Cambodia, and Laos will be able to unite to form a single Party: the Party of the Vietnam-Khmer-Laotian Federation."[3] Twenty years later,

Cambodian communists did build an autonomous communist party. In the early 1950s, however, the forces behind that movement—idealistic students named Saloth Sar (later known as Pol Pot), Ieng Sary, and Son Sen—were traveling in Marxist circles in Paris.

The end of the French protectorate in 1953 provided Norodom Sihanouk with the perfect political opening. By declaring himself the father of Cambodian independence, he simultaneously attracted broad popular support and deprived the Issaraks of the one issue that had united their movement. Many Issaraks who had been motivated by the struggle for independence rather than communism and who were not members of the Khmer People's Revolutionary Party returned to civilian life. The communists, meanwhile, had to contend with larger geopolitical forces. In 1954 the historic Geneva Conference granted independence to Cambodia and Laos and divided Vietnam. Unlike their Vietnamese and Lao comrades, the Cambodian communists did not participate in the conference and were left with no internationally recognized territory of their own. The Cambodians resented the outcome and, years later, cited it as confirmation that their revolutionary struggle could be sacrificed to the immediate interests of other communist powers, specifically Vietnam.

The Geneva Conference also divided the Cambodian revolutionary movement. Saloth Sar and the other French-educated communists took up residence in Phnom Penh, where they hoped to challenge Sihanouk politically while retaining ties to the few communist Issarak militants still operating in the countryside. Another contingent—more than a thousand Issarak troops—hid themselves among the Viet Minh being withdrawn from southern Vietnam, and headed to Hanoi. A few, including future Khmer Rouge leaders Nuon Chea and Sao Phim, returned to Cambodia a year or so after the conference. The rest joined Son Ngoc Minh for what became an extended period of Vietnamese political, military, and technical education. Twenty-five years later, the survivors of this group returned to Cambodia on the heels of the Vietnamese invasion, assuming positions as powerful ministers in the People's Republic of Kampuchea. For the time being, though, they remained isolated from events inside their country, watching at a distance as they became marginal figures in the Cambodian revolution.

INDEPENDENT CAMBODIA

Sihanouk took advantage of his moment of glory by solidifying his personal rule. The most threatening of his rivals was Son Ngoc Thanh, who, denied a place in the new regime, went into exile in Thailand. The rest Sihanouk hoped to bring under his control. Abdicating the throne to his own unambitious father in 1955, the prince threw himself into politics and formed a new political entity, the Sangkum Reastr Niyum (People's Socialist Community), a populist movement that sought to absorb and dissolve all other political parties. Through intimidation, violence, and relentless propaganda and with the help of his own personal popularity among Cambodian peasants, Sihanouk easily won elections against the remnants of the Democrats and a more left-leaning party, Pracheachun (The People). The Sangkum launched the prince into fifteen more years of power while co-opting much of Cambodian society. It rarely demanded ideological conformity from its members, merely absolute loyalty. As such, it offers a model that has reemerged in the nonideological but frequently ruthless power struggles of postrevolutionary Cambodia.

In foreign policy, Sihanouk sought to secure Cambodia's neutrality while accepting financial support from rival powers. This strategy, frequently referred to as the prince's "tightrope," allowed for both American military assistance and Cambodian participation in the international Nonaligned Movement. Political considerations eventually pushed Sihanouk away from the Americans, however. Having co-opted the cause of independence from Cambodian nationalists, Sihanouk attempted to isolate the left by stealing what remained of their platform—namely, anti-imperialism. His rejection, in 1955, of the anticommunist Southeast Asian Treaty Organization (SEATO) won him economic assistance from China and the political support of the Viet Minh. Meanwhile, he appointed prominent leftists such as Khieu Samphan to his cabinet and began calling himself a socialist.

The late 1950s and early 1960s would be remembered by many Cambodians, during and after the Khmer Rouge regime, as Cambodia's golden moment. The country enjoyed neutrality and relative peace while maintaining a functioning, if inequitable, economy. Cambodia exported rice, rubber, and pepper and received foreign aid from France, the United States, and the Sino-Soviet bloc. This assistance not only helped build hospitals, schools, and a transportation infrastructure but also ensured that, despite corruption and inefficiency, enough money trickled down to ward off hunger and discontent. Phnom Penh buzzed with cultural glories, all of which owed their patronage to Sihanouk. There was the royal ballet, the National Museum, and a lavish palace, built by the French, to which the elite could expect to be invited. On one level, the affable, accessible Sihanouk was extremely popular, especially in the countryside, where Cambodian peasants adored him, not just as royalty but as the embodiment of Cambodia itself. In the capital and in the larger towns, however, many Cambodians blamed him for condoning corruption and political intimidation.

Sihanouk's Cambodia was also a land in which ethnicity was frequently associated with social and economic roles. The vast majority of Khmers worked in the rice paddies of the Cambodian countryside, satisfying Sihanouk's vision of his happy "children." At the opposite end of the socioeconomic spectrum was the aristocracy—the Khmers and mixed Sino-Thai-Vietnamese Khmers who dined with the prince and provided his supporting cast. Important segments of society, including a majority of the residents of Phnom Penh, were either Chinese or Vietnamese. The Chinese dominated the economy, particularly its trading and informal banking sectors. Sometimes assimilated through marriage into Khmer society, Sino-Khmers, along with full-blooded Chinese, presented a near impenetrable wall that prevented poorer Cambodians from entering commercial life. The Vietnamese were more insular, divided from the Khmers by cultural and language differences and by racial antagonism. In the cities the Vietnamese worked as artisans, small traders, clerks, or domestic servants for Western residents; in the countryside they lived as fishermen along rivers and the Tonle Sap lake. The rest of the Cambodian population consisted of Cham Muslims and the northeastern minorities, who remained isolated and largely untouched by modern life.

CAMBODIA UNBALANCED

In the late 1980s, when Cambodia's communist leaders were bent on reforming the economy and were looking to the past as a model, the few intellectuals who had not emigrated or been killed served as their memory. "How was it under the old regime?" the communists asked. What the questioners sometimes missed, however, was that the "old regime," the Sihanouk era, was not a fixed moment but a fluid series of events.

In 1959 the Vietnamese Workers Party decided to promote armed struggle in South Vietnam and set out to build a supply route through Laos and Cambodia: the Ho Chi Minh Trail. This project and the traffic that flowed along the trail greatly increased the number of Vietnamese communist troops on Cambodian soil and resulted in expanded cooperation between the two countries' revolutionary movements. At the same time, the Cambodian communists suffered serious setbacks, as Sihanouk successfully infiltrated their rural networks and forced them to concentrate their efforts in the capital. Encouraged by the

VWP, they met secretly in a Phnom Penh railway station in September 1960, organizing themselves as the Workers Party of Kampuchea and selecting as the Party's leaders the future rulers of Democratic Kampuchea. Saloth Sar held the number three position; two other future Khmer Rouge leaders, Nuon Chea and Ieng Sary, were numbers two and five, respectively.

Hoping to neutralize the anti-imperialist rhetoric of his critics, secure support from communist powers, and preempt a communist revolution, Sihanouk embarked on a series of leftist economic reforms. Beginning in 1963, private banks were nationalized; foreign trading companies were either closed or absorbed into a state-administered National Company for Export and Import; foreign investment was restricted; and prices were fixed in an effort to ward off competition from imported goods. These gestures failed, however, to appease the increasingly radicalized leftists. Worse still for Sihanouk, the reforms generated a new set of enemies. By nationalizing commercial and banking interests, the prince had specifically intended to undermine the influence of the Sino-Khmer commercial elite, whose ties to capitalist Thailand and to South Vietnam he had long feared. The foreseeable effect of these policies was the political alienation of the country's biggest businesspeople, who resented Sihanouk even as they found ways to corrupt and profit from the new system. The prince also managed to anger an urban elite who had depended both on the private economy and on the U.S. aid that he now rejected, and liberals who decried the power and corruption of the state.

Apart from the political effects that Sihanouk's policies had on Cambodia and on his own future, this period offers a preview of later transitional moments. By attempting to quash Chinese economic dominance, by nationalizing banks and import-export companies, and, later, by attempting to distribute rice through state channels, Sihanouk was taking tentative half-steps toward socialism. Intended to protect his own political power without actually overturning Cambodian society, these policies ultimately failed and were overwhelmed by a utopian regime that was committed to an absolute struggle against the free market. A few years later, in 1979, the economic history of Cambodia began to rewind. Promising more freedom than had been granted by the Khmer Rouge, the PRK attempted a tentative half-step back toward once-familiar economic patterns. Like Sihanouk, the PRK's leaders hoped that ambiguously centrist policies would gain the support of a maximum number of Cambodians while ensuring economic and political control. Like Sihanouk, they failed. The difference was that the PRK had to contend not with a revolution but with a population that was, by the 1980s, thoroughly disillusioned with communism.

Sihanouk and the PRK faced similar obstacles to administering socialism, including a particularly debilitating form of corruption. Whereas Cambodia's traditional Chinese-dominated commercial order had been greased by private-sector bribes to state officials, Sihanouk's new state-dominated economy presented his officials with opportunities to steal state resources and accept ever-larger bribes from Chinese and Sino-Khmer businesspeople. Civil war also created inopportune conditions for socialist experimentation. Under Sihanouk and the PRK, military units acted according to their own nonideological interests, ignoring efforts by Phnom Penh to promote a centrally planned economy.

Ultimately, geopolitics dictated Sihanouk's steps toward socialism as well as the PRK's eventual acceptance of its demise. Sihanouk, faced with the rise of Asian communism, imagined a future in which Cambodia maintained economic and political ties with Hanoi and Beijing and adjusted his economic policies accordingly. By the late 1980s, however, the international communist movement had collapsed, and it was clear to most of the PRK leadership that economic survival now required investment from the capitalist nations of Southeast Asia.

Throughout the mid and late 1960s Sihanouk floundered politically in an increasingly polarized political environment. Security forces responded to anti-Sihanouk demonstrations in 1963 with harsh suppression, forcing many communists, including Saloth Sar, now running the Workers Party of Kampuchea, to flee Phnom Penh. While Sar was spending time in Vietnam and China, South Vietnamese communists (the National Liberation Front, or NLF) operated freely in Cambodia, nurturing the Cambodian revolution while trading with Sino-Khmer merchants and the Cambodian military. The ascendance of Sihanouk's conservative defense chief, General Lon Nol, to prime minister marked an increasing militarization of Cambodian politics and economics. Soldiers responsible for the collection of rice committed widespread abuses and inspired violent demonstrations. Threatened with arrest, Khieu Samphan and other leftists who previously had served in Sihanouk's cabinet joined Saloth Sar in the countryside. Meanwhile, in South Vietnam, the war escalated, and, in March 1969, the United States began bombing Cambodia.[4]

COLLAPSE

In January 1970, Norodom Sihanouk left Cambodia on a trip to France, entrusting the country to Prime Minister Lon Nol and his pro-Western deputy prime minister, Prince Sisowath Sirik Matak. Unhappy with how Sihanouk had been handling the war, Lon Nol and Matak promptly launched attacks on Vietnamese communist positions, organized anti-Vietnamese demonstrations, and reestablished ties with various noncommunist groups, including the South Vietnam–based Khmer Serei (Free Khmer) and the long-banished Son Ngoc Thanh. From Paris, Sihanouk criticized the "capitalist imperialist" motives of the government and made private threats against his cabinet. Under heavy pressure from Sirik Matak, Lon Nol agreed to depose Sihanouk. On March 18, 1970, the National Assembly, by a secret vote of 89–3, brought Cambodia's thousand-year-old monarchy to an abrupt end.

Five days later, speaking from Beijing, Norodom Sihanouk declared war against the new regime and announced the formation of the National United Front of Kampuchea (known by its French acronym, FUNK); a government-in-exile, the Royal Government of National Union of Kampuchea (GRUNK); and a National Liberation Army. Enraged, Sihanouk agreed to an alliance with China, North Vietnam, and the the National Liberation Front of South Vietnam, as well as with his long-standing adversaries the Cambodian communists, whom he had dubbed the Khmer Rouge.

Cambodia soon came apart. In Phnom Penh, decades of repressed anger against Sihanouk burst forth. In Phnom Penh and the major towns, liberals and the bourgeoisie held out hopes for more democratic rule. The leaders of the new regime, more concerned with opposing the communist insurgency and the NLF than with political reform, promoted anti-Vietnamese hatred and orchestrated massacres of ethnic Vietnamese. Fervently nationalistic recruits filled the ranks of the army. In the countryside, peasants, students, and plantation workers held pro-FUNK demonstrations, which the government violently suppressed. Leftists such as Khieu Samphan changed course and united behind Sihanouk, inspiring tens of thousands of Cambodians to join the FUNK.

Social and economic life in Phnom Penh deteriorated as a result of the war and the sudden influx of U.S. military assistance. This aid, which by the beginning of 1971 had reached $180 million, found its way to corrupt generals and to officials in control of fuel, medicine, and other elements of the economy connected to the war effort. Lon Nol himself focused almost entirely on spiritual aspects of the war, convinced that superstitious as well as traditional Buddhist forces would propel his troops to victory against the communist nonbelievers. He promoted racial theories for Cambodia's historical greatness, attacking not only the Vietnamese but the Sino-Khmers and all who had diluted what he called the Khmer-Mon ethnic and national traditions of Cambodia. Despite suffering a stroke in early 1971, Lon Nol managed to arrange for constitutional amendments creating a powerful presidency, organize fraudulent presidential elections, and hold practically uncontested elections to the National Assembly.

The military struggle was still dominated by the Vietnamese communists. A hardened fighting force, the NLF scored easy victories throughout eastern Cambodia. The April 1970 invasion of Cambodia by some thirty thousand U.S. troops and forty-thousand-plus South Vietnamese seeking to root out their opponents in South Vietnam had little effect other than to drive the Vietnamese communists further into the Cambodian interior. The Hanoi-trained Cambodian communists—those who had gone into exile in 1954—now played a direct role in liberating their country. Although a few stayed behind to work with the FUNK's propaganda units in Hanoi, about a thousand, including many of the future leaders of the PRK, left Vietnam and followed the Ho Chi Minh Trail into Cambodia.

Upon their arrival, the Hanoi veterans discovered that the Khmer Rouge were refusing to integrate their troops with the Vietnamese forces. Somewhat more symbolically, the Workers Party of Kampuchea, to which the veterans had remained loyal while in exile, had changed its name. Now referred to as the Communist Party of Kampuchea (CPK), the Party was not only distancing itself from its patrons, the Vietnamese Workers Party, but testing the loyalty of the new arrivals, who were expected to approve of the name change. Instructed by Son Ngoc Minh to respect the directives of the Party in Cambodia, the returnees had no choice but to endorse the new name and accept whatever positions were granted them in the revolutionary organization. Those who had received military training in Hanoi were deemed useful by the CPK leadership and were given relatively low-level command positions. Others were disarmed. Few were given any actual authority within the Khmer Rouge political structure.

The real split came in September 1971, when the CPK held a congress at which it formalized its name change and selected a Central Committee that included none of the returnees from Vietnam. By the end of the year the Khmer Rouge were organizing anti-Vietnamese demonstrations, forcing both NLF soldiers and ethnic Vietnamese civilians to leave Cambodia. The CPK also began purging the "Hanoi Khmer." Where these veteran revolutionaries were isolated from their colleagues and from the Vietnamese, the Khmer Rouge killed them secretly, one at a time. Others were sent to "reeducation camps," although they, too, were eventually murdered, in 1976. A few managed to return to Vietnam. One who fled in the opposite direction, an ethnic Thai revolutionary named Say Phouthang, held out in the remote Cardamom Mountains of Koh

Kong province, along the Thai border, for six years. Phouthang later became one of the most powerful figures in the PRK.[5]

After North Vietnam and the United States signed peace accords in January 1973, Vietnamese forces withdrew from Cambodia, with the exception of the border area of Kampong Cham and the Ho Chi Minh Trail in the northeast. The Khmer Rouge were now openly denouncing both the Vietnamese and Si-hanouk and were engaged in skirmishes with Vietnamese forces still on Cam-bodian territory. Free at last to conduct the revolution as they saw fit, the Khmer Rouge began treating "liberated zones" as they would the rest of the country. In the southwest they evacuated towns, murdered educated Cambodi-ans, and enforced a policy of radical collectivization.[6]

Before the U.S. Congress put an end to it, in August 1973, U.S. planes had dropped three times as much tonnage of bombs on Cambodia as they had on Japan in World War II. The bombing, the resulting lack of available farmland, and the insurgency drove more than 750,000 rural Cambodians into the cities, hundreds of thousands coming to Phnom Penh alone. Refugee camps were in-fested with disease; the desperate begged on the streets; social services ceased to function; and all elements of the administration rotted with corruption. Dis-gusted by life in Phnom Penh and attracted to the apparent purity of the revo-lution, students demonstrated under the covert leadership of the CPK. All around, the insurgency gathered strength, gradually turning the capital into a political island. It all ended in April 1975. First Lon Nol left Cambodia, as did hundreds of wealthy Cambodians. Then the American embassy personnel folded their flag and boarded their helicopters. Finally, on April 17, the people of Phnom Penh became the last of the Cambodians to see the Khmer Rouge.

DEMOCRATIC KAMPUCHEA

Dressed in black or green pajamas and heavily armed, the Khmer Rouge sol-diers marched into Phnom Penh, offering a vision of the years to come. Serious, aloof, seemingly angry even in victory, they patrolled the strange urban land-scape without a hint of jubilation. The new occupiers of the capital were, like so many of the Khmer Rouge, thoroughly indoctrinated, utterly obedient to the revolution, and filled with contempt for whichever enemies were placed before them.

Unlike these odd-looking peasants in the streets, the people of Phnom Penh mostly felt relief. Life in the city had grown worse; the economic crises, the cor-ruption, the refugees, and the violence had led even the most anticommunist among them to hope for improvements. Urban Cambodians expected that they would be permitted to accommodate the revolution and planned to offer their services and skills to the new regime. The Khmer Rouge soldiers, however, pointed their guns at the residents of Phnom Penh and instructed them to move out, explaining that an American bombing of the city was imminent and that immediate evacuation was necessary. Preparing for an uncertain journey, middle-class and wealthy Cambodians desperately stitched jewels and gold into their clothes and hid valuables in and around their houses for when they might return. Hundreds of thousands of Cambodians paraded out of the city and into the countryside. Deprived of medicine, food, and water, the old and the sick died along the way. Khmer Rouge soldiers shot many who complained.

Military officers, ordered to identify themselves, were systematically executed. Other evacuees were told to produce "biographies." Unaware of the consequences, politicians, police, civil servants, teachers, engineers, and doctors revealed their professions, usually at the cost of their lives. Urban residents who survived the trek were treated with outright contempt. Many Khmer Rouge had a deep-seated, visceral distrust of city people, whom they saw as reactionary, corrupt, and degenerate, as well as inherently disloyal to the revolution. "To keep you is no gain, to lose you is no loss" was the chilling mantra applied to Cambodia's urban residents. By May 1975 they had been dubbed "new people" or " April 17 people" and had been escorted to the rural cooperatives that now controlled the whole of the Cambodian population.

The separation of the new people from their urban lives occurred simultaneously with the country's self-imposed isolation from the rest of the world. Under the new regime, which named itself Democratic Kampuchea in 1976, there would be no international telephone calls, no telegrams, cables, or mail. International flights were discontinued except for official visits back and forth to Beijing and, for the moment, Hanoi. The regime closed all borders; foreigners, save for Chinese advisors and the staffs of a mere eight embassies, were expelled. Diplomats allowed to live in the capital were prohibited from moving around the empty streets of Phnom Penh.

The Khmer Rouge leadership remained invisible. At a congress held on April 25, 1975, Sihanouk, who was still in China, was referred to as president of the FUNK and head of state. There was no mention of the Party or its ideology. And, in a decision designed to obfuscate, the new rulers were identified only as *angkar,* the Organization, while its leadership was described only as the Upper Organization (*angkar loeu*).

Sihanouk returned to Cambodia in late 1975, in time to see the promulgation of a new constitution. The document called for the collectivization of "all important means of production" and offered one constitutional right: the "right to work." It also described a People's Representative Assembly, which would meet once, and courts, which would never convene. There was still no mention of socialism or the Party or a head of state, an omission that did not augur well for the prince. Just six months later, the Khmer Rouge placed Sihanouk under palace arrest and forbade him to travel, make public statements, or receive visitors.[7]

By this time, the leadership of Democratic Kampuchea was unquestionably in the hands of Saloth Sar, known to his colleagues as Pol Pot, or Brother Number One, and Nuon Chea, who, as Brother Number Two, was responsible for Party organizations and for helping Pol Pot oversee the national security police. Three veteran regional leaders—Sao Phim (East), Ruoh Nheam (Northwest), and Ta Mok (Southwest)—and three French-educated Cambodians—Ieng Sary (foreign minister), Son Sen (defense minister), and Khieu Samphan (head of state)—rounded out the leadership. Two of Samphan's former colleagues in Sihanouk's more leftist cabinets, Hou Youn and Hu Nim, were out of favor. Hou Youn was killed in April 1975, Hu Nim less than two years later.

LIFE UNDER THE KHMER ROUGE

In the countryside, Cambodians heard from fervent young cadres the nature of the task ahead of them. Haing Ngor, a medical student who successfully hid his identity and survived to write of his experiences (and to star in the film *The Killing Fields*), described the speech that greeted his arrival in the cooperative. "We have won the revolution but the war still goes on!" a cadre exclaimed. "Now we are in a new phase of struggle. We warn you that it will not be easy. We must maintain a mentality of struggling against all obstacles. If Angkar says to break rocks, break rocks. If Angkar says to dig canals, you must dig canals. If Angkar says to farm, you must farm. Struggle against the elements! When there are obstacles, smash them. Only in this way can we liberate the country and liberate the people!"[8]

Nowadays the policies pursued by the Khmer Rouge are well known, from scholarly literature and from first-person accounts, such as that of Haing Ngor. At the time, though, they baffled Cambodians. Abolishing currency, markets, and privately owned goods, the regime took over the distribution of all food. Obsessed with uniformity and the eradication of "reactionary" culture, it defrocked Buddhist monks and sent them to work in the fields, forbade all religious rites, destroyed and desecrated pagodas, and burned or shredded books. Cambodians, with the exception of Khmer Rouge cadres and soldiers, worked in the fields through the daylight hours and, in parts of the country, much longer. Cooperatives ate together. Evenings, spent in the communal dining halls, were taken up with political education, self-criticism, and criticism of others. Life was structured and regulated down to the smallest detail, including the length of one's hair. The Khmer Rouge frequently separated men from women and organized mass forced marriages for single people as well as for the ever-increasing number of widows and widowers. Children often lived separately and were encouraged to spy on and betray their parents. The only family bonds actually encouraged by the Khmer Rouge were bonds of guilt; to be related to the former bourgeoisie and civil servants, whom the regime designated "class enemies," was to be suspect.

Where had these policies come from? Although the basic notions of Marxism-Leninism absorbed by Pol Pot and the other Khmer Rouge leaders in France provided the foundation for the Cambodian revolution, many of the policies of Democratic Kampuchea relied on more specific and more radical inspirations. Stalin's Soviet Union and Mao's People's Republic of China had engaged in continual purges and killings of those with real or imagined links to foreign states. Both had also experimented with rapid collectivization, a legacy echoed by the Khmer Rouge, who called their agricultural policy a "Great Leap Forward." The Chinese Cultural Revolution promoted a hatred of intellectuals and the bourgeoisie and took the old revolutionary precept of "red" over "expert" to new levels. (The Khmer Rouge emulated this model by killing off professionals and permitting those with supposedly pure ideological stances, including children, to serve as doctors and nurses.) North Korea had established a precedent for the Khmer Rouge's isolation and extreme self-reliance. And from the Vietnamese revolution, Democratic Kampuchea borrowed its political and administrative structure, some of the collectivization policies of the 1950s, and the distinction between "old" and "new" people.[9]

But the "struggle against the elements" was failing. By 1977 almost all Cambodians were suffering from malnutrition. The rice that the newly "self-sufficient" Cambodians produced disappeared, trucked away to meet unrealistic production goals and to feed the leadership or the army. Some of it was exported to China in exchange for aid and Chinese advisors. The rice that remained in sight was eaten mostly by local Khmer Rouge cadres and by the peasants, who were now known as the "old people." Most of the former urban residents, the new people, consumed riceless gruel. Every object, including wild edible plants and fruit, was considered communal property. Private vegetable gardens and livestock were strictly prohibited. Secretly, a few new people bought food with the gold and valuables they had stashed away, but such transactions were dangerous. Most Cambodians who survived Democratic Kampuchea recall meals of insects, scorpions, and vermin nabbed surreptitiously in the rice fields. They also remember the diseases that thrived in these conditions: diarrhea, dysentery, typhoid, and, especially in the northwest, malaria. In many places, there was little or no real medicine.

Few complaints were voiced. Not only were direct appeals for better treatment cause for execution; so, too, was the expression of discontent. Indoctrinated children listened carefully to conversations, even among family members. "Angkar has a thousand eyes, like a pineapple," it was said. Silence did not guarantee survival. Executions occurred almost randomly, inspired by the slightest suspicion of disobedience or of bourgeois background. Khmer Rouge cadres killed with impunity. "He had a sharp eye for mistakes," recalls Someth May, another survivor who wrote of his experiences, of one young cadre. "A boy from the Old People stepped on some paddy by mistake. Comrade Thol beckoned him away. A woman, also from the Old People, broke a sickle. Comrade Thol observed the incident. She never came back."[10] Killings occurred out of sight. Later, villagers would sometimes find the bodies dumped unceremoniously in the fields and forests.

The Khmer Rouge considered foreignness of any kind a threat and set out to create a pure Kampuchean revolutionary worker-peasant. The revolution forbade use of foreign languages or the practice of "foreign cultures," including those of Cambodia's minority groups. Particularly vulnerable were the ethnic Vietnamese, who were murdered or chased into Vietnam. Other minorities, subject to the same cultural nihilism, saw their traditions obliterated. Khmer Rouge cadres executed Muslim Cham religious leaders, destroyed mosques, and forced the Cham to wear Khmer peasant clothes, shave their beards, and take "Khmer" names. The revolution also targeted the Chinese and Sino-Khmer because of their role in Cambodia's private economy. To the Khmer Rouge, Chinese ethnicity became practically synonymous with a bourgeois class background.

After the initial wave of killings came a lull, which was followed by spasms of violence. In 1976, with Sihanouk "retired," the Khmer Rouge began purging intellectuals, many of whom had returned from overseas to serve the revolution. The regime also intensified its class warfare, killing family members of people associated with the old regime and formerly rich peasants serving in the Khmer Rouge army. Economic failings only exacerbated suspicions. The leadership, seeking to explain disappointing harvests, reasoned that bad cadres and insufficiently vigorous revolutionary organizations were to blame. By 1978 anyone without a proper class background—anyone who had not been extremely poor—was suspect, including Party members. Eventually, top Party leaders, including several cabinet members, fell victim to the rages of the revolution.

REGIONALISM AND DISINTEGRATION

The central leadership attempted to monopolize power from Phnom Penh. Information and goods moved between the capital and the regional zones, but rarely between zones. This hub-and-spoke system proved to be extremely inefficient, impeding what the Khmer Rouge claimed to want most, the integration of its various regions into a seamless cooperative system. It was also counterproductive in that it undermined the leadership's efforts to ensure centralized control. Without any influence from other provinces and in the absence of any local bureaucracies or indeed of decent communications with Phnom Penh, the individual zone secretaries rose to positions of unprecedented regional power. In the end, the Party had only one way to control events in the countryside: the removal and execution of the zone secretaries and the appointment of new leadership.

While disparities in conditions among the various zones are the subject of ongoing debate, a few generalizations are possible. In the North and Northwest, Cambodians lived under especially unbending and violent cadres who often forced new people to build villages in inhospitable and malaria-infested jungles. In the Southwest, the zone secretary, Ta Mok, demonstrated particular enthusiasm for collectivization and purging of class enemies. The Eastern Zone, from which many of the future leaders of the PRK defected in 1977 and 1978, has, not surprisingly, generated the most intense debates among academics and politicians. Home to somewhat more experienced cadres and a large rural population (which helped cushion the dislocations of urban evacuation), the Eastern Zone offered better living conditions, relatively speaking. On the other hand, collectivization, the prohibition on private property, and class warfare all occurred. The actual extent to which Eastern Zone leaders were complicitous in implementing Democratic Kampuchea's more heinous policies, including the killing of minorities and the use of violence and terror, continues to generate controversy.[11]

By the middle of 1976, Pol Pot and others in the leadership were looking at the various zones and sensing betrayal. First in the North and then in the Northwest, zone cadres were removed, killed, and replaced, usually by cadres from Ta Mok's Southwestern Zone. The purges culminated, however, in the East, where zone secretary Sao Phim, a veteran revolutionary and a member of the Party's Standing Committee, came to personify Pol Pot's fears of conspiracies and Vietnamese agents. Despite having been close to Pol Pot in the 1950s and 1960s and having participated in attacks on ethnic Vietnamese and in the purges of the Hanoi-trained Cambodian communists, Phim was suspected of ties to the Vietnamese and of disloyalty to the central leadership. Implicated by various cadres during interrogation sessions as early as July 1976, Sao Phim was initially too powerful to arrest.

While Phim remained in control of the Eastern Zone, zone commanders and Party figures were being called to Phnom Penh for "meetings." There they discovered the dark center of the Khmer Rouge security apparatus, the infamous interrogation center, Tuol Sleng. Inside the innocuous three-story building that was once a high school, the regime detained suspected enemies, tortured them, extracted elaborate and often fantastical confessions, and eventually murdered them. By 1977 the number of prisoners had soared to more than six thousand. An increasing number of the detainees were Party members, including those accused of being too closely linked to Vietnam and to the revolution's internationalist past. Suspicions of pro-Vietnamese sentiments began to dominate the logic of the purges and the interrogations.[12]

As Democratic Kampuchea engaged Vietnamese troops in a series of border skirmishes, losses suffered by Eastern Zone troops provided, for Pol Pot, final confirmation of the zone's betrayal. After several years of low-level tension, fighting had escalated in mid and late 1977. Following Cambodian massacres of Vietnamese civilians, Vietnam retaliated with an extended incursion into the southeastern province of Svay Rieng. Announcing a "temporary" severing of diplomatic relations until the "aggressor forces" had withdrawn, Phnom Penh actively searched for scapegoats. The Vietnamese withdrawal in January 1978 did not repair Cambodian-Vietnamese relations, nor did it ease the Party Center's suspicions of the Eastern Zone. In March 1978, Sao Phim called together zone leaders, warning them to be careful. Within a month, however, approximately four hundred Eastern Zone cadres were imprisoned at Tuol Sleng.[13]

In May troops under the command of Pol Pot and Nuon Chea fought with Eastern Zone units, forcing top Eastern Zone cadres to flee to the jungle. Among them were Heng Samrin, whose own brother had been "invited" to

Phnom Penh and had not returned, and Chea Sim. Sao Phim himself refused to defect. Called by Pol Pot for a "meeting" in Phnom Penh, he shot himself.

Ordinary Cambodians living in the Eastern Zone, accused of having "Cambodian bodies and Vietnamese minds," also suffered. The Khmer Rouge evacuated thousands of people west across the Mekong, farther away from the Vietnamese, and massacred tens of thousands.

TO THE EAST

Far away from the volatile border, in Hanoi, Beijing, Moscow, and Washington, geopolitical forces were leading to war. For years, Vietnam's relations with China had been deteriorating, first as a result of the Sino-Soviet split and Hanoi's eventual acceptance of Soviet assistance and influence and then from ideological divergences brought about by the Chinese Cultural Revolution. After the reunification of Vietnam, China complained about Hanoi's treatment of its ethnic Chinese both in northern Vietnam, where they were suspected of loyalties to the PRC, and in the south, where the new communist leaders sought to dismantle Chinese-dominated commercial networks. China's alliance with a now hostile Democratic Kampuchea was the final straw. From Hanoi's perspective, the border clashes with Khmer Rouge forces represented an imperialist threat from China.

The fate of Cambodia was being decided in Washington as well. As Nayan Chanda explains in *Brother Enemy: The War After the War,* the United States faced a fundamental diplomatic dilemma: whether to recognize China or Vietnam first. The conclusion—the United States chose to recognize Beijing—solidified Vietnam's alliance with the Soviet Union and convinced Hanoi that its problems with Democratic Kampuchea (and, by extension, China) required a military solution. The pieces were in place for a decade-long geopolitical stand-off pitting China, the United States, the West, and the capitalist countries of the Association of Southeast Asian Nations (ASEAN) against Vietnam, the Soviet Union, and the Eastern Bloc.

The Vietnamese planned their invasion for December 1978, when the terrain would be dry and when Cambodia's rice harvest would be available to an invading army. To construct a Cambodian front for the invasion, Vietnamese authorities set about mobilizing Cambodian refugees who had fled to Vietnam after 1975. Equally important to the future of Cambodia, Vietnamese officials started working with Cambodian communists to establish a post–Khmer Rouge regime.

Cambodian revolutionaries who had lived in Hanoi since 1954 emerged from years of political oblivion. After the betrayal of the early 1970s, when they joined the revolution only to be purged and chased back to Vietnam, the Hanoi veterans were eager to rally against the Khmer Rouge. Among their leaders was Pen Sovan, a gaunt, sunken-cheeked, austere cadre who had arrived in Hanoi as a teenager, received his education in Vietnamese Communist Party and army schools, and risen to the rank of major in the Vietnamese army. Sovan, who is fluent in communist jargon and who speaks crisply and authoritatively even in informal settings, worked for the FUNK's radio service in the early 1970s. Like his Hanoi-based comrades, he also made an attempt to rejoin the Cambodian revolution. The trip was apparently deeply dispiriting, although he still describes it in largely ideological terms, explaining that the Khmer Rouge "were practicing Maoism and a cultural revolution." In January 1974, Sovan returned to Vietnam, where he monitored developments in Democratic Kampuchea. Embittered, he contacted other Hanoi veterans in an attempt to form a new anti–Khmer Rouge communist movement. He also sought support from Vietnamese authorities but found them reluctant, at least initially, to disrupt Hanoi's outwardly cordial relations with Democratic Kampuchea.[14]

In 1977, as the first group of Khmer Rouge cadres and soldiers defected from the Eastern Zone, Sovan and his colleagues were assigned to debrief their compatriots. Among the first arrivals was Hun Sen, a military officer from Region 21 of the Eastern Zone whose involvement in recent border clashes led to his immediate arrest by Vietnamese authorities. Employing veteran Cambodian revolutionaries from Hanoi as translators, Vietnamese military officers interrogated Hun Sen for several months before releasing him.[15]

Only in 1978, as Vietnamese-Cambodian relations were collapsing, did Hanoi's alternative to Democratic Kampuchea take shape. In February the Vietnamese Communist Party, led by Le Duc Tho and Party secretary Le Duan, began planning the reestablishment of a pro-Vietnamese Cambodian communist party. To rally Cambodians around a new regime and to justify an invasion, the Vietnamese cobbled together the Kampuchean United Front for National Salvation (the Front) out of the refugees who had fled Democratic Kampuchea and the Eastern Zone defectors. The turning point came in May, when intensifying purges finally prompted Eastern Zone forces to rebel. According to diplomatic correspondence with the Soviets, the Vietnamese had originally hoped to recruit Sao Phim himself. Phim's death, however, required that they consider a number of other defectors, some of whom were more enthusiastic than others at the prospect of Vietnamese patronage.[16]

In August and September 1978 various figures in the Eastern Zone uprising, all of them future leaders of the PRK, met to assess their options. Heng Samrin, division commander and deputy chief of staff of Military Region 203, was the most senior of the military officers. Two other members of the military region's staff committee also joined the discussions: Pol Sareun, who ran an ammunition factory, and Mao Phok, a logistics officer. Politically, the highest ranking was the deputy secretary of Region 21, Uk Bunchheuan.

According to Bunchheuan, he, Mao Phok, and three other Eastern Zone cadres had already been to Ho Chi Minh City to negotiate an agreement with the Vietnamese authorities, meeting both Le Duc Tho and General Le Duc Anh, the man who eventually coordinated the invasion of Cambodia. Having asked the Vietnamese for material assistance, Bunchheuan and the others returned to Cambodia unconvinced of the bargain they were being offered. Their hesitation prompted the Vietnamese to turn to Heng Samrin, who was pulled out of Cambodia by Vietnamese troops in October, and to Chea Sim, a Party leader from the Eastern Zone's Region 20 who crossed the border on his own, along with three hundred Eastern Zone people. By the time Uk Bunchheuan and Mao Phok arrived in Vietnam, it was too late for them to curry favor with the Vietnamese. Neither assumed leadership positions in the Front.[17]

By November all of the future leaders of the PRK were in place. Pen Sovan considered himself to be the leader of the Front and, within the bounds of Vietnamese scrutiny, wielded a great deal of influence over the promotion of Hanoi veterans. Sovan also understood, or at least claims now to have understood, the strategic importance of staying in the background while the Khmer Rouge defectors (and, to a lesser extent, noncommunist refugees) were promoted in an effort to appeal to the "forces within the country." Heng Samrin thus became the public face of the Front as Sovan worked behind the scenes to ensure his eventual appointment as secretary of the newly reconstituted Kampuchean People's Revolutionary Party. (Ros Samay, Pen Sovan's cousin and fellow Hanoi veteran, was the Front's less visible secretary-general.) Most of the other Khmer Rouge defectors who became Front members and PRK leaders were selected from Chea Sim's broad network of Eastern Zone Party and security cadres.[18]

On November 30, 1978, Vietnamese authorities arranged for the Front to meet in Ho Chi Minh City to officially designate its leadership. At six the following morning, Heng Samrin, Chea Sim, Hun Sen, Ros Samay, the other

Front members, and hundreds of refugees climbed into Vietnamese vehicles and headed for the border. Twenty-four hours later, they were in Snoul, in Kratie province, where they announced their intention to overthrow the "reactionary Pol Pot gang."[19]

THE FIGHT FOR HISTORY

Everyone was constructing history. The speech that Heng Samrin gave that day at Snoul, in which he extolled the "glorious victory of April 17, 1975," was an attempt to mythologize the revolution and to blame its implosion on the actions, taken "a few days after liberation," by "the reactionary Pol Pot–Ieng Sary gang and their families." The Vietnamese and the Cambodians who had taken refuge in Hanoi in 1954 were looking further back into Cambodia's revolutionary past, seeking to re-create a period when the two countries' communist movements were more united. They were also attempting to cover up current and historical Vietnamese domination.

Heng Samrin's speech at Snoul also signified the beginning of Cambodians' efforts to retrieve their own history. The promise that they could "return to their old native land" and enjoy "freedom of thought, association, and religion" was an invitation to look back, past the "glorious victory of April 17, 1975," to an easier time. Sihanouk, the monarchy, the period before the war, even the French, created a sense of nostalgia among Cambodians. Now Samrin was telling them that they could return to the past.

The river could finally reverse course. Where, then, was it headed? Cambodia's new leaders and their Vietnamese patrons were pointing in one general direction—toward an imagined history of revolutionary glory. Most Cambodians, however, were imagining a past that included neither communism nor Vietnamese occupation. They were also focused on rebuilding their lives and on surviving the challenges of Cambodia's new era. Less interested in the nation's destiny than in the safety and welfare of themselves and their families, they made their own choices and, in so doing, routed Cambodia's historical waters in a million different directions.

Part Two **The Second Revolution, 1979–1981**

Chapter 3 Blood Debts:

Transition and Continuity

Under a New Regime

Someth May, making his way across northwestern Cambodia in the immediate aftermath of the Vietnamese invasion, witnessed a gruesome drama. "A young woman ran across my path, pursued by a group of men armed with *parangs,* axes and sticks. She ran quite a good distance before she fell to the ground, screaming. 'No, it wasn't me, I was told to do it. Please don't kill me. Please don't kill me. . . .' It took them five seconds to kill her and cut off her head. The man with the axe held it up by the hair. He yelled into her face, 'I've got you now. Why did you starve me and my children? I'll get your husband next.' He took the head with him and went off with the group."[1]

Accounts from other Cambodians recall similar spontaneous acts of violence. Loung Ung, who was a child at the time, describes pushing her way to the middle of a crowd where a Khmer Rouge soldier, tied to a chair, sat helplessly. Loung recalls several women emerging from the crowd to accuse the prisoner and, ultimately, to kill him.

"'I know this Khmer Rouge soldier!' [one] screams. In her left hand she holds a nine-inch knife. It is copper brown, rusty, and dull. 'He was the Khmer Rouge soldier in my village. He killed my husband and baby! I will avenge them!'

"Another woman then pushes her way out of the crowd. 'I also know him. He killed my children and grandchildren. Now I am alone in this world.' The second woman is older, perhaps sixty or seventy. She is thin and wears black clothes. In her hand she holds a hammer, its wooden handle worn and splintered.

"The old woman's hands shake as she raises the hammer high above her head and brings it crashing down into the prisoner's skull."[2]

Officially at least, neither the Vietnamese nor the Front promoted revenge. "Enemy troops who are captured or who surrender," read the Front's pronouncements, "are considered children of the people who were deceived or forced to work for the enemy. All acts of reprisal against prisoners of war and those who have given themselves up, such as torture or humiliation, are strictly prohibited." Cambodian Front soldiers, dispatched to the countryside along with the Vietnamese troops, were given orders to protect the Khmer Rouge, as, presumably, were the Vietnamese. During the fighting, however, there was little opportunity, much less inclination, to stop the killings. Vietnamese soldiers, anxious not to incur the rage of Cambodians, sometimes surrendered Khmer Rouge prisoners to vengeful mobs.[3]

MOVEMENTS

Cambodians scattered in all directions. Thousands went with the Khmer Rouge to Thailand, most of them abducted at gunpoint. The rest seized the food stocks of the Khmer Rouge cooperatives, eating their fill for the first time in years. With little thought to the future, they slaughtered pigs, cows, and buffaloes. Then they grabbed pots and pans, farm tools, wagons, and any remaining animals, and took to the road.

With Vietnamese planes overhead and Vietnamese and Khmer Rouge troops waging bloody ground battles, Cambodians zigzagged across the countryside looking for lost relatives, seeking to return to their homes, or simply trying to avoid the fighting. Once the Vietnamese army had overtaken them and the fear of rearguard Khmer Rouge attacks had subsided, most found themselves relatively free to move around, assured by Front soldiers and representatives that they could "return to their places of birth." Traveling mostly by foot, individuals, families, and whole communities followed dusty roads and longneglected highways, frequently retracing the paths of the Khmer Rouge deportations. There was little or no food available; survival depended on whatever rice, fruit, or animals had been taken from the cooperatives and whatever was found along the road. The journeys often lasted for months. Cambodians crossed paths, met, and moved on. Loung Ung describes a moment in the confusion: "The small red gravel roads are swarmed body to body with people in their black shirts and pants. The traffic does not stop and continues to move, everybody dragging their feet slower and slower. Those who cannot move any farther sit at the side of the road, some curl up in a fetal position and sleep. Others leave the traffic to scavenge for fruits and berries a few meters from the road, all the time keeping themselves close to the traffic."[4]

The upheavals caused by this migration left strange demographic holes throughout the country. In parts of the east, the Khmer Rouge had evacuated entire communities in anticipation of the Vietnamese invasion, leaving villages deserted. Elsewhere, particularly in the northwest, fighting forced people to flee. In the months after liberation, it is likely that as many as half the villages in the country were empty.[5]

Searching for food or transportation or looking to return to their homes, tens of thousands of Cambodians headed toward provincial capitals. Initially, refugees found shelter in empty, dilapidated houses not occupied by Vietnamese soldiers and officials. In some parts of the country, particularly in Battambang, however, Vietnamese troops evicted squatters and ordered them to return to the countryside, prompting Cambodians to construct makeshift camps on the outskirts of the towns. Throughout the summer of 1979, as food shortages pulled tens of thousands of rural Khmers out of their villages and toward the towns (where they hoped that rice might be distributed), the camps grew. Attempting to stem the exodus from the countryside, the regime began requiring travel documents and authorizing Vietnamese and Cambodian soldiers to stop and search travelers and squatters. These directions had little effect on the flow of hungry people toward the towns.[6]

The biggest collection of internal refugees could be found around Phnom Penh, which had been blocked off by Vietnamese soldiers since the taking of the city on January 7. Just outside the barricades, Cambodians built shanties or camped in the open air, searched for family and friends, exchanged rumors about the new regime and the Vietnamese, and engaged, for the first time in almost four years, in relatively open trading of rice, consumer goods, and gold. The camps also proved useful to the Front as it searched for educated Cambodians to work in the regime's skeletal administration. For several months Front members, most of whom had just been plucked from the crowds themselves, identified former lawyers, bankers, and professors, as well as old colleagues, classmates, and friends. Assigned positions in ministries, the new civil servants were permitted to leave the camps and move into the empty houses of the city.[7]

A few less well educated people were also finding their way into Phnom Penh. Those who had connections to people working in the government or who could afford to bribe an official secured jobs in factories and ministries. The need for manual laborers also required that the regime permit a few Cambodians to take work in the city as waiters, construction workers, cyclo (bicycle rickshaw) drivers, porters, servants, bicycle repairmen, mechanics, and small-scale merchants. Still, hundreds, if not thousands, had to sneak into the city, often at night, to obtain household goods, firewood, or whatever else they needed to survive. Some were retrieving family belongings; most simply looted unoccupied houses. "In principle, [entering the city] was prohibited," wrote Y Phandara, a former diplomat who was briefly in Phnom Penh but who soon fled the country, "but surveillance was not tight and every day I saw people making off with all kinds of objects that they'd retrieved. Some returned to see their old houses and to leave messages on the walls for family members from whom they'd been separated."[8]

These trespasses provoked fear of enemy infiltration among Vietnamese officials and the new Cambodian leadership. In June 1979 the regime stepped up security around the city, increasing the number of checkpoints and rerouting those who intended to pass through Phnom Penh on their way to their native villages. Access remained strictly prohibited, and in September and October an estimated hundred thousand people were still living on the outskirts of the city.[9]

FLIGHT TO THAILAND

The world's image of Cambodia in 1979, conveyed largely by television, was of the tens of thousands of refugees who crossed into Thailand in the first few months of the year. Their stories, told and retold in refugee camps (and, later, in France, the United States, and Australia), offer a look into the agonizing choices that compelled Cambodians to choose exile.

At first, the refugees were simply searching for food or attempting to avoid the fighting. Former residents of Phnom Penh who had been evacuated by the Khmer Rouge to the northwest were closer to Thailand than to home. For them, the border offered better prospects than a long and potentially treacherous journey into the Cambodian interior.

Many refugees had grown tired of living in Cambodia. Educated people and former city dwellers, some of whom had family or friends in the West, could imagine a life overseas and had some reason to believe that Thailand would not be their final destination. Others wished to escape a country they associated with war, hunger, and brutality. The arrival of the Vietnamese seemed to confirm a dismal future. Despite a general understanding that the Vietnamese had liberated Cambodia from the Khmer Rouge, the mere thought of foreign occupation inspired fear and pessimism. Accounts of the behavior of the Vietnamese soldiers varied. Some refugees described the soldiers as helpful or indifferent. Others experienced hostility from the Vietnamese who, in their efforts to identify Khmer Rouge soldiers, interrogated Cambodians with varying degrees of patience. There were accounts of cruelty and of looting by the Vietnamese, none of which can be conclusively documented. In any case, almost all refugees considered an extended Vietnamese presence a threat to the nation.

The policies and the rhetoric of the new regime persuaded many Cambodians to flee. The relief and elation that had accompanied the invasion was a product of an expectation, promoted by the Front itself, that Cambodia was returning to something like its prerevolutionary self. But as former townspeople fled the rural collectives and arrived at the barricades that surrounded Phnom Penh and the provincial capitals, they saw a continuation of the antiurban policies of the Khmer Rouge. The Front's vague promise that they would be permitted to enter the towns "when the overall situation in the whole country permits" was not reassuring given the Khmer Rouge's past deceptions. Red flags, revolutionary slogans, and communist jargon also reappeared, carrying terrifying associations.[10]

The dilemma for the regime was that the Cambodians whose defections it could afford least were the ones most likely to flee. Newly installed civil servants readily understood the extent of Vietnamese control. Educated Cambodians, whom the regime desperately needed to staff the bureaucracy, were likely to interpret the promotion of uneducated Cambodian communists as a continuation of the policies of the Khmer Rouge. The arrival in Thailand of these people dealt a sharp blow to the regime as it struggled to project an image of stability and inclusiveness.[11]

Refugees attempting to cross the border into Thailand faced threats of extortion and violence from newly formed village militias, bandit groups, the Khmer Rouge, and, as they arrived at the border, Thai soldiers. In June 1979 the Thai army forced tens of thousands of refugees back into Cambodia, literally pushing them over the cliffs of northeast Thailand and into the minefields of

Cambodia's remote Preah Vihear province. Those who survived were met by Vietnamese troops, who escorted them south. Because of their decision to flee and their brief stay in Thailand, the Vietnamese viewed them as a potential security threat.[12]

Despite these risks, emigration intensified, reaching its peak in the second half of 1979. By then, the main catalyst was food. With rice stocks in Cambodia shrinking, Cambodians became aware of humanitarian assistance being distributed at the border. In some parts of Cambodia this push-and-pull effect led to the complete breakdown of local authority. Newly appointed village chiefs not only left for Thailand but permitted entire villages to flee. Village militias abandoned defense tasks, sometimes to form bandit groups to steal rice. A web of paths and trails soon twisted through the forests along the Thai-Cambodian border as refugees and smugglers attempted to avoid bandits, the Khmer Rouge, and Vietnamese and Thai soldiers. By the end of October 1979 three hundred thousand Cambodians were living along the border.[13]

THE WORLD TAKES SIDES

For the next twelve years, this exodus divided not only Cambodians but, politically at least, much of the world. In regional capitals and in Beijing, Washington, and Moscow, the Cambodia conflict was seen and often referred to as a "proxy" for Cold War antagonism. Almost immediately, the dispute over Cambodia pitted Vietnam against Thailand, which in turn matched Moscow and the Eastern Bloc against China, the United States, and the capitalist countries of the Association of Southeast Asian Nations (ASEAN).[14]

The Khmer Rouge, after years of self-imposed isolation, now looked to the international community for diplomatic support while fashioning a message that blended anti-Vietnamese rhetoric with warnings of a global Soviet conspiracy. Cambodians, they asserted, were "seething with national and racial hatred against the Vietnamese aggressors, Soviet international expansionists, and the Warsaw military pact." Hanoi, for its part, initially characterized Khmer Rouge accounts of an invasion as "slanderous" before settling into what would be a long pattern of hailing Cambodia's newfound independence.[15] As the editorial page in the Vietnamese Communist Party newspaper proclaimed on January 7, 1979, "Heroic Kampuchea has revived and entered a new era, the era of independence, freedom, and advance to socialism. The danger of fascist genocide has been eliminated. From now on, the Kampuchean people will forever be the absolute masters of their homeland and destiny."[16]

Within a week, the rest of the world had taken sides. On January 9, Soviet Party Secretary Leonid Brezhnev sent a letter to Heng Samrin applauding the "complete victory" of the Front and of "patriotic Kampucheans who have risen up to firmly struggle for their fatherland's freedom and independence. . . . This victory puts an end to the painful and dark days of the Kampuchean people under the domination of the reactionary dictators." The following day, the rest of the Eastern Bloc recognized the new regime in Phnom Penh: the People's Republic of Kampuchea.[17]

On the other side, China accused Vietnam of attempting to annex Cambodia and "set up an 'Indochina Federation' under its control." According to Beijing, Vietnam's invasion of Cambodia also furthered "the Soviet drive for hegemony in Asia and the Far East." In Bangkok, ASEAN foreign ministers met to "strongly deplore the armed intervention against the independence, sovereignty and territorial integrity of Kampuchea." The United States accused Vietnam of being "guilty of aggression."[18]

As the U.N. Security Council met, on January 11, to discuss a draft resolution from China condemning the Vietnamese invasion, Sihanouk reappeared. The Khmer Rouge leadership having chosen to disappear (the press reported that Ieng Sary and his family had been airlifted from Thailand to China, while Pol Pot's whereabouts remained unknown), the prince became the public face of Cambodia. After several years of palace arrest in Phnom Penh, he arrived in New York blasting both the internal policies of Democratic Kampuchea and the "criminal aggression" of Vietnam. Supporting China's resolution, the prince explained that it was "no longer a question of political differences or human rights, but a question of whether Cambodia shall disappear from the map, to become a province of the Vietnamese imperialists and their Soviet masters." The resolution, supported by the United States, France, and Britain, was vetoed by the Soviet Union.[19]

U.S. policy makers saw Cambodia primarily in terms of America's antagonism toward Vietnam and its hopes that warming relations with China could help stem Vietnamese and Soviet expansion in Asia. Although the United States did not directly assist the Khmer Rouge resistance, it condemned neither China's resuscitation of its forces nor China's February invasion of northern Vietnam, an incursion intended as retaliation for the occupation of Cambodia. The U.S. State Department also walked a fine line in its criticism of the Khmer Rouge, carefully avoiding the word "genocide" in order to finesse the judicial and diplomatic implications of the Genocide Convention. The United States attempted to isolate Vietnam and Cambodia as well. Throughout the summer of 1979, American diplomats lobbied other countries, charities, international aid organizations, the International Monetary Fund, and the World Bank to suspend aid to both countries.[20]

In September the diplomatic game came to a head. Critical of both sides, Prince Sihanouk insisted that Cambodia's seat in international organizations remain vacant, a position that prevailed at the summit of the Nonaligned Movement in Havana. Two weeks later, however, at the U.N. General Assembly, China, ASEAN, the United States, and their allies adopted a recommendation from the credentials committee granting the Cambodian U.N. seat to the exiled government of Democratic Kampuchea. The vote was 71–35, with 34 abstaining.[21]

On the ground, the West's interaction with Cambodia was limited to the border camps into which Cambodian refugees were herded. The first camps, established under the watchful eye of the Thai military in 1979–80, served as military bases for the Khmer Rouge leadership and for the Cambodians they conscripted. Elsewhere, though, entire new cities were emerging out of refugee camps controlled by noncommunist resistance forces.

Recipients of Western assistance and hosts to both aid workers and a revolving corps of journalists and politicians, camps such as Khao I Dang—population 120,000—became political and military bases for the resistance. The noncommunist camps also developed close ties with Cambodian communities in the West, serving for many as a launching point for a new life overseas and, as such, the preferred destination for thousands of Cambodian defectors yet to come.[22]

Back in Phnom Penh, Vietnamese and Cambodian officials had settled upon words and phrases with which to describe the regime, its enemies, and, ultimately, its legitimacy. The PRK stood in opposition to all "expansionist genocidal Pol Potists," the "reactionary clique," and the "Chinese expansionists." The resistance, both outside and within the country, became the "enemy" or "Pol Pot." As the bellicose lyrics of the PRK's new national anthem made clear, the regime would find purpose and unity in its struggles against a monolithic, genocidal, and as-yet-unidentified opponent.

> The people of Kampuchea make up a resolute force,
>   determined to destroy the enemy.
> We draw our strength from our unity and stand ready
>   to shed our blood for victory.
> The Kampuchean army marches valiantly forward, setting
>   adversity at defiance,

To destroy the despots who threaten our people
with extermination
And bring prosperity to the heroic Kampuchean people!
The Kampuchean people, fighting stubbornly will make
the enemy pay his debt of blood!
The blood-red flag with the towers is raised and
will lead the nation to happiness and prosperity.[23]

THE "HENG SAMRIN REGIME"

Amidst the diplomatic posturing and revolutionary rhetoric, the PRK was taking shape. Guided by Vietnamese military and civilian advisors, the regime established itself along typical communist lines. Although the first pronouncements from Phnom Penh described only the state apparatus—the Kampuchean People's Revolutionary Council (KPRC)—power in the PRK, to the extent that it was wielded by Cambodians, was in the hands of an as-yet-unnamed communist party (generally referred to in internal documents simply as "the Party"). The Party leadership, whose members were eventually organized as a Politburo, were, for the moment, grouped into a small Central Committee. An assortment of Khmer Rouge defectors and Hanoi-trained revolutionaries, they were known collectively, by external critics who preferred not to recognize the PRK and by Cambodians accustomed to personifying power, as the Heng Samrin regime.

Heng Samrin, the former Khmer Rouge commander whom the Vietnamese selected to be president and head of state, was virtually unknown to Cambodians. An Eastern Zone defector, Samrin was referred to by the Voice of Democratic Kampuchea as a "cattle rustler" and a "cheap Vietnamese lackey who sold himself to the Le Duan–Pham Van Dong clique [Hanoi]." Whatever his exploits (or, conversely, his treacheries) in resisting Pol Pot forces, Heng Samrin wielded little political power. Despite his lengthy revolutionary career (Samrin joined the revolution as a courier in the last 1950s), his prominence was due in part to his older brother, Heng Sam Huoy, another Eastern Zone officer, who was executed by the Khmer Rouge in May 1978. Uneducated and yet rigidly Marxist in outlook, Samrin was politically and ideologically reliable. His background as a former Khmer Rouge cadre also allowed Hanoi to present the new regime as being led by "forces inside the country," as opposed to Hanoi-trained communists. Later, it became apparent that Samrin was dependent on Vietnamese support and that he lacked the political skills necessary to develop a personal power base.[24]

If any Cambodian might have objected to Heng Samrin's appointment, it would have been Pen Sovan. After spending his entire adult life in Hanoi and much of the late 1970s immersed in frustrated political scheming, Sovan harbored a compulsive, driving ambition. His acceptance of Heng Samrin as president was predicated on an understanding that Samrin was basically guileless, experienced in military matters but politically weak. As Sovan explains now, Heng Samrin "was incompetent, but I would teach him." Pen Sovan's intelligence, energy, apparent ideological conformity, and, most of all, his long association with Vietnam rendered him more than suitable from the perspective of Hanoi. Behind the scenes, Vietnamese officials attempted to bolster Sovan's power, organizing a Party congress in Ho Chi Minh City at which he was elected first Party secretary. Publicly, however, the Vietnamese promoted Heng Samrin and the Front while Sovan's role as Party secretary and the existence of the Party itself remained a secret. Government reports referred to Pen Sovan by his state titles: vice president and minister of defense.[25]

Among the former Khmer Rouge cadres, Minister of the Interior Chea Sim wielded the most power. Sim, who joined the revolution in the late 1940s, initially as an organizer among Cambodian monks, was an old-fashioned Cambodian politician who understood how to nurture a patronage system and how to inspire loyalty in his followers. His tendency to sit quietly in official meetings as other leaders expounded on policy, ideology, and legislation masked his actual authority. Behind the scenes, he ran the Ministry of the Interior and those parts of the country where he was most influential as he had his former Khmer Rouge district. Valued by the Vietnamese for his ability to co-opt Khmer Rouge defectors, Chea Sim recruited large numbers of Eastern Zone cadres and quickly constructed a personal power base. His status as minister of the interior also served to counterbalance Pen Sovan's authority as minister of defense.[26]

Fourth in the Party hierarchy was Say Phouthang, the Hanoi veteran who returned to Cambodia in 1970 and later rebelled against the Khmer Rouge. Phouthang had spent the period of the Democratic Kampuchea regime in the southwestern province of Koh Kong or in Thailand itself. Fifty-four years old at the time of the Vietnamese invasion, Phouthang wasn't even in Phnom Penh in January 1979. Contacted through Vietnamese networks in Koh Kong by a Thai-speaking Vietnamese cadre, he arrived in the capital at the end of March.[27]

For the Vietnamese, Say Phouthang was a blessing. Isolated throughout the 1970s from his former Hanoi-based colleagues and the Khmer Rouge, he was the kind of solitary, autonomous revolutionary with whom the Vietnamese au-

thorities could develop a direct relationship unadulterated by factional intrigue. The fact that Phouthang was ethnic Thai also helped to assure the Vietnamese that he would not be subject to the kinds of ethnically motivated resentments from which Cambodian-Vietnamese relations had suffered for so
long. In this regard, Phouthang proved them right, neither demonstrating nor
engendering loyalties outside a few old comrades—fellow ethnic Thais from
Koh Kong. A committed communist, Say Phouthang became, in June 1979,
chair of the Party's powerful Central Organization Committee, a position
through which he was able to control appointments to the state and Party apparatuses while enforcing Party discipline. Unlike most of his colleagues, the
rather elusive Say Phouthang had no position in the government and no public
role for several years.[28]

The fifth man in the leadership, Bou Thang, also relied on Party positions
and regional influence, rather than a government ministry, for his personal
power. Thang, a member of the Tapuon minority from Cambodia's northeastern hills, left Hanoi in 1970 and rose in the ranks of the Khmer Rouge military
structure before taking refuge in Vietnam in 1973. After twenty-five years with
the Vietnamese Communist Party, he retained a deep appreciation for Cambodian, Vietnamese, and Laotian revolutionary history and joined the PRK's
power structure as chair of the Party's Central Education and Propaganda
Committee, through which he directed the regime's relentless political study
sessions. Respected by members of the isolated hill peoples and proficient in
several of their languages, Bou Thang was considered useful by the Vietnamese
in ensuring the loyalty of these minority groups.[29]

The youngest of the top leaders was Foreign Minister Hun Sen. Relatively
well educated for a former Khmer Rouge soldier, Hun Sen came from a large
family from Kampong Cham and had been sent to Phnom Penh for a high
school education. Enlisted into the revolutionary movement by a cousin in the
late 1960s, he served as a Khmer Rouge courier. After rising to the ranks of commander in the Eastern Zone military, he suffered a series of injuries, the most
serious being the loss of his left eye. Without anything like Chea Sim's power
base, it was his early arrival in Vietnam—in 1977—that gained him the trust of
Vietnamese authorities. Equally important, however, were personal qualities
that distinguished him from his colleagues. Completely unfamiliar with international affairs, he proved to be a quick learner. "He remembered things," explains a now-retired Hanoi-trained communist, "unlike Heng Samrin." Initially responsible only for the "Youth Movement," Hun Sen demonstrated
ambition, motivation, and, most of all, the verbal skills necessary for diplo-

macy. He proved an adept messenger for the regime, articulating Hanoi's position on Cambodian-Vietnamese relations and arguing on behalf of the PRK's international standing. In speech after speech he attacked the resistance and extolled solidarity with Vietnam. The appointment of Hun Sen, which close associates describe as an "experiment," proved to be one of Vietnam's most astute decisions.[30]

THE PARTY

In keeping with communist tradition, the Vietnamese constructed two separate bureaucracies around the Cambodian leadership: a Party structure and a state apparatus. The former was built around the Party Central Committee, the institution that is technically the central decision-making body but that is generally controlled by the members of the Politburo. Because there were initially so few Party cadres, however, the Central Committee consisted merely of the top leaders (there was no point in establishing a Politburo) and a set of committees that served as extensions of each leader's personal authority, including Say Phouthang's Central Organization Committee and Bou Thang's Central Education and Propaganda Committee. In an effort to consolidate control over the PRK's most sensitive political matters, the Vietnamese also established Party committees for internal security, national defense, and diplomacy—to be chaired by Chea Sim, Pen Sovan and Hun Sen—and granted direct control over these areas to the Party, as opposed to the state.[31]

The building of the Party posed unique problems for the PRK. Unlike most communist regimes, the PRK did not ride to power atop a sustained and coherent movement but was installed, abruptly, by an outside power. The Party, which considered itself the heir to Cambodia's revolutionary history, thus inherited next to nothing. At the outset, it had a mere two hundred cadres—the Hanoi veterans and former Khmer Rouge cadres who had participated in the 1978 uprising—many of whom were not Party members. No one else with revolutionary experience had yet demonstrated any opposition to the Khmer Rouge.[32]

In time the Cambodian leadership and its Vietnamese advisors sought to replicate the vast, ubiquitous structure of the Vietnamese Communist Party, establishing Party branches in every state institution, from ministries to local government offices, military units, schools, and hospitals. Initially, however, the lack of Party members forced the regime to rely on the next best thing: core groups (*krom snoul*). Like the Party branches, the core groups enforced Party discipline, encouraging members to discuss the "attitudes of the masses" and offer up self-criticisms and criticisms of others. The core groups were also testing grounds for Party membership and thus a means to expand the Party and increase its presence in the administration. Yet in April 1979, the Party had managed to field core groups in only a few central ministries and were desperately scouring the state administration, the Cambodian military, and the Front for acceptable cadres.[33]

Recruitment was proceeding so slowly in part because of the Party's obsession with political purity. In addition to the dutiful execution of Party orders, core group candidates were expected to have a "clear personal history." "If the personal history is not clear," one of the Party's April directives read, "a person may be mistakenly admitted into the group who comes from the ranks of the enemy or the bad elements or has been [the subject of] an accusation concerning his past that would prevent him from entering the core group or the Party." Three months later, as Say Phouthang took control of the Central Organization Committee, the directives grew more specific, excluding "secret agents and spies of all kinds, leaders in the apparatus of the [former] state authority at all levels from commune leaders up and military officers from the Sihanouk, Lon Nol, and Pol Pot–Ieng Sary periods." The exceptions were those who, like Heng Samrin and other former Eastern Zone cadres, had "risen up and struggled before the day of liberation and who surely walk with the revolution."[34]

Cambodians, most of whom were deeply disillusioned with communism, were suspicious of the Party. Even those who were tempted to join out of pure opportunism had reason to balk, aware that the Khmer Rouge had executed thousands of its own Party members. As a result of these misgivings and the restrictive core group qualifications, Party membership remained low, particularly outside Phnom Penh, where, in the summer of 1979, there were fewer than seven members per province. Seeking to correct this situation, the Party began inducting Cambodians who had previously belonged to the Vietnamese or Laotian Communist Party while accelerating the induction process for former Cambodian Party members who had rebelled prior to 1979. This policy, in effect, formalized the Party's general sense of historical continuity, linking the new regime to Indochina's communist past and to the Khmer Rouge revolution.[35]

THE STATE

The state apparatus, the KPRC, dominated by Hanoi veterans, reflected the influence of Pen Sovan as well as Hanoi's desire to work with predictable Vietnam-trained administrators. Other than President Heng Samrin, Minister of the Interior Chea Sim, Minister of Foreign Affairs Hun Sen, and, later, Minister of Agriculture Men Chhan, there were no former Khmer Rouge.[36] Regardless, the composition of the cabinet offered little indication of what was actually happening in the country in 1979. Without specific mandates, a functioning bureaucracy, or even, in most cases, buildings and furniture, the ministers could do little other than appoint a handful of staff and wait for outside assistance.

Communist revolutionaries tend, upon victory, to politicize and gradually restaff the bureaucracies of their predecessors. Both Democratic Kampuchea and the PRK were exceptions to this pattern, however—Democratic Kampuchea because it chose to eliminate and then do without a normal administration, the PRK because the Khmer Rouge left nothing behind. In the starkest physical terms, the lack of functioning ministries required that each minister and his staff scout the city for a proper physical site, negotiate with Vietnamese officials for each office building, and hire crews to clean up the long-abandoned buildings, collect the trash, and clip overgrown weeds and bushes. The tiny ministry staffs then went out in search of chairs, desks, pens, paper, typewriters, and other supplies. "We collected whatever old books were still around and brought them back to the Ministry in wheelbarrows," recalls Chan Ven, the minister of education. Re-creating each detail of a functioning administration was time consuming and constantly overshadowed by the regime's military, diplomatic, and economic crises.[37]

Once the bureaucracy began to function, Cambodian ministers and their Vietnamese advisors encountered confusion over the roles of the various ministries. The Khmer Rouge's extermination of civil servants had nearly erased a national memory of how government worked. With few experienced bureaucrats and with ministers who themselves had no administrative background, the civil service succumbed to the natural bureaucratic tendency to appropriate power and assume overlapping responsibilities. The administrative chaos frustrated those within the regime who understood the problem, and upset the Vietnamese. "Each central ministry should prepare drafts establishing its structure and work regime and send them to the higher level," one Vietnamese advisor instructed Heng Samrin in late December 1979, "because, so far, most act independently without [first receiving] any decision or circular from the [KPRC] to implement."[38]

To bring some clarity to the situation, the Vietnamese government sent teams of advisors from the central ministries of Hanoi, each responsible for duplicating Vietnamese administrative structures within their counterpart ministries in Phnom Penh. Under the control of Le Duc Tho and answerable to the Party leadership in Hanoi, these advisors formed a separate bureaucracy known as B68. They drafted the documents creating the KPRC and its ministries or else received them from Hanoi and arranged for their translation into Khmer. The most influential of these advisors was "Dao Duc Chinh," who worked at the KPRC instructing the Cambodians on how to run a central bureaucracy.[39]

The man to whom much of Chinh's advice was directed, Ung Phan, was a former Eastern Zone cadre who defected in 1977 alongside Hun Sen. Rewarded with the position of minister in charge of the KPRC (which later became the Council of Ministers), he oversaw the formation of the administration, the hiring of state cadres, and the distribution of salaries. Like many ordinary Cambodians, Ung Phan credited the Vietnamese with overthrowing the Khmer Rouge and permitting certain basic freedoms. "Our new regime," he exclaimed at one Party meeting, "is as different from the Pol Pot regime as the sky is from the earth." Within a few years, he would be grumbling about Vietnamese intentions in Cambodia, but for the time being, he kept his mouth shut. In contrast to his old comrade, the loquacious Hun Sen, Ung Phan was prone to impassive, sometimes intimidating silences. Although this guardedness may have helped him survive politically, it often inhibited his efficiency. In the early years of the PRK, questions related to staffing were directed to Phan, and, as his colleague at the KPRC, Meas Leas, complained, Ung Phan's personality deterred recruitment. "There are some problems with regard to the selection of people to come here to work which have not been resolved," Leas told the Party in early 1981. "People don't dare ask Comrade Ung Phan because he doesn't really answer right away but rather usually sits there quietly." Leas pleaded with Phan to "offer his views a little more quickly because remaining quiet and not answering makes people not dare to ask."[40]

Ung Phan notwithstanding, Cambodia's bureaucrats were eager to begin hiring. With all of Cambodia impoverished and with no salaried work outside the civil service, the priority of the ministers and their staffs was not policy or planning but the distribution of positions to family and friends. The ministries ballooned as ministers took on new staff members with regard neither to bureaucratic structure nor to Party scrutiny. The leadership soon became concerned. In June 1979, around the same time that the regime hardened its stance toward Cambodians attempting to enter Phnom Penh, the Party issued a circular asking ministries to report on the numbers of people they had hired. A few months later, it ordered an immediate freeze on hiring. According to the Party, unqualified cadres and staff and people who came to the ministry simply to eat would be removed and offered an allotment of rice so that they could "return to their village of birth and join in [agricultural] production or seek some other work so as to make a living." All new hiring would henceforth require an official request to the KPRC.[41]

The regime saw nepotism as a serious security risk. State officials, warned one Party document, were "selecting people according to their own sentiments and regionalism . . . such that there are increasing intervals of carelessness that allow bad people and enemies to enter the [state] offices and enterprises."[42] To control who entered the state apparatus, the Party ordered that every civil servant complete a "personal biography" (*bravat roup,* a phrase previously used by the Khmer Rouge), account for his or her whereabouts and activities since childhood, and list the names and backgrounds of family members and "close friends." Understandably, Cambodians demurred: they had survived the Khmer Rouge only because they had refused to respond to such inquiries. Many left whole sections blank. The most common response to questions about "close friends" was "none." Frustrated, the Party ordered ministers and Party secretaries to become more personally involved in the investigations. A directive issued in August 1979 stated, "When it is time to write [the biographies], it is necessary to go and help directly and to resolve, in a timely manner, any reluctance on the part of our brothers and sisters. [It is necessary] to stir them up and raise their level of consciousness and responsibility and demonstrate . . . loyalty to the Party, to the Front, and to the revolutionary state authority."[43]

As under the Khmer Rouge, the Party attempted to discern "loyalty" through a thorough examination of a candidate's background and relations. Ties to people associated with prerevolutionary regimes or to people who had fled to the border were grounds for suspicion and, frequently, rejection. "The examination of cadres' connections is important, as are investigations into social and family circles and examinations of the influence of these contacts on the cadres," read one 1980 decree.[44]

Uninterested in subjecting new employees (many of whom were family and friends) to vigorous political vetting, state officials frequently ignored these exhortations. Reporting to the Party in early 1981, Ung Phan complained that "the selection of people to enter the ministries [is made] without a clear understanding of their personal histories and is instead based only on requests from particular persons that they come work." According to Phan, the bureaucracy was growing uncontrollably because state officials were making "decisions to put people to work with a salary without any clear discussion as to how many will enter each organization."[45]

The Party expected that the Vietnamese would oversee hiring and instructed ministers to "invite Vietnamese advisors to participate and offer opinions at all ministerial meetings, including discussions on appointments." In effect, the Vietnamese were standing in for nonexistent Party branches. Meanwhile, the Party Central Organization Committee and its Vietnamese advisors pored over stacks of personal biographies, failing either to meet the state's needs or to keep up with the tendencies of officials to hand out positions. More than three years after the establishment of the PRK, ministers were still complaining that the Central Organization Committee's deliberate review process virtually forced them to search for cadres and staff on their own.[46]

THE PROVINCES

The Vietnamese were in a bind. Maintaining Vietnamese authority in the Cambodian countryside required working with the existing power structure, which in 1979 meant the Khmer Rouge, specifically the Eastern Zone defectors. Yet only a few months before, the Eastern Zone cadres had belonged to a rabidly anti-Vietnamese regime. Their PRK biographies may have described them as "having clearly understood the traitorous maneuvers and activities of the reactionary Pol Pot–Ieng Sary group," but the fact remained that they had fled to Vietnam only to avoid being purged. Nonetheless, Vietnamese authorities had ideological reasons for promoting former Khmer Rouge cadres. The cadres shared the Vietnamese authorities' communist leanings and revolutionary rhetoric. There was also a deep historical relationship between the two revolutions; after thirty years of fraternal anti-imperialist struggle, a few years of tension could be overlooked.[47]

Communists trained in Hanoi offered the best prospects for ideological conformity, but they were needed in the central government, and there were too few of them to send to the provinces. From a strategic point of view, the Hanoi veterans would not have served Vietnamese purposes in any case. Having gone into exile as young men, they had little understanding of what it took to wield power in the Cambodian countryside. The Hanoi communists also lacked actual connections with which to build a provincial administration. As one Party document explained, the Hanoi veterans, "whether they are well qualified or not, have all, generally speaking, studied for a long time. But their weakness is in their lack of actual experience inside the country."[48]

The backgrounds of the Hanoi veterans were, in fact, a liability in the provinces, where the regime's overriding strategic goal was to reassure and co-opt anti-Vietnamese Khmer Rouge cadres. As local power brokers and as the public face of the PRK, the Eastern Zone defectors were deemed vital to winning the war and consolidating power. They, the Party concluded, had "experienced military struggle, and whether they worked a lot or a little, they understood the situation within the country."[49]

Throughout the country, former Eastern Zone cadres became governors and provincial Party secretaries. While Vietnamese authorities were ultimately responsible for these appointments, in practice they sought the advice of the PRK's top leaders both when inquiring about the loyalty of individual cadres and when attempting to ensure that the leadership in Phnom Penh was invested in what was happening in the provinces. The Vietnamese authorities' primary liaison to the Eastern Zone defectors was Chea Sim. Promoted to the leadership precisely because of his broad network of former comrades, Sim promptly identified a range of relatives and close associates, assembling a large and loyal power base.[50]

The Vietnamese made sure to appoint a few local authorities close to other Cambodian leaders. In Say Phouthang's native Koh Kong province, an old comrade from the anti–Khmer Rouge uprising and a fellow ethnic Thai, Rong Keysan, became Party secretary and governor. In the southern port of Kampong Som, Hun Sen agreed to the appointment of his former Khmer Rouge superior Chum Hol. In Svay Rieng, Heng Samrin's older brother, Heng Samkai, took power. And, in the northeast, Bou Thang's years of military activity as well as his ethnic affinity to local people allowed him to take control over the appointment of local leaders.[51]

Hanoi veterans were appointed to positions of strategic importance, as in Phnom Penh, where Minister of Economics Mok Sokun became mayor. Following Sokun's death in April, another Hanoi-trained revolutionary, Minister of Propaganda Kaev Chenda, took charge of the city. Elsewhere, special crises required immediate assurances of loyalty: in Battambang, the fighting, the stream of refugees heading for Thailand, and the defection of the first governor, a former Eastern Zone cadre, required that a trusted Hanoi veteran, Lay Samon, step in. In the few provinces where previously noncommunist Cambodians (those who had fled to Vietnam and joined the Front) were selected as governors, they were overshadowed by more powerful provincial Party secretaries.[52]

Although the Vietnamese authorities had worked out a structure for local administrations—the People's Revolutionary Councils overseen by Party Committees—they had trouble identifying suitable Cambodians to staff them. After the Khmer Rouge defectors, the Vietnamese tended to prefer Cambodians who had been refugees in Vietnam or who spoke Vietnamese. The problem was that they found fewer Cambodians who met these qualifications the further down the administrative pyramid they went. There were tens of thousands of positions to fill and no obvious candidates. To complicate matters, there were almost no Vietnamese advisors below the district level to guide the appointment process and ensure the loyalty of newly designated officials.[53]

"GETTING THE MASSES TO BUILD STATE AUTHORITY"

The emergence of local leadership immediately after liberation was a chaotic, spontaneous, and often autonomous affair. In initial pronouncements, the Front urged the Cambodians to rise up, overthrow the Khmer Rouge, and form "people's self-management committees." Practically anyone could participate. "The people's self-management committee is elected by the people and composed of those who have suffered at the hands of the Pol Pot–Ieng Sary clique, those who have done meritorious services to the revolution, and patriarchs trusted by the villagers," Cambodians were told. Before long, people who had been village chiefs and civil servants during the Sihanouk and Lon Nol regimes emerged. There was no actual state to administer, but there were houses and land to redistribute, food to divide up, and countless other disputes to settle. Cambodians, eager to return to more familiar ways of doing things, found the judgments of these people, if not impeccable, then preferable to the existing chaos and certainly to the Khmer Rouge.[54]

For the first few months of 1979, the Vietnamese were too preoccupied with military matters to address issues of local leadership. Given the immediate choice between a power vacuum—into which the Khmer Rouge might reassert itself—and the relatively unthreatening authority of village and commune elders, the Vietnamese preferred the latter. The regime thus permitted a generally autonomous selection of local leaders, describing the process as the "people's movement" or "getting the masses to build state authority."[55]

Gradually, however, Vietnamese and Cambodian officials inserted themselves into the selection process. "In villages where there is not yet state authority," read a vaguely worded Party document, "examine the situation in the village and then come up with a plan to push the masses to select decent people of good character and sufficient qualifications to join the state." In practice, the regime's capacity to "push the masses" varied greatly. Although Vietnamese advisors were clearly in charge at the district level, there was no permanent Vietnamese presence in the communes and villages. Local "elections" were overseen by roving groups of Vietnamese and Cambodian authorities, including district-level officials, "Executive Teams" of Front representatives (responsible for "educating the masses"), and Cambodian soldiers. The selection process generally involved Cambodians raising their hands or applauding for leaders chosen from a preapproved slate.[56]

Where Vietnamese advisors and Cambodian officials were able to supervise the selection of local leaders, they were careful not to allow the administration to be dominated by former officials from the Lon Nol and Sihanouk regimes. (The mere presence of Vietnamese and Cambodian communists also deterred some of these officials from stepping forth as candidates.) Nonetheless, the Vietnamese did not wish, at such a delicate moment, to alienate the Cambodians by denying them their choice of leaders and thus did not entirely exclude prerevolutionary officials. The reemergence of these officials was seen as an indication that the horrors of Democratic Kampuchea were really over and that the PRK would protect the victims of the Khmer Rouge. Furthermore, the immediate goal of consolidating power required that the Vietnamese tolerate any local leadership that was recognized and respected by the Cambodians.[57]

REMOVING THE "REACTIONARIES"

The PRK's initial indulgence of prerevolutionary leaders was on a slow collision course with the regime's security concerns and its ideological biases. According to refugees at the Thai-Cambodian border, the purges began with the disarming of local militias which had been established—or had arisen spontaneously—in the wake of the invasion. The initial strategy having been to encourage Cambodians to defend themselves against Khmer Rouge counterattacks, Vietnamese soldiers had permitted anyone who was not Khmer Rouge to join. Village and commune militias had thus included prerevolutionary officials and even some Sihanouk and Lon Nol soldiers. Once the military threat from the Khmer Rouge had dissipated and the Vietnamese military occupation had grown stronger, however, it was possible to disband the militias.[58]

The regime was somewhat slower to reconfigure the composition of civilian leadership and used the first half of 1979 mainly to investigate the activities of local officials.[59] By March, judging from a broadcast report, Phnom Penh was already thoroughly disgusted. A number of local officials, it was announced,

were guilty of favoritism, materialism, laziness, and failure to communicate
with or obey superiors. Degenerates were apparently running the country.
"[Some] cadres and party members have become greedy and blinded by material wealth. They collect all kinds of property for their own use and for the use of
their families. Because of this pleasure-seeking abandonment, some have violated women, raping the daughters of the people." The broadcast also contained plenty of class resentment. "Many [officials] have shown a lack of spirit
in learning from the masses. They refuse to listen to the masses and even behave
like mandarins toward the masses. They mistreat the people, scorning them or
showing off their better positions and possessions to the people. . . . [In selecting other cadres] they do not make any effort to discover or enroll the children
of poor peasants, the children of cadres and those who helped the revolution. In
some areas, these people are just ignored or even rejected." The political consequences were dire. "All these shortcomings," concluded the broadcast, "may
cause the masses to revive the feudal system, which embraces the same acts of
hooliganism and debauchery committed by certain cadres. Therefore, they
produce the most evil consequences and exert an absolutely malignant influence on the Party, the revolution, and the people."[60]

The regime also had problems with the general population. The euphoria
and gratitude that had accompanied the Vietnamese liberation was quickly
eroding, in part because of the desperate conditions in the country but also because of Vietnamese control and communist ideology. In some parts of the
country, Cambodians launched demonstrations against foreign occupation.
Party documents described the problem in both political and military terms.
"In places where the enemy has provoked the people to rebel or demonstrate,
we should use political propaganda to make the people disperse. If there are organizers who are obstinate, we should use severe methods."[61]

By the spring, events on the border had influenced how the regime perceived
local leadership and how Cambodians, in turn, perceived the regime. Small
bands of resistance fighters led by or associated with former Lon Nol officials
had joined forces, forming a movement called the Khmer People's National
Liberation Front, or KPNLF.[62] Militarily insignificant, the KPNLF nonetheless represented a noncommunist alternative to the PRK and therefore a political threat. Facing defections, uprisings, and armed insurrection, the Party concluded that the appeal of the noncommunist resistance had contaminated local
leadership. "Now, apart from the defeated Pol Pot troops, there are many
groups and units of armed forces, including the reactionary Lon Nol, In Tam
[prime minister in 1973], and Sihanouk, who are conducting activities and co-

operating with each other in order to expand their war of espionage over a broader area. . . . Among these reactionary parties, especially among the nationalists and the Khmer Serei [noncommunist, or "Free Khmer"] Front, there are a large number of French, American, and Chinese spies, many of whom have taken the opportunity, while we are filling empty positions and are not paying attention, to infiltrate our state authority, the ministries, the offices, and military organizations at all levels."[63]

As the regime's anxieties mounted, qualifications for local leadership tightened. In contrast to the initial pronouncements of the Front, it was no longer sufficient to have suffered under the Khmer Rouge. "If we want to examine and consider a cadre correctly, we should rely on the principles of the working class," read one Party resolution. "Everyone experienced suffering and misfortune [under Pol Pot]. If we rely only on this, we will accidentally end up employing the cruel remnants of the destructive machine of the Lon Nol and Sihanouk era."[64] By July 1979, the leadership had decided to "clean out and remove the bad elements." According to Party documents, "Places where there are two-faced elements or bad elements who have infiltrated should be investigated carefully to see whether these elements are real reactionaries or whether the enemy has coerced or intimidated them. Check carefully and examine the views of these elements. If they are reactionary types, they should be arrested. Those who have been coerced should be educated and replaced by 'new people.' This change in personnel is necessary."[65]

For several months, while the regime attempted to implement this policy, many villages, communes, and districts actually had multiple leaders, some chosen locally, others by Party, Front, or Vietnamese officials. Although many "reactionary" local leaders were eventually arrested, the Party feared that if it failed to involve the provincial authorities in the arrests, the regime's actions would appear arbitrary and would further alienate the local population. Unclear cases, warned the Party, "cause confusion among the masses."[66]

By the end of the year, Phnom Penh had lost patience with the "masses building the state authority." Party documents complained that Cambodians "insert people [into the state] in a disorganized fashion, taking those who used to be in repressive apparatuses, such as military officers, [those in] security networks, spies, and many authorities from the old state apparatus of Sihanouk and Lon Nol." But "even though they really were oppressed by Pol Pot and Ieng Sary, we mustn't use them in our revolutionary organizations."[67]

Purging local leadership on the basis of background created political havoc. Given the absence of records, suspicions of "reactionary" backgrounds were unprovable. "There are people who, out of vindictiveness, trade accusations back and forth," read one Party report. Unsure how to resolve all the unsubstantiated charges, the Party offered unhelpful instructions: "We must be careful to listen to the views of the masses, but not 'follow the tails of the masses.'"[68]

Many Cambodians resisted the purges out of a desire to choose their own leadership, a generalized suspicion of the new regime, or their resentment of the Vietnamese occupation. Some local officials refused to participate—"bad elements," the Party later called them, "who were afraid and didn't dare push (*bomphos*) the masses because they feared that the masses would suddenly push back and denounce them." Phnom Penh's disagreements with these local officials frequently centered around the role of the Vietnamese. The Party line was that the Cambodian people had selected their new leadership "autonomously under the guidance of the Executive Teams or our armed forces" and that "the armed forces of [our Vietnamese] friends" had participated "only by helpfully guiding us." The "bad elements," on the other hand, "looked for ways to obstruct and falsely claimed that the commune and district state authority just established had been built by the Vietnamese."[69]

The Party concluded that those who questioned its description of the Vietnamese role were inherently disloyal: "This assistance from our [Vietnamese] friends is absolutely important and necessary, so these words are false accusations by the bad people and the traitors whom we must struggle to wipe out (*komchat*)."[70] This kind of logic soon created mutual mistrust between the Party and much of the population. In 1979 many Cambodians agreed that the Vietnamese presence was "absolutely important and necessary." But by characterizing those who resented Vietnamese political domination as "traitors," the Party committed itself to a permanent campaign, not just against the regime's opponents but against the very perception that Cambodia was occupied.

The removal of prerevolutionary leaders created a power vacuum which the Party hoped to fill with "core people," Cambodians who had suffered under the Khmer Rouge but had not been associated with the Sihanouk or Lon Nol regimes. In theory, the core people would be identified by the "mass organizations"—classic communist groups, such as the Women's Association and the Youth Association, established under the Front—and then "built" through political education, a process that required that they be removed from their villages and communes and sent for several months of training in Vietnam. Throughout the latter half of 1979, the Party and its Vietnamese advisors inspected the biographies of prospective state cadres, identifying six qualifications.[71] Obedience was paramount: "First, loyalty to serve the revolution unconditionally. Second, activities in accordance with all domestic and international edicts of the Party, the government, and the Front, including respecting the Party's revolutionary disciplinary organizations. Third, having close relations with the masses and being loved, esteemed, and trusted by the masses. Fourth, living cleanly and appropriately. Fifth, having competence and personally guaranteeing the work of the Party, the government, and the Front. And sixth, must have clear personal history."[72]

From the beginning, the prospect of relying solely on the core people posed ideological and pragmatic problems. Not only did they lack previous communist training, but, having served neither the prerevolutionary regimes nor the Khmer Rouge, they offered no administrative experience.[73] The core people also lacked political connections to the PRK's provincial leadership and thus failed to contribute to the regime's efforts to consolidate power. For strategic and ideological reasons, the Vietnamese had appointed former Khmer Rouge cadres as provincial Party secretaries and governors. Those officials, looking to build patronage networks with family members, friends, and former comrades, naturally appointed other Khmer Rouge veterans to positions in the districts, communes, and villages. Far from offending the Vietnamese, these attempts to establish personal fiefdoms made the PRK's provincial apparatus more cohesive and therefore stronger. The presence of former comrades in positions of power reassured members of the Khmer Rouge resistance that they could safely surrender and would even be rewarded for throwing their support behind the PRK. With a civil war to fight, the co-optation of the remnants of Democratic Kampuchea became the regime's overriding strategic goal, one that would guide the Party for the next twenty years. It would also require the appointment, throughout Cambodia's state apparatus, of former Khmer Rouge cadres. The problem was that the entire justification for the PRK's existence was to serve as a clean break from Cambodia's cruel past.

THE TRIAL

The leaders of Cambodia's second revolution had a lot of explaining to do. Cambodians were horrified by what had been done to Cambodia in the name of communism, and now thousands were fleeing to Thailand in part because of the unsettling reappearance of communist slogans and iconography. What was required, quickly, was carefully constructed language by which the People's Republic of Kampuchea could distinguish its ideology from that of Democratic Kampuchea. The PRK's propaganda thus described the Khmer Rouge as

Maoist rather than communist, sparing Marxism-Leninism the taint of genocidal associations. It also sought to distinguish between Khmer Rouge leaders responsible for the crimes of Democratic Kampuchea and the thousands of Khmer Rouge cadres and soldiers whom the regime hoped to co-opt. The culprits were therefore "Pol Pot," "Pol Pot–Ieng Sary," "Pol Pot–Ieng Sary–Khieu Samphan," and their "cliques." The failure to mention other top Khmer Rouge leaders (Nuon Chea, for instance) suggested that they, too, might, at some point, be co-opted.

The PRK's efforts to gain international recognition had also turned into a debate about the legacy of the Khmer Rouge. By portraying Democratic Kampuchea as genocidal, Hanoi and Phnom Penh hoped to undermine diplomatic and military support for the resistance. The Khmer Rouge leadership, of course, defended its record. The disagreement was quantitative as well as qualitative. In April, Pen Sovan declared that three million Cambodians had died during the Pol Pot regime. Two months later, Ieng Sary questioned this figure, arguing, "You have to lack some common sense to believe that three million people—almost half the population—have been killed." Asked how many were killed, Sary responded, "Several thousand," adding that he hoped to "forget the past to start afresh." It was in this context that the Vietnamese and Cambodian leadership decided that they had to prove their point. In July the PRK's official news agency, SPK, began releasing pictures of mass graves, piles of bones and skulls, and bloody bodies chained to beds in Tuol Sleng prison. Phnom Penh was also preparing a grand gesture, a trial that would convince the world of Pol Pot's crimes and promote the legitimacy of the PRK.[74]

It was first necessary to reassure those in the Khmer Rouge resistance that they were not on trial. In April the regime issued guidelines on the legal status of Khmer Rouge cadres and soldiers, the "Circular on Punishment for Those Who Committed Offenses Against the People During the Pol Pot–Ieng Sary Regime." Despite references to crime and justice, the circular merely formalized the Front's policy of co-optation. The fate of Khmer Rouge cadres "who killed people directly or who signed orders to have people killed" depended entirely on the defendants' attitude toward the new regime and on their value to the ongoing military campaign. Those unfortunate enough to already have been arrested and detained were of little use to the regime and were stuck with a prison sentence of between three and five years, perhaps longer if they failed to become "honest persons." Khmer Rouge cadres and soldiers not yet in detention were more valuable and could earn a reduced sentence through such "achievements for the revolution" as convincing resistance fighters to surrender or reporting their whereabouts to the military. Those who were not yet under the control of the state authority were luckiest of all. "Soldiers and cadres of Pol Pot–Ieng Sary who come join the local revolutionary state authority, as individuals, units, or groups, and apologize to the people for their past offenses shall, after careful examination and education to make them [politically] aware, be permitted to return to work and make a living with their families as normal people." The real crime, then, was not so much the past killings as continued "obstinate" resistance to the new regime, an offense that would be "punished severely."[75]

The accusation, launched by Khmer Rouge radio, that the trial was being organized by the "Vietnamese–Le Duan–Pham Van Dong clique" was essentially correct. A document dated May 10, 1979, describes in a cursory manner the high-level Vietnamese deliberations that preceded the trial: "After the exchange of opinions and the agreement of the fraternal leaders of Cambodia, the Central Committee of the Vietnamese Communist Party has decided to create an Executive Team for a Cambodian court in order to help Cambodia convene a trial to sentence the Pol Pot–Ieng Sary clique." The team, which consisted of a number of Vietnamese officials with legal experience, was headed by Tran Huu Duc, a seventy-five-year-old member of the Central Committee known mostly for his background in economics.[76]

As the indictment took shape, the organizers of the trial decided to drop two of the initial charges—"betraying the revolution and fatherland" and "creating war by invading Vietnam"—which would have drawn attention to the communist ideology of the PRK and to the Vietnamese occupation. Instead, they limited the indictment to the crime of "genocide," a charge that included the evacuation of the towns; forced labor and the killing of civilians; the purging of certain communist cadres ("intellectuals," those with connections to Vietnam, and those who had operated in the Eastern Zone); the abolition of religion and the extermination of religious leaders; the killing of ethnic minorities; the "sabotage" of the economy; and torture. Notwithstanding the Khmer Rouge's claim that the trial was "part of [Vietnam's] trick to shift the responsibility for their widely known and glaringly monumental crimes onto the shoulders of Democratic Kampuchea," almost all Cambodians could agree that the Khmer Rouge had grossly mistreated the civilian population. The suffering that occurred under Democratic Kampuchea also provided the Vietnamese with a moral justification for their invasion and occupation of Cambodia.[77]

By May the organizers of the trial had begun to collect evidence of these crimes, prepare witnesses, and draft documents, including reports, prepared testimony, and the verdict. The plan was to have finished these tasks by the end of June 1979 so that sympathetic lawyers from other countries could visit Cambodia in July and lend legitimacy to the proceedings. It was also necessary to create a venue for the trial. There were no courts in Cambodia, nor had the regime established a Ministry of Justice. Instead, as befits a show trial, the proceedings would be run by officials from the Ministry of Propaganda, with Vietnamese advisors to the ministry serving as advisors for the trial. The minister himself, Kaev Chenda, acted as president of the court.[78]

Chenda was one of the PRK's earliest public faces. Along with fellow Hanoi-trained communists Pen Sovan and Ros Samay, he had helped explain the horrors of the Khmer Rouge to the Soviet Union and Eastern Europe while assuring them that Marxism-Leninism was still the answer to Cambodia's suffering. "Comrade Pen Sovan was the one who led us," he told East German filmmakers in 1980 as he clutched oversize pictures of both Marx and Lenin. Chenda was also a spokesman for the Front's policy of co-optation. At a July press conference at which he distributed the law establishing the tribunal, he explained that while those "who served in the repressive machinery of the Pol Pot–Ieng Sary clique" will have to "pay many blood debts to the people," they would be judged less severely than their leaders "to give them a chance to reform." "At the same time," he continued, "the people's power continues its policy of leniency towards all those who are sincerely repentant and gives appropriate rewards to those who have contributed to the revolution."[79]

Chenda was something of an intellectual and had even written a Marxist-Leninist political novel, *Happiness in the Family of Travelers,* during his exile in Hanoi. Known for his affinity with other educated Cambodians, Chenda staffed the court accordingly. Among the other judges was a thirty-eight-year-old jurist named Chhour Leang Huot, who had posed as an illiterate bookseller in Kampong Cham during the Khmer Rouge period and had survived the purges of the east only because of a late relocation to Kampong Thom, west of the Mekong. Animated and excitable, Chhour Leang Huot had offered himself to the new regime with few reservations and was serving in the Ministry of Propaganda with Chenda when he was selected as a judge. Besides Huot, the judicial panel included a former educator, a pediatrician, a former classical dance instructor, and several former Khmer Rouge cadres.[80]

The opposing sides were represented by three men with very different backgrounds. The prosecutor, a forty-nine-year-old veteran revolutionary named Mat Ly, had been a top Khmer Rouge cadre and vice president of Democratic

Kampuchea's nonfunctioning National Assembly. On the other side were two men posing as defense attorneys: Yos Por, a Hanoi-trained veteran cadre, and Dith Munty, a former jurist. Serious, restrained, and discreet, Munty had survived the Khmer Rouge by posing as a pharmacy employee, hiding his real profession even from a former medical student whom he met in the fields and eventually married. After the overthrow of the Khmer Rouge, Munty had been tempted to flee the country. "I was concerned about the Vietnamese," he explains now, "so I decided to stay and see what would happen." Dith Munty was working at the Ministry of Propaganda when he was recruited to participate in the trial. Not surprisingly, he was reluctant to defend Khmer Rouge leaders, whom he blamed for the deaths of some thirty-eight family members. He was therefore relieved to learn that he would not be required to claim Pol Pot's and Ieng Sary's innocence, but rather to raise the culpability of the "hegemonist Beijing reactionaries." Nor did his role as defense attorney preclude Munty from testifying as a trial witness.[81]

In the days before the trial, Vietnamese authorities made elaborate preparations for teams of foreign journalists and other observers, driving them in from Ho Chi Minh City and renovating a Phnom Penh hotel for their comfort. An American lawyer who had been invited to testify by Vietnamese lawyers with whom he had been in contact during the Vietnam War recalled that his "initial reaction upon arriving in Phnom Penh was to wonder why anyone was bothering to hold a criminal trial, when so much needed to be done to restore normal life."[82]

The whole event, which began on August 15, lasted four days. The American lawyer describes the scene: "Around the auditorium where the trial was held, an overflow audience milled, anxious to talk with anyone who would listen about what they and their families had suffered under the Khmer Rouge. Security in Phnom Penh was uncertain, as the Khmer Rouge still operated in many parts of the country. Along with other foreign participants, I traveled each day to Chakdomuk Hall, the venue of the trial, in a military-style convoy, with armed vehicles at the head and rear."[83]

At the trial, witnesses read "investigative reports" written by surviving intellectuals like Minister of Education Chan Ven, a former teacher, and Vandy Kaon, the sociologist. Witnesses—surviving intellectuals, peasants, former Buddhist monks, and ethnic Vietnamese—testified to their own experiences; many did so in tears. There were also "confessions" from three "criminal figures" (low-level Khmer Rouge cadres who had repented) and visits to the "crime scene" at Tuol Sleng prison. The morning of the 19th, the prosecutor and defense attorneys presented their final arguments. That afternoon the judgment was read: more than three million Cambodians "were killed or otherwise succumbed because of torture or the poor conditions of life under the Pol Pot–Ieng Sary regime." Pol Pot and Ieng Sary were found guilty on all charges, including genocide, and were sentenced to death in absentia.[84]

The role of the foreign lawyers was mainly political. Representatives of socialist countries or jurists personally sympathetic to the Indochinese revolutionary struggle, they came from Syria, Cuba, India, Japan, Laos, Algeria, Vietnam, the Soviet Union, and the United States. Their assignments varied. Mohammed Hikmet Turkmanee of Syria acted as counsel for the plaintiffs in the concurrent civil action. John Quigley, the American who had been invited by Vietnamese lawyers, testified to the commission of genocide by Pol Pot and Ieng Sary. Mostly the foreign lawyers offered a veneer of international legitimacy through their presence and participation. Their testimony, which provided some of the trial's most heated revolutionary rhetoric, was also intended to place the verdict squarely in the context of the Cold War. Francisco Varona de Estrade, vice president of the Cuban People's Supreme Tribunal and representative of the Cuban Association of Lawyers, complained of the Khmer Rouge's "betrayal of their people, of their comrades, of the liberation movement of the oppressed people and of the Marxist-Leninist principles they claimed to profess." Another American, Hope Stevens of the National Conference of Black Lawyers of the United States and Canada, blamed "the manipulators of world imperialism, the profiteers of neo-colonialism, the fascist philosophers, the hegemonists, who are supporting Zionism, racism, apartheid and reactionary regimes in the world," and the "false socialist leaders of fascist China." After stressing the importance of "due process of law" and "presumption of innocence," Stevens concluded, "It is now clear to all that Pol Pot and Ieng Sary were criminally insane monsters."[85]

The regime had succeeded in formulating a verdict that was part historical truth and part political strategy. The "Pol Pot–Ieng Sary clique" was characterized as genocidal, and the crimes of Democratic Kampuchea were described as having arisen not from radical communism but from "fascist methods" and "extremely reactionary" policies. The verdict also cited China's ties to Democratic Kampuchea, implicitly criticizing Beijing's ongoing military and diplomatic support for the Khmer Rouge resistance. Overseas, the PRK hoped to use the trial to discredit the Khmer Rouge and its patrons. (At the United Nations, where Democratic Kampuchea occupied Cambodia's seat, the Vietnamese representative delivered a copy of the judgment to the secretary-general for distribution.) Domestically, the trial helped the PRK define its enemies while reassuring the population. All strata of society, including surviving intellectuals, were now classified as victims of Pol Pot, an implicit promise that they would no longer face extermination and that their contributions to the new regime were welcome. The trial also served to describe the suffering of the purged Eastern Zone cadres, a matter of particular importance to the former Khmer Rouge cadres in the PRK leadership. Though not suggesting that Pol Pot's crimes had not occurred in the east, the verdict absolved individual cadres from personal responsibility.[86]

BLOOD DEBTS

By coming up with sentences only for Pol Pot and Ieng Sary, the trial concealed a debate within the Party over the role of former Khmer Rouge cadres in the new regime. Party insiders recall a clear division between the Hanoi veterans, led by Pen Sovan and Ros Samay, and the former Eastern Zone Khmer Rouge cadres. The Hanoi veterans, whose only personal experience with the Khmer Rouge had been the purges that met them on their return from Vietnam in the early 1970s, distrusted many of the former cadres of Democratic Kampuchea (D.K.) and considered their inclusion in the PRK state and Party apparatus as potentially dangerous. These concerns are expressed vividly in a Party document, apparently from 1980, that was intended for the signature of Pen Sovan. The opposite view, that of Eastern Zone defectors, who naturally favored their former D.K. comrades, is revealed in an equally vehement document from July 1979, unsigned but attributed to the Party Central Committee.[87]

On some issues, including the purging of former Lon Nol and Sihanouk officials, the Party leadership was united. The documents do reveal, however, a preference on the part of the Hanoi veterans for the core people. Having spent their lives away from Cambodia, Pen Sovan and his colleagues empathized with the new recruits, characterizing them as "cadres who have just sprouted up from the revolutionary movement of the masses following liberation, who were oppressed and suffered terribly and have a lot of anger against the old regime and are working hard at implementing the duties of the new revolution."[88]

Sympathy for the core people was matched by a suspicion of former Khmer Rouge cadres. While acknowledging the recent defectors' military experience and their understanding of the "actual situation in the country," the Hanoi veterans doubted their loyalty and their ability to work with the Vietnamese. "The attitudes of many [former D.K.] cadres is still vague, which creates problems for the nation and for international solidarity because of the long-term absorption of [Khmer Rouge] political education and the attitudes of Pol Pot–Ieng Sary and because up to now they have not studied much [from us]."[89] By contrast, the document associated with the Eastern Zone defectors insisted that "although there are a few people of this kind who are not good, a definite majority are good people, so we should straighten them out in order that they can become good cadres of the Party."[90]

The main point of disagreement was the culpability—blood debts—of former Khmer Rouge cadres and what to do about them. The perspective of the Hanoi faction was clear: "We cannot use [cadres with blood debts] in the apparatus of the state authority or in the committees of the mass organizations." To Pen Sovan and the other Hanoi veterans, it mattered little when the former Khmer Rouge cadres had defected. Those who were "only removed following liberation" were held in contempt by the people, they said. "The masses hate them and have a lot of anger because it was just yesterday that [these cadres] were forces oppressing the masses, and they can't just snap back and become revolutionaries."

Those who had defected before the invasion, which included the former Eastern Zone cadres in the PRK leadership, were not much better: "Among cadres, Party members, and the masses who rose up and struggled, there are some who have blood debts, who killed with their own hands or issued direct orders to kill cadres and people or who made lists of cadres, Party members, and the masses and reported them to the higher level to be killed. Cadres from the security sector all have blood debts. The political program of the Party has clearly indicated that none of these people with blood debts should be inserted into the Party committees and ministries. It is especially important that the Party clearly examine each person, consider whether they committed heavy offenses or light offenses, and punish them according to appropriate regulations."[91]

As for the political ramifications of appointing former Khmer Rouge with blood debts, the Hanoi group feared the worst. "If we keep these cadres in the Party and state leadership at all levels and in important ministries and state offices, the masses will be suspicious and will not believe in the leadership of the Party. This would scar the relationship between the Party and the masses. They will lose hope and not implement the goals and duties put forth by the Party. The Party has always considered its relationship with the masses as its constant livelihood. If the Party moves too far from the masses, it will have no strength and, at a certain stage, will be destroyed. The Party can become popular only if it has a close relationship with the masses and the masses trust the Party. The lesson, so far, of the Pol Pot–Ieng Sary reactionaries is that they couldn't get the people's support and so were defeated."[92]

The document associated with the Eastern Zone defectors expresses an entirely different perspective. From their point of view, Democratic Kampuchea was a morally confusing place where good people sometimes killed. "Examining and considering [the issue of blood debts] is extremely complicated because under Pol Pot there were some people who acted directly and some who acted from a distance, some people with a lot of blood debts and some with a few, some people who were compelled to do things and some who did them of their own accord. There are some other people who truly have a blood debt but were not moved by malice."[93]

The Eastern Zone defectors also insisted that Khmer Rouge cadres could be redeemed, regardless of what they had done. "Because their families were mercilessly killed by Pol Pot, some people have blood debts, but in the end, Pol Pot harmed them, and they rose up and opposed the Pol Pot–Ieng Sary clique and produced achievements for the revolution. . . . Therefore, we cannot speak generally of 'blood debts.'"[94]

Even the Eastern Zone defectors acknowledged how Cambodians felt about many of their comrades. Their solution, however, was not to disqualify cadres with blood debts from leadership positions but to transfer them to localities where their constituents would not recognize them or to sectors "where there isn't so much contact with the people." This policy was directed at cadres who had participated in the 1978 rebellion, and was designed "to protect cadres and their families from revenge, to not allow the enemy to cast doubt on the purity of state authority, and to avoid criticism from the masses, which could have a bad effect on trust in the revolution."[95]

Although the debate within the leadership was never formally resolved, the PRK was extremely reluctant to remove former Khmer Rouge cadres from positions of responsibility. Their power in the countryside and the strategic importance of co-opting the resistance required that Phnom Penh act cautiously. "In proceeding," read the Hanoi faction's document, "we must conduct examinations carefully. If it is not done appropriately, it will cause the cadres to panic."[96] In fact, these cadres, once in power, were almost never removed. The Party feared their defection back to the Khmer Rouge. More important, the investigations were conducted by local officials who were themselves mostly former Khmer Rouge officials, and were directed by Chea Sim, minister of the interior (and former D.K. district chief).[97]

Throughout Cambodia, former Khmer Rouge cadres remained in power, working alongside Hanoi veterans and newly recruited core people with no previous revolutionary experience. According to the document associated with the Hanoi faction, the cadres "torment[ed] each other." The Hanoi veterans were "not yet convinced of the positions and attitudes" of the Khmer Rouge defectors, whereas the Khmer Rouge defectors didn't trust the Hanoi veterans and considered them "inexperienced and unrealistic." Both groups "look[ed] down on and discriminate[d] against" the new recruits, whom they considered "unrevolutionary" and who, in turn, were suspicious and fearful of the former Khmer Rouge cadres. Concerned that rancor was undermining the stability of the regime, the Party warned that "whether cadres unite or divide determines whether the revolution prevails or is defeated." Internal solidarity, the leadership concluded, was the key to the survival of the PRK. "Cambodia's previous revolutionary experience was that the reactionary clique of Pol Pot–Ieng Sary constantly divided cadres and made them commit offenses against each other, even killing each other, which led to the defeat of the revolution. This is the painful and pitiful lesson of the Cambodian revolution."[98]

THE FRONT

The institution tasked with holding the revolution together was the Kampuchean United Front for National Salvation. Having promised to unite "all patriotic forces regardless of political and religious tendencies," the Front initially set forth the ideal of a liberal and pluralistic country.[99] Soon, however, it offered the sort of inclusion espoused throughout the communist world. Under the PRK, all components of Cambodian society would be mobilized and organized under the Front and controlled by the Communist Party. The principle was a familiar one, employed not only by the NLF and, later, the Socialist Republic of Vietnam but by Cambodian and Vietnamese communists in the 1950s and by Sihanouk during the time of the Sangkum Reastr Niyum. The most recent and troubling example of a united front was Sihanouk's alliance with the Khmer Rouge, the FUNK, whose promises of inclusion ended in purges and executions.

Nonetheless, after the Khmer Rouge's attempts to eradicate all vestiges of Cambodian diversity, the Front's relative tolerance constituted true liberation. As Cambodians traveled around the country in 1979, they sought to regain the social, economic, and cultural traditions that had previously defined them, their communities, and their families. They practiced Buddhism and Islam, resumed fishing, small-scale commerce, and other familiar trades, spoke Chinese and Vietnamese, and otherwise asserted their ethnic identities. The Front, which was responsible for rallying the country around the new regime and against the Khmer Rouge, generated goodwill simply by indulging Cambodians in their return to these prerevolutionary practices. Its members "educated" Cambodians on the evils of "Pol Pot" and conducted surveys of the death toll, a task intended to reassure Cambodians and to counter Khmer Rouge claims that only twenty to thirty thousand people had died during the D.K. regime. Many of the Front's earliest recruits were educated Cambodians with noncommunist pasts who could articulate the PRK's message of change. Despite their suspicions of the communist, Vietnamese-dominated regime, Front members generally found the Front's work rewarding and even cathartic.

Within a year, the Front had evolved into a bureaucracy, complete with central authorities, local branches, and units in every political, economic, and social institution in the country. In keeping with Vietnamese and Cambodian communist tradition, there were mass organizations, including a Women's Movement, a Youth Movement, and a National Salvation Trade Union, which would act as bridges between the Party and the "masses" and serve as training grounds for future Party members and state cadres. In theory, the mass organizations would also represent ordinary Cambodians in their dealings with the state and Party. In the end, however, they turned out to be weak partners in local governance and rarely dared to report, much less oppose, the abuses committed by local authorities. In time, representatives of the mass organizations came to feel used by the leadership, forced to implement some of the regime's most unpopular policies, such as conscripting soldiers, without adequate compensation or recognition.[100]

The Front was expected to channel Cambodians' newly discovered freedoms and ensure that certain traditions—reverence for the monarchy, animosity between Khmer and Vietnamese—did not reappear. The Party also directed the Front to control the Buddhist clergy and the educated, two groups that were historically noncommunist. "We should pay close attention and train and use them to build the nation appropriately and truly," read one Party document. "But among these people are a small number who are still under the strong influence of Sihanouk, including those [loyal to] other reactionaries—In Tam, Lon Nol, and, from before, Son Ngoc Thanh—who have established reactionary parties. So in selecting and using [educated persons and monks], we should maintain the maximum of caution and not permit bad elements to sneak in."[101]

RELIGION

In the months following the overthrow of the Khmer Rouge, the regime's decision to permit Cambodians to practice Buddhism inspired both goodwill and support. Most Cambodians found comfort in the resumption of traditional rituals, as well as some spiritual peace in the midst of devastating personal losses. The chaos of the moment also permitted the almost immediate reemergence of a clergy. Spontaneously, men who had been monks prior to the revolution or who saw the religious life as the answer to the emotional and material void left behind by the Khmer Rouge began donning the maroon and saffron robes of the monkhood. The regime found these developments disconcerting. Cambodians were ordaining themselves, the Front recalled later, "in accordance with their own wishes; people just followed what they saw as their own needs. . . . These ordinations were confused and in accordance with inappropriate conditions."[102] The leadership feared, accurately perhaps, that newly ordained monks might "take advantage [of the situation] and use Buddhism and the beliefs of the people to go and conduct activities to destroy the principles of the pure revolution or to propagate and divide national solidarity."[103]

The Party attempted to bring Cambodia's religious revival under control. On the one hand, it presented monks in positions of leadership, most notably the Venerable Tep Vong, a forty-nine-year-old former refugee in Vietnam, who served as a founding member of the Front and, later, as vice president of the National Assembly. At the same time, however, the regime built a new religious hierarchy under the control of the Front. The process began, according to Front documents, in Vietnam.

The [PRK] invited a set of monks from Vietnam to come and ordain seven former monks in Wat Unnalom in Phnom Penh on September 19, 1979, in order to sow the first seeds of the monkhood. After that, the state took an interest in organizing religion in a unified, correct, and appropriate [fashion]. First, central monks were set up, and a provisional Ministry of Religion drafted Circular 1 on November 1, 1979, in order to allow faithful people to be ordained so that there would be but one unified system in accordance with monk solidarity and without any sectarianism. . . . [By June 1981] ordinations had increased in every province, and the central monks could not go out to ordain others just because the people so requested it. The Central Committee of the Front and the Kampuchean People's Revolutionary Council agreed that the central monks would [ordain] high priests (*ubochha*) and monks in all the provinces in order to meet the desires of the people.[104]

Provincial priests and monks were required to be "loyal to the revolution," to have "clear personal histories," and to be recognized by local state authorities. Echoing the Khmer Rouge's efforts, in the early 1970s, to create a Patriotic Monks' Association, the Front announced that "in order to glorify patriotic consciousness, monks in all the provinces and municipalities must be designated by the Monks' Association; the Monks' Association is under the guidance of the Kampuchean United Front for National Salvation."[105]

Other religions experienced varying degrees of control. Publicly, the regime said that no Christians were left in Cambodia. "One may presume that as a consequence of the policy of genocide pursued by the Pol Pot–Ieng Sary clique, all Christians and their clergy in Kampuchea have been exterminated," asserted documents from the Pol Pot–Ieng Sary trial.[106] Many of the Christians in Cambodia had been ethnic Vietnamese and had, in fact, been killed or chased into Vietnam. Those who remained, however, were severely oppressed.

Islam, on the other hand, enjoyed an immediate, if highly controlled, rebirth. Practiced by Cambodia's minority Cham population, the Islamic traditions of Cambodia included an important role for local religious leaders, the *hakem*, in teaching Islamic principles and handling family disputes. Permitted once again to take their positions in the Cham villages of eastern Cambodia, the *hakem* were subject to control by the Front, which reviewed their personal biographies, and by local state authorities, whose "recognition" was required. The traditional national leader of the Chams, the *mufti*, did not return under the PRK; he had been replaced, in effect, by the Front. The leadership hoped, however, that Chams would take some comfort from the visibility and apparent authority of Mat Ly, a Cham whose presence in the Front, like that of the Venerable Tep Vong, was intended to demonstrate the religious tolerance and inclusiveness of the new regime. It is unclear how many Chams knew that Mat Ly, the former vice president of the National Assembly in Democratic Kampuchea, had earlier been given the same role by the Khmer Rouge.[107]

THE INTELLECTUALS

Education in Cambodia had nowhere to go but up. Under Democratic Kampuchea, schools had been closed, children and university students had missed four years of education, and thousands of schoolteachers had been murdered. The education system required rebuilding, and a whole new corps of teachers required training. "Those who know a lot teach those who know little" was the motto of the Ministry of Education. "Those who know little teach those who know nothing." In this spirit, and with a strong dose of political education included, the ministry opened a School of Pedagogy in Phnom Penh, which offered one month's training to teachers. In the next few years, under the guidance of Vietnamese, Soviet, and other foreign professors and curriculum advisors, the PRK managed to reestablish a network of schools and university faculties. It was one of the regime's greatest achievements.[108]

There is a Khmer saying, "The stupid person, scorned by neighbors, may suddenly become wealthy and wise" (*Trok trok neak srok moel ngeay; rolaos kouth khchay nean ud mean phoan*). So it must have seemed to educated Cambodians. No other ethnic Khmers had suffered more under Democratic Kampuchea than the "intellectuals" (a term used by both the Khmer Rouge and the PRK to refer to those with a high school education). According to Party estimates, a mere 15 percent of educated Cambodians had survived.[109]

Their mistreatment by the Khmer Rouge should have endeared educated Cambodians to the liberating regime. The Front had issued its appeals to "patriotic intellectuals," and over the first weeks and months following the overthrow of the Khmer Rouge, educated Cambodians came to trust that their backgrounds were no longer grounds for execution. The problem for the Front, however, was that none of them were communists. One of the many sad ironies was that the more leftist a student, teacher, or professional had been at the time of the revolution, the less likely he or she was to survive. Only those suspicious enough of the revolution to have hidden their identities rather than offer their services to the Khmer Rouge remained alive in 1979, leaving the PRK with a particularly skeptical contingent of educated elite.

The "intellectuals" heard different sets of messages from the Cambodian leadership. In a series of "political education" sessions, Minister of Health Nou Peng, Minister of Propaganda Kaev Chenda, and Minister of Education Chan Ven commiserated with educated Cambodians for their suffering and assured them of their role in the new regime. Pen Sovan also offered reassurances. "Cast away all the doubts you may have about our revolution," he told a group of educated Cambodians on March 5, 1979. "We will never mislead our people. We will never turn white into black. It is enough for our nation to have endured the danger of extermination. It is more than enough that it has had to suffer such destruction and devastation. Let us rebuild our nation. Your active contribution is needed."[110]

Sovan's message was undercut, however, by the speeches of other leaders. On

April 17, the anniversary of the Khmer Rouge's victory, the PRK held what it called its Fourth National Day. Cambodians who turned on the radio heard Heng Samrin speak as if Democratic Kampuchea had never been overthrown: "On April 17, 1975, our Kampuchean people launched a heavy assault on the last den of the U.S. imperialists and Lon Nol puppets, liberating Phnom Penh and all of our beloved Kampuchean land. April 17, 1975, has become a great historic day in Kampuchea, the day on which the ferocious war of the U.S. imperialists and their lackeys was brought to an end." Samrin went on in full revolutionary mode, lashing out at Cambodia's former "colonialist," "neocolonialist," and "feudal" regimes and promising a "protracted struggle." He then offered a communist and fundamentally rural vision for Cambodia's future. The "most urgent tasks at present," said Samrin, were obtaining material assistance and "prepar[ing] seeds and tools for the cultivation of rice and other crops in time for the coming rainy season." The Front would "mobilize the masses in a great revolutionary movement, strengthen revolutionary power, organize mass organizations. and consolidate the mass organizations in hamlets, villages, and districts."[111]

Even as the Front attempted to recruit educated Cambodians into the state apparatus, these hard-line communist messages strongly implied that the PRK intended to repeat the policies of Democratic Kampuchea. Thousands of educated Cambodians headed for the Thai border; those who stayed behind were disillusioned. As one Vietnamese advisor reported back to Hanoi, the "intellectuals" were ideologically unsound, "isolated from the public," and uninterested in the "collective benefit." His report accurately described the prevailing sentiment: "I actually asked one hundred intellectuals, and all one hundred of them talked with pessimistic attitudes about the country, their ancestry, and also about themselves." In fact, educated Cambodians were frustrated, not only by the reappearance of communist policies and rhetoric but by being once again under the direct control of uneducated revolutionaries. This, too, the Vietnamese advisor reported to Hanoi. "They don't believe in the current contingent of cadres," he wrote. "And they don't respect the officials in the current administration. They say that they cannot understand how people with so little knowledge can lead the country."[112]

THE POLICE

Toward the end of 1979, Phnom Penh was awash with agents loyal to the noncommunist resistance and with Vietnamese officials seeking to thwart them. A variety of Vietnamese institutions were responsible for ensuring order in the capital, including A50, which was established specifically to manage urban affairs, and 7708, a special Vietnamese police unit operating in Phnom Penh. In cooperation with Vietnamese military units, 7708 security officials were arresting hundreds of suspects, interrogating them, and detaining them in a prison network that the Vietnamese established in Cambodia.[113]

Vietnamese officials also established and consolidated a Cambodian security apparatus, including police forces in the provinces, municipalities, districts, wards, and communes. At the top of this pyramid was Chea Sim's Ministry of the Interior, which was responsible for reviewing all important political cases, government secrecy, local police training, and, increasingly, the interrogation of prisoners. Most important to Sim, however, was control over applications to join the police. This process, which the ministry oversaw either directly or through its representatives, reflected the biases and personal connections of Chea Sim. The police forces would include no police, soldiers, or officials from the prerevolutionary regimes nor any ethnic Chinese or Sino-Khmer. Rather, the chief qualification for membership in the security apparatus was a "proper class background." No former Khmer Rouge cadre would be excluded, so long as he had defected by May 1978 and was "known to be obedient to Party cadres." Even former Khmer Rouge police were welcomed into the PRK's security apparatus, despite their presumed blood debts.[114]

It was becoming increasingly clear whom the regime was willing to co-opt and whom it saw as a threat. At the end of 1979, the Party ordered the release from prison of all former Khmer Rouge officials and soldiers (including those who had "engaged in offenses against the people," so long as they had "reformed") while at the same time cracking down on suspected members of noncommunist groups.[115] Dozens of such groups had emerged in opposition to both the Khmer Rouge and the Vietnamese and were developing ties to larger resistance movements, including the Khmer People's National Liberation Front and the pro-Sihanouk Mouvement de Libération Nationale du Kampuchea (MOULINAKA). The existence of one such network led by a resistance agent named Haem Kroesna prompted several waves of arrests, many of which were based on the flimsiest of pretexts. As Heng Samrin acknowledged nearly a decade later, "In 1979 and 1980, with regard to the Haem Kroesna group, there were some whom we knew to have contacts with the group and some whom we merely suspected and yet arrested. When we prepared a case later, no [evidence] appeared."[116]

THE CITY

The regime's fears of noncommunist infiltration had a lot to do with the gradual return of urban culture. The Party's efforts to stop state officials from hiring friends and family had failed, offering thousands of Cambodians the opportunity to live in the city. Others bought state positions, bribed the soldiers and police manning the checkpoints around Phnom Penh, or sneaked in. In the summer of 1980 the regime attempted to reverse the flood by ordering municipal officials to send people back to the countryside and by compiling a list of families authorized to stay. It was too late; by the end of the year Phnom Penh was home to more than three hundred thousand people.[117]

The city did not return to normal. Although former residents of Phnom Penh went in search of family homes, the larger and less dilapidated houses were generally occupied by Vietnamese or Cambodian soldiers, Vietnamese advisors, or Cambodian state cadres. Newly appointed civil servants were assigned housing by their ministries or by Vietnamese officials. Others took whatever was available. Cambodians tended to cluster together, often with multiple families to a house and five or six people to a room. This pattern reflected a cultural familiarity with close quarters and, likely, a psychological yearning for proximity after the wrenching separations imposed by the Khmer Rouge. Politics and economics, past and present, also played a role. Having just survived a regime in which possession of property was a capital crime, Cambodians were initially reluctant to accumulate wealth in a conspicuous form. Nor did the ideological rhetoric and opaque policies of the PRK and the presence of Vietnamese communists encourage ordinary Cambodians to appropriate houses and land. Even if possession was tolerated, the lack of recognition of private property precluded the financial incentives—the right to rent, to sell, or to use property as collateral—that would have encouraged people to take more than was necessary. The only motivation for occupying an entire house, then, was the immodesty of living well, an indulgence that few but the most powerful and secure cadres were willing to risk.[118]

The city appeared chaotic. Many of its residents had never lived in Phnom Penh before and were unfamiliar with city living. Cows and buffaloes stood tied to houses. Trash and animal waste accumulated everywhere. The streets, buildings, waterworks, and electrical grid lay in ruins. Cars, horses, carts, cyclos, and motorcycles ferried people around the city, unrestrained by traffic rules.

An informal urban economy emerged. Unable to feed state workers, the leadership had no choice but to permit private merchants to operate in Phnom

Penh. Defying the state's efforts to control their activities, these merchants moved back and forth between downtown Phnom Penh and the markets they had established outside the city limits. Many were ethnic Chinese or Sino-Khmer and therefore suspicious in the eyes of a regime fixated on Beijing's support for the Khmer Rouge. With Cambodians of all ethnicities entering the city practically at will, and with city residents gathering informally around noodle shops and coffeehouses, the leadership feared that infiltration and conspiracies were rife throughout Phnom Penh.[119]

Like the Khmer Rouge, the PRK leadership and its Vietnamese advisors equated urban life with counterrevolution. They assumed, accurately, that bourgeois city dwellers returning to Phnom Penh after four years in the Khmer Rouge collectives would be disillusioned with the Vietnamese-dominated communist PRK and attracted to the idea of an anticommunist alternative. But they also mistrusted urban culture itself: the music, drinking, idle youth, chance encounters of citizens, and the opportunity to cause trouble. These concerns helped inspire the regime's campaign against those it suspected of undermining its authority or its ideology.

BETRAYING THE REVOLUTION

In early June 1980, Phnom Penh radio suddenly announced the trial of seventeen noncommunist agents associated with the resistance leader Haem Kroesna, almost all of whom had been arrested the previous August or September. Their crimes included forming a "government" and successfully infiltrating the regime. "In particular," announced the broadcast, "they persuaded to their side a number of persons in the ranks of ministries, departments, factories, and some units of the revolutionary armed forces, as well as local administration at the district, commune. and village levels." The Haem Kroesna agents were sentenced to three to twenty years in prison.[120]

The following month, the government authorized the Ministry of the Interior to take direct control of "reform offices" throughout the country and to detain large numbers of suspected Cambodians, including two thousand in one district of Kampong Cham alone. Terrified of infiltration, the Party and the state reminded authorities to counter "psychological warfare," calling for increased vigilance against enemy infiltration and against the theft of state secrets. The Party also announced new rounds of political education intended to remind Cambodians of the dangers of those who "betray the revolution."[121]

The regime then issued a law, Decree-Law 2 Against Betraying the Revolution and Other Offenses, which granted the security forces expanded powers and revealed the PRK's ideological biases. Convoluted and self-referential, the decree-law was practically undecipherable. According to an accompanying circular, however, "betraying the revolution" meant the dissemination of any anti-Vietnamese propaganda or, as the circular described it, anything that "destroys the ties of national solidarity, divides the people internally, [or] divides solidarity between nationalities on Cambodian territory." The circular also prohibited literature, music, even clothes, that the regime associated with prerevolutionary Cambodia. In language that revived the puritanical views of the Khmer Rouge, the circular made it a crime to import, distribute, or trade in "newspapers, magazines, and other forms of reactionary [literature] and pornography," to engage in "propaganda and cultural activities that disseminate a degenerate lifestyle, [to wear] big pants, long hair, or skimpy skirts, or to play songs from the old society that destroy revolutionary morality, good traditions, and the growth of the people."[122]

The revolution was once again a revolution. Like the D.K., the PRK had identified as its primary enemies the imperialists, the bourgeois, and even the hippies. Having purged the state of prerevolutionary officials and investigated the "connections" of all new civil servants, the regime was now arresting thousands of Cambodians suspected of links to the noncommunist resistance. Unlike the D.K., the PRK tolerated some diversity within the population, but only so much as could be controlled by the Front. Indications of civil society, such as the spontaneous reemergence of the Buddhist monkhood, were repressed. Meanwhile, refugee camps in Thailand were filling up with former officials from the Sihanouk and Lon Nol regimes, their families, and others who had little faith in a Vietnamese-occupied communist Cambodia.

Whereas the PRK's definition of the noncommunist threat gradually expanded to include an entire culture, its communist enemies, the Khmer Rouge, were reduced to one name: Pol Pot. Despite consternation from the Hanoi veterans in the Party leadership, former Khmer Rouge cadres and soldiers, even those with blood debts, were appointed to positions in the Party, the state apparatus, and the security forces. The ongoing military threat posed by the Khmer Rouge did not discourage the PRK from promoting former D.K. cadres. Rather, the desire to co-opt the Khmer Rouge resistance was the rationale for this policy. Many Cambodians, inside the state and in the general population, found these developments disorienting and deeply disturbing. All the rhetoric of "solidarity" notwithstanding, the dawn of Cambodia's second revolution was a divisive moment.

Chapter 4 The Birth of an Economy

When the Khmer Rouge retreated in the face of the Vietnamese on-slaught, they left behind a country that, for close to four years, they had systematically driven beyond poverty into a precommercial state of chaos. A partial list of the devastation, culled from PRK reports, only hints at the suffering endured by Cambodians under Democratic Kampuchea and at the challenges ahead.

According to one such report, approximately one third of the country's rice fields had been left fallow, in part because the Khmer Rouge had diverted much of the labor force toward water projects and in part because so many Cambodians had died. This land was not, in 1979, immediately usable. Only a small amount of rice seed was left for the next harvest, and an estimated two thirds of Cambodia's cows and buffaloes had died or been slaughtered in the immediate aftermath of the Vietnamese invasion. Agricultural tools and tractors had fallen into disrepair. The commercial infrastructure lay in ruins; roads, bridges, railroads, stores, and warehouses were seriously damaged, and most vehicles had broken down or been destroyed. The ports of Kampong Som and Phnom Penh lacked workable equipment. The telephone, telegraph, and postal networks all required repairs, if not complete reconstruction.[1]

Worst of all, the treatment of the people by the Khmer Rouge had rendered them unable to resume normal economic activity. The killings and the starvation brought upon the educated class had decimated Cambodia's small corps of technocrats. The rest of the population was not in a position to immediately produce economically. Having been forced to work from twelve to fourteen hours a day with little food, the vast majority of Cambodians suffered from malnutrition and general weakness.

Internal migrations exacerbated the food crisis. The Vietnamese timed their invasion for December, when the main rice harvest would be available to feed their army and the Cambodian people, yet most Cambodians seized the opportunity to abandon the Khmer Rouge cooperatives, leaving much of the rice crop in the fields. By April and May, when planting was supposed to begin, the limited rice stocks were dwindling, and malnutrition, disease, fighting, and shortages of rice seed, carts, draft animals, and arable land were all disrupting the planting. With starvation setting in, Cambodians left the rice fields for towns in search of food. By the end of the year, the regime estimated that between three and four million people faced serious shortages and that parts of Cambodia lacked food entirely.[2]

For political reasons, the first rescue efforts came from Vietnam, the Soviet Union, and Eastern Europe. A July 1979 report stated that the PRK had received approximately ten thousand tons of rice seed, ten thousand tons of rice, nine thousand tons of fuel, and large shipments of tools and equipment from Hanoi and Moscow. None of this assistance, especially not the perishable goods, would have been of any use to Cambodia without warehouses, which were rebuilt with Vietnamese assistance. Technicians from the Soviet Union, Eastern Europe, and Vietnam, along with Cambodian and Vietnamese workers and soldiers, also rebuilt roads, bridges, and railroads. Among the most urgent projects were the road and railroad connecting Phnom Penh and the port of Kampong Som, through which assistance would arrive from the Soviet Union and, later, from the West. Soviet dockers and East German mechanics began repairs on the port itself. Elsewhere, Vietnamese authorities directed the reconstruction of major routes, motivated in large part by the need to transport soldiers and military equipment.[3]

THE POLITICS OF FOOD

Ros Samay was the kind of man who, to celebrate May Day, would lecture illiterate Cambodian workers on nineteenth-century American labor movements. Slight, delicate-looking, and precise, Samay was a refined communist in every sense. Yet underneath a rather fragile exterior lay an urgent desire to make the most of his newfound authority. Like his cousin Pen Sovan, Ros Samay had waited patiently in exile for a quarter-century, and like Sovan, Samay harbored independent tendencies that eventually led to his downfall.[4]

For the time being, he had a lot on his plate. From mid-1977, when he participated in the debriefing of the defector Hun Sen, to December 1978, when he emerged as secretary-general of the Kampuchean United Front for National Salvation, Samay served as an important interlocutor for the Vietnamese authorities. Immediately prior and subsequent to the establishment of the PRK, he acted as a key representative and spokesperson for the new regime, describing the Front and its policies to African and Asian representatives gathered in Hanoi, and traveling to Moscow and Eastern Europe to explain Vietnam's invasion of Cambodia. Following this show of loyalty, Samay returned to Phnom Penh, where he accepted more responsibilities than he could handle. As head of the Ministry of Religion, he oversaw the ordination of monks, visited newly restored wats, and published tracts with names like "Buddhism and the Motherland." He was also minister in charge of justice, a role that later included the drafting of the constitution in 1980. And, as minister of economics and livelihood, a position he assumed in May 1979 following the death of fellow Hanoi veteran Mok Sokun, Ros Samay faced the huge challenge of building an economic bureaucracy in response to an urgent crisis and in the midst of political chaos.[5]

In theory, the responsibilities of the Ministry of Economics and Livelihood included accepting foreign assistance, determining how much assistance went to each province, and dispatching cadres to the countryside to help Cambodian soldiers distribute food. Fourteen months after becoming minister, however, Samay reported that he had accomplished nothing other than establishing the ministry itself. "Up to now," he wrote, "I've appointed, on a permanent basis, the ministry's cadres, staff, and workers. I've prepared the ministry for work. There are sufficient tables, chairs, lighting, and so on." He described how he had "educated" his staff on political matters and organized a few working groups. "Other than this, there are a lot of other units [of the ministry] that are not functioning," Samay acknowledged, blaming the failure of the ministry on the absence of Vietnamese advisors and a lack of support from the central bureaucracy.[6]

The Ministry of Economics and Livelihood also faced bureaucratic competitors, including the Economic Office of the KPRC and Minister of Commerce Tang Sareum, whom the leadership and the Vietnamese advisors authorized to negotiate directly with the Soviet Union for the delivery of food and other assistance. There was little or no coordination. When Sareum bothered to report on his arrangements with the Soviets, he informed the Vietnamese or Heng Samrin and Pen Sovan, rather than Ros Samay. Meanwhile, other bureaucracies were accepting assistance directly from representatives of socialist countries. As one Vietnamese advisor complained to Heng Samrin at the end of 1979, "We need to receive assistance from the Soviet Union and many other socialist countries, but what ministry does this assistance go to? Which ministry takes care of it? First, do vehicles go to the Ministry of Commerce or to the Ministry of Communications? Do tractors go to the Ministry of Commerce or to the Ministry of Agriculture? Does medicine go to the Ministry of Commerce or to the Ministry of Health? I have already described some of this problem to you."[7]

The urgency of Cambodia's economic crisis and the bureaucratic turmoil that accompanied the establishment of the new government excused much of this confusion. Cambodian ministers were free to negotiate economic assistance with a variety of socialist countries. Later, rivalries evolved among Cambodia's patrons, in particular between the Soviet Union and Vietnam. For the moment, these were subsumed by the rush of fraternal concern. The more immediate political tensions over foreign aid arose over the reception of assistance from the West.

"IMPERIALIST" ASSISTANCE

Images of starving Cambodians crawling over the border into Thailand soon filled television screens across the world, creating the impression of widespread famine and prompting one of the biggest international humanitarian campaigns in history. Food, clothing, and household goods, not to mention hundreds of development experts and volunteers, headed for Thailand. Represented by the International Committee of the Red Cross and UNICEF, the West also made its first overtures to Phnom Penh. From the perspective of Vietnamese officials and some of the PRK leadership, however, Western offers of assistance were suspect. Humanitarian activities in Thailand had already helped resuscitate the Khmer Rouge and strengthen the noncommunist groups, feeding the PRK's opponents and luring to the border tens of thousands of Cambodians who eventually joined the resistance.

The Red Cross and UNICEF representatives met with delays and, at times, outright hostility. Although their requests to enter Cambodia began on January 4, three days before the Vietnamese entered Phnom Penh, and were repeated frequently thereafter, they were not permitted into the PRK until the summer of 1979, and then only for forty-eight hours. Faced with indifference from Cambodian and Vietnamese officials, the Red Cross and UNICEF finally found a helpful interlocutor in Ros Samay. On September 23, Samay approved the organizations' proposals and granted them permission to establish permanent offices in Phnom Penh.[8]

Ros Samay, whose tendency to meet with foreign representatives without consulting the leadership irked even Pen Sovan, either did not speak for the regime or was unclear as to its shifting policies. Samay's timing was also unfortunate. The U.N. General Assembly had just voted to recognize an exiled Democratic Kampuchean government (the vote occurred on September 21), infuriating leaders in Hanoi and Phnom Penh and prompting *Nhan Dan,* the official newspaper of the Vietnamese Communist Party, to characterize proposed international assistance to the PRK as "a cover for intervention and aggression." On September 26, Foreign Minister Hun Sen met with the Red Cross and UNICEF representatives and effectively reversed Samay's decision.[9]

Eventually, a tacit agreement emerged. The PRK would continue to denounce what was happening on the border but would permit the Red Cross and UNICEF to operate in Cambodia. The agencies, for their part, would not attempt to monitor the internal distribution of international humanitarian assistance. The regime was ill equipped to distribute the aid, however, and throughout the remaining months of 1979 and into 1980, it accumulated at the port. In December 1979 a Vietnamese advisor complained to Heng Samrin: "Goods are piling up in Kampong Som these days. Everything has not been brought to Phnom Penh. There must be a way to get the state's Ministry of Communications to deliver it immediately. There are perhaps 25,000 tons in Kampong Som."[10]

Nineteen-eighty was a frustrating year for the Westerners in Cambodia. Aside from watching food pile up in Kampong Som, they experienced delays and obstacles from Vietnamese and Cambodian officials in securing visas, flying into the country, and arranging meetings. Although logistical problems and bureaucratic inefficiency were to blame, internal political developments created additional obstacles. Throughout 1979, Minister of Economics Ros Samay and Minister of Commerce Tang Sareum had competed for control of foreign assistance. Then, at the end of the year, the leadership conferred on Ros Samay the full-time responsibility of drafting the constitution and made Sareum responsible for foreign aid.[11]

Tang Sareum was a crafty survivor, a Hanoi veteran who returned to Cambodia in the early 1970s, lived through the purges, and remained in Democratic Kampuchea until 1978. At times ideological, Sareum usually perceived economic bureaucracies in terms of internal power struggles, a tendency that led him into conflict with other ministers. Sareum also developed an antagonistic relationship with Western donors, who saw him as distant and indifferent.[12]

With Ros Samay out of the way, PRK policies began to reflect Sareum's less accommodating approach. Western assistance was to be treated not as immediate relief from a desperate economic situation but as a stream to be exploited according to political expediency. By the summer of 1980, Cambodian authorities were acknowledging to Western aid representatives that food was being warehoused, explaining that it would be held until the end of the year, when stocks would be low. At the end of the year, however, the leadership was still discussing the option of limiting the distribution of international aid. At a January 1981 meeting of the KPRC, attended by the Cambodian leadership and all the top Vietnamese economic advisors, a series of proposals, attributed in the minutes to no one in particular, were made. One idea put forth was that "the KPRC should grant ministries that receive assistance from international or humanitarian organizations the authority to accept and keep the assistance but not to distribute it." The government would then make a political calculation. "The KPRC should distribute a portion of the assistance to the ministries that were the original recipients so that they can distribute it in the direction [suggested by] the donors. In this way, we can elicit (*teak teanh*) a lot more assistance in the future." Whether the failure to distribute all the aid was the result of this policy or simple incompetence, Western donors did not respond as the leadership had hoped. In late 1980 and early 1981 assistance fell off, largely because of the regime's failure to distribute what had already been provided.[13]

Continued suspicion of the West's political motives, shared by most of the PRK leadership, also soured the relationship. Among the most forceful skeptics was Nguyen Con, the chief economic advisor to the PRK and head of A40, the Vietnamese organ guiding the regime's policies on economics and other technical matters. Con, a member of the Central Committee of the Vietnamese Communist Party, a former deputy prime minister and chair of the State Planning Commission, was a hard-liner who had rarely traveled outside northern

Vietnam.[14] Speaking to Heng Samrin in December 1980, he offered an unforgiving assessment of the international organizations.

> We should consider the intentions of the international organizations that are providing us assistance. Most of them are imperialists who seize everything. Providing assistance to Cambodia is just one part [of what they are doing]; a second portion [of their assistance] goes to Thailand and to Pol Pot. The provision of assistance [to our regime] is only a pretext. Their goal is to impose their influence on cadres and staff of the ministries and offices and on the people. First, they know that our country is socialist, and yet they try hard to impose their influence. Second, helping Cambodia is a pretext for helping Pol Pot.
>
> . . . Providing assistance is an opportunity for them [to make] domestic contacts and deeply infiltrate various localities, factories, and ministerial offices. Some enter the houses of cadres and staff and give them equipment in order to recruit them. This is in their self-interest; their intentions are not honest, even though there are also a small number of good people among them. Sometimes while providing assistance, they take the opportunity to conduct business. Seeing this kind of opportunism, we shouldn't be afraid, but should be extremely vigilant and use the opportunity to request valuable assistance from them.[15]

This vigilance was apparent not only to the international aid workers but to the residents of Phnom Penh. Westerners were housed in a single hotel and restricted even in their movements around the capital, not to mention the rest of the country. The government also controlled who could work with Western organizations and prohibited all other contact between Cambodians and foreigners. "Cambodian citizens and residents governed by the state of Cambodia," read one directive, "are not permitted to send letters or documents on their own accord, or to contact directly by phone international organizations based in Cambodia or international guests who have come to work in Cambodia, and are not permitted to invite foreigners into their houses."[16]

By late 1980 the world's attention had shifted, largely because the economic crisis appeared to have dissipated. Not only had rice harvests doubled from those of the previous year, but some development experts were questioning whether their initial reports of catastrophic famine had not been overly pessimistic. The food aid had helped, of course, but so, too, had political and environmental factors. Cambodians suffering from malnutrition had managed to mitigate rice shortages by doing precisely what the Khmer Rouge had forbade: plant vegetable gardens and forage for fruit, lotuses, roots, fish, lobsters, and frogs.[17]

Western aid organizations were also frustrated with the regime, its failure to distribute much of what had been delivered, its hoarding of food aid, and its deliveries of rice to Vietnam. Some redirected their attention to other parts of the world. Some stayed on, however, annoyed by PRK politics and the restrictions placed on their activities but more outraged by the West's politically motivated economic embargo of Cambodia. Particularly infuriating both to Western aid workers and to the regime was the ban on long-term development aid. "This goes against the adage: 'Give a man a fish and he will eat for a day, give him a fishing net and he will eat for the rest of his life,'" argued a Western development worker in *Punishing the Poor,* a 1988 Oxfam publication intended as a critique of the embargo. Despite this sympathetic attitude, the regime's leadership barely modified its view of the Westerners. "Advisors from capitalist countries," reported the government in 1985, include "a small number in the ministries who are engaged in imperialist acts and who are seizing the opportunity to insert spies into our country to buy hearts, recruit, or infiltrate, dressing up as advisors to conduct their activities. We should personally maintain careful attention." Restrictions on contact between Cambodians and Westerners continued through the 1980s.[18]

THE POLITICAL LEGACY OF FOOD AID

Many of the patterns of Vietnamese-Cambodian relations were established in the first six months following the invasion. Vietnamese soldiers, scattered around the countryside, were positioned both to help distribute foreign food aid and to control the politics of distribution. Long after the distribution of food had ended, the Vietnamese military continued to participate in the Cambodian economy, especially with regard to the exploitation of natural resources.[19]

Just as immediate was the intervention of Vietnamese provincial authorities. According to a mid-1979 report, Cambodia had received "assistance from Vietnamese provinces and municipalities that have built a bridge of friendship with Cambodian provinces and municipalities and that are still providing assistance according to contracts they have signed." These economic ties, later formalized as part of a policy of promoting "sister provinces," facilitated the delivery of goods from Vietnam but also decentralized Cambodian-Vietnamese economic relations. For years Cambodian bureaucrats in Phnom Penh expressed gratitude for this assistance while complaining that they had little control over the direct relations established between provincial authorities in the two countries.[20]

The Vietnamese also dictated the terms of Soviet and Eastern European assistance. Prior to the repair of Kampong Som and, to a great extent, even after the port began operating, most foreign assistance to Cambodia passed through Ho Chi Minh City. Once inside the country, European goods were distributed under the direction of Vietnamese soldiers and civilian officials. The contrast between the roles of Moscow and Hanoi, between provider and distributor, set in place practical relationships that were often more important than the proprieties of fraternal diplomacy.[21]

Foreign assistance helped to stabilize and legitimize the regime. It offered Cambodian leaders their first opportunity to project statesmanship and power; their status was enhanced by their agreements with Western humanitarian organizations and with Soviet and Eastern European dignitaries. More important, international assistance helped the PRK consolidate power. Apart from overthrowing the Khmer Rouge, neither the Vietnamese army nor the PRK had much to offer. By distributing rice and other goods, however, the regime demonstrated its desire and ability to help its citizens, instilling the minimum of goodwill necessary to govern and to fight off a civil insurgency. Food aid also made it possible to create an administration. Without a functioning economy, a currency, or any actual assets, the government had no way of paying its employees. Taxes or confiscations of rice from the peasants were not only politically impossible but were themselves dependent on a state apparatus of some kind. The PRK thus directed much of the rice it received from overseas to Phnom Penh and the provincial capitals to pay its officials, soldiers, cadres, and state workers.

International aid gave birth to a food distribution network and, concomitantly, to confusion and corruption. The regime anticipated that distribution would be coordinated in Phnom Penh. Each province would maintain a representative in the capital charged with accepting aid and bringing it back to the countryside. From the beginning, however, onerous bureaucratic requirements impeded the process, for provincial officials were required to obtain the signatures of Ros Samay, Tang Sareum, and a representative of the KPRC before taking possession of any goods. In the provinces, the process was obscure. Despite plans to appoint representatives from central ministries to help coordinate distribution, a sufficient number of cadres was never available. Soldiers, local Front members, and local state officials filled the void, distributing, selling, or seizing rice according to local conditions and their own impulses.[22]

Local officials, paid in rice, had a hard time distinguishing between food assistance, which was to be distributed to the people, and their own salaries. Later this kind of confusion was called "theft of state property" and "corruption." For the time being, the obvious benefits of participating in the distribution system set a precedent: the value of a state job lay in access to state goods. State officials also sold rice in a flourishing black market, blurring the lines between socialist state commerce and the private sector. Neither the decentralization of economic decision making nor the flow of state property into private hands ever abated.

THE EMERGENCE OF THE BLACK MARKET

The economic crisis and the flood of hungry refugees to Thailand forced the PRK to take a nonideological approach to feeding its people. One 1979 state planning document, marked "secret," reveals the regime's tentative and grudging indulgence of a free market. "In response to the need to trade, purchase, and sell goods between the state and the people, and while money is being printed [there was not yet a Cambodian currency], the conditions for production, transportation, and the exchange of goods are not yet normal, and the [state] market has not yet arisen, we permit the people to trade freely with one another and to buy and sell freely."[23]

Survival for most Cambodians was a matter of personal initiative rather than state intervention. In camps set up around Phnom Penh and the provincial capitals and on the sides of roads, everything was for sale: vegetables, fruit, meat, fish, noodles, and old clothes. The currency was rice, available to soldiers, state officials, and a few ordinary Cambodians lucky enough to receive more than a small allotment of internationally donated food aid. Rice itself was for sale, its value determined according to the currency that came to dominate the economy: gold.

Almost immediately after the Vietnamese invasion, much of Cambodia's prerevolutionary wealth emerged, from homes and yards in towns and from secret hiding places in cooperatives. Sometimes the original owners had returned. More frequently the gold found its way into the hands of Cambodians for whom searching every possible hiding place was an act of desperation. Graves, where one might find gold-capped teeth, were frequently dug up.[24]

The regime made halfhearted efforts to control the trade in rice, gold, and Vietnamese money (dong), which was also circulating in Cambodia, particularly in the east. Prohibitions on these currencies were vague, leaving open the question of whether Cambodians could trade in small quantities. Government directives granted broad discretion to state officials to "educate" and warn traders and to confiscate gold and other precious metals, policies that enriched these officials without bringing order to the economic chaos. As for the trading of goods, the regime looked the other way. Lacking a socialist bureaucracy, the leadership recognized the necessity of "temporarily" encouraging a private sector, although they hoped eventually to bring it under control. "We have the goal of maintaining private commerce and free market activities," read a report issued in January 1981, "but there must be the means to guide and inspect [these activities]."[25]

TRADING WITH THE ENEMY

Reluctantly the regime also accepted the biggest factor in Cambodia's economic rebirth: Thailand. In the months following the invasion, refugees and resistance soldiers traveled back and forth over the border carrying consumer goods that Cambodians had not seen since 1975. The decision by international organizations to distribute rice to refugees at the border further encouraged this trade, creating a "land bridge" by which Cambodians could enter Thailand to pick up food aid and then return to Cambodia. By the end of 1979, Thai border towns contained huge open-air markets where Cambodians bought dishes, forks and knives, bottles, cloth, string, shoes, matches, candles, alcohol, cigarettes, prescription drugs, cosmetics, radios, cameras, guns, mechanical parts, soap, shampoo, toothpaste, and canned food. On scales set up around the markets, Thais and Cambodians weighed gold and jewels, often in the form of rings and bracelets. On some days, up to half a million dollars in gold came across the Cambodian border into Thailand.[26]

Tens of thousands of Cambodians were directly involved in transporting and trading Thai consumer goods and the rice distributed by the international organizations. Many were Chinese or Sino-Khmer who, blocked from returning to the cities and to traditional urban commercial activities, nonetheless rediscovered old trading partners or found new ones. Crowded camps surrounding western provincial capitals became vital commercial centers, and with the repair of the railroad connecting Battambang and Phnom Penh, Thai goods were soon available throughout the country.

The leadership harbored deep qualms about the reemergence of capitalism. It understood that Thai-Cambodian trading was enriching networks of merchants whose contacts extended from Bangkok to Phnom Penh to Ho Chi Minh City, while also allowing resistance agents to enter the country. Party leaders and their Vietnamese advisors were particularly suspicious of ethnic

Chinese, whom they viewed both as capitalists and as agents of Beijing. For economic and political reasons, however, they could not afford to deny Cambodians much-needed goods. As one state plan declared, "It is necessary to immediately reestablish exports and imports through Thai border crossings. We may use the private sector to buy and import some manufactured goods and raw materials that have value for the growth of the Cambodian economy."[27]

There were financial incentives to permitting private trading. At the local level, "using the private sector" meant authorizing soldiers (both Vietnamese and Cambodian), police, and state officials to stop or delay travelers and exact fees in exchange for passage. In Phnom Penh the leadership considered ways to collect revenues, including the establishment of customs offices at the border. At a meeting of the KPRC in January 1981, the Cambodian leaders and Vietnamese advisors decided to continue permitting private trading with Thailand while collecting a portion for the state and its officials. Observed one unattributed participant, "In fact, we are losing between fifteen and twenty kilograms of gold a day" by failing to more aggressively or systematically tax cross-border trade.[28]

This decision would have far-ranging impact. The regime's pragmatism would eventually enrich local and national leaders, military figures, and thousands of other state and Party cadres for whom cutting off the border would have meant economic suicide. Trade with Thailand also built economic empires, channeling money into patronage systems that connected local authorities with a hand in the trade to some of the most powerful people in Phnom Penh. Finally, the ongoing economic relationship between the two countries would ensure that Cambodia remained connected to its capitalist neighbor in ways that imposed a constant influence on the evolution of the PRK's economic policies.

BACK TO THE COLLECTIVES

Under the Khmer Rouge, the supposed glories of agricultural collectivization were the subject of song.

> O Solidarity Group, working in unison, happy and self-assured! Dry-season rice,
>   wet-season rice, light and heavy varieties of rice: our husbandry
>   is successful everywhere.
> O Solidarity Group, you are the new kind of family, special, beautiful,
>   and unique. Our happiness is enormous, and we struggle to expand
>   and solidify it even more.[29]

Now, with significantly less fanfare, the PRK was planning to move Cambodians back into cooperatives. "To get agricultural production back on its feet with the shortest possible delay," Hun Sen told a Western journalist in March 1979, "we are hoping to employ a form of collective exploitation."[30]

The regime and its Vietnamese advisors had many reasons to collectivize. By getting Cambodians to work in the fields, they hoped to generate rice production, rescue the economy, and resolve the food crisis. They also had humanitarian concerns. In the power vacuum created by the Vietnamese invasion, individuals, families, and armed groups had seized tools, animals, seeds, carts, and land. The losers included the tens of thousands of widows and orphans left behind by the Khmer Rouge, as well as elderly people with no means to feed themselves.

The question was whether to force Cambodians into cooperatives. Despite the reemergence of the Khmer Rouge phrase "Solidarity Groups" (*krom samaki*), the leadership attempted to distinguish its own agricultural policy from that of Democratic Kampuchea. "We will not force farmers into participating, and those who are capable of farming individually may do so," said Hun Sen in March 1979. "Therefore, collective exploitation [is our policy], but without the methods of Pol Pot, which were nothing but a monstrous caricature of collectivization." He added, however, that "because of shortages in seed, farm tools, and work animals, we think these special cases will be rare, and we have no intention of favoring them at the expense of the majority."[31]

The Solidarity Groups suited the leadership ideologically. As in newly unified Vietnam, collectivized agriculture in the PRK was expected to form the backbone of a socialized economy, channeling food to a state commercial network that would, in turn, distribute goods throughout the country. For the top Cambodian leaders, all of whom were versed in the virtues of socialist collectivization, this system would permit a benevolent state to distribute resources equally and fairly. It also offered the only long-term possibility for feeding state cadres and soldiers.

But on December 8, 1979, when a Vietnamese advisor met with Heng Samrin to discuss how collectivization was going, it was apparent that the PRK's collectivization policies were being driven primarily by strategic considerations. The Solidarity Groups, the advisor and Samrin agreed, were intended to draw Cambodians away from the resistance and keep them under the regime's control. Within the Solidarity Groups equal distribution of rice, regardless of individual contribution, was also intended to keep Cambodians in the fold. According to the Vietnamese advisor, "In each Production Solidarity Group, there are some people who work, plowing, harrowing, and transplanting seed-lings, some people who enter [the Solidarity Groups] only when the rice is ready, and some people who have just returned from the enemy. So the distri-bution of rice should follow a system that avoids harming the solidarity of our people." In this context, "solidarity" meant both equality and the consolidation of PRK power.[32]

Heng Samrin, an enthusiastic supporter of collectivization, called for "an at-titude of mutual assistance" whereby those who had reclaimed prerevolution-ary animals and tools would "want to help people who only show their face at harvest time and people who have only just returned from the enemy in order to have some food. Help each other, and don't allow some to have nothing and be hungry. Everyone should distribute together and live together." The advisor was pleased. "I am happy with your views," he told Samrin.

Later in the meeting, the advisor reported that other Vietnamese advisors were working with the Ministry of Agriculture to explain the collectivization policy to the provinces and that he himself was helping draft a circular. With-out collectivization, he warned, "there will be a division of solidarity, which will result in our people not working and the rice falling into the hands of Pol Pot." Samrin agreed. "I also know that this circular is in the spirit of preventing the division of solidarity of the people and doing what we can to get the people to share a desire to help each other and to all eat together." Again, the advisor of-fered his approval. "I accept (*totuol yual srab*) this attitude."

The advisor then described two problems. The first was that many Cambo-dians, especially those in possession of cows and buffaloes, were not interested in collective farming. The second was that there was no consistent policy. "Based on what we've been able to grasp," he told Samrin, "Mondolkiri, Rat-tanakiri, Kratie, and Battambang [provinces] . . . all are doing things com-pletely differently from each other."

The situation was indeed confusing. Local state cadres and Solidarity Group leaders included newly recruited Cambodians, former Khmer Rouge cadres, and, for a while, former Sihanouk and Lon Nol officials. Their implementation of the Solidarity Group policy, the collectivization of land, tools, and animals, and the distribution of rice varied according to the ideological biases of these local leaders. Still, a few generalizations are possible. First, in a departure from Khmer Rouge practices, Cambodian families were permitted to live and eat by themselves and to resume the kinds of normal social interactions that had de-fined traditional rural life. Second, the regime discouraged Cambodians from leaving the cooperatives but did not strictly enforce collectivization. And third, there was often little or no rice.[33]

Cambodians voted with their feet. The lack of food compelled tens of thousands to head for the cities or for Thailand. Thousands of former urban dwellers, unwilling to endure further years of agricultural bondage but unable to enter the cities, fled to the border. Others squatted around the towns, particularly Phnom Penh, and joined the informal economy. Peasants, too, had no choice but to leave the cooperatives in search of food. An official document from June 1980 describes the situation. "From the January 7 liberation to now, our Cambodian people throughout the country have regained their rights and freedoms. As a result, we have seen that most people, including Khmers, Chinese residents, and brothers and sisters of the Cham nationality are coming from all provinces to gather together and live in and around Phnom Penh. A number of these brothers and sisters were clearly born there. But others who were born in rice fields and plantations in the provinces have abandoned their provinces to come gather in Phnom Penh to conduct other business, including trading, smuggling, fishing, slaughtering cows and buffaloes to sell [their meat], and so on. This situation is intensifying every day."[34]

In the same document city officials were instructed to send "anyone who has fled the countryside, plantations, and villages in the provinces" back to the Solidarity Groups. To deal with the lack of rice available in the Solidarity Groups, the regime recommended greater discipline: "Pay attention and forcefully push the production movement to raise the standard of living and rebuild the country. Freely conducting love affairs and playing sports during work hours affect production, and [such behavior] should be corrected and reduced. Do whatever you can to constantly increase production."

Instructions like these were familiar to the former Khmer Rouge cadres who, by the summer of 1980, had been assigned to many positions of local authority. Whether conditions in the Solidarity Groups were affected by policies issued from Phnom Penh or by the habits of these cadres is unclear. In any case, the leadership apparently began to fear that the similarities between the Khmer Rouge collectives and the policies of the PRK were contributing to the flight from the countryside. In August 1980 there was a shift in tone as the government issued a series of directives intended to protect Cambodian peasants from Solidarity Group leaders and from local state authorities. According to one policy document, "The Groups should meet democratically to discuss and decide on such important matters as the distribution of produce and the system of dis-

tribution. Cadres from the Groups, villages, and wards shall respect these democratic rights and shall not compel the Groups to follow the cadres' personal
judgments."[35]

Voluntary participation or forced collectivization? Discipline or democracy?
The regime swung back and forth, issuing contradictory instructions in an attempt to find an appropriate, nuanced policy. As the Vietnamese advisor had
warned Heng Samrin in December 1979, the distribution of food was a crucial
element of the Solidarity Group policy, and it, too, presented the PRK leadership with a dilemma: distribute equally and undermine any incentive to work,
or distribute unequally and lose "solidarity." According to government reports,
the Groups had failed to find the proper balance. "In a lot of places, [distribu-
tion] has not yet been in accordance with the desire to work or with mutual assistance. There are some places where distribution is not yet equal and not yet
considerate, and this has caused a rise in jealousy among the people."[36]

To resolve this problem, Vietnamese advisors at the Ministry of Agriculture
set to work devising complex mathematical formulas by which produce would
be distributed according to workers' strength and the number of days they
worked while also taking into account care for the old and infirm. The system
was doomed to failure. The regime expected Solidarity Group leaders to classify
the workforce of the Groups, keep records on work participation, and implement the food distribution formulas, yet there were no trained agricultural
cadres below the district level available to interpret these policies. Moreover, the
economic crisis gripping Cambodia rendered the entire system unworkable.
Permitted to forgo the food distribution formulas whenever there were rice
shortages—an exception that applied to most of the country most of the
time—the Solidarity Groups had little to offer Cambodians by way of incentives to work.[37]

Little by little, the regime retreated from collectivization. With similar discussions occurring within the Vietnamese Communist Party, the environment
was right to contemplate the distribution and "lending out" of land to individual families. As with rice allotments, land distribution was supposed to proceed
according to complex instructions developed by the central bureaucracy. This
time, however, policy documents authorized local officials to do as they wished.
The land distribution instructions were "important guidelines for distribution," read one such document, "but the situation on the ground is more realistic and is different in each location and during each production season.
Therefore, in proceeding with this distribution, don't act in exact accordance
with these [guidelines]. We must be alert to the actual situation in each loca-

tion." By issuing such flexible directives, the regime ensured that there would never be a consistent application of agricultural policy.[38]

Land distribution did not constitute private ownership. As the regime had made clear from the start, state property included anything in the possession of "organizations, enterprises, localities, and various sectors." The state also appropriated to itself "the property of the old state authority," thereby claiming inheritance of the confiscations effected in the radically collectivized economy of the Khmer Rouge.[39] Nonetheless, by parceling out land to individual families, the PRK leadership hoped to create sufficient incentives to achieve economic growth.

The regime also began recognizing small-scale private-sector activity, or the "family economy." The idea was not new: the collapse of the southern Vietnamese economy in the late 1970s had prompted Hanoi to tolerate a limited private sector. In the Cambodian context, however, economic loosening was intended to encourage former city dwellers to stay in the countryside. "For all families who used to live in the cities and provincial and district capitals and have become rural people," explained a state directive, "it is necessary to provide each such family a place to build a house and have a family garden." There were also limits to the "family economy." Farm equipment remained the property of the Solidarity Groups, whereas cows and buffaloes were effectively collective property (their owners were "made to understand" that they had to "volunteer their [animals] to help the Solidarity Group"). Cambodians were nevertheless permitted a range of new economic activities, including the production of textiles, clothes, mats, baskets, pots, and pans, all using raw materials that they were encouraged to find for themselves. They were also allowed to sell their goods in the private market.[40]

The "family economy" conflicted not only with more rigid directives coming from Phnom Penh but also with the general ideological biases of the PRK's local and national leadership. Throughout the country, at every administrative level, officials responded to the new policy with resounding ambivalence. Some local cadres resisted, prompting the central government to remind village chiefs "not to issue orders prohibiting [the family economy]." Among provincial governors, former Khmer Rouge cadres such as Heng Samrin's older brother, Heng Samkai, refused to accept the notion of private property. And, in Phnom Penh, the leadership remained hopelessly unsure over how much to promote its own policies. Read one government directive: "Don't let the family economy obstruct the cooperative economy, and don't let the cooperative economy obstruct the family economy, either."[41]

THE SOCIALIST ECONOMY

Hanoi's third priority in Cambodia, after fighting the war and promoting loyal Cambodian leadership, was the establishment of a communist economic system in the PRK. After its unexpectedly quick victory over the Khmer Rouge, however, Vietnam was unprepared to field economic advisors to the new regime. Throughout 1979, despite the presence of a few top Vietnamese Party and state leaders in Phnom Penh and the pervasive role of Vietnamese military authorities in the countryside, technical advisors were notably absent, especially in the provinces. That left the reemergence of the Cambodian economy to the impulses of its citizens and subject to the discretion of local leaders. With the arrival of economic advisors delayed for more than a year, the regime's efforts to establish a state sector ended up playing a permanent game of catch-up against a decentralized, unplanned, and nonideological market economy.[42]

The system envisioned by bureaucrats in Phnom Penh included a state commercial network that would purchase rice and other agricultural goods from the people and establish state stores at which these goods would be sold along with clothing, textiles, mosquito nets, paper, books, and other consumer products. The obstacles were immense. In the beginning of 1980 there were few buildings suitable for state trading and no state transportation network. Political confusion in the countryside prevented officials in Phnom Penh from even knowing who was responsible for local commercial matters. And although the state had made efforts to staff the commercial sector with remaining technicians from the prerevolutionary era, most had either died or fled to Thailand. Within a couple of years the ministry and its Vietnamese advisors hoped to identify new economic cadres and to train them in Phnom Penh. For the moment, however, inexperienced local cadres struggled to understand the shifting nature of their roles, from the distribution of international food aid to the management of state commerce. They had no training other than that offered by a few roving teams of Vietnamese advisors.[43] According to reports written by central government officials, local cadres often broke or stole equipment, used their positions to engage in personal business, and generally neglected their duties. With no regulations directing the distribution of food and other goods and no effective dissemination of policy, the central leadership was unable to discipline local officials or stem the flow of goods into the free market. The regime had thus created a state apparatus, bestowing upon its cadres power and access to goods without making them accountable. The system was "anarchic" (*anathibatey*), according to government reports.[44] Yet a functioning state commerce system was a prerequisite for the regime's most dramatic policy initiative: the injection of money.

INTRODUCING THE RIEL

In her account of her childhood under the Khmer Rouge, Loung Ung describes how, during her family's evacuation from Phnom Penh, the economic policies of the revolution first came to her attention:

> "I have to go to the toilet," I tell Ma urgently after dinner.
>
> "You have to go in the woods."
>
> "But where?"
>
> "Anywhere you can find. Wait, I'll get you some toilet paper." Ma goes away and comes back with a bunch of paper sheets in her hand. My eyes widen in disbelief, "Ma! It's money. I can't use money!"
>
> "Use it, it is of no use to us anymore," she replies, pushing the crisp sheets into my hand.[45]

Overnight the national currency, the riel, had become worthless. Middle-class and wealthy Cambodians who carried money on the journey out of Phnom Penh ended up discarding it on the ground. In Phnom Penh the former Cambodian National Bank lay in ruins, destroyed either during or immediately after the Khmer Rouge takeover. In Beijing, Chinese authorities printed new Khmer Rouge currency, red notes adorned with stirring pictures of peasants and workers, but it was never used. Although the Chinese eventually delivered the money to Cambodia, the Khmer Rouge had decided to do entirely without a currency and never distributed it to the population. Commercial activity under Democratic Kampuchea thus consisted of illicit attempts to buy food with hidden gold and family jewels. Those who were caught were almost always beaten and were sometimes executed.

Throughout 1979, as Cambodians openly traded in gold, rice, Thai baht, and Vietnamese dong, the leadership waited before reintroducing the riel. The delay was not political (the arrival of the riel was seen as an important symbol of the new regime's legitimacy) but logistical. In February 1980, just getting money from the Soviet Union (where it was printed) to Cambodia was a complicated affair. Nguyen Con, chief economic advisor to the PRK, took control, arranging for an initial shipment of one hundred million in new riels, its receipt by Vietnamese soldiers in Kampong Som, and its transport to Phnom Penh, where Vietnamese security cadres guarded the worksite where the Cambodian

National Bank was being rebuilt.[46] Then it was time to convince Cambodians that the riel had value.

Injecting a new currency into a moneyless economy is like changing the side of the street on which people drive: it works only if everyone agrees simultaneously. The government would have to start paying state workers, cadres, officials, and soldiers in currency rather than rice. Civil servants would have to accept the riels on the assumption that the money could be used to purchase rice and other goods in state stores. The state stores would have to accept the riels with the expectation that the currency could be used to purchase rice from farmers. And the farmers would have to be willing to sell their rice to the state, something that they would agree to only if, after almost five years of bartering, they suddenly accepted the value of the new currency.

The first step was to distribute riels as salaries for civil servants. Daunting problems were soon apparent. Many state workers, especially those with some technical training like doctors, nurses, midwives, and pharmacists, refused to work for a salary of thirty riels a month. The introduction of salaries also resulted in increased violence within undisciplined military and police units. More generally, the absence of state stores rendered riel salaries effectively worthless. Even where a state trading system did exist, commercial cadres could hardly accept the riel before they themselves had adapted to the new currency. And to do that, every office, every trading store, and every warehouse would have to first find a way to value its assets, establish and manage budgets, put accounting systems in place, track revenues and expenditures, price goods, and pay salaries. Almost no cadres were trained to implement any of these tasks.[47]

The second step was to convince peasants to sell their rice to the state in exchange for the riel. This posed a fundamental dilemma. The PRK had no functioning state trading system with which to purchase rice. If the riel were ever to circulate through the countryside, it would therefore have to pass through the private market. In resolving this problem, the leadership decided that its desire to launch a money economy was stronger than its preference for socialism. Preparing for the introduction of the riel, central planners allowed that provincial authorities could "use purchasing companies and selling companies in the private sector in some communes [as long as they were] under the control of the state authority and Executive Teams." In April 1980, to encourage Cambodians to use the riel and stop trading in Vietnamese dong, the Party reiterated the policy, permitting the "use of private companies if it is deemed necessary to convince [people] to inject the riel into the purchase of agricultural produce, food, and manufactured goods at mutually agreed upon prices."[48]

"Mutually agreed upon prices" included, however, the price of the riel itself. Unlike other revolutionary regimes, the PRK did not have the option of offering a new currency in exchange for an old one. The closest the state could come was an exchange program in the east, where Cambodians were encouraged to trade in Vietnamese dong for riels, although at a rate much lower than they could get on the black market. Elsewhere, the regime had to convince people that the value of rice and other goods, bartered or purchased in gold for years, could now be expressed in these new notes. Many Cambodians, unfamiliar with the new currency, either refused to accept it or valued it well below the state's expectations.[49]

If the riel were to ever stand on its own, it would have to reflect the value of goods produced within the country, the hard currency that those goods gained on the international market, and the country's assets, specifically gold. But in early 1981 none of these supports was in place. Cambodia produced almost nothing of value. The only source of hard currency was the export of rubber to the Soviet Union and kapok to Japan. Meanwhile, gold continued to pour out of Cambodia into Thailand. For years the regime struggled to stabilize its currency, looking for goods to export and attempting to achieve the politically difficult and logistically impossible goal of suppressing smuggling.[50]

Tolerance of "mutually agreed upon prices" also disagreed with the regime's vision of central planning. A fixture of socialist regimes throughout the world, artificial pricing had a particularly long history in Vietnam, where Soviet aid had allowed the Vietnamese Communist Party to ignore economic forces and rely on outside assistance to keep prices manageable. After Vietnamese reunification, reductions in external aid resulted in vast disparities between official and black market prices, but this did not prevent Vietnamese authorities from importing the system into Cambodia.

The PRK's primary strategy was to set prices on goods low enough that Cambodians, particularly state workers, could afford them. As a Vietnamese advisor reminded Heng Samrin shortly before the introduction of currency, "If we don't determine the price of goods appropriately, we won't be able to ensure the standard of living of the people, cadres, and staff, and they won't obey us, either." Two weeks later, the same advisor was more specific. "It is absolutely necessary that we determine the prices of rice, salt, and cloth at which cadres and staff will trade with the state. The state should determine a fixed price and not let it go up or down, because these three goods are extremely special. If prices go up and down, it will clearly cause political harm."[51]

The immediate effect of these policies was to encourage state officials to sell state goods on the black market, where they could get a better price. Even before the introduction of the currency, Vietnamese officials could foresee the bleeding the system would endure. "Soap and fuel, for example, should be priced above normal and not be too cheap," explained the advisor to Heng Samrin, "because if it is sold too cheap, the capitalists will buy it all up and take it to [southern] Vietnam. We must have a clear and agreed-on system to prevent the concealing of goods, indeed, not permit it at all."[52]

Even as Vietnamese advisors were instructing Cambodian bureaucrats in the art of socialist pricing, Cambodian peasants were refusing to sell their rice to the state below black market prices. Again, the regime was willing to bend its socialist principles, instructing local officials to buy rice at close to market prices while issuing only maximum and minimum prices. In a country with extremely uneven economic conditions, this policy presented enormous opportunities for graft and corruption to the bureaucracy, thereby ensuring that alongside the state commercial network's expanding authority lay the seeds for its own disintegration.[53]

THE LATE REVOLUTION

The perspective of the Cambodian leadership and the Vietnamese advisors was that the Khmer Rouge had imposed a "monstrous caricature" of collectivization and that the PRK was offering Cambodia its first opportunity to enjoy socialism. Most Cambodians did not see it that way. Former urban residents interpreted the Solidarity Groups and other elements of Phnom Penh's economic policies as a resumption of Khmer Rouge practices. Peasants who managed to gain possession of farm animals and equipment hoped to farm privately. The rest were left behind in nonfunctioning cooperatives in which food was scarce or nonexistent. Tens of thousands of Cambodians looked to black market trading as the only means of survival.

Pragmatism softened many of Phnom Penh's economic policies. To bring some economic stability to the country, to feed and clothe its cadres, and to reintroduce the riel, the PRK tolerated a certain amount of private-sector activity, including private commerce, the "family economy," the distribution of land, and even private trading with Thailand. These accommodations were intended to be temporary, a brief experiment until the crisis was over, Vietnamese economic advisors were on the ground, and Cambodian cadres had been properly trained in operating a socialist system. For years, however, the leadership would struggle to rein in an informal economy that they had liberated from Khmer Rouge strictures.

From their own experience in socializing the southern Vietnamese economy, the Vietnamese advisors could have predicted (and sometimes did predict) the future of the PRK's state economy: disparities in state and black market prices and the bleeding of state goods into the private sector. Factors unique to the Cambodian economy, such as the sudden infusion of international humanitarian assistance, also contributed to the emergence of a state commercial sector that operated according to the needs of its cadres rather than socialist principles.

The year 1979 was an odd and inopportune time for a communist revolution. Mired in Brezhnev-era stagnation and corruption, the Soviet Union was no model. In China, Deng Xiaoping was launching what would be a long, persistent, and ultimately successful transition toward a market economy. Hanoi's efforts to bring the southern Vietnamese economy in line with the socialist system of the north had brought the country to a standstill and had prompted the Communist Party to begin considering more flexible policies. Cambodians, who had their own historic reasons for viewing communism with suspicion, were thus part of a global trend away from centrally controlled collectivized economies. The communism imposed by the PRK was not quite the last such experiment (the Sandinista revolution in Nicaragua came a few months later), but it was probably the least resolute.

Chapter 5 Comrades and Traitors: Political Intrigue in the Shadow of Occupation

In the northwestern province of Siem Reap, the Vietnamese were having problems with their former Khmer Rouge cadres. Second in military importance only to the neighboring province of Battambang, Siem Reap was under threat of attack from nearby resistance forces. In the hopes of luring some of these forces to the regime, Vietnamese authorities had named, as Party secretary, a former Eastern Zone district secretary and one of the most powerful and important of the Eastern Zone defectors, Haem Bau. To further clarify their intentions, they selected two other 1978 defectors as top provincial leaders: Em Chheum, as provincial governor, and Hong Han, as a member of the provincial People's Revolutionary Committee.[1]

By June 1979 the Vietnamese were regretting these appointments. Haem Bau had recently married a third wife, a morality issue generally forgiven among the new leaders—except that Bau's wife was the former spouse of a Lon Nol soldier and a former resident of Thailand. According to Party investigations, Bau also drank, was corrupt, and "was not a revolutionary." Even more troubling was the suspicion that he moved in noncommunist resistance circles (the Sereika), distributing state rice, medicine, cloth, and other goods to the enemy. Indeed, all three provincial leaders, Bau, Chheum, and Han, were thought to have ties to the Sereika and to an underground anti-Vietnamese, anti–Khmer Rouge group that called itself Khmer Consciousness (Praloeng Khmer). According to Party documents, "They were becoming increasingly immersed in secretly opposing and disputing the edicts of the revolution. There is ample evidence that they intentionally released Sereika and Khmer Consciousness cadres arrested by Siem Reap armed forces and security officers." Eventually Bau, Chheum, and Han defected, an event described by the Party thus: "On December 18 and 19, 1979, in Siem Reap, Em Chheum and Hong Han, on the authorization of Haem Bau, met secretly with two people, the chief and deputy chief of the Khmer Consciousness movement, in order to agree to a plan for Haem Bau, Em Chheum, and Hong Han to run off with the Sereika traitors. On December 21, on the pretext of going to a cadres' meeting in Phnom Penh, Haem Bau drove to Chi Kraeng district, where the Khmer Consciousness met him and led him into the forest. At eight that evening, Em Chheum and Hong Han sneaked away, too, in accordance with the plan prepared by the detestable Khmer Consciousness."[2]

In January 1980, as the Permanent Committee of the Party met to officially expel the Siem Reap defectors from the Party and call for their arrests, the leadership could look back at a series of disappointments. Throughout the western portion of the country, lower-level officials were abandoning their new positions and heading for the border. Only a few months earlier, Kao Ty, the first governor of Battambang and another former Eastern Zone cadre, had fled to Thailand.[3] And in Siem Reap, all of the provincial leaders were seemingly going their own way. According to Party documents:

> Since the beginning, there hasn't been good solidarity within the Siem Reap provincial committee. Even though the Permanent Central [Party] Committee has frequently met with and expressed its views [to the provincial leadership] and frequently recalled and rebuilt people, the provincial leaders still hold a grudge, and there is deep hatred within the Siem Reap provincial committee. The problems are not dissipating; rather, divisions are becoming more profound. The working relationships between Cambodian cadres and Vietnamese advisors and soldiers stationed in Siem Reap, despite a strong basis, still [suffer from] misunderstandings and failings. But [Haem Bau, Em Chheum, and Hong Han], because of their incorrect stance and views, refused to appropriately correct any of the situations that arose.[4]

Recognizing that resentment of Vietnamese control was behind many of the regime's problems, the Party called on cadres to exercise "revolutionary caution," "strengthen Cambodian-Vietnamese solidarity," and "resolve the various issues that have arisen in the relationships among Cambodian cadres, Vietnamese advisors, and Vietnamese soldiers."[5]

IMMORALITY, NEPOTISM, AND DISLOYALTY

As the Vietnamese authorities and the Cambodian leadership entered the second year of the PRK, they were not impressed with the quality of the local leadership. The cadres whom they had selected had little administrative experience, other than those who had been Khmer Rouge district chiefs. Equally damaging to the functioning of the administration were the psychological effects of years of deprivation and horror, described in the West as post-traumatic stress syndrome and manifested, among Cambodian officials, in numbness and inefficiency. And then there were the morality problems that were exhibited not only by the new people, who had been subject to the full force of Khmer Rouge oppression, but also by former Khmer Rouge cadres, who, despite their privileged positions in the D.K. regime, had to ascribe to a relatively ascetic lifestyle while under the constant threat of purges. The sudden release from these constraints, the achievement of a certain amount of power, and a general atmosphere of chaos and uncertainty that permitted indulgences tempted many of them away from "revolutionary morality." As with the Siem Reap defectors, there were heavy drinking, multiple wives, and theft.[6]

Most local leaders who exhibited this behavior were not removed. With a limited number of trusted cadres available to fill positions, Vietnamese authorities felt that they had no choice but to be patient with Cambodian officials. As one Vietnamese advisor reported to Hanoi in June 1980, "In my opinion, although the current cadre contingent in Cambodia currently has good and bad characteristics, this is only normal. It is not necessary to feel impatient with the process. From local officials to central officials, problems such as corruption, bribery, and failure to love the people are not unusual. It is inevitable with a newly established country. At present we should try to maintain the country with this cadre contingent, even though it exhibits some weak points."[7]

While the Vietnamese and the Cambodian leaders indulged the personal weaknesses of the local leadership, they were obsessed with what the Party referred to as "regionalism," "organizationalism," and "nepotism." This menace, otherwise known as patronage, posed a challenge to central authority and to the ideology and ideologically based policies of the Party. The fear in Phnom Penh was that police, soldiers, and civil servants, rather than exhibit loyalty to

the regime, would look to more immediate authorities for guidance—a provincial or district Party secretary, governor, or other local leader, the head of a
ministry, department, or office, or whatever friend or relative had given them a
job. Given the weakness of the central Party and the widespread disillusion-
ment with communist ideology, the leadership was right to be concerned.[8]

The Siem Reap defections had also raised the specter of collaboration and rebellion. In the spring of 1980 the Party issued a policy stating that PRK officials
"who are afraid of the enemy or who are serving the enemy" would be removed
from their positions and that those against whom there was "clear evidence of
their activities in betraying the revolution" would be arrested and detained. Actually removing these officials was complicated, however. If a few local cadres
left the regime, the political and military consequences would be manageable.
Provincial leaders, on the other hand, had been appointed precisely because of
their broad contacts among former Khmer Rouge cadres and their ability to
command a network of loyalists. The Vietnamese thus feared that any action
taken against these officials might prompt widespread defections or at least serious instability.[9]

THE PROBLEM WITH CHEA SIM

Chea Sim, who had vouched for the Siem Riep leadership as well as other troublesome local leaders, maintained a relationship with the Vietnamese that vac-
illated between deep suspicion and grudging reliance. At the provincial level,
the Vietnamese demonstrated their ambivalence toward the PRK's well-connected minister of the interior by dealing with his Eastern Zone loyalists on a
case-by-case basis. In Siem Reap, Chea Sim's influence continued unabated despite the defections. In Kampong Thom, the Vietnamese came to suspect Chea
Sim's nephew, provincial Party secretary and governor Ros Chhun, for his close
association with the Siem Reap defector Haem Bau. The site of heavy Khmer
Rouge activity, Kampong Thom was one province where the Vietnamese were
especially watchful and where they could not afford high-level defections. Protected by his connection to Chea Sim, Ros Chhun soon found himself in
Berlin, struggling to understand his role as the PRK's newly appointed ambassador to East Germany. Meanwhile, the Vietnamese turned the province over
to a series of harmless governors, including a French-educated intellectual, an
elderly Hanoi veteran, and a former teacher.[10]

Back in Phnom Penh, tension was rising between the Vietnamese and Chea
Sim himself. Almost immediately after the establishment of the PRK's police

forces, Sim had demonstrated a disconcerting autonomy, prompting a warning from the Party Central Committee. "All policies and methods of the struggle against betrayers of the revolution and violators of the law shall be decided by the central Party," it read. "The Ministry of the Interior has no right to issue orders or resolutions concerning the above issues."[11] The root of the problem was patronage, which Sim was promoting through the appointment of fellow Eastern Zone veterans to the ministry. Patronage was also apparently the source of tension between Sim and the top advisor to the Ministry of the Interior, Tran Vien Chi, a deputy minister of the interior in Hanoi who had directed security forces of his own and who expected to dominate the ministry in Phnom Penh.[12]

The Vietnamese were keeping watch over all the Cambodian leaders, requiring members of the Central Committee to report the length and purpose of all trips out of the capital and scrutinizing the political loyalty of all personnel assigned to them, including servants and cooks. Vietnamese authorities were somewhat less controlling of bodyguard contingents, providing guards to Hanoi-trained leaders while permitting some of the former Khmer Rouge cadres to recruit their own.[13] Nevertheless, Vietnamese surveillance of Cambodian leaders was assured by the presence of the Vietnamese soldiers who guarded their houses. Among the reports delivered by these soldiers to the Vietnamese authorities was one that, according to a former well-connected Vietnamese advisor, accused Chea Sim of meeting with Cambodians from the countryside whom the Vietnamese authorities considered suspect. Two top Vietnamese generals, Nguyen Thuan and Le Chiau, reportedly responded to this news by organizing a tour of the country for Sim, removing him from Phnom Penh in order to search his house and personal papers. When Chea Sim returned, says the former advisor, he complained to Le Duc Tho, who, to appease him, sent the two generals responsible for the flap back to Hanoi.[14]

A CONSTITUTION "ACCORDING TO OUR IDEAS ALONE"

The sensitivity shown by Le Duc Tho in the Chea Sim affair contrasted sharply with the severity with which Vietnamese authorities dealt with troublesome members of the PRK's other set of leaders, the Hanoi-trained revolutionaries. The first of these veterans to annoy the Vietnamese was Ros Samay, who, following his negotiations with Western humanitarian organizations, had acquired a reputation for excessive independence. Nonetheless, in October 1979 he was asked to oversee the drafting of the PRK's constitution, a task he took on with enthusiasm and apparently without regard for the Vietnamese.[15]

The drafting of the constitution required the participation of the country's few surviving jurists, which suited Samay, who had shown a preference for educated Cambodians over former Khmer Rouge cadres. In January 1980 he formed a secretariat for the Constitutional Drafting Council, a team of former judges, law-trained officials, and other former professionals, most of whom were working in the PRK's skeletal administration. Some had participated in the trial of Pol Pot and Ieng Sary, including the former judge Chhour Leang Huot, the sociologist Vandy Ka-on, and Lueng Chhai, a former judge who had feigned poverty and illiteracy throughout the D.K. period and had served as a French-Khmer translator for the tribunal. In all, there were nine men and two women assigned to the secretariat. None had survived the Khmer Rouge without having to watch their children, their siblings, or their spouses die or disappear. And none were communists.[16]

Although Heng Samrin was the president of the Constitutional Drafting Council, the drafting itself came under the purview of Ros Samay, who, after a brief presentation by Vietnamese advisors, operated largely without external input—not that the overall direction of the document was ever in doubt. The members of the secretariat understood that a communist system was in place and were given copies of the constitutions of the Soviet Union, Vietnam, East Germany, Hungary, and Bulgaria (in addition to previous Cambodian constitutions) to use as models. Samay divided the secretariat into subcommittees and outlined the general principles of each chapter, establishing a four-month schedule for completion of the draft. Working within the ideological constraints set before them, the members of the secretariat met in the subcommittees and then as a group to reach consensus on each article and to gain the ultimate approval of Samay. A draft was completed on April 7, 1980, and approved by the secretariat on April 11. The next day, it was endorsed by the KPRC and passed to the Party.[17]

The Party leadership (now grouped in a Permanent Committee) convened on the morning of April 18 to review and amend the draft constitution. Present in the room were Pen Sovan, Chea Sim, Say Phouthang, Bou Thang, and Hun Sen, as well as Ros Samay and most of the noncommunist jurists of the secretariat. Absent from the meeting, which was chaired by Party secretary Pen Sovan, was the president of the Constitutional Drafting Council, Heng Samrin, who was on a mission overseas. No Vietnamese advisors were in attendance.[18]

At 7:45, Pen Sovan opened the meeting with a forthright assertion of independence. "Our Constitution," stated the veteran of a quarter-century of Vietnamese training, "is *truly* (*pit pit*) our achievement and is not a copy of any constitution and was drafted according to the actual conditions of our people." Sovan stressed the primacy of Marxism-Leninism as the guiding principle of the constitution and invited the members of the secretariat to read chapters and the members of the Permanent Committee to propose amendments. First, though, Ros Samay reaffirmed Sovan's statements. "Comrade Pen Sovan is absolutely right that our draft Constitution is not a copy of the constitution of any country." Referring perhaps to the absence of Vietnamese advisors from the drafting process, Samay added, "This draft constitution was drafted according to our ideas alone, with assistance and support of all kinds from Comrade Heng Samrin and Comrade Pen Sovan." Apparently assuming that the Party would quickly approve the draft, Samay asked for permission to disseminate it.

Samay was right. The debate that morning covered neither the complexities of governance nor the checks and balances that are usually central to the drafting of constitutions. Instead, there was discussion over whether to make explicit reference to the Party and a semantic exchange over the meaning of "democracy" and "socialism." The afternoon also went smoothly as the Party leadership considered the rights, freedoms, and responsibilities of Cambodian citizens. According to the minutes of the meeting, there were no amendments other than those proposed by Pen Sovan, all of which were accepted.

Sovan's control over the meeting reflected not only his personal confidence but also his political biases. His invitation to secretariat members to explain civil liberties to the Party leadership—the former judge Leung Chhai even argued that two or more witnesses were required before security forces could conduct a search of a house, an almost comical proposition to make to men like Chea Sim—demonstrated a desire to include noncommunist intellectuals in internal political debate. At the same time, however, Sovan's own suggestions reveal a reluctance to embrace democratic freedoms, as in his removal of the "freedom to demonstrate," and a strain of puritanism, as with his inclusion of "corruption and pornography" in a general prohibition on "reactionary culture." But far and away the most significant issue raised by Sovan, at least with regard to his own political future, was that of international economic cooperation, which, he said, should be conducted not only with socialist allies but with "other countries without political conditions in order [for Cambodia] to receive assistance and to engage in trade." This attitude, precisely the one that had caused Ros Samay trouble as minister of economics, was soon to be a source of friction between Sovan and the Vietnamese authorities.

At five in the afternoon the meeting adjourned. The draft constitution had been read in full to the Party's Permanent Committee; few changes had been made, and few members of the committee had raised questions. Ros Samay asked for permission from the committee to print and disseminate the draft to cadres throughout the country for study, and as Samay had anticipated, the committee agreed. Shortly thereafter, the secretariat published the draft, bound in a bright pink cover and accompanied by a French translation, and distributed approximately ten thousand copies to ministries and provincial and municipal administrations.[19]

FRATERNAL INTERVENTION

As members of the secretariat set out on a trip around the country to discuss the draft, the French translation provided Vietnamese authorities with their first chance to read it. They were not impressed. According to Pen Sovan, the Vietnamese were not only irritated by the substance, which conformed neither to the Vietnamese constitution nor to their understanding of how Cambodia should be governed, but by the fact that the Cambodians had drafted the constitution themselves and distributed it without their permission. Internal reports, not surprisingly, were more diplomatic, stating only that "the Vietnamese advisors saw that the draft constitution still lacked words, and some substance was not yet right, and some sentences were not yet in accordance with the wishes of the people." The Vietnamese had also had enough of Ros Samay and were ready to replace him with a man they figured would exhibit less independence, the former Khmer Rouge cadre Uk Bunchheuan.[20]

Bunchheuan's relationship with the Vietnamese was complicated. In the final months before the invasion, his reluctance to join forces with the Vietnamese had aroused Hanoi's suspicions. After January 7, when many of his former Khmer Rouge colleagues returned to Cambodia to take over ministerial or provincial positions, Bunchheuan remained in Ho Chi Minh City for more than a year of intense political education. Trained in economics as well as political theory, Bunchheuan had no idea what he was being prepared for, and, after returning to Cambodia in February 1980, he was not granted a position for two months. Then, on April 4, Say Phouthang signed a Central Committee resolution appointing Bunchheuan minister of justice, effectively removing Ros Samay from his authority over law and the courts. A couple of weeks later, on

April 20, two days after Pen Sovan had so heartily endorsed Samay's draft constitution, Sovan approved Bunchheuan's appointment.[21]

The next order of business, the amending of the draft constitution, still required Ros Samay's participation. The process began one morning in late May when Vietnamese advisors arrived at the office of the secretariat. For three and a half hours they sat alone with Samay, methodically rewriting the preamble before allowing him to meet with the rest of the secretariat in the afternoon. For the veteran revolutionary who had exhibited such proud independence the previous month, it was the beginning of a difficult time. With one month to redraft the constitution, Samay spent all of June meeting with the Vietnamese advisors in the morning and reporting their amendments to the secretariat in the afternoon. Not surprisingly, the manner in which the Vietnamese advisors had taken over the drafting of the constitution and had imposed their own vision over that of the Cambodians was deeply resented by the members of the secretariat. As one member said later, distinguishing between the April draft and the final version of the constitution, "This one is Cambodian. That one is *yuon* (Vietnamese)."[22]

Ros Samay was frightened by the decisiveness demonstrated by the Vietnamese authorities and yet reluctant to leave his position. In the end, he went quietly, submitting his last report on July 7 and disappearing from the ranks of the PRK leadership. Samay was apparently resentful, however, and was the subject of a rumored defection. Either his impetuous nature or else the following he commanded among certain members of the PRK administration convinced some in the leadership that, even removed from all positions of authority, Samay remained a threat. Sometime over the next year, Samay was discreetly arrested. By the end of 1981 he was back in Vietnam, where he had lived so much of his life, only this time he would spend ten years in detention.[23]

Meanwhile, the political career of Uk Bunchheuan began again. In contrast to Ros Samay and Pen Sovan, who had received decades of communist training in Vietnam and considered themselves ready to make independent decisions, Bunchheuan was still compensating for his anti-Vietnamese past. Reporting in July 1980, shortly after the redrafting of the constitution, Bunchheuan assured his superiors that "Vietnamese advisors helped provide their views, in a loyal manner, to the Secretariat for Drafting the Constitution and joined in amending the draft constitution so that it had substance in accordance with socialist countries." According to Bunchheuan, the secretariat was "happy and thankful for the instruction and teaching of the Vietnamese advisors, which is of high fraternal revolutionary quality and represents broad international solidarity."[24]

What exactly were the contributions of the Vietnamese advisors? As Samay learned on the morning of May 29 (and as the secretariat learned that afternoon), the Vietnamese were keenly interested in the impact that the constitution would have on domestic and international politics. They inserted the names Pol Pot–Ieng Sary–Khieu Samphan to "emphasize the names of the genocidal clique." They also overruled the Cambodian leadership and removed the name Communist Party of Kampuchea, which had been used by the Khmer Rouge. Their explanation was that "in the current situation, the people would be startled by the [appearance] of the Communist Party of Kampuchea because they are afraid of more communism like that of the Party of Pol Pot." The Vietnamese advisors' solution was to "educate the people so that they thoroughly understand the Party and to then announce its name." For now, the draft constitution would refer to the Party of the Working Class (*bak robas vonnah kammokar*).[25]

There were more rhetorical amendments, including provisions denouncing "betrayers of the revolution" both domestic and outside the country and "imperialist invaders" and a mention of support for revolutions throughout the world. Removing Pen Sovan's provision on broad international cooperation, the advisors tightened language governing foreign relations, changing "socialist" countries to "friendly" countries, thereby excluding China.

The Vietnamese advisors also made substantive modifications whose effect was to delay the development of democratic institutions. From the legislature they removed the authority to "interpret laws" or to renew debate on a law after promulgation, the right to dissolve itself, the obligation to field a quorum, and the requirement that its sessions be public and the proceedings published. Popular control over the legislature was also eliminated—the dismissal of members of the National Assembly and the replacement of the president of the National Assembly were no longer subject to democratic processes. Finally, the advisors removed from the draft provisions allowing for popular elections of provincial and municipal assemblies, as well as all provisions related to those assemblies' selection of their own leadership.[26]

According to Uk Bunchheuan's reports, these changes were "in accordance with the situation in our country following the war." The security problems faced by the regime and the threat of infiltration, explained Bunchheuan, required that there be a minimum of political transparency and democratic choice. Rather, the war required that there be a Supreme Organization (*angkar kompoul*) to select representatives of the people before the people elect them. "It shall be done like this so that the enemy cannot infiltrate [the country]." If

Bunchheuan heard the echoes of the Khmer Rouge's secret rule by angkar and its Upper Organization (*angkar loeu*), he apparently wasn't disturbed.[27]

The Vietnamese advisors also removed human rights provisions that the secretariat had inserted into the draft. These included equality before the law without regard to political position, prohibitions on forced confessions, punishment for those responsible for harming detainees, the invalidity of forced confessions, the presumption of innocence and the requirement that detainees merely suspected of a crime be released, requirements that witnesses be present for searches of homes, and prohibitions on retroactive applicability of criminal law. Although the secretariat had allowed for a suspension of certain rights in cases of emergency, it had included a six-month time limit on that suspension; in the redrafting this time limit was removed. The advisors also significantly restricted the ability of prosecutors to pursue human rights violations and malfeasance of any kind by removing provisions allowing them to investigate state bodies. The only human rights that the Vietnamese added to the constitution were for minority populations, including respect for the languages and traditions of all nationalities. They also removed a provision requiring that court proceedings be conducted in Khmer.

These amendments took place in a political environment that was becoming increasingly hostile toward the noncommunist resistance and toward ideological opposition to communist rule in general. During the summer of 1980 the regime announced the "trial" of the Haem Kroesna agents, authorized thousands of arrests, and promulgated the decree-law against "betraying the revolution." Cambodian officials were subject to intense political education, including lessons on "betrayers of the revolution," and mounting official condemnation of prerevolutionary culture.[28] In this context, bourgeois civil liberties were apparently unacceptable, at least to the Vietnamese. Nor was it an opportune time to exhibit national independence. In June the KPRC responded to increasing tension between Cambodians and Vietnamese advisors by reminding its officials to cooperate more closely with the Vietnamese.[29]

After the secretariat wrapped up its work under the scrutiny of Uk Bunchheuan and the Vietnamese advisors, the leadership met again to approve the draft. A week later, Heng Samrin granted permission to disseminate it and to hold local study sessions originally planned for April. From the middle of August to September, the members of the secretariat patiently explained and defended the various provisions of the new draft to the staff of the newly established Ministry of Justice, to city officials at Phnom Penh's old City Hall, and to provincial cadres in nearby Kandal and Kampong Speu. Outside the Ministry of Justice whoever was organizing the sessions made sure that trusted officials controlled the agenda. In Phnom Penh, Minister of Propaganda Kaev Chenda chaired the proceedings. In Kandal and Kampong Speu provincial Party secretaries ran the sessions, with Minister of Education Chan Ven helping out in Kandal. The members of the secretariat were so mistrusted by the Party that they did not participate in the group discussions that followed the presentations, and although they were permitted to field written questions on the "framework" of the constitution, "political questions" were to be directed to the provincial officials.[30]

These restrictions reflected the Party leadership's suspicions of the noncommunists in the administration. As Heng Samrin told a gathering of Party and state leaders and Vietnamese advisors, "Many of our leadership cadres who have lived in feudal, colonial, imperialist society are still wrapped up in old ideas, ideas that are exploitative, envious, and disloyal." By the end of 1980 the members of the Constitutional Drafting Secretariat—who now had been absorbed into the Ministry of Justice—were subject to daily "political study sessions concerning class and class struggle." East German jurists were visiting, bringing with them French-language treatises on "socialist legal systems" and "socialist legality" for the Cambodians to translate into Khmer. Meanwhile, Uk Bunchheuan, who had recently returned from a trip to Vietnam, where he received training for his new position as minister of justice, reassured the leadership that the noncommunists in his ministry were under control. In a report he delivered in December 1980, he explained, in practiced jargon, that "throughout the ministry, our staff and cadres are absorbed in and implementing well the political tactics, strategies, and policies of the Kampuchean United Front for National Salvation. Employing the edicts [of the Front] as principles in implementing all duties conferred by the KPRC, they are trying hard to serve the revolution with absolute care and loyalty." Nonetheless, Bunchheuan was forced to acknowledge that "there are a small number of colleagues who do not understand [the policies of the revolution] deeply and so just do this or that and frequently do whatever they wish."[31]

A couple of months later, as the constitution drafting process resumed, Bunchheuan promised at a meeting of Party leaders that there would be no more problems from the secretariat. "In June 1980 there was some conflict, but now it's been resolved, and [the ministry] can keep secrets," he said, perhaps recalling the disputed dissemination of the first draft. Bunchheuan expressed frustration, however, with the deliberation with which the members of the secretariat approached their work. "The drafting of the constitution is slow," he complained, "because the people have never done this kind of work before. When they don't understand a sentence, they run to compare it with the treatises and don't go according to the actual situation in Cambodian society."[32]

What the "actual situation" required, it turned out, were more amendments similar to those imposed by the Vietnamese advisors in June 1980. Institutions envisioned in the original draft, including some that existed in Vietnam, were removed entirely, including a Supreme Court, a general procurator, and local legislatures (whose duties were transferred to unelected People's Revolutionary Committees). The National Assembly was weakened further, and its leadership and that of the government were to be selected by even more opaque processes. The implication of these amendments was that Cambodia was not yet ready for any level of democracy or transparency, even for the communist tradition of legislative rubber stamping of Party decisions. As A40 chief Nguyen Con explained to Heng Samrin, "The experience in Vietnam and other socialist countries is that economic plans should go through the Center, and the National Assembly decides. But the current situation in Cambodia is such that they can go through the Center, and the National Assembly [receives] reports on important goals later. Details are not necessary."[33]

The amendments of early 1981 also continued the trend of removing the civil liberties that had been written into the original draft, including the right to choose a profession, the right to travel and to choose a place of residence, the right to a legal defense "throughout the duration of the penal process," the right not to be tortured, and the remaining restrictions on searches of homes. (The only victory won by the members of the secretariat was the inclusion of a provision stating, "In the case of an arrest with evidence, records must be immediately transmitted to the competent organ for decision.") Finally, the assumption that overseas Cambodians and Cambodians at the border were hostile to the PRK was reflected in the removal of prohibitions on banishing Cambodians and on depriving them of their nationality. Overseas Cambodians, according to the amended draft, still enjoyed state protection, but only so long as they were "genuinely patriotic." (With the removal of references to the country's "neutrality," this meant supporting the PRK and its allies.) The draft was now acceptable to the Vietnamese.

The constitution became a part of a larger campaign to present a successful regime, domestically and internationally. Now in the hands of the Party Central Education and Propaganda Committee, the draft was circulated, read over the radio, and taught in political study sessions.[34] Eventually the campaign was reduced to a few official slogans: "All the people and the entire army come together to understand and build the constitution!" and "Congratulations on the draft constitution of the People's Republic of Kampuchea!"[35]

THE POLITICS OF 1981

The spring of 1981 was a busy time, filled with pronouncements and ceremonies, political education and tension. As usual, the military and diplomatic struggle drove internal events. The West, which blamed the Vietnamese occupation for the ongoing conflict in Cambodia, was calling for an international conference. Hanoi and Phnom Penh, on the other hand, preferred a regional approach involving direct negotiations between the PRK and Thailand. As the Vietnamese and the Cambodians knew, such negotiations would require Thailand first to recognize the legitimacy of the PRK, a prospect rejected outright by China. The standoff was exacerbated by a military incursion: even as Hanoi was arguing for a demilitarized zone along the Thai-Cambodian border, Vietnamese army units were crossing into Thai territory. The trespass hardened Thai opposition to the Vietnamese occupation and brought ASEAN even closer to China. The PRK's global diplomatic situation was suffering, too. In October 1980 the General Assembly of the United Nations had voted, by an even greater majority than in the previous year, to continue to seat the exiled regime of Democratic Kampuchea.

The eventual resolution of the Cambodia problem lay in the proposals of China and ASEAN: a withdrawal of Vietnamese forces from Cambodia followed by a United Nations–sponsored election. At the time, however, this was not a solution. The Vietnamese continued to describe the establishment of the PRK as "irreversible" and rejected multiparty elections. Its troops were necessary to thwart a "Chinese threat," they said, and could not be removed until the Khmer Rouge were disarmed, another proposal unacceptable to the Chinese.[36]

Both sides were settling in. There were stirrings of unity in the resistance and increased cooperation between the PRK and Vietnam. In January 1981, the president of the Khmer People's National Liberation Front, Son Sann, formed a common front with the royalist resistance, MOULINAKA. The following month, Sihanouk was talking of a "United Front against Vietnamese colonization of Cambodia." In response, Vietnam consolidated its military presence in Cambodia, concluding a series of defense agreements with the PRK in June 1981. Hanoi and Phnom Penh were also responding to the political threat posed by a resistance coalition. Hoping to improve its international standing and discourage Cambodians from defecting, the PRK sought to present the trappings of a more consolidated, permanent, and democratic regime, with elections, a legislature, and a constitution.[37]

THE TRAPPINGS OF DEMOCRACY

Every decision that followed represented a trade-off between a show of democracy and the fear of internal opposition. Discussing preparations for elections, Ung Phan, minister in charge of the Council of Ministers, and Uk Bunchheuan tersely summed up the issues. "I am fearful that free campaigning may conceal the beginning of something that could lead to the damaging of national interests and of society," said Phan. "This free campaigning has a good meaning in the context of international politics," Bunchheuan reminded his colleague. "Foreign observers will recognize that election campaigning can occur freely and plentifully. Also, with regard to domestic politics, this freedom in election campaigning must respect the national interest and individual honor. So there is nothing to be afraid of."[38]

Bunchheuan's confidence was well placed. The election process was a tightly controlled, one-party affair directed by Say Phouthang, chair of the Party Central Organization Committee, and orchestrated by Bou Thang, chair of the Party Central Education and Propaganda Committee. The local officials responsible for conducting the elections were also tested. In March the PRK organized elections for commune-level officials in about 30 percent of the communes. The elections were marked by extreme caution in selecting candidates and by the heavy involvement of Vietnamese advisors and local military officers. "The election to select the state authority in the communes and urban areas," the Party told provincial authorities, "is a severe and complicated struggle between us and the enemy."[39]

On May 1, having successfully conducted the commune elections, local officials, members of the core groups, and members of the mass organizations managed to mobilize much of the Cambodian population to vote in national parliamentary elections. For the ballots the Party had constructed lists of candidates with the current top leaders first. Generally, there was only one more candidate than there were seats to be filled; Cambodians were instructed to cross off the name (or names) of the candidate (or candidates) they did *not* prefer. By crossing off the last name on the list, voters produced a highly satisfying result. Despite the almost absolute anonymity of the Cambodian leaders among the general population (the names had been announced on April 26), the top leaders were elected overwhelmingly and in close proportion to their standing within the state and Party hierarchy. Heng Samrin gained 99.75 percent of the vote, Pen Sovan 99.63 percent, Chea Sim 99.61 percent, and so on. As Say Phouthang reported to the Election Committee, "There were no complaints at all concerning the results of the election."[40]

The next few events—the Fourth National Party Congress, the promulgation of the constitution, and the opening session of the newly elected National Assembly—offered little suspense. The Party congress, which Pen Sovan had been calling for since late 1980 but which Vietnamese officials had put off until after the election, took place at the end of May, by which time the fundamental political and economic policies of the regime had been set. The selection by the congress of a Politburo and the expansion of the Party Central Committee to twenty-one members presented few surprises: no one from the top leadership was dropped, no new faces moved to the top, and the balance between the Hanoi group and the former Eastern Zone cadres remained comfortably even. Nor were any of the speeches astonishing. Pen Sovan spoke at length (eighty-four pages in the French translation) and without any apparent divergences from Vietnamese positions on, among other things, the history of Cambodian independence, the previous two years of reconstruction and defense, and the building of the Party.[41]

The promulgation of the constitution led to a brief, ineffectual discussion. In early May, after the elections, the government sent copies of the draft to cadres in various provinces, requesting their comments. The cadres, who, unlike the members of the Constitutional Drafting Secretariat, had never received legal training or higher education of any kind, nonetheless raised fundamental human rights concerns, recommending that detention be limited to twenty-four hours, that there be a "right to a defense when the home is violated," and that privacy of the mail be guaranteed. These suggestions were rejected by Uk Bunchheuan, who promised that they would be addressed in subsequent laws and regulations.[42]

Cambodians heard other important pronouncements that spring. In recognition of the stability of the regime and the economic challenges ahead, the Kampuchean United Front for National Salvation was renamed the Solidarity Front for Building the Cambodian Motherland. There was also a newly elected National Assembly, to be headed by Chea Sim, and a Council of State, which would serve as the permanent committee of the assembly and which would be led by Heng Samrin. Although Samrin would continue as head of state, the administration of the country was now under the control of a new government, a Council of Ministers, to be headed by a prime minister, Pen Sovan. Most important, the Party had emerged, not as the Communist Party of Kampuchea, as Pen Sovan, Hun Sen, Say Phouthang, and Bou Thang had recommended in April 1980, but as the Kampuchean People's Revolutionary Party (KPRP).

The political theater in Phnom Penh did nothing to improve the PRK's standing overseas. A few weeks after the first session of the National Assembly, an international conference on the Cambodian conflict was convened in New York under the auspices of the United Nations. Boycotted by the Soviet Union, the Eastern Bloc, Vietnam, Laos, and the PRK, the conference concluded with a call for a ceasefire, a U.N.-supervised withdrawal of foreign forces, and free elections. American officials, who walked out on Khmer Rouge representatives, nevertheless announced that there would be no economic assistance to Vietnam so long as it occupied Cambodia. Chinese, ASEAN, and French officials also lashed out at Vietnam. From Hanoi, Vietnamese Foreign Minister Nguyen Co Thach struck back, accusing the conference of interfering in Cambodia's internal affairs. In Phnom Penh the PRK news agency echoed these sentiments, adding that the conference was using the name of the United Nations "to consecrate the genocidal Pol Pot clique and serve the interests of the Beijing expansionists." In regard to supervision of a Vietnamese withdrawal or elections, Phnom Penh was adamant. "To demand U.N. intervention in a country like this is to trample underfoot basic principles of international law, insult the U.N. Charter, and, more dangerous, scorn the sovereignty and independence of a small country, thus setting a detrimental precedent with respect to the current struggle waged by national liberation movements." The PRK's perspective was straightforward: "there is no Kampuchea problem and hence no solution to be found for it."[43]

DEMOTING THE INTELLECTUALS

Beneath the ceremony and expressions of solidarity lay serious tensions both among various Cambodian officials and between elements of the Cambodian leadership and their Vietnamese advisors. The former jurists and intellectuals whose contribution to the drafting of the constitution had been overruled by the Vietnamese were disgruntled, as were many other noncommunists who had hoped for a more open and democratic country and who instead faced an onslaught of political education. PRK officials attended study sessions in newly opened political schools in Cambodia; almost all were sent to Vietnam for up to six months of political education. Still, Party leaders considered many of the civil servants to be potential security risks. As Minister of Commerce Tang Sareum warned, the regime should be "extra careful with regard to some staff, cadres, and workers who ask permission to leave their houses and who then turn around and go serve the enemy's schemes, returning to engage in economic sabotage and kill the leadership cadres of our revolution."[44]

Vietnamese authorities used the summer of 1981 to chip away at the power of ministers whose views were different from their own. Ros Samay had been removed from power and was now in detention. Minister of Health Nou Peng and Minister of Education Chan Ven were more fortunate and were transferred. With the establishment of the National Assembly and the Council of State, legislative bodies with very little real power, the regime could safely move potentially independent ministers into prestigious but weak positions. Peng, a veteran revolutionary who had studied medicine and health administration in Vietnam and who had associated himself with Pen Sovan's overtures to educated Cambodians, was named vice president of the National Assembly. Chan Ven was made secretary-general of the Council of State.[45]

The case of Chan Ven suggests some of the tensions and divisions within the leadership. In the first two years of the PRK, Ven had personified the regime's effort to rally intellectuals. His unique role had begun with his flight, in July 1978, from a Khmer Rouge cooperative in Svay Rieng to Vietnam, where he was detained in an "education camp" and interrogated by Kaev Chenda and Ros Samay. Satisfied with his explanation for his flight—"I couldn't live with the Khmer Rouge"—the Cambodian communists invited him to serve as the representative intellectual of the Front. Chan Ven was also a spokesperson for the new regime, substituting for Ros Samay as chief of delegation during visits to the Soviet Union and Eastern Europe. Returning to Cambodia in early February 1979, he became minister of education as well as president of the Cambodian-Vietnamese Friendship Association, serving as a symbol of prerevolutionary Cambodia's accommodation to the new political situation. His bourgeois background caused some concern; filling in Chan Ven's personal history in late 1979, Ung Phan remarked that he was "determined to have a nonrevolutionary spirit." The Party nonetheless considered him loyal, and in July 1980 he was appointed mayor of Phnom Penh.[46]

Chan Ven's application for Party membership split the leadership. Pen Sovan tended to see educated Cambodians like Ven as potential leaders who were not only competent but, subjected to the right mix of political education, amenable to the kind of socialism to which he himself adhered. Sovan also hoped to establish a political base of Party and state officials who would be loyal neither to the Vietnamese nor to the former Eastern Zone cadres in the leadership. In early 1981, Sovan directed that Chan Ven be granted Party candidate status. For more than a year, however, Ven's entry was delayed by those who saw insubordination, even treason, in his nonideological positions. One such leader was Finance Minister Chan Phin, an ideologically rigid Hanoi veteran who was suspicious of noncommunist intellectuals. According to Phin, Chan Ven had made visits to his native Svay Rieng, where he told Cambodians that they needn't sell rice to the state—behavior that, according to Chan Phin, "caused Heng Samrin a lot of heartache." In the spring and summer of 1981, complaints such as these derailed Chan Ven's career, overriding Pen Sovan's patronage. Two months after the Party congress, Ven dutifully attended a Communist Party congress in Mongolia and accepted a study mission in the Soviet Union. Upon his return in July, he learned that he had been removed as both minister of education and mayor of Phnom Penh and had been appointed to the powerless Council of State.[47]

The demotions of intellectuals were costly. The decision by thousands of educated Cambodians to flee to the border had deprived the regime of technocrats and had inflicted serious damage to the PRK's international image. Rumors that prominent intellectuals had given up on the regime could only exacerbate the problem. Heng Samrin described the prevailing mood: "Some intellectuals are listening to a lot of foreign radio and only studying our revolutionary politics a little. They are also unhappy with the situation. Some cadres are saying, wrongly, that various cadres who are uneasy want to flee [to Thailand]. For example, they say that Comrade Nou Peng, Comrade Vandy Ka-on, and Comrade Ros Samay have prepared to flee to Thailand. This is the psychological [manipulation] of the enemy, which undermines our trust in each other."[48]

The secrecy with which Ros Samay was arrested and the decision to grant Nou Peng, Chan Ven, and Vandy Ka-on high-profile positions in the legislature (Ka-on, the former sociologist, became chair of the Legislation Commission) were intended to stem the perception that the PRK was hostile to intellectuals. As we shall see, what these officials did in their new positions was, to a certain extent, up to them. Some would serve in these positions quietly, afraid that they might be arrested as a result of some political misstep. Others would see the regime's decision to retain them as an opportunity to express their opinions—internally and always within the bounds of acceptable political discourse—in the hopes of effecting incremental change.

PEN SOVAN AND THE SEARCH
FOR TRADING PARTNERS

Perhaps the most troubled of the Cambodian leaders was Pen Sovan himself. Having praised Cambodia's "intellectuals" in his speech to the Party congress in May, he was now witnessing their isolation at the hands of rival leaders and the Vietnamese. Sovan's own power was slipping as well, beginning with the loss of his military portfolio. In the months before the promulgation of the constitution, last-minute changes to the draft included the removal of a National Defense Council, a military organ that presumably would have been headed by Sovan. With the establishment of the new government, the Ministry of Defense went to Sovan's fellow Hanoi veteran Chan Si. Heng Samrin became chief of staff.

By all accounts, Pen Sovan's independent attitude bothered the Vietnamese. After a quarter-century of communist military and political training, he considered himself equal to the top Vietnamese leaders and did not appreciate what he perceived as condescension. Many Cambodians who were politically active in the early years of the PRK can tell at least one story related to Sovan's defiant resistance to Vietnamese control, his efforts to oppose directions from Hanoi, and his expressions of irritation with heavy-handed Vietnamese behavior. Although many of these stories describe purely symbolic gestures or Pen Sovan's prickly, contemptuous manner, it is clear that Sovan was also pursuing policies that ran counter to Hanoi's plans for Cambodia and the Vietnamese-Cambodian relationship. In particular, the Vietnamese were increasingly concerned about his search for economic independence and his contacts with alternative trading partners within the Eastern Bloc and with the capitalist world. Some of the first such initiatives came out of trips, taken in 1980, to the Soviet Union and East Germany, during which he concluded agreements on the export of Cambodian rubber. According to Pen Sovan, these deals prompted Le Duc Tho, in March 1981, to issue what Sovan now calls his "first warning." Whereas the Vietnamese encouraged much of the trade being established between Cambodia and Eastern Europe, rubber was an area of some competition. The 1980 deals thus complicated not only Cambodia's relations with Vietnam but relations between Vietnam and the Eastern Bloc.[49]

Sovan also set out in pursuit of hard currency for the PRK. Initially, the export of Cambodian goods for currency had been the responsibility of the Vietnamese. But Pen Sovan was actively looking to reduce Cambodia's financial dependence on Vietnam, and, as the Cambodian Central Bank reported in July

1981, the possibilities were there. To broaden the PRK's global economic ties, the Central Bank had contacted the banks of ten socialist countries, a private bank in Paris, and two overseas branches of a Soviet bank. The private bank, the Commercial Bank of Northern Europe, had assisted Vietnamese banks in retrieving assets frozen by the United States and had helped the Vietnamese find French bank officials to train cadres in Vietnam. This kind of assistance, along with help in getting Cambodians living in France to send hard currency to their families in Cambodia, would have been much appreciated by Phnom Penh. So, too, would relations with the Moscow Narodny Bank, whose branch in London would have helped the inexperienced Cambodians in their financial transactions with capitalist countries.[50]

The Cambodians were especially eager to establish a relationship with the Moscow bank's Singapore branch, which, according to Central Bank officials, would "allow access to the international market in the area." The appeal of regional trade, neither restrained by Vietnamese control nor corrupted by infiltration from Thailand, was undeniable. "Goods in Singapore are cheaper than in neighboring countries, such as Thailand," bank officials told Sovan. "Also, we can export our goods to sell in Singapore." The Cambodians expected the Soviets, not the Vietnamese, to facilitate this relationship.[51]

CHEA SIM, KHANG SARIN, AND THE
REBELLIOUS MAO PHOK

Chea Sim was also on the minds of the Vietnamese. By 1981 he had appointed hundreds of police, prison officers, interrogators, and other security officials, loyal subordinates whom Cambodians referred to as Chea Sim's *konchau* (literally, "children and grandchildren"). Thanks to Sim, they had been effectively cleared of any wrongdoing committed during the D.K. regime and had been given clothes, food, and housing, as well as power. According to Pen Sovan, Sim's *konchau* also appreciated their patron's relatively independent stance toward the Vietnamese, including his opposition to perceived encroachments on the Vietnamese border and his resistance to Vietnamese appointments within the Ministry of the Interior. Whether it was Chea Sim's independence that concerned the Vietnamese or his disconcerting accumulation of power, it was time for him to go. In June, Chea Sim was removed from his position as minister of the interior and assigned the ceremonial role of president of the National Assembly.[52]

His replacement, Khang Sarin, was more to Vietnam's liking. Trained in

Hanoi, Sarin had been an officer in the Vietnamese army, spoke fluent Vietnamese, and, as one story goes, absentmindedly saluted Vietnamese officers even after becoming an official of the PRK. Immediately after liberation, he had served as the commander of the First Brigade for the defense of Phnom Penh, a position he left in 1980 to pursue military training in the USSR. Upon his return, Sarin became not only minister of the interior but also deputy minister of defense, deputy chief of staff, and, eventually, a member of the Party Central Committee Secretariat.[53]

Khang Sarin was actually much weaker than this list of titles might suggest. Having never commanded any Cambodians, Sarin was ill equipped to develop a power base at the Ministry of the Interior. Although the Vietnamese attempted to help him impose his influence at the ministry, the transition did not go smoothly. "When Comrade Chea Sim was replaced by Comrade Khang Sarin, lower-level comrades had feelings about the selection of sixty of Khang Sarin's people to replace people at the Ministry of the Interior," said Heng Samrin diplomatically at one Party meeting. Sarin's lack of control over the security forces was apparent in a state document issued later in the year: "The Ministry of the Interior and state authorities at all levels have not yet fully absorbed the principles of leadership and management of the police forces."[54]

In the rubber plantations of Kampong Cham, a far more direct threat to the regime was taking shape. The crisis had its origins in the plantation town of Memot, where, in the fall of 1978, Eastern Zone cadres Uk Bunchheuan and Mao Phok had spurned the Vietnamese. Having incurred the suspicion of Hanoi, Bunchheuan accepted extended political training in Vietnam and later returned as a powerless and deferential minister of justice. Phok rejected these compromises, however, refusing to attend political education and seeking powerful positions within the PRK. Like many other former Khmer Rouge leaders, Phok was respected and feared for his appeal to "forces within the country." After granting him a position under Chea Sim at the Ministry of the Interior, Vietnamese authorities attempted, at the end of 1979, to move Mao Phok to a civil position (deputy minister of agriculture for aquatic production) where he could not betray the regime militarily. Phok refused, insisting on the portfolio for rubber plantations.[55]

Although no objective account exists for what happened next, the regime's investigative reports reveal what the leadership *feared* Mao Phok was up to. According to those reports, Phok embarked on a spree of malfeasance, pilfering state property, overestimating the number of workers in the plantations and pocketing the allocated salaries, stealing state gold and silver, selling off state property, using state workers for the construction of his house and cooperative ponds for personal fish farming, renting state land, and generally attempting to profit from the plantations. But the alleged corruption itself was not the problem. As Say Phouthang later conceded, "If it was only mismanagement of state property, we could have educated him, but what can't be tolerated are the traitorous activities of Mao Phok." The real problem, it turned out, was his purported accumulation of personal power, which, the regime's reports claim, he accomplished by paying plantation personnel (with money gained from the sale of state property), forcibly removing plantation cadres not personally loyal to him, and refusing to accept Party appointments. "No one can control Mao Phok," bemoaned Say Phouthang.[56]

By the end of 1980 the leadership even suspected Mao Phok of having participated in the assassinations of PRK officials. Around the time of the Fourth Party Congress in May 1981, Party leaders understood Phok to be "making contacts with reactionary groups hiding in the forest around the rubber plantation area . . . to oppose the revolution" and "creating armed forces on the rubber plantations that are growing in strength and becoming personal forces that would live or die with Mao Phok." According to the state's investigation, "Mao Phok ordered his faction to gather provisions and store them for when there is an opportunity to oppose the revolution." Even then, the weakness of the regime (and of the Vietnamese) was such that, despite these accusations, Mao Phok was not arrested for another twelve months.[57]

DEBATING VIETNAMESE IMMIGRATION

One complaint that united the intellectuals and the former Eastern Zone cadres was the apparent impunity with which Vietnamese officials seemed to be operating in Cambodia, particularly their tolerance of Vietnamese immigration. The issue was complicated. Some ethnic Vietnamese immigrants had previously lived in Cambodia and were returning from exile. Many came with spouses, children, or other family members who were new to Cambodia. Other immigrants were fleeing political repression in Vietnam. A final group was seeking greater economic opportunities. The numbers associated with these frequently overlapping categories, as well as the overall scope of Vietnamese immigration, were (and remain) vague. By 1980, however, provincial officials were registering their concerns with the central government and complaining that the immigration of Vietnamese and ethnic Chinese from southern Vietnam was "illegal."[58]

Although Pen Sovan had been addressing the issue since late 1979, when he instructed Ung Phan to check travel documentation of Vietnamese entering Cambodia, it had become clear that the PRK could do little to stem the flow. Sovan thus turned to the two top Vietnamese authorities in Cambodia for help. The first was Vietnamese ambassador Ngo Dien, a veteran diplomat and former journalist. The other was Tran Xuan Bach, Le Duc Tho's replacement as Vietnamese Communist Party representative in Cambodia and head of B68. As a subsequent Cambodian Party document put it, Pen Sovan intended to discuss "a resolution on the increasing [numbers] of Vietnamese nationals coming illegally to Cambodia" in the spirit of "restrengthening the ties of pure friendship and solidarity between Cambodia and Vietnam."[59]

According to Sovan, Ngo Dien and Tran Xuan Bach told him that they would have to take the issue up with the Vietnamese Communist Party in Hanoi. A week and a half after the meeting, however, the Cambodian Party leadership issued a policy on Vietnamese immigration. It was a bold document. On the one hand, the new policy supported Hanoi's efforts to control the exodus of those southern Vietnamese who were attempting to escape anticapitalist campaigns and forced reeducation. On the other hand, it asserted Cambodian jurisdiction over immigration matters, including the authority to confiscate the property of ethnic Vietnamese or expel them from Cambodian territory. According to the policy, "Any bad person who conducts business dishonestly, disseminates . . . divisive propaganda, promotes narrow-minded, nationalistic views, contacts bad people, leads people to flee overseas or looks for routes to flee overseas . . . shall be rounded up, guided, educated, and, within a short time period to be determined, forced to return to Vietnam."[60]

The Party leadership took a lenient approach to ethnic Vietnamese deemed to be engaging in productive economic activity. "Vietnamese nationals who have come to Cambodia illegally but who are now conducting business honestly as artisans, as rice [farmers], or [as workers] on plantations" would be permitted to remain in Cambodia so long as they received the permission of local officials and "the approval of the people." The policy took aim, however, at purported economic exploitation by ethnic Vietnamese, in particular by Vietnamese fishermen.

This was an old complaint. During the Lon Nol and Khmer Rouge regimes, ethnic Vietnamese who lived and fished along Cambodia's rivers and the Tonle Sap Lake were accused of exploitation; most were either killed or forced to flee to Vietnam. There is no indication that PRK officials intended to repeat the violence, nor would the regime expel any "Vietnamese residents who had lived for a long time in Cambodia." Instead, the Cambodians were simply asserting that they, rather than Vietnamese authorities, would decide who would stay and who would go. According to the new policy, provincial officials would be permitted to "hire" Vietnamese fishermen, who would not be permitted to cross from one province to another. Fishermen not hired by the officials and not "approved" by the people would be "rounded up for education and returned to Vietnam."[61]

Regardless of the policy, Cambodians lacked the power to expel immigrants. Just a few days after Pen Sovan's meeting with Ngo Dien and Tran Xuan Bach, the leadership received a letter from Chan Ven, then mayor of Phnom Penh. By Chan Ven's estimates, there were 954 Vietnamese and ethnic Chinese from Vietnam living "illegally" in the capital. Municipal officials, he explained, had already discussed the problem with Vietnamese advisors and had "explained" to the immigrants that they were to return. A few volunteered, he said, but most did not, claiming that they had previously lived in Cambodia or had a Cambodian spouse. Chan Ven asked the KPRC to intervene. The response, which came shortly after the Party had issued its policy, was that "the Vietnamese and Chinese residents . . . shall be sent back to their country because they did not actually live here before [the revolution]; they came only in 1979, after the Pol Pot period, and they have all sneaked in (*luoch ruat mok*) illegally." The leadership did not offer Chan Ven much of a solution, however, proposing merely that he "cooperate with the Vietnamese advisors to facilitate in some way the return of those who have come illegally back to their country."[62]

As Pen Sovan and his colleagues prepared for the Party congress, the promulgation of the constitution, and the establishment of a new government, they deferred their concerns about Vietnamese immigration. By August 1981, however, Cambodians working in a variety of different state institutions were again discussing the issue.

One institution whose internal debates came around to the issue of immigration was the awkwardly named Committee for the Establishment of Social Order and Security for the Capital of Phnom Penh, an interministerial body established by the Party Central Committee to confront the unchecked repopulation of the capital. This committee, chaired by Minister of the Interior Khang Sarin, was not originally tasked with resolving the problem of Vietnamese immigration. Its first few meetings were devoted to reurbanization and to concerns related to the growth of the private sector. Discussions related to the ethnic composition of the city's growing population focused squarely on the "Chinese capitalists" and "Beijing Chinese hiding themselves as spies." At the committee's third meeting, however, Sarin broached the subject of Vietnamese immigration. "There should be a firm procedure for those elements from Vietnam who steal, swindle, and trade illegally. But the two states agree to provide assistance to Vietnamese residents who come to conduct normal business."[63]

Peng Pat, a 1977 Eastern Zone defector who had replaced Khang Sarin as military chief of Phnom Penh, was the first to voice objections. "[I recognize] the victory of Cambodian-Vietnamese solidarity as a factor, but the Vietnamese people are entering Cambodia illegally and what kind of procedure do we have? . . . What are we going to do? Are we going to do nothing? We have procedures only for the Chinese and the Khmers who are in the city and who have no work and must be sent to the countryside. For Vietnamese residents who have come illegally, do we respond in the same manner? We let the Vietnamese residents enter Cambodia without management, and they scurry around (*daoer kakaur kakay*) as they wish, from province to province, from Cambodia to Thailand, to Vietnam, and so on. How are we to solve this? Do we determine them to be refugees or not?"[64]

The chief of the Phnom Penh police, Khoem Pon, also had strong feelings about the Vietnamese. Pon was a Khmer from southern Vietnam, a member of the Vietnamese Communist Party, and a former police officer in Vietnam's Cuu Long province.[65] Despite, or perhaps because of, his background, Pon did not look favorably on Vietnamese immigration. "With regard to Vietnamese residents who have come without permission, the following [problems] must be resolved: trade in Vietnamese currency, theft, prostitution, desertion by soldiers who then form armed gangs, smugglers of medicines, opium . . . and smugglers of people. The noodle shops in the corners of the New Market are all Vietnamese, and I ask that there be a procedure to resolve this problem. In Vietnam and Kampuchea Krom [southern Vietnam], the youth are disappearing, running away to go live temporarily in Cambodia on their way to Thailand."[66]

A week later, when the committee reconvened, Khang Sarin was prepared. He described the offenses he said were being committed by Vietnamese residents in Cambodia, including prostitution, theft, gambling, smuggling, and "destroying the economy," concluding: "We should direct any Vietnamese who are clearly seen to be a bad element to return to their country." Political cases, he said, would be handled directly by the Vietnamese and by Cambodian security forces. "Officers, spies, and government officials of the Thieu-Ky puppets [i.e., the former leaders of South Vietnam] should be arrested and sent to the Vietnamese state authority, Organization 7708 [the Phnom Penh–based Vietnamese security organ]. Any Vietnamese who has come seeking refuge in Cambodia to prepare to flee overseas shall be rounded up and handed over to the police."[67]

Khang Sarin reiterated aspects of the Party's 1980 policy, including the authority of local state officials to return ethnic Vietnamese to Vietnam and the right of former residents to stay in Cambodia. He also reminded the committee that immigration was, diplomatically speaking, a sensitive matter. "In order to appropriately implement this policy and avoid harming politics between the two countries, Cambodia and Vietnam, we should carefully examine and consider [each case] before distinguishing among different kinds of Vietnamese."[68]

The Cambodians were frustrated by their inability to make these distinctions. "We don't yet have a law to implement with regard to prostitution, smuggling, or destroying the economy so now we should first round them up and gradually educate them and wait until we can tie together some appropriate law," suggested Uk Bunchheuan, adding, "We should implement policy with regard to the Vietnamese alertly and not swerve too far right or too far left but rather use the opportunity to attract some Vietnamese technicians to come serve our work." Khoem Pon then recommended that local Cambodian officials "keep statistics and investigate carefully" the activities of Vietnamese immigrants. Once again, Peng Pat was the most outspoken. "What should we do about Vietnamese residents who don't speak Khmer?" he asked. "More and more, they are coming [to live] together, which is causing our state authority complicated problems. So, should we gather together the Vietnamese in one place or not?"[69]

The members of the committee were fearful of acting unilaterally. Uk Bunchheuan recommended the establishment of a Joint Cambodian-Vietnamese Committee to handle immigration matters, a proposal with which Khoem Pon agreed. Peng Pat was also cautious, warning, "We should resolve this problem based on the limitations of solidarity between Cambodia and Vietnam." Heum Chhaem, a former teacher working in the Ministry of Propaganda, was most blunt. "We shouldn't implement the rounding up of the Vietnamese. Does our country want to start a war?"[70]

The committee did not meet for another month, during which time the political climate in Phnom Penh became increasingly stifling. As the various resistance factions moved toward a unified anti-Vietnamese coalition, the leadership responded by ordering more political education intended not only to counter the "psychological warfare" of the enemy but also to instill an appreciation for Indochinese revolutionary history. Debates on sensitive subjects like

Vietnamese immigration were squelched. When Khang Sarin finally reconvened the Phnom Penh committee in early September, the topic of discussion was the use of motorcycles in the capital. "As for Chinese and Vietnamese residents," remarked Sarin, "I ask Comrade Uk Bunchheuan to amend and draft a policy previously brought up at the meeting to send to the Council of Ministers for decision." The following week, Sarin announced the results: "The policy with regard to Chinese and Vietnamese residents is the same as it is for our Cambodian people who have no work to do." In other words, ethnic Vietnamese would not be sent to Vietnam unless Vietnamese authorities chose to do so.[71]

Meanwhile, hundreds more Cambodians were fleeing to Thailand, encouraged by the promise of a united resistance. By late September 1981, as Sihanouk, Son Sann, and Khieu Samphan were hammering out the details of a coalition, the Party began asking ministers how many of their cadres had already gone to the border, demanding reports on the defections of Party and core group members, and inquiring what effect these defections were having on the functioning of the state.[72]

State cadres who stayed behind in the PRK were increasingly resentful of the Vietnamese. "Some comrades have suspicions and charge that the Vietnamese are doing [everything]," complained Heng Samrin at a Party meeting in October. According to Samrin, the sense that the Vietnamese were dominating Cambodia was widespread, infecting those without firsthand knowledge of Vietnamese activities. "Other comrades follow [those who charge that the Vietnamese are doing everything] and speak as if they've been roused by some drug and have realized this themselves, until they're asked, and they respond that they're following others." As the situation became increasingly untenable, it was clear that the Vietnamese would have to do something. They decided to start at the top.[73]

THE LAST DAYS OF PEN SOVAN

Pen Sovan, the man the Vietnamese had come to trust least, continued to pursue policies contrary to Hanoi's interests. On October 16 he signed a resolution permitting the civil aviation agency of Cambodia to levy taxes on foreign planes landing in Phnom Penh. This policy (which exempted the Red Cross and planes carrying "special delegations" with prior tax exemption approved by the Cambodian Ministry of Foreign Affairs) was potentially costly to the Vietnamese, who were responsible for most of the air traffic in and out of Cambodia. It would also have required the Vietnamese to request permission, on a case by case basis, to land planes in Phnom Penh tax free. According to Pen Sovan, this decision prompted Tran Xuan Bach to issue him his "second warning," on November 20. Looking back, Sovan says that while he knew the Vietnamese might arrest him, "I wouldn't listen to them. I was the leader of Cambodia."[74]

Pen Sovan's overtures to Moscow provided the backdrop to his final days in office. Despite having been warned by the Vietnamese once before, after his 1980 rubber deals with the Soviet Union, Sovan was not backing down. From his perspective, the Party secretary and prime minister of the PRK was just as entitled to deal directly with Moscow as the Vietnamese leadership was. On November 21, the day after his conversation with Tran Xuan Bach, Pen Sovan signed a Council of Ministers decision appointing a government delegation to go to the Soviet Union to negotiate and sign a commercial agreement. He spent the last week of November in Battambang and Pursat provinces giving speeches in which he extolled the Soviet people's commitment to the PRK.[75]

Sovan's political problems ran deeper than his defiance of the Vietnamese. After a quarter-century in Vietnam, he had relatively few connections in Cambodia and thus no real power base. Those most loyal to him—old comrades from Hanoi and the intellectuals he promoted—had no independent authority and were subject, as the arrest of Ros Samay made clear, to removal at any time. Unlike Chea Sim, Sovan had no *konchau*. His one opportunity to develop such a network, his position as minister of defense, had not proven conducive to patronage, largely because the Cambodian armed forces were an extension of the Vietnamese army and their personnel were controlled by Vietnamese officers. Even if Sovan had managed to develop a personal network within the military, such plans would have been undermined when he lost his military portfolio in 1981.

Even those Politburo members who shared Pen Sovan's feelings about the Vietnamese did not support him. Chea Sim, in particular, was far too different in personality and background to find common cause with the erudite and haughty Sovan. Indeed, Sovan's attitude—"I was the teacher, they were the students" is how he describes his relationship with other PRK leaders—sums up why his colleagues took a dislike to him. Rivalries also helped bring him down. It was not a surprise to learn that two Politburo members who had a lot to gain from loyalty to the Vietnamese, Say Phouthang and Hun Sen, were meeting with Tran Xuan Bach and Ngo Dien in the closing weeks of November 1981.[76]

On December 2, 1981, Vietnamese troops arrested Pen Sovan. In an account provided by Sovan but difficult to confirm, Hun Sen accompanied the Vietnamese and read the charges. Pen Sovan, Hun Sen purportedly said, had pursued political and economic policies that "betrayed communist principles," had engaged in "narrow-minded nationalism" in opposing Vietnam, and, most specifically and immediately, had taxed Vietnamese airplanes. The troops blindfolded and handcuffed Sovan and flew him to Hanoi, where he was detained, without trial, for ten years.[77]

Outside the Politburo, no one in the government knew what was happening. Kong Korm, the Cambodian ambassador to Vietnam, was told by Vietnamese officials during a visit to Mongolia that Sovan was "ill." Back in Phnom Penh, state cadres were informed that Sovan had "left the ranks of the revolution," a phrase that left them guessing whether he had retired or was, in the classic communist tradition, expunged from history. Cambodians listening to the Party's public explanations along with the outside world learned only that Pen Sovan was in for a "long rest."[78]

The arrest changed the direction of the PRK. Many of Pen Sovan's policy initiatives, particularly his pursuit of economic independence, came to an immediate halt. Sovan's removal also reminded the Cambodian leadership that they served at the behest of Vietnamese authorities. The Vietnamese demonstrated their distaste for the accumulation of authority by any one Cambodian leader by dividing Pen Sovan's responsibilities: Heng Samrin was named Party secretary, and Chan Si, a forty-seven-year-old Hanoi veteran, became prime minister.

THE CHAN SI GOVERNMENT

Chan Si was the safe choice. Described by those who remember him as clever, mild-mannered, and accommodating, he exhibited none of Pen Sovan's steely autonomy. Chan Si was also more fluent in Vietnamese than Sovan was and, according to a former Vietnamese official, enjoyed an easy relationship with Le Duc Tho. After years in the Vietnamese army, Chan Si served the PRK as chief of the army's Political Department before rising to deputy prime minister and minister of defense in June 1981. Now, however, Chan Si was expected to help the Vietnamese control an extremely volatile internal situation, not only by stepping in as prime minister but also by taking on oversight responsibilities for the municipality of Phnom Penh and two of the PRK's more independent ministries, Interior and Justice.[79]

To bring some control over the provinces, Vietnamese authorities appointed three deputy prime ministers each of whom was granted "responsibility" (*totuol bantuk*) for several provinces. The first was Foreign Minister Hun Sen, to whom the Vietnamese assigned Kampong Som (where his former Khmer Rouge commander, Chum Hol, was already in charge) and Kampong Cham, the most populous and resource-rich province. Administratively unstable, Kampong Cham had seen a parade of governors and Party secretaries, including both Hanoi veterans and Eastern Zone defectors. It was also the base for a suspected rebellion by forces loyal to Mao Phok. Hun Sen, whose loyalty and performance as foreign minister had already earned him the position of deputy prime minister in June 1981, was expected to impose some personal authority over the province.[80]

The Vietnamese had similar hopes for Chea Soth, the minister of planning. White-haired and rail thin at the age of fifty-three, Chea Soth brought with him an extensive revolutionary résumé going back to Prey Veng in the mid-1940s. After taking refuge in Hanoi in 1954, Soth served as an editor for the Vietnam News Agency and spent time in the People's Republic of China, where he studied radio broadcasting. In 1979 he became the PRK's first ambassador to Hanoi, a position he relinquished a year later in order to serve as minister of planning. Granted broad authority over the economic bureaucracy, Chea Soth had personal responsibilities that included exports and imports, foreign economic cooperation, salaries, prices, and statistics. As deputy prime minister, a position he first assumed in June 1981, Soth oversaw the National Bank and the Ministries of Agriculture, Commerce, and Finance. His most daunting new assignment, however, was the as-yet-undefined "responsibility" for two provinces: Prey Veng, whose governor, an Eastern Zone defector, had recently been replaced by a schoolteacher, and the vital battleground of Battambang.[81]

The rest of the leadership remained largely in place. Bou Thang, the third deputy prime minister and the newly appointed minister of defense, remained chair of the Party's Central Education and Propaganda Committee and was personally responsible for Cambodia's northeast. Say Phouthang assumed more power as a result of Pen Sovan's removal, using his position as chair of the Central Organization Committee to control state and Party personnel decisions. Phouthang also ensured that Koh Kong, an increasingly lucrative smuggling portal, remained in the hands of associates and fellow ethnic Thais. Chea Sim held no position at all, other than his Politburo seat and the ceremonial presidency of the National Assembly.[82]

In the spring of 1982, as Cambodian leaders moved to fill the vacuum left by the arrest of Pen Sovan, the Vietnamese learned a few things about power in Cambodia. On the afternoon of March 20, Dang Dinh Long, a former deputy finance minister from Hanoi serving as advisor to the Council of Ministers, met with Chan Si, Hun Sen, Chea Soth, and Ung Phan. As was apparent during the meeting, the Vietnamese had failed to recognize the respect or fear with which the Cambodian leadership viewed Chea Sim. "So far, Comrade Bou Thang has been afraid to infringe on the mass organization duties of Comrade Hun Sen and Comrade Chea Sim," Ung Phan reported to Dinh Long. Hun Sen was equally deferential. "I propose giving all of the mass organization work within the country to Comrade Chea Sim." According to the minutes of the meeting, Dinh Long did not respond. The following month, however, Chea Sim was named president of the Front.[83]

Though conceding Chea Sim's power in the Party, Hun Sen used the meeting to outline his own ambitions. "I will continue to deal with organizational issues related to foreign affairs," he told Dang Dinh Long. Describing the Vietnamese decision to assign multiple ministries and provinces to each deputy prime minister as a "very heavy" responsibility, which "we must accept," Hun Sen explained that he and his colleagues would need a lot of help if they were to assume such a burden. "We can resolve these difficult conditions by taking on a corps of assistants so that each comrade has a personal secretary and at least one person to help with the work of the Council of Ministers. If we take on the work of a separate ministry, there should be one or two personal secretaries for the ministry, and there should be at least one more assistant for each deputy prime minister to allow work to function smoothly and to [help us] get a grasp of every situation."[84]

Hun Sen was demonstrating an affinity for bureaucratic patronage, and Dang Dinh Long liked what he heard. "I agree with what Comrade Hun Sen has suggested, that there be at least one assistant for every comrade. So it is necessary to request more cadres to help the Council of Ministers. In the future, each comrade deputy prime minister shall have two or three assistants who will be cadres with good, firm [political] stances, who know how to keep secrets, and who are highly educated and have clear expertise." Dang Dinh Long made sure, however, to remind the Cambodians of his own role. "When it comes time to request sufficient [numbers of] cadres, I will help guide them by leading them to study on the job and by sending them to study and gain experience in Vietnam."

Hun Sen was also taking his new provincial duties seriously. "There must be leadership," he told Dang Dinh Long, "meaning that we must actually go to the provinces and satisfy all requests. It's not just about appointing people and then [assuming that] everything will be quiet and still. I propose that comrade prime minister and the deputy prime ministers . . . visit, examine, and follow the situation in the provinces and that, in accordance with this work system, we visit the provinces two months out of the year."

According to the minutes of the meeting, none of the other Cambodians had any further suggestions on the matter. Their silence was telling. Over the next several years, Hun Sen appointed numerous deputies and assistants, many of whom were educated Cambodians, and nurtured an extensive patronage system within the central bureaucracy. He developed close provincial relationships, too, particularly in Kampong Cham, where his younger brother was eventually made governor. Granted similar opportunities, neither Prime Minister Chan Si nor Deputy Prime Ministers Chea Soth and Bou Thang had the ambition or political instincts to expand their personal power.

The new leadership reflected Hanoi's biases, agendas, and compromises. Policy differences over the constitution, Vietnamese immigration, and external economic relations had prompted the Vietnamese to remove two of the PRK's most important figures: Ros Samay and Pen Sovan. That Samay and Sovan were Hanoi-trained revolutionary veterans had not protected them; instead, it had made them more vulnerable. Lacking connections to former Khmer Rouge cadres in the countryside, they could be purged without fear of sparking an uprising or encouraging defections. By contrast, the Vietnamese were more cautious in dealing with former Eastern Zone cadres, including Ros Chhun, who, despite being suspected of disloyalty, was only transferred overseas, and Mao Phok, who was permitted to operate an allegedly corrupt and murderous fiefdom for more than a year prior to his arrest. Chea Sim, meanwhile, continued to develop his own patronage system in the provinces and among loyalists in the security apparatus. Unlike the other top Cambodian leaders, he was not promoted by the Vietnamese but simply tolerated.

The new prime minister, Chan Si, died in late 1984, having served a mere four years. To this day, Chan Si's death, which paved the way for Hun Sen's promotion to the premiership, is clouded by rumors of foul play. No one has ever produced any evidence that Si was murdered, nor does his tenure as prime minister—during which he remained loyal to the Vietnamese—suggest any reason why Hanoi would have wanted him eliminated. If conspiracy theories persist, however, it is because the events of 1981, when Vietnamese authorities arrested the prime minister of Cambodia and pronounced him "ill," suggest that anything is possible.

Phnom Penh, January 1979

Cambodian soldiers, Phnom Penh, January 1979

Internal migrants, 1979

The Cambodian National Bank, destroyed during or after the 1975 Khmer Rouge takeover of Phnom Penh, 1979

The leadership (*clockwise from top left*): Hun Sen, Chea Sim, Chea Soth, and Say Phouthang

Heng Samrin (*left*) and Pen Sovan shaking hands; behind them (*left to far right*), Chea Sim, Ros Samay, and Meas Samnang

The visit of Prime Minister Pham Van Dong (*front left, with white hair*) to Phnom Penh in February 1979, here accompanied by Pen Sovan (*center in cap*), Vietnamese General Van Tien Dung (*behind Pen Sovan, in cap*), Heng Samrin (*front right*), and Hun Sen (*back right in glasses*)

Chu Huy Man, chief of the Political Department of the Vietnamese army, honoring (*left to right*) Say Phouthang, Chea Sim, and Hun Sen

Ngo Dien, Vietnamese ambassador to the PRK (*left*), and Bou Thang

Mai Chi Tho, chair of the Ho Chi Minh City People's Committee (*left*), and Ros Samay

Le Duc Anh,
commander of the
Vietnamese forces
in Cambodia

Tran Xuan Bach,
chief of B68

Kaev Chenda

Uk Bunchheuan

Tea Banh

Speaking at the National Assembly (*top to bottom*): Ung Phan, Vandy Ka-on, and Sin Song; seated behind each speaker (*left to right*): Chan Si, Chea Sim, Heng Samrin (*obscured*), Say Phouthang, and Bou Thang

Hok Longdi (*front left*) and Sar Kheng (*second from right*)

It Leau (*front left*) and Nheum Vanda (*center, with scarf*) inspecting the border

Public ceremonies marking the Vietnamese withdrawal from Cambodia, September 1989: a Vietnamese soldier; and soldiers lining up at the Cambodian-Vietnamese-Lao Friendship Monument

Part Three **Battlefields, 1982–1987**

Chapter 6 The Vietnamese: Soldiers, Advisors, and "Bad Elements"

In early 1982, in a commune in the southeastern province of Svay Rieng, old women tied threads around their wrists in the hope that this would hasten the end of the Vietnamese occupation. The idea apparently came from four local schoolteachers. The threads were sacred, the teachers explained, and would help bring about the salvation of the Khmer people by the Buddhist spirits and by Sihanouk. Invoking mystical names—Entrathirach, Souphavongs, and Sivata—along with the prince's familiar title, Samdech U, they painted a pure, nationalistic, and profoundly spiritual picture of Cambodia under the yoke of Vietnamese occupation. The "*yuon*" (Vietnamese) were evil (*abot*), warned the teachers, who instructed the women to use "Sihanouk money" (leftover prerevolutionary riels) rather than "*yuon* money" (PRK riels). In perhaps a year, they said, Sihanouk, along with the West, would rescue Cambodia.[1]

Local state authorities responded quickly to this threat, detaining the teachers, interrogating them about their "network," and "educating" them on the Party line on the Vietnamese. (According to official reports, three of the teachers were then released; there is no mention of what became of the fourth.) From the perspective of the PRK security apparatus, the teachers had conducted "psychological warfare." To the old women, however, the exercise had offered some hope. As investigators noted, some had even affixed the sacred threads to their cows.

The Svay Rieng episode hints at what the Vietnamese authorities and the PRK leadership were up against. The anti-Vietnamese rhetoric that the Lon Nol and Khmer Rouge regimes had disseminated throughout the 1970s, the unremitting anti-Vietnamese propaganda coming from the resistance, and the semi-mythical stories of Vietnamese atrocities from the nineteenth century inspired a nationalistic, racist opposition to the Vietnamese occupation. The charges, expressed openly in the border camps and whispered inside Cambodia, were endless: the *yuon* were colonizing Cambodia; the *yuon* were taking Cambodian rice and starving the Khmers; more than a million *yuon* were in Cambodia, with more to come; the *yuon* were committing a "genocide" against the Khmers, forcing Khmers to speak their language, even taking Khmer orphans back to Vietnam to turn them into *yuon* spies. Most Cambodians, resentful of the occupation but unable to separate truth from myth, inferred from these accusations a larger conspiracy to absorb and destroy Cambodia and its people.

Internal government documents reveal a more nuanced picture of the Vietnamese occupation and of Cambodian sentiments inside the country. First, the resentment that Cambodians felt toward the Vietnamese was not constant; it intensified and diminished in response to specific actions taken by Vietnamese officials, the PRK leadership, and the resistance. Second, the occupation was not monolithic. A wide assortment of Vietnamese operated in Cambodia, including generals and footsoldiers, government ministers and low-level cadres. Depending on their professional backgrounds, their personalities, or their origin, from the north or the south, the Vietnamese operating in Cambodia experienced the occupation differently, behaved differently, and promoted different policies. Third, although Vietnamese officials did promote the export of Cambodian rice and natural resources to Vietnam, the nature and effects of this policy varied. Fourth, there were more ethnic Vietnamese in Cambodia than the PRK acknowledged, but far fewer than the resistance claimed. Fifth, accusations that Cambodia was undergoing Vietnamization were overblown, in large part because the Vietnamese lacked the people and resources to change Cambodian society. And sixth, although Vietnamese officials repressed Cambodians, they were also suspicious of Cambodia's ethnic Vietnamese, few of whom were communists.

"NATIONALISM AND NARROW-MINDEDNESS"

The hope among the PRK leadership was that Cambodians, grateful for the overthrow of the Khmer Rouge and the relative freedoms that the regime had conferred on them, would forgive the sometimes heavy-handed actions of the Vietnamese. After the arrest of Pen Sovan, however, what remained of this gratitude was quickly evaporating, particularly among state cadres. In a May 1982 Party meeting, Ung Phan attempted to reassure his colleagues. During the coming Khmer New Year celebration, he noted optimistically, cadres would be enjoying "the vacation, the family get-togethers, walks with siblings, children, and grandchildren, popular games, art, and sports. . . . When they are happy, they will think of the achievements of the Party and the Front and the achievements of our Vietnamese friends, whose assistance has allowed us to live, to enjoy, to eat and drink, and to have good fortune."[2] In fact, state cadres were anxious, not just because Sovan's disappearance carried an implicit warning, but also because the regime responded to discontent in an oppressive and ultimately counterproductive manner. Subjected to political education sessions two evenings a week, state employees pursued their day jobs with increasing trepidation. Fear and self-censorship led to bureaucratic paralysis. As Ung Phan reported to the Party on another occasion, "The work of the ministries has not yet been properly prepared because some tasks are not yet understood and because some tasks are understood but [cadres] don't dare act for fear of violating outside views."[3]

A unified anti-Vietnamese resistance exacerbated the PRK's problems. On June 22, 1982, Sihanouk, Son Sann, and Khieu Samphan agreed to an alliance and formed the Coalition Government of Democratic Kampuchea (CGDK). A united political front as well as a shadow cabinet, the CGDK gained for the Khmer Rouge the indirect support of Western countries. For Sihanouk and Son Sann, both of whom came under heavy pressure from the United States, ASEAN, and China to form the CGDK, the coalition provided an opportunity to wed their own Western support with the assets of the Khmer Rouge, namely, Chinese military assistance and Cambodia's U.N. seat. All that really united this collection of royalists, republicans, and communists was their shared opposition to Vietnamese occupation and the "puppet" PRK government.

Publicly the PRK dismissed the CGDK as "cosmetic surgery to make up the face of the Beijing Dracula." Within the leadership, however, there was deep concern that a united movement headed by Sihanouk would draw large numbers of Cambodians into the resistance. Their fears were well grounded. In the 1950s and 1960s, Sihanouk ruled Cambodia as monarch, head of state, and self-proclaimed father of national independence. To many Cambodians, he was the embodiment of the country. His removal from power in 1970 and the subsequent disintegration of the country only added to his radiant image. While Sihanouk was in exile, the war escalated and the Khmer Rouge came to power. His disappearance during the D.K. regime (he was under palace arrest) was associated, by many Cambodians, with atrocities and social upheaval, and his second exile, which began in 1979, occurred during the Vietnamese occupation. For more than a decade, Cambodians inside and outside the country had looked to Sihanouk as a national savior. His absence suggested a certain incompleteness, an unsettledness, that no amount of PRK propaganda could soothe. The PRK's counterargument—that Sihanouk was allied with the Khmer Rouge —had some appeal. The problem was that the Vietnamese occupation instilled in many Cambodians a sense of political and cultural disorientation and a suspicion that Cambodia had suffered a loss of nationhood.[4]

Vietnamese policies seemed to confirm the notion that the occupiers were undermining at least some of what it meant to be Khmer. Vietnamese officials placed restrictions on prerevolutionary Cambodian culture and on the importation of art and film in order to protect what the government called the "new culture and the new socialist persons in accordance with pure Marxism-Leninism." The "propaganda and education campaign" with which the PRK responded to the formation of the CGDK engendered alienation and anti-Vietnamese resentment rather than loyalty and solidarity, yet neither the Vietnamese nor the more ideological members of the Cambodian leadership seriously contemplated the counterproductive nature of the campaign. As Prime Minister Chan Si said in July 1982, "The people, the masses, at the ministries and offices" should be made to "understand clearly" the regime's political line, "because they have nationalist ideas and are narrow-minded."[5]

COUNTERING THE RESISTANCE

Hanoi responded to the formation of the CGDK with an important public relations maneuver. Two weeks after the announcement of the coalition, at the Sixth Meeting of the Indochinese Ministers of Foreign Affairs, Vietnamese officials broached with the Cambodians the idea of publicly withdrawing some troops. "Before, we withdrew some Vietnamese soldiers," Prime Minister Chan

Si told the Council of Ministers shortly thereafter, "but didn't announce it openly." This latest pronouncement, said Chan Si, was necessary to counter "the confused views of some of the masses" and "international opinion that charges that the Vietnamese army will absorb Cambodia."[6]

The ceremonies that marked the withdrawal of Vietnamese troops concealed two fundamental assumptions held by the Cambodian leadership. The first was that the withdrawal was tentative and contingent on the course of the war against the resistance. "For example," said Chan Si, "we are withdrawing one unit, but if the enemy uses its forces to pressure us, we will immediately increase [the Vietnamese presence] by two or three units." The second assumption was that "the Vietnamese army will be withdrawn when Cambodian society has sufficient stability, the Cambodian state authority is strengthened, and the Cambodian army is stronger and can take over by itself."[7]

Building this "stability," in Hanoi's view, required the strengthening of relations between the Cambodian and the Vietnamese security apparatuses. In an agreement signed on June 26, 1982, just four days after the formation of the CGDK, the two Ministries of the Interior pledged to cooperate in the areas of "political security" and "social order." The agreement formalized the Vietnamese police presence in Cambodia, ensured that Vietnamese security forces would continue to protect Cambodian Party and state leaders, and called for an intensification of Vietnamese training of Cambodian security cadres both in Cambodia and in Vietnam. On the day of the signing, the first of 258 additional advisors from the Ministry of the Interior in Hanoi arrived in Cambodia, of whom 70 would be stationed at the central Ministry of the Interior, 21 with the municipality of Phnom Penh, 51 in the provinces, and 116 in important districts throughout the country. The two countries also agreed on training to be conducted in Vietnam, including short courses at the Vietnamese Ministry of the Interior for more than 200 leadership cadres and more than 300 military cadres and long-term training at the Vietnamese Police Academy for 22 Cambodians, mostly children of police and soldiers.[8]

Vietnamese dominance was apparent to most Cambodians. In addition to the 180,000 Vietnamese troops stationed in Cambodia, Vietnamese security officials periodically flexed their muscle. In 1983 fears of infiltration prompted Vietnamese officials in Siem Reap to arrest several hundred suspected resistance sympathizers, including provincial officials and security officers. This purge prompted thousands of Cambodians to head for the border, many of them arriving at refugee camps accusing Vietnam of "colonialism." To mitigate these sorts of charges, the Vietnamese attempted to operate covertly. "Keep the work of the advisors secret," urged a 1985 Council of Ministers document. "Don't express freely [the PRK's] policies regarding the advisors." This was nothing new—Vietnamese communists had been operating secretly in Cambodia for fifty years—but it had the effect of breeding suspicion and cynicism.[9]

THE SOLDIERS

The Vietnamese military experience in Cambodia depended a great deal on rank. For those in the central Vietnamese command, service in Cambodia proved to be a fruitful career move. The Vietnamese Communist Party had always rewarded military success, and with the reunification of the country, the struggle against the "Chinese expansionists" offered one of the last remaining proving grounds for politically ambitious generals.

Le Duc Anh, commander in chief of the occupying Vietnamese forces was one of the beneficiaries. Born in the central Vietnamese city of Hue, Anh served under Le Duc Tho as deputy commander of the Central Office for South Vietnam, rose to four-star general in 1974, and was eventually selected by Tho to command the invasion of Cambodia. As chief of 478, the central Vietnamese command center, he not only directed the occupation and the war against the resistance but advised the Cambodian general staff and shaped the formation of the Cambodian army.[10]

Conservative and ideologically rigid, Le Duc Anh equated war with revolution. Speaking of Cambodia at the end of the 1984, he stated that the revolution "must undergo a comprehensive struggle politically, militarily, economically, and diplomatically in order to defeat the counterrevolution and protect national independence and revolutionary gains and to build the fatherland on its transitional path toward socialism. This is a very decisive national and class struggle." These views helped catapult Le Duc Anh into the highest echelons of the Hanoi leadership, where he become minister of defense, Politburo member, and, eventually, head of state.[11]

Le Duc Anh was not the only Vietnamese general in Cambodia to be rewarded politically. Doan Khue, political commissar of the Vietnamese forces in Cambodia, joined the Politburo in 1986 and became chief of staff of the People's Army of Vietnam. Le Kha Phieu, chief of the Political Department for the occupying forces and Le Duc Anh's equally conservative protégé, held the position of Party secretary from late 1997 to early 2000.[12]

Lower-ranking officers and soldiers were less fortunate. Outside Phnom

Penh, troops from military regions in central and southern Vietnam set up military structures in southeast and northeast Cambodia, respectively. In Battambang and Siem Riep soldiers from Organization 779 took on the brunt of the Cambodian civil war. Made up of southern troops from Military Region 7 near Ho Chi Minh City, 779 (the number of the region, along with the year of the Cambodian invasion, formed its name) offered living conditions that the Vietnamese army newspaper described as "austere and hard." "Daily life is full of hardship," reported the paper in 1981. "There are nutritional deficiencies, a shortage of vegetables. . . . There is malaria, and the constant search for medical plants to treat it. . . . [There are] many misunderstandings between the friendly [Cambodian] people and our troops."[13]

The troops of the Vietnamese Volunteer Army, as the occupying forces were called, settled into the rhythms of Cambodian warfare, launching dry season offensives against the resistance, deploying tanks and artillery, and absorbing losses during the monsoons, when the mud made conventional warfare impossible. In a frank radio essay a Vietnamese helicopter pilot described what it was like to deliver supplies to the troops. "During the rainy season, forward bases look like small desolate islands surrounded on all sides by dense jungle; all the trails leading to them seem to be impassable. No one can refrain from feeling sorry for those infantrymen dressed in rags, puritanically fed, mostly disease-ridden, and devoid of news from the rear."[14]

In September 1989, when the Vietnamese army finally withdrew from Cambodia, a Ministry of Defense spokesman announced that approximately 55,300 Vietnamese soldiers had died in Cambodia since 1978. The number was slightly lower than the number of Americans who died in Vietnam.[15]

THE ADVISORS

Every so often, a PRK defector arrived at the border camps in Thailand with an account of life under the Vietnamese, and each time the CGDK reiterated its accusation that Vietnam was dominating Cambodia politically.[16] The resistance was essentially right. Long after Vietnamese advisors had set up the PRK, its Party structure, and its state bureaucracy, they continued to wield tight control over the regime. Deference to the advisors was a matter of official policy: "We should discuss all tasks with the fraternal advisors . . . weigh heavily the opinions of the fraternal advisors. . . . At all levels and in all sectors, we should hold discussions with the fraternal advisors in order to agree on weekly and monthly programs and planned activities. . . . We should take the opportunity to ask the opinions of the fraternal advisors, and the fraternal advisors should offer their ideas and their opinions to us."[17]

Initially, the occupation was dominated by Le Duc Tho. Remembered now for his condescending lectures to the Cambodian leadership, Tho was seen by Cambodians and Vietnamese alike as the embodiment of Vietnamese arrogance. In 1981 he began spending more time in Vietnam and, by all accounts, was not missed. His replacement, Tran Xuan Bach, was a more enigmatic figure. He had solid revolutionary credentials and, like Le Duc Anh, rose within Hanoi political circles during and after his stint in Cambodia, joining the Central Committee, becoming secretary of the Party Secretariat in 1982, and ascending to the Politburo in 1986. Poised, it seemed, to become Party secretary, Tran Xuan Bach suffered an abrupt fall from power after what the leadership of the Vietnamese Communist Party (VCP) perceived to be a flirtation with political liberalism. Although there is no evidence that he harbored reformist views while in Cambodia, PRK officials describe him as having a different temperament than Le Duc Tho. "Of the top Vietnamese officials, Tran Xuan Bach was most inclined to let Cambodia help itself," recalls Kong Korm, a former minister of foreign affairs.[18]

Tran Xuan Bach's duties in Hanoi and his replacement, in 1985, by a lower-level Party figure left much of the governance of Cambodia to the Vietnamese bureaucracy. A fully staffed administration that oversaw all the Vietnamese advisors operating in Cambodia, B68 was led by a committee of Vietnamese officials and was connected to Vietnamese security units through its Information Office. Underneath B68, two sometimes overlapping hierarchies of Vietnamese advisors extended through the Cambodian bureaucracy and out into the provinces: one responsible for Party matters (including Party branches and core groups) and personnel (including matters related to loyalty and solidarity), the other responsible for the technical work of the ministries and other state institutions.[19]

The Party advisors worked within the KPRP Central Committee bureaucracy, the Front, the mass organizations, and the Party branches and core groups of ministries and other state bodies. Drawn from parallel Vietnamese institutions, they oversaw Cambodian personnel issues for both the Party hierarchy and the state apparatus. At the top of this particular network were three powerful Vietnamese revolutionaries who operated out of the Central Organization Committee. Vu Van Day, who had previously served as chief of the cabinet of the Communist Party of Ho Chi Minh City, was an expert on internal

Party structures. "Phoc" and "Tun Lem" were unusual in that they had previously worked in Cambodia.[20]

These latter two men, elderly veterans of previous Indochinese revolutionary struggles and fluent speakers of Khmer, were familiar with the volatile history of the Cambodian revolution and with the whole assortment of Cambodian communists. Although neither held high positions in the VCP, they were valued for their understanding of Cambodia. Phoc, or "Ta" (Grandfather) Phoc to the Cambodians with whom he worked, was also fluent in Lao and had been active in the northeast prior to the Khmer Rouge victory. Tun Lem, who spoke Thai, worked closely with Say Phouthang and had been responsible for bringing him back to Phnom Penh in 1979. Among the more popular of the Vietnamese advisors for their knowledge and appreciation of Cambodian traditions, Phoc and Lem remained in Phnom Penh until 1989.[21]

The technical specialists and economic experts who advised Cambodian state institutions ranged from deputy ministers, seconded from ministries in Hanoi, to low-level bureaucrats. Organized under a separate Vietnamese institution known as A40, most worked out of Cambodian ministries and state agencies. With bureaucratic mandates vague and the PRK's policies in flux, they frequently found themselves arbitrating among the Cambodians. As veteran Hanoi bureaucrats, however, they were also prone to conflict among themselves. When, as was often the case, Cambodian ministries engaged in disputes over the scope of their authority, Vietnamese advisors frequently sided with their Cambodian counterparts in opposition to rival Cambodian bureaucrats and rival advisors.

Ideologically, Vietnamese advisors rarely, if ever, strayed from the Party line. Educated in Vietnam and, in some cases, the Soviet Union, they tended to approach their role from the perspective of doctrinaire communism. Two of the most powerful and longest serving of these advisors, "Pham Van Kath" and "Fang You" of the Council of Ministers, faithfully promoted Vietnamese and, at times, Soviet models. As economic policies shifted in Vietnam, however, their advice became increasingly tentative and incoherent.[22]

The Cambodian leadership often had little idea what the Vietnamese were doing in Cambodia. Individual ministries made direct arrangements with their Vietnamese counterparts, provincial authorities with their sister provinces. In 1984, when the Council of Ministers finally created a special department to track and coordinate the movements of advisors, it was too late. "Because of a failure to keep statistics on the advisors who came before," read one council report, "we are now unable to figure out the number of advisors who've come year by year. . . . Because there are no reports from the central ministries and offices nor from the provinces and municipalities, the number of long-term and short-term advisors in these localities is not yet clear."[23]

There were other, non-Vietnamese advisors, on whom the Council of Ministers kept relatively accurate statistics. The most diverse representation could be found at the Ministry of Health, where advisors from numerous communist countries worked alongside twenty-five representatives of international organizations. Eastern Europeans were most active at the Ministry of Education, to which professors were sent; the Ministry of Communications, where thirty-five Soviets and two East Germans helped reconstruct the ports of Kampong Som and Phnom Penh; and the Ministry of Industry, where seventy-nine Soviets and fourteen Czechs attempted to prop up Cambodia's state-owned factories. There were also forty-one Soviets at the Ministry of Agriculture and nineteen at the General Department of Rubber Plantations. Altogether, in late 1985, some three hundred and ten Soviet advisors were working in Cambodia, along with twenty-two Czechs, eleven Cubans, seven Germans, five Laos, four Bulgarians, and three Indians and, at the international organizations, five Swiss, three French, three Swedes, four Filipinos, two Belgians, two Canadians, a Netherlander, an Australian, and a Finn.[24]

Vietnamese officials attempted to limit the number of Soviets and Eastern Europeans working in Cambodia. In late 1985, "Ngiem Van Ky," the Vietnamese advisor to the Council of Ministers' Advisor Department, told the Cambodians that a Cambodian-Soviet agreement reached by Pen Sovan should be renegotiated. This would not be easy, Ky acknowledged, noting that Cambodian cadres "feared losing [Soviet] friendship" and were reluctant to "find reason to struggle with friends."[25]

The complaints lodged by the Vietnamese against the Soviets and Eastern Europeans were mostly financial. The Cambodian government was taking on increasing debt to pay for salaries that ranged from the lowest Soviet salary of 300 rubles to the highest Czech salary of 3,000 rubles a month (U.S.$1,980, according to official exchange rates) and per diems of up to U.S.$28. Other costs included hotel rooms (at 3,840 riels a month per advisor) for the less rugged of the Eastern European advisors, and Cambodian translators, many of whom, once trained, either demanded compensation comparable to that afforded their foreign colleagues or refused to leave Phnom Penh and work in the provinces. In 1985, when Cambodia was already spending about 2 million rubles a year on its Soviet advisors, Moscow suddenly proposed that the salaries be doubled. The demands placed the Cambodians in a difficult position. As Ty

Yao, a Soviet-educated cadre at the Council of Ministers, reminded his colleagues, "It's hard to reduce the number of Soviet advisors because . . . we are afraid of losing the ties of solidarity." He also noted, "They come with the equipment."[26]

The Vietnamese cost money, too, but a lot less. According to reports of the Council of Ministers, Cambodian ministries frequently subjected their Vietnamese advisors to "student conditions," crowding them into communal houses far from the center of Phnom Penh, depriving them of water and electricity, and providing them with stingy stipends of food and spending money. Vietnamese advisors resented the disparity between their living conditions and those of the Eastern Europeans, yet the Cambodians valued the Vietnamese precisely because they were so inexpensive. Vietnamese advisors, officials at the Council of Ministers noted, conformed to a "traditional standard of living which is like that of the Cambodian people."[27]

Despite being paid so little, the Vietnamese advisors were much more influential than the Soviets or the Eastern Europeans were, both in Phnom Penh and in the countryside. At the Council of Ministers, the Ministries of Finance, Planning, and Commerce, the National Bank, and Cambodian Party organs, there were only Vietnamese advisors. Although it is unclear how many Soviets and Eastern Europeans were working in the Ministries of the Interior and Defense, they would have been far outweighed by the hundreds of Vietnamese security officials and the thousands of Vietnamese military officers operating throughout the country. In the provinces the Vietnamese oversaw the Cambodian commercial administration through a network of advisors at state-run commercial entities, including trade and equipment companies. Other than a few strategic provincial capitals—Battambang, Siem Riep, Kampong Cham, Kampong Som, Takeo, and Kandal—there were no non-Vietnamese advisors operating outside Phnom Penh at all.[28]

THE ECONOMIC RELATIONSHIP

Early one morning in March 1982, Prime Minister Chan Si, Minister of Planning Chea Soth, and two officials from the Ministry of Commerce met with a team of top Vietnamese advisors to hear a report on the future of Cambodian-Vietnamese economic cooperation. The messenger was "Pham Chong Tuoc," the chief advisor to the Cambodian Ministry of Finance. "Assistance not requiring repayment has now been stopped," Tuoc informed the Cambodians. "The parties should negotiate regarding the exchange of goods, various businesses, and transportation and agree upon the exchange annually. As for the workers and technicians whom Cambodia hires from Vietnam, the Cambodians must pay for everything. Contracts will be signed annually. Repayment must be in rubles."[29]

The Cambodians had seen this coming. Since 1979 the PRK had received Vietnamese rice, medicines and other goods, Vietnamese advisors, and assistance in the reconstruction of the communications, industrial, hydrological, and transportation infrastructures. Beginning in May 1981, however, economic planners began to anticipate a reduction in direct assistance from Vietnam and a corresponding increase in bilateral trade. Now Cambodia would pay for all goods, equipment, advisors, and labor from Vietnam. "If we need them," stated a 1982 report, "we will get them through commercial exchanges."[30]

Tuoc had other, more abrupt announcements. Putting an immediate stop to Pen Sovan's quest for economic partners in Singapore, Paris, and London, Tuoc told the Cambodians that "Vietnam will facilitate commerce with all capitalist countries." He listed the goods that Cambodia would export through Vietnam. "[Cambodian] farmers have rubber, rice, corn, agricultural products, timber, and other natural resources . . . which are not only intended to help the standard of living of the [Cambodian] people but must also be stored and exported for sale overseas for hard currency. . . . Exports to capitalist countries go through Vietnam." Tuoc's proposal received qualified support from the Cambodians. "I agree with this cooperation policy," said Prime Minister Chan Si, "but it must go through the Central Party and be disseminated throughout the country." The Party apparently acquiesced. Within a few months Cambodian currency holdings amounting to some U.S.$1 million had been transferred to Vietnam for the purchase of fuel and equipment from the United States.[31]

Cambodia's trade relations with other socialist countries, another matter over which the Vietnamese had disagreed with Pen Sovan, remained politically delicate. Soviet political and economic support was vital, not only to the PRK but to Vietnam itself, and the Vietnamese authorities were reluctant to undermine Cambodian-Soviet economic ties in too sudden or obvious a manner. In the months following Pen Sovan's arrest, the Cambodian government and its Vietnamese advisors quietly conducted an overall reassessment of the PRK's other bilateral relations.[32]

In June 1982 the Council of Ministers finally convened to establish the basis for Cambodia's economic ties to the Soviet Union and Eastern Europe: the currency exchange rate between the Cambodian riel and the Soviet ruble. As PRK officials prepared for negotiations with Moscow, they sought to promote a strong riel so that riel-denominated goods could buy a maximum of ruble-de-nominated Soviet goods. The danger was that if the Cambodians insisted on too favorable an exchange rate, the Soviets would walk away from the table. The end result of a breakdown in negotiations would be that the PRK would have to tie the riel to the Vietnamese dong.

This appeared to be what the Vietnamese wanted. Coaching the Cambodi-ans on how to approach the Soviets, a Vietnamese advisor attached to the Min-istry of Finance (identified only as "Tui") suggested that the Cambodians "make clear that Cambodia wants to sign an agreement with the Soviet Union first before signing an agreement with Vietnam" but also that they insist on an exchange rate that was far more favorable than a reasonable assessment of the value of the riel would warrant. "If we determine the value of goods according to the free market, we see that our money is much less valuable, meaning that one ruble may be equivalent to many tens of riels. . . . If our Soviet friends pro-pose that one ruble be more than eight riels, we should sign an agreement with Vietnam first. If Cambodia [signs] with Vietnam first, we can then move to-ward a settlement with the Soviet Union more easily."[33]

The result of this advice was that the riel was tied first to the Vietnamese dong, its international value determined according to the dong-ruble exchange rate. The Cambodian economy was thus further integrated into the Viet-namese economy in the same manner as Eastern Europe was tied to the Soviet Union. In effect, what both Tuoc (who had told the Cambodians that they must export their goods through Vietnam) and Tui were insisting on was a satellite relationship in which Vietnam served as an intermediary for Cambo-dia's other economic relations.

THE SISTER PROVINCES

Cambodia's economic relationship with Vietnam was supposed to be guided by the usual communist preference for centralized control. As Tui told the Coun-cil of Ministers in June 1982, the plan was to establish a Joint Economic Com-mission whose staff would be selected by Vietnamese officials and whose agenda would be guided by advisors from A40. As chair of the commission, the Vietnamese selected Planning Minister (and Deputy Prime Minister) Chea Soth, a Hanoi veteran and former PRK ambassador to Vietnam. Yet from the start, Soth and his colleagues in the central bureaucracy were frustrated by provincial officials who were already trading directly with their Vietnamese sis-ter provinces.[34]

Relations between the sister provinces were originally intended to facilitate the delivery of emergency economic assistance to the Cambodian countryside and were not necessarily intended to be permanent. As Cambodia's economic crisis subsided and as the PRK and its Vietnamese advisors drew the blueprints for a centrally planned economy, the Cambodian leadership expressed hope that bilateral economic relations would be controlled by the Cambodian Ministry of Commerce and its Vietnamese counterpart. In early 1981, however, the central government's limitations remained apparent, prompting the leadership to conclude that "if the Ministry [of Commerce] lacks the capacity [to conduct trade], it should permit the provinces to communicate directly with the Vietnamese provinces with which they have cooperated."[35]

Over the course of the year, Cambodian provincial authorities traded, inconsistently and in small quantities, with Vietnamese sister provinces. Meanwhile, the Ministry of Commerce continued to sign agreements with Vietnam that it could not implement (the ministry was incapable of either collecting goods for export to Vietnam or distributing goods imported from Vietnam). With provincial authorities complaining that their needs were not being met, the leadership decided to formally decentralize Cambodian-Vietnamese economic ties. According to a September 1982 circular, the provinces were permitted "to open broad commercial and economic relations [with their Vietnamese counterparts] in the spirit of equality and mutual assistance and in the name of comradeship."[36]

Henceforth, Cambodian provinces could sell agricultural goods and natural resources such as fish and timber to Vietnam. (Strategically important goods such as rice, rubber, and farm animals and imports such as fuel, chemicals, and vehicles could not be exported without permission from the Council of Ministers.) In exchange, the provinces would receive Vietnamese advisors, workers, technicians, factory managers, and mechanics, as well as Vietnamese goods. Provincial authorities were also granted autonomy in conducting this trade, operating their own accounts, financing exchanges through loans from the state banking system, and selling materials and equipment to state and private enterprises in the provinces. The only requirements were that the provinces first meet their obligations, established by the Ministry of Planning, to deliver a certain amount of produce to Phnom Penh and that they report the details of their sister province exchanges to the Council of Ministers.[37]

Over the next few years, as trade between the sister provinces expanded, the central government found it impossible to keep track of these exchanges or to reconcile them with its centrally planned economic policies. There was disagreement, however, over whether this was a bad thing. Bureaucrats at the Ministries of Commerce and Planning considered decentralization dangerous both to their understanding of the country's administrative hierarchy and to the public welfare in whose service they purported to operate. As a frustrated deputy minister of planning, Ty Yao, warned in May 1984, "Some provinces have plans to enter into too many agreements with the sister provinces without thinking of the needs of the people inside the country and have done too much already without the agreement of the higher levels." But the sister province policy had an advocate in Foreign Minister Hun Sen. "In the future, we need not allocate too many goods for [centralized] cooperation," he told the Council of Ministers in 1982, "but should find markets to sell [our goods] and then allow the provinces to [trade]." In the years to come, Hun Sen continued to promote the sister province policy and economic decentralization in general with increasing success.[38]

EXPORTING RICE

Cambodian-Vietnamese economic cooperation included the export of rice, the linchpin of Cambodia's economy and the staple of its citizens' diet. Few aspects of the occupation were as controversial. Having endured years of hunger under the Khmer Rouge and immediately following the Vietnamese invasion, the country continued to contend with pockets of malnutrition. The notion that under such circumstances Cambodian rice would be sent abroad was naturally disturbing. The PRK had acknowledged as much at the Pol Pot–Ieng Sary trial, the verdict of which condemned Pol Pot for sending between 100,000 and 150,000 tons of rice to China.[39]

Although it is unclear whether exports from the PRK to Vietnam ever reached comparable levels, government reports show that the Ministry of Commerce sent 23,000 tons of rice to Vietnam in the first half of 1981, with another 17,000 tons planned for the remainder of the year. By late 1982 rice exports had become an integral part of the Cambodian-Vietnamese economic relationship, in part because Cambodia lacked warehouses in which to store its rice and could export it to Vietnam in exchange for consumer goods but mostly because Vietnam was looking to alleviate its own rice shortages.[40]

A 1982 circular set forth the pretense that rice exports were in Cambodia's immediate interest: "This is a necessary task in the special economic relationship with our Vietnamese friends in order to serve the future interests of the people throughout the country." Disagreement was considered treasonous.

"The enemy can seize the opportunity to poison the ranks of the people in order to spread propaganda and falsely blame our Cambodian revolution. Comrades at all levels of the state authority, especially those at the Ministry of Commerce and the Ministry of Communications and Transportation and the comrade governors of Kampong Cham, Prey Veng, Svay Rieng, and Kampong Thom, are responsible for using all means to disseminate [the Party's justification for the policy] to cadres, for guiding the provinces so that the people understand clearly the policy of our Party and state, and for crushing all enemy propaganda schemes concerning this problem."[41]

In 1983 and 1984, Cambodia was exporting what Hun Sen described, years later, as "tens of thousands of tons" of rice to Vietnam, even though as many as one out of ten Cambodian households still lacked sufficient food. Despite complaints from Minister of Commerce Tang Sareum that exports should "depend on the domestic situation," the Cambodian leadership could do little to reverse the policy.[42]

Before rice could be exported to Vietnam, it had to be collected by the state, either through the purchasing networks of the Ministry of Commerce or through a mandatory "Patriotic Contribution." (The Patriotic Contributions, begun in 1984, were inspired by Vietnamese policies and by the "voluntary contributions" of the Sihanouk era. The word "tax" was not used, said Hun Sen, "so as not to allow the enemy to criticize our policies.") Cambodians, however, refused to cooperate. Farmers handed over inferior-quality rice or avoided state officials altogether and sold on the black market. State officials sold whatever rice they had collected rather than deliver it to Phnom Penh. As a result, the Ministry of Commerce failed to amass sufficient rice either for internal distribution or for export to Vietnam.[43]

In other words, the main limitations on exports of rice to Vietnam were popular resistance and the inefficiency of the state collection system. As Chea Soth acknowledged to Nguyen Chanh, the Vietnamese deputy minister of foreign trade, in early 1983, "Cambodia's failure to meet the plan for exporting overseas in a timely fashion is the result of the management of the economy, which so far has been complicated by the lack of experience among the cadres." "I relate to Cambodia's problems," replied Chanh, noting that reunified Vietnam was facing similar challenges. "There are more problems in southern Vietnam than in northern Vietnam because the South has just been liberated and the people don't yet have a spirit of awareness, so state rice collection has not been good."[44]

. . . AND RUBBER

The Vietnamese had always competed with other foreigners for control over Cambodia's fifty thousand hectares of rubber plantations. Designed and managed by the French and operated with Vietnamese labor, the plantations provided the Indochinese Communist Party with its first recruitment opportunity in the Cambodian protectorate. After independence in 1954, the rubber industry remained in French hands, even as Cambodian and Vietnamese communists operated nearby. Under Democratic Kampuchea, Chinese experts helped operate the plantations and exported rubber back to China, a practice that the PRK and its Vietnamese advisors considered a crime. Like the export of rice to China, the export of rubber—some twenty thousand to twenty-five thousand tons of it—was cited in the verdict of the Pol Pot–Ieng Sary trial.[45]

Soon after the invasion, the Vietnamese were again considering the potential of Cambodian rubber. In December 1979 a Vietnamese advisor approached Heng Samrin. "Before starting up the rubber plantations again, the following should be examined. In Kampong Cham, how much has been destroyed? How much has been cut down by the people? I don't have a handle on this yet." The advisor told Samrin what would be required: "According to the experience in Vietnam, five hundred workers are required for every hectare. Processing workers, electricity workers, drivers, planning cadres, accountants, factory bosses, and bosses for each sector are needed. . . . I propose that the provincial committee select workers, and I will help with technical training." The advisor concluded the meeting with an explanation of where the rubber would go and who would control it. "Rubber is a big resource for Cambodia to sell overseas for a lot of dollars to build up the country. Before proceeding, Vietnamese advisors should be sent to investigate in Chup and Memot [two plantation areas in Kampong Cham], and [we] should wait for them to draft a plan to send to the [Cambodian government] to examine."[46]

Neither Heng Samrin nor the advisor mentioned the Europeans. Yet two months later, Pen Sovan flew to Moscow, where he offered the same plantations and the same rubber to the Soviets in exchange for automobiles, medicine, food, and dollars. During the summer of 1980, Sovan also visited Berlin, offering fully one third of Cambodia's rubber in exchange for rubber-processing machines and the reconstruction of the country's rubber infrastructure. Within months, Russian and German technicians were touring Kampong Cham, inspecting Cambodia's ruined rubber industry and planning its rebirth. "This made the Vietnamese angry, but they [the Vietnamese] just weren't helping Cambodia in terms of modern agricultural techniques," says Pen Sovan.[47]

After Sovan's arrest, the Cambodian leadership and their Vietnamese advisors attempted to extricate themselves from at least some of these overlapping commitments. The East Germans, who wielded little clout in Phnom Penh, could, with some finesse, be turned away. In a Council of Ministers meeting in July 1983, Nuch Than, director of the General Department of Rubber Plantations, explained that it was also possible to play the Soviets off against the Germans. Speaking of one agreement to confer 20,000 hectares to the Germans, Than explained that the agreement "definitely offends our Soviet friends because [they] have helped us more than the Germans have." Ung Phan agreed with Nuch Than, suggesting only that the Germans be approached diplomatically: "In discussions with the German friends, we should be polite and take careful positions." Later in the meeting, Nuch Than and Ung Phan discussed another 10,000-hectare plantation in Prey Kok that had been promised to the Germans but which Vietnamese advisors had counseled the Cambodians to hold on to. "Will [keeping the plantation for ourselves] affect our politics or our friendships?" asked Ung Phan. "In fact, our [German] friends have not helped us a lot in the area of economics, but in other areas, they have offered us broad support. Particularly with regard to [rubber], when we hold discussions with the Germans, we should speak in the name of the technicians first, not in the name of the government, in order to avoid having the [Germans] blame our government."[48]

The Soviets were in a stronger position than the Germans because of their political power in Phnom Penh and their contribution of start-up capital for the plantations. The Cambodian General Department of Rubber Plantations was also filled with Soviet advisors—nineteen at one point in 1985—without any documented Vietnamese, much less German, colleagues. Yet the Vietnamese, despite never arriving at a formal nation-to-nation agreement, continued to export Cambodian rubber to Vietnam. Rubber plantations in Rattanakiri were too isolated to be included in central plans, and Vietnamese advisors consigned their production for direct export to nearby Vietnamese provinces. Vietnamese advisors and workers also controlled the day-to-day operations of the rubber plantations, even those whose output was officially allocated to the Soviets. As one 1982 Council of Ministers report stated, "Cambodian rubber for which start-up capital has been borrowed from the Soviets should receive Vietnamese assistance with regard to technical cadres and the training of workers and managers, including the efficient use of this borrowed money. We have drafted a letter to the Vietnamese requesting this help, and the Soviets have agreed. This is provided for clearly in the agreement between Cambodia and the Soviet Union."[49]

. . . AND FISH

Control over the fishing sector was a purely bilateral issue, between Cambodians and Vietnamese. For several years, advisors working within the Cambodian Ministry of Agriculture promoted the collectivization of fishing villages while bemoaning the Cambodian state's inability to transport fish from one site to another. Formal trade began in 1982, when the ministry signed agreements with the Vietnamese Ministry of Fishing for the export of thousands of tons of fish, and expanded in 1983, when the Ministry of Commerce arrived at a series of export agreements of its own. Almost immediately, the implementation of these pacts prompted bitter complaints from lower-level cadres. According to bureaucrats from both ministries, the Vietnamese were "stealing" approximately 1 percent of the hard-currency value of the fish, charging the Cambodians another 4–5 percent for transport, "quality certificates," and "stamps of exchange" and requiring that the Cambodians pay for warehouse, transportation, fuel, and port expenses.[50]

The Vietnamese were also fishing in Cambodia. Prior to 1975, tens of thousands of Vietnamese had lived on Cambodia's riverbanks and lakeshores, their lives organized around traditional fishing practices. Gathered together along waterways, on the shores of the Tonle Sap, or in floating villages of houseboats connected by plank walkways, they proved easy targets for the purges of the Lon Nol and Khmer Rouge regimes. According to Vietnamese advisors, all but 20 percent of the ethnic Vietnamese fishermen died during the 1970s; almost all the rest fled to Vietnam. The reemergence of Vietnamese fishing villages—now called Fishing Solidarity Groups—was therefore presented to the Cambodians as a partial correction of earlier brutality. As was apparent in the Party's 1980 immigration policy and the debates of 1981, at least some Cambodian leaders were unconvinced. "Along the banks of the river, there are only Vietnamese," noted the chief of the Phnom Penh police, Khoem Pon. By 1982, Cambodian officials were also complaining about the government's inability to control the coming and going of larger Vietnamese fishing vessels and the fishing activities of Vietnamese military units posted along the Tonle Sap lake.[51]

In 1984, when the Council of Ministers met to discuss "fishing offenses"—overfishing, fishing without permits, the use of oversized or otherwise prohibited nets, the cutting of timber along waterways, and fishing in "prohibited areas"—the leadership understood that, when it came to ethnic Vietnamese fishermen, they could not act unilaterally. "We should have a strict system for dealing with offenders who are Cambodian nationals," said Chan Si, "[but] for our Vietnamese friends, we should establish a joint Cambodian-Vietnamese commission to inspect and resolve [the problem]." No such commission was ever formed, however. What is more, Vietnamese advisors and military officers were actively encouraging the decentralization of the fishing sector. To the frustration of the leadership in Phnom Penh, provincial officials consistently failed to report on the fishing activities of either the Khmer or the ethnic Vietnamese.[52]

. . . AND TIMBER

In recent years, the exploitation of Cambodian timber has raised serious concerns about deforestation. Deals have been struck between foreign companies and Cambodian officials, including provincial authorities, military figures, and top leaders, yet little revenue has flowed to the central coffers. Now part of the public dialogue among the Cambodian government, international lending institutions, and nongovernmental organizations, these environmental and financial issues appeared in the early years of the PRK, when control over Cambodian timber was officially decentralized.

Timber, Cambodia's most valuable natural resource, was quickly identified by PRK officials and their Vietnamese advisors as a potential source of income. By the end of 1980 some 20,000 cubic meters had been cut and sold. Fearing environmental damage, the leadership authorized the Ministry of Agriculture to bring some order to the situation. The ministry was undermined, however, by its own provincial offices, which sold timber to politically connected private-sector interests, and by powerful institutions in Phnom Penh—including the cabinet of the Party Central Committee—which were often the end buyers.[53]

In 1984, Vietnamese advisors decided to formally decentralize the timber industry. Pham Van Kath, an advisor to the Council of Ministers, explained that it was a matter of efficiency. "Because the [Ministry of Agriculture] has many responsibilities and can't handle the situation in time, decisions are slow," he pointed out. "Responsibility for the distribution of felled timber should be granted to the provinces and municipalities." The result of this decision was greater Vietnamese control over Cambodian timber. Although the Ministry of Agriculture had been cutting its own deals with the Vietnamese Ministry of

Timber, exports increased as decision making devolved to the provinces. Vietnamese advisors and the Cambodian leadership instructed provincial authorities to develop local timber industries, to export directly to Vietnamese sister
provinces, and to permit direct Vietnamese participation in the Cambodian
timber sector. Where forests were located in insecure areas, moreover, local
Cambodian officials were expected to allow Vietnamese soldiers and workers to
log directly.[54]

A variety of Vietnamese institutions and persons were involved in the export of Cambodian timber to Vietnam. Vietnamese officials established "mixed
Cambodian-Vietnamese timber companies" in the provinces and permitted a
level of private-sector activity along the border. As Tien, advisor to the Ministry
of Commerce, explained, "There is a set of big [Vietnamese] businesspeople
who go to buy timber from Kratie [province] and then go and sell it in Vietnam. We should have an appropriate way of controlling this problem, but we
mustn't prohibit such buying and selling."[55] The Vietnamese army, which
oversaw the cutting of trees along roadways (to deny the resistance hiding
places) and which used timber to build shelters for its soldiers, also transported
timber to Vietnam. According to reports from the Kampong Speu provincial
timber office and from cadres at timber inspection sites around Phnom Penh,
Vietnamese soldiers responsible for the southeastern sector of the country and
Phnom Penh–based Vietnamese security officials were moving logs "by land,
water, and rail . . . without any permission whatsoever from the timber organizations." The reports depicted the local Cambodian cadres as entirely helpless.
"Usually these soldiers are armed when transporting timber along roads and
waterways and don't slow down or stop to allow the inspection teams of the
timber organizations the possibility of examining the timber."[56]

After 1985, when the Party designated the timber sector as the country's
number one economic priority, the situation became even more chaotic. As one
official from the Ministry of Cooperation complained, we are "cutting down
timber without any strategic direction, for example, defense, replanting, or
maintenance." Direct Vietnamese control over timber continued up through
1988 as both the Vietnamese Ministry of Timber and the sister provinces felled
trees in "cooperative work sites." Throughout the 1980s, Cambodian officials
complained of Vietnamese overcutting, selective exports of only the best wood,
and the inability of the state to collect revenue from the timber industry. According to one 1987 Ministry of Industry report, 70 percent of all timber went
to Vietnam prior to processing, thereby depriving Cambodia of the opportunity to export a value-added product. A significant amount of timber simply

disappeared, its whereabouts uncontrolled by any state authorities. The Ministry of Communications attributed some of these losses to nighttime theft by Vietnamese forces. Much of the rest fell into the undocumented black market.[57]

THE NORTH AND THE SOUTH

As part of a policy to decentralize Cambodian-Vietnamese relations, central advisors, almost all of whom had come from Hanoi, encouraged Cambodian provincial authorities to invite large numbers of advisors from southern Vietnamese sister provinces. Although a few of these local advisors were northerners who came to Cambodia having already served as communist advisors to post-reunification southern Vietnam, most were southerners who, prior to 1975, had never lived under a communist regime. To many Cambodians who worked closely with the Vietnamese, these southerners seemed culturally and politically different from their northern compatriots.[58]

In language that echoes how Vietnamese people often describe their own cultural divisions, Cambodians generally describe the northerners as more "disciplined," as well as more "rigid" and "dogmatic" ideologically. Surprisingly, perhaps, the same Cambodians often preferred their comrades from Hanoi. Relatively austere in demeanor and spending habits, the northerners came across as more honest and consequently less interested in using their tenure in Cambodia to conduct personal business. Well educated, northern Vietnamese cadres also appealed to those Cambodians for whom a certain amount of technical competence was a prerequisite for respect. While most Cambodians chafed under the political and ideological supervision imposed by Hanoi, they generally viewed the northerners as more professional, more formal, and more polite.

Vietnamese advisors from Hanoi also appeared to many Cambodians to harbor fewer cultural and ethnic biases. Northerners, they felt, saw Cambodia as a foreign nation and Cambodians as a foreign people, to be respected even in the midst of imposing a communist system. By contrast, southerners represented a historical threat based less on ideology than on economic domination and territorial expansion. There were Cambodians who maintained good relations with the southerners, who saw in southern Vietnamese culture an openness and looseness, an "ability to be happy," that bore similarities to their own. But many others saw the southern Vietnamese advisors' use of the black market economy as evidence of economic exploitation or the presence of their families as proof of uncontrolled immigration. Worse still, many Cambodians perceived the southern Vietnamese as direct heirs to Vietnam's historical takeover of Khmer-held territory. There was a sense that the southern Vietnamese seemed to treat Cambodians less as a sovereign people than as ethnic minorities in a Vietnamese world—in short, like the Khmer minorities of the Mekong Delta, the Kampuchea Krom.

These perceptions corresponded with gradual changes in the nature of the Vietnamese occupation and the mission of the advisors. Vietnam's initial efforts to build a central Cambodian state were dictated from Hanoi and governed by Le Duc Tho and the VCP Politburo. Hanoi-trained Cambodian revolutionaries like Pen Sovan took power in Phnom Penh while hundreds of central Vietnamese bureaucrats set out to build the PRK's administration. Having successfully installed a communist regime loyal to Hanoi, the Vietnamese Party leadership was now willing to leave the occupation of Cambodia to southern Vietnam. The promotion of sister province relations brought not only southern Vietnamese advisors but also the economic and political agenda of the South. From the perspective of many Cambodians, this meant trading in Cambodian natural resources, permitting Vietnamese immigration, and shielding ethnic Vietnamese from the jurisdiction of Cambodian officials. This historically resonant, nonideological, *ethnic* threat came to be described, at least by Hanoi's more vociferous critics in the resistance and in the West, as "Vietnamization."

VIETNAMIZATION

In October 1982, KPNLF President Son Sann summed up the accusations associated with Vietnamization. The Vietnamese have "impose[d] the teaching of the Vietnamese language in Cambodian schools, sent thousands of young Cambodians for 'advanced education' in Hanoi, and indoctrinated the population and the youth," he told his supporters, concluding that "Hanoi is attempting to kill off the Khmer identity and the Khmer soul."[59]

Many Cambodians believed these charges in part because of historical precedent. Officials from the Nguyen dynasty had aspired to a certain amount of cultural colonization. As Emperor Minh Mang wrote in the 1830s, "[The Cambodians] should be taught to speak Vietnamese. [Our habits of] dress and table manners must also be followed. If there is any out-dated or barbarous custom that can be simplified or reprised, then do so." There was another historical lesson, however, one that Son Sann and other alarmists generally failed to recall, and that was that the Nguyen occupiers had failed to Vietnamize Cambodia. As the emperor himself complained, "The customs of the barbarians are so different from our own, that even if we were to capture all their territory, it would not be certain we could change them."[60]

There was little opposition from the PRK leadership to Vietnamese offers to help educate Cambodians. The first minister of education, Chan Ven, who talks now of having "struggled with the Vietnamese" over human rights issues, did not complain either about general Vietnamese assistance in the area of education or about the teaching of Vietnamese. To Ven and to the rest of the Cambodian leadership, Vietnamese was simply another foreign language whose introduction to Cambodia would help the country reconnect to the outside world. They also figured that if the Vietnamese government offered teachers at a reasonable cost, Phnom Penh could hardly refuse. As Pen Navuth, Chan Ven's successor, said in 1986, "The Ministry of Education starts with Vietnamese because it's easy to get teachers of Vietnamese in terms of housing and stipend." Outside the Council of Ministers, there were plenty of Cambodians who saw Vietnamese language training as a symbol of repression and isolation. Prohibitions on the teaching of English and French, languages that the regime associated with its capitalist enemies, only perpetuated these resentments. In the end, though, Cambodians did not experience the kind of linguistic imperialism suggested by the resistance, mainly because limited resources prevented Vietnamese from being taught more than one day a week.[61]

Vietnamese officials made a concerted effort to teach Vietnamese to Cambodian soldiers, police, and bureaucrats, often in conjunction with political education. In the army the ability to communicate with Vietnamese officers and soldiers was sometimes vital. Among civilians there was less urgency, and even though Vietnamese speakers were promoted within the bureaucracy, there was very little interest in language study. Explained Ung Phan in May 1982, Cambodian cadres have "already been studying Vietnamese, but we have not yet seen anyone speak it such that it has become a habit."[62]

State and Party cadres, doctors, and teachers were required to attend political education in Vietnam, sometimes for as long as six months. Many resented the training and the time spent away from home, and it is unlikely that these efforts succeeded at "indoctrinating" Cambodian officials beyond providing an understanding of the acceptable boundaries of political discourse. More closely connected to Vietnam itself and therefore more complex in their sympathies were the Cambodian students, many of them the children of Party officials, who received long-term training in Vietnam. Carefully vetted for loyalty by

Vietnamese advisors, Cambodian Party officials, and the Ministries of Education and the Interior, these students nonetheless tended to avoid political courseloads and chose instead to pursue technical education. "There was an intellectual life in Hanoi that didn't exist in Phnom Penh," recalls one former student. "You could buy books." Comfortable with Vietnamese culture, they often returned to Cambodia as literate and cosmopolitan Khmers whose education, exposure to the outside world, and, in many cases, fluency in English soon drew them toward a larger world outside Indochinese solidarity.[63]

Vietnamese authorities have also been accused of more insidious efforts to co-opt Cambodians. Accounts of Cambodian orphans secretly raised in Vietnam and then inserted into the Ministries of Defense and the Interior—circulated by Cambodians with close ties to Vietnam as well as by those for whom conspiracies are central to their view of the Vietnamese—have fed the darkest suspicions about Vietnamese machinations in Cambodia. These sorts of stories recall the ethnically charged accusations launched by the Khmer Rouge against Khmers who had "Cambodian bodies and Vietnamese heads." On the other hand, the Vietnamese political control over the Cambodian government and the complete secrecy with which they operated raised questions for many Cambodians as to whether Vietnam was concealing a long-term plan by which to expand its influence. The repressive and highly opaque nature of the regime and the occupation thus perpetuated the conspiracy theories and general paranoia that fed Cambodian nationalism.

"MASTERS OF THE LAND"

No accusation against the Vietnamese occupation was repeated more frequently or was subject to more debate than Vietnamese immigration into Cambodia. Inside Cambodia and in refugee camps, Cambodians speculated about the numbers of immigrants. There were also accusations concerning the alleged control that ethnic Vietnamese wielded over Khmers and over the country. "In its scheme, Hanoi has moved hundreds of thousands of Vietnamese nationals into Cambodia as new masters of the land," asserted one typically heated *KPNLF Bulletin.*[64]

In 1982 the PRK was taking a more forgiving approach to Vietnamese immigration. Chastened by the arrest of Pen Sovan, the leadership had stopped suggesting that immigrants return to Vietnam. Other matters prompted internal debate, however—in particular, the hiring of Vietnamese to work in factories, warehouses, and rubber plantations and on infrastructure projects, frequently alongside Cambodian workers but under the control of Vietnamese supervisors. Although Vietnamese advisors promoted this policy, they were aware of how it might be perceived. Warned Tui, the Vietnamese advisor to the Ministry of Finance, "There may be accusations when we bring in a lot of Vietnamese workers, so we want to avoid other contact between the Cambodian people and the Vietnamese workers."[65]

The Cambodian leadership had similar qualms. In June 1982, in a Council of Ministers meeting attended by Tui and Dao Duc Chinh, advisor to the Council of Ministers, the normally accommodating Chan Si wondered if Vietnamese workers were more trouble than they were worth. "We've seen that cooperation with Vietnam, where we work together and distribute [the results among Cambodians and Vietnamese], causes big problems because the enemy can make various kinds of accusations. So don't bring Vietnamese workers into Cambodia." The minutes of the meeting do not record any response from Tui or Chinh, nor did the policy change.[66]

The PRK's immigration policy was, in fact, loosening, as was apparent in an October 1982 Council of Ministers circular entitled "The Organization and Management of Certain Vietnamese People Who Have Come to Mix Together and to Work and Live in Cambodia." Whereas Pen Sovan had attempted to limit Vietnamese immigration to those who had fled Cambodia during the Lon Nol and Khmer Rouge regimes, the circular said that "Vietnamese with friends [in Cambodia] who know them or close family who will help them and want them to come to Cambodia to live and work or visit family" would be permitted to immigrate. The regime's only apparent concern was the effect that immigration would have on its image. According to the circular, local officials were to exercise caution in permitting ethnic Vietnamese to live in Cambodia in order to avoid giving ammunition to the anti-Vietnamese message of the resistance, or what the circular referred to as the "psychological warfare that divides the two peoples."[67]

A 1983 border agreement between Cambodia and Vietnam further encouraged the movement of people, permitting both Khmers and Vietnamese living in border regions to engage in cross-border trade, to check on family members, and, with the permission of local authorities from both countries, to "build houses, farm, take timber, herd and kill animals . . . and conduct fishing in the other country's territory." The agreement also recognized, as legal residents, Vietnamese immigrants who had "lived in border areas of [Cambodia] for a long time already," so long as they "respected the laws and traditions of the host country."[68] To the frustration of the Cambodian Ministry of the Interior, there was almost no policing of the border. According to a ministry report from 1984, the two parties had not yet produced a plan to document border crossings and had failed to instruct the provinces on how to implement the 1983 agreement. The ministry pleaded with the Vietnamese for assistance. "For several years, the PRK Ministry of the Interior has asked the Ministry of the Interior of the Socialist Republic of Vietnam to help in exchanging experience to strengthen the people's police forces from the ministry down to the localities, to expand and guide systems with expertise in espionage and counterespionage, and to establish systems for managing border crossings and foreigners and for issuing border-crossing letters to cadres and people."[69]

To Vietnamese officials, who estimated that some 600,000 ethnic Vietnamese had once lived in Cambodia, this new wave of immigration barely made up for the killings and expulsions that had occurred during the Lon Nol and Khmer Rouge regimes. From the perspective of the resistance, however, the PRK's immigration policies had succeeded in flooding Cambodia with ethnic Vietnamese in numbers that far exceeded prerevolutionary demographics. It became, in the end, a war of numbers. In the mid-1980s, Sihanouk and the KPNLF estimated that 700,000 ethnic Vietnamese were living in Cambodia. The PRK, for its part, insisted that there were only 56,000. Less exaggerated and less politically fraught outside estimates put the number between 100,000 and 250,000, figures that generally comported with the PRK's own internal calculations. Although no overall estimate is available, the municipality of Phnom Penh and the nearby province of Kandal endeavored, in 1985, to determine the size of their Vietnamese populations. The resulting figure for the two jurisdictions—43,000—suggests, if accurate, that overall numbers exceeded Phnom Penh's public claims but fell short of not only resistance figures but the prerevolutionary numbers against which the PRK measured Vietnamese immigration.[70]

The difference between the two eras, in the minds of many Cambodians, was the favoritism that a Vietnamese-dominated PRK offered the immigrants. In Phnom Penh, where more than 19,000 Vietnamese were engaged in trade, crafts, small repairs, fishing, and animal husbandry, municipal authorities built Vietnamese-language schools, distributed rice and other goods, and provided land and housing to approximately one fourth of the ethnic Vietnamese families. The municipality also created an infrastructure to help its Vietnamese residents, establishing branches of the Cambodian-Vietnamese Friendship Association and designating representatives of the Vietnamese community to work with city officials.[71]

In 1986, as the leadership began discussing a national policy concerning the ethnic Vietnamese, Phnom Penh—along with Kandal, which had also issued directives to provide "assistance to Vietnamese residents who are conducting business in a nice fashion"—provided a model of cooperation. Speaking to the Council of Ministers, a representative of the Vietnamese embassy reminded the Cambodians that "life has not been easy for ethnic Vietnamese living in Cambodia" and that anti-Vietnamese sentiments among the Khmer were partly to blame. He nonetheless praised the assistance that local officials had given the Vietnamese. "The Vietnamese embassy, like the Vietnamese Party and government, are pleased with these results and with the Cambodian Party and government, which have concerned themselves with this issue."[72]

Not all the Cambodians were enthused. Citing the limited capacity of Phnom Penh to house its residents, Ung Phan complained that there were "Vietnamese residents who have come to Cambodia without a profession and without housing and have asked the state to help them. . . . If assistance can't be provided to them, I propose that they should be sent to the provinces. On the other hand, if they have certificates and houses, then they should be granted permission [to stay in the city]." Phan added, on a somewhat discordant note, "Some Vietnamese residents buy identity cards. Some have never lived in Cambodia. I ask for a reexamination of this issue. With regard to those who've come to live illegally, it is the role of the police to investigate, and if [their status] is not appropriate, they should be sent back to Vietnam."[73]

Notwithstanding Ung Phan's protestations, the policy issued by the Council of Ministers the following month called for greater material assistance to Vietnamese residents in Phnom Penh. Local municipal officials were directed to find land for ethnic Vietnamese. Those Vietnamese who already had homes would be issued family identity cards, and those without a profession would be assisted in finding work. The circular setting forth this policy contained no provisions for repatriation, nor did it amend the PRK's policies on immigration and border crossings. It was the last official word on Vietnamese residents for the duration of the occupation. Meanwhile, refugees leaving Cambodia arrived at the border complaining that they had had to build houses for the Vietnamese and characterizing the situation as similar to that of Kampuchea Krom.[74]

THE "BAD ELEMENTS"

Generally overlooked in examinations of Vietnamese immigration was the degree to which Vietnamese officials distrusted the loyalties of their compatriots.

Official documents refer repeatedly to "bad elements" whose activities or backgrounds supposedly posed a threat to the Cambodian and Vietnamese revolutions. These included hundreds of defectors from the Vietnamese army who, after a period of detention, frequently stayed in Cambodia "keeping long hair and driving motor scooters in Phnom Penh." There were also Vietnamese who were attempting to escape southern Vietnam and make their way overseas. Like the hundreds of thousands of boat people who fled the South by sea, the Vietnamese who crossed into Cambodia aggravated Vietnamese authorities. "We should prohibit businesspeople from conducting business in Cambodia," a Vietnamese advisor instructed the Council of Ministers in 1982, "because we are afraid they will flee to Thailand." According to PRK documents, Vietnamese who attempted to flee were to be "detained, disciplined, or forced . . . to return to Vietnam."[75] One Vietnamese woman who attempted to flee southern Vietnam via Cambodia recalled the suspicions of the Vietnamese soldiers. "It would be all right if we had to pass the checkpoints where Cambodian soldiers were in charge. However, it would be more difficult if we had to deal with the Vietnamese soldiers. As a routine, they checked carefully. They also questioned you if they suspected something. At the checkpoints near the rivers, the Vietnamese military group always took charge of the bridges. As a result, we were informed ahead of time to prepare ourselves when we approached checkpoints with Vietnamese soldiers."[76]

Worst of all, from the perspective of Hanoi, were the anticommunist South Vietnamese, the "soldiers from the old army and other bad people." Sensitive to any threats to reunification, Vietnamese authorities employed a variety of institutions in Cambodia, including 7708, the Phnom Penh–based Vietnamese police, in seeking out former officials of the old South Vietnamese anticommunist Thieu regime. Civilian institutions, including A40 and A50, the special advisor unit for Phnom Penh, claimed responsibility for investigating and suppressing "illegal" activity on the part of Vietnamese residents and immigrants. The Cambodian Ministry of the Interior, too, was expected to "cooperate in fighting counterrevolutionary Vietnamese." Between 1983 and 1985, Vietnamese and Cambodian authorities claimed to have uncovered nine conspiracies of "Thieu Vietnamese traitors," involving more than a hundred people.[77]

Vietnamese officials, fearful of infiltration and unauthorized economic activities, attempted to mobilize ethnic Vietnamese in Cambodia in revolutionary units—political cells, or *snoul*—whose role was to lead "the movement of the Vietnamese people." Vietnamese civilians were also made to live in Solidarity Groups, which were arranged sometimes along professional lines but often according to ethnicity, hence the names Vietnamese Resident Solidarity Groups or Vietnamese Solidarity Villages. Designed to protect Vietnamese cultural practices and to provide Vietnamese-language education, these villages also served, in the words of one Council of Ministers circular, to "consolidate the Vietnamese residents in order to teach the policies of the Cambodian revolution and the Vietnamese revolution, mutual assistance, ceaseless solidarity, etc." Vietnamese authorities monitored the political backgrounds of Vietnamese village leaders and schoolteachers. Within the villages, Vietnamese were expected to participate in the policing of their own community against the "bad elements."[78]

Among the most persistent suspicions held by Cambodians during the occupation and long afterward was that Vietnamese authorities controlled the ethnic Vietnamese in Cambodia. Judging by official PRK documents, they certainly tried. The Vietnamese embassy in Phnom Penh considered itself the representative of all Vietnamese residents living in Cambodia, overseeing a network of representatives of various ethnic Vietnamese communities. Vietnamese advisors—political officials answerable to B68—assumed leadership roles within the ethnic Vietnamese community, "explaining, leading, and educating the Vietnamese people in all places where there are Vietnamese people living and working." But were the ethnic Vietnamese responsive to this leadership? Were they, as the resistance and critics of the regime charged, a fifth column loyal to the Vietnamese authorities? In fact, very few of the immigrants were communists. A large number had crossed the border precisely because they had found it difficult to make a living in newly communist southern Vietnam. If they felt loyalty toward Vietnamese authorities in Cambodia, it was based less on shared ideology than on the protective umbrella offered by the occupation.[79]

PROTECTING THE VIETNAMESE

As a recognized minority in Cambodia, the ethnic Vietnamese enjoyed a certain civic equality, participating in small numbers in the Cambodian military and police and voting in supplemental National Assembly elections. (Keenly aware of how such activities would be perceived by Cambodians and by critics of the occupation, the Cambodian leadership entertained convoluted ideas of how to disguise Vietnamese voters, including insisting that they drop a syllable from their names before voting.) The question of whether ethnic Vietnamese could become Cambodian citizens was, however, never resolved. Instead, their status under the law depended on the ad hoc intervention of Vietnamese mili-

tary and civil officials. With the establishment of Cambodian security and judicial institutions, this legal ambiguity became more complex, as demonstrated
in two very different cases.[80]

The first involved "Ne Hoth," a Vietnamese resident of Kampong Thom
province convicted of smuggling by the provincial court. As was the practice
throughout the country, the court solicited the prior opinion of the provincial
Party committee, which had conducted its own investigation and had already
decided to convict. "Ty Khieth," a Kampong Thom–based Vietnamese advisor, also exerted pressure on the court, reportedly telling the prosecutor that "if
it were my country, the people would have cut off his head already." A dispute
arose after the expected conviction, when the same Vietnamese advisor instructed the provincial Party committee to release Hoth and return all confiscated gold and other property to him. Writing to the Ministry of Justice, the
provincial Party secretary, So Hean, explained his dilemma: "If we don't act according to our fear of [the Vietnamese], they will not protect the province [militarily]." Lacking the capacity to order an arrest, Justice Minister Uk Bunchheuan brought the case to the Council of State, saying, "This is a problem of
relations with the advisors." In response, Say Phouthang reiterated the long-
standing policy of the PRK. "Among our people it must be resolved according
to the law. If it relates to a [Vietnamese] resident, [the advisor] can intervene."
Any problems with this policy, Phouthang explained, should be taken by
provincial Party secretaries to the Vietnamese authorities at B68, not the Cambodian leadership.[81]

A year and a half later, Hoth remained free, had built himself a new house,
and had, according to Uk Bunchheuan, resumed smuggling. The chief judge of
the provincial court had fled in fear to Phnom Penh, and the Council of State
continued to vent its frustration. "We should call the Kampong Thom Party,"
said Say Phouthang, "to ask if it will continue like this and if another hundred
years will pass without the verdict being implemented."[82]

Two years later another case revealed how the Vietnamese occupation offered some protection for more vulnerable ethnic Vietnamese. The targets of
prosecution, in this instance, were Vietnamese prostitutes in Phnom Penh
whom municipal authorities had arrested and sent to a reeducation camp. Vietnamese officials complained to the Cambodian Ministry of Foreign Affairs that
old women and children had been rounded up indiscriminately and that prostitutes had suffered beatings and rapes and had, in some cases, died in police
custody. Phnom Penh Mayor Thaong Khon denied the charges: "Some prostitutes say slanderous things. It isn't true." Apparently indifferent to humanitar-

ian concerns but aware of the diplomatic consequences, Deputy Minister of Foreign Affairs Long Visalo reminded Khon that "if it is true that Vietnamese prostitutes are harmed in [the reeducation camp], then there may be revenge against the Cambodians from Vietnamese [soldiers in] army barracks who are relatives of those prostitutes."[83]

The Vietnamese military withdrawal from Cambodia in 1989 spelled the end of this threat and of the protections the occupation had offered to ethnic Vietnamese. For Cambodians the withdrawal meant a taste of sovereignty and independence. For Vietnamese civilians, scapegoats for Vietnamese government policies, the departure of the troops was a disaster, permitting the anti-Vietnamese attacks conducted by the Khmer Rouge in the early 1990s, as well as the periodic anti-Vietnamese violence that continues to this day.

DEFINING THE OCCUPATION

The political legacy of the Vietnamese occupation is clear enough. More than a decade after the Vietnamese withdrawal, opposition figures continue to ascribe the derogatory adjective "*yuon*" to the ruling Party, recalling that its leaders were installed by the Vietnamese and implying that they are still under the influence of Vietnam. The current leadership, for its part, refuses to acknowledge the control that Vietnam wielded over the PRK. In the middle of the debate is a vacuum, a missing consensus with regard to Vietnam's role in Cambodia that permits stark characterizations ranging from "salvation" to "genocide." The historical record, to the extent that it has become available, suggests something more subtle.

Vietnam's role in Cambodia was not exactly colonial. Its reason for occupying Cambodia was more strategic (to protect Vietnam from China) than economic. Its justification for the occupation (to protect Cambodians from the Khmer Rouge) also seems more valid to modern historians than the racist theories spun by colonial Europeans. As neighbors with an intertwined history, the peoples of Vietnam and Cambodia had a relationship very different from the one between Europeans and their Asian, African, and Latin American subjects.

The experience of ethnic Vietnamese in Cambodia was also vastly different from that of Europeans in their colonies. Fishermen, small-scale merchants, and repairmen, they maintained a sometimes tense relationship with communist Vietnamese authorities. Indeed, the influx of ethnic Vietnamese into Cambodia was as much a part of a larger wave of refugees fleeing southern Vietnam in the early 1980s as a systematic populating of Cambodia per se. Like European colonial authorities, however, Vietnamese military and political officials protected their compatriots.

Vietnam's economic relationship with the PRK, which included the exploitation of Cambodia's natural resources and the manipulation of its currency, was similar to the Soviet Union's domination of Eastern Europe. Like the Soviet Union and its satellites, Vietnam and Cambodia couched their agreements in terms of "friendship" and "solidarity," but in fact, benefits flowed mostly to the stronger party. The bilateral relationship was uniquely complicated, however, by Cambodia's being a satellite of a satellite, which created tensions between Vietnam and the Soviet Union over issues such as Soviet advisors and control of Cambodian rubber plantations.

Cambodia also differed from Eastern Europe in that an active resistance along the border was engaged in a permanent campaign to convince Cambodians to take up arms against the occupiers. Many Cambodians heeded the call, but the majority engaged in passive resistance, refusing to help the Vietnamese achieve their goals for Cambodia. For the occupation must be understood not just in terms of control but in terms of the imposition of ideology, or rather two ideologies, the first being Indochinese solidarity, the second being communism. Neither ideology took hold. Despite years of propaganda and political education aimed at nurturing fraternal bonds and instilling an appreciation for socialism, Cambodians remained stubbornly nationalistic and ideologically apathetic.

Nowadays the harshest critics of the Vietnamese occupation insist that, whatever failures the Vietnamese may have encountered during the occupation, they *intended* to conquer, subjugate, and Vietnamize Cambodia. The secret nature of Vietnamese politics prevents scholars from confirming or disproving grand schemes of demographic or cultural colonization. Even if Vietnamese Politburo documents revealed a vast plot, however, one must ask whether it would matter. The Vietnamese occupation of Cambodia was decentralized, deliberately so since Vietnamese advisors promoted the sister province relationships. Immigration was mostly a matter of individual choice, facilitated by an unregulated border. Economic policy in the provinces was not controlled by Hanoi but rather by southern Vietnamese officials whose political views often differed from those of the Phnom Penh–based northerners. Furthermore, if Hanoi were ever to make a real colony out of Cambodia or to impose its vision of society on the Cambodian people, it would first have to arrive at some consensus as to what Vietnamese society should look like. As Vietnam's own painful reunification has revealed, this task may never be fully accomplished.

Chapter 7 The Chinese:

Racial Politics in the PRK

Despite its daily condemnations of Democratic Kampuchea for, among other crimes, systematically repressing Vietnamese, Chinese, and Cham Cambodians, the PRK was preparing to persecute people for their ethnicity. This time the sole target was the Chinese. As Chea Soth explained in a speech in October 1982, the problem, as he saw it, was global. "Throughout the world, countries are extremely concerned about the Chinese," he expounded, ticking off the details. "There are so many Chinese living in Singapore that now the country has lost its nationality. . . . In Burma, Malaysia, Thailand, Laos, Cambodia, and Vietnam, there are complex problems related to the Chinese. . . . They conduct business and control the economy. In capitalist countries, they control the entire economy, as well as state officials at every level, whom they are always trying to buy off. Especially in Vietnam, during the Ngo Diem period, nothing could be done [about the Chinese]. . . . Eighty percent of Thailand is Chinese, most of whom conduct business. . . . [The attempted communist coup in Indonesia] was fomented and poisoned by a Maoist communist party. In general, the Chinese there are still poisonous."[1]

Soth, whose own studies in China had apparently generated little warmth for the country or its people, spoke of the local situation. "At first, these Chinese arrived [in Cambodia] with empty hands, but then [they revealed] their capacity to commandeer our workers and our nationals and take steps toward engaging in pure capitalism. . . . In Cambodia the Chinese are creating insecurity and are destroying the national economy."

Although similar sentiments had guided the decisions of Vietnamese advisors and PRK officials since 1979, Chea Soth's dire assessment reflected the political atmosphere of 1982, when the Party and the government came closest to absolute repression of the ethnic Chinese. Before the Cambodians could arrive at such a crossroads, however, they first had to see their own history in a particularly dark light and then feel the full weight of Vietnamese-Chinese tensions.

COMMERCE AND COMMUNISTS

In the fifteenth century, immigrants from Guangdong (Canton), Fujian, and other parts of China began arriving in what is now Cambodia. Connected to ancestral villages and family lineages in China, they nonetheless assimilated, often through intermarriage, into Cambodian society. Occasionally they even joined the court as ministers. As in other Southeast Asian countries, ethnic Chinese dominated trade, a state of affairs that French colonial authorities regarded as politically threatening. "In Cambodia, as everywhere else, [the Chinese] are insolent . . . [and] rely on the weakness, the corruption or the [lack of] firmness of the authorities," reported Résident-Supérieur Aymonier in 1875, conjuring up familiar stereotypes.[2]

After independence, Cambodian leaders of all political stripes began to imagine a Chinese menace. In the 1950s and 1960s, Sihanouk attempted first to place restrictions on the kinds of professions available to the Chinese and then, through socialist reforms, to nationalize Chinese-controlled import-export and banking enterprises. After the coup of 1970, Lon Nol perceived a different threat: ethnic Chinese loyal to communist China. In the midst of a civil war against the Beijing-backed Khmer Rouge, Lon Nol's Republic of Cambodia shut down Chinese schools and newspapers. Democratic Kampuchea was the worst of all for the Chinese, who were again seen as degenerate urban capitalists. In line with their own quasi-political, quasi-racial obsession with creating a new worker-peasant society devoid of ethnic diversity, the Khmer Rouge eradicated Chinese bourgeois culture and forbade the speaking of foreign languages, including Chinese. Rural as well as urban Chinese came under suspicion. The more assimilated Sino-Khmers attempted to hide their background.[3]

The history of the Chinese in Vietnam is equally complex. A by-product of the Sino-Soviet split, the tensions that divided Hanoi from Beijing were explained, in official propaganda, as profound ideological divergences. The Chinese understood Vietnam to be serving the Soviet Union's "hegemonist" ends. Vietnam, for its part, followed Moscow's lead, referring to the Chinese as "reactionaries" who, by virtue of the Sino-American rapprochement, now had "imperialist" ambitions. Inevitably perhaps, Hanoi identified as infiltrators in its own backyard the ethnic Chinese of North Vietnam. In the early and mid 1970s the VCP began discriminating against the Hoa, as the Chinese are known in Vietnam, eventually purging them from the Party, the state administration, and strategic industries.[4]

After communist victories in Cambodia and Vietnam, Hanoi found its Cambodian comrades retreating into isolation and hostility and almost entirely dependent, militarily and economically, on China. Hoping to reestablish what they saw as an Indochinese revolution, Vietnamese authorities continued to approach the new rulers of Cambodia. Once border skirmishes between the two countries had intensified to a point where tensions were irreparable, however, Vietnam came to believe that its worst fears of Chinese power and influence had been confirmed.

A different kind of Chinese threat emerged in southern Vietnam, where Hanoi's prescriptions for communist economics ran headlong into an unexpectedly resilient commercial culture. Like the people of Phnom Penh, many residents of Saigon had greeted the end of the war with qualified relief, hopeful for peace and stability and yet suspicious of communism. For merchants and for their customers, private commerce was the rhythm of daily life. An estimated half of South Vietnam's money and most of its gold and dollars circulated through Saigon. Few of the city's residents, even those who welcomed reunification, wanted the economy turned upside down.

As in Cambodia and many other Southeast Asian countries, ethnic Chinese had traditionally dominated South Vietnam's import-export business, banking sector, and wholesale and retail trade. Most vexing to Hanoi was Chinese control over the sector by which it judged the success of the revolution: the rice trade. As Saigon's new administrators failed to deliver this trade into the hands of state institutions and as the economy faltered, they blamed the Chinese for inflation, for food shortages, and for the lack of consumer goods. They also attempted to uproot the urban Chinese, conscripting them into the military or relocating them to rural New Economic Zones. Repression reached its peak in 1978, when police conducted raids of Cholon, Saigon's Chinese district. Private Chinese businesses were shut down, and new currency laws wiped out generations of Chinese savings. These decisions eventually led to the flight and exile of hundreds of thousands of ethnic Chinese, as well as Vietnamese urban residents.[5]

Throughout this period, Beijing complained of Hanoi's treatment of ethnic Chinese, yet it was only Vietnam's decision to invade Cambodia—a violation of China's direct political and strategic interests—that prompted a military response. On February 17, 1979, a quarter of a million Chinese soldiers swept into North Vietnam in a bloody adventure that gained no territory for China but that succeeded, by Beijing's reckoning, at teaching Vietnam "a lesson."[6]

A COMMON ENEMY

For all the historical similarities between the South Vietnamese and Cambodian economies, the struggles to suppress capitalism waged by the Vietnamese Socialist Republic and the PRK were conducted on very different terrain. In Saigon the Vietnamese communists found a disconcertingly vibrant merchant community, networks of anticommunist officials from previous regimes, and an educated bourgeois class whose loyalty to the revolution was dubious at best.[7] By contrast, when the PRK took power in Cambodia, Phnom Penh was virtually empty. The evacuation of the capital by the Khmer Rouge presented serious problems for the new regime, from the chaos of dislocation to the costs of reestablishing the municipal infrastructure. But the willingness of Democratic Kampuchea to implement cruel and sweeping anti-urban policies spared the PRK from having to pursue the kinds of unpopular practices applied by Hanoi in Saigon. There was no capitalism to quash nor urban counterrevolutionaries to weed out. The PRK, inspired by Vietnam's revolutionary policies, had no revolution of its own to wage. Its policies toward the cities and the Chinese merchant class were aimed solely at preventing the resurgence of the capitalists.

Even without capitalism, the PRK had political reasons for suspecting the Chinese. Having supported the government of Democratic Kampuchea and rallied behind an exiled Khmer Rouge leadership, the People's Republic of China had succeeded in inspiring fierce antipathy among many top PRK leaders. *All* Cambodian officials were expected, however, to express a certain amount of outrage. The forms on which cadres completed their personal biographies

told them as much. Nheum Vanda, a former Khmer Rouge cadre working at
the Ministry of Planning, either really hated Beijing or else knew the routine.

> *What was your political attitude toward Pol Pot–Ieng Sary? (State clearly what your*
> *activities were.)*
> At that time I absolutely opposed the Pol Pot–Ieng Sary Group, who were the out-
> and-out slaves of Peking Chinese.
> *What was your attitude toward the Chinese hegemonists?*
> I had a hot burning hatred for the Chinese reactionaries, absolutely opposing
> them at all times.[8]

Vietnamese advisors were convinced both that Cambodians really felt this way
and that they projected this hatred onto Cambodia's ethnic Chinese. As one internal Vietnamese report pronounced in June 1980, "In general, the attitude of
young people and intellectuals is that they hate Cambodian-Chinese."[9]

From the beginning, the Vietnamese and some of the PRK leadership promoted discriminatory policies. The Party prohibited state institutions, police
forces, and state industries from hiring ethnic Chinese. In Phnom Penh intellectuals of Chinese descent were denied positions in the new government, regardless of their political stance. Pen Sovan and other former officials who today claim to have opposed the Vietnamese on such policies were either silenced
or ineffective.[10]

Outside the top leadership, however, many officials resisted the anti-Chinese
policies. Occasionally they spoke up, questioning, for example, the inclusion of
"Beijing, China" in the constitutional provision referring to the struggle against
"reactionary and imperialist enemies." More frequently, local officials circum-
vented the policies, failing to investigate the ethnic backgrounds of applicants
and accepting those who went by Cambodian names. As one Party official in
Battambang commented, "If [the directives on the Chinese] had been implemented forcefully, no people would have been appointed as district chiefs."
Even in Phnom Penh, directly under the eyes of the leadership, directors of
state institutions and enterprises hired ethnic Chinese as staff and as cadres.[11]

The geopolitical threat so vivid to the Vietnamese advisors was an abstraction to most Cambodians. After generations in Cambodia, ethnic Chinese bore
little association with China. At most, only one in seven was *not* a Cambodian
citizen, and only one in twenty-three had been born in China. Whatever role
the People's Republic of China had in supporting "Pol Pot and Ieng Sary," it
had been Khmers who had carried out the policies of Democratic Kampuchea.
The regime's attempts to draw a connection between Pol Pot and the ethnic

Chinese were further complicated, moreover, by the obvious suffering inflicted by the Khmer Rouge on the ethnic Chinese community.[12]

The leadership's confusion over how to deal with this contradiction was apparent during the Pol Pot–Ieng Sary trial. One of the trial's purposes was to confirm the victimization of large segments of the Cambodian population, from Cham Muslims to intellectuals to Eastern Zone defectors. By recognizing their suffering, the PRK was implicitly inviting these groups to join the regime. Conversely, the PRK's enemies were those who had inflicted the suffering: the "Pol Pot–Ieng Sary clique" and the "Beijing reactionaries." It was unclear to the organizers of the trial where the ethnic Chinese fit. One document submitted to the court, entitled "Report on Crimes Committed by the Pol Pot–Ieng Sary Clique Against National Minorities in General and the Cham Muslims in Particular," reflected this uncertainty: "Finally, we should mention that the minorities of Chinese origin or the Chinese themselves were killed in 1975, as they were labeled 'bourgeois elements.' However, since 1976, their lives in the communes became less difficult due to the effective intervention of the Government of the People's Republic of China on their behalf."[13] There has been little or no evidence of this intervention, and, in the end, the final verdict included the ethnic Chinese among the victims of "Pol Pot–Ieng Sary": "Foreign residents like the Chinese, Vietnamese and those who were close to them, like mixed Chinese-Khmer, or mixed Vietnamese-Khmer, were killed. Pol Pot and Ieng Sary killed or deported hundreds of thousands of Chinese and Vietnamese. As a consequence, tens of thousands of Chinese took refuge in Vietnam."[14]

If the verdict represented a victory of history over geopolitics, it did not erase the suspicion, among some in the leadership and among the Vietnamese advisors, that ethnic Chinese were acting as spies for the PRC. Nor, paradoxically, were the regime's fears of Maoist infiltration lessened by the resurgence of Chinese capitalism.

CHINESE MERCHANTS

Within the first two to three years after the overthrow of the Khmer Rouge, Phnom Penh's retail economy grew from a few stalls selling noodles to state cadres and staff to a complex, regionally connected market with imported consumer goods. Having spent months living on the outskirts of Phnom Penh trading in gold and Thai goods, Cambodia's ethnic Chinese and Sino-Khmers saw reurbanization as an opportunity to return to familiar commercial activities. Throughout the city (as well as in the provincial capitals), they sold gold and silver, U.S. dollars and Vietnamese dong, meat, dried fish, noodles, cigarettes, shoes, dishes, cloth, fruit, and lotuses. As in the Khmer merchant community, women minded the storefronts; larger enterprises, including transportation and import-export businesses, were run by men. As the state's investigations later revealed, these "big businesspeople" established commercial networks that connected Phnom Penh to the ports of Koh Kong and Kampong Som, to Vietnam, and to Thailand. Along the way, they hired private transport and bribed soldiers and border patrols. To the leadership, these practices cast suspicion on all Chinese merchants; behind every noodle shop, they feared, hid a capitalist network.[15]

The private economy was not only selling consumer goods but making them. In January 1981 there were at least 2,000 private "manufacturing" operations in the country. In Phnom Penh alone, Chinese, Khmer, and Vietnamese residents were rolling cigarettes and sewing clothes in 712 separate sites, using their own capital to buy raw materials and selling their products on the free market. To the regime, which had managed to establish only 60 comparable state-run operations throughout the entire country, the success of these private ventures was embarrassing. In May 1981, when the Party convened its Fourth Party Congress, participants passed around privately manufactured cigarettes, an act that Heum Chhaem of the Ministry of Propaganda referred to as a "symbol of freedom [that] can have a bad effect on our politics."[16]

THE ESTABLISHMENT OF SOCIAL ORDER
AND SECURITY

After the Party congress, the elections, and the promulgation of the constitution in June 1981, the regime directed its attention to the problem of urban commerce—specifically, the Chinese. In creating the Committee for the Establishment of Social Order and Security for the Capital of Phnom Penh, the Party hoped to construct a state-run urban economy and rein in a galloping private sector. The leadership also began discussing the deportation of ethnic Chinese from Phnom Penh, an idea inspired by the Vietnamese policy of sending Saigon residents to New Economic Zones and by the Khmer Rouge evacuation of April 1975.

Minister of the Interior Khang Sarin set out the committee's agenda. "We should have a plan for how many markets there will be in Phnom Penh in order to meet the needs of the people. . . . Each market will be clearly divided into sections for trading in distinct kinds of goods, with sections for selling cloth, vegetables, [and] meat." Sarin also announced a crackdown on the private sector and the social vices that the leadership associated with unrestrained economic freedom. The municipality, he urged, should "gather statistics on the Chinese segment [of Phnom Penh commerce], businesspeople, prostitutes, and people with no appropriate work."[17]

Other members of the committee elaborated. "We can't do everything at once," said Peng Pat, the former Eastern Zone cadre who was chief of Phnom Penh's military. The committee's priorities were, first, to establish municipal government; second, to expel (*chonlies chenh*) "big businesspeople" and give their houses to the state; and, third, to "break up the big noodle houses, the small markets, and the motor scooter and car repair shops." Mok Mareth, a former biologist with a doctorate from the University of Toulouse in France, had been appointed deputy mayor of Phnom Penh and was thus one of the officials who would have to implement this policy. Despite his cosmopolitan background, Mareth agreed with his colleagues. "There is a way," he promised, "to close noodle shops and remove those with no work and Chinese capitalists and then to break up the coffeehouses."[18]

The committee's plans resembled Hanoi's approach to Saigon. This convergence was in part a by-product of the political tensions of late 1981, when Vietnamese authorities responded to anti-Vietnamese sentiments among PRK officials by stressing solidarity and the common threats faced by the nations of Indochina.[19] The PRK's policies on the Chinese also reflected the perspectives of Vietnamese advisors like Tran Vien Chi, advisor to the Ministry of the Interior. Vietnam's deputy minister of public security, Vien Chi, had played an important role in suppressing bourgeois culture in southern Vietnam and establishing the reeducation camps. The author of articles with titles like "The People's Security Forces Are Determined to Implement the Decrees Punishing the Crimes of Encroachment upon Socialist Property," Vien Chi was instrumental in formulating the PRK's policy on the ethnic Chinese.[20]

Tran Vien Chi's Cambodian counterpart, Khang Sarin, tended to put the problem in rigid ideological terms. "The Ministry of the Interior," he told the committee at a meeting on August 3, 1981, "should distinguish among different kinds of people based on proletarian class tendencies." To explain what this meant, Sarin listed the various categories into which the Party was now classifying the ethnic Chinese. There were "new Chinese" (those who had not "lived in Cambodia for a long time"), "Chinese advisors" (former advisors to Democratic Kampuchea whom the regime feared were still in Cambodia), "Chinese agents or Beijing Chinese hiding themselves as spies," and "capitalists who've just come from Thailand" (merchants engaged in cross-border trade). "There should be a way to suppress, divide, or arrest them," insisted Sarin, delegating the assignment to the Phnom Penh municipality, to be undertaken "in cooperation with the Vietnamese advisors."[21]

Sarin also set out a convoluted prescription for dealing with Chinese economic activities. Those engaged in the service sector or in small repair shops would be permitted to continue, under state supervision. The rest fell under an ambiguous policy. "Those Chinese who are trading should be directed by the state to change [jobs] and to go increase rural production," explained Sarin. Yet in the next breath he stated that merchants could engage in commerce so long as they "make accounts of their goods and pay heavy taxes to the state." Sarin's muddled speech revealed a fundamental tension within the PRK. So long as the the state commercial network could not feed and clothe Phnom Penh, the regime needed private merchants, most of whom were Chinese. The accommodation was meant to be temporary. "When our state commerce increases a lot," Khang Sarin assured the committee, "private commerce will be cut off and discarded." This never happened. As we shall see, the state sector was soon overwhelmed by the free market, forcing the PRK to abandon its anticapitalist campaigns. For the time being, however, the leadership was still contemplating a serious crackdown.[22]

According to Khang Sarin, the removal of ethnic Chinese from the city was to be effected with a minimum of political backlash. "If it is not done smoothly, it will harm politics and [economic] production." What this meant was that the municipal government, because it consisted of cadres and mass organizations that were ostensibly sensitive to the response an evacuation might elicit from Phnom Penh residents, would be responsible for arresting (*chap*) evacuees. The police, whose involvement would lend a more oppressive tone to the whole operation, were to be used only as a last resort—"to provide security when protests occur," was how Sarin put it.[23]

Khang Sarin seemed somewhat apprehensive about the fate of the evacuees. "There should be a way to educate them so that they understand the policies, [there should be a way] to educate their spirit. Prepare in advance places for them to go [in the countryside], communicate with the provincial People's Revolutionary Councils to prepare for [their arrival], and give them some rice. Those who are sick should have a place to go and heal and be taken care of." Sarin even expressed concern for Chinese prostitutes, who, upon dispatch to the countryside, "should have someone responsible for them and someone to train them in another profession and give them land on which to produce."[24]

On August 10, 1981, the municipality launched a limited crackdown. It did not immediately evacuate anyone from Phnom Penh (at least not systematically), nor did it strike at larger commercial networks. Rather, the move was intended to shut down eating and drinking establishments. (The municipality closed twelve of the capital's one hundred and forty noodle shops, ten of its thirty coffeehouses, and all twenty-seven of its bars, confiscating goods and equipment and issuing warnings to the others.) Apparently the leadership was ultimately more concerned about counterrevolutionary culture than it was about capitalism.[25] As Khang Sarin boasted to the committee in early September:

> So far, we've been successful in wiping out degenerate, corrupt culture, especially the playing of songs from the old society and foreign songs of weak quality, some of which we've eliminated already.
>
> As for coffee shops, we can reopen some in order to serve the needs of the people, but we should call [the owners] in for study, and they should submit an application to open their shop. . . . [The shops] should have traditional order; there should be no degenerate women in the shops, no playing of foreign music or music from the old society. . . . The production of Buddhas will be limited. Other religions, such as Christianity and Catholicism, must be prohibited, and [their status must] not be permitted to remain unclear.[26]

According to Deputy Mayor Mok Mareth, owners and employees of the noodle shops and bars responded to the sweep with "some protest" and with efforts to hide their activities. In fact, many of Phnom Penh's residents had begun to fear evacuation. Waitresses, cooks, and other targets of the crackdown pleaded with state officials to hire them rather than send them back to the countryside. Yet Mareth, despite having once been evacuated from Phnom Penh himself, was steadfast in his intention to rid the city of unwanted residents. "In the first three months of 1982, we will remove people with no work to do from Phnom Penh," he assured the leadership.[27]

DEPORTATIONS

On December 29, 1981, the Council of Ministers, now under Chan Si, issued a circular regarding the repopulation of Phnom Penh. "Vagrants," as the document called the city's new residents, were coming in from all over the country. "Among them, there are young and old, men and women, some who are healthy and some who are disabled." The circular portrayed a legion of people sneaking into Phnom Penh "to beg and then to stay and sleep all over the place." Yet those who were making a living were also considered a menace. Having entered "without letters of permission," they "work as water carriers or cyclo drivers, or engage in various vices that cause harm to order, discipline, and the security of society in the capital." The circular set forth what the Party felt should be done. "As for people who have entered Phnom Penh and have no clear work and are living as vagrants [and for] disabled persons who have no shelter, the Phnom Penh People's Revolutionary Committee shall have a system for rounding them up, educating them, and sending them back to their provinces and cities of birth."[28]

Over the next six months, this policy was enforced only sporadically, and the city's population continued to balloon. By August 1982 nearly half a million people were living in Phnom Penh. At a meeting of the Council of Ministers, Mok Mareth reported on the situation. "So far, there have been some people who have left the capital to go live in the countryside, but there are still some who come back," he explained. "The problem that we are most concerned about is the Chinese residents who are constantly entering the city, especially from Kampong Cham and Koh Kong."[29]

The few Phnom Penh residents who had actually volunteered to leave the city were headed to the ports of Kampong Som and Koh Kong, where trade with Thailand had nurtured a thriving private sector and where smuggling seemed to offer an opportunity to earn a living. The leadership, focused on increasing rice production, preferred that people leaving the city relocate in the Cambodian countryside, specifically in the southeastern province of Svay Rieng. Underpopulated since 1978 as a result of Khmer Rouge evacuations and the Vietnamese invasion, the province had been identified by Vietnamese advisors in 1979 as being unproductive agriculturally. Provincial authorities, led by Heng Samrin's brother, Heng Samkai, appealed to Phnom Penh's municipal authorities to send people to work in the fields, and in one instance of forced evacuation, Phnom Penh Mayor Kaev Chenda sent five hundred families to Svay Rieng without even informing the Council of Ministers. As Mok Mareth reported, Phnom Penh residents were doing everything they could to avoid deportation. "No one wants to be sent to Svay Rieng, even though we are trying hard to disseminate propaganda in the [city's] wards. The people turn around and try hard to work and produce constantly because they are afraid of being put on the list to go to Svay Rieng."[30]

Before engaging in a genuine deportation campaign, the leadership was forced to consider the painful legacy of the Khmer Rouge. If the PRK was going to repeat the unpopular policies of Democratic Kampuchea, could it soften the blow? Were Phnom Penh residents expected, once again, to abandon their personal possessions? How should evacuations proceed? Would urban residents be expected to settle in unwelcoming cooperatives? Mok Mareth, who now seemed to be having second thoughts, began asking these kinds of questions: "What should we do about the problem of their property, the houses that they have attempted to repair, their tools, tables, chests, telephones, and refrigerators? In moving people out, should our state help transport them to the locality or let people arrange for [transportation] themselves? After they've arrived at the locality, does our state have a policy of helping them? In each locality, there is the responsibility for building shelter for people, for providing sufficient agricultural tools, schools, and hospitals. Should the state provide rice only when people are leaving, or can it sell some more later, given that for the first four or five months people won't be producing?"[31]

Mat Ly, a Khmer Rouge veteran, asked different questions, which were eerily evocative of D.K. policies. "Sending people out of Phnom Penh is related to re-purifying new land," he said. "So should we take these people and mix them in with the old village and commune people or build new villages for these people?"[32]

Prime Minister Chan Si attempted to draw distinctions between PRK policies and those of the Khmer Rouge. "The Party and the Council of Ministers do not [want] to make the people be vindictive toward each other nor to divide the old people from the new people." he explained. During the evacuation "the state should provide transportation and distribute rice," and out in the provinces, officials should not greet the evacuees as they had under Democratic Kampuchea but rather "provide land and agricultural tools, construct houses, and, especially, make sure that the new people and the old people understand close solidarity." Chan Si then explained the difference between these plans and the unpopular deportations of the Saigonese. "We are not sending them to create New Economic Zones; we are taking [the evacuees] and dividing them among communes, four or five families per commune, and then dividing them among villages, mixing them in with the old people to facilitate management and assistance."[33]

The regime could not possibly arrange the logistics for such an operation, nor could it ever afford the transportation, rice, and rural housing that Chan Si was calling for. Nonetheless, Party officials remained obsessed with the threat of urban capitalism and, in particular, the Chinese. "As for the policy regarding the Chinese residents," Chan Si reminded Deputy Mayor Mok Mareth, "the [municipality] is really not the one that resolves this. In fact, it's our Party and state [that does]."³⁴ Two months later, as promised, the Party arrived at a policy.

CIRCULAR 351

The morning of October 24, 1982, a crowd of sorts had gathered at the old Royal Palace. Ministers, deputy ministers and their assistants, representatives from various state institutions, provincial Party secretaries and deputy secretaries, other Party leaders, and Vietnamese advisors attached to the Council of Ministers, thirty-seven people in all, waited for Deputy Prime Minister Chea Soth to announce the regime's new policy on the Chinese. Soth began his speech with some recent history: "After liberation, there were perhaps 40,000 Chinese in Cambodia who had survived [the Khmer Rouge]. Before, they were scattered all around the countryside and the cities. After the overthrow of the Pol Pot regime, because of their own character, the Chinese began to conduct business, to buy and sell, and to open stores and work as small merchants. They have avoided working in the rice fields. . . . Wherever there is an opportunity to conduct business, the Chinese have rushed in, for example, in [the ports of] Kampong Som, Kampot, and Koh Kong. This has confused our national economy and created insecurity and chaos. In Phnom Penh they have opened shops all over." He said that Chinese wealth and independence also undermined the state. "Cadres with little competence don't dare go to investigate [Chinese activities], because [the Chinese] are at an advantage and are defended by people with weapons. Some of our cadres have abandoned their original class stance as a result of the Chinese enticing them, even giving them young girls or bribing powerful people in order to defend their interests. When there are problems, our Khmers turn around and defend and help the Chinese."³⁵

But what to do? Immediate deportation was not the answer. "If we move them out, where do we put them?" Soth asked. "If we send them to China, they won't go. If we send back the Chinese who fled Vietnam, they won't go. . . . If we act too strongly or too broadly, it will harm political relations among the nationalities." Returning to ideology, Chea Soth reminded his audience that "this is a class struggle, not a struggle between the Khmer nationality and [the Chinese]." The first step, then, was to gather information on the nature of Chinese capitalism. "For example, in Prey Veng, how many Chinese are conducting business? How many families? What kind of work do they do? How much capital do they have? What are their business connections? Where were they born?

Those who have lived [in a particular location] a long time, since their parents conducted business there—what business do they do now?"

Soth then read a set of Party and state documents setting out the regime's policy toward the Chinese and the establishment of something called the Central Committee to Examine and Research and Guide Implementation of the Policy Regarding the Chinese in Cambodia. He concluded his speech with a revealing statement. "I stress that when the committee examines and conducts research and when we act, there will certainly be a reaction. If our actions are directed toward the Chinese, the reaction won't be any problem. But if Khmers react, we will have to analyze [our actions] and reconsider."[36]

The Party circular read by Chea Soth, which was distributed to provincial and municipal Party officials, central ministries, and some district chiefs, was mostly an investigative exercise, intended to uncover Chinese networks in the country. As the first widely distributed description of the regime's attitude toward the Chinese, "Circular 351" also became shorthand for years of discriminatory policies.[37]

Circular 351 instructed state officials to inquire into Chinese people's citizenship status, geographic origins, the amount of time they had lived in Cambodia, their families, overseas connections, language abilities, political leanings, and past affiliations, including whether they had ever worked in the police, military, or courts of the Sihanouk, Lon Nol, or Pol Pot regimes. It also revealed the Party's fascination with and fear of Chinese commerce, inquiring into the profession of every Chinese person and the ownership of every "photo shop, copy shop, radio repair shop, publishing [house], stamping [business], dentist's office, noodle shop, etc." By uncovering this information, the Party hoped for a glimpse at the flow of money in Cambodia—the Chinese trading companies operating between Phnom Penh and Thailand and between Cambodia, Singapore, and Hong Kong. "Are they trading privately or as a company? What goods do they have? What is the source of the goods? Where are goods distributed? Are there companies or intermediaries that give them the goods? How much initial capital is there?" Officials were told to collect information on means of transportation, number of employees, salaries, sources of equipment, raw materials, capital, and the organizational structures of Chinese enterprises, including forms of equity, capitalization, distribution of capital among partners, and even "management efficiency." Armed with this data, Cambodian authorities were then expected to determine whether to send urban Chinese families to the countryside based on whether they were "conducting inappropriate business" or lacked a "clear profession." The cadres were also expected to carry out this task without overly upsetting the Chinese or engendering "heavy agitation."[38]

The committee responsible for guiding this impossible policy was headed by Finance Minister Chan Phin, a Hanoi-trained hard-liner, and Deputy Minister of the Interior Sin Song, a former Eastern Zone cadre. In the provinces, teams of cadres, chosen from the police and various sectors of the administration, conducted investigations and directed local leadership on how to deal with the Chinese. In Phnom Penh, where nearly all the urban Chinese resided, Police Chief Khoem Pon oversaw a set of team leaders whose job qualifications revealed the sensitivity of the committee's work. According to state documents, these cadres were supposed to be of "good political quality with working-class stances" and devoid of "narrow-minded nationalism," that is, anti-Vietnamese attitudes. The regime's greatest fear, however, was that its personnel might be vulnerable to "propaganda and destructive acts, tricks to buy trust, bribery, and threats." Team leaders were thus expected to be a disciplined lot, willing to recall and "build" cadres, resist bribes, and refuse to keep secrets from their superiors or defend wrongdoing on the part of their colleagues.[39]

The leadership and the Vietnamese advisors were so concerned about subversion that they imposed on cadres implementing Circular 351 a set of rules against corruption that were more specific and absolute than any law or circular the PRK would ever set forth. "It is prohibited to fraternize with offenders and bad elements or fraternize with inappropriate women," read the regulations. "It is prohibited to take the opportunity to receive gifts or take bribes of any form." The committee also recognized the corollary to corruption: extortion. "It is prohibited to use one's position to intimidate people, especially Chinese people. . . . It is prohibited to hide or protect offenders or accuse those who have done nothing wrong."[40]

Even before implementation, it was apparent that cadres didn't understand the policy. In study sessions they expressed confusion as to how exactly they were expected to treat the Chinese. Their written instructions—which told them to "take the opportunity to ask the opinion of the [Vietnamese] advisor in [your] sector" for an explanation of the policy—were of little help. The fundamental question thus remained: Was Circular 351 an ideological policy, intended to draw fine distinctions between "classes," or a nationalist policy and a license for racial repression?[41]

Most cadres assumed the policy to be racial. The leadership, in announcing Circular 351, had blurred its anticapitalist and anti-Maoist sentiments so thoroughly that the enemy, in the end, was simply the Chinese. The regime had also injected Circular 351 into a country with a venomous racial history. The class struggles of the Khmer Rouge had engendered suspicion of ethnic groups considered "bourgeois," including the Chinese. The cadres responsible for implementing Circular 351, most of whom were uneducated, would have been more familiar with these prejudices than with the PRK's nuanced class distinctions. Like Khmer Rouge cadres, they would have found it easier to identify racial, linguistic, and cultural characteristics than to define a "working-class stance." When the committee finally sent its cadres out into Phnom Penh to question ethnic Chinese about their backgrounds, their politics, and their economic activities, most Chinese, expecting prejudice or worse, either hid from the cadres or withheld information.

Meanwhile, international tensions inflamed the regime's anger against China. In March 1983 the Chinese Foreign Ministry reiterated calls for an unconditional Vietnamese withdrawal from Cambodia. The PRK responded by comparing the Beijing regime to the Ming dynasty imposing its will on its vassals. In April the PRC launched more border attacks against northern Vietnam.[42] In this environment, the Cambodian leadership and its Vietnamese advisors became even more committed to investigating the activities of the ethnic Chinese.

"What's been done already has been good but is not yet sufficient," said Tran Vien Chi, the Vietnamese advisor to the Cambodian Ministry of the Interior, at an April meeting of the Council of Ministers, adding, "Our failings are that we haven't conducted secret investigations." Aware that the implementation of Circular 351 had succeeded only in upsetting people, Chan Si also felt a need for new tactics that were simultaneously more subtle and more thorough: "We've [attempted] to implement this policy on the Chinese two or three times already but have not yet succeeded because we use methods that are too aggressive. . . . [Circular 351] stated clearly that we should not create conflict and turn the Chinese into enemies. Based on the proletariat stance, our Party has advanced a correct method, which is much different from Pol Pot's. . . . The organization of the committee should be clearly divided between offices responsible for direct [investigations] and those responsible for secret [investigations]. If overt [investigations] are not successful, we should proceed secretly. . . . [Circular 351] can be taught openly because it has no provisions that reveal us to be taking steps to harm the Chinese residents, but any tasks that are secret shall be conducted secretly."[43]

Phnom Penh's Chinese residents were understandably unconvinced of the regime's good intentions. As progress reports came in, it became clear that many Chinese were still withholding information regarding their ethnicity, personal histories, citizenship, occupation, and wealth. The Chinese had many reasons to do so. For one, the language by which the committee referred to this information—the Chinese were expected to produce a "confession" (*sarapheap*)—recalled the horrors of Khmer Rouge investigations. More specifically, the Chinese were attempting to avoid deportation. There was also extortion. The regime had begun to impose taxes on the private sector, and although the Circular 351 cadres were not technically collecting the taxes, they were reporting instances of evasion. To the ethnic Chinese being investigated, there was little practical distinction: the investigator was likely to view the discovery of unreported property as an opportunity to extract a bribe from the owner. The greater the value of the property, the greater the incentive to keep it unreported, and the bigger the bribe. This logic was all too clear, and, as the Party had warned, wealthier Chinese merchants corrupted PRK cadres and even hired soldiers to protect themselves.[44]

Over the course of the next year or so, the implementation of Circular 351 abated. After a period of intense scrutiny and sporadic evacuations, police and state cadres established more predictable and more accommodating relationships with Chinese merchants. There were no more mass deportations. Instead, the Chinese-dominated private sector continued to grow, to the benefit of Phnom Penh residents. Only within the Party and the Council of Ministers, where the leadership continued to discuss the need to bring the Chinese into the Marxist-Leninist fold, did ideologically motivated ethnic politics persist.[45]

QUIET RESISTANCE

Revolution should have come easily to the PRK. As Chan Si told the Council of Ministers in April 1983, "The unique thing about Cambodia is that Pol Pot annihilated all the capitalists, and we must do whatever we can not to allow them to raise their heads again." Yet the same extraordinary history obstructed efforts to suppress capitalism. On the one hand, the leadership pledged to be firm with the Chinese capitalists. "They are opposing us in the areas of economics, culture, and psychological warfare," warned Chan Si. "As Lenin said, 'Socialist revolution must make use of the dictatorship of the proletariat.'" At the same time, however, the desire of the leadership to distinguish itself from the Khmer Rouge precluded full-scale evacuations.[46]

The regime's cadres were more interested in taking bribes from ethnic Chinese than in building socialism. Oppressing capitalists was more lucrative than shutting them down and replacing them with state institutions. Again, in the words of a frustrated Chan Si: "When we conduct a national democratic revolution [the first anticapitalist stage of communist revolution], our cadres participate and applaud, but when we take steps toward a socialist revolution, they oppose us and move far away from us."[47] Over time, PRK cadres became less and less interested in repressing the Chinese. As we shall see, the economic reforms of the late 1980s and the active participation of PRK officials in Phnom Penh's private commercial sector ensured that the state would become increasingly dependent on Chinese capitalists.

Ultimately, the indifference of Phnom Penh's population guaranteed the failure of Circular 351. The ethnic Chinese resisted the policy, of course, but, as Chea Soth had feared, so did the Khmers. Despite Beijing's ongoing support for the Khmer Rouge resistance and its border incursions in northern Vietnam, most Khmers refused to see ethnic Chinese as potential spies. Nor had they much interest in the Party's theories of class struggle. After Democratic Kampuchea, communism was a permanently discredited ideology. Once it became clear to the residents of Phnom Penh that the state could not feed them, they concluded that the private, Chinese-dominated commercial sector offered the only solution to the country's economic problems. Cambodians thus approached the Party's policy toward the Chinese as they did communism: by ignoring it.

Chapter 8 Cities and Markets

Almost eight years after the Khmer Rouge evacuated Phnom Penh and the provincial and district capitals and four years after the overthrow of Democratic Kampuchea, the PRK was finally ready to acknowledge that Cambodia was not a purely rural country. As Council of Ministers advisor Fang You reported to the Cambodian leadership in early 1983, "The provinces have provincial capitals and the districts have district capitals that are, in fact, economic, cultural, and political centers."

On their own, Cambodians had come together and re-created cities and towns. Defying efforts to keep them in the countryside, they had returned to old population centers, which the regime now found itself unprepared to govern. By January 1983, when the Council of Ministers met to consider a constitutional amendment to provide for urban administration, the situation was already out of control. "If we don't create [administrations for] provincial capitals, district capitals, precincts, districts, suburbs, and population centers, they will be difficult for us to manage," said Minister of the Interior Khang Sarin, who considered tight control of the cities as a necessary component of revolutionary authority. Prime Minister Chan Si agreed, citing "Vietnam's wartime experience" to stress the importance of properly administering district capitals. The Vietnamese advisors Dao Duc Chinh and Fang You were just as pragmatic. "When we drafted the [1981] constitution," You recalled, "there were few people in the city. Now there are more than 400,000 people, and it could go up to 500,000 or 600,000." The leadership and its Vietnamese advisors were still suspicious of urban culture, which they considered degenerate and counterrevolutionary, and were still contemplating evacuations of ethnic Chinese from Phnom Penh. Nevertheless, they were not so unrealistic as to believe that it was possible or desirable to prevent people from living in towns. Governing Cambodia thus required a clearheaded acknowledgment that towns existed and that an expanded bureaucracy was necessary.[1]

The regime's capacity to control the reurbanization was challenged by the failure of the state commercial sector to feed those who had come to live in Phnom Penh and in district and provincial capitals. "The truth is that there is a [state] trading store in every single district," said "Tien," an advisor to the Ministry of Commerce in early June 1982, "but every month, regardless of whether there are goods or not, we see that they don't really open their doors to sell goods to the people." According to Tien, local commercial cadres preferred to sell state goods to private traders rather than to ordinary customers and paid off higher-level officials whenever they came to investigate. The whole commercial system was at stake, Tien warned. "If the goods that our state sends to the districts to sell to the people are not sold [to the people], the work of buying agricultural produce from the people cannot proceed well, and this will have bad political effects on our Party and our state."[2]

Aware that capitalist networks (and, in particular, Chinese capitalists) were buying goods wholesale from state officials, the leadership and the Vietnamese advisors attempted to curtail these transactions from both the demand and the supply sides. On the demand side, the regime issued Circular 351 and stepped up its surveillance of Chinese private-sector activities. On the supply side, it hoped to build a more disciplined state commercial system. The problem was that even as the PRK's anti-Chinese policies were reaching their zenith, key members of the Council of Ministers were openly acknowledging their willingness to deal with private merchants.

As Party leaders and Vietnamese advisors considered their options, the debate was shaped by two important trends. The first was the indifference with which local officials received Phnom Penh's socialist edicts. The second was the economic and political transformation taking place in southern Vietnam.

FEEDING OFF THE MARKET

Revenues generated from the private sector had weakened the regime's resolve for building socialism. Although the leaders had begun contemplating taxes as early as April 1980, they waited two more years, until after the riel had stabilized, before issuing decrees on business taxes and import taxes. Once the regime had begun levying these taxes, however, it became financially dependent on the private sector. To a certain extent, this was true of the central government, although its ability to collect revenues was always extremely limited.[3] More important were the tax schemes devised by local authorities. As the Council of Ministers reported, these tended to be arbitrary. "Some localities have issued, by themselves, revenue-generating plans of differing types (market profits, contributions, grants, . . .) But in fact [these plans] have the characteristics of tax collection on the business, commercial, food, and service sectors and on the production, artisan, industrial, transportation, and other sectors. Other localities and sectors have set up, by themselves, checkpoints on roads used for transporting goods in order to collect some money or seize and confiscate goods and use them however they wish and without any policy."[4]

Within the central government, opinions on taxes varied. Harder-line communists, who managed to overlook the tendency of state officials to become economically dependent on those they taxed, saw taxes as a means to suppress the private sector. Noncommunists working as technocrats in the Council of Ministers took the exact opposite view, describing arbitrary interference in the free market as "unethical." In the countryside, local officials had no interest in any ideology whatsoever. Having undergone only a few weeks or months of Marxist-Leninist training in Vietnam, they returned to Cambodia with a superficial understanding of socialist economics. They had also experienced communism as practiced by the Khmer Rouge and lacked any personal investment in a system that Hanoi-trained ministers like Chan Phin had spent their lives studying. Yet they were hardly capitalists. In the end, local officials were inclined neither to suppress the private market nor to leave it alone. For them, the market represented the only source of state revenue and, more important, private income.[5]

Cambodia's trade with Vietnam contributed to the growth of the private sector. In theory, state commercial organizations were supposed to monopolize commerce between Cambodian and Vietnamese sister provinces.[6] In reality, local Cambodian officials permitted private individuals and state cadres to trade directly with the Vietnamese. As a Council of Ministers document reported in June 1982, "There are still some ministries, offices, and provincial and municipal [authorities] that are not respecting the rules, leading to dishonest people taking advantage and conducting activities harming the interests of our people and those of Vietnam. These ministries, offices, and provincial and municipal [authorities] are issuing letters allowing staff, cadres, and other people to go to Ho Chi Minh City directly without going through the responsible [state] organizations."[7]

Central Party and state institutions were helpless to stop these activities. Border agreements concluded between Cambodia and Vietnam expressly permitted citizens to trade freely. To the extent that these agreements granted authority to Cambodian officials to control this trade, it was to district and commune-level authorities with little appreciation for socialism. On the other side of the border, local Vietnamese authorities did little to discourage private trading. Like their Cambodian counterparts, they ignored the socialist policies designed by distant bureaucrats. For southern Vietnam was engaged in its own struggle over decentralization and the private economy.[8]

THE SOUTHERN PATH

Throughout the early 1980s, Hanoi confronted challenges to its economic policies from an unexpected source: the South Vietnamese revolutionary leadership. During the war, as North Vietnam and the National Liberation Front joined forces to reunite the country, economic disagreements had laid dormant. Following reunification, however, when Hanoi communists attempted to impose an unfamiliar socialist system on the south, many National Liberation Front cadres were bewildered. Most had fought the war for nationalist rather than ideological reasons and had not anticipated an abrupt economic revolution. For years, southern Party officials expressed ambivalence, if not opposition, to policies such as agricultural collectivization and the suppression of private traders, and in the early 1980s they launched Vietnam's first experiments in economic reform, the "Southern Path."[9]

Changing the name of Saigon to Ho Chi Minh City had not succeeded in crushing the city's capitalist spirit, nor had the appointment of loyal southern communists to run the city. Mai Chi Tho, Le Duc Tho's southern brother, began the reform process in late 1980 with efforts to register and tax private businesses. The following year, the Party appointed Nguyen Van Linh Party secretary for Ho Chi Minh City and chair of the city's Socialist Transformation Commission, positions through which he expanded the registration process, permitted private rice merchants to purchase directly from farmers at market prices, and even entrusted certain ethnic Chinese to establish import-export companies. Along with another reformer, Vo Van Kiet (who later became Ho Chi Minh City Party secretary), Nguyen Van Linh challenged the north's efforts to wipe out private enterprise. Years later, Linh and Kiet, as Party secretary and prime minister, led the whole of Vietnam toward market reform. In 1982, however, they encountered a backlash from Hanoi that resulted in the cancellation of various reform initiatives in Ho Chi Minh City and the temporary removal of Nguyen Van Linh from the Politburo.[10]

Vietnamese advisors in Cambodia were well aware of these vacillations, and it impeded their ability to offer coherent policy guidance. Although they sat in on all important meetings, they frequently talked in broad generalities and made only vague references to Vietnamese practices. When they commented directly on Cambodian policies, they shifted back and forth between rigid ideological prescriptions and looser, more pragmatic approaches. Furthermore, they did not always agree with one another. According to the minutes of these meetings, the Cambodians did not expressly contradict the Vietnamese, but the failure of the advisors to present workable solutions to the PRK's economic problems left room to maneuver.

THE DEBATE

In June 1982, Tien, the Vietnamese advisor to the Ministry of Commerce, described to the Council of Ministers how Chinese merchants were ruining southern Vietnam and threatening Cambodia. "In Ho Chi Minh City there is a big problem with Chinese businesspeople that requires us to employ a policy of centralized economics," he explained. "So far in Cambodia the Chinese have bought up the dried fish, sesame, and tobacco, causing us difficulties in the economic sector. They have money and can pay off soldiers and commercial [cadres] and exert a political influence on our state as well." Tien then offered some typically vague and contradictory advice, "We mustn't prohibit trading, but must simply have the means to control it appropriately," adding, "In Vietnam implementation is done like this." Deputy Prime Minister Hun Sen seemed to understand what he was getting at: "The management of the market requires first that we manage the Chinese businesspeople. We should keep the small middlemen and allow them to continue to conduct business. In using and managing these businesspeople, we should always be cautious because, up to now, the Thais can grasp our situation very well through Chinese business-people and through some of our cadres who provide them information."[11]

Hun Sen did not suggest abandoning the state sector. Rather, he spoke of the state's failure to distribute consumer goods and urged that more state trading stores should be built. In other words, he adhered to the notion that a state commercial system could be established, while tentatively (and with support from advisors like Tien) recommending that the regime recognize and "use" the private sector. This was the safe way to frame a policy shift, and it did not im-mediately upset his more conservative colleagues. The meeting ended with Chan Si's reiteration of socialist policy. The highest-ranking Vietnamese advi-sor at the meeting, Dao Duc Chinh, remained silent.

Over the next few weeks, Hun Sen took a moderate position on another eco-nomic issue—private cross-border trade between Cambodia and Vietnam—and again he stuck close to the position of a Vietnamese advisor. This time, the advisor was "Tui" from the Ministry of Finance, who told the Cambodians that "we [should] allow the peoples [of Cambodia and Vietnam] to exchange goods with each other." As minister of foreign affairs and the signatory of Cambo-dian-Vietnamese border agreements, Hun Sen was positioned to elaborate for his colleagues. Skirting the question of larger businesses, he urged his col-leagues to permit "Cambodian people and Vietnamese people" to trade directly with each other. This position did not have universal support among the Cam-bodians: Minister of Finance Chan Phin and Minister of Commerce Tang Sareum both felt that Kampixim, the state trading company, should control cross-border trade. At this particular meeting, however, there were no objec-tions to the positions taken by Tui and Hun Sen. Again, Dao Duc Chinh sat quietly.[12]

At an October 1982 meeting of the Council of Ministers, the debate became more heated. Notwithstanding his efforts to defend Kampixim's monopoly over foreign trade, Minister of Commerce Tang Sareum was now openly pro-moting the role of private merchants in domestic commerce. His ministry and the Ministry of Agriculture, he said, had already "lent" more than 100 million riels in fertilizers, rice, seed, and money to private individuals "to increase pro-duction." The reason, Sareum acknowledged, was that the state commercial sector could not feed Cambodia by itself. "These days, with the state unable to control the sale of goods to the people, I request that we confer a portion [of the economy] on the private sector to help us and that we permit businesspeople to accept goods from the state . . . to sell to the people in distant locations."

Speaking next, Hun Sen expressed, in the most direct terms yet, his willingness to accommodate the private sector. "Send some rice to be sold on the free market in order to lower the price of rice and free up the warehouses [where state officials were hoarding rice]." By this point, the more doctrinaire communists had apparently heard enough. Finance Minister Chan Phin called for the suppression of "enemy opportunists" and distanced himself from the "loans" issued by the Ministries of Commerce and Agriculture. Minister of Inspection Sim Kar, a former Khmer Rouge cadre, also spoke up, explaining that "middlemen were purchasing from the state because the army and police have not yet taken a strong stance."[13]

Vietnamese advisor Dao Duc Chinh spoke next. Tang Sareum, Hun Sen, Chan Phin, and Sim Kar had arrived at a fundamental policy disagreement; here was an opportunity for Chinh to offer some direction. Instead, he spoke of hectares of land, tons of rice production, and the importance of balancing the state budget. Rather than address the question of the private sector, Chinh provided the kind of technical instructions with which he felt most comfortable.[14]

The Cambodians resumed their discussion. For Finance Minister Chan Phin, one of the most troubling aspects of the current situation was the tendency of local state officials to permit private individuals to collect rice directly from the people, a development that was particularly prevalent in the more agriculturally productive provinces of Battambang and Kampong Cham. The answer, as far as Phin was concerned, was to impose greater discipline on, and offer increased incentives to, the provinces. Local officials were responsible for buying rice, he reminded the council. "This is the duty of Comrade Chan Si because he can order the provincial Party secretaries [to comply]. Goods that are to be sold to the people should be distributed largely to provinces that buy a lot of rice. Don't give a lot of goods to provinces [that don't purchase rice from the people]."[15]

Chan Si concluded the meeting with an even more direct solution: involve soldiers and police in rice purchasing. "The Ministry of Defense and the Ministry of the Interior should cooperate with the Ministry of Commerce to help defend security in the battle to buy rice," he urged, adding: "We should find a good way to suppress the middlemen." Whether he knew it or not, Chan Si was recommending a policy similar to the one employed by Sihanouk and his defense minister, Lon Nol, in the late 1960s. Perhaps he believed that PRK soldiers would appreciate socialism more than Sihanouk's soldiers had.[16]

Other Cambodian leaders participated in the debate. Ung Phan, minister in charge of the Council of Ministers, was one of the earliest, and most independent, advocates of economic flexibility. In May 1982, he even told the Council of Ministers (when no Vietnamese advisors were present) that the Vietnamese had made mistakes in suppressing their private sector. "In fact, back in 1976, Ho Chi Minh City did not allow rice into the city, and the price of rice went up. But when they repealed the prohibitions, the price of rice fell. [Guards posted] in locations around the city do nothing but sit and wait to take money for themselves from those transporting [rice] in and out."[17]

After an early career marked by reticence, Ung Phan was becoming more outspoken and more direct. Unlike Hun Sen, Phan did not qualify his support for economic reform with assurances that the state would "use" or "manage" the private sector. Describing the state as useless or even abusive, he offered a humanitarian perspective that contrasted sharply with those of his more conservative colleagues. Deputy Interior Minister Sin Song, for one, disagreed strongly with Ung Phan's tolerance of private transportation. "The enemy can use this to destroy us," Song warned the Council of Ministers in February 1983. Responded Ung Phan, "Cars belonging to the private sector or to Solidarity Groups are transporting travelers at a time when the state does not yet have sufficient capacity and lacks the means to serve the needs of the people. If we shut down [the private transportation businesses], what kind of difficulties will the people face? Conducting a revolution means to serve the interests and needs of the people." Phan was even willing to obliquely challenge a Vietnamese advisor, Fang You. Having heard You stress the importance of state control over the transportation sector, Ung Phan concluded the meeting by criticizing "corrupt elements who use their positions to extort money from the people."[18]

Hun Sen was more tactful, and a week later, at a meeting of the Council of Ministers, he reintroduced the idea of recognizing the private sector in purely pragmatic terms. "The actual situation now is that private businesspeople are taking the opportunity to compete to buy agricultural goods [from the people], regardless of whether the state has issued a circular prohibiting it or not." Complaining that lower-level cadres were ignoring Council of Ministers policies and that various ministries lacked a "socialist cooperative spirit," Hun Sen called for a "general policy that would confer the means of production on the private sector."[19]

As the discussion rambled on, the Vietnamese advisor, Fang You, remained studiously neutral. You was far from happy with what was happening in Phnom Penh (at a later meeting, he bemoaned the "trading and pornography near the houses of leaders and the problem of casinos"), but, like Dao Duc Chinh, he was reluctant to step in and prescribe policy. His refusal to get involved may have reflected Vietnamese uncertainty about Cambodia's economic problems. It also suggested a growing sense that Hun Sen could be trusted to sort them out.[20]

In the provinces, Vietnamese advisors were even less interested in promoting doctrinaire communism. Most came from southern Vietnamese sister provinces, where local officials often ignored Hanoi's economic proscriptions. Once in Cambodia, they were equally indifferent to the policies developed by their northern Vietnamese compatriots, the A40 economic advisors sent from Hanoi. In a sense, Vietnam's internal tensions had been transferred to Cambodia. The effect was an increased disregard for central planning, state commerce, artificial pricing, and agricultural collectivization.

This disregard was most apparent in Phnom Penh, where the municipality's advisors came directly from the capital's "sister province," Ho Chi Minh City. In linking the cities, the Vietnamese leadership hoped that Ho Chi Minh City officials would call upon their experience in urban management and policing and help bring Phnom Penh under control. What they did not expect was that advisors from Ho Chi Minh City would promote economic liberalization in Phnom Penh and that their Cambodian counterparts would be receptive to this message. Nor could they have imagined how quickly the two cities would return to their traditional economic relationship, which was dominated by private, primarily Chinese commerce.

THE "KAEV CHENDA CRISIS"

"Bored with communism" is how one former colleague described Kaev Chenda. Independent, ideologically flexible, and, in the eyes of the leadership, dangerously permissive, the man who had once been one of the regime's most eloquent spokesmen was quickly becoming one of the Party's biggest headaches. Although he had served as minister of propaganda, chief judge of the Pol Pot–Ieng Sary trial, and minister of industry, it was as mayor of Phnom Penh that he touched off what Heng Samrin referred to as the "Kaev Chenda crisis."[21]

According to official documents, Chenda first caused trouble at the Ministry of Industry, where relations with Vietnamese advisors were apparently tense. As the deputy minister recounted in a typically diplomatic report, "The perspectives of the Cambodians and the Vietnamese related to some areas of work were different from each other, which required that a lot of time be expended in gradually gaining experience from each other." By the end of 1981, however, the Party was accusing Chenda of selling state property without consulting the central government.[22]

Like his patron Pen Sovan, Chenda was also prone to making deals with the Soviets without consulting the Vietnamese or the rest of the leadership. As mayor of Phnom Penh, he invited the Soviets to contribute to the defense of the city, an initiative that would certainly have intruded on Vietnam's monopoly over Cambodian security matters and that elicited complaints from Prime Minister Chan Si. He did not bother to inform the leadership before expelling five hundred families from the city to Svay Rieng, nor did he request permission to celebrate the April 1982 Khmer New Year by decorating one of Phnom Penh's most famous sites, the hilltop pagoda of Wat Phnom, and allowing residents a large outdoor party. By July 1982 the leadership (or the Vietnamese) had had enough. Chenda, who had spent most of his life receiving political education from the North Vietnamese, was sent once again to "study" in Hanoi.[23]

Shortly afterward, the Party stepped up its investigation into malfeasance at the Ministry of Industry and recalled Chenda to Phnom Penh to answer for the scandal. Then, in August 1982, in anticipation of the arrests of several lower-level cadres, the Party removed him entirely from the ministry. Thus, by the time Kaev Chenda returned from Hanoi at the end of 1982, his only state position was mayor of Phnom Penh.[24]

In some respects, he was powerless. When the Vietnamese convened Phnom Penh's Joint [Military] Command Committee in November 1982, Kaev Chenda, though technically chair of the committee, was in Hanoi. Upon his return, he had little awareness of security matters in his own city. As he told the Council of Ministers in February 1983, "People are arrested and then disappear, and we don't know where they've been taken."[25]

On economic matters, Chenda's more flexible propensities began to emerge. At Council of Ministers meetings, he reassured his colleagues that he would not tolerate the vices of Phnom Penh. "There is an increase in hidden prostitution, gambling, disorderly trading. . . . I will have ways of dealing with this bit by bit." Yet Chenda himself had a reputation for womanizing and was considered personally responsible for promoting gambling and commerce. He also had a record of economic experimentation, including tolerating private merchants (and taxing them heavily). Most disconcerting, from the perspective of the leadership, was that Chenda's "study" in Hanoi had failed to curb his tendency to act independently. His decision to permit private vehicles in Phnom Penh without consulting the Council of Ministers prompted complaints not only from conservatives but from Hun Sen and Ung Phan.[26]

By the spring of 1983, as the Party was struggling to implement Circular 351 and considering the deportation of Chinese merchants, Kaev Chenda was openly promoting the private sector. At a Council of Ministers meeting in April, Deputy Minister of the Interior Sin Song cited Chenda as part of the problem. "Methods for managing the market and the traffic in goods are complicated. If we compare the substance of [Circular 351] and the proposals of Comrade Kaev Chenda, we see that they are exactly opposite. The second provision of [Chenda's] proposal reads, 'I request the [authority to] use a set of businesspeople as representatives of the state.' If we don't think about this problem, there may be danger."[27]

Chenda was off on his own again, this time in cooperation with Vietnamese advisors from Ho Chi Minh City. "Phnom Penh has drafted a plan without communicating with the ministries," he acknowledged to the Council of Ministers in July 1983. "Working with Ho Chi Minh City can make Phnom Penh increasingly fresh and beautiful," he said by way of explanation. Deputy Mayor Mok Mareth was more specific. "Up to now economic and cultural cooperation between Phnom Penh and Ho Chi Minh City in all sectors has raised the standard of living of the people to a higher level, has resulted in the repair of buildings, and has compensated extremely well for the lack of capacity of the Center [the central ministries]."[28]

With Phnom Penh delivering corn, beans, fish, pigs, lotuses, hemp, timber, and other goods to Ho Chi Minh City, its exports actually exceeded those of the Ministry of Commerce. Fearing that the country's only source of currency would fall out of the hands of the government, Cambodian officials and Vietnamese advisors from the Ministry of Planning insisted that Phnom Penh remit its agricultural products to the central bureaucracy. "I suggest that foreign relations go through the Ministry of Planning and that these activities be entered into the state plan," said a concerned Commerce Minister Tang Sareum.[29]

Phnom Penh was also competing with the Ministry of Commerce domestically. As Sin Song had warned, the municipality was "using" private merchants to purchase rice from farmers at market prices and bring it into the city. This was a policy employed by Nguyen Van Linh in Ho Chi Minh City, and it had been adopted in Phnom Penh. As Mok Mareth assured the Council of Ministers, "The two cities can manage the free market." To Commerce Minister Tang Sareum, however, the whole arrangement was somehow unfair. Having previously called for a loosening of the relationship between the state and private sectors, Sareum was being beaten at his own game, by merchants who made no pretense of sticking to state prices and who were not bogged down by an inefficient bureaucracy.[30]

There were two ways of looking at the problem. From Tang Sareum's perspective, Phnom Penh's private merchants were undermining the state's ability to purchase and distribute goods and produce. From the point of view of Kaev Chenda, the failures of the state left the city no choice. Despite rousing slogans—"To sell rice to the state is patriotic"—the Ministry of Commerce was barely functioning. Its provincial network lacked vehicles, warehouses, and equipment, not to mention cadres with financial, accounting, or management training. Barely paid, state officials had no incentive to collect rice. When they tried to do so, Cambodian peasants refused to sell at low state prices, keeping their produce for themselves or selling it on the free market. Although statisticians from the Ministries of Commerce and Agriculture were having trouble even estimating how much rice was being collected and by whom, the figures looked bleak. Despite higher and higher yields, total state purchases were actually declining, and as a percentage of overall collection, the state's share was looking skimpy. As Minister of Agriculture Kong Samol reported to the Council of Ministers, Cambodians in one heavily populated province—Kampong Cham—were selling a mere 7 percent of their rice to the state.[31]

In June 1983, Ministry of Commerce officials took their concerns to the Council of Ministers. Acknowledging that the ministry had collected insufficient rice to meet the needs of Phnom Penh, they nonetheless insisted that the municipality put an end to private rice purchasing. "We must avoid competitive purchasing above state prices," asserted Tang Sareum. The director of Phnom Penh's Commercial Office responded with a frank acknowledgment of the situation. "Phnom Penh has many businesspeople, which requires that there be a different plan and different prices." Kaev Chenda also defended the city's policies. "Phnom Penh is not growing in competition with the Center. But should we purchase [rice] or not? I stress that Phnom Penh has no intention of haggling with the Center, but if we buy at state prices, there will be no goods entering Phnom Penh."[32]

Vietnamese advisor Fang You then offered a compromise. In circumscribed "collection areas," he said, the Ministry of Commerce would have the first opportunity to buy rice from the peasants. If the ministry failed, Phnom Penh's merchants could step in. In effect, You was encouraging competition, but with a head start for the Ministry of Commerce. This formula, which was later employed by Hun Sen, did nothing for the fortunes of the ministry.

Within a year, Phnom Penh's economy was entirely out of the state's control. Yawning disparities between state and free market prices sucked almost everything out of the state system. Cloth, medicine, alcohol, cigarettes, soda, ice, and other household goods, even cement and fuel intended for sale to state workers and institutions at subsidized prices, were sold off by state officials to private interests, appearing on the market with average price hikes of 20 percent and, in some places, 70 percent or 100 percent. In August 1984, Phnom Penh authorities estimated that the private sector accounted for 90 percent of all commercial activity in the city, half the distribution of rice, and 100 percent of other food, tools, cooking fuel, and household goods. With no goods available through state channels, cadres, workers, and even Vietnamese advisors bought from the free market. Salaries were ludicrously low, prompting even ideologically flexible ministers like Hun Sen and Ung Phan to call for price controls. Cadres and their families were forced to supplement their incomes by working in the free market, frequently borrowing state equipment and vehicles. Cadres also took advantage of the state's restrictions on commerce by selling off letters of permission to private interests, while soldiers and police extorted money from merchants at checkpoints in and around the city. As the municipality acknowledged in a report to the leadership, state officials were being "recruited" into "illegal businesses" and "given a share" of the profits. Corruption and bribery were prevalent and were "damaging" cadres, soldiers, and police.[33]

THE PARTY STRIKES BACK

The Party's conservative leaders were getting concerned. They were also baffled by the complexity of the country's economic and social problems and incapable of disengaging from outdated, irrelevant ideology. Unable to consider realistic policy options, they continued to hold discussions on whether to officially recognize or formally condemn the irreversible.

One such discussion involved the recognition of the market towns, or "population centers," that were already dominating the national economy. In January 1984, a year after the Council of Ministers had accepted the repopulating of the towns, Heng Samrin was still not convinced. "We shouldn't allow there to be district capitals and population centers," the former Khmer Rouge cadre told the Council of State, "because, over time, we will lose [agricultural] workers." Say Phouthang feared that formal recognition of towns and markets would encourage Cambodians to leave the countryside. Chea Sim concluded simply that "it is not necessary to create district capitals and population centers," a position with which at least one of his provincial allies (Kampong Chhnang Party Secretary Dok Narin) agreed. Even some Vietnamese advisors were arguing against urbanization. Pham Van Kath, an advisor to the Council of Ministers, insisted that the formation of population centers had contributed to lower agricultural production, and Vuong Dinh Chau, an advisor to the Council of State, proposed that "small provinces" not be permitted to establish provincial capitals. Among the top Party leaders, only Hun Sen continued to repeat the obvious, that "even if we don't create [population centers], they exist already."[34]

Inspired in part by economic retrenchment in Vietnam, the Party leadership decided to launch a rearguard action against Phnom Penh's private sector. First, it intensified its rhetoric concerning "reactionaries among Chinese residents and nationals." Then, in July 1984, the Politburo announced that the small-scale manufacturing or "artisan" sector would be brought under control. Private artisans would henceforth be required to join Solidarity Groups or, in certain cases, to operate privately through contracts with the state.[35]

Phnom Penh municipal authorities responded defensively to the campaign, issuing a lengthy report to the leadership on the "increase in the activities of socialist commerce." Acknowledging the dominance of the private sector, the municipality framed the problem in ideological terms. "This situation requires us to be cautious of the Chinese imperialists who operate through the bad elements among the big businesspeople. . . . They destroy us by creating confusion in the market, which leads to political confusion." According to municipal authorities, the private sector was undermining the state's ideological underpinnings. "The sale of many consumer goods makes the Phnom Penh market request too much," read their report, "creating hallucinations of a struggle between two roads: capitalist and socialist."[36]

The Council of Ministers also took an ideological turn. Policy documents prohibiting cadres from using state resources to conduct private commerce referred to "the schemes of Beijing reactionaries" and "building the revolutionary forces." Cambodian bureaucrats were apparently in need of more indoctrination. "Concentrate on feeding the essential theory to the political sector," read one policy paper, "especially to the most important cadres, staff, and leaders in the [commercial] sector." At one council meeting, Minister of Commerce Tang Sareum blamed the crisis on Phnom Penh municipal authorities, who, he said, had ignored state prices and had refused to cooperate with the state's system for distributing agricultural goods. "Phnom Penh seems to consider itself outside the family of Cambodia," he said to Kaev Chenda. On the defensive, Chenda responded meekly. "The capital is still weak in controlling goods and in implementing administrative methods and has not yet followed the policies of the state."[37]

Neither the intensified rhetoric of the Party nor the new policies of the Council of Ministers were having any effect on the private economy of Phnom Penh. The leadership needed a scapegoat, and that person was Kaev Chenda. Rumors already abounded within the Party that Chenda had alcohol and woman problems, that he had profited personally from the city's economic re-birth, and that he was "out of control." Whether these charges were true or not, or whether they distinguished him from other top leaders, Chenda was clearly on his way out. First, though, there would be an occasion to criticize him and his record as mayor of Phnom Penh before a gathering of Party members.[38]

On the morning of August 8, 1984, on the second day of a National Cadres Congress, Kaev Chenda rose in front of 120 Party leaders, ministers and deputy ministers, provincial Party and state officials and cadres from both the Party and state apparatuses. After reading the Party Central Committee's determina-tions regarding the Phnom Penh economy, Chanda spoke for three hours on what the minutes of the congress describe as the "good experiences and short-comings of Phnom Penh's implementation [of Party policies]." After lunch, the participants broke into "discussion groups," reconvening at 4:30 to hear a lengthy account of the municipality's failings. According to the report, some urban Solidarity Groups were actually "groups of individuals and families"; "dishonest businesspeople" were pretending to respect the state but were se-cretly engaged in price competition; and private small-scale manufacturing sites had "harmed the rights and health of neighbors, damaged houses and state property, and damaged social order." There was apparently some debate over these findings. "All participants of the congress," read the minutes, "agreed with the spirit of the Politburo's [determinations]. But some cadres do not yet understand clearly the following: that artisanship in Phnom Penh has already expanded enormously and does not need to expand any more; and that the strong growth in artisanship can engender a reborn belief in capitalism." The minutes do not identify the dissenters.[39]

A couple of months later, the Party removed Chenda from his position as mayor of Phnom Penh, although he retained his position in the National As-sembly and was listed for years among the top leaders of the PRK. Politically invisible for the remainder of his life, Kaev Chenda died in 1989.

HANOI TURNS ITS BACK

Having removed Chenda, the Party continued its rhetorical campaign, issuing, in November 1984, a resolution calling for the "immediate wiping out of the private sector" and invoking a "struggle between two roads, socialism and cap-italism." In Phnom Penh, however, capitalism was winning. Kaev Chenda had been replaced by a series of newcomers to the Party who, though lacking Chenda's independent streak, shared his disinterest in socialism. They were also free to govern the city as they saw fit, thanks to a May 1984 decision by the Council of Ministers to officially grant Phnom Penh (and the provinces) finan-cial and budgetary autonomy.[40]

By late 1984, Hanoi had ceased to care. Much of the VCP leadership had ac-knowledged Vietnam's economic failures and was promoting reform, including a partial abandonment of wage and price controls. Southern Vietnamese offi-cials were permitted to make more economic decisions, a move that coincided with a more tolerant approach toward ethnic Chinese. The Vietnamese leader-ship was also feeling the financial and diplomatic costs of its occupation of Cambodia. Hanoi, it seemed, was slowly retreating from the entire Mekong Delta, loosening its hold on both Ho Chi Minh City and Phnom Penh.[41]

Toward the end of 1984, the VCP decided to transfer control over Cam-bodian-Vietnamese economic relations to Ho Chi Minh City. Not only was Phnom Penh free to reach autonomous arrangements with its sister province, but the Cambodian Ministries of Commerce and Industry—the very institu-tions that had opposed the decentralization of Cambodian-Vietnamese eco-nomic relations—were now told to go to Ho Chi Minh City for assistance, rather than to Hanoi. The result of this decision was a more flexible approach to Cambodian economic policy. Hard-line communists from Hanoi, men like A40 chief Nguyen Con, receded in influence, while other advisors, including Fang You, promoted the growth of the market economy.[42]

MEKONGIZATION

To the dismay of the Cambodian Party leadership, citizens and state cadres alike welcomed the return of the private sector. The state commercial system had failed, and only private merchants were bringing food and consumer goods into Phnom Penh and the other towns. In the provinces, local officials came to rely on the private sector for tax revenues and for personal profits. Vietnamese advisors based in the provinces, most of whom had come from relatively liberal southern Vietnamese provinces, were equally indifferent to socialism. Meanwhile, the shifting economic policies of Hanoi and Ho Chi Minh City kept the Vietnamese advisors at the Cambodian Council of Ministers off guard, permitting a certain amount of room for Cambodians to debate their own economic future. Protected by the changes taking place in Vietnam, Deputy Prime Minister and Foreign Minister Hun Sen became an influential voice for the proposition that controlling the economy required that the government use the private sector. Reluctant to acknowledge that Cambodia had cities or that the state commercial sector had failed, other Party leaders became irrelevant to the debate.

Realistic, clearheaded, yet never outside the bounds of Vietnam's own policy directives, Hun Sen was looking like a candidate for prime minister. For several years he had been impressing the Vietnamese with his bureaucratic and diplomatic skills and his willingness to support a series of controversial, pro-Vietnamese border agreements. But his economic maneuvering bears notice as well. In December 1984, as Chan Si lay ill, Hun Sen began speaking conservatively of "suppressing price competition with the state" and "ensuring implementation of the policy of increasing state artisanship." It was a shrewd move, reassuring the Party leadership that he was still, after all, a communist. Less than two weeks later, on December 27, the Politburo met and declared him acting prime minister. Almost immediately after the National Assembly voted him in, however, Hun Sen again demonstrated his preference for flexible, decentralized economic decision making. On January 19, 1985, the Council of Ministers dispatched a telegram formally granting provincial officials (and the Phnom Penh leadership) authority to conclude agreements with Vietnamese sister provinces without prior central approval. A month later, the council asked Ho Chi Minh City to send an economic representative to serve at the Vietnamese embassy in Phnom Penh.[43]

Hun Sen's acceptance of decentralized economics was less an ideological decision than a concession to history. Long before Cambodian and Vietnamese independence, merchants—Khmer, Vietnamese, and especially Chinese—had moved back and forth along the Mekong between Phnom Penh and Saigon. Rather than suppress these trading networks, the Indochinese communist movement that emerged in the 1930s and 1940s relied on them for produce, equipment, and arms. Now, in the wake of Hanoi's economically disastrous and widely unpopular anticapitalist campaigns of the late 1970s, southern Vietnamese leaders were once again looking to the private sector. Together with Kaev Chenda, they gradually permitted the Chinese-dominated merchant class to re-create the traditional economic relationship between Saigon and Phnom Penh. Chenda, of course, was purged for the resulting failure of socialism. But by transferring to Ho Chi Minh City authority over Cambodian-Vietnamese economic relations and by promoting the nonideological Hun Sen, Hanoi was abandoning its original mission, to bring communism to the Mekong Delta.[44]

Chapter 9 Hun Sen
and the Hidden World
of Phnom Penh Politics

On February 2, 1985, four officials from the Party Central Organization Committee and their Vietnamese advisor made their way over to the Council of Ministers, where they found Hun Sen alone. "This was supposed to be a meeting of the Permanent Committee of the Council of Ministers," explained the man who had held the position of prime minister for all of three weeks. "But since both comrade deputy prime ministers are busy, I must now work alone with you, comrades of the Central Organization Committee, and I will provide the comrade deputy prime ministers the minutes [of our meeting] later."[1] It was a banal and yet important moment. A masterful bureaucratic infighter, Hun Sen was quietly taking charge of a country that the rest of the world thought of only in terms of violence and open conflict.

In the mid-1980s, Cambodia's international image was formed, in large part, by *The Killing Fields,* Roland Joffe's 1984 film about the *New York Times* correspondent Sydney Schanberg and his assistant Dith Pran. The movie, which takes place immediately before and during the Khmer Rouge regime, has a happy ending. The year is 1979, Vietnam has invaded, and Pran has escaped from Cambodia. His family in the United States is alerted, and Schanberg flies to Thailand for an emotional reunion. For many of the Westerners who saw *The Killing Fields*, the story of Dith Pran (and the Oscar-winning performance of Dr. Haing Ngor, himself a survivor of the Khmer Rouge) instilled a rare connection to a distant country, its people, and its history. The film ends, however, as Dith Pran begins his life as a refugee. *The Killing Fields*—and its Western audience—leaves Cambodia behind.

The absence of information about events inside Cambodia was a result of the country's international isolation and the PRK's own political system. Throughout the mid-1980s the regime's patrons in Hanoi and Moscow remained locked in a diplomatic stalemate with the Chinese and Western supporters of the Cambodian resistance. Aside from a handful of humanitarian relief workers, almost no Westerners were in Cambodia, and certainly no journalists. News of the regime, as recounted by refugees, focused on the Vietnamese occupation, conscription, and rumors of a wall being constructed at the behest of the Vietnamese to separate Cambodia from Thailand. Radio broadcasts from Phnom Penh railing against China and the West and touting the achievements of the revolution provided little information on the power struggle being played out in the capital.

In many respects, the situation was in actuality how it appeared from the outside. The Vietnamese military campaign and the effort to end the PRK's diplomatic isolation dictated the terms by which Cambodian leaders were permitted to govern. But because the Vietnamese were focused primarily on war and diplomacy, more ambitious leaders had space to maneuver. Jaded by their experiences with Pen Sovan and Ros Samay, Vietnamese leaders no longer believed that their interests were best served by Hanoi-trained communists. Nor did they care whether the PRK was constructing a perfect socialist system. What mattered was the ability to accumulate power, the willingness to wield it in ways that supported the regime's military and diplomatic campaigns, and the capacity to construct a power base that could withstand a partial or complete Vietnamese withdrawal. Hun Sen managed all of this, using whatever positions the Vietnamese granted him as a base for future advancement while carefully timing his challenges to political rivals. As was apparent in his early meeting with Party cadres, he was a deft practitioner of communist institutional politics, deferential to the Party apparatus when necessary, proactive whenever an opening appeared.

The delegation that greeted Hun Sen that February afternoon was headed by one of the Party's most experienced cadres, Chey Saphon. A Hanoi veteran fluent in Vietnamese, Saphon had been responsible for debriefing Hun Sen in 1977. After liberation, he held the number eleven position in the Party Central Committee and assumed authority over much of the PRK's information system, serving as director-general of the state news agency, chair of the Kampuchean Journalists Association, and editor in chief of the newspaper *Kampuchea*. As deputy chair of the Central Organization Committee, he reviewed the personal histories of applicants for Party and state jobs. Initially close to Pen Sovan, Saphon worked mostly with the chair of the committee, Say Phouthang, although the latter's frequent illnesses often left Saphon in charge. Now, six and a half years after his interrogation of Hun Sen, Saphon got a taste of the energy and ambitions of the new prime minister.[2]

Saphon's colleagues stayed quiet during the meeting, as did Phoc, the Vietnamese advisor to the Central Organization Committee. Saphon began by briefing Hun Sen on the Politburo and Party Secretariat's appointments and transfers of ministerial cadres. Agreeing with these decisions, Hun Sen offered his own ideas. He was well prepared. "I propose that we focus on the transfer of cadres from the Social Works Committee to the Ministry of Disabled Veterans and Social Works, for there are many people whom we are not yet using, and there are some qualified people who should be transferred to empty ministries." He continued in that vein, proposing that more cadres be hired at the Ministry of Overseas Economic and Cultural Cooperation and that cadres be transferred from the Ministry of Commerce.[3]

Having shown a desire to micromanage the central bureaucracy, Hun Sen listened as Chey Saphon reported on the Politburo and Party Secretariat's decisions regarding provincial personnel. There was only one issue to be decided: the transfer of Steung Treng governor Bun Chan. According to Saphon, the removal of Chan was opposed by Central Organization Committee chair Say Phouthang. Hun Sen, who likely had no personal interests in Steung Treng, saw no value in challenging Phouthang. "Keep him there," he told Saphon.

THE MINISTER

Hun Sen had learned a few things about bureaucracy at the Ministry of Foreign Affairs. In many ways, the ministry was a typical place to build a patronage system. Apart from implementing foreign policy, ministry officials wielded day-to-day power over Cambodians by controlling their contact with foreigners and foreign organizations. In 1984 the ministry also began regulating tourism, an embryonic sector from which the PRK hoped to gain some hard currency.

The authority to grant or refuse permission to work for an international organization or open a guesthouse provided impoverished low-level cadres the opportunity to accept bribes. There was also the black market, where a number of
the Ministry of Foreign Affairs personnel earned outside income. As Heng
Samrin told the Party in 1982, the ministry under Hun Sen seemed a relatively
relaxed place. "There is eating, drinking, quarreling, and a lot of messing
around (*roe kakay*). There is also an increasing problem of collusion (*sum
krolum knea*) with the Liberation Cigarette Factory, which makes cigarettes and
sells them outside [in the black market]."[4]

The Ministry of Foreign Affairs, by virtue of its role, needed educated, literate Cambodians to read and draft diplomatic documents and English and
French speakers to interpret and translate. Desperate to put an articulate face
on the regime, Party leaders and Vietnamese advisors directed qualified cadres
to the Foreign Ministry. Meanwhile, Hun Sen made personal appeals to intellectuals to join the ministry. The first former Khmer Rouge leader to extend
such an invitation, Hun Sen offered ambitious noncommunists a career opportunity. Because policy emanated from Hanoi, diplomacy gave these Cambodians a chance to prove their political loyalty, as well as their technical competence. Later, after Hun Sen had become prime minister, several former Foreign
Ministry cadres became powerful ministers in an increasingly nonideological
regime. In the early 1980s their skills and education offered Foreign Minister
Hun Sen advantages not enjoyed by other ministers. Ung Phan, for one, was
jealous, as was apparent in his conversations with Council of Ministers advisor
Dang Dinh Long. His subordinates, he complained, were "ordinary cadres"
who "don't understand the directions we give them." By contrast, Hun Sen's assistants were "all more educated than at other departments," had "expertise,"
and could represent Hun Sen in an official capacity. It was not lost on Ung
Phan that all those qualified cadres were educating their boss. "In other words,
they can offer advice on the substance of official documents to Hun Sen, who
listens and understands."[5]

Hun Sen's other teachers—and his most important constituents—were the
Vietnamese. Utterly unprepared for the position of foreign minister, Hun Sen
relied heavily on Ngo Dien, the Vietnamese ambassador to the PRK. As the senior Vietnamese diplomat in Cambodia, Dien served not only as Hanoi's representative but as the chief advisor to the Cambodian Ministry of Foreign Affairs. Every morning he received Hun Sen at the Vietnamese embassy to give
him lessons in global politics and basic diplomacy. Dien, who also accompanied Hun Sen on interviews with foreign journalists, recognized the intelli-

gence of the young Cambodian and was willing to overlook his lack of formal Marxist-Leninist education. In return, Hun Sen demonstrated loyalty, promoting Hanoi's positions to the outside world and defending sensitive bilateral decisions to other Cambodian leaders.[6]

THE BORDER

Inside the PRK, Hun Sen's most delicate task was his ministry's negotiation of Cambodia's eastern border with Vietnam. Suspicions that the Vietnamese were taking advantage of the occupation to encroach on Cambodian territory abounded in the border camps, where refugees from eastern provinces complained that border markers were being moved, and in Cambodia. To counter the charge that Vietnam was absorbing Cambodia and to resolve outstanding disputes left over by Democratic Kampuchea, the Vietnamese sought to conclude a series of border agreements with the PRK. It was important to Hanoi, however, to present a picture of a normal bilateral relationship, for which they needed Cambodian leaders who would accept and defend the agreements.

Ocean waters, a subject that helped destroy relations between Vietnam and Democratic Kampuchea in 1976, was the first matter to be resolved. A July 1982 agreement concluded by Hun Sen and Vietnamese Foreign Minister Nguyen Co Thach included a recognition of what is known as the Brevié Line, an ocean boundary drawn by French colonial authorities in 1939 as an administrative convenience rather than a division of sovereignty. The basis of a 1966 agreement between Sihanouk and the National Liberation Front, the Brevié Line is resented by many Cambodians who consider it overly generous to Vietnam. (The line extends westward from the coastline and gives to Vietnam the island of Phu Quoc, which lies due south of the Cambodian province of Kampot.) Hor Namhong, a Sihanouk-era diplomat who was serving as the PRK's ambassador to the Soviet Union in July 1982, was among the PRK officials dissatisfied with the agreement. Years later, after he became minister of foreign affairs, Namhong, complained that "in fact, the Brevié Line is not a border. In fact, this area is ours, beginning in [the French] period and continuing to the present. But because of our laziness (*nhaoey khchoel*), [the Vietnamese] took it for themselves, and our laziness in doing nothing to claim it pleases them."[7]

The 1982 agreement also covered "historical waters," which were even closer to the Cambodian shore. Decrees issued by the PRK at the time of the signing proclaimed that Vietnamese use of these waters would be limited to defense purposes and that Cambodia retained rights regarding natural resources over the continental shelf. The agreement itself was more circumspect, stating that the "two parties shall cooperate" with regard to natural resources and "decide in a [subsequent] agreement." (Years later, after the U.N. election, Cambodia and Vietnam disagreed over access to oil deposits in these waters.) The agreement also included a provision allowing the "people of the region" to "continue to engage in fishing and bring in various ocean products in the area according to traditions that continue up to now." This proved to be a source of serious contention, as Vietnamese military units fished not only in "historical waters" but directly off the Cambodian coast. Officials of the Foreign Affairs Ministry complained at length to Hun Sen about these activities. Minutes of such meetings show Hun Sen listening quietly.[8]

In 1983, Hun Sen signed an agreement with Vietnam on the land border based on a mutually acceptable map from 1954. As has historically been the case, the details of the border and the actual placement of the border markers were what mattered. After selecting cadres from the Ministry of Foreign Affairs for a Joint Commission to Determine the Cambodian-Vietnamese Border, Hun Sen and the ministry's Vietnamese advisors guided the subsequent negotiations attentively. The chair of the commission, Dith Munty, was sent to Hanoi for a period of unspecified "study" and replaced temporarily by the deputy minister of foreign affairs and former ambassador to Vietnam, Kong Korm. At the commission's first meeting, a Vietnamese advisor to the Ministry of Foreign Affairs identified as "Tun" explained to the Cambodians what was expected of them. Cambodia's negotiating position, he said, should be "based on the spirit of friendship, solidarity, and cooperation." Tun also stressed confidentiality. "Our future duties, starting now, are secret. I ask that there be no negligence in [keeping] secrets." Despite complaints from the Cambodians regarding a lack of money and relevant documents, Tun urged them to prepare quickly for upcoming negotiations. "In comparison to the Vietnamese, our work is four months behind. I inform the meeting that in the view of Comrade Minister Hun Sen with regard to this matter, the Cambodians should shorten their meetings some." Two months later, in a meeting choreographed by Vietnamese advisors, Hun Sen touted the commission's progress to the Council of Ministers, even as the commission's Cambodian members complained of insufficient funds to visit the border and a lack of modern surveying equipment.[9]

In 1985, after Hun Sen became prime minister, he consolidated control over border issues within the Council of Ministers. He also concluded a final land-border treaty, at the end of 1985, which he was forced to defend to skeptical members of the government and the National Assembly. At one meeting of the

Council of State, Hun Sen acknowledged various compromises made by the Cambodians, including the use of a 1924 map more favorable to the Vietnamese. This prompted a response from Heng Samrin. "During the colonial period, both the Vietnamese and the Cambodians supervised [the border], so the border markers have already been put in place, but [the Vietnamese] want to place them [again], regardless of whether they're accurate." Chan Ven, who had just been complaining about lost territory in Svay Rieng, concluded the discussion by stating simply, "I ask Comrade Prime Minister to prepare to explain this to the members of the National Assembly."[10]

Such was the price of power in the PRK. As foreign minister, Hun Sen was expected to defend the border agreements not only to the world but within the regime. Despite grumblings and complaints from other members of the leadership and from cadres within his own ministry, Hun Sen pushed ahead, demonstrating to the Vietnamese that he was willing to accept personal responsibility for one of the more unpopular aspects of the bilateral relationship.

THE BUREAUCRAT

From the moment, in 1982, when he was appointed deputy prime minister, Hun Sen saw the Council of Ministers as an opportunity to extend his influence beyond his base at the Ministry of Foreign Affairs. The council also happened to be run by his old friend Ung Phan, on whose behalf Hun Sen promoted an expanded and more powerful bureaucracy with responsibility over economic policy and foreign economic cooperation. The result was that, by the time Hun Sen became prime minister, he had already begun to build a formidable state administration.[11]

The bureaucracy, like its patron, was fundamentally nonideological. As Ung Phan had reminded the Vietnamese, the state apparatus was desperate for cadres with technical expertise and administrative experience. Such people were hardly ever communists. Indeed, thousands of Cambodians flocked to the bureaucracy, not out of Party loyalty but as the only means of survival in a fragile economy. Although the new civil servants were generally inept at regulating the country's increasingly private economy, they were able to intervene in day-to-day matters, collecting taxes and bribes and passing the revenues on to their superiors. The state thus turned into a sprawling and heterogeneous network of ministries, agencies, and provincial and local administrations whose members adhered to the rules of patronage.

Gradually the bureaucracy began to function independently of the Party. Although Party membership had increased, from one thousand in May 1981 to seven thousand in October 1985, there were still far too few Party branches and core groups to oversee all the institutions and agencies that made up the state apparatus. The Politburo and the Central Committee still determined the principles by which the country was governed. But in an environment of constantly shifting economic and social conditions and near extemporaneous policy responses, state officials made decisions faster than the Party leadership could follow. Even when the ministries were forced to issue circulars conforming with Party economic prescriptions, bureaucrats were rarely required to implement them with any vigor. Party discipline was almost nonexistent, and so long as an immediate boss or some other bureaucratic patron was satisfied, it was almost impossible to lose a state job.[12]

THE FALL OF THE HANOI VETERANS

The Party leadership was in flux as the remaining Hanoi veterans were removed and replaced by former Khmer Rouge cadres, military figures, and technicians. The reasons for the turnover had to do with domestic Cambodian politics and the changing nature of the Vietnamese occupation. As the removal of Pen Sovan had demonstrated, the Hanoi veterans were unprepared to establish personal power bases in Cambodia. Having spent most of their lives outside the country, they did not fully appreciate the importance of patronage and were easily isolated. The former Khmer Rouge cadres, on the other hand, had already survived political battles that were more treacherous and deadly than those they faced under the PRK. They had learned over the course of their revolutionary careers that whereas ideologies are subject to unpredictable shifts, loyal patronage systems are the key to political survival. In general, they did not allow the tenets of socialism to prevent them from enriching themselves and their followers.

The Vietnamese actually had everything to gain by allowing the Cambodian power struggles to play themselves out. Support for what Hanoi was trying to accomplish in Cambodia, militarily and diplomatically, was still a prerequisite for power in the PRK; besides that, it was a case of survival of the fittest. This was a change. In the first three years of the regime, Hanoi needed powerful former Khmer Rouge cadres but feared them as well. Now, six years (and several key arrests) later, the Vietnamese were no longer worried about betrayal. Instead, they were contemplating withdrawing from Cambodia, a prospect that depended on the consolidation of the regime by self-sufficient (and by now thoroughly vetted) power brokers like Chea Sim.

In short, the Vietnamese no longer needed the Hanoi veterans they had installed in 1979. Those who were still in power in 1984—Central Organization Committee chair Say Phouthang and Deputy Prime Ministers Chea Soth and Bou Thang—served mainly at the behest of Vietnamese patrons. Their dependence on Hanoi had originally been a political asset, assuring the Vietnamese that they would remain loyal. Now their nominal hold on power served only to delay the day when the PRK could stand on its own. No other event proved this more than the promotion of Hun Sen. Having defended Vietnam's strategic interests as minister of foreign affairs, Hun Sen had shown himself to be as least as trustworthy as his colleagues Chea Soth and Bou Thang, yet he was also capable of accumulating power on his own. Here was a man who was ambitious and flexible enough to govern Cambodia without direct Vietnamese support. Why get in his way?

Around the time Hun Sen became prime minister, the composition of the Party leadership shifted dramatically. In late 1984, at the National Cadres Congress, the Party elected eight new candidate members of the Central Committee, all either former Khmer Rouge cadres or new Party members. A year later, at the Fifth Party Congress, the balance tilted for good. One Hanoi veteran after another lost his position on the Party Central Committee. Chey Saphon, said to be sick, dropped from eleventh in the Party hierarchy all the way out of the Central Committee. Khang Sarin, minister of the interior, was removed from the Central Committee, as was Suy Keo, a former deputy minister of defense and chief of staff; Lim Nay, chief of cabinet of the Party Central Committee; and Lay Samon, Party secretary of Battambang.[13]

The most important of the Hanoi veterans, Say Phouthang, apparently showed little loyalty to his old comrades. Says one now-retired revolutionary, Phouthang "tricked" the old communists, leading them to trust him and then betraying them. But Phouthang himself was slipping, receiving the fewest Central Committee votes of any Politburo member and falling to ninth in the Party hierarchy. More important, the Party removed him as chair of the Central Organization Committee and placed him in charge of the less important Inspection Committee. Soon, says his disgruntled former comrade, Phouthang was "following Hun Sen and making him happy."[14]

By the end of the Party congress, former Khmer Rouge cadres had gained a majority in both the Politburo and the Central Committee. Say Phouthang's position as chair of the Central Organization Committee was taken by Men Sam An, a former nurse and a new member of the Central Committee. Close to neither Hun Sen nor Chea Sim, and a woman in a very male arena, Sam An was never as powerful as her predecessor. Sar Kheng's career, on the other hand, was on the rise. Chea Sim's brother-in-law, Kheng had recently become chief of cabinet of the Central Committee and was now a full member of the committee. The Party congress promoted other kinds of leaders as well. The rise of military figures was attributable to the importance of the war effort and to the power that many generals wielded in the provinces. And the appearance in the Central Committee of state ministers with no pre-1979 revolutionary experience coincided with a more pragmatic personnel policy and a preference for technocrats.[15]

Within months of the Party congress, the composition of the Council of Ministers began reflecting the Party's change in direction, as veteran Hanoi communists left their ministerial posts to their technocrat deputies. At Finance, Chan Phin was replaced by Chhay Than, a former student at the Faculty of Commerce. At Interior, Khang Sarin stepped aside for Ne Penna, a thirty-eight-year-old former teacher who, prior to coming to the ministry, had served as Party secretary of the isolated and sparsely populated province of Preah Vihear. And at Planning, Chea Soth relinquished his ministerial post in favor of Chea Chantho, a former employee of the Cambodian National Bank who would become a vocal supporter of economic reform.

The regime was sufficiently consolidated to permit technicians, as opposed to revolutionaries, to run the administration. The leadership was also acknowledging that the Vietnamese answer to the PRK's bureaucratic chaos—the assignment of a small number of leaders to multiple state and Party functions—had failed. Deputy Prime Ministers Chea Soth and Bou Thang, overcommitted and incapable of accomplishing their various duties, were the subject of criticism. Bou Thang, said Say Phouthang of his old Hanoi comrade, "hasn't really done the work of the Council of Ministers because he can't do it all." Chea Soth was so busy reviewing documents for both the Ministry of Planning and the Council of Ministers that he "cannot examine them closely and must rely heavily on the minister and deputy minister of the cabinet of the Council of Ministers." Heng Samrin agreed, noting that Bou Thang and Chea Soth were more focused on core group activities than on state functions. Removed from their positions at the Ministries of Defense and Planning, Thang and Soth concentrated on Party work. Within the state apparatus they each retained the post of deputy prime minister, a position whose power depended on what Hun Sen decided to delegate.[16]

HUN SEN CONSOLIDATES
BUREAUCRATIC POWER

Leaving the Ministry of Foreign Affairs to his deputy, Kong Korm, Hun Sen concentrated on strengthening the Council of Ministers. One of his first acts as prime minister, in February 1985, was to take control of the distribution of humanitarian assistance away from the Ministry of Commerce and reassign it to the council. Over the course of the year he expanded the size and responsibility of the council, adding a Department for Planning of Overseas Economic and Cultural Cooperation; a Department of Commerce, Finance, and Banking; a Department of Industry and Construction; a Department of Education, Culture, and Social Affairs; a Department of Communications and Electricity; a Department of Agriculture; and a Department of Internal Affairs. To fill these offices, Hun Sen recruited educated Cambodians, including the first set of students returning from Vietnam, the Soviet Union, and Eastern Europe. He also attempted to prevent the Party apparatus from taking his bureaucrats, warning that "if [the Party] takes 100 percent all at once, we'll lack [sufficient] cadres for state tasks."[17]

Hun Sen considered it time to undo one of the peculiar features of the PRK bureaucracy: the bottleneck at the Ministry of Justice. In most communist systems the Council of Ministers (after receiving policy guidance from the Party) delegates to individual ministries the responsibility for drafting laws, circulars, and other official documents. In Cambodia, however, few people knew what a legal document looked like, much less how to draft one. The regime had originally resolved this problem by assigning Cambodia's few remaining jurists to the Ministry of Justice. But by 1986, Hun Sen had become irritated with the ministry, partly because of its insistence on inserting human rights provisions into legislation (as will be discussed in Chapter 11). Others within the Council of Ministers complained that the ministry's obsession with legality was slowing everything down. Removing some of its authority would, said Meas Leas, "avoid lots of negotiations over the forms and meaning of each legal document." Vietnamese advisor Fang You agreed. "According to our current revolutionary situation, we don't have to be too rigid; we should issue a legal document in order to control our urgent situation. We should streamline the work system in whatever way that allows it [to function] faster than before." In early 1987, over the protests of the Ministry of Justice, the Council of Ministers established its own Legislation Office responsible for "conducting research and drafting or offering opinions on all legislative documents."[18]

THE NATIONAL ASSEMBLY

As in other communist countries, the authority of the Cambodian legislature existed only in theory. Twice a year, members of the National Assembly convened in strictly orchestrated events at which Assembly president Chea Sim presided over unanimous reaffirmations of Party and state policies and post facto appointments of new ministers. Behind the scenes were Vietnamese advisors, who assured that disagreements did not arise in Assembly sessions.[19]

The members of parliament themselves had been elected in 1981 and were not subject to subsequent contests. In January 1986, toward the end of the Assembly's mandate, the leadership and the Vietnamese advisors decided to extend the session for another five years. "To hold an election, we would have to spend a lot of money," explained Heng Samrin, reminding his colleagues of their other priorities. "And we must decide on the economic agenda that the Fifth Party Congress has established; and a system for defending the [Thai] border must be determined." Vuong Dinh Chau, an advisor to the National Assembly and a former secretary-general of the Vietnamese Assembly, cited precedent. "In the experience of Vietnam, in order to vote for the members of the National Assembly there must be at least six months' preparation, and the forces of many people must be mobilized. Vietnam has delayed elections, too, and many elections have waited for opportune times."[20]

The Party replaced members, when necessary, through elections that, for security and budgetary reasons, were often limited to provincial capitals or selected communes. To at least one member of the Assembly, this practice undermined what little democracy existed in the PRK. It was simply "wrong" to hold elections in one small subset of a constituency, insisted Vandy Ka-on in August 1986. "This is because afterward these members will not appear to be representatives of the people throughout the constituency." Ka-on added a strategic consideration: "Also, this can have a bad effect on politics outside our country." Say Phouthang acknowledged some of Ka-on's concerns. "The connection to politics outside the country is one issue, but inside our [country], we should take care to explain to our people because if we hold an election only in that one locality, the people in other localities in the constituency are unable to recognize the new member of the Assembly as their representative." Heng Samrin ended the discussion tersely: "What's important is our actual situation."[21]

THE COUNCIL OF STATE

These discussions took place within the Council of State, the permanent body of the National Assembly. Of the top four Party leaders, three served on the council: Assembly president Chea Sim, Say Phouthang, and the president of the council, Heng Samrin. Chea Sim, who preferred to wield power through informal personal connections, rarely attended meetings, and when he did, he sat quietly. But Samrin and Phouthang, whose careers were in decline, took the Council of State seriously.

Perhaps because the council was powerless, it offered some of the liveliest debates inside the PRK. In addition to the Party leadership, the council included former Minister of Health Nou Peng and former Minister of Agriculture Men Chhan, both of whom complained periodically of the lawlessness they saw engulfing the country. Some of the PRK's more liberal figures, including Chan Ven and Vandy Ka-on, had also been assigned to the council. Insufficiently loyal for state positions, Ven and Ka-on were nonetheless useful to the Party leadership as symbols: reassuring Cambodians of the regime's inclusiveness. Their capacity to speak out within the council also suggests that the Party had an interest in what these intellectuals thought of the PRK's policies, even if their recommendations were rarely followed.[22]

Chan Ven, who, after his period of "study" in Hanoi, finally achieved full Party membership, gamely promoted the role of the legislature in drafting legislation and reviewing political appointments. "The National Assembly is the supreme state organization," he argued on one occasion, in reference to the national budget. "[Its members] want to know about defending and rebuilding the country. Nothing should be hidden from the members of the Assembly." "Usually," responded Chea Sim, "our National Assembly approves just a general budget, meaning general revenues and expenditures. Detailed expenditures are up to the Ministry of Finance."[23]

Vandy Ka-on built a career on ineffectual internal argument. After participating in the Pol Pot–Ieng Sary trial, Ka-on spent September 1979 attending conferences in the Soviet Union, Vietnam, and Australia, recounting the horrors of the Khmer Rouge. Upon his return he was assigned to the Council of State, where he expressed liberal positions without questioning the regime's one-party system. Ka-on also served as chair of the Legislation Commission of the

National Assembly, a position from which he sometimes commented on draft laws. In many cases, however, important legislation bypassed the commission, with an explanation from Heng Samrin or Chea Sim that the Politburo had already made its decisions or that there was "too little time." Ultimately Ka-on's only influence came from exploiting his symbolic value to the regime. If things got too bad, he told the leadership, he would resign and go to France.[24]

THE LANGUAGE WARS

Vandy Ka-on was also engaged in a battle to resurrect Cambodian culture. The situation was bleak. There was little art of any kind that was not political: artists were put to work painting socialist billboards of virtuous peasants and workers, musicians were hired to write revolutionary songs, and the radio broadcasts were mostly propaganda. The literature coming out of the Ministry of Culture also conformed to the Party line. Novels with titles like *We Resolutely Decide to Make Every Sacrifice to Save the Nation and the Motherland* depicted the horrors of Democratic Kampuchea, the Eastern Zone uprising of 1978, and the struggle against Thailand. In this context, Vandy Ka-on's 1987 book, *Island of the Evil Spirits* (*Koah besach*) was a welcome change. An invocation of life under the Khmer Rouge, it was at least allegorical.[25]

Besides glorifying the revolution, PRK propaganda sought to fuel anger against Pol Pot. The radio played lugubrious music punctuated by crying, which was intended to recall the horrors of the Khmer Rouge; theatrical productions reminded audiences of the massacres in detail. Beginning in 1984, Cambodians were treated to an annual national holiday devoted entirely to these sorts of events. According to a National Assembly declaration, May 20 would be commemorated as the National Day of Hatred.[26]

The regime's public criticism of the noncommunist resistance was less effective. Despite frequent reminders on the radio and in the newspaper that Sihanouk and Son Sann were now allied with Pol Pot, many people continued to look to prerevolutionary leaders as an alternative to communism and occupation. Attempts by PRK propagandists to use traditional Khmer culture to disseminate the Party line—for example, by organizing dance performances around anti-Sihanouk themes—only highlighted the regime's fundamental dilemma. Cambodians, especially educated ones, welcomed the revival of Khmer culture and, to some extent, appreciated the fact that the PRK had overthrown the profoundly anticultural Khmer Rouge regime. Yet much of what Cambodians thought of as their cultural inheritance reminded them of Sihanouk and of the royalist movement against which the PRK was struggling militarily and politically. The police and the propaganda apparatus thus attempted to make distinctions between, for instance, "songs from the old society" (Sihanouk songs) and "traditional songs," as if Cambodians could skip their feudal, royalist history and return to some ancient, apolitical past. The challenge, in short, was to re-create Khmer traditions without generating nostalgia. The Vietnamese occupation further complicated this task. A visible cultural revival helped the PRK counter the resistance's accusations that Cambodia was undergoing Vietnamization. And yet the narrowest of gaps separated celebrations of national culture from assertions of nationalism.[27]

Vandy Ka-on moved cautiously. Soon after his trips overseas and after extensive political reeducation, he requested permission from the Party to establish a research committee to collect documents and literature on Cambodian culture. When receiving researchers visiting from communist countries, Ka-on assured them that the committee was just a personal project and that he had nothing against Marx. Despite rumors of his planned defection, Ka-on believed himself to be protected by powerful elements in the Party. Hun Sen and Chea Sim, he now says, appreciated him and "listened politely" to his views, even if they rarely followed his advice. Bou Thang, he jokes, was his "ideological professor." To the extent that Ka-on felt threatened, it was only by mysterious pro-Vietnamese forces whom he is still reluctant to name.[28]

Ka-on's colleague Thun Saray had no powerful patrons. One of the few intellectuals in the country not to join the government or the Front, Saray considered his work at the Institute of Sociology (the eventual name of the research committee) as a defiant, symbolic act of independence. "There were no Vietnamese advisors there," he says.

The Party, which wished to demonstrate its acceptance of Cambodian intellectual culture, permitted Ka-on and Saray to establish an office in central Phnom Penh. Avoiding political subjects, the two men began writing articles on biology, environmental science, medicine, and other academic subjects. Around 1983 they obtained a manual mimeograph machine and began publishing journals, limiting their distribution to about two hundred "researchers." Eventually, three or four thousand copies circulated around the capital and were read by intellectuals throughout the government.

Most of the subscribers, aware that the regime remained suspicious of all noncommunist intellectuals, were too afraid to come anywhere near the institute. In its efforts to recruit educated Cambodians to staff the government, the Party began, in 1986 and 1987, to officially tolerate "original class background, previous relations with the old regime, and current ties to family and friends living in capitalist countries." At the same time, however, it used the Front to monitor "revolutionary intellectuals," organizing all educated state cadres into "intellectual teams" and assigning one member to report on the "activities, situation, views, positions, attitudes, virtues, failings, and requests of the intellectuals." Many of the city's educated noncommunists sensed that basic attitudes had not changed since the Khmer Rouge. "We had the same car, only we had changed the driver," explains Ang Eng Thong, a former jurist who joined the Institute of Sociology in 1989. "If you stuck out your arm, it got cut off."[29]

It was also hard to move around the city. On the alert for conspiracies, security officials followed anyone suspected of anticommunist sentiments. The number of political arrests offers an indication of the repressive climate. From 1983 to 1985 municipal police reported 11 cases connected to Sihanouk, leading to 72 arrests; 35 Son Sann cases, for which 120 people were detained; and 13 other cases "related to politics," for which 71 people were arrested. Hundreds more were being watched.[30]

Logistical obstacles contributed to the feeling of isolation among Phnom Penh's educated class. For years residents had neither telephones nor bicycles and therefore had little opportunity to extend their connections beyond their families, neighbors, and work colleagues. With conversations and meetings monitored, most Cambodians had little to gain and much to lose by associating themselves with the Institute of Sociology. Ka-on and Saray were sympathetic. Saray had witnessed the arrests of several friends and family members involved in resistance networks, including a cousin who was detained and tortured for two years, and he scrupulously avoided associating the institute with anyone whom the regime might consider the opposition.[31]

Working in isolation and under close scrutiny, Vandy Ka-on and Thun Saray issued publications that supported the regime's politics, including articles that described the country's "liberation" and its struggle against "American imperialism" and Pol Pot "Maoism." There were cultural pieces on the "Marxist aesthetic" and legal treatises on the role of the Council of State and the Council of Ministers. In addressing historical issues in depth, however, the articles sometimes wandered out of sight of the official Party line. One issue reported on Khmer Rouge purges of royalists in the early 1970s, reminding readers of the long association between Sihanouk and Pol Pot but also revealing that the revolution had betrayed its followers *prior* to 1975. The article even included citations to CIA sources. Another piece, discussing sixteenth-century Siamese-

Cambodian relations, referred, disconcertingly perhaps, to foreign invasions and disloyal Khmer leaders.[32]

The institute's publications were intended as assertions of the Khmer culture. There were romantic short stories and essays on Khmer rural traditions. Mostly, however, the institute promoted apolitical intellectualism. Ka-on wrote articles with titles like "Structural Analysis" and "General Theory on Systems," dropping in abundant French as well as Khmer footnotes with references to Copernicus, Claude Lévi-Strauss, and *structuralisme transformationnel.* Aggressively esoteric, Ka-on's writings had little to offer a perplexed readership. In the aftermath of the Khmer Rouge and in the midst of stultifying political education, however, the mere exertion of intellectual energy was itself liberating, not least for the author, who had recently spent three years feigning mental retardation.

Ka-on waged his biggest battles over the Khmer language. As the PRK struggled to rebuild an education system and to re-create a literate, if ideologically conformist, educated class, the complexities and irregularities of the Khmer written word were deemed expendable. State and Party newspapers simplified Khmer spelling, and the regime established an interministerial commission to create new words. The debate was fierce, with Chea Soth complaining of "anarchy" in writing and Say Phouthang warning of a "language war." The issue was so intense that it was eventually submitted to the Politburo, although it was eventually dropped for more urgent priorities. Vandy Ka-on felt that Khmer culture was at stake. "The spelling of words means that they cannot be changed," he insisted to the Council of State. "Can anyone change a word that already has a history?"[33] Reasserting traditional spellings in the Institute of Sociology publications, Ka-on produced pages of Khmer words and their French equivalents, thereby providing Cambodians words for such abstract concepts as "chromosome," "existentialism," and "anorexia."

THE EYE OF THE STORM

Phnom Penh was at once the center of the Cambodian conflict and a distant player. Hun Sen's bureaucratic maneuvering and his promotion to prime minister, as well as changes in the Party's leadership and the composition of the Council of Ministers, had little immediate impact on most Cambodians. Only a handful of cadres were aware of the debates taking place in the Council of State, and few outside the capital read the publications of the Institute of Sociology. The conversation taking place in Phnom Penh among Hun Sen, Heng Samrin, Vandy Ka-on, and Thun Saray covered the most important questions of the post–Khmer Rouge period. How much democracy could Cambodia afford? What was the PRK's relationship with Vietnam? What was Khmer culture? These discussions were directly relevant to all Cambodians, and yet few ever heard them.

Phnom Penh's political and cultural struggles were hidden and, from the perspective of the Vietnamese, safely under control. In Hun Sen they had found a Cambodian leader who could be entrusted to protect Hanoi's interests yet who was not overly dependent on Vietnamese support. That he was not a doctrinaire Marxist was, by now, unimportant. Nor were the Vietnamese bent on suppressing internal debate so long as no one challenged the legitimacy of the regime or the value of the occupation. The limited freedom granted to Vandy Ka-on and Thun Saray also served a purpose, helping the PRK present a more inclusive image and perhaps convincing some educated Cambodians to stay in the country.

Political life in Phnom Penh had arrived at a tense equilibrium. The capital's elite were under constant surveillance but were nonetheless encouraged to work for the state, regardless of their backgrounds. Communist propaganda continued unabated, yet ideological conformity had become less important to the leadership than loyalty. These modest accommodations were necessary if the regime was to have a functioning bureaucracy. They also permitted the leadership and the Vietnamese to focus on what they perceived to be immediate security threats and to direct attention and resources on their primary objective: winning the war against the resistance.

Chapter 10 Wartime:

Conscription, Profiteering,

and K5

Toward the end of each year, as the rains stopped and the muddy roads dried out, the Vietnamese army went on the offensive. Capable of moving its artillery from place to place, the Vietnamese could pursue the Cambodian resistance and destroy its bases. Then, each spring, as the rains resumed, the resistance would strike back, destroying railroads, bridges, and fuel facilities and forcing the now immobilized Vietnamese to defend hard-earned territory. Such was the case in early 1984, when the Khmer Rouge burned buildings around the outskirts of the provincial capital of Siem Riep, and units of various resistance forces launched attacks in Pursat, Kampong Thom, Kampong Speu, Kampong Chhnang, and Koh Kong provinces.[1]

At the end of the year, the Vietnamese army initiated its largest and most successful dry season offensive. Taking territory along the border, Vietnamese units attacked and destroyed refugee camps belonging to all three resistance groups, thus depriving them of their "liberated zones." The offensive also forced some 230,000 refugees over the border into Thailand.[2]

As the resistance struggled to establish bases among newly expanded refugee camps on Thai soil, it looked to the West for help. In the spring and summer of 1985 a major debate ensued within the United States over Cambodia policy, culminating in congressional approval of $5 million in aid to the noncommunist resistance. Meanwhile, to repair its image, the Khmer Rouge announced that it was working toward a liberal capitalist system and that Pol Pot would be retiring as commander in chief, a move that Hanoi promptly labeled a "cheap deceitful trick." Outside observers generally agreed with Radio Hanoi's analysis, that "Pol Pot may still use his power among the Khmer Rouge leaders even though he has loudly proclaimed his resignation." Nonetheless, the PRK, having personalized Democratic Kampuchea, was now forced to issue a clarification. "We demand the elimination of Pol Pot politically and militarily," Hun Sen told a Vietnamese newspaper in August 1985. "This means that it is necessary to eliminate Pol Pot not as a person but as an organization."[3]

Cambodia's role on the international stage remained unchanged. As it had every year since 1979, the U.N. General Assembly passed a resolution that called for the "withdrawal of all foreign forces" (that is, the Vietnamese) while accepting the credentials of the CGDK. The resistance was nonetheless in disarray. In February 1986 efforts by top KPNLF officers to take control of the movement prompted Son Sann to demote his commander in chief, General Sak Sutsakhan, and his chief of staff, General Dien Del, and to expel two other prominent KPNLF leaders. On the defensive militarily, the coalition government was becoming more accommodating diplomatically, speaking of a Vietnamese withdrawal in "two phases" (thereby removing total withdrawal as a precondition for a political settlement) and of a four-party interim government (which would include the PRK leadership as well as the three resistance groups). "In the past we did not talk to Heng Samrin," said Sihanouk from Beijing, "but now we accept that Heng Samrin and his followers could hold talks with us and then, together, we must organize and establish a quadripartite government and free elections."[4]

The Vietnamese military victories of 1984–85 changed the nature of the war. Unable to defend territory inside Cambodia, resistance soldiers divided into small groups and headed into the interior. According to PRK estimates, 15,300 "enemies" were operating inside the country in 1984, and 21,000 in 1987. Trade between Thailand and Cambodia made infiltration hard to control, prompting the leadership to equate merchants with the resistance. Citing his own province of Koh Kong as a major transit route, Say Phouthang said, "Regardless of whether they are Chinese, Khmer, or Vietnamese, they have committed an offense and should be punished because [their travels back and forth] serve the politics of the enemy, which has a network in Thailand that can enter [Cambodia] anywhere and knows everything. They are all the same."[5]

THE MISLED PERSONS MOVEMENT

Ever since December 1978, when Heng Samrin extended his promise to "warmly welcome" Khmer Rouge cadres and soldiers into the new regime, defections had been the primary strategic goal of the PRK. In 1984 and 1985 the regime intensified its efforts. Broken up into small, disconnected, and ill-equipped groups, resistance soldiers operating deep inside Cambodia were coming into contact with Cambodian civilians living under PRK rule. Capable of spreading resistance propaganda, gathering intelligence, and recruiting defectors of their own, these units were also vulnerable. Far from their base camps, the soldiers were frequently tempted to give up and rejoin family and friends in Cambodia. "Most of the people in the ranks of the armed forces of Pol Pot, Ieng Sary, Khieu Samphan, Son Sann, and Sihanouk are the husbands, children, and younger siblings of our Cambodian citizens," reported the Council of Ministers in 1984. The PRK thus encouraged its citizens to "pull" family members out of the resistance. It also instructed local authorities to "protect the lives of and provide assistance" to resistance soldiers who "confessed," to refrain from taking their personal property (other than weapons and enemy documents), and to provide education on the "important policies of the Party and state." Defectors, said Phnom Penh, should be "asked to join the local state authority." Labeled the Misled Persons Movement, this policy was intended to divide the resistance by promising favorable treatment upon surrender.[6]

Not all defections were thought to be sincere. By July 1985 more than two thousand Cambodians were reported to have defected from the resistance, yet the Party leadership suspected that many were spies. As Heng Samrin told the Council of State, "Among the 2,176 confessors, we see only 676 weapons. We should be cautious of this for fear that these people are surrendering so that they can return to live among us and conduct activities. [This is a concern] because every single enemy soldier [normally] carries a weapon." The man responsible for coordinating the defection policy, Un Dara, defended the regime's successes, saying that Vietnamese advisors had reported the confiscation of 1,268 weapons. Besides, he added, defectors would not necessarily bring their weapons with them. "Enemies who come and surrender don't dare carry weapons because they are afraid their commanders will see them. Also, if they carry weapons with them, they are afraid that we will shoot them."[7]

Encouraging defectors while weeding out spies was tricky business, requiring a balance between a "warm welcome" and a thorough investigation. "The enemy is afraid that we don't trust them," noted Say Phouthang, adding that "we've had examples in many places which provide sufficient experience for us to always be cautious." To Heng Samrin, exercising caution meant interrogating all defectors. In a number of provinces, he told the Council of State, resistance soldiers had surrendered and confessed and yet only after "education and guidance" was an "honest confession" elicited. This second confession, said Samrin, revealed that the soldiers had originally been ordered by their superiors to feign defections in order to "communicate with their internal networks."[8]

Vietnamese and Cambodian authorities focused their attention on Khmer Rouge military officers, thirty-three of whom had defected by the end of 1985. As Minister of the Interior Sin Song explained in 1988, the regime was willing to expend significant resources in an effort to entice the enemy. "So far, when fearful Pol Pot regiment or battalion commanders (*thnak voreah*) come and surrender," Song told the Council of State, "we give them houses and sometimes reward them further."[9]

TO "DEFEND THE MOTHERLAND"

The first step in getting Cambodians to defend the PRK was to rebuild the militias, which had been disbanded in 1979 largely because they included former Sihanouk and Lon Nol soldiers. The new militias, based in the villages, communes, and urban neighborhoods, were intended to turn Cambodian civilians into vigilant revolutionaries. As Deputy Chief of Staff Chay Sang Yaun told the Joint Command Committee of Phnom Penh in 1982, the PRK hoped to "promote the movement of the masses in whatever manner necessary to get each person to become a soldier and a police officer." As we shall see in Chapter 11, the role of civilians in policing society was the subject of debate within the leadership.[10]

The Kampuchean People's Revolutionary Army did not grow out of the militias but rather from a set of operation teams (later called armed propaganda teams), which had originally been set up by the Vietnamese to protect local authorities, to "propagate the political principles of the revolution," and to "seek out enemies of all kinds." Around the middle of 1980, Vietnamese authorities began organizing these teams into district and provincial command committees and incorporating them into an overall military structure. Over time, the Cambodian army took shape and grew, from a force of six hundred in 1979 to three thousand in 1980, to five thousand in 1981. Cambodian soldiers nonetheless remained under Vietnamese orders. According to agreements drafted in June 1981, "The Cambodian Ministry of Defense confers rights on the big Vietnamese military organizations with regard to the plans for establishing actual military cooperation . . . and coordination of orders in each region." Vietnamese military advisors also conducted training down to the commune-level armed propaganda teams while gradually deploying Cambodians in more battle situations.[11]

For several years, the distinction between recruitment and conscription remained vague. The PRK's propagandists did not attempt to portray military service as anything but sacrifice. The army, they said, wanted "young people with revolutionary ideals and a militant core who are absolutely courageous and unafraid of suffering and dare to give up their lives for the revolution, for the people, and for supreme glory."[12] Not surprisingly, most Cambodians had little or no interest in joining the military. According to a Vietnamese advisor named Nguyen Thu, they despised the whole idea of being a soldier. In a report to Hanoi, Thu wrote, "It is difficult to recruit new troops because, under previous regimes, military salaries were high so that the soldiers could pay family expenses. To get money [now], they extort from other people, and that happens frequently. The bad things that happened in the past still continue in the present. People don't want to join the army because they think of soldiers as bad people who threaten others."[13]

With few Cambodians volunteering, the PRK turned to conscription. In 1982 the Council of Ministers issued instructions to local authorities to take men between the ages of seventeen and twenty-five, as well as a few unmarried women. Conditions were difficult and morale was low. In the spring of 1984, Vietnamese officials estimated that the Cambodian army was losing 2,000 soldiers a month to death or defection, even though Vietnamese soldiers were doing most of the fighting. Still, Vietnamese authorities hoped to increase the size of the Cambodian army so that it could help in the 1984–85 dry-season offensive and so that the Vietnamese army could eventually withdraw from Cambodia. The PRK stepped up its conscription efforts, and by April 1985 internal Vietnamese reports claimed that 80,000 Cambodians were enlisted. Although this number is difficult to confirm, the Kampuchean People's Revolutionary Army was now at least proximate in size, if not skill, to the resistance's purported 40,000 Khmer Rouge troops, 14,000 KPNLF troops, and 10,000 troops of the Armée Nationaliste Sihanoukienne (ANS).[14]

In the summer of 1985, when the leadership met to formalize its conscription policy, there was little outright opposition, although a few officials attempted to impose limits. On one side of the debate were Heng Samrin, Hun Sen, the rest of the Party leadership, and the Ministry of Defense, who proposed drafting men aged eighteen to thirty. On the other were Minister of Education Pen Navuth, Justice Minister Uk Bunchheuan, and Vandy Ka-on, who suggested starting at age twenty-one or twenty-two in order not to interrupt the soldiers' education. Bunchheuan also complained that a five-year tour of duty would prevent people from caring for their parents and ultimately encourage defections.[15] Vandy Ka-on cited the country's need for educated people. "Five years' service in the army seems too long because when the young people get out of school, they haven't yet worked in the area of expertise that they studied but must go serve in the army for five years first. After five years, they will have forgotten all the subjects they studied, and it will be as if their studies were useless. Also, the situation in our country is not like in Vietnam. In Vietnam, there are a lot of educated people. In our country, there are very few educated people, and if those few must go serve in the army and return having forgotten everything, what will happen in the future?"[16]

The arguments presented by Ka-on, Bunchheuan and Navuth were rejected by the Ministry of Defense and by the leadership. "The Ministry of Defense has discussed this issue of length of service many times already," said Bou Thang, closing the discussion. "We've discussed a two-year period, a three-year period, and a five-year period. In the end, the Party's Military [Committee] and Chairman Heng Samrin agreed on five years because when we have too much turnover, the quality of our soldiers is not strengthened. In enlisting soldiers, what's important is that we turn people into tough fighters."[17]

Most Cambodians were looking for ways to avoid conscription. Fifteen years had passed since the country had enjoyed peace and stability, and Cambodians were only just beginning to live normal lives with what was left of their families. Many had fought for the revolution or against it and were, by now, immune to ideological appeals. This particular conflict, in which Vietnamese occupiers were fighting a Khmer resistance headed by Sihanouk, seemed particularly pointless. (Among the more effective lines propagated by the resistance was the appeal for "Khmer not to fight Khmer.") Cambodians thus went to great lengths to avoid conscription, prompting the Council of Ministers to issue guidelines for punishing "anyone who is obstinate in avoiding their military duty; those who intentionally maim themselves, damage their health or damage the health of someone else, or flee overseas without permission in order to avoid their military duty; and those who use status and position to prevent citizens from fulfilling their duty to protect the motherland."[18]

Some of the leadership understood the effect that conscription was having on the PRK's popularity. According to Ung Phan, families who had received "certificates of sacrifice" (notices that their relatives had been conscripted) "don't know where they have been taken. They ask and the commune doesn't know, the district doesn't know, and the provincial office doesn't know. This results in protests. There are cries that our state authorities know when their husbands and children are alive, but when they die, no thought is given to that."[19]

AN AUTONOMOUS MILITARY

In fact, Phnom Penh had little control over local military authorities. The most aggressive defense minister, Pen Sovan, served only until mid-1981, when the Cambodian military was still a small appendage of the Vietnamese army. Subsequent ministers, Chan Si and Bou Thang, had received extensive training in Vietnam but did not have the capacity to command a military bureaucracy. Nor was Koy Buntha, a former Khmer Rouge soldier, particularly skilled in patronage. The line of command also undermined civilian control. As in Vietnam, the army bypassed the Council of Ministers and answered directly to the Party's Military Committee, which, in the PRK, was headed by the mostly ineffectual Heng Samrin.[20]

In the field Cambodian military units operated under the direct control of the Vietnamese command. Where Cambodian units operated independently, they guarded roads and bridges—in effect, acting as tax collectors for their commanding officers or local authorities. The military thus evolved into a lucrative patronage system that supported itself and propped up local civilian authorities. Once Cambodian field officers began accepting battlefield assignments from their Vietnamese counterparts, their autonomy vis-à-vis local civilians was unquestioned. In strategically important provinces like Battambang, military chiefs were appointed as Party secretaries. Elsewhere, local civilian authorities had little hope of controlling the activities of free-ranging military units moving easily from one jurisdiction to the next. Hun Sen explained the situation to the Council of Ministers: "The first reason that there is no control by state authorities is that it isn't a provincial military. Another reason is that the divisions of the army are not under the provinces, meaning that they go set themselves up in locations that no province can manage."[21]

With military autonomy came the pursuit of revenues, specifically the exploitation of natural resources. Cambodian soldiers, like their Vietnamese colleagues, engaged in fishing either independently or under the control of higher military authorities. "These days," Ung Phan told the Council of Ministers in 1985, "we have conferred to the army fishing areas in which the security situation is not assured for them to conduct business on a temporary basis, especially in the Tonle Sap." As soldiers fished, they sometimes turned to unorthodox fishing techniques, including grenades.[22]

In many parts of the country, local military authorities also controlled the timber business. Since 1983, the Ministry of Agriculture had been complaining of unauthorized timber commerce by a wide range of Cambodian military organizations, including units from Phnom Penh, the central armed forces bodyguard organization, the military's political branch, its technical finance school, and even the Army Arts Organization. Like fish, timber was available to the military wherever civilians could not get to it. As Ung Phan told the Council of Ministers in 1985, "There is timber in places where we cannot ensure security and timber whose surroundings pose problems for the conduct of business. Because of a lack of means of production, we should confer the authority to the army stationed there to manage and conduct business and to fight the enemy." In the coming years, when the leadership discussed the problem of deforestation, senior military figures defended the right of local military units to engage in the timber business. "If we prohibit [logging]," warned Defense Minister Koy Buntha, "there will be consequences; for example, if the army [unit] stationed in one place can't log at all, they will encounter difficulties."[23]

The autonomy enjoyed by local military units was most apparent in their capacity to smuggle goods and to extort money from merchants. "When the military smuggles, it smuggles big," acknowledged Chea Sim in July 1987. "Also, they have guns to protect them every time." The prevalence of military checkpoints also concerned the leadership. "The elimination of this problem requires correct disciplinary measures," insisted Heng Samrin. "We already have a law, but the law hasn't yet been fully implemented." Samrin then described the troubled relationship between the military and the local civilian authorities. "All these failures consistently rest with the army, but responsibility [should lie with] our local state authorities. These days, local state authorities are not so happy with our army because when we station soldiers and remove soldiers or do anything in their area, we don't tell them. We don't respect [the local state authorities], and we provoke them."[24]

Party leaders saw these issues from the perspective of their own revolutionary pasts. According to Heng Samrin, the military was more disciplined when it was fighting the Lon Nol regime. "During the period of fighting the Americans," recalled the former Khmer Rouge officer, "we really respected the local state authorities, and the army was afraid of the militias (*chhlop*), and militia units searched soldiers." Say Phouthang's point of reference was Vietnam. "When the [Vietnamese] army wants to station [troops] somewhere," he reminded his colleagues, "it must first ask permission from the state authority in that area. If the state authority does not permit them to be stationed, they don't dare go. If we act the way [we have so far], the people will hate us and they won't report the enemy's activities to us. So far, we've acted like this a lot."[25]

Whether Samrin's recollections of the early 1970s or Phouthang's description of Vietnam were accurate, the unflattering comparison to the PRK military reveals how powerless Cambodia's civilian leadership felt. It also suggests that whether field officers were bravely fighting the resistance, exploiting natural resources, or extorting money from the local population, they did not see the war as a revolution guided by the Party. If the PRK leadership was to maintain some control over local military officials, it would be through personal connections and mutually beneficial arrangements—patronage—rather than Party discipline.

THE WALL

The most unpopular aspect of the war, perhaps the single most resented policy of the PRK, was the conscription of Cambodians for a vast construction project along the Thai border. The program had begun gradually, in 1982 and 1983, when Vietnamese military authorities began constructing roads with which to consolidate newly acquired territory and barriers with which to hold off the resistance. In the summer of 1984, however, as the Vietnamese were planning their biggest offensive yet, the Politburo met to discuss the mobilization of several hundred thousand Cambodian civilians to chop down forests, construct more roads, and lay down hundreds of kilometers of earthen walls, two-and-a-half-meter-deep spiked ditches, barbed wire, and minefields. The idea was to build a Berlin Wall of sorts that would stretch along the Thai-Cambodian border and prevent resistance soldiers from infiltrating.

The planners of K5—which the program came to be called—envisioned somewhere between 146,000 and 381,000 Cambodians engaged in intense labor for upward of six months. Conscription, which was conducted by provincial state officials, military and police officers, and Vietnamese soldiers, began immediately. By the end of 1984 there were already 50,000 K5 workers at the border, a number that exceeded Phnom Penh's expectations. Even though there were only enough equipment, food, and provisions for 33,000 at a time, newly appointed K5 officials continued to request more conscripts on the logic that more men would speed up the work. At the end of 1985, Vietnamese officials estimated the total number of K5 workers for the year at 150,000, and still the program grew. In April 1986, at the end of another dry season offensive, Vietnamese advisors ordered the expansion of the program, explaining, "The enemy has infiltrated." The result was a personal windfall for some politicians and a heavy human cost for the Cambodian population.[26]

"The budgetary issue isn't important" in building the wall, explained Hun Sen to the Council of Ministers. "What's most important is the equipment, which we don't have in our hands and so must import from overseas." "Overseas" generally meant Moscow. Bulldozers, excavators, construction steel, petroleum products, logging trucks, dump trucks, dumpsters, and even textiles were all arriving from the Soviet Union, a contribution that, along with budgetary support, eventually totaled in value 13 million rubles (almost U.S.$18.5 million, according to official 1986 exchange rates). The Cambodian K5 budget, originally set at 100 million riels for the end of 1984 and all of 1985, was rapidly being adjusted upward. By the end of 1985, Vietnamese advisors were discussing a 300 million riel annual budget.[27]

These funds, along with the equipment, were channeled into an enormous distribution pyramid consisting of a Central K5 Committee and various interested ministries. The Ministry of Defense was responsible for distributing materials and equipment and overseeing road construction, the Ministry of Communications for transporting personnel and materials to the front, and the Ministry of Planning for K5 budgetary allocations. Following Chea Soth's departure from the Ministry of Planning, the ministry's K5 responsibilities fell to Deputy Minister Nheum Vanda.[28]

Whereas the new minister, Chea Chantho, represented the PRK's new corps of technocrats, Nheum Vanda offered a different vision of nonideological pragmatism. Born into a family of rubber plantation workers in Prey Veng, he joined the revolution in 1970 and changed his name—Nheum Huon—to his *nom de geurre*. Initially responsible for "educating" Lon Nol prisoners of war, Vanda—who lost his left arm somewhere along the way—eventually became, under Democratic Kampuchea, a militia chief and a district-level cadre. Under the PRK he was assigned to the Economics and Livelihood Ministry, despite an economic background that consisted entirely of a brief stint as chair of a Khmer

Rouge printing plant. He became chief of cabinet of the Ministry of Planning in 1980 and was promoted to deputy minister of planning in 1983.[29]

Former colleagues describe Vanda as a "realist" who was "less into theory than in doing things" and a skilled practitioner of patronage politics. Initially closer to Chea Sim, Vanda demonstrated a nonideological approach that appealed to Hun Sen. In late 1986 the Party appointed him chair of the Central K5 Committee, a position he held concurrently with that of deputy minister of planning. Later he served as deputy minister of defense for finance and supplies and minister of commerce.[30]

Nheum Vanda's oversight of K5 funds, equipment, and provisions coincided with widespread confusion, inefficiency, theft, and corruption. Deliveries of equipment and food were delayed or failed to arrive at all. Irritated by the chaos, Vietnamese advisors instructed the Cambodians to rely more on provincial contributions to the overall effort, and within a few years, Vanda was encouraging an overall decentralization of the entire K5 network. Provincial authorities gradually took over direct control of K5 infrastructure projects, raising their own revenues through logging and gem mining. As a result, K5 evolved into an enormous network of self-supporting economic ventures involving provincial authorities and branches of the Ministries of Defense, Communications, and Commerce.[31] As Vanda told the Council of Ministers in October 1988, "The provinces, municipalities, and ministries have really emerged in 1988 after the Party and state conferred duties for them to conduct [K5 activities] directly. They believe wholeheartedly and are very happy that we have clearly given them the work. Before, when it was still centralized, it was difficult for them to act. But since we conferred [duties] on them, they have worked well."[32]

The fate of K5 was similar to that of the state commercial network: decentralization and privatization. For officials who participated in the distribution of equipment and funds, K5 had the added benefit of a constant infusion of foreign capital. For the workers, however, K5—and, specifically, the effects of the corruption—was a disaster.

LIFE UNDER K5

Throughout the country, convoys of trucks transported K5 workers to the border. Dropped off wherever the roads ended, the conscripts walked for two or three days until they arrived at their worksite. Guarded by Vietnamese or Cambodian soldiers, they labored for eight to ten hours a day, cutting down trees, digging trenches, mining and de-mining, building roads, and transporting ammunition, equipment, and corpses. Twice a day they ate together, although there was rarely enough food.[33]

Conditions were deplorable, in large part because necessary goods disappeared on their way to the border. According to internal reports, food, clothing, shoes, medicine, and mosquito nets arrived late or not at all. One K5 worker, interviewed by a Western medical professional, described his arrival at the worksite in stark terms. "When we got there," he said, "thousands of workers had preceded us. We were maybe two thousand in number and we'd come from numerous provinces. There was no shelter, and it was useless to look to build oneself a hut, because we were moved every day. Some had hammocks, others nothing. They slept on the ground, on a piece of plastic or even on the dirt." These conditions and their effects on the K5 workforce were known to the leadership. In late 1985, Deputy Minister of Planning Ros Chhun (he also served as vice chair of the Central K5 Committee) reported that workers from Takeo were defecting en masse because of a lack of food. PRK leaders did not, however, acknowledge the similarities between K5 and life under Democratic Kampuchea. Another K5 worker, describing the wait for supplies, remarked on the parallels. "At the end of two weeks, nothing came," he said. "When new workers arrived, we were forced to share whatever was left with them. There was less and less to eat. A number of people died of starvation. It was like under Pol Pot."[34]

Malaria was the greatest danger faced by the K5 workers. Although it is rampant along the border, it is not common in other parts of Cambodia. As a consequence, most K5 workers, like the Cambodians whom the Khmer Rouge had deported to the west, had no immunity and were extremely vulnerable once exposed. Reports from the Central K5 Committee acknowledged that "high rates of malaria have seriously debilitated the workforce, and there are places where there have been deaths from malaria." Yet these reports strove for a level of optimism: "We know already that in some areas around the border, there is malaria and that this has an effect on the health of the workers, but in fact, there are some [military and K5] organizations working in dangerous areas whose workers and soldiers have remained healthy. In sum, even though there are difficult and complicated situations, if we have a careful policy of protecting and curing [the workers], we can in fact reduce illnesses."[35]

There were no antimalarial medicines, few doctors, and no hospitals. According to official estimates, only 30–40 percent of K5 workers slept under mosquito nets. The toll rose quickly. Six hundred and sixty workers from Kampot, whose mosquito nets had disappeared in transit, fell ill in 1985. In Battambang the figure was 995 workers; in Siem Reap, 440 workers. At the end of the year, a new strain appeared in Preah Vihear, quickly killing 100 people. In Phnom Penh, Ministry of Health officials were estimating the overall rate of malaria among K5 laborers at 80 percent.[36]

As infected workers made their way home, either in K5 trucks or under their own power, Western health professionals saw tens of thousands of cases of malaria. "Everywhere we went," reported one aid worker, "in the provinces and in the districts, 80–90 percent of the 'volunteers' returned sick. Mortality was extremely high, on the order of 5 to 10 percent. In Kandal, out of 12,000 workers, there were 9,000 cases of malaria and 700 deaths. In one district of Takeo, out of 1,000 participants, we counted 900 cases of malaria and 56 deaths. In a district of the province of Kampong Cham, 10 percent of the 'volunteers' succumbed to the illness." International humanitarian organizations, asked for medicine by the Ministry of Health, imported large amounts of quinine and tetracycline. There was still not nearly enough, and much of it was quickly diverted into private hands, appearing for sale in the markets. New hospitals were established in Phnom Penh, Kandal, Prey Veng, and Kampong Chhnang, but most patients relied on family members to bring them medicine.[37]

The Party leaders and their Vietnamese advisors were less than sympathetic. "It's true that there is a lot of malaria," Hun Sen acknowledged to the Council of Ministers at the end of 1985, "but it is easy to cure." "Dan Eung," a Vietnamese advisor to K5, doubted whether there really was so much malaria, concluding that the "enemy" was responsible for reports of an epidemic. "The hand of the enemy is mixed in with the workers. The activities of the enemy stir up and intimidate the workers, leading them to a consciousness that is not right. In fact, in similar areas there are [workers from] some provinces with little illness and [workers from other] provinces with a lot. The reason is the activities of the enemy in stirring up workers. In provinces where the enemy is stirring up the workers, there is a lot of illness. . . . I propose that the Council of Ministers permit the police of the Ministry of the Interior to go investigate the activities of the enemy among the workers."[38]

In fact, so many workers were suffering from malaria that provinces like Takeo, Kampong Cham, Prey Veng, Kampong Thom, and Battambang were reporting shortages of healthy men to produce rice. Agricultural production was suffering, yet still more K5 workers were being sent to the border. Eventually the regime made a few accommodations, permitting provinces to briefly delay further conscription.[39] As Hun Sen noted in late December 1985: "Takeo has 2,000 workers, of whom 1,700 are ill, so the [K5] Plan to send 600 more workers can't be implemented. If they send more workers, there will be an effect on the harvest. . . . So tell Takeo to permit the workers it still has to continue to work [in the rice fields] and not force them to go, and to wait until January 1986, when there will be a turnover."[40]

Overall, estimates of deaths from malaria run into the tens of thousands. If the mortality rate was a conservative 5 percent and if half a million Cambodians participated in K5 (some estimates are twice as high), then 25,000 died of malaria. One defector from the Ministry of Defense who arrived in Thailand reported that 30,000 K5 workers had died.[41]

The other great danger was landmines, which K5 workers both laid and removed, depending on whether they were constructing barriers or advancing on minefields laid by the resistance. De-mining is a complicated, delicate task, yet there was little technical instruction. Invariably, deaths and injuries occurred. Although the numbers are hard to calculate, the Centre d'Appareillage en Prosthèses in Phnom Penh reported receiving at least sixty new amputees a month, almost all from the border. There were certainly many more; most maimed K5 workers would not have known of the center or been able to get there.[42]

As a concentrated effort to wall Cambodia off from Thailand, K5 relied heavily on mines. By the end of the 1984–85 dry season, 464,000 antipersonnel mines had been planted along the border, with plans to lay another 1,618,400 the following year. The number of resistance soldiers operating inside Cambodia increased, however, suggesting that the resistance had found ways to avoid the minefields. Nonetheless, the authorities responsible for K5 considered their work a success in preventing infiltration. As one 1985 report reveals, they also viewed landmines as an effective way to demoralize the enemy. "There are many places where they've stepped on our mines, and this has destroyed their lives. In Region 1, eight hundred mines have exploded. There are places where the enemy has entered minefields and died. We discard the bodies, confiscate weapons, and take lots of prisoners. . . . In Region 4, north of Yeang Dangkum, more than five hundred enemies have died and a certain number have been wounded by mines. . . . In Region 3 there are many places where the enemy has stepped on our mines. . . . We can conclude that in the future, many more enemies will die or be wounded as a result of our barriers. The sound of exploding mines along the Cambodian-Thai border is still echoing in the ears and striking fear in the minds of our enemies and their leaders."[43]

THE POLITICS OF WAR

No one within the central government ever expressed dissatisfaction with K5. Vandy Ka-on says that he was warned that not even Party members were allowed to question the policy and claims that his own troubles with the regime began in 1987, when he opposed K5 conscription. Justice Minister Uk Bunch-heuan, the most outspoken member of the Council of Ministers, was equally reticent. "I didn't dare have an opinion about K5."[44]

Of all the things the Vietnamese were trying to accomplish in Cambodia, the conduct of the war was the least negotiable. Some Vietnamese policies were actually effective: by the time they withdrew from Cambodia in 1989, Vietnamese army officers had built a sizable Cambodian army capable of matching up to Khmer Rouge, KPNLF, and ANS forces. Others were failures: it would be hard to argue that K5 was worth the human cost. The irony is that conscription and K5, two policies intended to bring about the end of the Vietnamese occupation, were so unpopular. One reason is that Cambodians played no part in their formulation.

The long-term impact of the conflict is evident today. Minefields laid years ago continue to claim victims. The result: an estimated one in 240 Cambodians is disabled. In the provinces Cambodian military authorities enjoy the autonomy they achieved under the PRK, selling timber and other natural resources and extorting money from Cambodian civilians. The Misled Persons Movement, in particular the rewards offered to high-level defectors, also affects contemporary Cambodian politics. After the U.N.-supervised election, former PRK leaders and the royalist party of Norodom Rannaridh (Sihanouk's son) competed to lure Khmer Rouge soldiers into their respective militaries. In the end, Hun Sen had more to offer: money, rank, and the right to command one's own forces. This policy extended even to top Khmer Rouge leaders, including Ieng Sary, who, in 1996, was granted control over the area of Pailin in Battambang province. The legacy of the war can also be seen in the state's obsession with internal security, its continued violations of human rights, and its reluctance to accept a loyal opposition.

Chapter 11 Law, Human Rights, and the Case of the Yens

In June 1988, at a meeting of the Council of Ministers, Minister of Justice Uk Bunchheuan was engaged in a lengthy tirade on human rights abuses in the PRK when he blurted out an unusual threat. "I will resign from the Ministry of Justice. I cannot work any longer because there is no justice at all, and it is better to go back to working in the fields, in order not to have one's name involved in all this."[1]

Bunchheuan (who did not resign) was an unlikely figure to be espousing such views. As deputy secretary of Region 21 in the D.K.'s Eastern Zone, he was reported to have persecuted a number of Hanoi-trained cadres and to have been involved in as many as ten executions. Yet he somehow became the most liberal member of the Council of Ministers and a frequent proponent of human rights and the rule of law. Asked about this personal evolution, Bunchheuan offers little introspection. Instead, he talks as if one day he simply started looking at Cambodia differently. "I saw that our police and our interrogations were not good," he says. "We'd impose the death penalty and later we'd see that the person was innocent. Executions are permanent. But we'd just kill people and then they'd be gone."[2]

A LITANY OF ABUSES

Uk Bunchheuan was not alone. Inside the Council of Ministers, a set of anonymous bureaucrats drafted a report in 1985 that described human rights conditions in Cambodia. It is worth quoting at some length.

> Arbitrary searches, arrests, detentions, and imprisonments occur practically everywhere. Arrests, detentions, and imprisonments are getting more abusive. There are arrests without actual evidence, without a clear investigation, and without a file. Most arrests are followed by imprisonment based only on the report of a single person or merely on suspicion. Some minors under fourteen years of age are also being arrested and imprisoned. There are some cases of arrests in civil and family cases, such as the failure to implement contracts or family morality cases. Illegal arrests and imprisonment occur in all the provinces and cities, and in each province and city there are hundreds of people detained for months or years. The arresting and detaining organizations have no intention of sending [detainees] to the organizations responsible for prosecution. Adjudications don't occur, because there are no files and no evidence at all, and [yet] [detainees] are not released. . . .
>
> People arrested, detained, and imprisoned in political cases, as for ordinary criminal offenses, are commonly hit with sticks and tortured by interrogating organizations until they confess. . . .
>
> [Officials] abuse their power, frequently assaulting people over small matters. Recently in Phnom Penh a cadre drew a pistol at a merchant in his house simply because the merchant refused to sell him a case of beer. After they argued face to face, the cadre beat him, breaking his face and his mouth and sending him to the hospital. That didn't satisfy him; the cadre used his personal influence to get the Phnom Penh police to arrest the merchant in the hospital, where he was still receiving serum. He is still in detention. In Kampot the chief of the provincial military beat a commerce cadre from Chhouk district and injured one of his eyes because he didn't provide some goods on time. . . . In Kampong Chhnang a policeman used his own gun to shoot and kill a schoolteacher over a case involving the teaching of children. So far, the [arresting] organization has yet to send the file to the prosecutor and the court for prosecution and adjudication. In Kratie a district police cadre shot and killed someone merely on suspicion of having connections to the enemy, and another police cadre in the province shot and killed another person while arresting four people drinking beer. So far, the competent organizations have not yet produced any case on these two people. The two offenders remain at their jobs and at the same positions. . . .
>
> Many searches of homes occur without proper authorization or beyond the limits of what the law permits. And the confiscation of objects [is not limited to] the tools

of the offense or the fruits of the offense. There is also the confiscation of family property and the property of other people who are present. These confiscations occur without reports or with unclear reports, and these confiscated objects are kept inappropriately and not in accordance with the law. Some organizations have not yet collected the files and have them in all corners and dare to distribute these confiscated objects as restitution [for offenses] before the responsible organizations arrive at a decision.

The authors of the report arrived at two troubling conclusions: first, that "respect for legality" had decreased over the past few years; and, second, that education had not helped. "Abuses of law are almost entirely committed by state cadres who have studied the law once or twice already," read the report. "That is to say, the abuses are not committed as a result of a lack of understanding. They are committed intentionally for the purpose of winning more absolute power."[3]

JUSTICE

After a decade in power, Minister of the Interior Sin Song was looking back at a long and complex relationship with revolutionary justice. Born into a peasant family in Prey Veng province, he had joined the revolution in 1965. Under Democratic Kampuchea he served as an economic cadre and as a soldier and was eventually promoted to the position of regimental political commissar. Stationed in Region 24 in southern Prey Veng, along the Vietnamese border, Sin Song was among the first suspects in Pol Pot's purges of the Eastern Zone and was arrested in January 1977. After six months in detention, he escaped and fled to Vietnam. In 1979, Vietnamese officials assigned him to the Ministry of the Interior, promoting him to deputy minister in 1981. From 1985 to 1988 he served as minister of inspection before returning to the security apparatus as minister of the interior.[4]

Shortly after this latest transfer, Sin Song reflected on the early years of the PRK. "Our arresting and detaining organs had to be created first, before the organs for creating law, because immediately after liberation, the enemies created more than fifty movements and parties against our revolution. In February 1979 we established the first prison, T3. At that time, there were no jurists and no legal institutions, such as the Ministry of Justice, which was created later. In that initial period, in order to have a basis to convict the Pol Potists, I, who am not a jurist, had to take on the duty of drafting Decree-Law 2 in only one week to send to the [Kampuchean] People's Revolutionary Committee for a decision, and I had to be the one to explain the decree-law, too."[5]

Sin Song was not being modest. Decree-Law 2, which was Cambodia's only criminal code until 1993, was barely a legal document at all. Confusing and impenetrable, it served to reveal the fundamental tautology that underlay the PRK's criminal justice system: anyone guilty of "betraying the revolution" was "Pol Pot," and "Pol Pot" was anyone "betraying the revolution." Only subsequent circulars clarified that "betraying the revolution" meant any act deemed to be in opposition to the regime, its ideology, or its Vietnamese patrons.[6]

THE JURISTS

Sin Song's recollection was wrong on one count: there *were* jurists in June 1980, when he drafted Decree-Law 2. They were busy redrafting the constitution. There was also a Ministry of Justice, staffed in large part by the members of the Constitutional Drafting Secretariat, prerevolutionary jurists, and intellectuals like Chhour Leang Huot, Lueng Chhai, and, by September, Heng Chi. The ministry also employed untrained Cambodians and at least one former Khmer Rouge cadre, an Eastern Zone veteran with whom Uk Bunchheuan had negotiated with the Vietnamese. As Bunchheuan told the Party, this diverse mix created "solidarity" problems among "old and new cadres with different political and professional competence."[7]

The Ministry of Justice, like other PRK institutions, was supposed to be led by the Party. Uk Bunchheuan and the ministry's Vietnamese advisors established a Party core group in which Party members and core group members could discuss their own and each other's political stances, as well as their work with the "masses." Criticism was the primary language and Bunchheuan was among the critics. "Possessions that come from power can infuriate the masses," he reminded one department head who owned a motor scooter and drove a car. Bunchheuan himself was not criticized, although core group members made oblique references to the minister's more intimidating associates. "I ask Comrade [Bunchheuan] to help strengthen those directly around him to have a stronger revolutionary stance so that they don't speak carelessly and not to allow those close to Comrade [Bunchheuan] to frighten cadres in the ministry."[8]

Most of the jurists and other surviving intellectuals in the ministry avoided Party activities, associating political activity with unqualified opportunists.

(The exception was Chan Sok, a former banker, who confessed to the core group that "my political level is still weak because I used to be a technical person, but now I am trying hard to study the political principles of the Party.") The jurists' experience in drafting—and redrafting—the constitution also contributed to their resentment of the Party, as did the intensified indoctrination that followed the arrest and disappearance of Pen Sovan. The curriculum included socialist economics and politics, the Fifth VCP Congress, Vietnamese language classes, and lessons in what the Party called "the principle of analyzing and determining friends and enemies of the revolution in current Cambodian society."[9]

THE CONVERSION OF UK BUNCHHEUAN

Uk Bunchheuan developed a reputation as a political loner. His isolation was attributable in part to his desire to survive politically. Having initially rejected Vietnamese patronage, Bunchheuan was never going to be the most trusted of the Cambodian leaders. He was also associated with Mao Phok, the former Eastern Zone cadre whose activities in the rubber plantations of Kampong Cham were perceived by the leadership as outright rebellion. Bunchheuan kept a low profile, telling Party leaders in February 1981, " I haven't really communicated with other ministries or other persons, and I haven't really communicated with any friends, either." But his difficulties in building a Party presence within the Ministry of Justice and his apparent failure to communicate with the leadership occasioned some self-criticism. "I, Uk Bunchheuan, do not yet understand the new politics deeply because I am still influenced a lot by the old politics, and I am lazy in studying. I haven't yet established detailed procedures in my work, such as monthly, trimester, semester, yearly routines, etc. I haven't yet created a core group or increased the number of new cadres because of obstructionist views and not wanting to grow. My reports to the council have not been punctual, so I have fallen into anarchy. I have been detached from solidarity because I have not gone to ask the opinion at higher levels [in the Party]."[10]

Bunchheuan also promised the Party leadership that he would track down "enemies" and offered a self-criticism in which he confessed to "protecting" the ministry staff. "There are some young men and women who are spreading the words of the enemy, disseminating them in the ministry, and yet I have no system for preventing this in time."[11]

Like other ministers, Uk Bunchheuan received the counsel of Vietnamese advisors, two men whom he and the other ministry personnel considered useful or at least friendly and inoffensive. The first, Nguyen Dam, was the former deputy chief justice of the People's Supreme Court of Vietnam. Despite having written such tracts as "Motivating the Masses to Participate in Party Building," Dam was neither overly rigid nor heavyhanded. The second advisor, Pham Vong Chi, was an elderly jurist who had been educated during the French colonial period. There were no permanent European advisors at the ministry.[12]

According to Uk Bunchheuan and the ministry's staff, it was the surviving Cambodian jurists—Chhour Leang Huot, Lueng Chhai, Uk Sary, and Heng Chi—who provided Bunchheuan with a personal legal education and who fed him documents, which he is said to have studied extensively. Bunchheuan also learned on the job, delegating to jurists like Uk Sary the right to chair meetings on important pieces of legislation and allowing Sary, Lueng Chhai, and Heng Chi to contradict both him and the Party leadership, at least on relatively abstract legal issues. Frequently convinced by their arguments, Bunchheuan championed their positions with the leadership. "I defended the Ministry of Justice against the other ministries," he says now with a sense of pride. His staff agree, recalling that Bunchheuan insulated them from outside pressure while nurturing internal debate.[13]

THE LAW AND THE COURTS

One of the first tasks of the Ministry of Justice was to organize the School of Cadres, Administration, and Legislation. The training ground for future judges, prosecutors, and clerks as well as hundreds of state officials and police, the school maintained a highly ideological curriculum designed by Vietnamese advisors. Still, the promotion by the regime of legal education was an improvement over the lawlessness of recent years. The venue, the old Faculté de Droit and its small library of Sihanouk-era legal documents, also invoked a prerevolutionary past, as did the Party's choice for managing director: the former judge Lueng Chhai. There were a number of obstacles, including a refusal by provincial officials to send cadres to Phnom Penh and a lack of texts and food, which required a certain amount of pleading from Chhai. Nonetheless, in June 1982 the school opened. Say Phouthang, Chea Soth, and Hun Sen gave speeches, as did Uk Bunchheuan. But as Bunchheuan points out now, he was also a student.[14]

By the time the Ministry of Justice assumed a central role in drafting legislation, the PRK's criminal law was already in place. With little chance of softening the regime's approach to political crimes, the ministry hoped at least to begin defining common criminal offenses as something other than "betraying the revolution." Concluding, in late 1982, that "Decree-Law 2 doesn't yet answer the needs of the current situation with regard to the struggle against crime," the Ministry of Justice began working on a four-hundred-article criminal code. (The draft, which was never entirely completed, had no support among the leadership and never left the ministry.) In the meantime, Uk Bunchheuan and other ministry officials complained frequently and specifically about the lack of substantive criminal law concerning violations of public order, theft of state property, rape, and prostitution, as well as the absence of any distinction between felonies and misdemeanors.[15]

The ministry had high hopes for the justice system. An undated thirty-five-page document entitled "Policy on the Establishment and Role of the Ministry of Justice" ambitiously included courts down to the district level, a Supreme Court whose appellate jurisdiction included a Supreme Military Court, a role for the Ministry of Justice in keeping birth, death, and marriage records, a provincial "justice system" to help reconcile small cases or bring them to court, and even private lawyers. To the chagrin of ministry personnel, however, the PRK's immediate plans included none of these goals. Instead, the regime set up a single court, in Phnom Penh, whose purpose was to conduct show trials of suspected resistance members. The Party did not invite the participation of Ministry of Justice personnel. As Ung Phan explained to the National Assembly in February 1982, "So far, we have just opened the court in Phnom Penh, which is the apparatus [of the Party] and is placed right near the [offices of the] Central Party. The opening of courts in the provinces is a complicated problem, and we don't have the capacity to do it." A year later, there were still no functioning courts outside the capital.[16]

Provincial judges and prosecutors were selected by local authorities and approved, first by the Ministry of Justice and then by the Party Central Organization Committee. Most were schoolteachers and other literate Cambodians with no connections to previous regimes. As Bunchheuan acknowledged to the Council of State, "The judges and prosecutors are practically all cadres who are newly appointed and are not yet skilled in socialist law and socialist procedure." The appointment process faced serious delays, for many of the educated people in Cambodia were already working for ministries or ministerial offices that were unwilling to authorize their transfer to the court system. Even after they were nominated, the Party was slow to approve them.[17]

Beginning in late 1980, to compensate for the lack of courts, Ministry of Justice personnel, including Lueng Chhai and Chhour Leang Huot, began interviewing crime victims and reporting the cases to provincial state authorities. They also tried to follow up on appeals from Cambodians whose family members had been arrested, and authorized newly appointed judges and prosecutors, whose courts were not yet functioning, to do the same.[18] A 1982 Ministry of Justice report was extremely discouraging. "When the people make an appeal to the [judges and prosecutors] or appeal to the Ministry of Justice, suddenly there are complaints from the local [authorities] that the people have 'thrown a fishing line across the mountain' [violated the chain of command], and [the local authorities] create conflict with the people making the appeals. When the Ministry of Justice receives appeals from the people, we note the responses of the victims [to our questions] and send them to the locality for examination and resolution in accordance with the competence [of the local authority]. Right away, there are complaints that the Ministry of Justice is interfering in the duties of the locality."[19]

These complaints offered a hint of the conflicts to come. For as the courts began to function, two separate conversations emerged: a relatively smooth discussion concerning internal procedure within the justice system and a rancorous dispute over the authority of the courts vis-à-vis other state institutions.

Within the justice system, Uk Bunchheuan intended to maintain a firm hand. The Ministry of Justice would act, in some respects, as an appeals court, examining verdicts and making recommendations to the Council of State either for a retrial or, in the case of the death penalty, for clemency. Defendants would not be permitted to make direct appeals, however, but would have to wait for the ministry to review their cases. Unlike the ministry's jurists, Uk Bunchheuan felt that the right of citizens to appeal was potentially dangerous. "The actual situation in our country," Bunchheuan told the National Assembly's Legislation Commission, "does not favor an overly broad distribution of rights. Otherwise, the enemy will force its way in and cause us difficulties in [our attempts to] defend and ensure security and social order."[20]

On matters of trial procedure, Bunchheuan deferred to the jurists. To a considerable extent, so did the Party leadership. When the Council of Ministers met in February 1983 to discuss the Decree-Law Concerning Trial Procedures in Criminal Cases, Chem Snguon, a former Sihanouk diplomat who had been appointed deputy minister of justice, and Heng Chi, now deputy director of the ministry's Criminal and Civil Department, explained such concepts as the role of criminal defenders, the presentation of evidence, and the invalidity of improperly conducted trials. Their most convincing argument, however, was one they had been making in their reports for a year—that "capitalist countries" were "looking for faults in our drafting and implementation of law." From the perspective of the regime, internationally isolated as it was, redrafting procedural laws to accommodate external critics made sense. Referring to a provision that implied a minimum twenty-year sentence for all accused, Hun Sen warned, "If we say it like this, when we disseminate this decree-law, foreign newspapers, especially Western newspapers, might judge us [negatively]. Also, [this provision suggests that] we have sentenced them before adjudication. To ensure political [security] and the rights of the accused, we should amend [this article]." Pham Van Kath, the Vietnamese advisor to the Council of Ministers, agreed. "If we decide [on a sentence] beforehand, it's as though we are violating human rights, and it is against international law."[21]

These two remarkable statements, by the PRK's future prime minister and one of its most influential advisors, reveal an awareness of human rights issues that observers outside Cambodia could not have divined. They also show that human rights were, for the leadership, a public relations problem to be considered whenever there were likely to be diplomatic consequences. In this respect, the leadership differed from Uk Bunchheuan, for whom the rule of law was becoming something of a guiding principle.

That Hun Sen and Pham Van Kath had conceded on matters of trial procedure was irrelevant so long as there were no trials. As Uk Bunchheuan reminded the Party leadership in April 1983, "We can only hold trials if the police first send people [to court]. The problem is that there are a lot of arrests but no documentation or files. I ask the Council of Ministers to immediately issue a circular concerning this problem and to communicate directly with the Ministry of the Interior." Prime Minister Chan Si responded, "I promise to take this up directly with the Ministry of the Interior."[22]

But Bunchheuan and the Ministry of the Interior were already far apart. In National Assembly discussions in 1982, Bunchheuan had attempted to insert, into the Law Establishing the Courts and Prosecutors, provisions that prohibited detention for more than twenty-four hours and that allowed prosecutors to conduct investigations and visit detainees in prison. These proposals prompted an unusually personal response from Deputy Minister of the Interior Sin Song. "If we follow these views of Comrade Minister of Justice, if we implement the law in this form, all the police who have detained accused people up to now will have committed an offense. The enemy could be released or criminals could mistakenly be released from detention." The Assembly agreed and rejected Bunchheuan's provisions. Increasingly frustrated with the security apparatus,

Bunchheuan told the Council of Ministers that "people who have been arrested illegally should be compensated for mental suffering."[23]

"TYING THE HANDS AND FEET OF THE POLICE"

Meanwhile, cadres in the Ministry of Justice were drafting a law that would impose rules and duties on the police. When, in the spring of 1985, the draft arrived at the Council of Ministers, Bunchheuan and Sin Song resumed their dispute. Although the Ministry of Justice had invited the deputy minister of the interior to participate in the drafting, Sin Song had not taken the process seriously, as he readily acknowledged to the council. "There was a five-day drafting meeting at the Ministry of Justice, but sometimes I didn't participate. And, with regard to some sections [of the draft law], there were long negotiations. I participated and signed my name, and so, in fact, I am responsible for the agreement. But the issues on which I am appealing arise from those sections where I did not participate but signed only to accelerate its being sent to the Council of Ministers. I signed my name as deputy minister, not as a representative of the ministry, and with the understanding that there would be further discussions at the Council of Ministers."[24]

At a subsequent meeting, Sin Song complained that the discussions were stacked against the Ministry of the Interior. "So far, there have been meetings at the Ministry of Justice at which there were many people from the Ministry of Justice but only one or two from the Ministry of the Interior," he noted. "There was no balance, so decisions did not represent an [actual] agreement [between the two ministries]. So, in the future, I propose that there be equal numbers of people participating. There should also be [Vietnamese] advisors from both sides." Minister of the Interior Khang Sarin supported his deputy. "So far, in discussions [with the Ministry of Justice], only Comrade Sin Song, all alone, was there from the Ministry of the Interior, and he couldn't outnegotiate them."[25]

Despite meetings between Vietnamese advisors from both ministries, disagreements persisted. Khang Sarin figured it would be easier to negotiate directly with Uk Bunchheuan, minister to minister, revolutionary to revolutionary, than to deal with French-educated intellectuals. Bunchheuan, however, was not interested in undermining his staff. Sarin later complained, "I have invited Comrade Uk Bunchheuan two times to come have a discussion, but he says he's busy." Insisting that the Ministry of Justice "completely ties the hands and feet of the police," Sarin then asked the Council of Ministers to act as an arbiter between the two ministries.[26]

The arbiter was Prime Minister Hun Sen, who, in reviewing the work of the Ministry of Justice, discovered a draft with which he had fundamental disagreements of principle. One provision in particular, requiring police to gain permission from a homeowner before conducting a search, prompted a general rebuke. "As for searches of homes, I don't know what law the Ministry of Justice relied on," he said. "In the socialist countries that I have visited, they have shown me how their police can arrest [people] or enter and search houses. . . . The Ministry of Justice has drafted this decree-law based on the situation of a country at peace, not in accordance with the current situation of our country."[27]

Hun Sen faced a dilemma. Because he agreed with the views of the Ministry of the Interior, he had invited the ministry to draft its own version of the law. Yet the Ministry of the Interior had no one who could produce a coherent legal document. As Hun Sen complained, "In general, the drafting system of the Ministry of Justice is appropriate according to law, but some of the substance is not in accordance with the current situation. On the other hand, the draft of the Ministry of the Interior has some substance that is appropriate, but the drafting does not yet follow correct legal form." Within the year Hun Sen resolved this problem by creating an office within the Council of Ministers that was responsible for drafting laws. In the meantime, he expected concessions from the Ministry of Justice.[28]

The Ministry of the Interior was ready to submit the dispute to the Politburo, where it was confident it would prevail. As Sin Song reminded the Council of Ministers, "The Politburo also sees that this law restricts [the police]. I know that the Politburo has conferred [the task of reviewing the draft] to Comrade Chea Sim, so when there is a subsequent meeting with the Ministry of Justice, we can invite him to be chair for a day or half a day."[29]

One by one, the disagreements between the Ministries of Justice and the Interior got resolved. The first dispute involved the Ministry of the Interior's preference—supported by the ministry's Vietnamese advisors—to report arrests to provincial Party committees rather than to local state authorities. The problem disappeared once the advisors realized that the provincial governors generally served as deputy Party chiefs anyway. The second issue arose from the Ministry of Justice's attempts to prohibit nighttime arrests and was resolved by making exceptions in cases of flagrant crimes, "a cry for help from within," or "exceptionally serious and emergency circumstances affecting national security." Another disagreement involved the Ministry of Justice's attempts to prohibit police from arresting minors, a restriction that was removed from the draft. Finally, the provision that had annoyed Hun Sen, the requirement that police seek permission of homeowners before conducting a search, was taken out.[30]

Although Uk Bunchheuan generally supported the liberal inclinations of the Ministry of Justice personnel, his own Khmer Rouge background had not been entirely repressed, as was apparent in discussions on torture. The Ministry of Justice's cadres had inserted a blanket prohibition on physical abuse and had even received the support of a Vietnamese advisor from the Ministry of the Interior. "My understanding is that 'Violation of any person shall be prohibited' is a general phrase related to torture," said the advisor. "Prohibiting [torture] during arrests is appropriate and according to law, and torture during police detention should [likewise] be prohibited. During detention and interrogation, there should be no hitting." He proposed that the provision be redrafted to read, "It is absolutely prohibited to torture during arrest, detention, or temporary imprisonment and interrogation." Bunchheuan, however, was apparently concerned that this prohibition was too broad. "The word 'torture' has a lot of meanings, from hitting with a stick to depriving of food."[31]

Having conceded the point at the Council of Ministers, Bunchheuan raised his concerns once more at the Council of State. "This issue of interrogation procedures is a secret. It is an internal issue of the investigative institutions and can't be included in a decree-law." On this issue, Uk Bunchheuan found himself less inclined to protect detainees than was Heng Samrin. "Interrogate however you want," said Samrin, "but don't permit hitting, don't permit harming the body and torturing it." Bunchheuan was not backing down. "The word 'torture' is extremely broad, and includes depriving of food, hitting," he repeated. Heng Samrin concluded the discussion by reiterating his position: "During arrests, if there is a struggle, [the police] must hit first, but after [the offender] is restrained, there should be absolutely no harm done."[32]

One debate that both highlighted the chaos of law enforcement in the PRK and brought out fundamental philosophical and ideological differences centered on whether civilians would be permitted to arrest and search each other. "If we grant the right to search, I'm afraid there will be problems," said Bunchheuan. "I'm afraid of problems related to the management of [confiscated] objects. Also, if there are enemy networks, they'll search people and take everything." Later, at the Council of State, Bunchheuan received the support of Chan Ven, who also warned of "criminal networks" using the right to search in order to steal from citizens, and Vandy Ka-on, who stressed the role of the police. Failing to authorize citizens to search each other, noted Ka-on dryly, "won't create further catastrophe for society."[33]

Uk Bunchheuan, Chan Ven, and Vandy Ka-on were up against a basic revolutionary principle: what Deputy Chief of Staff Chay Sang Yaun had referred to back in 1982 as "the movement . . . to get each person to become a soldier and a policeman." In Vietnam and in Democratic Kampuchea (where peasants were encouraged to repress the new people and expose their offenses against *angkar*), the revolutionary duties of citizens included informal police work. Argued Deputy Defense Minister Meas Krauch, "We are granting broad rights to the people to search [each other] in order to expand the mastery (*set tvoe mchas*) of the people." The disagreement was stark. While Bunchheuan argued that "the people are not actually the state authority," more ideological leaders like Heng Samrin insisted that Cambodian citizens *become* the state authority. "In general, the people do not dare to arrest [other citizens]," bemoaned Samrin, "because we have established state authority everywhere, meaning village councils, police, and military officers. Only if [citizens] dare to arrest will they join with these forces."[34]

Although the decree-law limited detention without trial to twelve months, it was understood that, in political cases, this period could be extended. "This provision relates to the issue of law and politics," Hun Sen reminded the Council of Ministers. "In some cases, when we imprison people we can't take them out [of detention] and sentence them. Such was the case of Ros Samay and Mao Phok." From the perspective of Hun Sen and the other leaders, the courts could never be entirely trusted. "If [people] can't be tried, then they can't be set free."[35]

In practice, extended detention, when not a matter of simple neglect and indifference, was determined by the Ministries of the Interior and Defense and their Party patrons. In drafting the law, however, the leadership was required to identify some other authority. (Communist legal tradition required at least nominal civilian oversight of the arresting authorities and precluded direct references to the Party.) In late August 1985 the Politburo, at the urging of Hun Sen, decided that the Council of Ministers would be authorized to extend the detention of political prisoners. Two months later, however, when the draft arrived at the Council of State and the Legislation Commission of the National Assembly, a major debate emerged. The arguments reflected both principled differences and an internal power struggle.[36]

According to Vandy Ka-on and Deputy Justice Minister Chem Snguon, authority should rest with the general procurator of the new and as-yet-idle Supreme Court. Snguon, who cited Soviet, East German, Hungarian, and Vietnamese precedent to bolster his argument, also raised the issue of the international human rights groups. In addition to low-level activities by Amnesty International, the Lawyers Committee for Human Rights had recently issued a report charging Vietnamese and PRK officials with undocumented arrests and torture. Employing the regime's communist rhetoric and echoing its defiant stance toward the West, the former diplomat argued that the regime should consider the influence of the two organizations. Confusing Amnesty International and the Lawyers Committee, Snguon said, "Recently, Amnesty International, which is an association of jurists, has achieved a level of influence over the international stage. . . . The association of capitalist jurists has written a letter to the Minister of Justice, using my name directly as deputy minister of justice, to Comrade Chan Ven as secretary-general of the Council of State, and to Comrade Vandy Ka-on and Comrade Sin Song as chair and secretary of the Legislation Commission of the National Assembly. [The letters ask us] to conduct research into a broad set of issues related to the drafting of [this law]. So the reactionaries are following extremely closely everything that we do that relates to the rights and freedoms of citizens. If we draft a law that has any omissions, they will use those provisions to immediately attack us on the international stage. . . . [Granting authority to the general procurator will mean that] the organization of reactionary jurists can't attack us."[37]

A few weeks later, at a meeting of the Council of State, Uk Bunchheuan took up the issue, characterizing the investment of detention power in Hun Sen's Council of Ministers as "unconstitutional" and "illegal." He also sought to reassure Heng Samrin and Say Phouthang that granting authority to the general procurator was tantamount to giving it to the Council of State, which had direct oversight over the judiciary.[38]

Bunchheuan may have been playing on Samrin and Phouthang's increasing suspicions that Hun Sen had gotten away with something. Just two weeks before, Hun Sen and Chea Sim had taken control of the Fifth Party Congress and had removed or demoted many of the Hanoi veterans, including Phouthang himself. Perhaps as a result of these developments, a number of officials were beginning to see the authority of the Council of Ministers in a different light. Minister of the Interior Khang Sarin, a Hanoi veteran, was about to be removed from the ministry and appointed president of the nonfunctioning Supreme Court. Having previously supported Hun Sen on the issue, Sarin now concluded that conferring authority to extend detention to the Council of Ministers was "not appropriate." Heng Samrin also considered the Council of Ministers the wrong institution in which to vest this power. With the support of the Vietnamese advisor to the Council of State, Vuong Dinh Chau, Samrin ended up agreeing with Uk Bunchheuan. "In order not to violate the constitution and not to relinquish the rights of the general procurator, I see that the general procurator should have responsibility for this area. But decisions should be sent to the Council of State because the Council of State decides collectively, and these decisions ensure the rights of the citizens better."[39]

Samrin, Say Phouthang, and the Council of State decided to send the question once again to the Politburo. The papers arrived at Party headquarters in the middle of November 1985 and included a constitutional analysis by Chan Ven. According to Ven's report, the Council of Ministers included the two institutions responsible for detentions—the Ministries of the Interior and Defense—and for the same body that detained people to then decide on whether to extend those detentions indefinitely was unconstitutional.[40]

Where Chan Ven saw constitutional problems, Hun Sen saw political advantage. Any law that vested authority in the executive branch, rather than the prosecutors or the Council of State, would have the support of the Ministry of the Interior. By protecting the power of the security forces against encroachment from rival branches of government, Hun Sen gained powerful allies. He also found common cause with Chea Sim, who was still the most important patron of the security apparatus. On the other side of this political fight were Heng Samrin and Say Phouthang, who were hoping to salvage some authority by empowering the Council of State, an impotent legislative body to which they happened to belong. The contest was lopsided. At the end of December 1985, the secretary of the Central Committee Cabinet, Sar Kheng (Chea Sim's brother-in-law), signed a letter announcing the Politburo's decision: authority to extend detentions would be vested in the Council of Ministers.[41]

The Ministry of Justice did win on one fundamental principle: the police were now required to send cases to the prosecutors. The debate had not gone smoothly, and it was not clear to what extent the Ministry of the Interior had agreed to be bound by the law. As Sin Song pointed out to the Council of Ministers, "The [Vietnamese] advisor from my ministry has clarified this issue. In cases where there is evidence for arrest, a report to the prosecutor should be sent. In political cases with no evidence, there will be no report. Only after the investigation will an investigative report be sent to the prosecutor." Besides, he said, this requirement went against the interrogation techniques used by the Ministry of the Interior. "We arrest offenders, at which point we hold them and arrest others to come answer everything, and only then can we send [the case on to the prosecutor]." In political cases—which, from the point of view of the Ministry of the Interior, was just about every case—it was especially important for the police to control the process. "In political cases," explained Sin Song, "a report cannot be sent until the investigation is completed, and we can't determine how long that will take. If we implement [procedures] in accordance with the [views of the] Ministry of Justice, all the police will end up in jail because they haven't [completed reports] in time."[42]

Sin Song's protests reflected how he and his colleagues saw their work. Suspects were to be detained with or without evidence, indefinitely or until other suspects implicated them. Nonetheless, the law promulgated in March 1986 and known as Decree-Law 27, Concerning Arrests, Holding in Custody, Temporary Detention, Release, and Search of Domicile, Possessions, and the Person, required the police to submit files to the prosecutors fifteen days "after the questioning of the offender."

VIOLATING THE LAW

The Ministry of Justice did not expect to participate in political cases but hoped instead that common, nonpolitical criminal cases would be sent to the courts. There was, however, an opposing viewpoint: that *all* crimes were inherently political, that to engage in any activity considered antisocial by the Party was to "betray the revolution." This attitude, engraved in Decree-Law 2—the only substantive criminal law on the books—persisted in the minds of most of the leadership. As Hun Sen told a visiting delegation from the East German Ministry of Justice in early 1986, criminal offenses "arise from the schemes of the enemy. . . . Up to now, we have followed criminal offenses closely. At first we thought that they were ordinary offenses. But later we concluded that criminal and other offenses arise from the schemes of the enemy. They create conditions for armed robbery everywhere, which can then be exploited by the imperialists, such as the Pol Potists. So we see that countries at peace have less complicated criminal situations. As long as Cambodia still has both war and peace, there will be a lot more crime. With regard to this issue, we understand that you will truly and certainly understand Cambodia because Germany has experienced conflict with capitalist countries."[43]

The war took precedence over the judicial process. Just as Hun Sen had characterized all criminals as "enemies," so, too, could all criminals be redeemed through loyalty to the regime. The Misled Persons Movement not only granted

amnesty to those engaged in violent opposition but offered the greatest rewards
to the most powerful among them. The movement thus created confusion as
police and provincial authorities ordered arrests of defectors who were under
the protection of military authorities.[44]

The regime also placed a number of Cambodians under the direct control of
the Ministries of Defense and the Interior. According to an August 1987 subdecree, these were unreformed "criminals, professional robbers, thieves and mur-
derers," and "people who had participated in traitorous activities against the
revolution that are not yet at the level necessary for arrest and detention but
who are considered a potential danger to national security, order, and the security of society." The Council of Ministers authorized the ministries to relocate
these "elements" away from Phnom Penh and bordering communes, provincial
capitals, and "important places having a direct relationship with battles with
the enemy." Like provisions in the Vietnamese penal code, the subdecree created a quasi-legal form of internal exile that further blurred the distinctions between the judicial process and martial law.[45]

A wide variety of Cambodian officials and institutions interfered in the judicial system. Provincial state officials controlled the courts, managing their budgets, determining when prosecutors could investigate, appointing judges, and
preventing the Ministry of Justice from removing judges loyal to local authorities. Military officers, who were legally authorized to make arrests, failed to document their reasons and obstructed efforts by civilian authorities to secure releases. In battleground provinces, such as Siem Riep, they ignored orders to
release prisoners from even the highest Party representatives. Finally, the Party
itself actively manipulated the judicial process, ordering arrests and issuing "secret policies" on the proceedings and verdicts of trials. As Uk Bunchheuan complained, "Sentencing depends on the influence of the person offering an opinion, not on the law." Party intervention even annoyed Minister of the Interior
Ne Penna, who charged the provincial Party secretaries with "sticking their
hands in and ordering the arrests of people . . . in violation of Decree-Law 27."[46]

The Ministry of the Interior, which systematically failed to turn cases over to
the courts, was most responsible for violations of the decree-law. The vast majority of Cambodians who had been arrested prior to the passage of the law
(many of whom had been detained since 1979 or 1980) continued to languish in
prison. Detainees were released at the whim of the ministry, not as a result of
acquittals. According to a Ministry of the Interior report, between 1983 and
1985 the Phnom Penh police arrested 532 "betrayers of the revolution," 3,203
people engaged in undefined "criminal cases," 1,377 people accused of "theft,

rape, gambling, etc.," and 1,842 people who had allegedly engaged in "social of-fenses from the old regime, such as drugs, prostitution, etc.," or "activities that have a strong effect on the youth, such as pornographic videos." During this period the police submitted a mere 23 cases to the courts. At the end of 1987, fewer than 6 percent of detainees had seen a courthouse.[47]

In 1988 the general procurator of the Supreme Court issued a report describ-ing lengthy detentions, arbitrary confiscations of property, and a wholesale in-difference to the justice system. "Most provinces and municipalities," wrote Chan Min, a former deputy minister of education, "don't allow state prosecu-tors to offer an opinion when deciding to place someone in temporary deten-tion or extending temporary detention, and the police don't report to the state prosecutors after arresting an offender. In Phnom Penh every order from the state prosecutor to release someone who has been arrested elicits a protest from the organization responsible for implementing the order."[48]

Uk Bunchheuan was the harshest and most frequent critic of the govern-ment's failure to implement the law. "Violations of Decree-Law 27 continue despite its dissemination. Local officials are called to study in the School of Law [in Phnom Penh] and then return to commit further abuses. How can we say this results from [the law] being too new? . . . It's not true that it results from [the law] being new; it results from doing or not doing [what the law pre-scribes]." Bunchheuan was pushing for an end to impunity. "We should im-pose some punishment on people who hold power and have violated the law. Now, we take the rights of the citizens and the lives of the citizens as pieces in a game for us all to play. We want to arrest people and do whatever we want to them. If we want to release them, we can. If not, we can."[49]

Uk Bunchheuan also attempted to invoke the international human rights organizations. In August 1987, two months after Amnesty International issued a report that the PRK's official news agency called "groundless," Bunchheuan acknowledged that the organization had a point. "So far, Amnesty Interna-tional has asked the Ministry of Justice to respond with regard to the imple-mentation of law in Cambodia, but Comrade Hun Sen says it is not necessary to respond. . . . Afterward, they asked Hun Sen if they could come and investi-gate human rights in Cambodia, and we didn't respond. We are not actually startled by [the issues] raised by this organization, but in our role as leaders of the state, we should also think seriously about these cases. . . . Amnesty Inter-national has 300,000 members in all countries, and they know everything, and every year they have a summary report on the whole world."[50]

At one level, this debate over human rights and the rule of law was about principle. Another constant theme, however, was institutional rivalry, or what Uk Bunchheuan described as "competition between the Ministry of Justice and ministries and institutions that have the authority to arrest and detain." Just as Bunchheuan, in the midst of ethical appeals and references to international human rights organizations, defended the interests of his own bureaucracy, so, too, did successive ministers of the interior.[51]

The perspectives of these officials changed, however, depending on whether they were in or out of the ministry. Former Minister of the Interior Khang Sarin, who once protested against "tying the hands and feet of the police," complained of warrantless and undocumented arrests after he was appointed to the Supreme Court. Even more astonishing was the apparent conversion of Sin Song. The former deputy minister of the interior had been reassigned, in 1985, to the Ministry of Inspection and was, for several years, an outsider. During that time, he frequently agreed with Uk Bunchheuan's assessment of legality in Cambodia, reporting to the Council of Ministers that "people used to have a lot of faith in the state authority, but now this faith has completely dwindled away because of some state authorities and ministries that, in arresting and detaining people, have frequently violated the law. The people are disappointed, and they complain. Most of their complaints are not really inaccurate, because our state authority is truly abusive." Citing cases of indefinite detention for civil offenses and misdemeanors, Sin Song said, "We have yet to firmly accuse a single violator of [Decree-Law 27]. For this reason, the people are not happy." Sin Song even began comparing the PRK's human rights record to that of the Khmer Rouge, telling the Council of Ministers that a "recent case of real torture reported in Kratie is not much different from that which occurred in Tuol Sleng prison during the Pol Pot period."[52]

For Sin Song, the former Khmer Rouge soldier and hard-line security cadre, to suddenly begin complaining about human rights abuses suggests that neither personal experience nor "cultural" disposition necessarily precluded Cambodian leaders from promoting a just society. Rather, Song's temporary conversion (his perspective changed again once he returned to the Ministry of the Interior) reveals the extent to which personal interests and political calculations dictated the terms of the debate. Ordinary Cambodians, of course, had no knowledge of the perspectives of individual ministers. Yet those caught up in the PRK's confusing, abusive criminal justice system were at the mercy of fierce institutional rivalries. Such was the case of the Yens, whose relatively minor infractions set off a yearlong debate within the leadership that culminated in a special screening of pornographic videos for the Politburo.

THE CASE OF THE YENS

At the end of October 1985, twenty-eight-year-old Yen Sok Ieng, a resident of Phnom Penh, attempted to launch a business. Purchasing two videos, one violent (later described by Ministry of Justice reports as involving "fighting between private companies") and one romantic ("free kind of love"), he rented a VCR and opened shop, charging fifteen riels a viewer. A few days later, Yen Sok Ieng decided to expand, renting a pornographic ("piglet") video from one Sok Bun for fifty riels and employing his younger brother, twenty-year-old Yen Sok Huot, to collect what was now a thirty-riel admission fee. He was quickly shut down. On November 4 the municipal police seized the videos and arrested the Yens. Sok Bun was picked up the next day.[53]

It seemed a normal case of police discretion. Since 1979 security forces had enjoyed broad authority to seize materials they deemed "reactionary," whether they contained resistance propaganda, pictures of prerevolutionary Cambodia, nonrevolutionary love stories, or pornography. In the spring of 1984, however, the leadership had become alarmed at the increase in videos circulating through the capital and authorized a crackdown. By the end of 1985 the police had confiscated 167 videos with "pornographic stories or stories from the old society," all under the authority granted to them by Decree-Law 2, Against Betraying the Revolution and Other Crimes. That purveyors like the Yens were merely trying to make money was irrelevant to the police. According to the Ministry of the Interior, the brothers had a "commercial network" that "secretly rented and showed videocassettes the content of which was in accordance with the substance of the psychological warfare of the enemy."[54]

The story of how the Yens and their videos became the subject of intense debate at the highest levels of the Party and the state begins on New Year's Day, 1986, when the police made an unusual decision: they delivered the Yen file to the Phnom Penh state prosecutor. Soon the case was out of their hands. After the prosecutor interrogated the suspects, he asked the opinion of the Ministry of Justice, which in turn decided that the Yens had not betrayed the revolution, that Decree-Law 2 did not apply, and that, in the absence of applicable law, a simple fine would suffice. The Ministry of Justice then forwarded the case to the cabinet of the Council of State, where Chan Ven took an uncharacteristically ideological but ultimately lenient position. The offenses committed by the Yens, said Chan Ven, "affect political and social morality and obstruct the Party and state movement of social and socialist ideological education" and further "the schemes of the enemy, who is continually planning to attack our revolution on the battlefield of ideology and consciousness." Nonetheless, he agreed with Uk Bunchheuan, concluding that a fine would do.[55]

By the time the issue got to the Council of State, on April 23, the Council of Ministers had issued a new Subdecree 9, which applied directly to the question of videos and distinguished between criminal offenses (which involved "political security" and invoked Decree-Law 2) and unauthorized showings of videos "for commercial purposes" (for which a fine and confiscation were the appropriate penalty). According to the minutes of the council meeting, however, the leadership concluded only that the case be decided "in accordance with" the new subdecree. The prosecutor, apparently encouraged by these ambiguous instructions, reconfirmed his earlier decision to fine the Yens and ordered the police to release them. The police, refusing on the grounds that the Yens had violated political security, demanded that the prosecutor return the file. The prosecutor rejected the police request, claiming that the file had already been delivered to the Ministry of Justice. Both the police and the prosecutor then appealed to the Phnom Penh municipal authorities and to the city's Party Committee.

In a case with more serious political impact, the Phnom Penh state and Party authorities would have rendered a decision, and neither the police nor the prosecutor would have lodged a protest. But with little at stake, the authorities ordered the police and the prosecutor to meet together to resolve the case. It was thus the very banality of the offense—and the inattention paid by mid-level leaders—that kept the issue alive and led to a larger institutional standoff. For the time being, though, the Ministry of Justice still had the file, and the police still had the Yens.

As was sometimes the case in the PRK, Vietnamese advisors attempted to mediate. But when various Cambodian officials from the Phnom Penh court and municipal government met at the courthouse, they found the Vietnamese also in disagreement. Nguyen Dam, the advisor to the Ministry of Justice, supported the ministry. "The Council of State did not permit prosecution," he insisted, "because these offenders who showed the video did not have the intention of opposing the revolution but were doing it only to make money. On May 30, 1986, I reported to the [Vietnamese] advisors' Leadership Committee on this issue, and it agreed with the solution of the prosecutor." "Nguyen Hoc," a police advisor, refused to budge. "I agree to [resolve the case] in accordance with Subdecree 9 but [only] because of Article 18, which has not been implemented by the prosecutor," he explained, referring to the provision of the subdecree that covered political security and mandated imprisonment.[56]

By now the Ministry of Justice was also emboldened by the promulgation of Decree-Law 27, which it felt gave the prosecutor, rather than the police, the discretion over whether to prosecute, detain, imprison, or release an alleged offender, and ultimately to decide whether a video "betrayed the revolution." In late August 1986, when the Council of State revisited the case of the Yens, the debate focused not only on the content of the videos but on fundamental questions of institutional authority.

The minister of the interior, Ne Penna, despite being new to the revolution, understood the ideological perspective and institutional interests of the ministry. The Yens' videos, he told the Council of State, had a "reactionary quality," and therefore "the commercial activities of this group were in accordance with the schemes and psychological warfare of the enemy, affecting the security and order of Phnom Penh." If the defendants are released, he warned, "the police will lose morale." Penna was equally offended by the actions of the prosecutor, who, he argued, had undermined the authority of the Party by sending "secret state documents" to the Ministry of Justice. From Penna's perspective, the authority of the police was at stake. "It was not right for the state prosecutor to have sent the file to the Ministry of Justice, because this case had not yet been adjudicated and was still at the stage of building the case. If the police, upon delivering the file to the state prosecutor, are out of the loop (*phot rongvong*) . . . then the police have a duty to implement the decisions of the state prosecutor. The Ministry of the Interior does not yet agree with these conditions because the police institutions are the ones that investigate and bring charges. The police are responsible from the investigative stage right up until the implementation of the verdict."[57]

Uk Bunchheuan responded sardonically. "If we are talking about law, then I can tell you [how the case should be decided]. If we are talking about practice up to now, I cannot speak to that." Bunchheuan insisted that Decree-Law 27 provided discretion to the prosecutor, not to the police. "Regardless of whether the state prosecutor resolves a case correctly or incorrectly, there is no further connection to the police but only to the Ministry of Justice and the Council of State, because that is in their area of competence." On substantive grounds, Bunchheuan lent his support to the prosecutor's view of the case. "Up to now, it has been the police who have interpreted the law, and so pornography got included in political security. [But] the view [of the Ministry of Justice] is that pornography is an issue of morality and not political security. . . . If these films had broadcast the voice of Sihanouk or the propaganda of the tripartite government [the CGDK], then they would affect political security. I think that if there were really an enemy network, the enemy would not need fifty riels. They would show [the video] for free. But they charged. So is the enemy selling its politics or what?"

Bunchheuan also took the opportunity to defend the "independence" of the court. The Ministry of Justice, he explained, was responsible for substantive legal matters, whereas the Phnom Penh Party and state apparatus were permitted to "manage the courts only in the area of politics and the consciousness of the personnel." Therefore, concluded Bunchheuan, "the Ministry of Justice has not interfered with the court or the prosecutor; it is the People's Revolutionary Committee and the Party Committee that has interfered with these institutions."

Avoiding the issue of institutional competence, the Council of State's two Politburo members sided with Bunchheuan on the merits of the case. "If we rely on the law," said Heng Samrin, "it is not necessary to put these three people in jail." Say Phouthang added, "Only videocassettes that broadcast Sihanouk or Khieu Samphan are included in cases of political security."

Two weeks later, however, Politburo members met to watch the videos themselves and were apparently deeply concerned. "Before, we had not yet made a determination as to whether this was a criminal case or a morality case or whether it was to be considered a political case," Heng Samrin told the Council of State. "The Politburo has [now] determined that the case serves the psychological warfare of the enemy. The Politburo has asked the Municipal Party Committee to have the court conduct research for adjudication." Samrin, who in the past had complained of cadres watching pornographic videos, described the whole experience in appropriately detached and revolutionary language. "The Politburo watched these videos and saw that they were obscene and would confuse our society."[58]

Uk Bunchheuan was annoyed, insisting that "there is no actual evidence that shows that this is an offense of betraying the revolution." Heng Samrin, ignoring Bunchheuan's challenge, acted as if the case had not yet been entirely resolved. "To be sure, we should wait for the Politburo to meet again, and invite all the institutions connected [to this case] to participate, especially all the [Vietnamese] advisors."[59]

No subsequent meetings are on record, and the entire case seems simply to have faded away. At some point, the Yens were released, although it is unclear whether the Municipal Party Committee ordered them rearrested. In the end, though, the Politburo had reasserted its ideological stance while leaving unresolved the dispute between the police and courts.

EXECUTIONS

The Council of State also saw clashes of principle over the imposition of the death penalty. Heng Samrin and Say Phouthang, who never disagreed on capital cases, at least not in front of the council, had the final word. Samrin, Phouthang, and, when he attended council meetings, Chea Sim, were also the least prone to grant clemency. Uk Bunchheuan, on the other hand, was the council's most vocal opponent of the death penalty. Although he had supported some executions before 1984, by the mid-1980s he was offering up a wide array of unsuccessful arguments for granting clemency. Defendants, he said, should be spared because of their "low level of education" or because they had been "tricked" or "did not yet understand the policies of the Party." Rarely did these defenses elicit sympathy from the leadership.[60]

Armed resistance was sufficient grounds for execution. One defendant, explained Heng Samrin, "has opposed the revolution since 1979. Our state authority has exposed him many times, but he returns to Phnom Penh to resume activities that destroy the revolution. Our state authority has investigated him for a very long time already and knows that he intended to attack and liberate T3 [prison] in Phnom Penh. This person has not only killed [a cadre] but also committed the offense of destroying the revolution." Chea Sim agreed with Samrin that in these kinds of political cases the defendants should be executed. "There actually are many murders similar to this one," noted Sim, "but this case is a special one because this person killed [the victim] with the intention of defending a traitorous counterrevolutionary organization in order to continue traitorous activities."[61]

Uk Bunchheuan's argument, that the defendant was "not a ringleader," did not convince the leadership. "If we rely on [whether the defendant] is a ringleader, then why are we fighting Pol Pot's young soldiers?" asked Say Phouthang rhetorically. Nor did the leniency of the Misled Persons Movement convince Phouthang, who applied its guidelines only to surrendering soldiers. The defendant "is not a Misled Person," stated Phouthang. "He was living among us, and he conducted activities to destroy us. So [the death penalty] is not in contradiction with the Party's policies."[62]

The underlying goal of the Misled Persons Movement—eliciting confessions and manifestations of loyalty to the regime—often determined who was executed and who was not. In the summer of 1987 the Council of State debated the case of Sok Ban and Uk Ly, two Khmer Rouge soldiers who had participated in a nonlethal attack on the Phnom Penh airport. Ban, a battalion commander, did the shooting. But Uk Ly received the death penalty, partly because he had been wounded in an earlier altercation and had nonetheless fled back to the Khmer Rouge and partly because he was "obstinate" during his interrogation.[63]

"Uk Ly has never lived under this new regime," noted Uk Bunchheuan, urging clemency. "He has lived with the enemy since the age of fourteen. The enemy has thoroughly indoctrinated him to the point where he dares to struggle and involuntarily takes risks by engaging in activities with the enemy regime." To Khoem Pon, the former Phnom Penh police chief who was now deputy minister of the interior, the fact that Uk Ly had chosen once before to return to the Khmer Rouge demonstrated that he "does not recognize the compassionate principles of our revolution." Pon spoke, too, of the defendant's reluctance to confess. "During the interrogations, Sok Ban confessed, but Uk Ly was obstinate and refused to answer. We should examine those whom we've arrested [to see] who confesses truthfully and politely and who confesses grudgingly and slowly." Khoem Pon concluded, "There can be no compassion, no amnesty, and no reduction of sentence for Uk Ly."

After another attempt by Uk Bunchheuan to argue for life imprisonment in lieu of the death penalty, Heng Samrin reminded the meeting that "what's important is our examination of the stance of the person at the time he is arrested—whether he confesses or is obstinate." In this case, the leadership concluded that Uk Ly could not be co-opted and should therefore be executed. "It is clear that he cannot live with our revolution," said Sin Sen, director of the Interrogation Department of the Ministry of the Interior. "Compassion for Uk Ly is like helping a wounded tiger. When the tiger recovers, it will turn and bite us again."

Eventually, the leadership found political reasons not to impose the death penalty. One concern was the impact an execution would have on the defendant's family members. "If we kill him, won't this have some effect on his father and mother and relatives? Won't this be difficult and affect our revolution?" asked Uk Bunchheuan with regard to one 1987 case. Say Phouthang and Heng Samrin agreed. "Execution . . . will surely have a political effect on [the defendant's] two siblings," cautioned Phouthang. "We should think about the future difficulties for these two younger siblings." Samrin added, "If we execute [the defendant] . . . we won't be able to keep them in the police force."[64]

Grudgingly, the leadership also considered international opinion. In one 1986 case, Uk Bunchheuan, Chan Ven, and Vandy Ka-on urged that the regime consider external pressures while insisting that doing so was not a capitulation to the enemy. Bunchheuan made the report:

Immediately after we pronounced a verdict, we broadcast it on television and radio, prompting a reaction from the members of Amnesty International. They sent letters from all over the place requesting clemency for the offender, Chea Saran. The Ministry of Justice received 169 copies. My view is in accordance with that of [Chan Ven]. These international letters have no relation at all to our decision to grant or not grant clemency, because even if none of these letters existed, we would still consider [granting clemency]. But if we agree to grant clemency to this offender, it would permit the following. International [actors] would understand that we respect human rights. Enemies who are conducting activities against us would see that our regime is understanding and compassionate and does not "grasp the hands and the feet" [act repressively]. And it would be seen that our regime is stable, because when our international friends see that we still have the death penalty, they say that our regime is unstable.[65]

Bunchheuan and Ka-on then appealed to history. Bunchheuan argued that the PRK should demonstrate a "humanitarian character," which "defends human rights and doesn't grasp the hands and feet, as the previous regime did." Ka-on's point was grander. "Granting clemency is in accordance with the politics of our country, which is a country that has had a great civilization."

Heng Samrin considered Western criticism hypocritical. "These days in other countries they have the death penalty, too, as in Indonesia. Even though our international friends look for our mistakes, they still hang people just the same." He reluctantly acknowledged, however, that although other factors, including the political loyalty of the defendant's family and the regime's efforts to co-opt the resistance, were more important, "we can be somewhat influenced by foreign countries."

In fact, the leadership was reconsidering the imposition of the death penalty as part of a larger effort to appeal to Cambodians both outside the country and within. In early 1989 the Party amended the constitution to prohibit the death penalty, an act that did not stop soldiers and police from summarily executing detainees but that nonetheless marked an important concession to a basic principle of human rights.

APPEALS

For the vast majority of Cambodians, the corruption and extortion, daily annoyances and frequent tyrannies imposed by local state authorities meant more than high-level debates over the death penalty. According to PRK law, citizens could lodge complaints of state malfeasance with the National Assembly, the Council of State, and the responsible state authorities. The regime also intended to establish a Ministry of Inspection with branches throughout the government. This network was aimed as much at informing the leadership, however, as at assisting citizens. As the chair of the Vietnamese State Inspection Commission told Hun Sen, "The People's Inspection Committees are the eyes, ears, and arms of the Party and the state."[66]

The Ministry of Inspection never truly functioned. Although many of the complaints voiced by Cambodians involved arrests, the ministry was prevented from investigating either the Ministry of the Interior or the Ministry of Defense. And, to the frustration of successive ministers of inspection, the state failed to establish local Inspection Committees. Much of the resistance came from the Party's Central Organization Committee. Huet Savy, director of the committee's State Personnel Department, warned the Council of Ministers that the Ministry of Inspection could "infringe on the rights of the other ministries." Savy also opposed the expansion of the inspection bureaucracy. "Small provinces, such as Rattanakiri and Mondolkiri," should be excluded, as should ministerial departments, factories, and district- and commune-level administrations. If the state wished to extend the inspection system, it could confer inspection duties on existing cadres. Savy did not explain how these cadres could be expected to investigate their own conduct.[67]

Cambodian citizens lodged only seventy-six complaints in all of 1985. The reason, concluded Uk Bunchheuan at the end of the year, was "oppression that makes the appellants afraid, fed up, and not daring enough to show their faces by appealing directly." There was little question that Cambodians feared retaliation. Say Phouthang told the Council of State in 1988 that Cambodians were more afraid to register appeals than Vietnamese citizens were. Vandy Ka-on's Legislation Commission, in its report to the National Assembly, was bluntest of all. "Some [state] institutions, when they receive an appeal or complaint from the people, not only refuse to do anything to resolve the appeal but pursue various schemes to suppress and obstruct the appeal."[68]

In accordance with "socialist legality," the rights of citizens were to be protected by a Supreme Court and its general procurator. In 1985, shortly after the passage of a decree-law creating the Supreme Court, the Party arrived at its choice of chief judge: former Minister of the Interior Khang Sarin. As a Vietnamese-trained military figure, Sarin had neither a legal background nor, given the rising power of Hun Sen and Chea Sim, an independent power base. For years he was almost entirely inactive other than appearing at meetings to complain. There were the usual delays in finding competent legal cadres and getting them approved by the Party Central Organization Committee. Finding a building also proved laborious, as the court wrangled with the municipality, the Ministry of Defense, and even the Training Center for Army Culture and Arts over small plots of land. Well into 1989 the Supreme Court was still not functioning. The general procurator, Chan Min, was only slightly more engaged. To the horror of the Ministry of the Interior, the procurator's responsibilities included oversight of "legality" in the PRK and investigation into the implementation of court verdicts. Min had few resources, however, and no authority to enforce his findings. With little to do other than draft reports on "violations of law" and resubmit cases to the violating authorities, the office of the procurator served as a consistent, if ineffective, critic of state conduct.[69]

INCARCERATION AND AMNESTY

Originally established by Vietnamese authorities and various units of the Cambodian military, the PRK's prison system came to include sites under the control of the Ministry of the Interior and, later, "reform centers" (*kola*) run by the Phnom Penh municipality. Conditions inside the prisons were chaotic. Women frequently brought their younger children with them into detention. Minors occupied the "reform centers," as did nonviolent offenders, such as the prostitutes swept up in Phnom Penh's periodic campaigns. Some prisoners were put to work, collecting rice and palm sugar, doing carpentry, and sewing clothes for export to the Soviet Union. Most suffered from a lack of hygiene, food, and clothing. With two ministries technically responsible for prisons— the Ministries of Defense and the Interior—and the Ministry of Finance in control of prison funds, the little money allocated for keeping prisoners alive frequently failed to arrive on time. "The three ministries should discuss this every year," said Sin Song in 1985, "and shouldn't wait until prisoners die before holding discussions."[70]

In 1984 the cost of incarcerating thousands of people, the regime's relative stability, and its desire to demonstrate benevolence led the leadership to release some of the prisoners detained in 1979. Not until 1988, however, did significant numbers of Cambodian prisoners see the light of day. Noting that "over many years, we have arrested and detained a set of people for no clear reason," Ung Phan explained to the Council of State that the recent decision to release prisoners was inspired by the PRK's policy of "national reconciliation" (that is, the effort to appeal to the resistance) and by the "new policy of the Vietnamese Communist Party in releasing some old state officials who also used to engage in counterrevolutionary politics," by which he meant the partial emptying of the southern Vietnamese reeducation camps. Releasing prisoners, he added, would also relieve some of the discontent felt by the families of detainees. "Many of the masses have also inquired about cases of people detained without basis, [including] suspects, thieves, other offenders and people who committed some small social infraction. They judge our [state] agencies responsible for arresting, detaining, and imprisoning people and say that [these agencies] have incorrect intentions."[71]

Under the new policy, prisoners who had served most of their sentence and who had "reformed themselves and studied to be good citizens" were eligible for amnesty or a reduction of their sentence. The Ministry of the Interior kept no records for most of its prisoners, however, so had little idea when they had been arrested or how much time they had served. What is more, the vast majority of Cambodian prisoners had never seen the inside of a courthouse and therefore had no sentence to reduce. Despite Uk Bunchheuan's plea that these prisoners could be released "at any time," the Party leadership was thinking more strategically. Prisoners who had never been tried were released during national holidays along with those eligible for amnesty. Explained Heng Samrin, "We should announce [the releases] to our domestic and international friends so they will know clearly that we have merciful policies." The Party also had no interest in a general amnesty, which might allow the release of political opponents. Despite arguments by Chan Ven and the office of the general procurator that Cambodians detained for spreading "enemy propaganda" posed no threat to society, Heng Samrin preferred a case-by-case review. "If there is a serious offense related to politics in which there is no file and no clear report, ask the opinion of the Council of State, because thus far it is difficult to release prisoners and difficult not to release them."[72]

The vagaries of the amnesty policy set off institutional struggles among the Ministry of Justice, the Council of State, and the Council of Ministers, all of which claimed authority to order releases. The Ministry of the Interior, which held the prisoners, blamed local officials for its failure to implement the new policy. "So far we've wanted to release [prisoners], but the provinces don't agree because they still believe that offenses were committed, even though the Ministry of Inspection has examined the cases and not found sufficient documentation," complained Sin Song on his return to the Ministry of the Interior. Song also blamed the military. "When soldiers arrest civilians, they send them to the police without any documentation at all. Even if the police want to release them, they don't dare, because they are afraid that the soldiers will accuse them of taking bribes." An interministerial committee created to overcome the inefficiencies of the Ministry of the Interior was even less successful and was ignored by the same local officials as well as by the police. In the end, prisoners were released according to the whims and agendas of local officials. The arbitrary nature of the entire process led the general procurator, Chan Min, to comment, "As they say, arrest in order to release."[73]

BUILDING THE RULE OF LAW

The struggle to build the rule of law and to protect the human rights of Cambodians (and of citizens of the developing world generally) has often been described as a kind of national or cultural evolution. Cambodia, it is typically said, is attempting to overcome a long history of abusive rule. There is some truth in the statement. Poverty and illiteracy are society-wide problems that impede the establishment of an effective judicial system. The institutions of civil society cannot be constructed overnight. And even in the most favorable political environments, years are required, if not decades, to change the way a police force and an army go about their jobs. Nonetheless, by attributing human rights conditions solely to long-term endemic problems, commentators risk ignoring the individuals involved.

Countries are not monolithic, nor are regimes or even ruling parties. Behind closed doors, there were PRK bureaucrats who attempted to instill a greater respect for law and human rights, and there were those who resisted. Within the leadership, too, there were arguments on both sides. Top Party leaders, who were actually well informed on legal and human rights issues, weighed their desire to appear merciful against security concerns or their own personal interests, making conscious choices about what kind of criminal laws to pass, how long to detain people, and whether to impose the death penalty. In assessing this history, we may judge these leaders according to the pressures and risks of the period, but they are, nonetheless, responsible for their own decisions.

Human beings change their minds, even former Khmer Rouge cadres. In the case of Minister of Justice Uk Bunchheuan, a newfound respect for human rights was due to his association with liberal-minded former jurists, a desire to protect the interests of his ministry, and a flexible mind that permitted him to absorb a new approach to governance. For Khang Sarin and Sin Song, being removed from the Ministry of the Interior occasioned a new outlook. Most of the rest of the leadership, however, were swayed only by political pressure—from the resistance, the Vietnamese, and the international community—and by the need to improve the regime's image.

Part Four **Adjusting to History, 1988–1991**

Chapter 12 The Politics
of Economic Reform

Thirteen years after the Khmer Rouge revolution and almost a decade after Cambodia's second communist experiment began, even the PRK's most ideological Party leaders were indulging themselves in a little hindsight. They were not ready to give up entirely on communism—some still believed that in other contexts it could work—but collectivization had failed in Cambodia, and there had to be some historical reasons. In June 1988, at a meeting of the Council of State, Say Phouthang attempted to draw a distinction between North Vietnam, where, he claimed, people understood the "virtues of the revolution and were even happy to pay taxes to the state," and Cambodia. "In North Vietnam, farmland used to be the property of landowners, and their peasants were truly slaves," he explained. "But the situation in Cambodia is different from the one in Vietnam because most Cambodian farmland was the inherited property of the peasants over a very long time. Cambodian peasants had farmland before liberation. After liberation we took the land that was their property and distributed it back to them according to the determinations of our state revolutionary authority, and they weren't happy with us."[1]

The other problem, said Say Phouthang, was that Cambodians had failed to appreciate what had been given to them. "Cambodian farmers are grateful to our revolution only for helping to liberate them completely from the murderous hold of Pol Pot. [But] the collectivization of farmland and plantations and the distribution of cows and buffaloes to the cooperatives have made our farmers unhappy."

THE FAILURE OF COLLECTIVIZATION

By early 1984, Cambodians had had enough of the Solidarity Groups. The Party, however, in its reluctance to accept the failure of collectivization, arrived at a set of euphemisms to describe the situation. Cambodia, which was headed "step by step in the direction of socialism," had three types of collectives: Type One Solidarity Groups, in which peasants worked the land communally; Type Two Solidarity Groups, in which land was distributed to individual families, who coordinated the harvesting and sale of rice to the state; and Type Three Solidarity Groups, which were really just private farms.

The collapse of the Solidarity Groups began with the regime's 1980 decision to permit local officials to distribute land according to the "actual situation in each location." As it turned out, conditions were rarely conducive to collectivization. The state had failed to create a commercial network capable of providing the Solidarity Groups with fertilizers, pesticides, fuel, or other agricultural equipment. Peasants already in possession of such inputs were disinclined to share them with the collective, leaving members of the collective with no incentive to stay. Even when inputs were available, the absence of competent cadres to assign work and distribute food prompted peasants to farm by themselves. By 1984 a mere 10 percent of the Solidarity Groups could be described as Type One. Still, at least some of the PRK leadership remained committed to total collectivization. "The state authority at all levels, the Party, and all the people should focus on strengthening the Type One [Solidarity Groups]," urged Heng Samrin, who was not so much misinformed as ideologically fixated. "So far, they always say that [if they] work in a Type One, there's no rice, but if they work in a Type Two or Type Three, there is lots of rice to sell to the state." Samrin's prescription was an increase in equipment for the Type One collectives, combined with greater vigilance. "Be careful not to allow Type One to fall into Type Two and then Type Three," he warned.[2]

Collectivization was failing in part because local state officials, whose ideological commitment to collectivization had always been weak, were selling off the land. Council of Ministers reports complained of those "among the ranks of the local village, commune, and district authorites" buying, selling, and renting land and hiring labor. Mat Ly, who in 1983 was serving as deputy minister of agriculture, told the Council of Ministers that "every meeting or assembly of the heads of the agricultural offices of all the provinces confirms the problems that result from some local authorities who take the land to sell," not to the people, through formal distribution systems, but to each other. The result of this malfeasance was that Cambodians still living in Solidarity Groups, whether Type One or Type Two, received the worst land. According to the Council of Ministers, "A set of local cadres compete to take nearby rice fields and plantations for their own families. Rice fields that are far away and of bad quality are distributed to the people in the Solidarity Groups."[3]

State and Party authorities at the provincial level were equally indifferent to the Solidarity Groups. By the mid-1980s many had stopped providing agricultural inputs or distributing land to the collectives. Pol Sareun, Takeo Party secretary and an old Eastern Zone comrade of Chea Sim, spoke bluntly during a National Assembly session in 1988. Beginning in 1985, he acknowledged, the province had determined that it had no more rice fields and stopped distributing land to members of the Solidarity Groups. "If it is crowded," people without land "are permitted to go live somewhere else."[4]

Toward the end of 1987, after several years of poor harvests, central officials began discussing agricultural policies in terms of "rights," that is, the "right" of Cambodian peasants to work the land as they saw fit. Autonomous decision making within the context of the collectives, Agriculture Minister Say Chhum reckoned, would create the incentives that would boost rice yields. The Solidarity Groups themselves were not the problem, he had decided. Interference by incompetent and corrupt local officials was. "The Solidarity Group policy truly has qualities that are extremely appropriate for the situation in Cambodia. But so far we have imposed overly rigid limitations on our Solidarity Groups, so they don't function. This has a bad effect on production. As for land policy, we have said that the land is the property of the state but have given the Solidarity Groups and families the work of conducting business. So the Solidarity Groups and families have rights as masters of the land, whereas the owner is the state. But so far some of our local state authorities don't understand this clearly and turn around and take these ownership rights and manage and distribute land inappropriately. This is why people are very disappointed."[5]

If local authorities had failed to understand these distinctions, it was because the regime had never officially articulated them. Not until the spring of 1988, after the Vietnamese Communist Party had begun reforming its land policies, did the Cambodian leadership really begin to consider reform. In April a delegation from the VCP Central Committee came to Phnom Penh to talk over the issue with Chea Soth. "Before, we misunderstood the distinction between ownership and rights, and we rushed into collectivization too quickly," the head of the Vietnamese delegation explained. Soth agreed that collectivization was unpopular. "After observing the people for nearly ten years, we can see that they prefer working privately. They've woken up to [the idea of] working for themselves and improving themselves."

Still, Soth could not help accusing the people of failing to "understand" collectivization and of having a low "consciousness." He was also reluctant to change policy: "We are still pondering whether to keep these three types [of Solidarity Groups]," he told the Vietnamese. "The Soviets have already reformed to some extent, and the Vietnamese have changed, too. [Party Economics Commission Chair] Comrade Chan Phin and I are still discussing [this problem] and haven't yet issued [a decision]."[6]

At the end of June, as the leadership launched a broader debate over agricultural policy, Uk Bunchheuan, Planning Minister Chea Chantho, and Ung Phan were calling for reform. Hun Sen, whose feelings were also clear, remained deferential to the Party. "This issue relates to the resolution of the Party Central Committee," he reminded the Council of Ministers, "so if the [council] has an opinion, we will send a report to the Central Party on the issue of the use of land—whether we leave the people in a state where they can't know what's theirs and they refuse to increase [production], or [whether we allow them to] take care of the land. This is an issue that should be amended gradually."[7]

The Party was dragging its feet, aware that collectivization was not working but afraid of the political and military ramifications of any bold pronouncements. Said Nut Than, deputy chair of the Party Economics Commission, "In my opinion, we don't need to announce the dissolution of the Solidarity Groups." The reason, he explained, was that if Cambodians understood that they didn't need the collectives, they would conclude that they did not need the revolution at all and would "put their weapons down."[8]

At the Council of State, Say Phouthang summed up the Party position. "If [the people] work in Type One Solidarity Groups and there's no rice, go down to Type Two Groups. If there's no rice in the Type Two Groups, go down to Type Three Groups. We shouldn't abandon [the policy]. We should push them into Solidarity Groups. But we should make sure they have something to eat."

Acknowledging that the farmers had already rejected the Solidarity Groups, Phouthang grudgingly conceded that "our people will be overjoyed with the policy of land reform."[9]

Two weeks later, when the Cambodian National Assembly met for its biannual session, the leadership divided some of the parliamentarians into groups for nonpublic discussions. Among other topics, the groups discussed the status of land distribution in the countryside. What the leaders learned from this exercise—if they didn't know it already—was that their own debates were largely academic, that the division among types of Solidarity Groups was a semantic fiction. According to Saom Keum Suor, a deputy from Kampot and a Central Committee member, "The issue of Solidarity Groups is actually just one of names. In fact, most are private." Several provincial Party secretaries and governors described the collapse of collectivization. "In fact, Prey Veng province has established Solidarity Groups that we call Types One, Two, and Three," said the province's governor, Cheam Yeap. "But really, Type One is Type Two, Type Two is Type Three, and there is no Type Three." As was apparent during the course of the meetings, provincial figures throughout the country supported reform, including all the former Eastern Zone cadres close to Chea Sim—Pol Sareun of Takeo, Chan Seng of Siem Reap, and Ros Sreng of Pursat.[10]

By the end of the year, Hun Sen had the Party ideologues on the defensive. At one Council of State meeting, he even personalized the issue. "Nowadays the people want another regime to replace the Heng Samrin regime," he proclaimed as Samrin listened. Land reform, he said, will "allow them to have a regime in which there are ownership rights over land. The people of Phnom Penh also want a new regime so that they can have houses as their personal property. This is because, in the Heng Samrin regime, they have no ownership of or rights over land and houses." Samrin could respond only that collectivization had never occurred anyway. "So far, land has not been collectivized. Most is [private] property. There are still people without rice fields or farms. We should fix this."[11]

Having more or less accepted the concept of rights, the leadership attempted to distinguish between autonomous management of land and actual ownership. "Only produce and houses can be sold," insisted Uk Bunchheuan at the Council of State. "If we confer ownership rights on the citizens, they'll have the right to sell and pawn off [the land]. If they possess land for a long time, this land is on loan from the state." Say Phouthang added, "If we permit too much selling, there will be confusion. The state loans [land] to be worked on for a number of years, but there is no right to sell it."[12]

In February 1989 the Party acknowledged the change in policy, amending the constitution to read, "Citizens have full rights to hold (*kan kap*) and use (*braoe bras*) land and have the right to inheritance of land that the state has granted them to live on and to conduct business on." The amendment also included a set of prohibitions on selling and renting land and on using farmland and forestland "arbitrarily and for a different purpose without permission from the competent authorities." Despite these provisions and subsequent Party and state regulations on land use, the regime soon lost control of the situation. The sale and rental of houses and land increased dramatically as state cadres and others ignored distinctions between the right to hold and use property and absolute ownership. Meanwhile, the state's administration turned its attention to registering privately held land, a monumental task for which a provincial bureaucracy was created only in mid-1990.[13]

PERESTROIKA COMES TO PHNOM PENH

The message of reform was finding its way from Moscow to Cambodia by various routes. In the Soviet Union, where Mikhail Gorbachev's economic restructuring was taking hold, Cambodians were learning about capitalism. One Ministry of Planning official who spent several years in Moscow remembers attending classes on Adam Smith, Japanese management techniques, and the economic successes of countries like South Korea and Taiwan. In the mid and late 1980s, about a thousand Cambodian students and officials were studying in Moscow. Many returned to Cambodia with academic as well as personal experience with *perestroika*. Bureaucrats who never left Phnom Penh were also exposed to new ideas in seminars taught by visiting Soviet economists. Most important, however, was the message sent by the Soviet Union's retreat from its overseas commitments. Toward the end of 1987, Cambodian officials complained that Moscow was not sending factory parts it had promised and was not responding to inquiries. The silence was clear enough: Phnom Penh should start thinking about economic self-sufficiency.[14]

There was plenty of rethinking in Hanoi as well. After deciding in the summer of 1985 to loosen price controls and adopt a single-price system, the Vietnamese Communist Party followed the Soviet lead in granting autonomy to state enterprises. With the death of Party secretary Le Duan in July 1986 and the rise of the southerners Vo Van Kiet and Nguyen Van Linh, the VCP was ready for its own reform project, known as *doi moi*. In 1988, Vietnam moved gradually toward accepting private industry, liberalized prices, looked to new investment priorities, and launched new policies on the allocation of land. At the end of the year, the Party held its Sixth Congress, at which Nguyen Van Linh became Party secretary and private property was formally recognized.[15]

"FROM LEFT TO RIGHT"

Never very ideological to begin with, Hun Sen was now in a position to understand the changes taking place elsewhere in the socialist world. As minister of foreign affairs, he traveled widely. His two most important counterparts, Soviet Foreign Minister Eduard Shevardnadze and Vietnamese Foreign Minister Nguyen Co Thach, were both pragmatic men and advocates, within their respective countries, of economic reform. Hun Sen was also paying close attention to Cambodia's peculiar international position.

In July 1986, Soviet Party secretary Mikhail Gorbachev gave a historic speech in Vladivostok in which he began to unravel the Soviet Union's entanglements in Asia. In the course of the speech, he announced the withdrawal of Soviet troops from Afghanistan, proposed negotiations with the Mongolian government on the withdrawal of Soviet troops stationed there, called for the delineation of the Sino-Soviet border along the Amur River, and offered a general invitation to the People's Republic of China to confer "at any time and at any level" regarding the establishment of "an atmosphere of good-neighborliness." Turning to Cambodia, Gorbachev stated that the conflict could be resolved by the Cambodians themselves and that there were no insurmountable problems separating the Indochinese countries and the capitalist countries of ASEAN. A month later, Deng Xiaoping told CBS News that whereas there was "something new" in the speech, the Soviet leader had not broached the subject of the Vietnamese occupation of Cambodia. Deng would be willing to meet Gorbachev, he said, if the Soviets could convince Hanoi to withdraw.[16]

In March 1987, Soviet Foreign Minister Eduard Shevardnadze set off on a tour of Southeast Asia, holding talks in Thailand with Foreign Secretary Siddhi Savetsila and in Indonesia with Foreign Minister Mochtar Kusumaatmadja. Shevardnadze then headed for Cambodia, where he met with Heng Samrin, Hun Sen, and Foreign Minister Kong Korm. According to a joint communiqué, the two countries would continue "to take active, effective steps to strengthen and expand the fraternal relationship," and the two ruling parties would remain unified on the basis of "the unswerving principles of Marxism." But Shevardnadze had left the most important leg of the trip for last: a visit to Hanoi for talks with the VCP's new and somewhat more flexible leadership on resolving the Cambodia problem. Canceling a television appearance and a visit to the Revolution Museum, the Soviet foreign minister offered little public indication of what he was up to, other than to tell *Nhan Dan*, the VCP's official newspaper, that "the most important factor" in bringing peace to Southeast Asia was "the unanimity and the solidarity of the three Indochinese countries and their readiness to embark on dialogue with the ASEAN countries, China, and all the other parties concerned." Five days later, Vietnamese Prime Minister Pham Van Dong announced that Vietnam would be out of Cambodia by 1990, no matter what.[17]

It was clear that the PRK would soon be on its own. Convinced that the regime could not prevail militarily once the Vietnamese had withdrawn, the Party began pursuing political and diplomatic ways of resolving the conflict. On August 27, 1987, Phnom Penh announced its Declaration on the Policy of National Reconciliation of the People's Republic of Kampuchea. According to the declaration, the PRK was prepared to discuss the repatriation of refugees, to invite overseas Khmers to return to Cambodia and serve the PRK, and to "meet with other groups of Khmers and their leaders, except the criminal Pol Pot and his close associates, in order to conduct discussions of national reconciliation based on the nonrecurrence, forever, of the danger of genocide." Hun Sen later referred to this new approach as "switching our struggle from the military to the diplomatic field."[18]

Hun Sen wanted to meet Sihanouk and to drive a wedge between the supposedly adaptable prince and his seemingly intractable Cambodian and foreign allies. Sihanouk was anxious to distance himself from both the Khmer Rouge and the Chinese. Taking a "leave of absence" from the CGDK and calling himself a "private citizen," he granted himself enough independence to begin negotiating with Hun Sen. Finally, in December 1987, at a four-star hotel in the French town of Fère-en-Tardenois, the two leaders shook hands and began talking. By all accounts, Hun Sen was thrilled by the meeting and the boost it had given his own prestige, and set out on a direct course of co-opting Sihanouk. Although no major diplomatic breakthroughs occurred during 1988, many of the economic reforms promoted by Hun Sen over the course of the year were intended to appeal to the prince and, by extension, to the thousands of noncommunist Khmers still living in exile and supporting the resistance.[19]

The politics of this appeal were complicated. Party leaders in Phnom Penh and Hanoi were still concerned that a renunciation of socialism would seem like a concession or a defeat. Hun Sen, speaking to the Council of Ministers in September 1988, advised caution, at least in terms of public pronouncements.

"Should we follow capitalism or socialism? We shouldn't say because there are a lot of factors concerning the international [scene]." That the resistance was not homogeneously capitalist but rather included the Khmer Rouge was also a concern. "The biggest issue is, Can we satisfy the far right and the far left, who have joined together to fight us?" Hun Sen asked the council. But the overall economic direction of the country was already clear. Citing the suppression of the ethnic Chinese as particularly misguided, Hun Sen called for a "reevaluation" of past policies. "We are using capitalist investment to develop the country, raise the standard of living of the people. and deprive the far right of a weapon."[20]

In the spring of 1988, Hun Sen proposed to the Politburo a series of economic reforms, including an injection of private capital into previously state-run economic sectors. Even though these proposals were already being pushed in some form in Vietnam by VCP Party secretary Nguyen Van Linh, the Cambodian Party leadership responded passively. On some issues, the Politburo agreed with Hun Sen. On others, it chose to submit questions to the Central Committee or even to the National Assembly. Mostly, the Party leaders simply allowed Hun Sen's state apparatus to experiment as it saw fit. It was thus up to Hun Sen to convince his ministers of the importance of the new policies.[21] In a discussion on private transportation, he gave them a pep talk:

> Now, during this period of reform, we are taking steps backward and looking to re-create private business, opening up not a small private sector but a reasonably large private sector. So there may be differences of opinion. But the issue that arises now is, Should we prolong this situation, or should we agree to recognize private ownership and the business of the private sector in transporting travelers and thus reduce the difficulties and dangers faced by our people? Discussions at the Council of Ministers have arrived at a point where [we are talking about] a lot of reform, and we should continue. We don't [discuss reform just] for one or two days. There is no quick effectiveness. It is a journey filled with difficulties, and it is long-term. So far, our cadres are afraid and won't say anything. . . . Now, don't be afraid of anything at all. No one is anyone else's socialist teacher because [Cambodian socialists] have practiced socialism for twenty years already, and they are starting to discard and dismantle it and are starting anew. They are agreeing that they were completely wrong.[22]

Hun Sen, who was not about to rely on the Party leadership to push reform, urged his ministers to act on their own. "If we wait for the Sixth Party Congress in order to change, the situation will get increasingly worse, and we will face more and more problems," he warned. "So we should take the opportunity to reform bit by bit any sectors that can be reformed."[23]

Throughout the fall of 1988, Hun Sen convened long meetings at the Council of Ministers at which he urged his ministers to accept reform. On September 14 he argued for a single price system as the only way for state industries to compete and to develop their own relations with the private sector. "Up to now, we've said we have a planned economy, but there isn't one, because our plans are based on inaccurate numbers. In fact, Cambodia's economy has evolved into a market economy. There should be a way to change state intervention [in the economy], which is [currently] excessive. There isn't a single country that has succeeded at a planned economy." Again, Hun Sen dismissed the Party. "We should understand clearly the ideals of the Party, which are to build socialism. But how can socialism be practiced? No one can answer. Today we have plenty of economic slogans, but where can they lead us?"[24]

A week later, Hun Sen argued for greater autonomy for state enterprises, prompting protests from Minister of Commerce Tang Sareum and the new minister of industry, Ho Non. "In cases in which production is hindered, [stronger factories] carry the burden in order to satisfy the [state] plan and help [weaker factories]," insisted Non, whose previous position was as head of a state-run textile factory in Battambang. Responded Hun Sen, "Many socialist countries are collapsing because the big help the small. This situation leads to negligence. Now we are imposing competition."[25]

Early in the morning on October 1, Hun Sen opened a meeting of the council with the following pronouncement: "Cambodia is quietly reforming the management of its economy. We are moving from the left to the right." There was no argument.[26]

THE END OF IDEOLOGY

What had happened to the Party's ideology? To begin with, the leadership had ceased to care. Veteran Hanoi-trained revolutionaries like Chea Soth and Say Phouthang were not only isolated (their Vietnamese patrons were heavily engaged in their own reform experiments) but had by now acknowledged that socialist policies were unpopular. Chea Sim, the PRK's quiet powerbroker, was even more disinclined to promote socialism. Responsive to the interests of provincial loyalists rather than abstract—and now demonstrably unworkable —theories, Sim was more or less supportive of, if not actively engaged in promoting, economic reform.[27]

More important than the views of the leadership was the fact that the entire regime, from the lowest clerks to the most powerful Party officials, had a singular reason to support economic loosening: they had a personal stake in the free market. Since 1979 state cadres and their families had been permitted, unofficially, to supplement their wages through private business activities. The economics were simple. In 1985 state salaries were 100–150 riels a month for a manual laborer and 250–450 a month for a cadre, whereas a family of four needed 2,000 a month to live in Phnom Penh. State doctors thus gave private consultations, teachers taught privately, and government workers and cadres of all kinds, as well as their families, made their living as barbers, tailors, and merchants in the free market. Throughout the mid-1980s the Party looked the other way so long as personal profits remained modest. But as the private economy grew and as state salaries lagged further and further behind market prices, the policy evolved from tolerance to actual encouragement. In September 1987 the Council of Ministers finally issued a decision "pushing and increasing the family economy among the ranks of cadres, staff, and workers."[28]

The Party was in the same boat as the state. Candidates for Party and core group membership were thus permitted a level of private-sector activity even as members continued to insist that the free market posed ideological dangers. As one mid-level cadre stated at a Council of State core group meeting in the summer of 1987: "[The candidate] still has ideas about conducting business and has the views of a businessperson. Although we talk like this, the situation has changed. If we consider the principles of the Party, [his activities] are not yet appropriate because many businesspeople have exploitative ideas. But if we don't allow this business to be conducted, it will harm the standard of living. This exploitation is not really capitalism. It depends on time and place and the lack of a standard of living."[29]

Cambodians returning from communist education overseas also headed for the private sector. Vetted carefully for loyalty by Party officials and Vietnamese advisors, most of these students had nonetheless arrived in Moscow, Warsaw, Prague, even Hanoi, looking for a nonpolitical, technical education. Upon their return, they demonstrated little devotion to the regime, and although the state desperately needed their skills, it could offer them no more compensation than the rest of its civil servants. "When [students] come back," complained Minister of Planning Chea Chantho, "they won't come to work, or they refuse to go to the localities to which they are assigned. They prefer to conduct business in the free market instead." Responded Say Phouthang, who had no illusions about the gratitude of these students, "When sending them to study overseas, there should be a contract such that if they come back and won't work [for the state], they will reimburse [us for their education]."[30]

Throughout the late 1980s increasing numbers of cadres requested that they work only part-time in the ministries or simply left their jobs, taking off for months at a time. In addition to trading in the markets, they now had the option of using their "rights of possession" over land and houses as a base for conducting business. State housing soon evolved into shops, factories, and sites for exchanging illegal currencies and quasi-legal imported goods. "We shouldn't be like Thailand, where every one of the restaurants and dancehalls is owned by a general," warned Kong Samol, a U.S.-trained former minister of agriculture who had become a deputy prime minister.[31]

But the leadership was also thinking ahead to the period after the Vietnamese withdrawal, when the PRK might have to compete politically with capitalists. The regime had survived only by allowing its cadres to work in the private sector; to reverse course on economic reform would be political suicide. As Hun Sen explained in June 1989 to a visiting delegation from Vietnam, reliance by state workers on the private sector "exerts pressures on our policies and forces us to go the path [of economic reform and national reconciliation], so that [workers] don't lose their personal benefits from the state and so that they will follow us politically. If we don't resolve this problem in time, then when there is an election, the [resistance] will come and take houses and land and campaign against us incessantly. [People] will understand that if they vote for [the resistance parties, those parties] will give them rights over the houses and land they used to possess. We will lose in the countryside and in the city."[32]

Profits earned by state and Party cadres in the free market filtered upward to powerful patrons and those with the authority to permit private business ventures. As the tenants of the larger houses, high-level officials also held some of the more valuable assets in Phnom Penh. Veteran communists soon found themselves justifying sudden accumulations of wealth. In mid-1988, Ros Chhun, the former Khmer Rouge cadre and the current secretary-general of the Front, had seemingly defected to the other side of the class struggle. "Some comrades are still narrow-minded, seeing people with land producing a lot. There has been an increase in accusations that they are capitalists, as if [these comrades] are afraid that the people have too much. . . . I say we shouldn't be afraid of those rich people, and if they conduct overseas business, we will have sufficient commerce."[33]

Uk Bunchheuan supported Ros Chhun, insisting that wealthy Cambodians were not nearly wealthy enough. "So far, we've been way on the left in this area, afraid, as Ros Chhun says, that there will be rich people. I say that there won't be rich people. There will be rich people only when the prime minister, the president of the Council of State, and the general secretary of the Party turn into big capitalists. And still we'll face hardships." Bunchheuan reassured the Council of Ministers that economic growth in Cambodia would never create the heartless conditions of the capitalist West. "Rich people in our country," he contended, "have better hearts than rich people in other countries. Rich people in Cambodia don't have bad hearts like rich people in France and England. Rich people in Cambodia see poor people in need and are happy to distribute land to them or help them have equal wealth."[34]

Socialism had been replaced by charity, class struggle by *noblesse oblige*. Apparently forgetting that there had ever been a revolution in Cambodia, the two former Khmer Rouge cadres, Ros Chhun and Uk Bunchheuan, were suggesting that there was something fundamentally generous about Cambodian culture that would prevent big discrepancies in wealth from appearing. The argument was self-serving and, from the perspective of ordinary Cambodians, wrong. Three years later, when anti-corruption demonstrations filled the streets of Phnom Penh, protesters ransacked and burned a house purportedly misappropriated by Ros Chhun.[35]

ATTRACTING FOREIGN INVESTMENT

The money would have to come from somewhere. Since 1982 the PRK had gained hard currency by exporting natural resources through Vietnam, an arrangement that limited the Cambodians' access not only to foreign currency markets but to their own assets. As Cha Reang, head of the National Bank, explained to the Council of Ministers in October 1989, "Our currency goes to our Vietnamese friends, and Vietnam takes it for deposit in East Germany. So we have an account only with Vietnam, and settlements are extremely slow." Without hard currency assets the riel remained weak and, in many parts of the country, nearly worthless. In the east, Vietnamese dong circulated well into the mid-1980s, while most of the Cambodian economy operated with Thai baht, gold, silver, and gems. As it had since 1979, the regime launched periodic campaigns in which ministries and local state administrations were ordered to collect foreign currencies, valuable metals, and gems. The problem was that these same state institutions tended to keep whatever they confiscated rather than submit their acquisitions to the National Bank.[36]

To tap into the capital circulating in the informal economy, the Party encouraged private investment in state enterprises, amending the constitution to include what it referred to as the "mixed economy." Still, the leadership was anxious not to appear too lenient. A report from the Council of Ministers to the National Assembly reassured the delegates that the state would still "guide all production activities, examine production decisions, and facilitate the private sector in functioning in accordance with goals determined by the Party and the state." Despite arguments from Ministry of Justice and Council of Ministers cadres, the constitutional amendment failed to include any acknowledgment of overseas private investment. Instead, it read, "Foreign commerce is under the management and organization of the state." It was understood, however, that economic reform was moving faster than the Party was willing to acknowledge publicly. As Hun Sen told the Council of Ministers, "I still remember that [while] the Politburo has said that the state controls overseas commerce, in this place and time we may use the private sector. But in the constitution it is difficult to say this."[37]

In late 1988 and throughout 1989, the PRK pursued foreign investment, in particular from Cambodia's Asian neighbors. Initially, investors sought merely to purchase Cambodian natural resources; the arrangements thus had little impact on the management of the overall economy. The larger challenge to the PRK's socialist ideology appeared when investors from Hong Kong, Thailand, France, Australia, and Brunei began seeking a more secure financial basis for their investments, namely, private banks and private insurance companies. Unwilling to accept full-scale privatization, the leadership was reluctant to turn away prospective investors, especially when those investors were overseas Khmers.[38]

PURE COUSINS

Since its inception, the PRK had been haunted by the Khmer diaspora, not only the hundreds of thousands of Cambodians living in Thai refugee camps but those now living in France, the United States, and Australia. Their absence from Cambodia symbolized the country's divisions; by remaining overseas, they supported, intentionally or not, the resistance's contention that the Cambodian conflict had not been resolved. By 1987 the PRK had concluded that if it were to prevail politically and diplomatically, it would have to extend an invitation to overseas Cambodians to return. The policy of national reconciliation, as put forward in August, guaranteed that full voting rights would be given to these Khmers, as well as assistance in repatriating and "positions in light of their personal capabilities and contributions." By announcing this new policy, the PRK hoped to undermine the resistance while bringing in desperately needed educated cadres. In return, the leadership would have to accept a bureaucracy with an increasingly bourgeois perspective. In a sense, it was the same bargain that the Front had promised in December 1978, before the suspicions and political indoctrination sessions of the early 1980s.[39]

In 1989, the regime stepped up its appeals, convincing several prominent exiles to return to Cambodia. The leadership was thrilled: the return of overseas Cambodians helped the PRK project an inclusive image and strengthened its position at the negotiating table. The less ideological leaders also reckoned that Western-trained noncommunists would help reform the economy, thereby encouraging yet more noncommunists to return. As Hun Sen told Chhang Song, a former minister of information during the Lon Nol regime and a resident of the United States, "I ask that our intellectuals overseas who have a high level of education or who have recently studied some global technology, when they come to visit Cambodia, help teach and conduct seminars for our students, university students, cadres, and staff so that they can absorb this new knowledge. If anyone sees that our government has shortcomings, they should offer an opinion. We ask for helpful advice. We don't cast any blame. Economic work is new for us. So implementation thus far has involved a whole lot of mistakes."[40]

Pung Peng Cheng, the most prominent prerevolutionary official to join the PRK, was the kind of Cambodian to whom economic reform was intended to appeal. A former government minister, secretary-general of the High Council of the Throne, and chief of cabinet for Sihanouk in the early 1970s, Peng Cheng also carried with him the hopes of his compatriots. "We have received telegrams from France sent to Mr. Pung Peng Cheng from a set of Khmers resident overseas who've asked to come and cooperate with us in the area of banking and insurance," reported Kong Samol to the Council of Ministers. As Samol pointed out, these proposals required that the PRK reconsider its economic policies. "Now we need a lot of insurance companies. Every property, hotel, and life has to have insurance. If our state does it, it will cost a lot. Should we do it ourselves, or have them do it? These days the big businesspeople really need insurance companies in order to insure their business investments."[41] The investment proposals presented by foreigners and overseas Cambodians divided the leadership. Private banking, for example, had the support of Hun Sen, who argued that the Vietnamese were already privatizing and that private moneylenders were operating in Cambodia anyway. Other Party leaders preferred "mixed" state-private banks, which were intended to bring hard currency under the control of the government, permit the government to monitor and control the activities of the investors, and even create a few jobs for idle, impoverished, and untrained state banking employees. Eventually, the advocates of privatization prevailed; the regime's economic survival depended on the injection of capital and its political survival on the co-optation of overseas Cambodians. As Hun Sen boasted in August 1991, "We are opening a whole lot of private markets that Prince (*Samdech*) Sihanouk recognizes and that allow those returning from overseas to see us as pure cousins again."[42]

THE OLD SOCIETY

Within the government, economic reform was frequently described as a return to the "old society." On tax matters, import-export laws, foreign investment, and insurance, Cambodian officials went in search of "old documents" and "old laws from Sihanouk and Lon Nol," texts that were mostly French colonial in origin. French-language materials were discovered around Phnom Penh or else sent from France by overseas Cambodians. But laws from other countries in the region also provided a basis for Cambodia's new economy; Deputy Prime Minister Kong Samol even returned from a seminar in Thailand with a draft of a new investment law. By the end of 1989, Hun Sen was issuing explicit instructions to his cabinet: "The Ministry of Commerce should immediately appoint expert cadres to draft commercial laws and regulations on imports and exports by private companies. [The ministry] should take laws from the old society and the laws of other countries as a basis [for the drafts] because commercial businesses and the framework of society [in Cambodia prior to the revolution and in capitalist countries] are similar [to those of modern Cambodia], requiring only that some inappropriate provisions be amended."[43]

The regime sorely lacked the "expert cadres" needed to draft and implement these new and amended laws. Having scoured Cambodia and Cambodian communities overseas for qualified people, the regime eventually looked to foreigners. Reflexively, Deputy Prime Minister Chea Soth continued to ask Vietnam for commercial advisors. At the same time, however, noncommunists like Deputy Justice Minister Chem Snguon were imploring the regime to look to the West. By 1990, French advisors were drafting commercial laws with Ministry of Commerce officials.[44]

As the leadership studied the economic policies of past regimes, they found Sihanouk's interventionist practices reassuring. "During the old period, private importers were all managed by the state," Commerce Minister Tang Sareum reminded the Council of Ministers, recalling Sihanouk's socialist experiments of

1963–69. "And even though the private sector exported and imported, the state also inspected." By contrast, the capitalism of the Lon Nol period seemed unacceptably dangerous. "If we take the model from 1971–72, we will be defeated," warned Uk Bunchheuan. "At that time, the private sector and the state came together. The private sector had the means [of production] and the state had none. But the private sector joined with the state, purchased raw materials, and [hired] workers, creating conditions that deteriorated over several years and damaged the state. At this point, [the situation] was very dangerous, and the Vietnamese [that is, the Vietnamese-backed Khmer Rouge] came in and overthrew [Lon Nol's regime]." Bunchheuan's point was that the mixed state-private economy with which the PRK was experimenting could be overwhelmed by the resources of the private sector. Yet, if there was another lesson from the past, it was that a mixed economy required a competent bureaucracy. "The experience of the Sihanouk era," continued Bunchheuan, "was that in some places what were called the Cooperative Trading Associations disappeared within three months, four months, or a year. This was because of the management system. [Likewise, the PRK's] state framework at the lower levels has no management that can handle accounting, managing coffers, or planning with regard to buying and selling." Uk Bunchheuan's historical analogies were apt: the private sector was undermining a resource-poor state sector with few trained personnel. The only difference was that there was no revolution.[45]

Where, then, was the Cambodian economy heading? The answer lay in far-flung provinces where economic forces depended not on theoretical notions of "socialism" and "capitalism," nor on legal documents from the "old society," but on geography and on Cambodia's rich neighbor to the west.

THE COAST

Cambodia shares a historically porous border with Thailand. In the southwest, the Cambodian province of Koh Kong is separated from Thailand by mountain ranges suited to undetected movements of rebels and smugglers. From the coast, where short stretches of beach are scattered among long miles of rugged, isolated shoreline, the short boat ride to Thailand can be equally clandestine, especially when undertaken at night. For hundreds of years, Thai, Chinese, and Khmer merchants have made the journey, openly and furtively, indifferent to diplomatic and military tensions between the two countries. As economic ties flourished, cultural distinctions blurred as well, especially for the tens of thousands of ethnic Thai fishermen and peasants who live in Koh Kong.

The rebellion waged in Koh Kong against the Khmer Rouge leadership was led by ethnic Thais and kept alive by Thai traders. Revolutionaries like Rong Keysan had been moving back and forth between Cambodia and Thailand since 1968, when an uprising in the province was suppressed by the Sihanouk regime, and hundreds of Thai-Cambodian and Khmer communists crossed over the border to safety. As these same communists rose within the Khmer Rouge military and political ranks—Keysan became the political commissar responsible for Party matters in a Khmer Rouge battalion—their economic ties to Thailand incurred suspicion. But it was also this relationship that saved them. Joined by Say Phouthang, who had recently returned from Hanoi, they found shelter from Khmer Rouge purges in the Thai village of Cham Yeam. There, the Thai-Cambodian revolutionaries survived economically and militarily by harvesting Cambodian timber, rattan, and beeswax and trading them for Thai rice.[46]

After the overthrow of Democratic Kampuchea, Vietnamese officials decided to grant control of Koh Kong to Rong Keysan and his ethnic Thai comrades. Whatever unsettling economic connections they may have had to Thai capitalists were less important than their revolutionary backgrounds and their proven animosity toward the Khmer Rouge. From Phnom Penh, Say Phouthang protected their interests, and in Koh Kong itself they enjoyed broad discretion over local Party matters and provincial economics. Not surprisingly, the province's ethnic Thai leadership tolerated a significant amount of trade with Thailand, prompting frequent, if ineffectual, complaints from Cambodian and Vietnamese authorities.[47]

The Vietnamese dry season offensive in 1984 and the construction of K5 barriers separating northwestern Cambodia from Thailand redirected more smuggling to the coast. The beneficiaries were the Koh Kong military authorities, who, taking advantage of a general policy of expanding Cambodian participation in the war effort, took on a larger role in patrolling the seas. Since Koh Kong had no real port and since docking required customs fees, Thai merchants were required to anchor just off the Cambodian shore, where they waited for the Cambodian navy or boats under the navy's protection to deliver timber and other goods. Soon, provincial military authorities and private importers and exporters working informally with the military were among the richest people in Cambodia.[48]

To the east of Koh Kong province lies the city of Kampong Som. As the only deepwater port in the country, Kampong Som provided the Soviets and international humanitarian organizations their only access to the Cambodian inte-

rior. The possibility of docking larger ships also made the Party leadership particularly fearful of infiltration from Thailand, and, citing the threat of enemy
arms shipments, they closed off the municipality to trade. Smuggling, as well as
the city's long mercantile history, nonetheless drew thousands of ethnic Chinese and bourgeois Khmers to Kampong Som. The city and its informal economy grew quickly, presided over by Chum Hol, the former Eastern Zone regiment commander who had once been Hun Sen's direct superior.[49]

By 1988 the regime was allowing Koh Kong and Kampong Som to openly
conduct and manage trade with Thailand and, in the words of Hun Sen, to
"compete for higher priced exports and lower priced imports." The two ports
quickly became the engines of the Cambodian economy as provincial authorities throughout the country established their own export-import companies
and delivered goods to the coast. These officials were required to deposit all foreign currency earned from this trade with the state Foreign Commerce Bank
and remit 10 percent of all export revenues to the central government, but as
trade became dominated by private merchants, Phnom Penh's demands were
routinely ignored.[50]

Kampong Som officials, after years of socialist trade and technical training
from Soviet port advisors, seized these new economic opportunities with con-
siderably more sophistication than did their Koh Kong counterparts. In contrast
to Koh Kong, where authorities attempted to monopolize the import-export
business, Kampong Som experienced a reemergence of bourgeois commercial
culture. "We export and import goods relying on the actual situation and relying on businesspeople," said Chum Hol in June 1988. Looking for revenues,
Kampong Som authorities opened the port to Thai boats and began collecting
docking fees. Municipal officials also requested permission to open a separate
dollar-denominated account, to spend hard currency earned from exports, and
to seize "illegal" goods from other provinces and export these goods themselves.
Hun Sen personally approved each of these requests.[51]

None of these decisions did anything to resolve the PRK's trade imbalance
with Thailand. As Chum Hol reported in May 1988, "We have serious problems with regard to exports and imports because we don't have goods for export. . . . We export 5 percent of the goods we import." Since 1979 and 1980,
when gold flowed out of Cambodia over the "land bridge" in exchange for Thai
goods, the regime had fretted about this imbalance. As the volume of trade increased, the government's ability to control its own economic destiny remained
elusive. Fixing, even influencing, the price of goods was beyond its capacity.
Meanwhile, the value of the riel continued to deteriorate. Choosing hard cur-

rency revenues over national pride, the regime permitted customs officials to tax businesspeople in U.S. dollars and Thai baht and granted the National Bank the right to buy and sell foreign currency. Still, revenues were hard to come by: Finance Minister Chhay Than estimated that smuggling deprived the government of between 40 percent and 50 percent of import-export revenues. For the central leadership, the only option was to negotiate directly with the Thais.[52]

MEETING BANGKOK

On January 25, 1989, Hun Sen and a twenty-four-member delegation visited Bangkok at the invitation of Thai Prime Minister Chatichai Choonhavan. In political discussions the Cambodians voiced their disapproval of the latest Sihanouk proposal, which had included an armed peacekeeping force and the dismantling of the PRK prior to elections. On economic matters, however, Hun Sen hoped to entice the Thai prime minister—who had called for turning Indochina "from a battlefield into a trading market"—with a series of concessions in the areas of gems, fish, and timber. The Cambodian delegation also focused their attention on the commander in chief of the Thai army, General Chavalit Yongchaiyudh. The Thai military, the delegates figured, would have an interest in Cambodian-Thai economic exchanges and might therefore encourage a shift in Thailand's diplomatic stance. A few days later, after the delegation had returned to Phnom Penh, the Council of Ministers established a Committee for Cambodian-Thai Cooperation in the hopes that a similar committee would be set up in Thailand. The Cambodians also selected, as chair of the committee, their ethnic Thai minister of defense, Tea Banh.[53]

Banh, who dates his revolutionary career from 1965, was serving as a Khmer Rouge military officer at the time of the 1974 rebellion. Along with Rong Keysan and Say Phouthang, he fled to Thailand and remained there until 1979, when he was appointed Koh Kong provincial military chief. Rising through the Party ranks, Tea Banh joined the Central Committee in 1984. In early 1985 he became minister of communications and transportation.[54]

As in Vietnam, the war in Cambodia prompted the Party to assign military officers to civilian ministerial positions. According to Say Phouthang, military experience was especially relevant to the communications post. "The [transfer] of Comrade Tea Banh is not incorrect, because communications requires some military expertise in order to organize the defense, say, of the construction of roads and bridges that serve the fighting." As minister of communications,

Banh accomplished precisely what Say Phouthang had intended: he created what amounted to the ministry's own armed forces, the Defense Committees, which worked with the Ministries of the Interior and Defense in protecting routes of transportation.[55]

As minister of defense and deputy prime minister, positions he assumed in late 1987, Tea Banh promoted better relations with Thailand, autonomy for state enterprises, a removal of price controls on rice, and a return to prerevolutionary economic practices. Banh also appreciated the economic interests of the military and defended revenue-generating schemes by local military units, including the sale of timber. This approach no doubt helped smooth negotiations with Thai investors, many of whom were members of or otherwise associated with the Thai military. Tea Banh's nonideological perspective also served Hun Sen's diplomatic strategies. "We see that we should decide to extract benefits from any group of [Thai] businesspeople that has an influence on the [Thai] government, especially the Thai armed forces because they control the [resistance]," Banh urged the Council of Ministers. "This serves to confront [the resistance] while also benefiting our people."[56]

Despite Tea Banh's obvious enthusiasm, the Thais kept their distance, refusing to send delegations so long as Vietnamese troops remained on Cambodian soil and failing to formally appoint officials to negotiate with the Cambodians. As Banh reported to the Council of Ministers in July 1989, "When Mr. Chatichai met me informally, his view was that it was not necessary to have a committee because there would be too many rules." Informally, however, business was booming. "Now there are a lot of Thai businesspeople," continued Banh. "Some come through Koh Kong, some through Kampong Som, and some by car. This creates a complex situation, which our [Cambodian-Thai Cooperation] Committee can't follow."[57]

To coordinate and centralize Thai investment, Hun Sen appointed the deputy minister of the Council of Ministers, Cham Prasith, as secretary-general of the Cambodian-Thai Cooperation Committee. Born Ung You Teckhor, Prasith came from a family of affluent Phnom Penh import-exporters. Though ethnic Chinese, the family pushed at the ceilings of political power. Prasith's father, Ung You Y, served as a member of parliament during the Lon Nol regime, representing the remote northern province of Steung Treng, where elections were noncompetitive. Teckhor himself studied commerce and economics and eventually went to work as the chief accountant at Crédit Foncier, a semipublic bank in Phnom Penh. Evacuated by the Khmer Rouge to the far northwestern corner of Cambodia in what is now Banteay Meanchey province, Teckhor lost his father to execution, his mother to dysentery, and dozens of other relatives to the various depredations and cruelties imposed by the revolution. His own survival, he explains, was due only to the ignorance of his captors. Teckhor, who wore glasses, convinced the Khmer Rouge that he was blind and therefore uneducated.[58]

For more than a year after liberation, Teckhor worked in the fields of Siem Reap. The PRK's own anti-Chinese policies were well known, and by the time his family moved back to Phnom Penh, he was going by the Khmer name of Cham Prasith. Soon his educational background and his French and English language skills landed him a position at Hun Sen's Ministry of Foreign Affairs, where he rose quickly, from interpreter to head of department, and, in 1985, to personal secretary to Hun Sen, now prime minister. Moving over to the Council of Ministers in 1987, Prasith assumed the position of deputy minister of the council in charge of trade, banking, finance, industry, communications and transportation, construction, foreign investment, and foreign affairs.[59]

At the council and at the Cambodian-Thai Cooperation Committee, Prasith took a dim, realistic view of the PRK's increasingly unproductive economic relations with the communist world, arguing that potential investment deals with the Thais would allow the regime to extract itself from its commitments to its Eastern European trading partners. Prasith did not, however, welcome all Western investors. Foreign-owned private banks, he warned, allowed foreigners to "conspire to steal from us" and impeded the state's ability to "monitor their tricks." He also sought to wrest control over Thai investment from overly independent ministries and provinces.[60]

Most of the Thais came looking for Cambodian natural resources—in particular, timber. Negotiating with local civilian and military authorities, they benefited from the policies and practices established in the early 1980s: the decentralization and militarization of the Cambodian timber industry. In many parts of the country, private businesspeople traded in timber under the constant threat of extortion by local security forces. Various forms of corruption abounded, including the forging or the sale of official letters of permission from the provincial timber offices, the military, and the police.[61]

In Koh Kong businesspeople working with local military and civilian authorities were already exporting timber to Thailand. Careful to remit a percentage of revenues to Phnom Penh, Koh Kong officials elicited praise from Cambodian officials and from Vietnamese advisor Fang You, who credited the province with "implementing more than the [state] plan [required]." By 1988, however, Thai timber companies were operating all along the border, in Steung

Treng, in Pursat, and in Battambang, where the Thais convinced the Cambodians to improve the railway from the provincial capital to the border town of Poipet, specifically to facilitate the export of timber.[62]

In Phnom Penh, the expansion of the timber industry prompted Cambodian officials to warn of environmental destruction. "If we have no good way to manage timber, we will become a country with no trees because we have been cooperating with Vietnam to the east and with Thailand to the west," remarked Boun Ouy, an official at the Council of Ministers in early 1989.[63] At the end of the year, Agriculture Minister Say Chhum urged the Party to change its policy of exploiting timber. "We have recalculated the damage of war. After the destruction of the Pol Pot period, there were an estimated eleven million hectares [of forest]. But now, in the middle of this past year, an international timber organization reevaluated timber areas in many countries, among which was Cambodia, which has only seven million hectares left. They further concluded that in the future Cambodian forests will be devastated and [Cambodia] could become like the Amazon region or areas in Kenya."[64]

Images of a desert Cambodia did not prevent the leadership from cutting its own deals with the Thais. After years of pleas from the Ministry of Agriculture and its Vietnamese advisors, ministry officials were finally permitted to engage in direct exports of timber. Almost immediately, the ministry conceded some 300,000 hectares of land to a Thai investor named Samphop Kongivikan, of which only 10,000 had been approved by the Council of Ministers. Despite complaints from Tea Banh, Cham Prasith, and others, the council actually expanded the ministry's authority and, in May 1990, granted it direct control over eight areas along the Thai, Lao, and Vietnamese borders for the purpose of exporting timber.[65]

In May 1989 another Thai investor, by the name of Samphan Sahavath, arrived in Phnom Penh to discuss timber directly with Hun Sen. Samphan, whose previous agreements had been concluded with Koh Kong provincial authorities, had his eye on three separate border areas in Battambang and Pursat provinces. For political as well as economic reasons, the leadership had little choice but to be accommodating. "We must cooperate and meet with Samphan's group," Tea Banh told the Council of Ministers, "because he has soldiers behind him." Thus, while the Thais were still supporting the Khmer Rouge, the PRK leadership was selling timber to a variety of Thai interests, in exchange, they hoped, for diplomatic support. Explained Tea Banh: "We've had four groups come to communicate with us. One was a government group that came only to assess [the situation] and has not yet produced any results, perhaps because it is waiting for the Vietnamese army to withdraw. Another group has the [Thai] Ministry of the Interior behind it. We have sold that group a little timber to get it to create favorable conditions with regard to political [relations] with us. So we should give further consideration to this group. Another group was from the Thai parliament. [And] we have sold a small amount of timber to the [Thai] province of Trat."[66]

Thai businesspeople arrived with other investment proposals, including the construction of restaurants and hotels near Angkor Wat and, to the chagrin of Cambodian officials hoping to bring hard currency to Phnom Penh, direct flights between Bangkok and Siem Reap. The Thais also had plans to invest in manufacturing, approaching Koh Kong officials and representatives of the Ministry of Industry to discuss the production of cement, plastic goods, tires, beer, milk, soda, ice, clothing, shoes, fuel, and blackboards. Their demands were steep. Seeking to build factories in Kampot, Kampong Som, and Koh Kong, Samphan Sahavath and a Thai-Cambodian businessman named Teng Bunma submitted requests to purchase land, which the Ministry of Industry granted. Electricity, housing for factory bosses, and multiyear tax holidays were also part of the package. Samphan even asked the Cambodian government for assistance in hiring Chinese technicians to oversee production at a cement factory. "I am concerned about the use of Chinese experts to help fix up the cement factory," said Commerce Minister Tang Sareum. "Are they really technicians? [I am worried] because they are the slaves of China (*apot chea kaun cheung robas chen*)." The more pragmatic Nheum Vanda responded, "If we don't use the Chinese technicians, there will be a lot of problems because the factory parts come from China."[67]

Five years after his losing battle against Phnom Penh's Chinese-driven private economy, Tang Sareum was now watching as the investment and import-export sectors fell into the hands of foreigners. "There has been some work in which we've been too quick to [accommodate the foreign investors] because of our sentiments toward them," he complained to the Council of Ministers. "We should get a handle on their tricks and be careful, as in the story of the monster who comes disguised as a holy man."[68]

INFILTRATION

At various locations along the border but especially in Koh Kong, Thais were entering Cambodia more or less at will. In 1989 the Thai government decided to encourage this influx, authorizing the construction of two roads from Trat to

Koh Kong. With the Cambodian Ministry of the Interior complaining of its lack of police at the southwestern border, the leadership was forced to acknowledge its inability to control the situation. As Dith Munty, now minister of foreign affairs, remarked, "These days, because we have the goal of expanding foreign guests' access to Cambodia, we face a lot of confusion."[69]

Once inside Cambodia, the Thais discovered that the private transportation sector made internal travel relatively easy. In Phnom Penh, Cambodian ministers were horrified to find Thai investors walking into their offices after making the trip by themselves. At the Council of Ministers, they blamed officials from Koh Kong and Kampong Som for failing to regulate travel outside their jurisdictions. Sun Heng, deputy governor of Kampong Som, defended the way his municipality had dealt with Thai investors who asked to visit Phnom Penh, explaining that waiting for permission would entail "long delays." Despite complaints from Cham Prasith, Tea Banh sided with the provincial authorities. "Even though [the investors] come inappropriately and no matter how [they get here], we should continue to receive them and the groups with which they arrive." For Banh, at least, the desire to attract Thai investment outweighed the security concerns.[70]

Not all the Thais came to Phnom Penh. "Some guests come to invest or come as tourists; but we don't know what others have come to do, where they go, or where they stay," said Kong Samol. "None of us can control it. If the guests come to invest, it's not such a problem, and we cooperate in order to help them. But if they hire people to come engage in activities against our revolution, it is dangerous because we can't manage them." Cham Prasith agreed. "A big problem that the Ministries of Foreign Affairs and the Interior have no control over is the Khmers who've gone to live in Thailand and taken Thai citizenship. They enter Cambodia speaking Thai, and we don't know what their intentions are. Even [Sihanouk's son, resistance leader Norodom] Rannaridh speaks and sings in Thai." It was an odd reversal of prejudice: the Thais were fine, but not Khmers disguised as Thais.[71]

THE NORTHWEST

One destination that the leadership did know about and which caused a great deal of consternation was Battambang. Recent victories by Vietnamese and Cambodian forces had brought valuable territory under PRK control—in particular, the gem-rich town of Pailin. Because Thai merchants could no longer buy gems from the Khmer Rouge, they endeavored to enter Cambodia through

Koh Kong and Kampong Som and to cut deals with PRK officials. In mid-1989, Deputy Minister of the Interior Khoem Pon complained that despite the ministry's checkpoints and its regular searches of travelers, "capitalist businessmen" from Thailand were buying gems. "Most are spies," he warned.[72]

Like their comrades in Koh Kong, Battambang authorities had always tolerated a certain amount of trade with Thailand. In the early 1980s provincial military figures smuggled, extorted money and goods from private smugglers, and thwarted tax officials sent by Phnom Penh. Battambang's Party secretary at the time, a Hanoi veteran named Lay Samon, received the blame, not so much for what was happening in the province but for harboring gold and not sending it to the capital. In 1984, around the time that many of his former Hanoi comrades were being purged, Samon was removed.[73]

Samon's dismissal did nothing to change the basic economic and political patterns in Battambang and only helped consolidate military control over the province. After Vietnamese military officials assigned a larger role to Cambodian officers and soldiers, the Cambodians enjoyed more discretion, more freedom of movement, and more economic opportunities. Not only did the Cambodian armed forces participate in smuggling; they controlled the distribution of K5 materials and, thanks to the successes of the Vietnamese military, acquired whole new tracts of land to develop or exploit.

Although the Party had been encouraging, and at times compelling, Cambodians to move to underpopulated areas since 1980, territorial gains made during the 1984–85 dry-season offensive permitted the regime to send Cambodians to the war-torn areas that it euphemistically called New Economic Zones. Inspired by the Vietnamese policy of the same name, the repopulating of these northwestern territories was no more popular in Cambodia than it was in Vietnam. Daunted by the isolation, the proximity of the war, and the complete lack of a functioning economy in the zones, Cambodians resisted, and it is unclear how many ever actually arrived. Nonetheless, the New Economic Zones fell under the control of both the military and the K5 authorities, who organized local residents into militias and, when necessary, mobilized labor forces.[74]

The Cambodian military was quick to seize the economic opportunities available in the new territories. In September 1988 the Council of Ministers decided to allow foreign companies, presumably Thai, to mine for gems in the Pailin area of Battambang and gave the Ministries of Defense and the Interior the responsibility of choosing mining sites and making other necessary arrangements. Much of this task went to Nheum Vanda, who by early 1989 was deputy minister of defense, deputy minister of planning, deputy chair of the

Committee for Cambodian-Thai Cooperation, deputy chair of the Committee for the Construction of the Cambodia-Thai Border, and a two-star lieutenant general. Visiting Pailin, Vanda surveyed the area's geography and demographics and laid plans for strict military control over gem mining and exports to Thailand.[75]

Declaring Pailin a "prohibited area," Vanda hoped to restrict the unauthorized influx of Cambodians into the area while maintaining the military's monopoly over the gem trade. By the middle of 1989, however, Cambodians and Thais were entering gem areas "furtively, through private channels," according to Khoem Pon. Government reports estimated that between 10 and 20 percent of all state workers in Battambang province were leaving their duties to dig for gems. As Cambodians and Thais paid bribes to local military and civilian officials, tax revenues from the region actually decreased. In October 1989, after the Vietnamese withdrawal, Pailin fell again to the Khmer Rouge, who immediately began exploiting the gem resources for themselves.[76]

OPENING THE BORDER

North of Pailin, the dusty town of Poipet presented the Cambodian leadership with one of its most confounding economic and political decisions: whether to open the border with Thailand. Ever since 1979, when the land bridge to international humanitarian aid transformed Poipet into the commercial capital of Cambodia, local and Phnom Penh officials had understood the revenue-generating potential of the border crossing. In the mid-1980s, Vietnamese military authorities launched the K5 program, closed off the border, and, to tighten its administration of northern Battambang, created the new province of Banteay Meanchey. Yet even as Poipet remained relatively quiet, the temptations of trade were on the minds of local leaders. In 1989, Banteay Meanchey governor It Leua asked the Council of Ministers to open the crossing at Poipet to "allow foreign guests to enter and leave and conduct business," suggesting that "the provincial [administration] keep all the revenues coming into the province during the first year after the opening in order to develop the province."[77]

After another year of smuggling, the leadership concluded that the PRK's inept border controls accomplished little other than depriving Phnom Penh of revenues. In Hun Sen's words, "Even if we keep it closed, we believe that it will burst open, but we won't know where; it will just burst open at some other pass." Under the new policy, provincial Party and state officials, top military officers, and K5 authorities were free to establish direct economic relations with

Thai military authorities. Traders now had an opportunity to import and export goods with fewer hassles, paying taxes at a single checkpoint rather than negotiating an undetermined number of costly obstacles. But common soldiers who had lived off smuggling faced a more uncertain future. According to Tea Banh, "Businesspeople with money hire [Cambodian soldiers] to sit on their trucks to protect [the smugglers]. With [the border] closed, the businesspeople have to employ these soldiers. If the border were opened and I were a businessperson, I'd be happy to pay someone else [other than the soldiers] because I'm already operating legally." Opening the border, he said, could "result in reduced [economic] activities by the armed forces."[78]

The leadership faced a dilemma. Open cross-border trade offered the possibility of regulating economic activity, even perhaps of establishing a functioning import-export tax regime. At the same time, however, channeling trade through a legal market would deprive soldiers and officials of smuggling revenues, without which the entire patronage system might collapse. As meetings at the Council of Ministers make clear, the leadership understood the paradox but could reach no consensus on what to do about it.

For Deputy Defense Minister Ke Kim Yan, the border crossing represented a chance to expand trade, increase tax revenues, and improve national security. Kim Yan, who had risen through the Battambang military on a reputation for competence and professionalism, argued that the proliferation of checkpoints deprived traders of their profits and resulted in low tax revenues. Kim Yan recognized the potential effects that a legalized trading system would have on local military units and proposed that a salary system replace the current profit seeking—in short, that Cambodia nurture a professional military. "It is necessary to distribute [a portion of tax revenues] to the organizations that maintain security in order to raise morale and get them to try harder to defend [the border]."[79]

Nheum Vanda was somewhat less inclined toward such formal arrangements. Having built a career along the blurry line between military authority and the informal economy, Vanda appreciated the need for personal discretion and ad hoc profit seeking by soldiers and low-level officials. He did not oppose the opening of the crossroads; he merely insisted that those who had previously benefited from smuggling not be deprived of their livelihood. As Vanda remarked some months later, "There are brothers there who complain that they can't work if an [open] market exists. But in fact they are afraid of losing their personal benefits. I raised this issue, so that percentages are distributed as before." These views found favor with Hun Sen, whose only concern was that local profit taking not choke off trade altogether. "How should imports and exports function?" he asked the Council of Ministers. "Profits from confiscation should not be everything—at most, 50 percent. Don't permit [local officials] to take it all." A few months later, Hun Sen appointed Nheum Vanda to administer the border crossing, in place of Ke Kim Yan.[80]

HUN SENISM

By the summer of 1990, Hun Sen had finally arrived at an economic system that made sense to him. He had long ago given up on communism as unworkable. But he had not embraced capitalism, at least not the kind that precludes arbitrary and unforeseen state intervention. Instead, he promoted the discretionary authority of local officials. As Hun Sen saw it, these officials would remain loyal to their superiors and to the regime only if they were permitted to benefit directly and personally from local economic activity. "A part of the profits must go to [local officials]," he told the Council of Ministers with regard to the border. "If there aren't any [profits, the system] won't work."[81]

For Hun Sen, the lessons of history were complex. Power was not based on ideology, which had repeatedly failed to motivate state officials or to inspire loyalty. Rather, a stable regime required the enrichment of its officials. This vision evoked patterns of patronage that had existed in Cambodia long before the revolution. It also recalled the curious communism of Democratic Kampuchea, in which general lawlessness permitted cadres to amass modest wealth, relative, at least, to ordinary citizens. Only Hun Sen—Khmer Rouge soldier, economic reformer, and defender of patronage—could criticize the ideology of Democratic Kampuchea while praising the freedoms the regime had conferred on its cadres. As he told the Council of Ministers: "Experience shows that political spirit alone doesn't work, that, no matter what, it fails. Communism in China will fail, no matter what. This is surely their story. Pol Pot communism [was doomed to] fail, no matter what. [Yet] we don't even have gruel to eat, whereas [the Khmer Rouge cadres] ate heartily, and their day-to-day power was greater than ours. During the Pol Pot era district chiefs were wealthier than our officials. They lived prosperously and had equipment, cars, motor scooters, everything, whereas we have nothing, and our officials have no day-to-day power."[82]

Hun Sen was not calling for a return of Khmer Rouge economics; he was simply encouraging the current regime to be as generous with its officials as had Democratic Kampuchea. He was also promoting what would be Cambodia's postcommunist economic system. In Phnom Penh, reform-minded bureaucrats and former Sihanouk and Lon Nol officials were pushing for capitalist investment, from which they hoped to generate personal wealth as well as state revenues. In the provinces, state enterprises were expected to survive without subsidies, and local authorities were permitted to import and export. Yet this was not exactly market economics. By encouraging competition within the state sector, Hun Sen and like-minded leaders were creating a kind of state capitalism in which officials were prone to consider the resources at their disposal—land, factory parts, timber, vehicles, soldiers—as assets to be exploited for profit. For Hun Sen and much of the rest of the leadership, a permissive system of this sort was the key to consolidating power. It created networks of happy officials whose loyalty the regime could count on, even after the Vietnamese withdrew and Sihanouk returned.

Chapter 13 The End
of the Occupation

Cambodians who tuned in their radios in April 1989 would have heard Chea Sim speaking of political change. "Our National Assembly must examine and amend the fundamental legislation of our state, namely, our constitution," he announced. "This has to be done. With or without a political solution, we should amend our constitution. This is the norm and basic principle in matters of political, economic, and ideological reform." There were no specifics, and Cambodians must have wondered what Chea Sim meant. The economic reforms had been clear enough. But political reform was an elusive concept. The Vietnamese were leaving. Hun Sen was speaking to Sihanouk. That they knew. But what was coming?[1]

A DIPLOMATIC SOLUTION

In February 1989 the two sides were still far apart. According to the latest Indochinese diplomatic communiqué, "The withdrawal of Vietnamese troops should go hand in hand with the end of all military assistance to various Cambodian parties; the nonreturn of the Pol Pot regime, guilty of genocidal crimes; the prevention of a civil war; an international control mechanism; and an international conference." Internal matters, the document continued, would be resolved by Cambodians themselves, meaning that the PRK administration would not be dismantled. For Sihanouk, these conditions were practically offensive. "I will not . . . participate in this cynical comedy performed unashamed by the colonialist Viets and their Phnom Penh puppets," insisted the prince, explaining why he was boycotting the latest round of negotiations.[2]

For the leaders of the Soviet Union, China, and Vietnam, the prospect of normalizing relations with each other was too important to let Cambodia get in the way. In early February, Soviet Foreign Minister Eduard Shevardnadze visited Beijing for talks on the Sino-Soviet relationship. In a joint communiqué, Shevardnadze and his Chinese counterpart, Qian Qichen, acknowledged Vietnam's intention to withdraw by September and accepted the principle that foreign military aid to all parties (including the Chinese-backed Khmer Rouge) would be terminated. Meanwhile, both China and Thailand were making conditional overtures to Vietnam. In January, Thai Foreign Minister Siddhi Savetsila arrived in Hanoi to discuss the Vietnamese withdrawal from Cambodia as well as diplomatic normalization and increased economic cooperation between Thailand and Vietnam. A month and a half later, the outgoing Chinese ambassador to Vietnam told Vietnamese President Vo Chi Cong that Sino-Vietnamese relations could be normalized after the Cambodia conflict was resolved.[3]

At the end of March 1989, at the Sixth Plenum of the Central Committee of the Vietnamese Communist Party, Hanoi effectively acknowledged its diplomatic motives for ending the occupation. "We are shifting the direction of leadership over the strategy of foreign affairs gradually to open new capabilities and favorable conditions for developing the relations of co-operation with regional countries as well as with other countries in the world." A week later, the governments of Vietnam, Cambodia, and Laos released a joint statement saying that Vietnamese troops would withdraw from Cambodia unconditionally.[4]

The pressure was on Phnom Penh to find a diplomatic solution. The plan to hold elections with the various Cambodian parties had long been a matter of mutual agreement. The problem, as far as Phnom Penh was concerned, lay in the resistance's vision of a neutralized preelection Cambodia in which the PRK administration had been replaced by a multiparty interim government headed by Sihanouk. Any suggestion that the regime be dismantled was, in the words of Hun Sen, "absolutely unacceptable." If the CGDK was going to demand an open, inclusive, multiparty Cambodia, Phnom Penh would provide one, on its own terms.[5]

PHNOM PENH SPRING

To appear as inclusive and nonideological as possible, the Party established a Constitutional Commission that included several prominent overseas Cambodians: In Tam, a prime minister during the Lon Nol period and a resistance leader in more recent years; Pung Peng Cheng, the former secretary-general of the High Council of the Throne under Sihanouk; and Madame Pung Peng Cheng, a former minister of health, labor, and social affairs. "In addition to the above membership," the Council of State stated rather hopefully, "the commission can expand and add more members . . . such as Cambodian political dignitaries overseas and other Cambodians among the ranks of the opposition that want to participate in the commission."[6]

Within the commission, the discussion was mostly about symbolism and semantics. When the overseas Cambodians were not in attendance, however, the Party leadership admitted how superficial the process really was. At the Council of State, Heng Samrin discussed whether to use the word "Revolutionary" or "People's" in front of the names of state institutions. "If we don't insert the word 'Revolutionary,' there isn't any problem," conceded Samrin. "What is important is 'People's.' The achievements of the revolution are the achievements of the people because it was the people who accomplished them. We'll say 'People's Army' because the people were the ones to conduct the revolution." Responded Sar Kheng, who had just been appointed to the Politburo, "The use of this word ['People's'] is important to serve domestic and external politics. Pol Pot has entirely ruined the meaning of the word ["Revolutionary"]. We won't use the word 'Revolutionary,' but we'll continue to conduct revolution."[7]

On April 29, Chea Sim convened an extraordinary session of the National Assembly to adopt the constitutional amendments. There were changes to the flag, the national anthem, and the coat of arms, all of which had been stripped of their ideological content. The word "Revolutionary" disappeared from the names of administrative bodies. Buddhism became the state religion, and the death penalty was abolished. The Party even agreed to change the name of the country itself, from the People's Republic of Kampuchea to the nonideological name preferred by Hun Sen: the State of Cambodia (SOC). Outside Cambodia, the response to these changes was tepid. CGDK spokespeople characterized the new constitution as the "maneuvers of the Hanoi authorities" and as "unworthy of notice." Inside the country, there appeared to be an atmosphere of relative openness. Some foreign observers referred to the moment as the Phnom Penh Spring.[8]

Were Cambodians freer? Culturally and economically, Cambodia, or at least Phnom Penh, had undergone considerable change. The markets were filled with products from Thailand, China, and Singapore, bought by healthy Cambodians in new clothes. Restaurants, coffeehouses, bars, and beauty salons were opening their doors. For the first time since 1975, Cambodians could talk openly to foreigners, including aid workers and journalists, and even study English and French. At home they listened to the radio and watched foreign videos on new television sets.

There was no political freedom; Cambodians who gathered in a "suspicious manner" were still subject to arrest. But the appearance of bicycles, motor scooters, and telephones made communications and meetings easier. The police, weakened and corrupt, had no ideological reason to prevent internal movements, although they were still prone to extorting money from motorists and pedestrians. City dwellers shopped, visited family and friends, and strolled arm in arm along the river, tasting what the Party had always referred to as reactionary culture. To some in the leadership, these developments were worrisome. Others felt it was time to leave the capital's residents alone. "Every day we make mistakes," Uk Bunchheuan reminded the Council of Ministers. "There are some young people who are in love, and yet we consider them prostitutes."[9]

Social vices were indeed on the rise, including gambling, drug abuse, theft, and prostitution. Cambodian girls arrived in Phnom Penh from the countryside, some sold into prostitution by their families. Periodic crackdowns by municipal authorities resulted in hundreds of arrests, detention in secret reeducation centers, beatings, and rapes. Vietnamese prostitutes were also caught in the web of the police and sometimes sent back to Vietnam. Prostitution corrupted the state as the more affluent prostitutes and madams paid off the police. The involvement by some government officials in the prostitution business complicated the regime's efforts to crack down. "If the madams are our staff or cadres or are related to our staff or cadres," said Deputy Minister of the Interior Khoem Pon, "we have a hard time [making arrests], and there might be a protest."[10]

Although there were no open political challenges to the regime, Vandy Kaon came closest to offering one. For several years he had been traveling to and from France and attending fewer sessions of the National Assembly and Coun-

cil of State. He was also testing the boundaries of artistic expression and freedom of association by applying to establish an independent filmmakers association, a request approved with the caveat that he seek permission before establishing "contact with international organizations." Deferential in person,
Ka-on let his feelings be known in the reports he submitted as chair of the Legislation Commission of the Assembly. By 1988 he was drafting lengthy condemnations of the regime, the government, and the security forces. Lawlessness
abounded in Cambodia, wrote Ka-on, "because all the police and military institutions are the instruments of absolute power of the lower class (*vonnah
athon*) of the Party."[11] Critical of the corruption and repression that he saw destroying the country, Ka-on struck out at the very legitimacy of the government. Referring to Cambodia as a "feudal society," he appealed to the National
Assembly to hold the leadership accountable. "If [ministers] don't serve the
people, do we dare to remove them from government? This is an issue that we,
as representatives of the people, should reconsider. The [Legislation] Commission observes that if we don't exercise our full rights as representatives of the
people, the people will be right to accuse us of not fulfilling our duties as representatives, and we should, according to the law, be removed by the people because we are not serving their wishes. . . . The Commission requests a vote of
no confidence and removal of members of the government who are not serving
the wishes of the people."[12]

It is unclear whether such uncautious political statements prompted Vandy
Ka-on's flight from Cambodia. In his final speech, at the July 1989 Assembly
session, he was more reserved, calling for the prime minister to "be granted
broad rights to select and replace members of the Council of Ministers." Ka-
on, who says he was chased out of the country, does not blame the Cambodian
leadership. Hun Sen and Chea Sim liked him, he still insists, attributing the
surveillance and intimidation he encountered to "mysterious people" within
the Ministry of the Interior or simply the "Party." Financial issues may also
have contributed to his departure. Kong Samol and Chan Ven accused him of
bilking a film production company, and Heng Samrin even called for the
seizure of his assets in Cambodia. Whether the charges were trumped up or
not, Ka-on left Cambodia for good in September 1989, settling in France with
his wife, children, and mother.[13]

In Ka-on's absence, Thun Saray took over the Institute of Sociology, publishing a journal called *Economics* (*Sedtakech*). With articles entitled "How Are
Socialist Economics and Capitalist Economics Different?" and essays on mon-
etarism, Keynesian theory, joint ventures, and the Asian economic experience,

Economics was well ahead of the Party with regard to economic reform. But with Cambodia submersed in an economic free-for-all, it was not the content of Saray's journal that eventually landed him in trouble.[14]

HINTS OF PLURALISM

In the spring of 1989, just prior to the constitutional amendments, Hun Sen announced that there would be elections in Cambodia shortly after the withdrawal of the Vietnamese. The resistance, still insisting on a neutral environment for elections, referred to any unilateral moves by the PRK to hold elections as "illegitimate." In Phnom Penh, however, the leadership was already hammering out its version of pluralism.[15]

"If there is no political solution, and [Cambodians] return from overseas and want to create political parties but don't want to join with our Party, are they permitted to create a party?" asked Chan Ven at the Council of State. "We recognize all political forces, but our Party is the core leader (*snoul deuk noam*)," responded Heng Samrin. "A politician may have a party but must cooperate with our Party." This, in fact, was the Vietnamese model: a set of "minority parties" controlled by the Communist Party. To Hun Sen, who considered the mere recognition of other parties a concession, this seemed fair. "In this society that we are currently guiding," he said, "we are not yet permitting the creation of political parties. If there is a political solution and if [opposition politicians] come [to Cambodia], there should be mutual give-and-take. They repay us by recognizing us as the central leader. We repay them by recognizing them as a legal party."[16]

On the surface, it appeared that the Party might tolerate democratic debate. In July 1989, Chea Sim opened a session of the National Assembly with a call for "rapid change in the conditions of openness and appropriate accommodation in the period of national people's democracy." Adding that "the reform of the economy is proceeding, accompanied by political reform," Sim assured the Assembly that the regime was "promoting the courage to think, the courage to act, the courage to take responsibility, and the spirit of speaking truthfully and correctly, [a spirit] that is increasingly taking hold at all levels."[17]

Internally, however, the Party was becoming less inclined than ever toward political reform. One reason was that Sihanouk, despite initial public praise for the new constitution, was raising concerns. Some were merely symbolic—including the use of "People's" before the names of state institutions—whereas others went to the heart of Phnom Penh's approach toward pluralism. In particular, Sihanouk took issue with article 4 of the constitution, which stated that the Party was "the leading force (*kamlang deuk noam*) of the Cambodian society and state and the core force (*kamlang snoul*) of great national solidarity and of all political forces." The SOC, he declared, should adopt a parliamentary, multiparty liberal democracy. Sihanouk also insisted on international supervision of elections and a provisional government and military that included the resistance factions. So long as the SOC continued to reject these proposals, he refused Hun Sen's offer to return to Cambodia as head of state. Political reform having thus failed to draw Sihanouk toward Phnom Penh, the Party saw little reason to push it further.[18]

The Party leadership was also busy assessing the military situation and liked what it saw. In places where the Vietnamese army had withdrawn partially and allowed the Cambodian soldiers to fight, the Cambodians had held their own. Despite initial fears that Battambang, Siem Reap, Kampong Thom, and Pursat would all be vulnerable to attack after the Vietnamese withdrawal, the Politburo now concluded that none of these provinces would fall. Reductions in military aid to the resistance forces from China, the United States, and Thailand could only improve the situation for Phnom Penh. Feeling optimistic, the leadership drifted away from thoughts of negotiated solutions and liberalized political regimes. On July 10, 1989, the day before Chea Sim's inviting speech to the National Assembly, Hun Sen told the ministers of the interior of Vietnam and Laos where the Party really stood. "Before, we didn't expect to win militarily, and we decided to choose a political solution," he told the visitors. "But then the balance of forces shifted, and the leadership came up with the strategy of 'no political solution concerning internal views.'" Hun Sen explained that because the Party was "still seeking a political solution with regard to international views," it was "playing both sides," meaning that publicly it would present a more liberal face. "This is an issue that is absolutely secret in the strategy of the Party," he added.[19]

The leadership was thinking long-term and preparing for the withdrawal of the Vietnamese. "There are only three months left before the Vietnamese withdraw," Hun Sen reminded the Vietnamese and Lao visitors, "and during this short period of time, we have no hope for negotiations with Sihanouk. What's important is that we must prepare so that when the fraternal [Vietnamese] army leaves entirely, we will still have a stable situation." Not surprisingly, a meeting between Hun Sen and Sihanouk at the end of July ended in stalemate, as did a much anticipated international conference in Paris. A frustrated Sihanouk went home to Beijing comparing the Vietnamese to the Nazi occupiers of France.[20]

A few members of the Politburo were wondering whether Phnom Penh should pursue a political solution at all. Heng Samrin opposed the peace process for ideological reasons and, no doubt, for personal ones—if Sihanouk were to return, he stood to lose his position as head of state. Chea Soth considered negotiating with Sihanouk a waste of time, as he explained to Phan Ngoc Tuong, a visiting Vietnamese minister.

> Sihanouk has a lot of debts. Without France, it's tough for him. Without China, without America, without ASEAN, and without Pol Pot and Son Sann, it's tough for him. It's especially hard for him to be heard in family disputes. And he can't discard Beijing, either. He can't choose a political solution with us. Only when he can push all of these groups away will he be able to come to us unencumbered. . . .
>
> In my personal opinion, I don't want there to be a political solution. If there is a political solution, there will be continued fighting and confusion throughout the country just as before. Also, according to our assessment of the people, they don't want any political solution either, because now, in Phnom Penh, the people are happy making money. . . . Some want Sihanouk to come back, but those who have lived with him are really sick and tired (*thun troan nas*) of him already.[21]

THE VIETNAMESE WITHDRAW

The regime braced itself for the withdrawal of the Vietnamese and for a resistance offensive with the knowledge that, if things got too out of hand, Vietnamese troops could always return. As Chea Soth reminded Phan Ngoc Tuong, "No matter what, if there is a major problem, our Vietnamese friends will not stand silently with their hands tied. I believe wholeheartedly that this would surely happen because for our two countries, if one has problems, the other is uneasy. So we will continue to cooperate in defending each other. Right or wrong and in whatever fashion, our Vietnamese friends will not be completely quiet."[22]

On September 21, 1989, the Vietnamese celebrated their service in Cambodia and their departure. Lines of troops and tanks filed ceremoniously past crowds of onlookers in Phnom Penh. Bands played, paper flags were waved, and flowers were distributed. Throughout the day and night, Cambodian and Vietnamese officials gave speeches and raised their glasses to solidarity.

In the months that followed, the resistance—in particular, the Khmer

Rouge—took territory previously held by the State of Cambodia, including the gem-rich town of Pailin. Still, the performance of Cambodia's armed forces exceeded the leadership's expectations. "By our estimate, we could lose up to 30 percent of our territory," Hun Sen told a visiting Lao dignitary in December. "We knew clearly that when the Vietnamese army left, we wouldn't be able to hold on to 100 percent of the territory, as we did when the Vietnamese army was here. We planned to hold on to 70 percent and to strengthen our forces to fight for 100 percent. But so far our losses haven't reached 30 percent."[23]

The resistance, along with the Chinese, the Thais, and the Singaporeans, expressed doubts that the Vietnamese had actually left. The Chinese charged that some 30,000 Vietnamese troops remained; Son Sann spoke of 100,000 armed Vietnamese civilians on Cambodian soil. SOC documents confirm the accusations, if not the figures. According to a Ministry of the Interior report from September 1990, there were "Vietnamese soldiers and Vietnamese people conducting military activities with a strategic plan in the battlefields to launch a campaign to mop up [the resistance]." As late as May 1991 the Council of Ministers was still issuing decisions on salaries for Vietnamese security advisors and on housing, travel, hospital care, and financial assistance for their families, but without reference to soldiers. There are no subsequent documentary records on the subject.[24]

LEFT ALONE

The Vietnamese advisors had stayed longer than anticipated. In mid-1982 Vietnamese authorities had told the Cambodian leadership that the advisors would stay for only another three or four years; five years later, they were still there. One of the reasons was that Cambodian state institutions continued to request more advisors, regardless of whether they were of any use. Cambodian bureaucrats were also exhibiting an uncomfortable level of dependency on their advisors. According to Say Phouthang, eight years of Vietnamese tutelage was just beginning to show dividends. "Gradually we're able to do the work ourselves, and some documents we're drafting ourselves and just passing them by the advisors for their opinion." Eventually, many of the Vietnamese lost patience with their Cambodian colleagues. "At the end of 1987 comrade advisors trusted us and took our hands and made us do things by ourselves," said Meas Leas of the Council of Ministers.[25]

Some Cambodian officials, including Planning Minister Chea Chantho, Finance Minister Chhay Than, and the chief of the Council of Ministers, Ung

Phan, argued for reductions in the number of advisors, particularly at Party organs such as the mass organizations, and in the number of visiting political delegations from Vietnam. The value of economic advisors and technicians was also in question, especially given their increasingly irrelevant socialist backgrounds. "In fact, we don't know what they've achieved," said Chea Soth, "because we go according to the proposals of B68, and B68 examines their achievements and then reports to us. I've seen that some comrade advisors don't really do a lot."[26]

In March 1988, after most Vietnamese advisors had gone home, the Party's Central Organization Committee sent out a letter ordering bureaucrats to meet and discuss whether their institutions could function on their own. The ensuing meetings revealed some of the mixed feelings held by Cambodian officials regarding the Vietnamese and regarding their own competence. Noncommunist technicians as well as some former revolutionaries—including the regime's highest-ranking bureaucrat, Ung Phan—welcomed independence. "We agree on the withdrawal of the advisors because we can rely on the many years of learning from them," Ung Phan assured the Council of Ministers.[27]

Cambodians were also confident that they could take over personnel and Party work. "We have expert cadres for this, too . . . who have studied at the Tu Duc School [in Vietnam]," explained Dom Hin, secretary of the Party branch of the Council of State. Other cadres "also have work experience with the Vietnamese advisors over many years. The Vietnamese advisors have evaluated the opinions they express and their actions and have agreed with them. Also, if there are any issues that are unclear, we can always ask the opinion of the Central Organization Committee. In addition, the Party branch has received much experience from working with the advisors. Comrade advisor Ba Thay [a veteran with pre-1975 experience in Cambodia] has concluded that we can do the work. If there is an unusual problem, we have a Central Ministerial Party Committee to help us. In summary, we can do the work, but we should maintain good internal solidarity and continue in the same fashion."[28]

Within the Party branch of the Council of State, only Chan Sok, the former Lon Nol–era banking official, was worried. "I'm concerned about [the role of the Council of State in organizing] national parliamentary elections, because we have gained only a little experience. Other than that, we can proceed, but we should continue to be extremely careful that solidarity continues to be good." But the secretary-general of the council, Chan Ven, was more than ready to see the Vietnamese go. "I have seen that all work plans that we have drafted get reviewed by comrade advisors, and not a single provision has contradicted the views of the comrade advisors. As for elections to fill the national assembly, we can handle it. Our internal work and personnel work is strong. Our internal solidarity is strong. Comrade [advisor] Vuong Dinh Chau always compliments us a lot when speaking of solidarity and internal unity. . . . I thank the comrade Vietnamese advisors who have helped our organization wholeheartedly."[29]

In September 1989, as the Vietnamese army was withdrawing, only two Vietnamese advisors remained with the Council of Ministers. Institutions that were not considered important for security, such as the Ministry of Agriculture, had no Vietnamese presence at all. The remaining advisors ended their missions quietly, sometimes under decidedly unceremonial conditions. In the early months of 1990 some eighty Vietnamese teachers and professors, along with a handful of advisors to the Ministry of Commerce, stopped receiving salaries. Despite agreements reached between the Cambodian and Vietnamese governments and reassurances from the Ministry of Finance that the money would eventually come, many lost patience and went home. A representative of the Ministry of Education described a sad end to a glorious fraternal bond. "[Vietnamese] specialists and professors are requesting, on their own initiative, to return to their motherland for a long rest and to help their children and grandchildren during the exam season and are asking for money to help them get back on their own. [But] it is not necessary for the ministry to help them out."[30]

ECONOMIC ENTANGLEMENTS

Though no longer reliant on Vietnamese economic advisors, Cambodia still depended on Vietnam financially. In 1989 the SOC owed Vietnam for goods it had promised Vietnam but never delivered, for Vietnamese military equipment it had received but never paid for, and for various loans from Vietnam that, despite several instances of forgiveness, had accrued well beyond its capacity to repay. Hoping to settle accounts, Hun Sen reminded a visiting VCP Central Committee member that Vietnam also had debts and that it owed Cambodia for the tens of thousands of tons of rice that had been provided to the Vietnamese army. Responded the visitor, "The Vietnamese Ministry of Defense has proposed to Comrade Prime Minister to help out [Vietnam] by demonstrating goodwill [by treating] the provision of rice as assistance to the Vietnamese army." Meanwhile, Cambodia continued to borrow from Vietnam, further limiting its economic independence. According to Finance Minister Chhay Than, "We have borrowed seven or eight times as much as they've borrowed from us. So it is difficult for us to refuse to lend to them. If we are tough with them, it will be difficult for us to borrow."[31]

Outside Phnom Penh, where local authorities generally ignored the leadership's policy prescriptions and bilateral trade agreements, Vietnamese economic power had depended on the presence of the Vietnamese military and civilian advisors. As soon as they began to withdraw, the Vietnamese found that Cambodians were engaging in small acts of disobedience. In the relatively peaceful eastern provinces, where local authorities enjoyed a certain day-to-day autonomy, Vietnamese officials got their first taste of Cambodian independence. One episode in the southeastern border province of Svay Rieng showed how annoying this could be.

In April 1987 a truck carrying 1,500 cases of beer and a generator—worth a total of $8,800—crossed the Cambodian-Vietnamese border into Svay Rieng. The driver, who worked for Sapixim, Ho Chi Minh City's commercial company, was prepared for a long trip, to the far northern province of Steung Treng. There he expected to deliver the beer and the generator to the Cambodian Region 1 Military Command Committee. The Khmer New Year, as well as the anniversary of the founding of the Cambodian armed forces, was coming up; the occasion apparently called for a lot of beer. The journey had barely begun, however, when Svay Rieng provincial police stopped the truck, arrested the driver, and confiscated the goods.

When word of the seizure reached Phnom Penh, the commercial advisor at the Vietnamese embassy, "Nguyen Cuc Binh," informed the Cambodian Ministry of Commerce that there had been a contract for the beer and for the generator and that the provincial authorities had acted inappropriately. The case went to the Council of Ministers, where it was decided that, without the prior approval of the council or the Ministries of Commerce or Foreign Affairs, the contract could not have been valid in the first place. Backed up by its own Vietnamese advisor, the council even rebuffed the complaints of Ambassador Ngo Dien. A year went by and still the Cambodians refused to compensate the Vietnamese. Exasperated, Nguyen Cuc Binh went to meet with the council's deputy minister, Cham Prasith. "I have worked for more than thirty years and have never faced a problem like this," fumed Binh.

Prasith did not apologize. The Council of Ministers had not approved the deal, nor had the Ministries of Commerce or Foreign Affairs, he reminded Binh. "An individual made this contract, not a Cambodian state organization." Besides, he added, "It's curious where Military Region 1 could have found dollars with which to pay, because the army doesn't have dollars." The minutes of the meeting, recorded by a rather wry secretary, depict a frustrated Binh. "After a discussion that lasted for almost two hours, Comrade Nguyen Cuc Binh was still complaining. . . . Because these stubborn complaints had a repetitive quality, Comrade Cham Prasith offered the following view: 'I will report to Comrade Prime Minister once again concerning this issue. But I wish to inform you that the Council of Ministers has already examined [the issue] and made a decision and has based its decision on law.' . . . The meeting ended at 10:50 A.M. in an atmosphere of intimacy."[32]

Cambodian-Vietnamese trade had become a private affair. Cambodian timber and rubber continued to cross the border, mostly in the hands of private businesspeople. For Cambodian officials, this smuggling was a source of serious concern. How the Vietnamese government felt about it depended on what was being smuggled. Private imports of goods that the Vietnamese state hoped to control were not welcome. "The theft of rubber is getting increasingly serious," reported Sam Saret, the minister responsible for the General Department of Rubber Plantations in June 1988, "to the point where the Vietnamese Rubber Department has asked Cambodia to help suppress this stream heading toward them." With regard to other goods, Vietnamese officials discouraged the Cambodians from restricting trade. Said Kong Samol in mid-1990, "If we strongly suppress smuggling over the eastern border, we will lose solidarity."[33]

Neither Hanoi nor Phnom Penh had any control over the smuggling. Cambodian security forces were involved. So were Vietnamese soldiers who had stayed behind following the withdrawal of the Vietnamese army and who were armed and looking for work. "Anyone can conduct business, including soldiers and police. In general, those with weapons conduct business," Chea Soth explained to Le Van Phat, Vietnam's deputy minister of commerce. "For example, those who export rubber or transport timber by boat all have weapons, which is why customs can't search them. We have arrested some armed businesspeople of whom some have come from Vietnam. We have confiscated forty weapons. When we arrest them, we interrogate them, and they respond that they have been hired to protect the goods and to prevent them from being searched along the way. . . . These days, there are a great many cases, and I can't describe them all to you."

Le Van Phat could empathize. "The problems that you have raised are not only in Cambodia. Vietnam has them, too." Complaining of "armed forces protecting" businesspeople, Van Phat offered a grim description of the road connecting Svay Rieng and southern Vietnam. "Along the Bavet–Ho Chi Minh City road, efforts to oppose smuggling have already resulted in fifteen bloody conflicts. If we act now, they will intensify their smuggling. . . . If we act force-fully, they will find ways to trick us, and there might be armed conflict. So we must employ long-term [solutions] to oppose these activities."[34]

VIETNAMESE WORKERS

The demobilization of its forces exacerbated Vietnam's serious unemployment problem. Vietnamese officials were thus eager to keep Vietnamese workers ac-tively employed in Cambodia. "If the State of Cambodia needs any construc-tion work, the Vietnamese will help," Vietnam's deputy minister of construc-tion told Bou Thang.[35]

In the spring of 1989, Vietnamese officials began promoting a policy of building "Party Schools" throughout Cambodia, a project whose official pur-pose was political education but which would also permit Vietnamese cadres, workers and soldiers to remain in the country. As Vietnamese Minister of Con-struction Pham Ngoc Tuong told Chea Soth, "In my opinion, it won't be nec-essary to send too many more Vietnamese workers and technicians to Cambo-dia. We can try hard to use the forces that are stationed in localities [where the Party Schools were to be built]. That would be better." Replied Soth, "Com-rade Party secretary Heng Samrin supports the progress of this work whole-heartedly." Over the next two years, however, the Cambodians' indifference to the project became apparent as ministers failed to provide building materials, electricity, or land."[36]

Cambodian officials greeted the prospect of Vietnamese workers with vary-ing degrees of enthusiasm. Bou Thang, thinking about his native northeast, en-couraged Vietnamese officials to send construction workers to dig wells. Hun Sen also saw uses for Vietnamese workers, proposing to the Council of Minis-ters that workers from Song Be province in Vietnam help construct a road be-tween the Cambodian provinces of Kratie and Mondolkiri. Other Cambodi-ans resisted. "We have been pioneers in the area already and should use our forces for construction," insisted Tram Iv Toek, deputy minister of communi-cations. "If our [Vietnamese] friends come to work, they will tap our rubber [trees] and will put down only a portion of the road." Tea Banh, now deputy prime minister and minister of defense, shared Toek's qualms. "We should re-examine the implementation of our economic self-sufficiency," he told the Council of Ministers, warning that an idle Cambodian construction sector would inevitably sell off its equipment and contribute to the demise of public works. Chea Soth was also skeptical. "The cabinet of the Council of Ministers should inform Song Be province that the State of Cambodia lacks the funds at this time and does not have the capacity to hire our friends."[37]

A CHANGED RELATIONSHIP

Given how the Vietnamese had dominated the PRK politically, it is not surprising that many Cambodians doubted that things had changed after their withdrawal. The resistance launched a number of accusations, some of which —the continued presence of Vietnamese soldiers on Cambodian soil—were true. In most respects, however, the Vietnamese relationship with Cambodia had indeed changed, to the point where the Vietnamese faced challenges and annoyances similar to those confronted by nationals of other countries.

The Vietnamese went from dictating Phnom Penh's economic policies to being just another exploiter of Cambodian resources. Like the Thais and later the Malaysians and Taiwanese, the Vietnamese relied on ad hoc arrangements with individual leaders. Like their capitalist rivals, the Vietnamese were also at the mercy of private, decentralized forces that frequently rendered their officials helpless. Having withdrawn their troops, they could not impose their will on local officials and were left to vent their frustration to their counterparts in Phnom Penh.

A frequently expressed, but as yet unproven, suspicion is that Vietnam still has advisors working in the Cambodian government. If true, what kind of influence would they wield? A few Cambodian leaders maintain close relations with their former patrons, but these ties do not imply subjugation; short of threatening another invasion, Vietnam has no way to force Cambodia to do anything. (Cambodia is now economically dependent on other foreign donors.) The Vietnamese influence thus depends on the loyalty of individual Cambodians. Yet in the late 1980s, different Cambodians perceived and treated the Vietnamese differently. Chan Sok (later president of the Supreme Court) was reluctant to see the Vietnamese advisors go. Cham Prasith (currently minister of commerce) stood his ground against an irate Vietnamese official. Bou Thang and Hun Sen invited the Vietnamese to expand their economic activities in Cambodia. Tea Banh (currently minister of defense) resisted. The Cambodians, in other words, came to treat the Vietnamese as unevenly as they treat investors and advisors from other parts of the world.

Chapter 14 Buying Power: Privatization, Corruption, and Patronage

The collapse of the Soviet bloc left the Cambodian government more impoverished than ever. By the end of 1989, Cambodia had lost some hundred million rubles in commercial credit and a long list of imports, including construction materials and parts, vehicles, pharmaceuticals, chemicals, and, most important, fuel. Short on cash, the regime failed to pay salaries owed to its state workers, and yet, for political reasons, the leadership refused to consider layoffs. As Hun Sen acknowledged to a visiting Vietnamese delegation, "The political situation prevents us from reducing our workforce because if we release them from the administration, where will they go? Sihanouk and Son Sann are recruiting people away from us."[1]

To pay salaries and in a last-ditch effort to rescue its moribund rice-purchasing system, the regime printed more money, which led to inflation. As the riel's value deteriorated, the state's meager assets evaporated. The provinces were failing to contribute money to the central government; importers and exporters refused to deposit hard currency in state banks. Worst of all, this financial crisis occurred precisely as the regime sought to increase military spending.[2] In December 1989, Hun Sen set out the challenges facing the government: "Now we are buying weapons and ammunition with which to fight, without a lot of assistance to compensate us as before. We have begun to buy a lot already, and in the future, if we cannot find a political solution, we will need a lot more money to buy weapons and ammunition to serve the fighting. We cannot wait for a political solution, either. So a serious problem is how to increase production and find sources of a lot of revenue to control a constantly deteriorating situation. . . . We should think about a level of self-sufficiency because of the inability of socialist countries to conduct business [with us], support us, or encourage us as before. This is a problem we must join together to resolve."[3]

For the Cambodian military, the most damaging effect of the Soviet collapse was the end of subsidized fuel imports. (In 1989, Moscow cut back significantly from the 200,000 tons of petroleum products it had previously delivered to Cambodia annually; in 1990 it stopped sending fuel to Cambodia entirely.) To compensate, the SOC looked to private Thai importers. Much of Cambodia's fuel would come from Vietnam, however, in particular from a private businessman named Sok Kong, who had close ties to the Vietnamese army. Kong, who eventually built a vast business empire in Cambodia, had been shuttling back and forth between the two countries, supplying the Cambodian army with such Vietnamese goods as aluminum, food, and clothes. By the middle of 1990, Kong's company, Sokimex, was also the main supplier of fuel to the Cambodian military.[4]

The SOC was desperate for hard currency. Increasing amounts were circulating in the market. Yet, despite periodic campaigns, the government was unable to collect any of it. As Chea Soth told a visiting delegation, "We invited the big businesspeople to come and receive guidance with regard to commerce and the problem of using U.S. dollars in the market. We asked them to exchange their dollars at the [state] bank, but they didn't comply and went and traded secretly." Soth was pessimistic. "In the coming year, 1991, we will be disseminating directives on this matter through television and radio in order to indoctrinate [the people]. But I don't know whether these measures will have any effect."[5]

In 1988, the regime began experimenting with a dizzying array of new taxes and revenue-generating schemes, including land registration taxes, taxes on visas, a national lottery, taxes on transportation and vehicles, taxes on official stamps, and the issuance of national or "patriotic" bonds. The leadership intensified its efforts to attract foreign investment, passing an investment law in 1989 and looking beyond the Thais to investors in Singapore, Malaysia, Taiwan, Hong Kong, and Europe. The need for revenue and investment even led them to abandon prohibitive tariffs on cigarettes, beer, videos, and other goods whose imports had been restricted on the grounds that they were unnecessary for economic development.[6]

SELLING THE STATE

The Party had many reasons to privatize industry. State enterprises lost money and drained the national budget. The regime also had a war to fight, which required quick revenues. It was the country's uncertain political future, however, that most inspired the sell-offs. In the spring of 1989 the leadership considered the possibility that a political solution might entail power sharing and that the resistance might lay claim to state assets. In anticipation of such a scenario, it decided to transfer the state's entire industrial sector over to the Party.

"If there is a political solution, we want all state factories to become private factories," Hun Sen told a visiting Vietnamese delegation, "because if we leave them with the state, we will face problems when the three parties [of Sihanouk, Son Sann, and the Khmer Rouge] come and spend money that belongs to our factories, which we have operated for ten years." The result, he warned, would be that state assets would no longer be available to support the Party and its cadres. Hun Sen detailed what he had in mind. "We want to set up the factories as follows. Take, for example, a factory worth 100 million. Our Party will own 50 percent of the shares, or 50 million, while the other 50 million will be distributed as shares to the three hundred workers in the factory." This plan had the advantages of maintaining Party control over the factory, gaining favor with workers, and precluding outside ownership. "If our Party loses an election and the three parties want to privatize (*toubniyokam*) the factories, the workers will be unhappy with these measures because they will have shares in the factory. This is our idea."[7]

At the end of 1989 and the beginning of 1990, when the Council of Ministers convened to discuss the sale or lease of the state's economic enterprises, there were few disagreements. At the more radical end of the spectrum were Hun Sen, who suggested selling state banks, and the now thoroughly nonideological Chea Soth, who promoted the privatization of the transportation sector and the Post Office. Minister of Finance Chhay Than strongly supported the sale of state industries, accusing the Ministry of Industry of squandering state funds and using them for "personal means of transport, such as cars." As for the minister of industry herself, Ho Non's main concern was where the money made by leasing factories would go.[8]

Privatization accelerated throughout the year and into the next. "We've decided to sell or lease the factories so that we can find revenue," said Planning Minister Chea Chantho in April 1991. "The important issue is that we do whatever we can to get revenue and put it into the hands of our military to defend the country. In every country, they think first about military battles." By December 1991 all but three of the Ministry of Industry's factories had been sold. Chan Phin, the orthodox Marxist chair of the Party's Economics Commission, had recently returned to the government as minister of industry, in time to witness the end of the state economy. "I say that if we sell any more of the ministry, there will be no more Ministry of Industry left," he remarked sadly.[9]

Management, for the most part, had not changed. The old state and Party apparatus simply took over the newly privatized enterprises, administrators, and accountants. Factory Party secretaries stayed on as bosses, joined by secretaries of the Party's Trade Union. Party meetings continued to be held three times a week. Privatization also failed to raise salaries, stirring tensions between workers and management. "Some factory bosses . . . don't dare to sleep at home or at the factories and say that the workers come to protest and to look for their motor scooters and their cars," reported Chan Phin.[10]

The leadership was less anxious to privatize its rubber plantations, which, unlike state factories, had the capacity to generate revenues. The plantations' assets were nevertheless disappearing. Having been granted a certain amount of autonomy, plantation managers and provincial officials sold off much of the rubber that was under their control. Plantation workers themselves joined the market. As Chea Soth told a Vietnamese visitor, "Rubber is not being stolen by outsiders. Workers, guards, warehouse officials, and businesspeople are stealing. But if we're talking about the motivations for [this theft], it's the extremely low standard of living."[11]

By 1990 a major battle was taking shape over control of the rubber plantations. Hun Sen and the Council of Ministers were granting control over tens of thousands of hectares to provincial authorities. The reason, said Planning Minister Chea Chantho, was that the General Department of Rubber Plantations could not provide the necessary investment capital. But Hun Sen, who was seeking to dismantle much of the department's bureaucracy, was also furious at its unauthorized sale of plantations to private interests. "Maybe you are not different from Yeltsin," he told Sam Sarit, director of the department, chastising him for his overly enthusiastic privatization policies. "And perhaps I am Gorbachev, but I am not yet Yeltsin. They consider Gorbachev a reformer, but Yeltsin goes further, meaning that he moves faster than the steps I am taking."[12]

Ordinary Cambodians were more interested in the privatization of land and houses. With a political solution and possibly an election approaching, the leadership, and in particular Hun Sen, viewed land distribution as an urgent priority. Basing land rights on post-1979 possession, the regime intended to preclude claims by Cambodians returning from refugee camps and from overseas. By granting private land ownership to the people, it also hoped to preempt campaign promises from the resistance.[13]

In the countryside, a new bureaucracy—the district cadastry offices—emerged to grant land titles and generate revenues. The offices, which had no resources, rarely conducted investigations into claims. Instead, they distributed papers and levied taxes on registration papers and official seals. The program was plagued by corruption, military land grabs, distribution to local officials, the use of false names, nepotism, and incompetence. Cadastry officials frequently issued land titles to people with competing claims. Bribes were necessary to secure land titles, pay off officials in cases of disputed claims, or pay neighbors to collaborate claims. (In January 1990, Heng Samrin estimated that false testimony to the cadastry office earned a peasant approximately seventy riels.) According to a study by Viviane Frings, the costs of the land-titling program forced peasants to borrow money at an average interest rate of 15–20 percent a month and, at times, to sell their land.[14]

The most urgent privatization and the biggest problems occurred in Phnom Penh, where property was most valuable. Encouraged by the regime to seek income in the private market, residents transformed their houses into hotels and guesthouses or rented them to international organizations, foreign companies, and individuals. Those who shared housing with other families now saw the financial incentives of sole possession. Disputes arose constantly. Many houses were sold multiple times to multiple buyers. When subsequent buyers were more powerful, intimidation usually resulted in the voiding of the first agreement. State assets were also for sale. As Heng Samrin complained in July 1990, "There are some institutions, organizations, and individuals who have taken land, funds, and buildings that are supposed to be state property to distribute to their factions or their families or to sell for their own benefit." According to Uk Bunchheuan, the corruption was similar to that during the Lon Nol regime. "We are in a war of houses and a war of land."[15]

CORRUPTION

Speaking to the Council of Ministers in August 1990, Kong Samol catalogued the crimes taking place in the State of Cambodia. "Smuggling by car, train, or boat; evasion of customs; failures at checkpoints, ferry docks, and licensing [agencies]; gambling and prostitution; the problem of videos; [corruption in the] hospitals; pornography; negligence and anarchy in the areas of electricity, water, and construction; and traffic that affects the beauty of Phnom Penh." Samol wasn't done. "Complications in the social order and in port warehouses, failure to implement decisions and court verdicts, problems related to travel documents and people's land, the unauthorized taking of weapons from people, illegal imports, food companies importing radios and televisions, and so on." Samol was not the only one making these observations. Corruption and lawlessness were out of control, yet despite complaints from some in the leadership, offenders were almost never punished.[16]

Since 1982, when the regime promulgated the Decree-Law Protecting State Property, its unwillingness to combat corruption had been apparent. To the jurists of the Ministry of Justice, the law was intended to thwart the theft of state property by cadres and officials. To the leadership, though, the campaign to "protect state property" was part of the struggle against "betrayers of the revolution" and was meant to punish those engaged in conscious acts of sabotage. The enemy was political opposition, not greed. The law, therefore, had little, if any, effect on corruption.[17]

Nor did Cambodia have institutions to combat corruption. The courts were ineffectual, subject to political pressure, and often themselves corrupt. The police were prohibited from arresting a state cadre on charges of corruption (or any other malfeasance) without first clearing the arrest with a minister, a requirement that only encouraged state officials to deliver protection money to powerful patrons. The Ministry of Inspection, theoretically tasked with rooting out corruption, found its mandate limited by the Party leadership, by the Council of Ministers (which arrogated to itself all high-level corruption cases), and officials like Finance Minister Chhay Than who resisted its oversight over their personal bureaucracies.[18]

Theft of state property was made easier by the lack of accounting. As was acknowledged in a July 1990 report of the Council of State, "We don't yet have any separate organization to manage state and public property. But we have instructed all state institutions and organizations to make a list of merchandise and state property that they manage and use, including movable and immovable property." Few institutions bothered submitting such a list. Meanwhile, pilfering elicited a minimal response from the leadership. Factory managers should be punished only after stealing three times, insisted Minister of Industry Ho Non, noting, however, that, "this approach has caused some concern because it seems too strong and too hasty."[19]

With economic reform came a shift in the role of the bureaucracy, from running the economy to regulating it. Given the absence of a professional civil service, arbitrary enforcement was inevitable. In the construction sector, provincial and municipal governments attempted to inspect buildings for faulty or dangerous construction, even though the state employed almost no engineers. Other sectors of the economy posed similar technical challenges. The regime estimated that 35 percent of the pharmaceuticals being sold in Cambodia were counterfeit and that much of the rest had expired, yet the Ministry of Health had few qualified cadres to investigate the problem. As a result, Phnom Penh municipal authorities dispatched untrained and frequently uneducated police to decide which pharmacies to close and which drugs to confiscate.[20]

As clerks, tax officials, inspectors, and other civil servants came into daily contact with ordinary citizens, bribes supplemented meager state wages. Unable to establish a professional salary structure, the regime created a system that explicitly authorized state officials to pocket a percentage of whatever fees and fines they levied. Tax officials were offered rewards for collecting vehicle taxes "outside the state plan." Post Office and customs officials responsible for preventing smuggling benefited directly from opening packages suspected of containing currency. Even the justice system offered incentives for extracting money: Uk Bunchheuan proposed a one-thousand-riel fine for disobeying court orders—less to punish noncompliant litigants than "to make sure that the clerks don't neglect the case."[21]

Cambodians were most familiar with the financial rewards available to the police. The leadership considered such rewards necessary to keep the security forces happy. The Party had already permitted former Khmer Rouge security cadres to become PRK police—a policy that placed the consolidation of the regime's authority above concerns about abuse of power and lack of accountability. Permitting the police to take a percentage of the fines they collected was an extension of this calculation. The only question was how much. If the police received too little, they would either refuse to work or else not report their activities and pocket everything. If they received too high a percentage, there would be incentives for heavy-handed policing and arbitrary shakedowns. A higher take for the police also meant lower revenues for the central government. For years, the leadership attempted to strike the right balance, beginning in 1981, when they decided that the police could take 20 percent of all fines. A decade later, with police extorting bribes from private motorists and the regime starved for revenues, the debate took on greater urgency. Finance Minister Chhay Than, whose primary concern was state revenues, proposed that the police receive 10 percent of all fines. Interior Minister Sin Song, looking out for the police, was more generous, suggesting a take of 50 percent. "This is different from the imposition of other economic penalties, such as the seizure of equipment or the levying of taxes. This involves a willingness to combat offenses that harm the social order and pose broad dangers. In some similar instances in Vietnam, they give [the police] more than 70 percent."[22]

Endlessly frustrated by police and bureaucratic extortion, most Cambodians saw the true evil of corruption in the wealth being accumulated by powerful officials. In private, the leadership appreciated some of the political implications of rampant high-level corruption. Yet the political system—the closed, anonymous collective leadership favored by communist regimes—precluded any but the most general complaints. Officials rarely mentioned particular ministries and almost never individual officials. Nor was the Party willing to pursue instances of high-level malfeasance. The few exceptions, and the punishments that were actually meted out, reveal why corruption thrived.

WARNINGS AND CENSURES

In October 1982, PRK police officers arrested a mid-level bureaucrat from the Ministry of Industry named Um Bunna. The case, based on suspicions that Bunna had "embezzled state property," presented the usual political complications. What were his connections? Were higher-level officials involved? How could the Party punish corruption in the bureaucracy without disrupting delicate understandings among powerful politicians? Prior to the arrest, the Party had recalled Minister of Industry Kaev Chenda, then studying in Hanoi, to Phnom Penh for questioning. Chenda defended Bunna. Investigators also discussed the case with Deputy Minister Nuon Saret, whose response was less clear. In any case, Bunna spent more than two years in detention before the leadership was ready to deliberate.[23]

The Party, it turned out, had no working definition of corruption. According to Sim Kar, the minister of inspection, Um Bunna had engaged in a wide array of commercial activities, including the distribution of state-made plastic and soap to private individuals. Whether Bunna personally received compensation for this generosity was uncertain, at least to Sim Kar. "According to the interrogation of Um Bunna," Kar told the Council of State in 1985, "he received five *chi* worth of gold, but it was his younger brother who took it and sold [the goods], not him." Uk Bunchheuan agreed that the case was ambiguous. "As Comrade Sim Kar has pointed out, this does not really have the qualities of bribery."

Um Bunna's offenses also fit the classic pattern of patronage in which powerful figures expected bureaucrats to generate income while they themselves remained distant from the transactions. Accused of smuggling cigarettes and currency between Cambodia and Vietnam, Bunna invoked his connections as a defense. "Um Bunna responded that these failings resulted from his fear of the minister," reported Sim Kar. The leadership was familiar with the practice. "In some cases," Kar continued, "when we conduct really deep research, there are a great many connections right up to provincial Party secretaries, and some soldiers are involved, too." From Uk Bunchheuan's perspective, prosecuting just Bunna would look like favoritism. "If a trial is held, they can claim that the little people went to jail and the big people got off with only an administrative penalty [demotion, transfer, or fine]. The Ministry [of Justice] has considered this case carefully. If a trial is held, Kaev Chenda, Meas Samnang [the new minister], and Nuon Saret would be called in for questioning. But if we impose [only] an administrative penalty [on Um Bunna], which we can do, it is not necessary to call these people."[24]

Not wanting to implicate top officials, the Party released Um Bunna with a warning. Kaev Chenda, whose tenure as mayor of Phnom Penh had by that time come to an ignominious end, was not prosecuted. Meas Samnang, whom Heng Samrin suggested should be "helped to recall his errors," remained at the ministry. Nuon Saret was transferred, serving later as deputy minister of agriculture and, ironically perhaps, as deputy minister of inspection. The rest of the ministry was convened to hear a general warning.[25]

For the remainder of the decade, the Party did little to suppress corruption. A few district chiefs lost their jobs for "failing to pay attention to the livelihoods of the people and not implementing the policies of the Party and the state." In many cases where cadres were removed for corruption, however, they quickly returned either to their old positions or to similar posts elsewhere in the bureaucracy. Actual arrests, such as that of National Assembly member Mam Ngon in 1988, required much more serious offenses. According to the prosecutor, Ngon's alleged crimes, committed in his role as a district chief, included not only theft of state property and bribery but extortion, arbitrary searches and arrests of citizens, "arresting and raping women," and "violating the Party organization so as to harm unity and the revolution."[26]

For a simple case of embezzlement to attract the attention of the authorities, the offenders had to somehow violate the rules of the patronage system. A pyramid of money and influence, this system linked tens of thousands of low-level officials to the leadership. Protection depended on respecting the hierarchy and ensuring that one's superiors were informed of and benefited from any profit seeking. As Duong Khum and Dy Phin, two deputy ministers of disabled veterans and social affairs, discovered, deviating from the normal chain of command could ruin a career. As Chan Ven explained to the Council of State in June 1989, their sale of state property (which included provisions intended for orphanages) was not itself grounds for prosecution. "As for the receipt of money for personal spending from the sale of equipment at favorable prices—Comrade Duong kept 10,000 riels and Comrade Dy Phin kept 8,000 riels—the amount is not so interesting in comparison to [amounts collected by] other ministries, where they sell expensive goods outside [the state system] and receive more money than this. Activities of this kind are extremely common. There are even some [state] organizations and individuals with important positions who have money to buy houses, cars, or other luxuries, and there is no problem at all. This case arises from their knowing how to cooperate and cover up."[27]

The offense, then, was conspiracy. As Heng Samrin reminded the Council of State, Duong Khum and Dy Phin had offended the system by establishing a clandestine, *horizontal* relationship. "There truly are violations [that is, corruption] in all the ministries and institutions," Samrin acknowledged. "But with regard to these two deputy ministers, it is not just [this] transgression. They committed many other offenses. The Party has thought about this and decided to punish [the offenders] and to instruct [them to change their behavior]. A big part of this episode is the ministry's collectivity, its wrongful collusion (*samouhopheap krasuong khos chea muoy daer*)."[28]

There were no arrests. Sparing the minister of disabled veterans and social affairs, Central Committee member Koy Buntha, the Party pushed one low-level official into retirement, censured Duong Khim and Dy Phin, and forced them to pay back the 10,000 and 8,000 riels that they had "spent for their own benefit." In a concluding report, Chan Ven wrote that he "does not understand clearly the level of punishment but simply points out to the Council of State [which formally issued the punishments] that in almost every ministry and office there are violations of management orders, a lack of oversight, and a lack of responsibility. It's only that some [ministries] have few [such violations] and some have a lot."[29]

By 1990 the scope of the corruption had become alarming. Almost every transaction with the government required a bribe. State hospitals accepted cash payments only. Schools and universities became profit-making institutions in which admissions, grades, and degrees were all for sale. Public anger was on the rise, especially in Phnom Penh. Still, the leadership was loath to acknowledge the problem. Any document that might be distributed publicly was stripped of references to corruption. Speaking of a Council of Ministers report, Kong Samol stated, "It is true, what this report says, but it relates to our internal problems, especially the failings of the leadership [with regard to] management of our cadres. This candor of ours should not be put in a report but should be kept an internal matter to resolve." Samol was also thinking about the SOC's image overseas. "If our reports weren't translated, there would be no problem. But we translate and disseminate this, and it could result in external opinions holding us in less regard."[30]

At the end of the summer, when complaints of corruption came up both at a Central Committee meeting and at the National Assembly, the Party decided to make a gesture toward suppressing it. In September the news agency SPK announced that forty officials had been suspended as part of "a vigorous struggle against corruption by taking measures to get rid of all negative phenomena in society." Internally, though, the campaign was anything but systematic. "In my opinion," said Khong Phirun, a former jurist working at the Council of Ministers, "we needn't issue a circular [to combat corruption] because it would be a confession that our cadres are committing acts of corruption and that the government is ineffective in suppressing it." Kong Samol reassured Phirun that issuing the circular did not constitute a confession. "Besides," he added, "[corruption] is clearly the product of the enemy and of foreigners, who take our weaknesses as their strengths."[31]

Samol was making two points. The first was that the resistance was somehow to blame for corruption. The second was that, despite the regime's public announcements, the leadership still considered any acknowledgment of the problem as a gift to the resistance. Before long, the "struggle against corruption" quieted down. The following year, large-scale anti-corruption demonstrations hit the streets of Phnom Penh.

POWER AND PATRONAGE IN THE PROVINCES

In the early 1980s, when international humanitarian assistance dried up, the regime assumed that provincial authorities would survive off "Patriotic Contributions," which they levied on rice yields. It was soon apparent, however, that the policy had been implemented arbitrarily and excessively. "Collection is really strict," complained Minister of Finance Chan Phin in early 1984. "We always take everything." Despite the widespread unpopularity of the policy, it remained in force. "We're still calling them 'Patriotic Contributions,' and yet the people still don't like them," said Men Chhan, the chair of the Economics Commission of the National Assembly in early 1988. "I ask the Council of Ministers to do whatever it can to lighten the contributions because the people are still saying they're too heavy."[32]

As Cambodians were well aware, "taxes" and "contributions" were indistinguishable from extortion by state agents. Using the words interchangeably, the leadership debated at length the checkpoints that clogged roads and bridges with teams of police, soldiers, and customs officials. "There needs to be a system to suppress individuals who are taking contributions from the people arbitrarily at checkpoints," said Prime Minister Chan Si in early 1984. Although the Party leadership recognized the anger that these checkpoints engendered among citizens, they also valued the control the posts gave the state over enemy infiltration and free market activity. Throughout the early and mid 1980s, the regime issued regulations permitting police and soldiers to seize dollars, gold, silver, and any goods being traded in "large quantities" in order to "defend against and suppress central businesspeople." The result, according to a 1985 report from the Council of Ministers, was that "checkpoints along the national routes, whose primary purpose is to guard against and impede the schemes of the enemy and fight for national security, have turned around and become sites for extorting [money and goods] from the people. They take goods and [the products] of small businesses that the people take from one district to another or from one province to another to trade and make their living."[33]

Even after the regime began to permit more market activity, local authorities profited from policies requiring travel documents. According to a circular issued in January 1985, soon after Hun Sen became prime minister, civilians could move around the country so long as they had a "clear purpose." To officials authorized to grant permission, a purpose was less convincing than a bribe. As Hun Sen complained the following year, "Ever since we conferred the authority to issue travel documents to the police, it has been difficult for our people to travel because if no money is given, the police just say they're busy or that they don't have the papers."[34]

The Patriotic Contributions, the business taxes, the checkpoint "taxes," and the money received from travel documents all stayed in the provinces. Year after year, the leadership complained about the failure of local officials to remit revenues to Phnom Penh, yet by the late 1980s the regime's finances were more decentralized than ever. Provincial authorities collected hard currency from imports and exports, sold licenses to private traders, and ensured that revenues went to local patronage systems rather than central coffers. "There are some places where pressure is placed on customs [officials] not to collect taxes [for the central government]; this rises to a level of ultimate competition between the Center and the provinces and municipalities," warned Hun Sen. "In the end, we will all die together. There will be no winners and no losers."[35]

In 1989, the Council of Ministers formally capitulated to the provinces by granting them autonomy over "the labor force, land, natural resources, and any property within each province or municipality in order to strongly develop the local economy." Provincial officials now enjoyed discretion over taxation and controlled the flow of revenues. Local offices of the Ministry of Finance and other central bureaucracies fell increasingly under the control of provincial officials while the central bureaucracies faded into irrelevance. "In the old society, [the central ministries] could hold discussions with each other and implement [policies]," said Kong Samol. "But now the provinces make the decisions, and the ministries are afraid."[36]

The money itself passed through provincial offices of the National Bank, which had also come under local control and which lent both to provincial governors and to private individuals with ties to local authorities. From 1989 to 1990 loans to the private sector increased from 50 million riels to 500 million riels. "Why is there so much lending to the private sector? Because there are a lot of connections with the borrowers," reported Finance Minister Chhay Than.[37]

The motives for issuing these policies sprang from the regime's own economic and political crisis. It was hard enough to pay salaries to cadres in the central ministries; in the provinces it was impossible. With the resistance appealing to disgruntled civil servants, the regime was also unwilling to reduce the size of local bureaucracies. The only solution was to encourage officials at every level of the administrative ladder—in the districts, communes, and villages—to become financially self-sufficient. The Council of Ministers thus authorized the communes to supplement their collection of Patriotic Contribu-

tions with revenue from state-owned land, taxes on timber and fishing products, fees on the use of markets and riverbanks, and unspecified "contributions
from administrative letters." The effect was to perpetuate a system in which local positions were valued according to their revenue-generating potential,
while higher-level officials wielded power and wealth in accordance with their
ability to distribute those positions. Authority was handed down; money was
passed upward.[38]

The Party apparatus and mass organizations proved to be inefficient vehicles
for patronage politics. The officials who ran these institutions may have
wielded formidable power, but the bureaucracies themselves did not generate
revenues—for the state, for the Party, or for their patrons. In the late 1980s, as
ideology waned and money was short, various branches of the Party structure
were deemed superfluous. First to go were the Women's and Youth Associations, which, with the exception of the Central Organization Committee chair,
Men Sam An, had few supporters in the Party or among the Party's Vietnamese
advisors. In a failed effort to hold off the inevitable, the heads of the organizations presented themselves as vital to various state policies, including K5 conscription. "The Youth and Women's Associations don't just do their own
work," insisted the head of the Youth Association. "The organizations of state
authority also use them whenever they are needed." Meanwhile, the organizations were disintegrating from below as increasing numbers of cadres quit their
jobs to join the private sector or to seek more lucrative positions in the state apparatus.[39]

Elsewhere in the Party system, cadres whose jobs had been to formulate and
propagate ideology or to investigate the class backgrounds of state and Party
employees were no longer needed. The regime searched for a politically suitable
way to cut them off. "Our newest dilemma," Hun Sen told a Vietnamese visitor in May 1989, "is our plan for negotiating a political solution, because when
[a solution is reached,] those who are working [in the state apparatus] will be receiving a salary, [but] those who have aided the work of the Party have no
salary." The resolution of this problem—the transfer of shares in state enterprises to Party cadres—simultaneously compensated them for their loyalty and
incorporated them into the quasi-private economic system.[40]

In the provinces the more powerful Party officials, those who also held state
positions or had informal ties to the state system, were indifferent to this trend.
As an institution, though, the Party became more fractious. Hiring decisions
were now devoid of ideological considerations or Vietnamese influence; personal relationships held the system together. Because the SOC still had enemies

and because an election loomed, state officials managed their patronage networks for the benefit of the Party. The difference was that the Party, as an institution, did not give anything back. Outside the vertical chains of money that bound one official to another, Party status by itself meant little. As the less adaptable members of the Politburo were discovering, the cold new logic of patronage applied at every level of the Party.

Party secretary Heng Samrin was becoming increasingly irrelevant. Ideologically rigid and opposed in principle to the peace negotiations, Samrin stood still as Hun Sen led the regime in new directions. Despite the appointment of his brother, Heng Samkai, as Party secretary of Svay Rieng, Samrin never demonstrated the ability or desire to nurture a provincial power base. His leadership of the powerless Council of State provided him with little but a forum for complaint. Samrin's best chance to wield influence derived from his role as commander of the armed forces, yet none of the ministers of defense or chiefs of staff owed their positions to his patronage. After years of provincial politics, military figures like Tea Banh and Pol Sareun had long since abandoned communist ideology and had adhered to the wealth-generating policies of Hun Sen or the indulgent indifference of Chea Sim. By 1990, Heng Samrin had little to do other than meet dignitaries from foreign Communist Parties.[41]

The Hanoi veterans, after a quarter-century of academic communism, never adjusted. Chea Soth's mandate within the bureaucracy—central economic planning and state-to-state Cambodian-Vietnamese trade relations—no longer mattered. In the two provinces handed to him by the Vietnamese in 1982, Prey Veng and Battambang, Chea Sim's dominance was unquestioned. Bou Thang, the keeper of the regime's now meaningless ideology, still maintained influence over some of the northeastern provinces, but these were economically stagnant areas with few resources, other than timber, to reward power. The last of the Vietnam-trained Politburo members, Say Phouthang, the man who many felt had once been the most powerful man in the country, had faded away, politically and physically. In declining health, he spent more and more time in Thailand.

SIN SONG, CHEA SIM, AND THE POLICE

Whether Sin Song meant it when, as minister of inspection, he called the police "truly abusive" is not clear. If he did, no one seemed to hold it against him. Back at the Ministry of the Interior, he quickly resumed his staunch defense of the security forces. From his previous run-ins with the Ministry of Justice, he had also learned a lesson about the details of draft laws. "Take, for example, the situation in Poland, where, without the police force, Poland would have been lost. The police force depended on one small provision that had not previously been of great interest. But when the situation got the way it did, the police took that small provision and implemented it. That small provision, written into the constitution, provided that in special cases the Ministry of the Interior has the right to prohibit travel. At that time, the Ministry of the Interior immediately issued a proclamation prohibiting travel throughout the country and forbidding anyone from going anywhere. Only then did the provision go into effect. Without it, Poland would have been in danger."[42]

Sin Song had returned, from his temporary exile in the Ministry of Inspection, to a much stronger Ministry of the Interior. After the Vietnamese military successes of 1984–85, the regime had turned its attention to the threat of infiltration by the resistance and to expanding "village, commune, and Solidarity Group" police forces. In the villages, the police were outnumbered by the regime's vast network of local militias. Unlike the unpaid conscripts who made up the militias, however, police recruits entered a hierarchical system built on obedience and loyalty. The police force functioned as a classic patronage system, with officers delegating to their subordinates specific responsibilities, from criminal cases to the management of family statistics, from which a decent living could be made. Mindful that police officers were closely tied to local civilian officials, the Ministry of the Interior allocated a special budget to pay village police directly, thereby ensuring that lines of communication and fealty also extended upward through the police hierarchy to the ministry itself. Without a coherent and motivated security apparatus, the leadership reckoned, the regime had little chance against the "psychological warfare" of the enemy.[43]

But Sin Song was growing anxious. In August 1988, when the Vietnamese were preparing to withdraw and the Cambodian armed forces were heading toward the front, it was time, he decided, to enhance the role of the Ministry of the Interior. Reminding the Council of Ministers that he had the support of Hun Sen, Song explained that "this period is a vital one in which the Ministry of the Interior, like the police forces, must start taking responsibility for sharing the heavy burden of our military." The ministry "should think hard about taking partial responsibility and gradually taking complete responsibility for the defense of the border, especially the Thai border. I have made preparations for the first trimester of 1989. I will send a number of small police units to be stationed along the border which will be capable of taking on important matters that relate to political work, such as the work of security and [maintaining] social order."[44]

Over the next two years, the Ministry of the Interior sent special police units known as A-Teams—A9, A71, A44, and so forth—to the northwest, where they patrolled the border and tracked suspected resistance activity. Granted broad authority to control internal travel, in both the northwest and other parts of the country, the A-Teams established checkpoints along roads and bridges. Along Route 4, where A3 units policed commercial traffic moving between Phnom Penh and the coast, ministry personnel were particularly prone to engage in extortion and theft. Deputy Interior Minister Khoem Pon nonetheless defended the checkpoints as necessary to combat infiltration by spies disguised as businesspeople. "We must understand that if these people were not [acting] in the interests of Thailand, Thailand wouldn't allow them to come," he told the Council of Ministers.[45]

Elsewhere in the regime, there was grumbling about the activities of the Ministry of the Interior. Deputy Defense Minister Ke Kim Yan was among several military officials to complain of an "excess" of checkpoints. Council of Ministers reports were more scathing: checkpoints resulted in "a loss of time and a loss of the property and money of the people, causing fear and emotional and physical suffering among the people and raising the price of goods in the market. . . . Even more dangerous is the influence on the political sector, where the enemy can use these failings to entice the people away from the Party and the state."[46]

Decisions related to the Ministry of the Interior's expanded duties, the A-Teams and the checkpoints were guarded closely by the Party. As Sin Song reminded the Council of Ministers, "If the Secretariat or the Politburo agrees, responsibilities will be conferred on the Ministries of Defense and the Interior to discuss what to do. The Council of Ministers doesn't know whether [the police] are placed here or there and doesn't understand everything. In fact, only the Ministries of the Interior and Defense communicate regarding the policies of the Politburo and the Secretariat."[47]

Almost everyone associated with the new policies had some close association with Chea Sim. The Party Secretariat, which oversaw the security apparatus, was now under the control of Sar Kheng, Chea Sim's brother-in-law. In Battambang, Sin Song worked closely with the new Party secretary, Chea Sim's nephew Ung Samy, and with a provincial apparatus that was increasingly aligned with Samy and with Chea Sim. And from the same group of former

Eastern Zone cadres came Um Sarit, the new Party secretary of Banteay Mean-chay.[48]

Chea Sim himself wielded power both in the Politburo and entirely outside any formal institutions. When he chose to intervene personally in security matters—for instance, by ordering the release of prisoners—Interior officials deferred. As for the A-Teams, there were few Cambodians outside Chea Sim's inner circle and outside the Politburo who fully understood what was going on. Describing distinctions among A9, A71, and A44, Defense Minister Tea Banh told the Council of Ministers, "I didn't know about this. I learned about it from Chea Sim."[49]

HUN SEN IN THE PROVINCES

On the other side of the country, in Kampong Cham, Hun Sen was building his own family empire. It had taken a few years. In March 1982, when Vietnamese advisors presented Hun Sen with the opportunity to oversee Cambodia's most populous and resource-rich province, his enthusiasm was apparent. "We should visit the locality two months out of the year," he had suggested to Dang Dinh Long. Still, it was not until December 1983 that Hun Sen's brother, Hun Neng, became a district chief. And not until June 1985, after Hun Sen's promotion to prime minister, did Neng rise to the position of provincial Party secretary.[50]

Hun Sen had other loyalists in the province, including Kun Kim, a well-connected former Khmer Rouge cadre who, in the early years of the PRK, had served as a liaison to local Khmer Rouge forces and as a juror during the Pol Pot–Ieng Sary trial. As deputy governor of Kampong Cham, Kim promoted the province's economic autonomy, an agenda that had Hun Sen's full support. Kim and Neng could also thank Hun Sen for protecting their interests in the lucrative provincial rubber plantations against the General Department of Rubber Plantations.[51]

Hun Sen developed a close relationship with the governor of Svay Rieng, a former provincial military chief named Hok Longdi. Despite serving under Heng Samkai, Heng Samrin's harshly ideological brother, Longdi was hardly a communist. Described by Party insiders as "clever at business" and willing to send provincial revenues back to Phnom Penh, Longdi represented the kind of nonideological, money-driven local leader whom Hun Sen could count on. In return, Hun Sen encouraged Longdi's efforts to gain control over the province's economic bureaucracy. Under the supervision of central ministries, local offices had stolen state funds and had "created anarchy" in the areas of finance, taxes, and customs, he told the Council of Ministers in late 1989. "The sword of authority should be given to the province to resolve these problems, because the Party secretary and the governor are the representatives of the state in the province." Longdi pushed ahead, reminding the council of Hun Sen's personal support. "During a meeting on economic planning, the prime minister responded to my interjections by allowing me to find a formula to resolve the issue of the right to manage and the right to appoint."[52]

Within a few months, he had taken control of the local economic offices, a move that prompted complaints from central officials, including Planning Minister Chea Chantho, who accused Svay Rieng provincial officials of overdrawing from local branches of the state bank. These allegations notwithstanding, Longdi was soon promoted to a position from which he controlled the most valuable assets in Cambodia: mayor of Phnom Penh. There, he operated under the direct guidance of Hun Sen, from whom he received orders regarding which houses to build, which to demolish, whom to evict, and whom to grant ownership to. As Longdi informed the Council of State in July 1991, "An appeal to the city is the same as an appeal to Comrade Hun Sen, because Comrade Hun Sen is the one who orders the city to act. The city does not act on its own."[53]

THE FOUNDATIONS OF POWER

Hun Sen was expertly negotiating yet another of Cambodia's post–Khmer Rouge political drifts. In the early 1980s, when the Vietnamese were most influential, he used his position as minister of foreign affairs to demonstrate his loyalty. In the middle of the decade, he became a skilled bureaucrat, building a base within the state apparatus that rivaled the power of the Party. In the late 1980s, he rode a global trend of economic reform, pushing aside his more ideological rivals and promoting a system in which state officials benefited from an increase in overall economic activity. Now, in the early 1990s, Hun Sen was playing Chea Sim's game, nurturing a network of loyalists in the provinces. He was not taking on Sim directly—say, by challenging his control over the northwest. With a peace accord coming, the two Party leaders needed each other. Besides, it had never been Hun Sen's style to antagonize strong rivals so long as there were other avenues to pursue power. In this case, there were Kampong Cham, Svay Rieng, and Phnom Penh, three constituencies that were less strategically important than Battambang but more profitable. Hun Sen also had a new set of loyalists, in addition to the technocrats who served him at the Council of Ministers. Hun Neng, Kun Kim, and Hok Longdi had become Hun Sen's connection to local authorities and would, throughout the 1990s, play essential roles in propelling him to a position of unrivaled power.

Hun Sen and the rest of the current Cambodian leadership are the beneficiaries of the political and economic system that evolved in the 1980s. Civil servants, whose salaries are still too low to support themselves and their families, are allowed to pocket a percentage of any fines, taxes, fees, or bribes that they impose on the citizenry. The rest of the money is handed up, sometimes for state or Party coffers but generally to individual patrons. The result is a power structure made up of vertical—and yet mutually dependent—relationships. Top officials engage in direct corruption when they conclude deals with foreign investors. But the leadership also promotes lower-level corruption by perpetuating a weak salary system and by making nepotistic appointments. Powerful patrons have little incentive to punish their own loyalists. As long as the money flows, officials act with impunity—engaging in theft, extortion, or worse.

Chapter 15 The Throes
of Peace

The Cold War came to a dramatic close. The Berlin Wall fell, and suddenly Germany was no longer divided. The Velvet Revolution in Czechoslovakia took over the streets of Prague and thrust an absurdist playwright and veteran dissident, Vaclav Havel, into power. Eastern Europe's communist leaders were removed from office; in Romania, Nicolae Ceausescu was hunted down and executed. Within the Soviet Union, there were rumblings of independence from the Baltics to Central Asia. The superpower that had stood behind Hanoi and Phnom Penh was rapidly coming apart.

Nothing so tumultuous was happening in Cambodia, where change was a matter of painstaking and protracted diplomatic negotiation. The withdrawal of the Vietnamese army had effectively removed the biggest obstacle to the peace talks. Elections had been accepted in theory by both sides. Disagreements persisted, however, over the shape of an interim government to administer the elections. The resistance coalition, the CGDK, had taken the position that a quadripartite government should be established, a concept rejected by the State of Cambodia on the grounds that it would return the Khmer Rouge to power. Not until November 1989 did a compromise emerge: a proposal by Australian Minister for Foreign Affairs and Trade Gareth Evans to create a transitional administration under the authority of the United Nations. The plan, which was not rejected by either Cambodian side, was quickly embraced by the international community. On January 15 and 16, 1990, the deputy foreign ministers of all five permanent members of the U.N. Security Council met in Paris for a special conference on Cambodia. Without any Cambodians present, they arrived at a consensus that the United Nations would administer the country, that there would be a cease-fire, that Cambodia's U.N. seat would be left vacant, that a quadripartite Supreme National Council would be established as the "repository of Cambodian sovereignty," and that the SOC would be dismantled.[1]

The Perm-5, as they were called, were well ahead of the Cambodians. When Hun Sen met Sihanouk in Bangkok in February, the two leaders could reach only the barest of agreements on a "U.N. presence" and the establishment of a supreme national body "to symbolize Cambodia's national sovereignty and national unity." Later in the month, at a meeting in Jakarta, the two sides remained divided, by the CGDK's charge that Vietnamese troops were still in Cambodia, by the SOC's opposition to the dissolution of its administration, and by the SOC's insistence that any agreement ensure "the prevention of the return of the genocidal regime." Still, the Perm-5 continued to negotiate, meeting in March to establish some of the details of what was now being called the United Nations Transitional Authority in Cambodia (UNTAC). Meanwhile, the SOC's primary patron, Vietnam, was bending, mostly in the name of normalizing relations with China. In early May, VCP Party secretary Nguyen Van Linh told a visiting Japanese dignitary that the United Nations and independent American organizations could visit Cambodia to verify the Vietnamese troop withdrawal and hinted that the Khmer Rouge could participate in the Cambodian peace process.[2]

INTERNAL CHALLENGES

Although the end of the Cold War pushed Vietnam to start repairing its relationships with China and the West, it also hardened the internal politics of the VCP. Responding fearfully to the fall of the Berlin Wall, the Party recommitted itself to one-party rule, cracked down on writers and journalists, and purged a Politburo member who had contemplated democracy. Ironically, two of the antagonists were men whose careers had been built in Cambodia. The first was the former chief of B68, Tran Xuan Bach, whose assessment of events in Eastern Europe apparently brought him dangerously close to pluralism. The other figure in the drama was Le Duc Anh, the former commander of the Vietnamese forces in Cambodia. Now minister of defense, Anh helped see to Bach's removal in March 1990.[3]

By all accounts, there was no internal Politburo struggle in Cambodia. Nonetheless, the lessons of Eastern Europe weighed on the minds of Cambodian leaders. In a discussion with the Lao minister of justice in December 1989, Hun Sen almost seemed to be contemplating political change: "Most of all, we can conclude that reform is better than no reform. If there is no reform, there is greater danger than if there is reform. What we have seen is that Hungary and Poland reformed before there was an uprising by any strong movement. In this way, they limited the level of opposition against them. Countries that suppressed political reform, such as Germany, were victorious for all of six weeks. Czechoslovakia and Bulgaria were like this as well. We should [learn from the] experience of Romania, where the state authority lost everything in six days. So we see that suppressing the people's reform movements results in greater dangers than [does promoting] reform."

Yet as far as Hun Sen was concerned, reform consisted mainly of land distribution and economic loosening. "Political reform," whatever Hun Sen meant by that, would wait. "It is necessary," he told the Lao visitor, "for us to maintain the [current] political and military situation right up to the time of the elections."[4]

Outside the top leadership, some Cambodian officials were ready for political change. Aware that the country was heading toward multiparty elections, they began to consider whether the time was right to test the Party to see whether a little democracy might be tolerated. They were emboldened, in part, by Chea Sim's rhetoric of the previous summer, when he called for a "national people's democracy." They may also have felt that Hun Sen was ready to accept some kind of political reform, for the man they counted on as their liaison to the leadership was Hun Sen's old comrade Ung Phan.

Phan, who early in his career was known for his sometimes unsettling reticence, had become relatively outspoken, at least with regard to the Vietnamese. He had always been somewhat critical of Hanoi's social and economic policies, including its practice of sending people to New Economic Zones and its suppression of the free market, and had opposed the application of these policies to Cambodia. "Up to now," he told the Council of Ministers in late 1989, "we've seen that in Vietnam they are managing [the economy] wrong, and yet we follow them." Ung Phan was also a critic of Vietnamese immigration and, by 1988, was expressing rather nationalistic sentiments. Discussing the New Economic Zone policy, Phan managed to evoke both the "lost territory" of Kampuchea Krom and the suspicion that Vietnam was secretly promoting immigration into Cambodia. "Here is an issue the Vietnamese haven't told us about," he said at one 1988 Council of Ministers meeting. "They sent away millions of people, and beginning in 1978, [these people] returned to Prei Nokor [the Khmer name for Saigon]. Among them were those who came into our country." Whatever Ung Phan's colleagues thought of these views, they remained silent.[5]

Ung Phan's break from the leadership came after he was transferred from the Council of Ministers to the Ministry of Communications. There, away from the scrutiny of the leadership, he met new colleagues like Nou Saing Khan, director of the ministry's Planning Department and a former Lon Nol official. Soft-spoken and unassuming, Saing Khan had been thinking and secretly writing about political reform and democracy since 1979, having managed to collect and keep at his home French and prerevolutionary Cambodian political literature. Generally opposed to the Vietnamese occupation and aware, by virtue of numerous missions to Eastern Europe, of the economic problems of global communism, Saing Khan drew close to liberals both within and outside the state apparatus, including Vandy Ka-on and Thun Saray. As Saing Khan explains it, he served as a bridge between Ung Phan, whom he assumed to be protected by his relationship with Hun Sen, and the various liberal intellectuals in the capital who had no such ties to the leadership. What followed was, in retrospect, audacious.[6]

Sometime in late 1989, Nou Saing Khan, Ung Phan, and ministry Chief of Staff Yang Hon agreed to form a political party—the Free Social Democratic Party, or FSDP—in which Ung Phan would be president, Saing Khan the general secretary, and Yang Hon number three. Having agreed on the principles and platform of the party, Saing Khan left on an official trip to the former Soviet Union, which he extended for an extra two months. During that time, Saing Khan visited the Estonian capital of Tallinn to see an old friend, a former Soviet advisor to the PRK Ministry of Communications and a staunch Gorbachev supporter. For fifteen days, in the midst of the Baltic uprisings and Soviet crackdowns, Saing Khan stayed in Tallinn writing the manifesto of the new party. Using his old French and prerevolutionary Cambodian documents as guides, he completed the writing in Leningrad and returned to Cambodia.

Back in Phnom Penh, Nou Saing Khan printed two hundred copies of the manifesto on the ministry's Soviet-donated photocopier machines. In April, during the Khmer New Year, when it was possible to see large numbers of friends and acquaintances on an informal basis, he and his two colleagues distributed fifty-six copies. Saing Khan even made a special trip to the Institute of Sociology, where he handed the manifesto to Thun Saray. "I knew this was dangerous," says Saray. "We agreed that if either of us was caught, we would not discuss the participation of the other."[7]

It was also at this time that Ung Phan decided to inform his old revolutionary comrades. Figuring that they would recognize the new party, Ung Phan personally gave copies of the manifesto to Hun Sen and to Chea Sim. Looking back, Nou Saing Khan is unsure how Hun Sen reacted, although he recalls that Chea Sim told Ung Phan that he "didn't have time" to consider the proposal. By early May, however, Saing Khan understood that his work had not been greeted with enthusiasm. He began to notice officials from the Ministry of the Interior following him on their motor scooters and photographing his movements. One day a ministry official—whom Saing Khan describes as an ethnic Khmer "Vietnamese agent"—came to his house to warn him that he would be arrested. The manifesto was merely "an expression," he assured the visitor, explaining that he was not opposing his country. The agent remained silent. At that point, says Saing Khan, he knew that it was too late to flee the country.

A week later, on May 15, Saing Khan received a letter from Ung Phan asking him to come to his house to discuss work. In the early evening, Saing Khan left home, putting one hundred dollars in his pocket and telling his wife he would be back later. Arriving at Ung Phan's house, he noted two cars parked nearby. Phan greeted him at the door. "Have you eaten?" Phan asked. "I have prepared everything already," Saing Khan responded. Both were nervous, and according to Saing Khan, Ung Phan was sweating.

Saing Khan recalls what happened next. "Phan invited me into the house and explained that the Party leadership [Hun Sen, Chea Sim, and the Politburo] had not agreed with our proposal. I told him that I thought they would agree in the future and that I had no regrets. It was silent. Then, at 6:45 P.M., I got up to leave. I left the house, got into my car, and drove as far as the gate, where four armed soldiers stepped in front of me." According to Saing Khan, the team, led by Lou Ramin, the director of the Investigation Department of the Ministry of the Interior, ordered him into the back seat of a ministry car, between two of the officers.[8]

Within ten days of Nou Saing Khan's arrest, Ung Phan and Yang Hon were in detention, along with various recipients of the party manifesto: Thun Saray;

Kan Man, deputy director of the American and European Department of the Ministry of Foreign Affairs; Khay Mathury, a former lieutenant colonel and architect working at the Ministry of Foreign Affairs; and Colonel On Sum of the Research Department of the Ministry of Defense.[9]

The Party needed to explain the purge. On the morning of May 25, Kong Samol convened a meeting of forty-two Council of Ministers bureaucrats. "We are disseminating to comrades the report and instructions of the leadership of the Politburo and the Party Secretariat concerning the problem of the creation of the Free Social Democratic Party, [which has] enemies standing behind those who created it." Referring presumably to Ung Phan, Samol told the council, "Those who committed this act include communists as well, but most were not communists. If they were communists, they wouldn't oppose communists unless they were Pol Pot." The American-trained Samol then launched into a tirade against the United States. "Now, do we want more democracy?" he asked. "I wish to tell you that these days the United States is using the word 'democracy' to pressure countries without a high educational level and to provoke (*banka kangval*) the people. Now, American spies have entered and are using words with the people that they don't clearly understand, such as 'democracy.'"[10]

Kong Samol went on to complain about the control that Western humanitarian organizations had over the distribution of rice and to argue against renting buildings to international organizations. Announcing an intensification in security precautions, he told his colleagues that "we must absolutely oppose any person who opposes the Kampuchean People's Revolutionary Party and keep under surveillance any brother or sister who colludes with any party. I ask comrades to provide information to our Secretariat or to our state authority. This is an issue we should pay attention to so as not to allow attitudes to develop."

The reverberations of the arrests were felt elsewhere in the city. The Institute of Sociology closed with the detention of Thun Saray. Khieu Kannarith, the moderately liberal editor of the weekly *Kampuchea,* was briefly removed from his position. Whatever discussions had been taking place on political reform went even further underground. Within the leadership, cadres closely associated with Chea Sim enjoyed promotions. Sim's nephew Ros Chhun replaced Ung Phan at the Ministry of Communications. Yem Chhay Ly, a brother-in-law, was appointed minister of health. Most important, Sar Kheng became chair of the Party Central Organization Committee, replacing Men Sam An, whose husband was among those arrested. The implications of these moves, beyond an immediate boon to Chea Sim, are still unclear. Had Hun Sen encouraged Ung Phan? Had he betrayed him? Did the purge represent a Chea Sim–Hun Sen power struggle? These questions remain unanswered.[11]

TOWARD PEACE

Outside Cambodia the arrests had little impact on the peace talks. On May 25, the day Kong Samol warned the Council of Ministers about the Americans and their "democracy," the Perm-5 met in New York for another round of talks on Cambodia. A week later, in Tokyo, Hun Sen, Sihanouk, and Son Sann all agreed to join a Supreme National Council (SNC); Khieu Samphan, the Khmer Rouge representative, boycotted the meeting, insisting that the SOC be granted one-quarter representation on the SNC rather than one-half.[12]

Although Samphan soon returned to the bargaining table, the Khmer Rouge was increasingly isolated internationally. The Tiananmen massacre of 1989 had distanced the United States from China, the Khmer Rouge's primary patron. With growing criticism in the press regarding indirect U.S. assistance to the Khmer Rouge and with the Vietnamese army no longer in Cambodia, some American politicians were now questioning U.S. support for the Cambodian resistance. On July 18, 1990, after several months of debate in the Congress, Secretary of State James Baker announced that the Bush Administraion would no longer recognize Cambodia's U.N. seat as belonging to the CGDK because the United States wanted "to do everything we can to prevent the Khmer Rouge from returning to power." With the United States ready to begin direct discussions with Vietnam and with the State of Cambodia, international support for the resistance—in western Europe, in ASEAN, and in China—crumbled.[13]

Throughout the summer, Cambodia was the subject of intense bilateral negotiations, between the United States and Vietnam, the United States and the Soviet Union, and China and Vietnam. The Chinese, in particular, were demonstrating a desire to remove Cambodia as an obstacle to their diplomatic relations. On August 22, at a meeting in Beijing of the Cambodian resistance, Chinese officials successfully pressured the Khmer Rouge and the noncommunists to agree to the formula established by the Perm-5. A few days later, the Chinese joined the rest of the Perm-5 in arriving at a "framework for a comprehensive political settlement of the Cambodia conflict," which included UNTAC administration of the country, a peacekeeping role for UNTAC, elections, human rights, and assurances that the various parties would respect Cambodian neutrality and refrain from interfering in its internal affairs. The following week, in Chengdu, China, Chinese and Vietnamese officials held a secret and highly important summit at which both sides made concessions related to Cambodia. The Vietnamese agreed to verification of their withdrawal and recognition of a comprehensive political settlement under the United Nations, while the Chinese accepted the position previously rejected by Khieu Samphan: that the SOC would provide six of the twelve members of the SNC.[14]

Their various foreign patrons all having agreed on a framework for peace, the four Cambodian factions met in Jakarta on September 9 and 10 and accepted the plan formulated by the Perm-5 . The following month, the U.N. General Assembly adopted by acclamation a resolution stating that the SNC would represent Cambodia at the United Nations.[15]

Later that fall, the Perm-5 met in Paris to hammer out the roles of the SNC—"the unique legitimate body and source of authority" in Cambodia— and of UNTAC, to which the SNC would delegate "all powers necessary to ensure the implementation" of an agreement. The Perm-5 also determined that the SOC's administrative agencies, in the areas of foreign affairs, national defense, finance, public security, and information, would be "placed under the direct control of UNTAC." On military matters, the parties agreed to the withdrawal of foreign troops, the presence of U.N. advisors and military personnel, a cease-fire, the cantonment of forces, and a process of arms control, storage, and reduction. There was also an understanding regarding the repatriation of Cambodian refugees.[16]

At the end of the year and into 1991, the Cambodian parties continued to squabble. The fiercest disputes involved the question of whether a final agreement would use the word "genocide" to refer to the Khmer Rouge and the extent to which UNTAC would control the SOC administration. Eventually "genocide" would be dropped in favor of a provision stating that "the policies and practices of the past shall never be allowed to return." As for the control over the SOC administration, the eventual language was less important than how the relationship between UNTAC and the SOC played itself out.

While these and other disputes delayed the signing of a comprehensive agreement, the world was distracted. In February 1991 the United States cobbled together a coalition to fight a war against Iraq's occupation of Kuwait. Shortly thereafter, the Thai military launched a successful coup d'état against Prime Minister Choonhavan. Meanwhile, the situation in the Soviet Union was leading up to the failed coup attempt against Gorbachev in August. Yet, in the shadow of these events, there was some action on Cambodia. On May 1, the cease-fire went into effect, and on June 24–26, the SNC convened in Pattaya, Malaysia. The meeting was presided over by Norodom Sihanouk.[17]

Finally, on October 23, 1991, the various Cambodian parties and regional and global powers met in Paris and signed the Accords on a Comprehensive Political Settlement of the Cambodia Conflict. In attendance were the members of the SNC; U.N. Secretary-General Javier Pérez de Cuéllar; and the foreign ministers of nineteen countries, including the Perm-5, the countries of ASEAN, Vietnam, Laos, Yugoslavia and Zimbabwe (representatives of the Nonaligned Movement), Japan, India, Canada, and Australia. French President François Mitterrand gave the opening speech, pronouncing that Cambodia could now take its destiny into its own hands. Pérez de Cuéllar remarked that UNTAC "will probably be the biggest and most complex [mission] in the history of the United Nations" and called on the international community to assist in Cambodia's reconstruction.[18]

The actual agreement set forth the role of UNTAC in ensuring a "neutral political environment conducive to free and fair general elections" and included the details of the election process, the withdrawal of foreign troops and verification thereof, the cease-fire and the cessation of outside military assistance, the cantonment of the various Cambodian military forces, human rights guarantees, provisions for the return of refugees, the release of prisoners of war, and principles for a new, post-election constitution. Calling for its "loyal and scrupulous implementation," Sihanouk declared that the agreement "shall guide and lead us, from a solid base, towards a future filled with peace, justice and true democracy." Thai Foreign Minister Asa Sarasin stated simply that "our high hopes and aspirations must be tempered by a sense of realism. . . . The conclusion of the conflict in Cambodia is not an end in itself. In more ways than one, the process has only just begun."[19]

DANGEROUS FREEDOMS

Two weeks before the signing of the Paris Accords, Nou Saing Khan was eating with some of the T3 prison guards. "They brought their radio with them when they came to eat, and that's how I heard about the peace agreement. A little while later, the Ministry of the Interior people who came to visit me every week informed me that I would be allowed to leave." Thun Saray, too, heard of the peace agreement and was abruptly told he would be sent home. "I never saw any documents related to my arrest, my detention, or my release," he says. After a year and a half of detention, some of it spent shackled in tiny, stifling cells, Saing Khan, Saray, Ung Phan, and the rest of the group arrested in May 1990 left prison.[20]

Cambodia's new era arrived quickly. On October 17 and 18, the Kampuchean People's Revolutionary Party held a congress at which it officially abandoned Marxism-Leninism, changed its name to the Cambodian People's Party (CPP), replaced Party secretary Heng Samrin with Chea Sim, and announced its commitment to a free market economy, separation of powers, "liberal democracy," human rights, and pluralism. On November 9, the first members of the U.N. Advance Mission in Cambodia (UNAMIC) arrived in Cambodia. Five days later, Prince Sihanouk made his triumphant return to Cambodia after thirteen years in exile. Arriving in the morning, he stepped from the chartered plane he had taken from Beijing, onto a red carpet and into a convertible with Hun Sen. As the two leaders drove into Phnom Penh, enthusiastic flag-waving crowds gathered along the road. In a move that Hun Sen had been pursuing for years, the SOC leadership awarded Sihanouk the position of head of state. That evening, from the balcony of the palace, Sihanouk called for an international tribunal to try the Khmer Rouge. On November 20 he presided over the festival celebrating the reversal of the Tonle Sap waters.[21]

On November 27, Khmer Rouge leaders Khieu Samphan and Son Sen arrived to a colder reception. That morning around ten thousand Cambodians converged on the building where they were staying. Shouting "Kill them, kill them," several hundred people climbed over the fences and into the building. Hundreds of security forces who arrived shortly thereafter stood by, intervening only when demonstrators strung up a wire with which to lynch Samphan. Rescued at the last moment, Samphan and Sen were escorted by SOC soldiers to a plane that whisked them out of the country. Photographs show Khieu Samphan bloodied, his head having been gashed in the course of the assault. Whether Party leaders had coordinated the incident is unclear. Publicly Hun Sen called it "regrettable" and "unplanned." "Attacks or murders of a few Khmer Rouge leaders cannot solve the problems of the entire nation," he said, adding that "what we need to resolve the present problems is nonviolence."[22]

Over the next three weeks, both Chea Sim and Hun Sen publicly took the position that nonviolent demonstrations would be tolerated no matter who they were directed against. "I have no right to ban people from demonstrating," said Hun Sen on December 17. "As for the government, which is in charge of social order, we do not want demonstrations to take place. However, if these occur spontaneously, what do we do? I categorically declare that we will not use violence or weapons to repress demonstrations."[23]

That day, students, state employees, and other residents of Phnom Penh began demonstrating against corruption. Although the protests were initially peaceful, the leadership was concerned. "In general," Hun Sen told the Council of Ministers on December 19, "the exercise of the human right to demonstrate cannot be suppressed. Demonstrations are one option for people in countries that practice democracy. But it is apparent that demonstrations in our country arise from incitement by political parties." Adding that "some of [the protesters'] demands are appropriate, and some are not," he accused workers at the printing press of the *Kampuchea* newspaper of extortion and suggested that students at the art school were demonstrating only because they had failed their exams. Demonstrations against corruption were legitimate, he concluded, so long as they did not escalate into general criticism of the SOC. "If [the demonstrations] relate directly to a minister, he should submit his letter of resignation. We cannot allow this situation to continue any longer. If it does, it will gather into opposition against our government."[24]

The following day, about 250 demonstrators set fire to a house they said had been misappropriated by Ros Chhun, Chea Sim's nephew and the minister of communications. The demonstration spread to a local market, and a few protesters engaged in looting. A few others prevented fire engines from coming to the scene or threw rocks at the police. Carrying shields and truncheons, police reinforcements eventually arrived and restored order. Meanwhile, the official news media carried an announcement by Hun Sen that Ros Chhun had been relieved of office. The following morning, December 21, Hun Sen gave a radio speech criticizing the demonstrations. "The people have the right to express their views, protest or make demands in accordance with the law. However, the demonstrations of the past few days were essentially not in accordance with democracy and human rights. They were strikes using violence in violation of the law, creating social instability, fear and confusion among the people in general, and seriously threatening the stability needed for implementing the peace agreement."[25]

The broadcast concluded with a promise by Hun Sen not to accept "unrest stirred up by a small number of people" or the possibility of a "coup d'état." The government, he said, would "take appropriate measures to maintain law and social order" and not "remain indifferent to acts that are against the law." As the speech was being broadcast, a scuffle occurred at the Faculty of Medicine in Phnom Penh between students and police, and a medical student was arrested. Angered, the students marched to traffic police headquarters, where police administered beatings, and then on to the National Assembly. That evening hundreds of demonstrators headed toward various police offices, where they were met by armed police. Some rocks were thrown, then shots were fired. At least seven people were killed.[26]

The next morning the Ministry of the Interior announced that the demonstrations had been "instigated by armed reactionaries." Foreign Minister Hor Namhong described the events as "an armed insurrection with a political aim." Later in the week, when the National Assembly convened to amend the constitution (removing the article that had given the Party its monopoly on power), the delegates passed a law prohibiting "meetings of groups or crowds in public places or on public roads, or marching demonstrations which can be detrimental to public tranquility, order or security."[27]

The new year nonetheless brought with it a sense of tentative optimism. The first UNTAC soldiers and administrators had arrived in Phnom Penh, and in the middle of January the SNC announced that any Cambodians wanting to form a political group would be permitted to do so. Choosing to forgo partisan politics, Thun Saray and Khay Mathury worked at home, preparing the bylaws of Cambodia's first human rights organization, L'Association des Droits de l'Homme Cambodgienne (ADHOC). Police arrived at Saray's house. "You're still engaged in political activities," they told him. "This is stupid, stupid politics!" Despite the warning, Saray and Mathury set out for SNC headquarters and, on January 16, registered their organization.[28]

Outright political opposition was more dangerous. Even as hundreds of political prisoners were being released, many suspected opponents of the regime were still under close surveillance or else were hiding out in the provinces. Nonetheless, Ung Phan, Nou Saing Khan, and Yang Hon were back in contact. On January 17, 1992, Phan gave his first public interview since his release from prison. Calling the Party leadership "millionaire communists," he stated that an opposition party was necessary to combat the corruption that infected "every single department in every single ministry." He added, "My family and I have been threatened many times since I was released. The death threats come from the government." He was right to be afraid. On January 22, Tea Bun Long, an official who had been critical of corruption, was abducted from in front of his home. He was later found in Takeo province, dead, with his hands bound behind his back and a bullet hole in his head.[29]

Undeterred, Ung Phan picked January 27 to submit a request to the Council of Ministers to open an office of his Free Social Democratic Party. The following day the council sent Phan a letter granting permission. Late that afternoon Ung Phan was driving on a main road just outside Phnom Penh when two jeeps approached. As six or seven gunmen opened fire, he was hit by two bullets. One grazed his back; the other lodged in his neck. Somehow, Ung Phan drove to the hospital. Hun Sen arrived shortly thereafter and was seen to weep.[30]

CAMBODIA'S TRANSITION

In three months Cambodia's one-party dictatorship had evolved into a confusing, shifting regime that promised democratic freedoms but subjected those who exercised them to threats and violence. The inconsistencies led to speculation about internal disagreements. To whom were the security forces responsible? Who ordered the killing of Tea Bun Long and the shooting of Ung Phan? The relative opening of Cambodia rendered the answers to these questions even more elusive: political leaders who now professed support for "democracy" could afford neither to leave a paper trail linking them to political violence nor to discuss the attacks in any but the most private and informal settings. Beginning with the signing of the peace accords and up to today, assassinations and assassination attempts have been followed by official denunciations, denials, promises to investigate, and then inaction.

Two other important patterns emerged in those first few months following the Paris peace agreements. The first was that, whoever was ordering or carrying out the attacks, the leadership would stick together in denying responsibility. The second was that Cambodians were protected against human rights abuses in direct proportion to the pressure placed upon the SOC by the international community and to the ability of UNTAC to monitor events in Cambodia. The regime needed foreign assistance and could not afford to be seen as destroying the peace process. This was the motive for restraint. As Hun Sen told the Council of Ministers in anticipation of Khieu Samphan and Son Sen's return to Cambodia, "We should be careful tomorrow. All the ministries should remain quiet so as not to allow Khieu Samphan and Son Sen to run away again, which is the reason that the peace plan has been so weak up to now and the U.S. Senate has not yet approved its budget [for assistance to Cambodia]."[31]

No Berlin Wall ever fell in Cambodia. No Vaclav Havel or Lech Walesa came to power. The regime did not collapse; it negotiated the terms of its survival. Impoverished and isolated, the SOC understood that it needed legitimacy and assistance from the United Nations and from the West. This meant complying with the expectations of the international community, when necessary, and protecting power in undemocratic and frequently violent ways, when possible. In Phnom Penh, where the streets were soon filled with UNTAC soldiers and Western journalists, opposition politicians set up offices and campaigned more or less freely. In the provinces, away from foreign eyes, A-Teams and other elements of the security apparatus terrorized citizens working with opposition parties.

Thirteen years after the overthrow of the Khmer Rouge, Cambodia was experiencing another invasion. Unlike the Vietnamese army, however, UNTAC was invited. Nonetheless, its arrival heralded a new set of foreign benefactors and yet another political system. The transition to (violent, repressive) internationally sanctioned pluralism thus represented the latest in a series of political twists and turns, each of which required Cambodians to accept events beyond their control and to adapt themselves accordingly.

The frequent policy shifts that marked the PRK-SOC period were not always easy to grasp. In the mid-1980s tolerance for private commerce gradually overtook the regime's anti-Chinese campaigns. Local officials permitted private farming despite Phnom Penh's rhetorical commitment to collectivization. Intellectuals were encouraged to join the state apparatus, even as they were scrutinized for possible disloyalty. Ordinary Cambodians, if they were to make a living—in the markets, the countryside, or the state apparatus—were forced to negotiate these overlapping, contradictory pressures.

Politically nimble politicans such as Hun Sen and Chea Sim anticipated ideological transformation and thrived. Others were caught off guard. As Kaev Chenda discovered, even top officials were expected to defer to the sensibilities of a conservative Party leadership. Yet as the Cambodian economy became increasingly privatized and more directed toward Thailand, as political power came to depend on the capacity to nurture patronage systems, and as the peace process began to dictate Phnom Penh's policy choices, ideologically rigid leaders like Heng Samrin and Chea Soth were left behind. They played it safe and, as a result, remained in power, but with greatly reduced influence.

The one constant during the PRK-SOC period was the military and diplomatic stand-off, which Cambodia's leaders learned was not a subject for debate. But if acquiescence guaranteed the political survival of top officials, it did not protect ordinary citizens. Hundreds of thousands of Cambodians were sent to war, regardless of their fealty to the regime.

There were those who chose to challenge some of the regime's practices. A tiny number, including Justice Minister Uk Bunchheuan, were government officials who used the safety of their positions to promote human rights and the rule of law. A few who operated on the margins of power, men like Vandy Ka-on and Thun Saray, explored the limits of the Party's tolerance. The vast majority of Cambodians, however, were required to mask their discontent and recite the Party line.

Ordinary citizens also had no say in the peace process. UNTAC came to Cambodia because multiparty elections were the only way for Vietnam, China, the Soviet Union, Southeast Asia, and the West to end a draining international conflict. The timing and terms of the elections were dictated by external forces—the end of the Cold War, the desire of regional and global powers to improve relations with each other—and by the decisions of unaccountable leaders. Yet it was immediately apparent that Cambodian citizens were deeply invested in the transition, and not just because they yearned for peace. Having dutifully subscribed to so many passing ideologies, they were nonetheless genuinely excited about democracy.

Epilogue

When I arrived in Cambodia in May 1994, the political environment had changed dramatically as a result of the UNTAC elections. The Kingdom of Cambodia, as the new constitutional monarchy was now called, had returned Norodom Sihanouk, a popular, culturally unifying figurehead, to the throne. The new prime minister, Prince Norodom Rannaridh, was the president of a royalist party, FUNCINPEC (the name is the French acronym for the National United Front for an Independent, Neutral, Peaceful, and Cooperative Cambodia), which controlled a plurality in the National Assembly. A coalition government, in which FUNCINPEC and the Cambodian People's Party shared control of the ministries and the provinces, offered prospects for stability. A new constitution promised market economics, parliamentary democracy, and respect for human rights. There were independent human rights organizations and newspapers aligned with various political parties. Phnom Penh was filled with foreigners, including aid workers, legal advisors, human rights advocates, and journalists. Assistance from the West and from international lending institutions was pouring in. Cambodians were optimistic.

The old power structure was still in place, however. Rannaridh, who was known as the "first" prime minister, shared the Council of Ministers with Hun Sen, the "second" prime minister. Within the bureaucracy, civil servants continued to answer to CPP officials, rather than to FUNCINPEC ministers. In the provinces, FUNCINPEC governors were equally powerless, as district and commune chiefs, police officers, and clerks ignored their nominal bosses.

UNTAC and its twenty thousand soldiers, police, and officials had pulled off an election. It had repatriated several hundred thousand refugees and had created a relatively open political environment in which opposing parties had access to the media. Yet it had never controlled the SOC administration. Corruption and intimidation marred the lead-up to the election. In the countryside, shadowy security units assassinated more than a hundred opposition political workers. The Khmer Rouge were even less cooperative. Disappointed by the failure of the Paris peace agreements to undermine the SOC, they violated the cease-fire, killed ethnic Vietnamese, and finally boycotted the election altogether. Nonetheless, election campaigns were held. Parties associated with the resistance factions, including FUNCINPEC and Son Sann's Buddhist Liberation Democratic Party (BLDP), disseminated their message, with its anti-Vietnamese themes, while the CPP sought to link its royalist and republican opponents to the Khmer Rouge. On May 23, 1993, Cambodians voted, peacefully and enthusiastically. Despite threats and rumors of Khmer Rouge disruptions, 90 percent of all eligible voters went to the polls. The results: FUNCINPEC won 45 percent of the vote, the CPP 38 percent, and the BLDP 3.8 percent. The CPP was not pleased. In early June, Sin Song and Prince Norodom Chakrapong, a son of Sihanouk who had joined the Party in 1991, threatened to secede with Cambodia's eastern provinces and refuse to recognize the election. In response, UNTAC and Sihanouk agreed that FUNCINPEC would share power with the CPP.[1]

As I discovered in the course of my work, neither Norodom Rannaridh nor Hun Sen was eager to incorporate the principles of the new constitution into legislation. Efforts by a FUNCINPEC finance minister, Sam Rainsy, to create a transparent approval process for foreign investors were undercut by the leadership. Anti-corruption laws, touted publicly by the government, were never sent to the legislature. Neither party expressed interest in establishing a Constitutional Court, as required by the constitution. The judiciary remained under the control of the executive branch. Members of the National Assembly were unable—politically, if not constitutionally—to initiate legislation. A handful of politicians earnestly attempted to reform the country. They requested my assistance and that of other Western lawyers in drafting and amending laws and establishing new democratic institutions. Watching the fatalism that overtook their efforts was dispiriting.

Pluralism in Cambodia did not evolve into a democratic exchange of ideas but into a tenuous compact among competing patronage systems. Most FUNCINPEC officials were more concerned with satisfying their superiors than with changing the way the country was governed. A notable exception was Finance Minister Sam Rainsy, whose complaints about unaccountable timber deals and other forms of corruption incurred the anger of Hun Sen. Rainsy's actions also annoyed Rannaridh, who removed him from office in October 1994 and ousted him from FUNCINPEC and from the National Assembly the following June. The only other party represented in the government, the BLDP, also split; encouraged by Hun Sen, an anti–Son Sann, pro-CPP faction claimed the party mantle. The lesson was clear. Hun Sen and the CPP leadership could tolerate the multiparty system imposed on them by the international community so long as the other parties did not directly challenge their interests.[2]

There were divisions within the CPP as well. In July 1994 elements of the Party that were uncomfortable with the power-sharing arrangement and disenchanted with Hun Sen organized and then aborted a coup d'état. In the aftermath of what was an extremely disorganized effort, Sing Song and fellow Ministry of the Interior veteran Sin Sen fled to Thailand, where they were arrested. Hun Sen emerged more powerful than ever before, having removed disloyal elements of his own Party and demonstrated to FUNCINPEC that only he could preserve the stability of the coalition government.

But tension was mounting between Hun Sen and Rannaridh, particularly after March 1996, when Rannaridh began complaining about the inequality of the coalition. The following year, when word spread of an alliance between FUNCINPEC, BLDP, and a new party launched by Sam Rainsy, violence erupted. First, unidentified assailants, whom human rights investigators concluded were protected by Hun Sen bodyguard units, threw several grenades at a Rainsy rally in front of the National Assembly, killing sixteen people and wounding a hundred. Then, in July 1997, troops loyal to Hun Sen conducted a coup d'état, sending tanks into the streets of Phnom Penh, engaging in bloody skirmishes with royalist troops, and chasing Rannaridh, Rainsy, and other non-CPP politicians into exile. The official justification for the events was that Rannaridh was about to cut a deal with the Khmer Rouge.[3]

After seventeen years of co-optation—the "warm welcome" issued by the

Kampuchean United Front for National Salvation in December 1978, the Misled Persons Movement, and the payoffs to Khmer Rouge military officers—the Khmer Rouge were finally capitulating. Soldiers were defecting to both the CPP and FUNCINPEC militaries, which had not been integrated. Top officers, however, preferred the CPP, which permitted them to retain both their rank and their units. Some in the Khmer Rouge leadership were also making their peace with the CPP. In 1996 former D.K. Foreign Minister Ieng Sary established a separate zone around Pailin with the support of Hun Sen. (Sary also received an amnesty from King Sihanouk related to his in absentia conviction in 1979.)

As the relationship between Rannaridh and Hun Sen deteriorated, both looked to the remaining Khmer Rouge leaders, based in Anlong Veng, in the far north. In one last fit of paranoia, Pol Pot ordered the murder of his long-time defense chief, Son Sen, and his family; Khmer Rouge military commander Ta Mok then placed Pol Pot under arrest and conducted a show trial for him. It was at this moment, when an alliance between the Khmer Rouge and FUNCINPEC seemed possible, that Hun Sen conducted his coup. As a result, by the time Khmer Rouge leaders Khieu Samphan and Nuon Chea had fled to Ieng Sary's autonomous region of Pailin, there was only one undisputed leader in Phnom Penh with whom they could do business. During a visit to the capital, Samphan and Chea were assured by Hun Sen that it was time to "bury the past." Pol Pot, who had for so long personified the Khmer Rouge, died in April 1998. Only Ta Mok and Deuch, the infamous chief of the Tuol Sleng interrogation center, have been detained. In February 2002, negotiations between the United Nations and the Cambodian government over the terms of a trial for the surviving Khmer Rouge leaders broke down. For Hun Sen, who has permitted Sary, Samphan, and Chea a comfortable retirement, one of the sticking points was whether foreigners or CPP-approved Cambodians would decide who would be indicted.

In early 1998, after almost a year of negotiations, Norodom Rannaridh, Sam Rainsy, and others returned to Cambodia to participate in another election. The circumstances were similar to those of 1991–93. Direct international pressure, denial of foreign economic assistance, and the stain of illegitimacy forced Hun Sen to permit the return of his rivals. The campaign, too, was reminiscent of 1992–93. Although Rannaridh, Rainsy and other political leaders could deliver their message, their supporters in the countryside were attacked for attempting to turn their homes into party offices. There were dozens of political killings. Unlike the UNTAC election, however, the July 1998 election was controlled by the CPP, which dominated institutions such as the Election Com-

mittee and granted opposition politicians little or no access to the media. Accusations that the process was unfair surfaced constantly in the lead-up to the
election and then again after the results were announced: the CPP had purportedly won a plurality of the vote while Rannaridh and Rainsy had split the
majority. Angry and incredulous, tens of thousands of people took to the streets
of Phnom Penh to protest. After a week of demonstrations and political uncertainty, the CPP trucked in iron-baton-wielding counterdemonstrators to disperse the protesters. Shortly thereafter, Hun Sen emerged as the sole prime
minister in another, even more lopsided coalition. Rannaridh now presides as
president of the National Assembly. Chea Sim, the previous president, heads
the Senate, a second house of the legislature created, it seems, mostly so that the
CPP Party secretary would have a prestigious position.

There are many indications of a budding civil society. Local human rights
organizations have offices in Phnom Penh and the provincial capitals. There is
a bar association and criminal-defender organizations. Opposition newspapers
insult the leadership. Buddhist monks practice and teach. Labor unions challenge employers. Serious problems such as AIDS and environmental degrada-
tion are addressed by nongovernmental organizations and are the topics of frequent seminars and conferences. Since UNTAC, human rights and democratic
freedoms are the subject of constant discussion. Thanks to training and teaching by international and domestic organizations, Cambodians are well informed of their rights. Cambodian human rights organizations and employees
(both Cambodian and foreign) of the U.N. Centre for Human Rights investigate suspicious murders, land seizures, and other possible human rights abuses
and submit their complaints to various state institutions.

Yet Cambodian democracy often seems like an abstraction. The government
ignores reports of corruption and human rights abuses. The courts remain corrupt, politicized, and, for most citizens, geographically inaccessible and prohib-
itively expensive. Soldiers and police are never prosecuted for abuses, prompting
nongovernmental organizations to write lengthy reports on the problem of impunity—reports that are themselves ignored. Unlike the PRK and the SOC,
the government of the Kingdom of Cambodia no longer has political control
over the economy, internal travel, communications, or the comings and goings
of foreigners. It is also dependent on foreign assistance and thus reluctant to engage in acts of open repression. As a result, political control has become more
subtle. Intimidation, especially in the countryside, still prevents opposition
parties from turning into effective movements.

Although the methods of control have changed, the personnel governing the country remain largely the same, from Prime Minister Hun Sen and CPP President Chea Sim, to the CPP provincial governors and the CPP district and commune chiefs, whose monopoly on power has remained mostly untouched since 1979. Local elections, conducted in February 2002, changed the status quo only in the margins; the CPP shares commune councils with opposition figures but still controls the chairmanship of all but 23 of the 1,621 councils. The security apparatus and the local police forces are also staffed by people installed shortly after the establishment of the PRK.

Cambodia's leaders have accepted a new level of political discourse, to be sure, but they do so only to the extent that it does not jeopardize their power. This strategic, self-serving adaptation has, in fact, been the hallmark of their rule since 1979. The PRK was a tolerant regime relative to Democratic Kampuchea in that it freed Cambodians from virtual slavery and permitted some internal debate. In the late 1980s the regime began allowing Cambodians greater economic freedom. Today in the Kingdom of Cambodia citizens openly discuss democratic principles and may even form political parties and nongovernmental organizations. Until Cambodian leaders willingly and peacefully relinquish power, however, these changes should be understood not as a commitment to democracy but as a new level of patience and indulgence.

Two other themes link the Kingdom of Cambodia to the PRK and the SOC. The first is the sometimes limited influence of foreign advisors. The second is the economic transformation of Cambodia and the effects of corruption.

Instead of Vietnamese and Soviet cadres, the advisors to the Kingdom of Cambodia are Western Europeans, Americans, Australians, and a few Asians, Latin Americans, Africans, and overseas Khmers. Some offer technical advice valued by their hosts. Others are tolerated as part of a larger assistance package; like their Soviet predecessors, they "come with the equipment." The advisors are also divided among themselves, more so than were the Vietnamese and Eastern Europeans. Americans and French argue over language and the direction of the legal system. More importantly, foreign donors differ over human rights, democracy, political stability, and corruption. Whether the question is the legitimacy of elections or the efficacy of administrative reforms necessary to secure assistance from the multilateral development banks, debate and disagreement continue. The advisors, and the diplomats who stand behind them, are no more capable of agreeing on the meaning of "democracy," "rule of law," and "capitalism" than the Vietnamese were of defining "socialism." The result is an incoherent approach to the country's problems that gives astute Cambodian politicians like Hun Sen room to maneuver.

Like the Vietnamese advisors, the Westerners wield influence over Phnom Penh's macroeconomic and monetary policies. As under the PRK and the SOC regimes, however, corruption and decentralization render many policy prescriptions meaningless. Natural resources—in particular, timber—are sold off to profit individuals rather than to support the state budget. The riel remains feeble; all large transactions are based in dollars. Like their Vietnamese and Eastern European predecessors, the new advisors frequently find that it is easier simply to support the government financially while eliciting a general and superficial allegiance to political and economic principles than it is to influence how the country actually operates.[4]

The economic evolution that took place in the 1980s has continued. Socialism, to the extent it ever existed in Cambodia, is gone. In theory, the free market reigns, except that corruption impedes economic development, discourages entrepreneurial activity, and deters foreign investment. Nonetheless, the Chinese community has flourished and again dominates much of the economy. As the PRK had once feared, the ethnic Chinese have established connections with other overseas Chinese, importing and exporting goods throughout the region. There is more private-sector employment than in the past. In Phnom Penh, Malaysian, Singaporean, and Taiwanese investors have set up cell-phone and car dealerships that hire a few Cambodians with English and computer skills. For the moment, though, such skilled workers are far outnumbered by the thousands of women working for a dollar a day in foreign-owned garment sweatshops on the outskirts of the city.

Wealth accumulates in the hands of officials, generals, and a few big businesspeople. The relationship between government ministers and big business has grown closer, and some of the first big investors have become kingmakers. Teng Bunma, one of the early investors from Thailand, became the first president of the Chamber of Commerce and grew so powerful and so close to Hun Sen that he boasted that he had funded the 1997 coup d'état. His successor as president, Sok Kong of Sokimex, expanded his fuel business to include a concession to manage the temples of Angkor Wat.

Low-level corruption abounds. Despite numerous efforts by foreign donors and multilateral lending institutions to promote administrative reform, the bureaucracy is still bloated, mired in nepotism and patronage. There is no effective tax system to redirect money toward priorities such as education and health. Salaries remain inadequate, requiring civil servants to supplement their income with bribes and "fees." Public services are nonexistent or cost money. Schoolteachers and university professors, for example, either teach privately outside work hours or accept money for grades. As a result, Cambodian society lacks the kind of meritocratic ladder that rewards education and creates the kind of middle class that, elsewhere in Asia, has toppled repressive regimes.

Along Monivong Avenue, Phnom Penh's main commercial strip, signs of Cambodia's second revolution are nowhere to be seen. Cars with tinted windows creep along, reminders of the new wealth. Foolhardy young men on motor scooters weave in and out of traffic. Cyclo drivers balancing furniture and home appliances on the passenger's seat inch their way across the street, gauging the intentions of each oncoming vehicle. Chinese-language signs advertise restaurants, nightclubs, and electronics stores. Down the smaller streets, prostitutes sit under the awnings of brothels waiting for the evening clientele.

Scattered reminders of the 1980s remain. A few blocks west of Monivong Avenue stands Tuol Sleng, which the Vietnamese and the PRK turned into a museum. Inside, several walls are covered with haunting photographs, taken by Khmer Rouge functionaries, of soon-to-be executed prisoners. Another exhibit presents an explanation for the Vietnamese invasion and occupation of Cambodia: a map depicting Democratic Kampuchea's attacks on Vietnam.

Due south of Tuol Sleng is the Russian Market, so called because that is where the PRK's Russian advisors shopped. Nowadays it is filled with Cambodians buying vegetables and kitchenware and Westerners browsing for gems and textiles. Political memorabilia are also popular among the tourists, especially Khmer Rouge currency. Crisp, red notes with stirring pictures of peasants, workers, tractors, and bountiful fields, the money, which was never used, is now just communist kitsch. Souvenirs from the PRK are harder to find. There are a few stamps tucked behind glass counters. Printed in the Soviet Union, they depict Russian cosmonauts and Winter Olympians and were apparently intended to reassure Cambodians of their role in the international communist movement. Yet the very incongruity of the stamps seems to reinforce the obscurity of Cambodia's political and cultural evolution. The history of the PRK and the SOC has little to do with icons of the Cold War. Cambodia did not arise from the ashes of the Khmer Rouge with anything approaching ideological clarity. Rather, it emerged—after twelve years of conflict and confusion—a product of many quiet struggles, among its leaders, its foreign patrons, and its citizens.

Notes

CHAPTER ONE. LIBERATION

1. Interview, Heng Chi, Phnom Penh, Dec. 17, 1996
2. Interview, Thun Saray, Phnom Penh, Dec. 9, 1996.
3. Interview, Vandy Ka-on, Paris, Aug. 12, 1997.
4. Howard J. DeNike, John Quigley, and Kenneth J. Robinson, eds., *Genocide in Cambodia: Documents from the Trial of Pol Pot and Ieng Sary,* Philadelphia: University of Pennsylvania Press, 2000, pp. 169–74.
5. Interviews, Thun Saray, Phnom Penh, Dec. 9 and 18, 1996.
6. Saportemean Khmer (SPK), Dec. 3, 1979, and Dec. 4, 1979, Foreign Broadcast Information Service (FBIS), Dec. 4, 1979.
7. Timothy Carney, "Heng Samrin's Armed Forces and a Military Balance in Cambodia," in David A. Ablin and Marlowe Hood, eds., *The Cambodian Agony,* Armonk, N.Y.: M. E. Sharpe, 1987. Nayan Chanda, *Brother Enemy: The War After the War,* New York: Collier Books, 1986. Bui Tin, *From Cadre to Exile: The Memoirs of a North Vietnamese Journalist,* Chiang Mai, Thailand: Silkworm Books, 1995, pp. 45–46. Le Duc Tho's presence is described in Chanda, *Brother Enemy,* p. 339.
8. Ben Kiernan, *How Pol Pot Came to Power: A History of Communism in Kampuchea, 1930–1975,* London: Verso, 1985, p. 79. Bui Tin, *From Cadre to Exile,* pp. 45–46.

9. Chanda, *Brother Enemy*, p. 339. SPK, Dec. 3, 1979, and Dec. 4, 1979, FBIS, Dec. 4, 1979.

10. An account of the invasion is in Chanda, *Brother Enemy*, pp. 341–46.

11. Vietnamese Foreign Ministry Statement, Jan. 6, 1979, FBIS, Jan. 8, 1979. SPK, Jan. 8, 1979, FBIS, Jan. 9, 1979. SPK, Jan. 11, 1979, FBIS, Jan. 11, 1979.

12. Y Phandara, *Retour à Phnom Penh: Le Cambodge du génocide à la colonisation,* Paris: A. M. Métailié, 1982. "Kampuchea, Death and Rebirth," H & S Studio, Montagebuch Film Protocol, 1980. Interview, Pen Sovan, Takeo, May 12, 1999.

CHAPTER TWO. TURNING WATERS: THE PATTERNS AND MYTHS OF CAMBODIAN HISTORY

1. See David Chandler, *A History of Cambodia,* 3d ed., Boulder, Colo.: Westview Press, 2000; Chandler, *The Tragedy of Cambodian History: Politics, War and Revolution Since 1945,* New Haven: Yale University Press, 1991; Chandler, *Brother Number One: A Political Biography of Pol Pot,* 2d ed., Boulder, Colo.: Westview Press, 1999; Ben Kiernan, *How Pol Pot Came to Power;* Kiernan, *The Pol Pot Regime: Race, Power and Genocide in Cambodia Under the Khmer Rouge,* New Haven: Yale University Press, 1996; Elizabeth Becker, *When the War Was Over: Cambodia and the Khmer Rouge Revolution,* 2d ed., New York: Public Affairs, 1998; Milton Osborne, *Sihanouk: Prince of Light, Prince of Darkness,* Honolulu: University of Hawaii Press, 1994; Chanda, *Brother Enemy,* 1986.

2. For two descriptions of Khmer nationalism and its frequent corollary, anti-Vietnamese racism, see Penny Edwards, "Imagining the Other in Cambodian Nationalist Discourse Before and During the UNTAC Period," in Stephen Heder and Judy Ledgerwood, eds., *Propaganda, Politics and Violence in Cambodia: Democratic Transition Under United Nations Peace-Keeping,* Armonk, N.Y.: M.E. Sharpe, 1996, pp. 30–72; and Jay Jordens, "Persecution of Cambodia's Ethnic Vietnamese Communities During and Since the UNTAC Period," in ibid., pp. 134–158.

3. "Remarks on the Official Appearance of the Vietnamese Workers' Party," US Mission in Vietnam, Captured Documents Series, no. 2, quoted in Kiernan, *How Pol Pot Came to Power,* p. 83.

4. The U.S. bombing and subsequent invasion of Cambodia is the subject of William Shawcross, *Sideshow: Kissinger, Nixon and the Destruction of Cambodia,* New York: Simon and Schuster, 1979. See also Chandler, *Tragedy of Cambodian History,* p. 204.

5. Stephen Heder, *From Pol Pot to Pen Sovan in the Villages,* Bangkok: Chulalongkorn University, 1980, pp. 4–6. Kiernan, *How Pol Pot Came to Power,* p. 373. Chandler, *Tragedy of Cambodian History,* p. 210.

6. Kiernan, *How Pol Pot Came to Power,* pp. 380–88. Chandler, *Tragedy of Cambodian History,* pp. 226–27.

7. The text of the constitution of Democratic Kampuchea is included in François Ponchaud, *Cambodia: Year Zero,* New York: Holt, Rinehart and Winston, 1978, p. 222.

8. Haing Ngor with Roger Warner, *A Cambodian Odyssey,* New York: Macmillan, 1987, pp. 133–34.

9. Karl D. Jackson, "The Ideology of Total Revolution," in Jackson, ed., *Cambodia, 1975– 1978: Rendezvous with Death,* Princeton: Princeton University Press, 1989, pp. 37–78.

Jackson, "Intellectual Origins of the Khmer Rouge," in ibid., pp. 241–50. Becker, *When the War Was Over,* p. 203.

10. James Fenton, *Cambodia Witness: The Autobiography of Someth May,* New York: Random House, 1986, p. 228.

11. For a general description of the zones, see Chandler, *Tragedy of Cambodian History,* p. 269; Becker, *When the War Was Over,* p. 179. With regard to the Eastern Zone, Ben Kiernan has described relatively tolerant conditions in *The Pol Pot Regime,* esp. pp. 205– 10, and in "Wild Chickens, Farm Chickens, and Cormorants: Kampuchea's Eastern Zone Under Pol Pot," in David Chandler and Ben Kiernan, eds., *Revolution and Its Aftermath in Kampuchea,* Yale University Southeast Asia Studies Monograph no. 25, New Haven, 1983, pp. 136–211, as has Michael Vickery in *Kampuchea, 1975–1982,* Boston: South End Press, 1984. Stephen Heder offers a different perspective in "Racism, Marxism, Labeling, and Genocide in Ben Kiernan's *The Pol Pot Regime,*" *Southeast Asia Research,* 5, no. 2 (1997), pp. 101–53.

12. David Chandler, *Voices from S-21: Terror and History in Pol Pot's Secret Prison.* Berkeley: University of California Press, 1999.

13. For an account of the border skirmishes, see Stephen J. Morris, *Why Vietnam Invaded Cambodia,* Stanford, Calif.: Stanford University Press, 1999; Stephen Heder, "The Kampuchea-Vietnamese Conflict," in David W. P. Elliott, ed., *The Third Indochina Conflict,* Boulder, Colo.: Westview Press, 1981; Chanda, *Brother Enemy.*

14. Chanda, *Brother Enemy,* p. 217. Kiernan, *How Pol Pot Came to Power,* p. 360. Interview, Pen Sovan, Takeo, May 12, 1999.

15. Interview, Pen Sovan, Takeo, May 12, 1999.

16. Morris, *Why Vietnam Invaded Cambodia,* p. 109, citing "Report of a conversation with General Secretary of the CPV [Communist Party of Vietnam] Le Duan, May 9, 1978." For a description of the Vietnamese role in reestablishing the Party and constructing the Front, see Chanda, *Brother Enemy,* pp. 215–17, 253–54.

17. Interview, Uk Bunchheuan, Phnom Penh, May 31, 1999. Chanda, *Brother Enemy,* p. 253. Kiernan, *Pol Pot Regime,* pp. 395–96, 440–41. Becker, *When the War Was Over,* p. 312.

18. Interview, Uk Bunchheuan, Phnom Penh, May 31, 1999. Interview, Pen Sovan, Takeo, May 12, 1999. Interview, Chan Ven, Phnom Penh, May 21, 1999.

19. Interview, Pen Sovan, Takeo, May 12, 1999.

CHAPTER THREE. BLOOD DEBTS: TRANSITION AND CONTINUITY UNDER A NEW REGIME

1. Fenton, *Cambodia Witness,* p. 241.

2. Loung Ung, *First They Killed My Father,* New York: HarperCollins, 2000, p. 206. See also Haing Ngor with Roger Warner, *Surviving the Killing Fields: The Cambodian Odyssey of Haing S. Ngor,* London: Chatto and Windus, 1987, pp. 353, 362; Kiernan, *Pol Pot Regime,* p. 455.

3. SPK, Jan. 6, 1979, FBIS Jan. 8, 1979. Interview, former Front soldier, Phnom Penh, May 1999. Ung, *First They Killed My Father,* pp. 203–4.

4. Ung, *First They Killed My Father,* p. 167.

5. Stephen Heder, *Kampuchean Occupation and Resistance,* Bangkok: Chulalongkorn University, 1980, pp. 29, 34.

6. Directive Circular, KPRC, June 26, 1979 (*Doc. 14–24*). *Doc. 1–1, Doc. 1–2*, etc., refer to PRK and SOC documents copies of which are in my possession. All translations from the Khmer are mine unless otherwise noted. Heder, *Kampuchean Occupation and Resistance*, pp. 19, 21, 23–24, 45. Heder, *From Pol Pot to Pen Sovan*, p. 45.

7. Bulletin, Office, KPRC, 1979, p. 1 (*Doc. 14–25*).

8. Y Phandara, *Retour à Phnom Penh*, p. 255. My translation from the French.

9. Directive Circular 4, KPRC, Oct. 79 (*Doc. 14–17*). Special Circular, KPRC, June 10, 1979 (*Doc. 14–22*). Directive Circular, KPRC, June 26, 1979 (*Doc. 14–24*). Letter, Party Permanent Committee, Sept. 25, 1979, p. 2 (*Doc. 9–6*). Heder, *From Pol Pot to Pen Sovan*, p. 48. William Shawcross, *The Quality of Mercy: Cambodia, Holocaust and Modern Conscience*, New York: Simon and Schuster, 1984, p. 209.

10. SPK, Jan. 6, 1979, FBIS, Jan. 8, 1979.

11. Heder, *Kampuchean Occupation and Resistance*, p. 11. Numerous Cambodians who eventually settled in France and the United States, including Loung Ung, Someth May, Y Phandara, and Haing Ngor, have written accounts of the trip into exile and the reasons behind it. See also Yathay Pin, *Stay Alive, My Son*, London: Bloomsbury, 1987; Molyda Szymusiak, *The Stones Cry Out: A Cambodian Childhood, 1975–1980*, New York: Hill and Wang, 1986.

12. Resolution 2, Party Central Committee, July 17, 1979, p. 6 (*Doc. 8–81*). Heder, *Kampuchean Occupation and Resistance*, pp. 25, 49.

13. Shawcross, *Quality of Mercy*, pp. 125, 131–32, 169. Ben Kiernan, "Kampuchea, 1979–1981: National Rehabilitation in the Eye of the International Storm," *Southeast Asian Affairs*, 1982, p. 175. Heder, *Kampuchean Occupation and Resistance*, pp. 43–51.

14. News reports related to the international aspect of the Cambodian conflict have been compiled by Patrick Raszelenberg and Peter Schier in cooperation with Jeffry G. Wong, in *The Cambodia Conflict: Search for a Settlement, 1979–1991*, Hamburg: Mitteilungen des Instituts für Asienkunde, 1995. Becker, *When the War Was Over*, pp. 437–507. David W. P. Elliott, "Deadlock Diplomacy: Thai and Vietnamese Interests in Kampuchean," in Ablin and Hood, *Cambodian Agony*, pp. 69–92.

15. Phnom Penh Domestic Service, Jan. 5, 1979, FBIS, Jan. 8, 1979. Vietnamese Foreign Ministry Statement, Jan. 6, 1979, FBIS, Jan. 8, 1979.

16. *Nhan Dan* editorial, Jan. 7, 1979, FBIS, Jan. 8, 1979. On February 17, 1979, Vietnamese Prime Minister Pham Van Dong visited Phnom Penh for the signing of a Treaty of Friendship, Peace, and Cooperation. Vietnam News Agency, Hanoi, Feb. 18, 1979, FBIS, Feb. 22, 1979.

17. Hanoi Domestic Service, Jan. 10, 1979, FBIS, Jan. 11, 1979.

18. *New York Times*, Jan. 8, 1979; Jan. 9, 1979; Jan. 11, 1979.

19. "Joint Statement, Special Meeting of ASEAN Foreign Ministers on the Current Political Development in the South East Asian Region," in *Documents on the Kampuchean Problem, 1979–1985*, Bangkok: Department of Political Affairs, Ministry of Foreign Affairs, undated. *Yearbook of the United Nations*, New York, 1979. *Far Eastern Economic Review*, Jan. 26, 1979, p. 7. For an account of Sihanouk during this period, see Chanda, *Brother Enemy*, pp. 363–70.

20. The United States continued to avoid the word "genocide" in describing the Khmer

Rouge for more than a decade. The Paris peace accords of 1991, which ended the civil war and were signed by the Khmer Rouge, referred to the "policies and practices of the past."

21. *Yearbook of the United Nations,* 1979. Norodom Sihanouk had proposed leaving both the Nonaligned Movement seat and the U.N. seat open. Sihanouk, "An Open Letter to the Member States of the United Nations Organization," in Peter Schier and Manola Schier-Oum, *Prince Sihanouk on Cambodia: Interviews and Talks with Prince Norodom Sihanouk,* 2d ed., Hamburg: Institut für Asienkunde, 1985, pp. 75–80. Sihanouk, "An Open Letter to the Summit Conference of the Non-Aligned Countries, Havana," Pyongyang, August 1979, in ibid., pp. 69–74.

22. Shawcross, *Quality of Mercy,* pp. 176, 227–29, 306. Heder, *Kampuchean Occupation and Resistance,* pp. 50–51. Michael Vickery, "Refugee Politics: The Khmer Camp System in Thailand," in Ablin and Hood, *Cambodian Agony,* pp. 293–331.

23. Shawcross, *Quality of Mercy,* pp. 31–32. The PRK anthem was similar in rhetorical tone to that of Democratic Kampuchea, which sang of the "sublime blood of workers and peasants" and a "resolute struggle." The D.K. anthem concluded with the words "Let us resolutely raise high / The red Flag of the Revolution! / Let us edify our Motherland! / Let us make her advance with great leaps / So that she will be more glorious and more marvelous than ever!" Becker, *When the War Was Over,* pp. 207–8.

24. Voice of Democratic Kampuchea, Mar. 27, 1979, FBIS, Mar. 30, 1979. Personal communication, Stephen Heder, September 2001. Kiernan, *How Pol Pot Came to Power,* p. 311.

25. Interview, Pen Sovan, Takeo, May 12, 1999. The Party congress was held as the Vietnamese were taking Phnom Penh. "Some Documents on the Situation in Cambodia," [Vietnamese] Expert Group, Political Committee, 1984 (*Doc. 3KN*). Doc. 3KN, Doc. MMM, etc., refer to Vietnamese documents located in a private archive. Copies of those referred to herein are in my possession. The translator wishes to be anonymous.

26. Personal communication, Stephen Heder, September 2001.

27. Interview, Central Party official, Phnom Penh, May 19, 1999. Interview, Pen Sovan, Takeo, May 12, 1999. Kiernan, *How Pol Pot Came to Power,* p. 380.

28. Interview, Central Party official, Phnom Penh, May 17, 1999. For Phouthang's Party duties, see Resolution, Party Central Committee, Apr. 12, 1979, p. 4 (*Doc. 9–1*); Resolution, Party Central Committee, 1979, p. 4 (*Doc. 10–69*).

29. Interview, Central Party official, Phnom Penh, May 19, 1999. For Bou Thang's history, see Kiernan, *How Pol Pot Came to Power,* pp. 374–75, 407 n. 330; Timothy Carney, "Heng Samrin's Armed Forces and a Military Balance in Cambodia," in Ablin and Hood, *Cambodian Agony,* p. 157. For Bou Thang's Party role, see Resolution, Party Central Committee, Apr. 12, 1979 (*Doc. 9–1*).

30. For Hun Sen's history, see Kiernan, *How Pol Pot Came to Power,* pp. 254, 294 n. 198; Becker, *When the War Was Over,* pp. 441–42. Characterizations of Hun Sen's rise are taken from Interview, Central Party official, Phnom Penh, May 14, 1999; Interview, former Ministry of Foreign Affairs official, Phnom Penh, May 19, 1999. For a description of Hun Sen's Party role, see Resolution, Party Central Committee, Apr. 12, 1979 (*Doc. 9–1*).

31. Resolution, Party Central Committee, 1979, p. 6 (*Doc. 10–69*). Resolution, Party Central Committee, Apr. 12, 1979, p. 8 (*Doc. 9–1*). Minutes 04, Office, Council of Ministers, Jan. 19, 1984, p. 2 (*Doc. 7–116*).

32. Document, Party Central Committee, undated, p. 1 (*Doc. 8–71*).

33. Directive, Party Central Committee, Apr. 4, 1979, p. 14 (*Doc. 2–8*). Interview, Central Party official, Phnom Penh, May 19, 1999.

34. Circular 18, Party Central Committee, July 1979, p. 8 (*Doc. 2–8*). Directive, Party Central Committee, Apr. 4, 1979, p. 17 (*Doc. 2–8*).

35. Resolution 2, Party Central Committee, July 17, 1979, pp. 31–34 (*Doc. 8–81*). Directive Circular 12, Party Central Committee, Dec. 6, 1979 (*Doc. 5–27*).

36. Pen Sovan (minister of defense), Nou Peng (minister of health), Kaev Chenda (minister of propaganda, information, and culture), and Mok Sakun (minister of industry) had all come from Hanoi. Sokun, who was also chair of the Economics and Livelihood Committee, died in April 1979. The following month, the committee became a ministry to be headed by the Hanoi-trained Ros Samay. Kaev Chenda became minister of industry. Chan Ven, the minister of education, was an educated noncommunist who had sought refuge in Vietnam. Over the course of the year, more Hanoi-trained cadres entered the government, including Khun Chhi (minister of communications), Tang Sareum (minister of commerce), Chan Phin (minister of finance), and Neou Samom (minister of social affairs). Minutes, Council of State, Aug. 28, 1987, pp. 2–3 (*Doc. 5–87*); Resolution, Party Central Committee, Apr. 12, 1979, p. 8 (*Doc. 9–1*); Decision, KPRC, Nov. 18, 1979, p. 2 (*Doc. 14–45*); Minutes, Council of State, Aug. 28, 1987, pp. 2–3 (*Doc. 5–87*); Interview, Pen Sovan, Takeo, May 12, 1999; Interview, Central Party official, Phnom Penh, May 17, 1999; Carney, "Armed Forces," p. 185; Chanda, *Brother Enemy,* p. 449 n. 38. Extremely valuable in identifying ministers, as well as local officials, are Michael Vickery, *Kampuchea: Politics, Economics and Society,* London: Pinter, 1986, pp. 44–45; JPRS Report, *State of Cambodia: Biographic Information on Officials and Lists of Cambodian Officials (By Organizations),* FBIS, 1990; Raoul M. Jennar, *Les clés du Cambodge: Faits et chiffres, repère historiques, profiles cambodgiens, cartes,* Aubenas d'Ardèche, France: Maisonneuve and Larose, 1995.

37. Interview, Chan Ven, Phnom Penh, May 21, 1999.

38. Minutes, Dec. 29, 1979, pp. 1–2 (*Doc. 13–112*). As a stopgap measure, the Vietnamese assigned Heng Samrin, Pen Sovan, and Hun Sen the responsibility of handling "issues that involve multiple ministries or that fall outside the mandates of the ministries." Resolution, Party Central Committee, 1979 (*Doc. 10–69*).

39. "Dao Duc Chinh," a transliteration from the Khmer, may have been Do Chinh, who served as deputy director of the Economics and Planning Department of the VCP. Directorate of Central Intelligence, U.S. Government, *Directory of Officials of Vietnam,* 1985. For Chinh's role within the KPRC, see Minutes, KPRC, Oct. 10, 1980, p. 3 (*Doc. 11–47*) ("Comrade Chinh offered further advice to the meeting regarding the experiences in Vietnam concerning the role of office heads, the work of the offices, and the relations among the offices").

40. For Meas Leas's comments, see Minutes, Party, Feb. 26, 1981, pp. 8–9 (*Doc. 5–48*). For Ung Phan's comments, see Minutes, Party Ministerial Committee, May 1982, p. 2 (*Doc. 10–123*). For Ung Phan's role in the KPRC, see Minutes, Meeting Between Vietnamese Advisor and PRK Head of State, Dec. 29, 1979, p. 2 (*Doc. 13–112*); Minutes, Party Ministry Committee, May 1982 (*Doc. 10–123*); Minutes 8, Party Branch 2, Sept. 9, 1983 (*Doc.*

10–117); Letter, Party Branch 1, May 12, 1979 (*Doc. 10–64*); Minutes, KPRC, Oct. 22, 1980, p. 3 (*Doc. 11–47*).

41. Circular 10, Party Permanent Committee, June 6, 1979 (*Doc. 10–77*). Letter, Party Permanent Committee, Sept. 25, 1979, p. 2 (*Doc. 9–6*). Decision, Head of State, 1979, p. 1 (*Doc. 14–40*).

42. Letter, Party Permanent Committee, Sept. 25, 1979 (*Doc. 9–6*). Decision, Head of State, 1979, p. 1 (*Doc. 14–40*).

43. Directive Circular 2, Party Central Committee, Aug. 17, 1979, p. 2 (*Doc. 9–3*).

44. Implementation Decree 132, Party Central Committee, June 1980, pp. 3–4 (*Doc. 5–29*).

45. Minutes, Party, Feb. 26, 1981, p. 4 (*Doc. 5–48*).

46. Minutes, Party Ministry Committee, Aug. 31, 1982 (*Doc. 5–53*). Minutes 04, Party Ministry Committee, April 1982, p. 4 (*Doc. 5–49*). Interview, Central Party official, Phnom Penh, May 17, 1999. For the policy on advisors, see Determination 145, KPRC, June 28, 1980, p. 3 (*Doc. 13–46*).

47. The characterization of the Eastern Zone cadres is from Hun Sen's official biography. Jacques Bekaert, *Cambodia Diary: Tales from a Divided Nation,* Bangkok: DD Books, 1987, p. 134. For Vietnamese-Cambodian revolutionary history, see Kiernan, *How Pol Pot Came to Power.*

48. Party Document, undated (est. 1980), p. 3 (*Doc. 8–71*).

49. Ibid.

50. The distinction between state and Party was poorly defined. In about half the provinces, the Vietnamese appointed the same person as governor and Party secretary. Where the positions were divided between two people, the Party secretary generally maintained stronger connections to central leaders and had broader responsibilities, including the disciplining of local cadres. The governors, themselves deputy provincial Party secretaries, were also granted important duties. The overlapping and ambiguous nature of these posts resulted in ongoing disputes between state and Party leaders. See Resolution 2, Party Central Committee, July 17, 1979, p. 32 (*Doc. 8–81*); Circular 21, Party Central Committee, Mar. 15, 1980, p. 5 (*Doc. 6–31*); Minutes, 04, Party Ministry Committee, April 1982, p. 3 (*Doc. 5–49*); Resolution, Party Permanent Committee, undated, p. 2 (*Doc. 8–87*); Interview, Pen Sovan, Takeo, May 12, 1999; Interview, Central Party official, Phnom Penh, May 17, 1999. Eastern Zone defectors included Pol Saroeun (Party secretary of Takeo), Sim Kar (Party secretary and provincial governor of Kampong Cham), Ros Chhun (Party secretary and provincial governor of Kampong Thom), Haem Bau (Party secretary of Siem Reap), Em Chheum (provincial governor of Siem Reap), Dok Narin (Party secretary of Kampong Chhnang), Daok Samol (Party secretary of Prey Veng), Ros Sreng (Party secretary of Pursat), Chum Hol (Party secretary and governor of Kampong Som), Heng Samkai (Party secretary and governor of Svay Rieng), and Kao Ty, alias Keo Sokon (governor of Battambang). Interview, Pen Sovan, Takeo, May 12, 1999; Interview, Uk Bunchheuan, Phnom Penh, May 31, 1999; Personal communication, Stephen Heder, August 2000.

51. Interview, Pen Sovan, Takeo, May 12, 1999. Keysan also goes by the names Rong Them Ea Chramhaysone and Phlam Keysan. Jennar, *Les clés du Cambodge,* p. 248.

52. According to a veteran Battambang provincial Party cadre, Kao Ty had "morality" prob-

lems and fled to the border after only two or three months. In his place, Lay Samon was made Party secretary and provincial governor. Interview, Battambang Party official, May 26, 1999. A noncommunist was appointed governor of Kampot province. Shawcross, *Quality of Mercy,* p. 32.

53. For the presence of Vietnamese advisors at the province and district levels and their hiring preferences, I have relied on numerous interviews. See also Resolution, Party Central Committee, undated (est. 1980) (*Doc. 8–71*); Heder, *Kampuchean Occupation and Resistance,* pp. 13–14; Heder, *From Pol Pot to Pen Sovan,* pp. 19–22; Carney, "Armed Forces," p. 193; Interview, Pen Sovan, Takeo, May 12, 1999. For the structure of the local administrations, see Resolution 2, Party Central Committee, July 17, 1979 (*Doc. 8–81*); Resolution, Party Permanent Committee, undated (*Doc. 8–87*); Resolution, Party Permanent Committee, undated (*Doc. 10–71*).

54. SPK, Jan. 6, 1979, FBIS Jan. 8, 1979.

55. Resolution, Party Central Committee, undated (est. 1980), p. 1 (*Doc. 8–71*). Resolution 2, Party Central Committee, July 17, 1979, p. 19 (*Doc. 8–81*). Heder, *From Pol Pot to Pen Sovan,* pp. 24–25. Heder, *Kampuchean Occupation and Resistance,* pp. 10–12.

56. Resolution, Party Central Committee, undated (est. 1980), pp. 2, 7, 19 (*Doc. 8–71*). Heder, *From Pol Pot to Pen Sovan,* pp. 22–24. Heder, *Kampuchean Occupation and Resistance,* pp. 14–15.

57. Interview, former provincial Propaganda Office official, Phnom Penh, May 24, 1999. Heder, *Kampuchean Occupation and Resistance,* pp. 15–16.

58. Heder, *Kampuchean Occupation and Resistance,* p. 18, 23–24; Heder, *From Pol Pot to Pen Sovan,* p. 26. Fenton, *Cambodia Witness,* p. 253.

59. Resolution 2, Party Central Committee, July 17, 1979, p. 19 (*Doc. 8–81*).

60. KPRC Review of the General Situation in Cambodia, 1975–1979, Phnom Penh Domestic Service, Mar. 13, 1979, FBIS, Mar. 15, 1979.

61. Resolution 2, Party Central Committee, July 17, 1979, p. 24 (*Doc. 8–81*).

62. Jacques Bekaert, "Kampuchea: The Year of the Nationals?" *Southeast Asian Affairs,* 1983, p. 167.

63. Resolution 2, Party Central Committee, July 17, 1979, pp. 20, 22 (*Doc. 8–81*). Sihanouk, speaking indiscreetly from Beijing, acknowledged that In Tam was receiving Chinese support. *Far Eastern Economic Review,* Mar. 27, 1979.

64. Resolution 2, Party Central Committee, July 17, 1979, p. 28 (*Doc. 8–81*).

65. Ibid., p. 19.

66. Ibid., pp. 22–23. Secret Plan, 1979, p. 2 (*Doc. 9–10*).

67. Resolution, Party Central Committee, undated (est. 1980), pp. 1, 6 (*Doc. 8–71*).

68. Ibid., p. 2.

69. Ibid.

70. Ibid.

71. Resolution 2, Party Central Committee, July 17, 1979, p. 19 (*Doc. 8–81*). Resolution, Party Central Committee, undated (est. 1980), pp. 1–3 (*Doc. 8–71*). Directive Circular 2, Party Central Committee, Aug. 17, 1979 (*Doc. 9–3*). Interview, Battambang Party official, Battambang, May 26, 1999.

72. Resolution 2, Party Central Committee, July 17, 1979, p. 29 (*Doc. 8–81*).

73. Resolution, Party Central Committee, undated, pp. 3 (*Doc. 8–71*).

74. *Far Eastern Economic Review,* Apr. 27, 1979, p. 5; June 22, 1979, pp. 10–12; July 20, 1979, pp. 40–41.

75. Circular 1, KPRC, Apr. 15, 1979 (*Doc. 14–46*).

76. Work papers, Pol Pot Court, May 10, 1979 (*Doc. 14–48*). Interview, Bui Tin, Paris, May 2, 1999. *Who's Who in North Vietnam,* pp. 89–91. Telephone interview, John Quigley, November 2000. Voice of Democratic Kampuchea Radio, Aug. 2, 1979, FBIS, Aug. 13, 1979.

77. Work papers, Pol Pot Court, May 10, 1979 (*Doc. 14–48*). Voice of Democratic Kampuchea Radio, Aug. 2, 1979, FBIS, Aug. 13, 1979. Stephen Heder, "Victims' Justice and Clemency in the People's Republic of Kampuchea," unpublished.

78. Work papers, Pol Pot Court, May 10, 1979 (*Doc. 14–48*). Interview, former Ministry of Propaganda official, Phnom Penh, May 19, 1999.

79. "Kampuchea, Death and Rebirth," H & S Studio, Montagebuch Film Protocol, 1980. Howard J. DeNike, John Quigley, and Kenneth J. Robinson, eds., *Genocide in Cambodia: Documents from the Trial of Pol Pot and Ieng Sary,* Philadelphia: University of Pennsylvania Press, 2000, pp. 47–49.

80. Chenda's book was published in Hanoi in 1961 and republished in 1983 in the *Phnom Penh Gazette: Ecrivains et expressions littéraires du Cambodge au XXème siècle,* vol. 2, ed. Khing Hoc Dy, Paris: Editions L'Harmattan, 1993, p. 116. Interview, Chhour Leang Huot, Phnom Penh, Dec. 16, 1996. Besides Leang Huot, the members of the tribunal were Pen Navuth, former head of the Adult Education Section, Ministry of Education and Training; Chea Samy, former teacher of traditional dance; Meas Savath, acting battalion chief, First Brigade; Nouth Savoeun, doctor of pediatrics; Nouth Thon, secretary, Central Committee, Kampuchean Youth Organization; Chhouk Chhim, vice president, Association of Kampuchean Women; Kun Kim, worker at the power plant of Phnom Penh; Kim Kaneth, worker at the power plant of Phnom Penh; Lek Sarat, official in the Department of Propaganda and Education of the Central Committee. Decree-Law 25, Appointment of Members of the Tribunal, KPRC, July 20, 1979; in DeNike, Quigley, and Robinson, *Genocide in Cambodia,* pp. 50–51. Heder, "Victims' Justice and Clemency."

81. Interview, Dith Munty, Phnom Penh, Dec. 31, 1996. Documents, People's Revolutionary Tribunal, A Group of Cambodian Jurists, pp. VI-256 to VI-264. Closing Argument of Attorney Yuos Por for Pol Pot and Ieng Sary, Accused of Crimes of Genocide, in DeNike, Quigley, and Robinson, *Genocide in Cambodia,* pp. 508–11. Closing Argument of Attorney Dith Munty for the Accused Pol Pot and Ieng Sary, in ibid., pp. 511–13..

82. John Quigley, Introduction, in DeNike, Quigley, and Robinson, *Genocide in Cambodia,* p. 1.

83. Ibid.

84. Working Schedule for the People's Revolutionary Tribunal During Its Present Session, in DeNike, Quigley, and Robinson, *Genocide in Cambodia,* pp. 67–69. Heder, "Victims' Justice and Clemency." Casefile of the Tribunal to Judge the Genocidal Pol Pot–Ieng Sary Clique, Phnom Penh: Ministry of Propaganda, Culture, and Information, August 1979, in DeNike, Quigley, and Robinson, *Genocide in Cambodia,* pp. 47–75, 542–49.

85. DeNike, Quigley, and Robinson, *Genocide in Cambodia,* pp. 504–8, 513–22. Two decades later, the Cambodian government (made up of many of the same leaders) sought the limited participation of U.N.-appointed lawyers in a second trial of Khmer Rouge leaders.

86. Stephen Heder, "Victors' Genocide in Cambodia," *Phnom Penh Post,* Mar. 5–18, 1999. People's Revolutionary Tribunal Held in Phnom Penh for the Trial of the Genocide Crime of the Pol Pot–Ieng Sary Clique, "Judgment of the Revolutionary People's Tribunal Held in Phnom Penh from 15 to 19 August 1979," August 1979, in DeNike, Quigley, and Robinson, *Genocide in Cambodia,* pp. 542–49. Quigley, Introduction, p. 8. *Letter Dated 17 September 1979 from the Permanent Representative of Vietnam to the United Nations: Address to the Secretary-General,* UN Document A/34/491, Sept. 20, 1979.

87. The different dates may also be significant and could be interpreted as indicating a shift in policy. During the summer of 1979, the Party was focused on removing prerevolutionary officials, filling administrative positions, and consolidating the regime. Later, as it became more apparent that many Cambodians resented the replacement of noncommunists by former Khmer Rouge cadres, the Party may have had second thoughts. On the other hand, former PRK officials clearly recall the factional disputes. Moreover, the documents were prepared for different leaders but never signed, an indication that they were intended to represent the perspectives of separate factions even if those perspectives could not be accepted by the leadership as a whole.

88. Resolution, Party Central Committee, undated (est. 1980), p. 3 (*Doc. 8–71*).

89. Ibid.

90. Resolution 2, Party Central Committee, July 17, 1979, p. 30 (*Doc. 8–81*).

91. Resolution, Party Central Committee, undated (est. 1980), p. 5 (*Doc. 8–71*).

92. Ibid., pp. 4–6.

93. Resolution 2, Party Central Committee, July 17, 1979, p. 28 (*Doc. 8–81*).

94. Ibid.

95. Ibid., p. 29.

96. Resolution, Party Central Committee, undated (est. 1980), p. 5 (*Doc. 8–71*).

97. Interview, Central Party official, Phnom Penh, May 17, 1999.

98. Resolution, Party Central Committee, undated (est. 1980), p. 3 (*Doc. 8–71*).

99. SPK, Dec. 3, 1979, and Dec. 4, 1979, FBIS, Dec. 4, 1979.

100. For the structure of the mass organizations, see Circular, Party Central Committee, September 1979 (*Doc. 9–2*); Decision 84, Party Central Committee, May 9, 1980 (*Doc. 9–93*). For the history of the mass organizations, see Kiernan, *How Pol Pot Came to Power,* pp. 129, 345. For later complaints from mass organization officials, see Minutes 79, Office, Council of Ministers, June 8, 1984, p. 3 (*Doc. 7–106*); Minutes 7, Office, Council of Ministers, Mar. 12, 1988 (*Doc. 12–65*); Minutes 48, Office, Council of Ministers, Nov. 16, 1987 (*Doc. 13–33*).

101. Resolution 2, Party Central Committee, July 17, 1979, p. 30 (*Doc. 8–81*).

102. Circular 24, Front, June 5, 1981, p. 1 (*Doc. 9–92*).

103. Circular 1, KPRC, Aug. 17, 1979, pp. 1–2 (*Doc. 14–16*).

104. Circular 24, Front, June 5, 1981, p. 1 (*Doc. 9–92*).

105. Ibid. Circular 1, KPRC, Oct. 1979, p. 2 (*Doc. 14–16*). See Kiernan, *How Pol Pot Came to Power,* p. 345.

106. On the Crime of Genocide of the Pol Pot–Ieng Sary Clique Against Religions and Believers in Kampuchea, April 17, 1975, to July 1, 1979, in DeNike, Quigley, and Robinson, *Genocide in Cambodia,* p. 370. For the oppression of Christianity, see Minutes 8, Phnom Penh Security Committee, Sept. 9, 1981, p. 6 (*Doc. 10–156*).

107. Interview, Haj Kamaruddin Yusef, Phnom Penh, May 28, 1999.

108. Interview, Chan Ven, Phnom Penh, May 21, 1999. By 1983–84 the Ministry of Education had established 3,218 schools for students in grades one to ten and hired 38,085 teachers. The Faculty of Medicine and Pharmacy was reopened at the end of 1979, the School of Health Cadres and the School of Fine Arts in 1981, the Kampuchea-Soviet Technological Institute in 1981 or 1982, the School of Languages in 1982, and the School of Agriculture in 1985. Vickery, *Kampuchea: Politics,* pp. 154–55. Kiernan, "Eye of the International Storm," pp. 179–80. Esméralda Luciolli, *Le mur de bambou: Le Cambodge après Pol Pot,* Paris: Régime Deforges—Médecins sans frontières, 1988, p. 195.

109. Circular 11, Party Permanent Committee, Nov. 22, 1979, p. 1 (*Doc. 10–74*).

110. Phnom Penh Domestic Service, Mar. 6, 1979, FBIS, Mar. 12, 1979. SPK, Feb. 12, 1979, FBIS, Feb. 13, 1979.

111. Phnom Penh Domestic Service, Apr. 17, 1979, FBIS, Apr. 18, 1979.

112. Nguyen Thu, "Characteristics of the Intellectual Class in Cambodia," Department of Propaganda and Education, June 4, 1980, p. 2 (*Doc. MMM*).

113. Pen Sovan, in a speech, spoke of groups attempting to "incite our cadres." Phnom Penh Domestic Service, Nov. 18, 1979, FBIS, Nov. 26, 1979. Interview, former student, Phnom Penh, Dec. 31, 1996. Regarding Vietnamese institutions operating in Phnom Penh, see Minutes 63, Cabinet, Council of Ministers, May 5, 1983, p. 1 (*Doc. 11–119*); Minutes 3, Cabinet, Council of Ministers, Jan. 13, 1986, p. 2 (*Doc. 7–99*); Minutes, Phnom Penh Command, Nov. 10, 1982 (*Doc. 8–64*). Regarding the Vietnamese prison network, see Resolution 2, Party Central Committee, July 17, 1979, pp. 24–25 (*Doc. 8–81*); Amnesty International, *Kampuchea: Political Imprisonment and Torture,* London, 1987.

114. Regarding the duties of the Ministry of the Interior, see Determination, Party Central Committee, 1979, pp. 2–4 (*Doc. 8–84*). For the composition of the PRK police forces, see Determination, Party Central Committee, 1979, p. 1 (*Doc. 8–85*). For presumptions of blood debts among Khmer Rouge police, see Resolution, Party Central Committee, undated (est. 1980), p. 5 (*Doc. 8–71*).

115. Circular 8, Party, Nov. 17, 1979 (*Doc. 11–5*). Letter 2, KPRC, 1979 (*Doc. 14–26*).

116. Minutes, Council of State, Sept. 1, 1988, p. 3 (*Doc. 1–32*).

117. Directive Circular 146, KPRC, June 30, 1980, p. 1 (*Doc. 11–99*). Determination 154, KPRC, July 8, 1980 (*Doc. 14–2*). Minutes 78, Cabinet, Council of Ministers, Aug. 6, 1982, pp. 1–2 (*Doc. 13–88*).

118. Vietnamese advisors also participated in the distribution of housing. Announcement 66, Council of Ministers, Dec. 12, 1981 (*Doc. 13–81*).

119. Minutes, United Leadership Committee, Apr. 20, 1980, p. 3 (*Doc. 11–50*).

120. Ministry of the Interior Dossier, Phnom Penh Domestic Service, June 10, 1980, FBIS, June 12, 1980. Michael Leifer, "Kampuchea in 1980: The Politics of Attrition," *Asian Survey* 21, no. 1 (1981), p. 98.

121. Regarding detentions, see Decision 178, KPRC, July 25, 1980 (*Doc. 11–54*). Regarding infiltration and theft of state secrets, see Circular, Party, July 27, 1980 (*Doc. 10–67.1*); Circular 216, KPRC, Aug. 10, 1980 (*Doc. 10–67.4*). Regarding political education, see Circular, Party, July 27, 1980 (*Doc. 11–4*); Circular 177, KPRC, July 28, 1980 (*Doc. 11–102*).

122. Circular 217, KPRC, Aug. 11, 1980 (*Doc. 10–67.5*).

CHAPTER FOUR. THE BIRTH OF AN ECONOMY

1. Report, January 1981, p. 2 (*Doc. 10–120*).

2. Report, January 1981 (*Doc. 10–120*). Heder, *Kampuchean Occupation and Resistance,* pp. 27–44. Shawcross, *Quality of Mercy,* p. 96.

3. Resolution 2, Party Central Committee, July 17, 1979 (*Doc. 8–81*). Report, January 1981 (*Doc. 10–120*).

4. Phnom Penh Domestic Service, May 1, 1979, FBIS May 3, 1979.

5. Report 22, Constitutional Drafting Council, Apr. 18, 1980, pp. 2–3 (*Doc. 8–55*). Report, World Peace Committee, July 7, 1980, pp. 2–3 (*Doc. 10–85*). Interview, Pen Sovan, Takeo, May 12, 1999. Interview, Chan Ven, Phnom Penh, May 21, 1999.

6. Report, World Peace Committee, July 7, 1980, p. 1 (*Doc. 10–85*). Ministry of Health cadres were also supposed to participate in the distribution. For the stated duties of the Ministry of Economics, see Letter 13, KPRC, July 13, 1979 (*Doc. 14–18*); Resolution 2, Party Central Committee, July 17, 1979, p. 14 (*Doc. 8–81*).

7. Minutes, Dec. 29, 1979 (*Doc. 13–112*). Decision, KPRC, Nov. 18, 1979, p. 5 (*Doc. 14–45*).

8. Shawcross, *Quality of Mercy,* pp. 141–43. See also "Dying for the Right to Live," *Far Eastern Economic Review,* Aug. 17, 1979, pp. 16–17; "The Rules of Malnutrition," *Far Eastern Economic Review,* Sept. 7, 1979, p. 10.

9. Shawcross, *Quality of Mercy,* p. 142–43. Interview, Pen Sovan, Takeo, May 12, 1999.

10. Report, January 1981, p. 5 (*Doc. 10–120*). Minutes, Dec. 22, 1979, p. 5 (*Doc. 13–115*). Shawcross, *Quality of Mercy,* pp. 163–64, 390.

11. Minutes 057, Office, KPRC, Jan. 18, 1981 (*Doc. 6–33*).

12. Shawcross, *Quality of Mercy,* p. 210.

13. Ibid., pp. 210, 280–81, 390. Minutes 057, Office, KPRC, Jan. 18, 1981, p. 5 (*Doc. 6–33*).

14. *Who's Who in North Vietnam,* pp. 60–61. See also Pen Sovan's speech, carried by the Phnom Penh Domestic Service in November 1979, in which he refers to "Carter, President of the U.S. imperialists." FBIS, Nov. 26, 1979.

15. Minutes, KPRC, Dec. 21, 1980, pp. 2–3 (*Doc. 11–48*).

16. Determination 220, KPRC, Aug. 11, 1980 (*Doc. 14–1*). Regulations, KPRC, Mar. 18, 1980 (*Doc. 13–45*). Shawcross, *Quality of Mercy,* p. 255.

17. Joel R. Charney, "Appropriate Development Aid for Kampuchea," in Ablin and Hood, *Cambodian Agony,* p. 248. Heder, *From Pol Pot to Pen Sovan,* p. 47. Shawcross, *Quality of Mercy,* p. 375. Kiernan, "Eye of the International Storm," p. 176.

18. Research Document, Cabinet, Council of Ministers, Dec. 16, 1985, p. 3 (*Doc. 5–20*). Eva Mysliwiec, *Punishing the Poor: The International Isolation of Kampuchea,* Oxford, U.K.: Oxfam, 1988. Shawcross, *Quality of Mercy,* p. 390. By May 1980 the PRK had delivered over 26,000 tons of rice to Vietnam. Report, Ministry of Planning, May 2, 1981, p. 2 (*Doc. 10–23*).

19. Resolution 2, Party Central Committee, July 17, 1979, p. 6 (*Doc. 8–81*). For more on the Vietnamese role in distributing assistance, see Heder, *Kampuchean Occupation and Resistance,* pp. 47–48.

20. Resolution 2, Party Central Committee, July 17, 1979, p. 6 (*Doc. 8–81*).

21. Seventy percent of fuel and food aid came through Ho Chi Minh City in 1980, after Kampong Som port was repaired. Report, January 1981, p. 11 (*Doc. 10–120*).

22. Resolution 2, Party Central Committee, July 17, 1979, p. 14 (*Doc. 8–81*). Special Circular, KPRC, July 27, 1979 (*Doc. 14–20*). Report, World Peace Committee, July 7, 1980, p. 1 (*Doc. 10–85*). For bureaucratic hurdles in Phnom Penh, see Special Circular, KPRC, July 27, 1979 (*Doc. 14–20*).

23. Secret Plan, 1979, p. 7 (*Doc. 9–10*).

24. Haing Ngor with Roger Warner, *Surviving the Killing Fields: The Cambodian Odyssey of Haing S. Ngor,* London: Chatto and Windus, 1987, p. 366. Heder, *Kampuchean Occupation and Resistance,* p. 20.

25. Report, January 1981, p. 32 (*Doc. 10–120*). Secret Plan, 1979, p. 1 (*Doc. 9–10*). Special Circular, KPRC, June 21, 1979, p. 21 (*Doc. 14–23*). Draft, 1983, p. 1 (*Doc. 10–112*).

26. For descriptions of the trade, see Shawcross, *Quality of Mercy,* pp. 236–37; Heder, *From Pol Pot to Pen Sovan,* pp. 51–54; Heder, *Kampuchean Occupation and Resistance,* pp. 27, 51.

27. Secret Plan, 1979, p. 12 (*Doc. 9–10*).

28. Minutes 057, Office, KPRC, Jan. 18, 1981, pp. 4–5 (*Doc. 6–33*). Report, January 1981, p. 39 (*Doc. 10–120*).

29. Ben Kiernan and Chanthou Boua, *Peasants and Politics in Kampuchea, 1942–80,* London: Zed Press, 1982, pp. 326–27.

30. Interview of Hun Sen by Jean-Pierre Gallois of Agence France Presse, AFP dispatch, Phnom Penh, Mar. 23, 1979, FBIS, Mar. 23, 1979.

31. Ibid.

32. Minutes, Dec. 8, 1979 (*Doc. 13–113*).

33. Heder, *From Pol Pot to Pen Sovan,* pp. 30–31. Heder, *Kampuchean Occupation and Resistance,* p. 18. Viviane Frings, *The Failure of Agricultural Collectivization in the People's Republic of Kampuchea (1979–1989),* Clayton, Australia: Centre of Southeast Asian Studies, Monash University, 1993, p. 10.

34. Directive Circular 146, KPRC, June 30, 1980 (*Doc. 11–99*).

35. Determination, Office, Head of State, Aug. 30, 1980, p. 2, 6 (*Doc. 11–141*).

36. Ibid., p. 1.

37. Decision, Office, KPRC, Aug. 30, 1980, p. 5 (*Doc. 11–141*). For the distribution formulas, see Minutes, Dec. 8, 1979, pp. 3 (*Doc. 13–113*); Determination, Office, Head of State, Aug. 30, 1980 (*Doc. 11–141*).

38. Decision, Office, KPRC, Aug. 30, 1980, pp. 6–7 (*Doc. 11–141*). Report, Jan. 1981, p. 6 (*Doc. 10–120*). Circular 21, Party Central Committee, Mar. 15, 1980, pp. 3–4 (*Doc. 6–*

31). Determination, Office, Head of State, Aug. 30, 1980, pp. 1–3 (*Doc. 11–143*). Heder, *Kampuchean Occupation and Resistance,* p. 18. Heder, *From Pol Pot to Pen Sovan,* pp. 70–71. For Vietnamese policy shifts, see Gareth Porter, "Vietnamese Communism: Internal Debates Force Change," *Indochina Issues* 31, December 1982, p. 2.

39. Circular, KPRC, 1979, p. 2 (*Doc. 14–44.1*).

40. Determination, Office, Head of State, Aug. 30, 1980, pp. 1, 3–5 (*Doc. 11–143*). Report, January 1981, pp. 6, 32 (*Doc. 10–120*). Minutes 107, Cabinet, Council of Ministers, Sept. 9, 1987, p. 1 (*Doc. 13–15*). Determination, Office, Head of State, Aug. 30, 1980, p. 4 (*Doc. 11–141*). Directive Circular 146, KPRC, June 30, 1980, p. 1 (*Doc. 11–99*). For early Vietnamese economic experimentation, see Lewis M. Stern, *Conflict and Transition in the Vietnamese Economic Reform Program,* Bangkok: Institute of Security and International Studies, Chulangkorn University, 1988, pp. 3–6.

41. Determination, Office, Head of State, Aug. 30, 1980, p. 4 (*Doc. 11–143*). For references to Samkai's position, see Proceedings, Second National Assembly Session, Feb. 5–10, 1982, p. 22 (*Doc. 9–87*).

42. Secret Plan, 1979, pp. 15–16 (*Doc. 9–10*). Report, World Peace Committee, July 7, 1980, p. 1 (*Doc. 10–85*).

43. Minutes, Dec. 8, 1979, p. 7 (*Doc. 13–113*). Secret Plan, 1979, pp. 2, 15 (*Doc. 9–10*). Report, January 1981, p. 46 (*Doc. 10–120*). Minutes, Dec. 22, 1979, p. 4 (*Doc. 13–115*). Minutes, United Leadership Committee, Apr. 20, 1980, p. 2 (*Doc. 11–50*).

44. Report, January 1981, pp. 25, 47 (*Doc. 10–120*). Minutes 057, Office, KPRC, Jan. 18, 1981, p. 3 (*Doc. 6–33*). Secret Plan, 1979, p. 13 (*Doc. 9–10*).

45. Loung Ung, *First They Killed My Father,* New York: HarperCollins, 2000, pp. 24–25.

46. Letter, KPRC, Jan. 26, 1980 (*Doc. 11–46*).

47. Minutes, United Leadership Committee, Apr. 20, 1980 (*Doc. 11–50*). Draft Plan, KPRC, 1979 (*Doc. 14–44.3*). Secret Plan, 1979 (*Doc. 9–10*).

48. The first printing of money involved 70–100 million riels, of which 30–35 million would go to salaries and expenses supporting cadres, workers, state officials, and soldiers. The rest would go to the purchase of agricultural produce. Secret Plan, 1979, pp. 3–5, 12 (*Doc. 9–10*). Circular 70, Action Committee, Central Party, Apr. 29, 1980, p. 2 (*Doc. 13–108*).

49. Minutes, United Leadership Committee, Apr. 20, 1980, p. 2 (*Doc. 11–50*). Report, January 1981, p. 14 (*Doc. 10–120*). For the dong-riel exchange efforts, see Circular 70, Action Committee, Central Party, Apr. 29, 1980 (*Doc. 13–108*); Resolution, KPRC, Apr. 29, 1980 (*Doc. 11–135*); Draft Bulletin, KPRC, undated (est. 1980) (*Doc. 11–52*); Report, January 1981, p. 13 (*Doc. 10–120*).

50. Secret Plan, 1979, p. 6 (*Doc. 9–10*). Report, January 1981, p. 16 (*Doc. 10–120*).

51. Minutes, Dec. 8, 1979, p. 6 (*Doc. 13–113*). Minutes, Dec. 22, 1979, p. 3 (*Doc. 13–115*).

52. Minutes, Dec. 22, 1979, p. 3 (*Doc. 13–115*).

53. Secret Plan, 1979 (*Doc. 9–10*). Report, January 1981 (*Doc. 10–120*). Minutes 057, Office, KPRC, Jan. 18, 1981 (*Doc. 6–33*). Minutes, Dec. 8, 1979 (*Doc. 13–113*). Circular 70, Action Committee, Central Party, Apr. 29, 1980 (*Doc. 13–108*).

**CHAPTER FIVE. COMRADES AND TRAITORS: POLITICAL INTRIGUE
IN THE SHADOW OF OCCUPATION**

1. For background on Haem Bau, see Kiernan, *Pol Pot Regime,* pp. 397–98.
2. Bulletin 20, Party Permanent Committee, Feb. 1, 1980 (*Doc. 10–122*).
3. Interview, Battambang Party official, Battambang, May 26, 1999.
4. Bulletin 20, Party Permanent Committee, Feb. 1, 1980, p. 3 (*Doc. 10–122*).
5. Ibid.
6. Circular 21, Party Central Committee, Mar. 15, 1980, p. 8 (*Doc. 6–31*). Interview, Central Party official, Phnom Penh, June 1, 1999.
7. Nguyen Thu, "Characteristics of the Intellectual Class in Cambodia," Department of Propaganda and Education, June 4, 1980, p. 3 (*Doc. MMM*).
8. Circular 21, Party Central Committee, Mar. 15, 1980, p. 8 (*Doc. 6–31*). Resolution, Party Central Committee, undated, p. 4 (*Doc. 8–71*).
9. Circular 21, Party Central Committee, Mar. 15, 1980, p. 5 (*Doc. 6–31*).
10. Interview, former Kampong Thom official, Phnom Penh, May 14, 1999. The new Party secretary and provincial governor of Siem Riep, Chan Seng, was a former Khmer Rouge cadre close to Chea Sim. Interview, Central Party official, Phnom Penh, May 19, 1999.
11. Determination, Party Central Committee, 1979, pp. 1–2 (*Doc. 8–84*).
12. Interview, Pen Sovan, Takeo, May 12, 1999.
13. Resolution, Party Central Committee, 1979, p. 5 (*Doc. 10–69*). Determination 205, Party Central Committee, Aug. 28, 1980, p. 3 (*Doc. 5–25*). Interview, Uk Bunchheuan, Phnom Penh, May 31, 1999.
14. Interview, Bui Tin, Paris, May 2, 1999. Other Cambodians remember movements of Vietnamese forces around Sim's house around that time. Author's interviews.
15. Report, World Peace Committee, July 7, 1980, p. 1 (*Doc. 10–85*). Report 6, Minister with Special Responsibilities, Apr. 11, 1980, p. 1 (*Doc. 10–89*).
16. The other former jurists named to the secretariat were Uk Sokun, Uk Sary, and Yith Sovan (who soon fled to Thailand). There were also a former bank official, Chan Sok; a former journalist and Ministry of Justice staff member, Khong Phirun; a former finance official, Kao Samuth; and two women, Minh Kosny and Ly Vouch Leng, the latter a former law student and Minister of Justice staff member. Interview, Leung Chhai, Phnom Penh, Feb. 14, 1997. Interview, Uk Sokun, Phnom Penh, May 24, 1999. Interviews, Yith Sovan, Phnom Penh, Jan. 22 and 24, 1997. Interview, Chan Sok, Phnom Penh, Dec. 31, 1996. Interview, Ly Vouch Leng, Phnom Penh, Jan. 2, 1997. Interview, Central Party official, Phnom Penh, May 17, 1999. Personal history of Kao Samuth (*Doc. 9–42*). Jennar, *Les clés du Cambodge.* Report 62, Ministry of Justice, July 5, 1980 (*Doc. 8–53*).
17. Report, World Peace Committee, July 7, 1980 (*Doc. 10–85*). Report 6, Minister with Special Responsibilities, Apr. 11, 1980 (*Doc. 10–89*). Report 22, Constitutional Drafting Council, Apr. 18, 1980 (*Doc. 8–55*). Report 62, Ministry of Justice, July 5, 1980 (*Doc. 8–53*).
18. Report 22, Constitutional Drafting Council, Apr. 18, 1980 (*Doc. 8–55*).
19. Draft Constitution of the People's Republic of Kampuchea, Constitutional Drafting Council, April 1980. Report 62, Ministry of Justice, July 5, 1980, p. 2 (*Doc. 8–53*). Re-

port, World Peace Committee, July 7, 1980, p. 2 (*Doc. 10–85*). Timothy Carney, "Kampuchea in 1981: Fragile Stalemate," *Asian Survey* 22, no. 1 (1982), p. 81.

20. Report 62, Ministry of Justice, July 5, 1980, p. 2 (*Doc. 8–53*). Interview, Pen Sovan, Takeo, May 12, 1999.

21. Interviews, Uk Bunchheuan, Phnom Penh, Jan. 10, 1997, and May 31, 1999. Resolution 45, Party Central Committee, Apr. 4, 1980 (*Doc. 11–51*). Bulletin, KPRC, Apr. 20, 1980 (*Doc. 11–51*). Report 158, Ministry of Justice, June 10, 1980, p. 1 (*Doc. 8–61*).

22. Report 158, Ministry of Justice, June 10, 1980 (*Doc. 8–61*). Report 62, Ministry of Justice, July 5, 1980 (*Doc. 8–53*). Minutes, Party, Feb. 21, 1981, p. 5 (*Doc. 5–48*). Interview, Yith Sovan, Phnom Penh, Jan. 22 and 24, 1997. Interview, former member of the Constitutional Drafting Secretariat, Phnom Penh, Feb. 17, 1997.

23. Report, World Peace Committee, July 7, 1980 (*Doc. 10–85*). Minutes 112, Office, Council of Ministers, Aug. 19, 1985, p. 6 (*Doc. 12–39*).

24. Report 62, Ministry of Justice, July 5, 1980, p. 4 (*Doc. 8–53*).

25. Report 158, Ministry of Justice, June 10, 1980 (*Doc. 8–61*).

26. Amended draft of the constitution (*Doc. 10–150*).

27. Report 75, Ministry of Justice, July 15, 1980, p. 2 (*Doc. 10–152*). See Chandler, *Tragedy of Cambodian History*, p. 246.

28. Circular, Party, July 27, 1980 (*Doc. 11–4*). Circular 177, KPRC, July 28, 1980 (*Doc. 11–102*). Circular 217, KPRC, Aug. 11, 1980 (*Doc. 10–67.5*).

29. Determination 145, KPRC, June 28, 1980 (*Doc. 11–53*).

30. Report 62, Ministry of Justice, July 5, 1980 (*Doc. 8–53*). Report 108, Ministry of Justice, July 28, 1980 (*Doc. 8–58*). Report 75, Ministry of Justice, July 15, 1980 (*Doc. 10–152*). Letter 142, Ministry of Justice, Feb. 2, 1980 (*Doc. 8–69*). Letter 242, Ministry of Justice, Sept. 13, 1980 (*Doc. 8–50*). Letter 281, Ministry of Justice, July 20, 1980 (*Doc. 8–70*). Report 296, Ministry of Justice, September 1980 (*Doc. 8–60*).

31. Report 596, Ministry of Justice, Dec. 13, 1980 (*Doc. 8–54*). For Heng Samrin's comment, see Minutes 057, Office, KPRC, Jan. 18, 1981, p. 6 (*Doc. 6–33*). For political conditions within the Ministry of Justice, see Work summary 333, Ministry of Justice, Oct. 10, 1980 (*Doc. 8–63*); Report 578, Ministry of Justice, Dec. 9, 1980 (*Doc. 8–62*); Documents (*Doc. 8–83* and *Doc. 8–84*); Minutes, Party, Feb. 26, 1981, p. 5 (*Doc. 5–48*).

32. Minutes, Party, Feb. 26, 1981, p. 6 (*Doc. 5–48*).

33. For Nguyen Con's remarks, see Minutes, KPRC, Dec. 21, 1980, p. 2 (*Doc. 11–48*). As a result of these changes, the National Assembly did not decide on issues of war and peace, referendums, provincial and municipal boundaries, or the right of members of parliament to call for special sessions of the Assembly. Provisions authorizing investigations into the activities of state institutions by individual MPs and special investigative commissions were removed. The Council of State, the legislature's permanent body, was also weakened as a result of the amendments, mostly to the benefit of the Council of Ministers. The Council of State no longer had "control of the activities of the Council of Ministers." To the responsibilities of the Council of State to appoint and remove ministers and diplomats and create and abolish ministries was added the qualifier "on the recommendation of the Council of Ministers." The Council of State, which lost the right to declare a state of emergency, did gain, however, the power to "examine adjudications and

the use of the authority of the prosecutor." The National Assembly's right to elect the president of the Council of State was expunged from the draft, as were provisions allowing the National Assembly to replace either the president of the National Assembly or the prime minister. Even the Council of Ministers, the organ of state power most detached from popular control, was denied appointment powers; provisions allowing it to appoint and revoke state cadres, at either central or local administrative organs, were removed from the draft. For the final version of the constitution, see *Constitution of the People's Republic of Kampuchea,* PRK, June 27, 1981, translated in Albert P. Blaustein, Gisbert H. Flanz, G. Thomas Bowen, and Scott Sheldon, eds., *Constitutions of the Countries of the World,* Dobbs Ferry, N.Y.: Oceana Publication, 1982.

34. Study Document, Central Propaganda Committee, undated (est. 1981) (*Doc. 10–83*). Document, Constitutional Drafting Council, undated (est. 1980) (*Doc. 10–90*). "Questions and Answers," Ministry of Justice, undated (*Doc. 11–1*). Report 21, Office, KPRC, Mar. 23, 1981 (*Doc. 11–87*). Bulletin 2, KPRC, Mar. 10, 1981 (*Doc. 13–86*). Carney, "Fragile Stalemate," p. 81.

35. Directive 500, Central Propaganda Committee, Mar. 6, 1981 (*Doc. 10–63*).

36. Michael Leifer, "Kampuchea in 1980: The Politics of Attrition," *Asian Survey* 22, no. 1 (1981). Justus M. van der Kroef, "ASEAN, Hanoi, and the Kampuchean Conflict: Between 'Kuantan' and a 'Third Alternative,'" *Asian Survey* 21, no. 5 (1981).

37. Carney, "Fragile Stalemate," p. 82. Kroef, "ASEAN, Hanoi and the Kampuchean Conflict," p. 533. Draft Agreement, Ministry of Defense, June 1981 (*Doc. 9–99*). Draft Agreement, Ministry of Defense, June 1981 (*Doc. 9–100*). Draft Agreement, Ministry of Defense, June 1981 (*Doc. 9–101*).

38. Minutes, Ministry of Justice, Oct. 3, 1980, p. 3 (*Doc. 11–185*).

39. Minutes, Ministry of Justice, Oct. 3, 1980 (*Doc. 11–185*). Letter 13, Central Operation Committee, Jan. 28, 1981 (*Doc. 5–4*). Report, General Office, KPRC, Apr. 1981 (*Doc. 10–86*). Report, Committee to Prepare Elections, March 1981 (*Doc. 5–36*).

40. Plan, Election Committee, March 1981 (*Doc. 10–84*). Minutes, Election Committee, May 1, 1981, p. 7 (*Doc. 10–82*). Stephen Heder, "The 1981 Elections: The Genesis of Polarization," *Phnom Penh Post,* June 5–18, 1998. David Chandler, "Strategies for Survival in Kampuchea," *Current History,* April 1988, pp. 149–53.

41. The Party dated its foundation and its First Congress to 1951 and its Second Congress to 1960. Ignoring the CPK's 1971 Congress, it cited the January 1979 Congress as number three. Michael Vickery, *Kampuchea: Politics, Economics and Society,* London: Pinter, 1986, pp. 60–61. For Sovan's sense of timing for the Fourth Congress, see Minutes, KPRC, Dec. 21, 1980, p. 1 (*Doc. 11–48*). The Politburo was composed of Pen Sovan, Say Phouthang, Bou Thang, Hun Sen, Chea Soth, Chan Si, Chea Sim, and Heng Samrin. SPK, May 27, 1981, and Radio Phnom Penh, May 20, 1981, in Raszelenberg and Schier, *Cambodia Conflict,* p. 40. For the composition of the Central Committee, see "Some Documents About the Situation in Cambodia," [Vietnamese] Expert Group, Political Committee, 1984, p. 1 (*Doc. 3KN*). For a description of Sovan's speech, see Vickery, *Kampuchea,* pp. 66–72.

42. Report, Constitutional Drafting Council, undated (*Doc. 8–48*). Circular 20, KPRC, May 8, 1981 (*Doc. 13–44*).

43. SPK, July 11, 1981, FBIS, July 13, 1981. Radio Phnom Penh, July 19, 1981, Raszelenberg and Schier, *Cambodia Conflict,* p. 43. For a description of the conference and the response from Vietnam and the PRK, see Raszelenberg and Schier, *Cambodia Conflict,* pp. 42–44; *New York Times,* July 14, 1981.

44. Minutes 1, Committee for Security in Phnom Penh, July 14, 1981, p. 2 (*Doc. 10–153*). For a description of political education, see Resolution 109, Party Central Committee, June 20, 1981 (*Doc. 8–92*); Kiernan, "Eye of the International Storm," pp. 172–73; Vickery, *Kampuchea; Politics,* p. 49.

45. Minutes 06, Party Branch 2, Aug. 1, 1981, p. 3 (*Doc. 10–70*).

46. Personal History (*Doc. 5–45*). Interview, Chan Ven, Phnom Penh, May 21, 1999.

47. Minutes 06, Party Branch 2, Aug. 1, 1981, p. 6 (*Doc. 10–70*). Personal History (*Doc. 5–45*). Letter 9, Party Ministry Committee, Feb. 6, 1981 (*Doc. 5–45*). Minutes 5, Party Ministry Committee, Branch 2, May 1982, p. 4 (*Doc. 5–56*). For Chan Phin's comments, see Minutes, Party Ministry Committee, Aug. 31, 1982, p. 9 (*Doc. 5–53*).

48. Minutes 06, Party Branch 2, Aug. 1, 1981, pp. 3–4 (*Doc. 10–70*).

49. Minutes 103, Office, Council of Ministers, July 28, 1983, p. 5 (*Doc. 11–108*). Interview, Pen Sovan, Takeo, May 12, 1999. Author's interviews.

50. Letter 1153, National Bank, July 23, 1981 (*Doc. 5–5*). Secret Plan, 1979, p. 12 (*Doc. 9–10*).

51. Letter 1153, National Bank, July 23, 1981 (*Doc. 5–5*).

52. Interview, Pen Sovan, Takeo, May 12, 1999.

53. Timothy Carney, "Heng Samrin's Armed Forces and a Military Balance in Cambodia," in Ablin and Hood, *Cambodian Agony,* p. 189. Interview, Bui Tin, Paris, May 2, 1999.

54. Resolution 143, Council of Ministers, Nov. 20, 1981 (*Doc. 13–54*). For Samrin's comments, see Minutes 06, Party Branch 2, Aug. 1, 1981, p. 3 (*Doc. 10–70*).

55. Report, Council of State, Aug. 10, 1982 (*Doc. 6–42*). Minutes, Council of State, July 9, 1982, p. 2 (*Doc. 6–48*).

56. Minutes, Council of State, July 9, 1982, p. 2 (*Doc. 6–48*).

57. Report, Council of State, Aug. 10, 1982 (*Doc. 6–42*).

58. Document 221, Party, Oct. 11, 1980 (*Doc. 8–49*).

59. Letter, Party Branch 1, Dec. 5, 1979 (*Doc. 10–64*). Document 221, Party, Oct. 11, 1980 (*Doc. 8–49*).

60. Minutes 4, Phnom Penh Security Committee, Aug. 11, 1981, p. 4 (*Doc. 10–155*). Document 221, Party, Oct. 11, 1980, p. 2 (*Doc. 8–49*). Provincial officials had been complaining of "bad elements who opposed the revolution and some people who had escaped reeducation in Vietnam and had come [to Cambodia] to contact bad people and lead people to flee overseas." Document 221, Party, Oct. 11, 1980 (*Doc. 8–49*). Interview, Pen Sovan, Takeo, May 12, 1999.

61. Document 221, Party, Oct. 11, 1980, p. 2 (*Doc. 8–49*).

62. Letter 2494 and accompanying table, Phnom Penh People's Revolutionary Council, Oct. 4, 1980 (*Doc. 11–45*). Letter 331, KPRC, Oct. 19, 1980 (*Doc. 11–45*).

63. Minutes 1, Phnom Penh Security Committee, July 14, 1981 (*Doc. 10–153*). Minutes 3, Phnom Penh Security Committee, Aug. 3, 1981, p. 3 (*Doc. 10–154*).

64. Minutes 3, Phnom Penh Security Committee, Aug. 3, 1981, p. 4 (*Doc. 10–154*).

65. Personal communication, Stephen Heder, Nov. 9, 1998.

66. Minutes 3, Phnom Penh Security Committee, Aug. 3, 1981, pp. 5–6 (*Doc. 10–154*).

67. Minutes 4, Phnom Penh Security Committee, Aug. 11, 1981, p. 2 (*Doc. 10–155*).

68. Ibid., pp. 2–3.

69. Ibid., pp. 3–4.

70. Ibid.

71. Minutes 8, Phnom Penh Security Committee, Sept. 9, 1981, p. 5 (*Doc. 10–156*). Minutes 9, Phnom Penh Security Committee, Sept. 16, 1981, p. 4 (*Doc. 10–157*). For the content of political education, see Report 35, Office, Council of Ministers, Aug. 31, 1981 (*Doc. 11–83*).

72. Letter 169, Party Central Committee, Sept. 22, 1981, p. 2 (*Doc. 10–121*). For defections, see Carney, "Fragile Stalemate," p. 83.

73. Minutes 8, Party Ministry Committee, Oct. 24, 1981 (*Doc. 5–46*).

74. Resolution 117, Council of Ministers, Oct. 16, 1981 (*Doc. 13–55*). Determination 1, KPRC, Jan. 6, 1981 (*Doc. 13–85*). The policy was reversed shortly after Sovan's removal. Kiernan, "Eye of the International Storm," p. 171. Interviews, Pen Sovan, Phnom Penh, Jan. 25, 1997, and Takeo, May 12, 1999.

75. Decision 147, Council of Ministers, Nov. 21, 1981 (*Doc. 13–53*). Interviews, Pen Sovan, Phnom Penh, Jan. 25, 1997, and Takeo, May 12, 1999. Phnom Penh Domestic Service, Nov. 30 and Dec. 1, 1981, FBIS, Dec. 3, 1981.

76. Interviews, Pen Sovan, Phnom Penh, Jan. 25, 1997, and Takeo, May 12, 1999.

77. Interview, Pen Sovan, Takeo, May 12, 1999.

78. Interview, Kong Korm, Phnom Penh, May 6, 1999. Ministry of Justice officials expressed confusion as to whether to remove Sovan's name from the laws. Letter 35, Council of Ministers, Nov. 17, 1982 (*Doc. 9–155*). Sophia Quinn-Judge, "Kampuchea in 1982: Ploughing Toward Recovery," *Southeast Asian Affairs,* 1983, p. 154.

79. Interview, Bui Tin, Paris, May 2, 1999. Chanda, *Brother Enemy,* p. 217. Bulletin 1, Office, Council of Ministers, Mar. 31, 1982 (*Doc. 10–5*). Draft, Council of Ministers, Jan. 15, 1982 (*Doc. 10–6*).

80. Bulletin 1, Office, Council of Ministers, Mar. 31, 1982 (*Doc. 10–5*). Kampong Cham governors and Party secretaries had included Sim Kar, Preap Pichey, and Kim Yin. Vietnamese authorities had tried this approach in the 1930s and 1950s, assigning provinces to loyal central leaders. Chandler, *History of Cambodia,* p. 111. Kiernan, *How Pol Pot Came to Power,* p. 80.

81. Draft, Council of Ministers, Jan. 15, 1982 (*Doc. 10–6*). Background on Chea Soth from Kiernan, *How Pol Pot Came to Power,* pp. 60, 70 n. 70, 179; Chanda, *Brother Enemy,* p. 217. Daok Samol was replaced, as governor of Prey Veng, by Cheam Yeap.

82. Draft, Council of Ministers, Jan. 15, 1982 (*Doc. 10–6*). Interview, Central Party official, Phnom Penh, May 17, 1999.

83. Minutes 13, Office, Council of Ministers, Mar. 23, 1982 (*Doc. 10–115*). Dang Dinh Long is mentioned in *Who's Who in North Vietnam,* p. xvi. Resolution 132, Party Central Committee, Apr. 24, 1982 (*Doc. 13–111*).

84. Minutes 13, Office, Council of Ministers, Mar. 23, 1982 (*Doc. 10–115*).

CHAPTER SIX. THE VIETNAMESE: SOLDIERS, ADVISORS, AND "BAD ELEMENTS"

1. Report of Investigation, Office, Council of Ministers, June 24, 1982 (*Doc. 13–19*).
2. Minutes, Party Ministerial Committee, May 1982, pp. 2–3 (*Doc. 10–123*).
3. Minutes 5, Party Ministerial Committee, Branch 2, May 1982, p. 3 (*Doc. 5–56*). Report 387, Ministry of Justice, May 7, 1982, p. 4 (*Doc. 9–125*).
4. For the response to the CGDK, see SPK, June 23, 1982, FBIS, June 24, 1982.
5. Minutes 64, Cabinet, Council of Ministers, July 19, 1982, p. 2 (*Doc. 13–92*). For cultural restrictions, see Directive Circular 16, Council of Ministers, June 15, 1982 (*Doc. 13–76*).
6. Minutes 64, Cabinet, Council of Ministers, July 19, 1982, p. 3 (*Doc. 13–92*).
7. Ibid.
8. Report, Ministry of the Interior, 1984, pp. 5–6 (*Doc. 10–129*).
9. Research Document, Cabinet, Council of Ministers, Dec. 16, 1985, pp. 6, 9 (*Doc. 5–20*). For the Siem Riep purges, see Interview, Bui Tin, Paris 1997; Elizabeth Becker, "Kampuchea in 1983, Further from Peace," *Asian Survey* 24, no. 1 (1984), p. 44; Bekaert, *Cambodia Diary,* pp. 39–40, 52–53. For numbers of troops, see Carney, "Armed Forces," p. 167.
10. Interview, Bui Tin, Paris, May 2, 1999. Timothy Carney, "Kampuchea in 1982: Political and Military Escalation," *Asian Survey* 23, no. 1 (1983), p. 80.
11. Hanoi Domestic Service, Dec. 30, 1984, FBIS, Jan. 4, 1985.
12. Ronald J. Cima, ed., *Vietnam: A Country Study,* Washington, D.C.: Federal Research Division, Library of Congress, 1987, p. 329.
13. *Quan Doi Nhan Dan,* Apr. 22, 1981, quoted in Douglas Pike, *PAVN: People's Army of Vietnam,* London: Brassey's Defence Publishers, 1986, p. 71. For a description of the structure of the occupation, see Interview, Bui Tin, Paris, May 2, 1999. See also Pike, *PAVN,* pp.l 69–70, 85 n. 20.
14. Le Thanh, "Flights Heading Toward Forward Bases," radio essay, Hanoi Domestic Service, Aug. 14, 1986, FBIS, Aug. 22, 1986.
15. Deutsche Presse-Agentur, Sept. 21, 1989, in Raszelenberg and Schier, *Cambodia Conflict,* p. 260.
16. See, for instance, *New York Times,* Oct. 9, 1982.
17. Document, undated (*Doc. 8–83*).
18. Bui Tin, a former Vietnamese advisor in Cambodia, describes how Tho used to sit in Sihanouk's seat during meetings at the palace. Bui Tin, *From Cadre to Exile,* pp. 122–23. Interview, Pen Sovan, Takeo, May 12, 1999. Interview, Kong Korm, Phnom Penh, May 6, 1999. Biographical information on Tran Xuan Bach is from Cima, *Vietnam,* p. 328; Interview, Bui Tin, Paris, May 2, 1999.
19. Minutes, Council of State, Mar. 3, 1986 (*Doc. 11–3*). Letter 13, Council of State, Mar. 29, 1988, p. 1 (*Doc. 9–4*). Minutes, Council of State, Dec. 20, 1985, p. 1 (*Doc. 6–18*). Tran Xuan Bach's replacement was Dong Bai, who was not a member of the Central Committee. Interview, Bui Tin, Paris, May 2, 1999.
20. Minutes, Cabinet, Council of State, June 10, 1986 (*Doc. 3–87*). Letter 13, Council of State, Mar. 29, 1988, pp. 2–4 (*Doc. 9–4*). Minutes, Council of State, Oct. 30, 1985, p. 11 (*Doc. 6–19*). Minutes 5, Cabinet, Council of Ministers, Jan. 13, 1984 (*Doc. 7–115*). Inter-

view, Bui Tin, Paris, May 2, 1999. Interview, Central Party official, Phnom Penh, May 19, 1999. "Phoc" is a transliteration from Khmer documents. "Tun Lem" is an approximate spelling based on interviews.

21. Interview, Central Party official, Phnom Penh, May 19, 1999.

22. "Pham Van Kath" and "Fang You" are transliterations from Khmer documents. The role played by Vietnamese advisors in the PRK's debates over economic policy is described in Chapter 8.

23. Report 135, Cabinet, Council of Ministers, Nov. 27, 1985, p. 2 (*Doc. 12–60*). Report 109, Committee on Chinese, Nov. 16, 1983, p. 4 (*Doc. 10–60*). Subdecree 10, Council of Ministers, July 4, 1984 (*Doc. 7–117*).

24. Report 135, Cabinet, Council of Ministers, Nov. 27, 1985, p. 8 (*Doc. 12–60*).

25. "Ngiem Van Ky" is a transliteration from the Khmer. Minutes 52, Cabinet, Council of Ministers, Dec. 13, 1985, p. 4 (*Doc. 12–63*).

26. Research Document, Cabinet, Council of Ministers, Dec. 16, 1985, p. 6 (*Doc. 5–20*). Report 135, Cabinet, Council of Ministers, Nov. 27, 1985 (*Doc. 12–60*). Minutes 52, Cabinet, Council of Ministers, Dec. 13, 1985 (*Doc. 12–63*).

27. Minutes, Office, KPRC, June 24, 1980 (*Doc. 11–49*). Minutes 3, Council of Ministers, Mar. 6, 1982, p. 3 (*Doc. 10–4*). Agreement, Ministry of Planning, April 1983 (*Doc. 10–9*). Report, Council of Ministers, 1982 (*Doc. 10–22*). Minutes 57, Cabinet, Council of Ministers, June 27, 1982, p. 10 (*Doc. 13–91*). Research Document, Cabinet, Council of Ministers, Dec. 16, 1985, pp. 8–9 (*Doc. 5–20*). Report 135, Cabinet, Council of Ministers, Nov. 27, 1985, pp. 3, 6 (*Doc. 12–60*). Circular 16, Council of Ministers, Dec. 20, 1985, p. 3 (*Doc. 12–48*).

28. Minutes, Council of State, Mar. 3, 1986 (*Doc. 11–3*). Report 135, Cabinet, Council of Ministers, Nov. 27, 1985 (*Doc. 12–60*).

29. "Pham Chong Tuoc" is a transliteration from the Khmer. Minutes 3, Council of Ministers, Mar. 6, 1982 (*Doc. 10–4*).

30. Report, Jan. 1981, p. 29 (*Doc. 10–120*). Report, Ministry of Planning, 1982 (*Doc. 10–23*). Report, Council of Ministers, 1982, p. 2 (*Doc. 10–22*).

31. Minutes 3, Council of Ministers, Mar. 6, 1982, p. 3 (*Doc. 10–4*). Regarding the purchase of fuel and equipment from the United States, see Minutes 64, Cabinet, Council of Ministers, July 19, 1982, p. 11 (*Doc. 13–92*).

32. Minutes 04, Party Ministerial Committee, April 1982, p. 4 (*Doc. 5–49*).

33. "Tui" is a transliteration from the Khmer. Minutes 57, Cabinet, Council of Ministers, June 27, 1982 (*Doc. 13–91*).

34. Ibid.

35. Minutes 057, Office, KPRC, Jan. 18, 1981, p. 5 (*Doc. 6–33*). Report, Council of Ministers, 1982, p. 3 (*Doc. 10–22*).

36. Directive Circular 31, Council of Ministers, Sept. 16, 1982 (*Doc. 9–26*). For provincial complaints, see Minutes 57, Cabinet, Council of Ministers, June 27, 1982, p. 8 (*Doc. 13–91*).

37. Report, Council of Ministers, 1982, p. 3 (*Doc. 10–22*). Directive Circular 31, Council of Ministers, Sept. 16, 1982 (*Doc. 9–26*).

38. Minutes 57, Cabinet, Council of Ministers, June 27, 1982, p. 13 (*Doc. 13–91*). For complaints about the sister province arrangements, see Minutes 61, Cabinet, Council of

Ministers, May 9, 1984, p. 3 (*Doc. 7–110*); Minutes, Council of State, Jan. 30–31, 1986, pp. 5–6 (*Doc. 4–12*); Circular 427, Party Central Committee, Dec. 18, 1984 (*Doc. 6–84*); Directive 1, Council of Ministers, Feb. 5, 1985, p. 1 (*Doc. 11–174*).

39. DeNike, Quigley, and Robinson, *Genocide in Cambodia,* p. 538.

40. For rice exports in 1981, see Report, Ministry of Planning, 1982, p. 2 (*Doc. 10–23*).

41. Circular 43, Council of Ministers, Nov. 13, 1982 (*Doc. 13–72*).

42. Minutes 6, Cabinet, Council of Ministers, Mar. 9, 1993, p. 35 (*Doc. 3–80*). Minutes 95, Cabinet, Council of Ministers, June 30, 1983, p. 2 (*Doc. 11–146*). For Sareum's comments, see Minutes 59, Cabinet, Council of Ministers, Apr. 28, 1983, p. 4 (*Doc. 11–120*).

43. Minutes 107, Cabinet, Council of Ministers, Aug. 31, 1983 (*Doc. 11–109*). See Kiernan, *How Pol Pot Came to Power,* p. 218.

44. Minutes 23, Cabinet, Council of Ministers, Jan. 25, 1983, p. 2 (*Doc. 11–129*).

45. DeNike, Quigley, and Robinson, *Genocide in Cambodia,* p. 538.

46. Minutes, Dec. 10, 1979, pp. 1–6 (*Doc. 13–114*).

47. Interview, Pen Sovan, Takeo, May 12, 1999. Interview, former Kampong Cham governor Kim Yin, Phnom Penh, May 14, 1999.

48. Minutes 103, Cabinet, Council of Ministers, July 28, 1983, pp. 4–5 (*Doc. 11–108*).

49. Report, Council of Ministers, 1982, p. 4 (*Doc. 10–22*). For advisors at the General Department of Rubber Plantations, see Report 135, Cabinet, Council of Ministers, Nov. 27, 1985, p. 8 (*Doc. 12–60*). For the role of rubber in the sister province arrangements and exports to Vietnam from Rattanakiri, see Minutes 3, Council of Ministers, Mar. 6, 1982, p. 3 (*Doc. 10–4*); Minutes 103, Cabinet, Council of Ministers, July 28, 1983, p. 4 (*Doc. 11–108*); Directive Circular 31, Council of Ministers, Sept. 16, 1982, p. 1 (*Doc. 9–26*). Later, as provinces and municipalities became more autonomous, the Phnom Penh municipal government exported rubber directly to Vietnam. Determination 1, Council of Ministers, Feb. 27, 1985 (*Doc. 11–173*).

50. Minutes, Ministry of Agriculture, Dec. 23, 1983 (*Doc. 11–9*). For 1979–81 policy, see Minutes, Dec. 10, 1979 (*Doc. 13–114*). For Ministries of Agriculture and Commerce agreements with the Vietnamese, see Report, Ministry of Agriculture, undated (est. 1982), p. 10 (*Doc. 10–142*); Letter 815, Ministry of Commerce, Oct. 15, 1983 (*Doc. 11–15*); Letter 747, Ministry of Agriculture, Sept. 23, 1983 (*Doc. 11–16*); Contract, Fishing Company of Cambodia, undated (est. 1983) (*Doc. 11–17*); Letter 626, Cabinet, Council of Ministers, Dec. 15, 1982 (*Doc. 11–19*).

51. Minutes 47, Cabinet, Council of Ministers, May 28, 1982, p. 9 (*Doc. 13–94*). Minutes 68, Cabinet, Council of Ministers, May 21, 1984, p. 2 (*Doc. 7–108*). For estimates of Vietnamese deaths, see Minutes, Dec. 10, 1979, p. 8 (*Doc. 13–114*). See also Jay Jordens, "Persecution of Cambodia's Ethnic Vietnamese Communities During and Since the UNTAC Period," in Heder and Ledgerwood, *Propaganda, Politics and Violence in Cambodia,* p. 136. For Khoem Pon's comments, see Minutes 4, Phnom Penh Security Committee, Aug. 11, 1981, p. 4 (*Doc. 10–155*).

52. Minutes 27, Cabinet, Council of Ministers, Mar. 22, 1984, pp. 2–3 (*Doc. 7–113*). Minutes 68, Cabinet, Council of Ministers, May 21, 1984 (*Doc. 7–108*). Letter 50, Vietnamese Army, Command Committee 479, Feb. 25, 1983 (*Doc. 5–13*). Draft Determination, Council of Ministers, 1982 (*Doc. 10–22.1*).

53. Decision, KPRC, July 12, 1980 (*Doc. 6–32*). Circular 100–80, KPRC, May 10, 1980 (*Doc. 6–23*). Letter 288, Ministry of Justice, Apr. 20, 1982 (*Doc. 9–157*). Letter, Timber Sector, Kratie, Nov. 6, 1983 (*Doc. 9–25*). Minutes 98, Cabinet, Council of Ministers, July 13, 1983, p. 2 (*Doc. 11–106*). Letter 8689, Ministry of Agriculture, Nov. 18, 1983 (*Doc. 9–39*). For the timber business in 1979–80, see Report, Jan. 1981, p. 8 (*Doc. 10–120*).

54. Minutes 73, Council of Ministers, May 29, 1984, pp. 3–5 (*Doc. 7–107*). Report, Council of Ministers, 1982, p. 4 (*Doc. 10–22*). Determination 1, Council of Ministers, Feb. 27, 1985 (*Doc. 11–173*). For Ministry of Agriculture deals, see Letter 640, Cabinet, Council of Ministers, Aug. 11, 1983 (*Doc. 9–28*); Letter 1634, Ministry of Planning, July 23, 1983 (*Doc. 9–27*); Minutes 68, Cabinet, Council of Ministers, May 21, 1984, p. 6 (*Doc. 7–108*).

55. For Tien's comments, see Minutes 51, Cabinet, Council of Ministers, June 11, 1982, p. 6 (*Doc. 13–93*). Minutes 57, Cabinet, Council of Ministers, June 27, 1982, p. 11 (*Doc. 13–91*).

56. Letter 8126, Ministry of Agriculture, Oct. 26, 1983 (*Doc. 9–34*). Letter 50, Vietnamese Army, Command Committee 479, undated (*Doc. 5–13*).

57. Minutes 56, Cabinet, Council of Ministers, May 12, 1988, p. 3 (*Doc. 13–1*). Minutes 113, Cabinet, Council of Ministers, Sept. 15, 1988, pp. 5–6 (*Doc. 5–43*). Minutes, Council of State, Jan. 28–29, pp. 3–4 (*Doc. 1–29*). Minutes, Council of State, June 27–29, 1988, p. 5 (*Doc. 4–15*). Minutes 126, Cabinet, Council of Ministers, Oct. 12, 1987, pp. 2–3 (*Doc. 13–16*). Minutes 118, Cabinet, Council of Ministers, Sept. 7, 1985 (*Doc. 12–38*). For the 1987 report, see Minutes 6, Cabinet, Council of State, Jan. 14, 1987, p. 2 (*Doc. 13–39*). For the designation of timber as an economic priority, see Report, Council of State, July 1988, p. 2 (*Doc. 3–78*).

58. Minutes 3, Council of Ministers, Mar. 6, 1982, p. 2 (*Doc. 10–4*). Interview, Bui Tin, Paris, May 2, 1999. Author's interviews.

59. *KPNLF Bulletin,* no. 10, Jan. 15, 1983, p. 7.

60. *Dai Nam Thuc Luc Chinh Bien,* vol. 17, p. 30, quoted in Chandler, *History of Cambodia,* p. 126.

61. Interview, provincial officials, May 1999. Interview, Chan Ven, Phnom Penh, May 21, 1999. For Pen Navuth's comments, see Minutes, Council of State, Oct. 29, 1986, p. 6 (*Doc. 5–79*). It was up to the Soviets to train a few Cambodians in English and French. Minutes, Council of State, Oct. 29, 1986, p. 6 (*Doc. 5–79*).

62. Report 387, Ministry of Justice, May 7, 1982, p. 4 (*Doc. 9–125*). Minutes 5, Party Branch 2, May 28, 1982, p. 5 (*Doc. 10–111*).

63. Interview, former student in Hanoi, Phnom Penh, May 14, 1999. For political education in Vietnam, see Minutes, Party Ministerial Committee, May 1982, p. 3 (*Doc. 10–123*); Minutes 13, Cabinet, Council of Ministers, Mar. 23, 1982, p. 3 (*Doc. 10–115*); Minutes, Council of State, June 23, 1983, p. 3 (*Doc. 9–74*); Directive Circular 04, Council of Ministers, Feb. 21, 1986, p. 2 (*Doc. 7–97*); Luciolli, *Le mur de bambou,* p. 156.

64. *KPNLF Bulletin,* no. 10, July 15, 1983, p. 7.

65. Minutes 57, Cabinet, Council of Ministers, June 27, 1982, p. 12 (*Doc. 13–91*). Report, Council of Ministers, 1982, p. 5 (*Doc. 10–22*).

66. Minutes 57, Cabinet, Council of Ministers, June 27, 1982, p. 15 (*Doc. 13–91*).

67. Circular 38, Council of Ministers, Oct. 9, 1982, pp. 2–3 (*Doc. 4–56*).

68. Agreement, Aug. 6, 1983, pp. 3–4 (*Doc. 10–27*).

69. Report, Ministry of the Interior, 1984, p. 3 (*Doc. 10–129*).

70. For Vietnamese estimates of the prerevolutionary ethnic Vietnamese population, see "Some Documents About the Situation in Cambodia," [Vietnamese] Expert Group, Political Committee, 1984, p. 8 (*Doc. 3KN*). For resistance estimates of Vietnamese immigration, see *New York Times*, Oct. 18, 1985; *KPNLF Bulletin*, no. 10, July 15, 1983, p. 7. For the PRK line on Vietnamese immigration, see Lao Mong Hay, "Kampuchea: A Stalemate?" *Southeast Asian Affairs*, 1984, p. 155. For more objective estimates, see Tim Huxley, "Cambodia in 1986: The PRK's Eighth Year," *Southeast Asian Affairs*, 1987, p. 168. For internal PRK counts in Phnom Penh and Kandal, see Minutes 3, Cabinet, Council of Ministers, Jan. 13, 1986, p. 3 (*Doc. 7–99*).

71. Minutes 3, Cabinet, Council of Ministers, Jan. 13, 1986, pp. 2–3 (*Doc. 7–99*).

72. Ibid., p. 4. For Kandal's policies, see Directive Circular 05, Council of Ministers, Feb. 26, 1986, p. 1 (*Doc. 7–98*).

73. Minutes 3, Cabinet, Council of Ministers, Jan. 13, 1986, p. 4 (*Doc. 7–99*).

74. Directive Circular 5, Council of Ministers, Feb. 26, 1986 (*Doc. 7–98*). Marie-Alexandrine Martin, *Cambodia: A Shattered Society*, Berkeley: University of California Press, 1994, pp. 227–229.

75. Minutes 64, Cabinet, Council of Ministers, July 19, 1982, p. 11 (*Doc. 13–92*). Minutes 3, Cabinet, Council of Ministers, Jan. 13, 1986, p. 2 (*Doc. 7–99*). Minutes 51, Cabinet, Council of Ministers, June 11, 1982, p. 6 (*Doc. 13–93*). Directive Circular 05, Council of Ministers, Feb. 26, 1986, pp. 2–3 (*Doc. 7–98*).

76. Kim Ha, *Stormy Escape; A Vietnamese Woman's Account of Her 1980 Flight Through Cambodia to Thailand*, Jefferson, N.C.: McFarland and Co., 1997, p. 81.

77. Agreement, Aug. 6, 1983, p. 11 (*Doc. 10–27*). Minutes 4, Phnom Penh Security Committee, Aug. 11, 1981, p. 4 (*Doc. 10–155*). Directive Circular 05, Council of Ministers, Feb. 26, 1986, p. 1 (*Doc. 7–98*). Report, Ministry of the Interior, 1984, p. 2 (*Doc. 10–129*). For alleged conspiracies, see Report 166, Ministry of the Interior, Office of the Phnom Penh Police, Feb. 12, 1986, p. 2 (*Doc. 9–76*).

78. Circular 38, Council of Ministers, Oct. 9, 1982, p. 3 (*Doc. 4–56*). Directive Circular 05, Council of Ministers, Feb. 26, 1986, p. 2 (*Doc. 7–98*). Minutes 3, Cabinet, Council of Ministers, Jan. 13, 1986, p. 2 (*Doc. 7–99*).

79. For the role of the Vietnamese Embassy, see Minutes 3, Cabinet, Council of Ministers, Jan. 13, 1986, p. 4 (*Doc. 7–99*). For the role of Vietnamese advisors in the ethnic Vietnamese community, see Circular 38, Council of Ministers, Oct. 9, 1982, p. 3 (*Doc. 4–56*).

80. For the role of ethnic Vietnamese in the military and police, see Minutes 3, Cabinet, Council of Ministers, Jan. 13, 1986, p. 3 (*Doc. 7–99*). For the discussion on Vietnamese voting, see Minutes, Council of State, Nov. 28, 1986, pp. 3–4 (*Doc. 5–58*). Regarding citizenship, see Circular 38, Council of Ministers, Oct. 9, 1982, p. 3 (*Doc. 4–56*). The issue of citizenship was even raised by cadres during the circulation of the draft constitution, but it was not taken up by the leadership. See Report, Constitutional Drafting Council, p. 8 (*Doc. 8–48*). With regard to such civil matters as marriage, divorce, and death, Vietnamese authorities discussed laws specifically protecting Vietnamese traditions but

never actually passed any. Minutes 3, Cabinet, Council of Ministers, Jan. 13, 1986, p. 4 (*Doc. 7–99*).

81. "Ne Hoth" and "Ty Kieth" are transliterations from the Khmer. Minutes, Council of State, Dec. 31, 1986, p. 7 (*Doc. 5–81*). Minutes, Council of State, Oct. 30, 1985, p. 13 (*Doc. 6–19*).

82. Minutes, Council of State, Feb. 27, 1987, pp. 11–12 (*Doc. 4–64*).

83. Minutes, Council of State, Mar. 15, 1989, pp. 9–10 (*Doc. 1–36*).

CHAPTER SEVEN. THE CHINESE: RACIAL POLITICS IN THE PRK

1. Minutes 117, Cabinet, Council of Ministers, Nov. 2, 1982, p. 2 (*Doc. 13–95*).

2. E. Aymonier, *Notice sur le Cambodge,* Paris: Ernest Leroux, 1875, quoted in William E. Willmott, *The Chinese in Cambodia,* Vancouver: Publications Center, University of British Columbia, 1967, p. 40. My translation from the French.

3. See Willmott, *Chinese in Cambodia.* Penny Edwards, "A Century of Chineseness in Cambodia," Paper presented at the Forty-eighth Annual Meeting of the Association for Asian Studies, Honolulu, Apr. 12, 1996.

4. Becker, *When the War Was Over,* p. 361. Stephen J. Morris, *Why Vietnam Invaded Cambodia,* Stanford, Calif.: Stanford University Press, 1999, pp. 167–96.

5. Gareth Porter, *The Politics of Bureaucratic Socialism,* Ithaca, N.Y.: Cornell University Press, 1993, p. 33*n*. Chanda, *Brother Enemy,* pp. 234–40. Becker, *When the War Was Over,* pp. 358–363. Morris, *Why Vietnam Invaded Cambodia,* p. 187.

6. Chanda, *Brother Enemy,* pp. 360–62.

7. See Lewis M. Stern, "District Development, the New Economic Zones, Cooperativization and South Vietnam's New Economic Policies of 1979," *Asian Profile* 9, no. 4 (1981), pp. 363–66; Becker, *When the War Was Over,* p. 354; Porter, *Politics of Bureaucratic Socialism,* p. 33.

8. Nheum Vanda, Personal history (*Doc. 5–44*). Translation by Rich Arant.

9. Nguyen Thu, "Characteristics of the Intellectual Class in Cambodia," Department of Propaganda and Education, June 4, 1980, p. 21 (*Doc. MMM*).

10. Letter, Permanent Committee, Sept. 25, 1979, p. 1 (*Doc. 9–6*). Determination, Central Committee, 1979 (*Doc. 8–85*). Resolution, Party Central Committee, p. 6 (*Doc. 8–71*). Interview, Cham Prasith, Phnom Penh, Feb. 10, 1997. Interview, Pen Sovan, Takeo, May 12, 1999. Interview, former Ministry of Foreign Affairs official, Phnom Penh, May 19, 1999. Interview, former Ministry of Justice official, Phnom Penh, Jan. 24, 1997.

11. Letter, Permanent Committee, Sept. 25, 1979, p. 1 (*Doc. 9–6*). Interview, Battambang Party official, Battambang, May 26, 1999. For discussions on the draft constitution, see Report, Constitutional Drafting Council, p. 3 (*Doc. 8–48*).

12. Report, Leadership Committee to Implement Decree 351, June 19, 1983, p. 2 (*Doc. 5–31*).

13. DeNike, Quigley, and Robinson, *Genocide in Cambodia,* p. 319.

14. Ibid., p. 531.

15. Report, Leadership Committee to Implement Decree 351, June 19, 1983, p. 7–9 (*Doc. 5–31*). For Chinese participation in the Thai border trade, see Heder, *Kampuchean Occupation and Resistance,* pp. 21, 35.

16. Minutes 3, Phnom Penh Security Committee, Aug. 3, 1981, p. 5 (*Doc. 10–154*). For statistics on manufacturing sites, see Report, Jan. 1981, pp. 7–9 (*Doc. 10–120*); Secret Plan, 1979, p. 2 (*Doc. 9–10*); Report, Ministry of Industry, Sept. 9, 1980, p. 3 (*Doc. 8–52*).

17. Minutes 1, Phnom Penh Security Committee, July 14, 1981, p. 2 (*Doc. 10–153*).

18. Ibid., pp. 3–4.

19. Report 35, Cabinet, Council of Ministers, Aug. 31, 1981 (*Doc. 11–83*).

20. Minutes 54, Cabinet, Council of Ministers, Apr. 21, 1983 (*Doc. 11–122*). *Who's Who in North Vietnam*, p. 48. Bui Tin, *From Cadre to Exile*, p. 90.

21. Minutes 3, Phnom Penh Security Committee, Aug. 3, 1981, pp. 1–2 (*Doc. 10–154*).

22. Ibid.

23. Ibid., pp. 2–3.

24. Ibid.

25. For details on the crackdown, see Minutes 4, Phnom Penh Security Committee, Aug. 11, 1981, pp. 4–5 (*Doc. 10–155*). Over the next few weeks, the state also issued a series of circulars prohibiting the search for gold, unauthorized possession of land and houses, and the sale of houses. To what extent these were enforced is unclear. Report 35, Cabinet, Council of Ministers, Aug. 31, 1981, p. 2 (*Doc. 11–83*).

26. Minutes 8, Phnom Penh Security Committee, Sept. 9, 1981 (*Doc. 10–156*).

27. Ibid.

28. Circular 55, Council of Ministers, Dec. 29, 1981 (*Doc. 6–25*).

29. Minutes 78, Cabinet, Council of Ministers, Aug. 6, 1982, p. 3 (*Doc. 13–88*).

30. Ibid., p. 2–4. For early discussions regarding Svay Rieng, see Minutes, Dec. 22, 1979, p. 1 (*Doc. 13–115*). Regarding Koh Kong and Kampong Som, see Minutes 59, Cabinet, Council of Ministers, Apr. 28, 1983, p. 3 (*Doc. 11–120*).

31. Minutes 78, Cabinet, Council of Ministers, Aug. 6, 1982, p. 3 (*Doc. 13–88*).

32. Ibid.

33. Ibid., pp. 3–4.

34. Ibid., p. 3.

35. Minutes 117, Cabinet, Council of Ministers, Nov. 2, 1982 (*Doc. 13–95*).

36. Ibid., p. 4.

37. Circular 351, Party Central Committee, Oct. 28, 1982, p. 4 (*Doc. 10–57*).

38. Ibid., p. 3. Document, Council of Ministers, Committee for the Chinese (*Doc. 10–56*).

39. Circular 40, Council of Ministers, Oct. 22, 1982, p. 4 (*Doc. 10–54*). Report 109, Committee on Chinese, Nov. 16, 1983 (*Doc. 10–60*). Other members of the committee included Nhem Heng, director of the Religion Department of the Party's Central Education Committee; and Khem Chan of the Ministry of Defense. Decision 212, Council of Ministers, Oct. 23, 1982 (*Doc. 14–27*).

40. Internal Rules, Central Committee to Examine and Research and Guide Implementation of the Policy Regarding the Chinese in Cambodia, Oct. 28, 1983, p. 2 (*Doc. 10–55*).

41. Ibid., pp. 1–2. Report 109, Central Committee to Examine and Research and Guide Implementation of the Policy Regarding the Chinese in Cambodia, Nov. 16, 1983, pp. 2–3 (*Doc. 10–60*).

42. *New York Times,* Apr. 20, 1983. Raszelenberg and Schier, *Cambodia Conflict,* p. 59.

43. Minutes 54, Cabinet, Council of Ministers, Apr. 21, 1983, pp. 3–4 (*Doc. 11–122*).

44. Report 109, Committee on Chinese, Nov. 16, 1983, p. 1 (*Doc. 10–60*). Document, un-dated, pp. 5–6 (*Doc. 10–59*).

45. Minutes 20, Cabinet, Council of Ministers, Nov. 13, 1984 (*Doc. 6–81*).

46. Minutes 54, Cabinet, Council of Ministers, Apr. 21, 1983 (*Doc. 11–122*).

47. Ibid.

CHAPTER EIGHT. CITIES AND MARKETS

1. Minutes 11, Cabinet, Council of Ministers, Jan. 19, 1983 (*Doc. 8–44*).

2. Minutes 51, Cabinet, Council of Ministers, June 11, 1982, p. 4 (*Doc. 13–93*). "Tien," a transliteration from the Khmer, may have been Trinh Xuan Tien, the former deputy minister of grain and food products. *Who's Who in North Vietnam,* p. 278.

3. For the PRK tax policy, see Minutes, United Leadership Committee, Apr. 20, 1980, p. 3 (*Doc. 11–50*); Congress Minutes 057, Office, KPRC, Jan. 18, 1981 (*Doc. 6–33*); Letter 27, Council of Ministers, Apr. 1, 1985, p. 1 (*Doc. 11–168*).

4. Report, Council of Ministers, Oct. 27, 1982, p. 1 (*Doc. 14–11*).

5. For the views of Council of Ministers technocrats, see ibid.

6. Directive Circular 31, Council of Ministers, Sept. 16, 1982, p. 2 (*Doc. 9–26*). Draft De-termination, Council of Ministers, 1982 (*Doc. 10–22.1*).

7. Directive Circular 17, Council of Ministers, June 21, 1982 (*Doc. 13–77*).

8. For the border agreement, see Agreement, Aug. 6, 1983 (*Doc. 10–27*).

9. Porter, *Politics of Bureaucratic Socialism,* pp. 123–24, 126n. Porter, "Vietnamese Commu-nism," p. 5. Becker, *When the War Was Over,* pp. 351–52. Robert Templer, *Shadows and Wind: A View of Modern Vietnam,* New York: Penguin Books, 1999, p. 115.

10. Stern, *Conflict and Transition,* pp. 5, 68–72. Porter, *Politics of Bureaucratic Socialism,* pp. 108–9, 125, 142. Porter, "Vietnamese Communism," pp. 5–6.

11. Minutes 51, Cabinet, Council of Ministers, June 11, 1982, pp. 5–6, 8 (*Doc. 13–93*).

12. "Tui" is a transliteration from the Khmer. Minutes 57, Cabinet, Council of Ministers, June 27, 1982, esp. pp. 10, 13 (*Doc. 13–91*). For the views of Phin and Sareum, see Min-utes 64, Cabinet, Council of Ministers, July 19, 1982, p. 10 (*Doc. 13–92*); Minutes 27, Cabinet, Council of Ministers, Feb. 22, 1985, p. 9 (*Doc. 12–56*).

13. Minutes 108, Cabinet, Council of Ministers, Oct. 15, 1982, pp. 3–4 (*Doc. 9–49*).

14. Ibid., p. 4.

15. Ibid., pp. 4–5. For developments in Battambang and Kampong Cham, see Minutes 106, Cabinet, Council of Ministers, Oct. 9, 1982 (*Doc. 13–98*).

16. Minutes 108, Cabinet, Council of Ministers, Oct. 15, 1982, pp. 5–6 (*Doc. 9–49*).

17. Minutes 47, Cabinet, Council of Ministers, May 28, 1982, pp. 5–6 (*Doc. 13–94*).

18. Minutes 24, Cabinet, Council of Ministers, Feb. 1, 1983, pp. 3–4 (*Doc. 11–128*).

19. Minutes 25, Cabinet, Council of Ministers, Feb. 11, 1983, p. 2 (*Doc. 11–127*).

20. Ibid., p. 3. For Fang You's views on Phnom Penh, see Minutes 63, Cabinet, Council of Ministers, May 5, 1983, p. 5 (*Doc. 11–119*).

21. Minutes, Council of State, Apr. 27, 1990, p. 6 (*Doc. 10–101*). Interview, former Ministry of Propaganda official, Phnom Penh, 1999.

22. Report, Ministry of Industry, July 9, 1980, p. 3 (*Doc. 8–52*). See also Chanthou Boua, "Reflections," in David Chandler and Ben Kiernan, eds., *Revolution and Its Aftermath in Kampuchea,* Yale University Southeast Asia Studies Monograph no. 25, New Haven, 1983, pp. 285–86.

23. Regarding Phnom Penh's defense, see Minutes 13, Cabinet, Council of Ministers, Mar. 23, 1982, p. 3 (*Doc. 10–115*). For the deportation of Cambodians to Svay Rieng, see Minutes 78, Cabinet, Council of Ministers, Aug. 6, 1982, p. 4 (*Doc. 13–88*). For the New Year's celebration, see Minutes 04, Party Ministerial Committee, April 1982, p. 3 (*Doc. 5–49*). For Chenda's study in Hanoi, see Minutes 64, Cabinet, Council of Ministers, July 19, 1982, p. 2 (*Doc. 13–92*).

24. Regarding the Ministry of Industry, see Report, Council of State, Aug. 12, 1982, p. 2 (*Doc. 5–32*); Minutes, Council of State, Apr. 5, 1985, p. 6 (*Doc. 4–65*). For Chenda's return to Phnom Penh, see Circular, Council of Ministers, 1981, p. 1 (*Doc. 8–64*).

25. Minutes 24, Cabinet, Council of Ministers, Feb. 1, 1983, p. 2 (*Doc. 11–128*). For the meeting of the Joint Command Committee, see Minutes, Phnom Penh Command, Nov. 10, 1982 (*Doc. 8–64*).

26. For Chenda's decision on private transportation, see Minutes 25, Cabinet, Council of Ministers, Feb. 11, 1983, pp. 1–2 (*Doc. 11–127*). For Chenda's statements on urban vices, see Minutes 24, Cabinet, Council of Ministers, Feb. 1, 1983, p. 2 (*Doc. 11–128*). For Chenda's approach to private merchants, see Minutes 47, Cabinet, Council of Ministers, May 28, 1982, p. 4 (*Doc. 13–94*); Minutes 4, Cabinet, Council of Ministers, Jan. 19, 1984, pp. 6–7 (*Doc. 7–116*). Chenda's reputation within the Party is based on various interviews. See also Boua, "Reflections," pp. 285–86.

27. Minutes 54, Cabinet, Council of Ministers, Apr. 21, 1983, p. 3 (*Doc. 11–122*).

28. Minutes 99, Cabinet, Council of Ministers, July 19, 1983 (*Doc. 11–107*).

29. Ibid.

30. Minutes 99, Cabinet, Council of Ministers, July 19, 1983 (*Doc. 11–107*). See Porter, *Politics of Bureaucratic Socialism,* p. 125.

31. Minutes 120, Cabinet, Council of Ministers, Oct. 1, 1983, pp. 2–5 (*Doc. 11–111*). Minutes 61, Cabinet, Council of Ministers, May 9, 1984, pp. 3–4 (*Doc. 7–110*). Minutes 95, Cabinet, Council of Ministers, June 30, 1983 (*Doc. 11–146*). Minutes 42, Cabinet, Council of Ministers, Mar. 13, 1983, p. 2 (*Doc. 11–124*).

32. Minutes 99, Cabinet, Council of Ministers, July 19, 1983 (*Doc. 11–107*). See also Minutes 95, Cabinet, Council of Ministers, June 30, 1983, p. 2 (*Doc. 11–146*).

33. Minutes, Council of State, Jan. 30–31, 1984, p. 4 (*Doc. 6–53*). Report 135, Cabinet, Council of Ministers, Nov. 27, 1985, p. 6 (*Doc. 12–60*). Minutes 180, Cabinet, Council of Ministers, Dec. 25, 1984, p. 5 (*Doc. 9–18*). Minutes 110, Cabinet, Council of Ministers, Sept. 7, 1983, p. 2 (*Doc. 11–110*). Draft Decision, Council of Ministers, 1984 (*Doc. 12–3*). Report, Phnom Penh People's Revolutionary Committee, Aug. 10, 1984 (*Doc. 11–187*).

34. For the comments of Hun Sen and Pham Van Kath, see Minutes 04, Cabinet, Council of Ministers, Jan. 19, 1984, pp. 8–10 (*Doc. 7–116*). For the comments of Heng Samrin, Say Phouthang, Chea Sim, and Dok Narin, see Minutes, Council of State, Jan. 30–31,

1984, pp. 7–8 (*Doc. 6–53*). For the comments of Vuong Dinh Chau, see Minutes 5, Cabinet, Council of Ministers, Jan. 13, 1984, p. 3 (*Doc. 7–115*).

35. Resolution 247, Politburo, July 27, 1984 (*Doc. 4–67*). Directive Circular 240, Politburo, July 24, 1984, p. 3 (*Doc. 6–59*).

36. Report, Phnom Penh People's Revolutionary Committee, Aug. 10, 1984, esp. pp. 5–6 (*Doc. 11–187*). See Porter, *Politics of Bureaucratic Socialism*, p. 142.

37. Draft Decision, Council of Ministers, 1984 (*Doc. 12–3*). Minutes 131, Cabinet, Council of Ministers, Aug. 30, 1984, pp. 2–3 (*Doc. 12–2*).

38. Interview, Central Party official, Phnom Penh, May 17, 1999.

39. Minutes 145, Cabinet, Council of Ministers, Sept. 21, 1984, pp. 7–8 (*Doc. 12–12*).

40. Resolution, Party, November 1984, p. 1 (*Doc. 10–140*). Decision 101, Council of Ministers, May 29, 1984 (*Doc. 12–6*). Letter 27, Council of Ministers, Apr. 1, 1985 (*Doc. 11–168*). Minutes 156, Cabinet, Council of Ministers, Oct. 18, 1984, p. 2 (*Doc. 11–26*).

41. Porter, *Politics of Bureaucratic Socialism*, pp. 35n, 120–21, 205. Stern, *Conflict and Transition*, p. 7.

42. Minutes 27, Cabinet, Council of Ministers, Feb. 22, 1985, pp. 6, 10 (*Doc. 12–56*). For Vietnamese views on the private sector, see Minutes 152, Cabinet, Council of Ministers, Oct. 4, 1984, p. 3 (*Doc. 9–19*); Minutes 156, Cabinet, Council of Ministers, Oct. 18, 1984 (*Doc. 11–26*).

43. Minutes 180, Cabinet, Council of Ministers, Dec. 25, 1984, p. 5 (*Doc. 9–18*). Telegram 48, Council of Ministers, Jan. 19, 1985, referred to in Directive Circular 04, Council of Ministers, Feb. 21, 1986, p. 1 (*Doc. 7–97*). The only limitation on the policy of decentralization was that the Center be informed, a requirement generally ignored by the provinces. Ibid., p. 3. See Minutes, Council of State, Jan. 30–31, 1986, pp. 5–6 (*Doc. 4–12*); Determination 1, Council of Ministers, Feb. 27, 1985 (*Doc. 11–173*). For Hun Sen's promotion, see Bulletin 4, Party Central Committee, Jan. 1, 1985 (*Doc. 5–7*).

44. See Christopher E. Goscha, *Thailand and the Southeast Asian Networks of the Vietnamese Revolution, 1885–1954*, Surrey, U.K.: Curzon Press, 1999, esp. chapter entitled "The Southeast Asian Commercial Networks of the DRV (1945–48)."

CHAPTER NINE. HUN SEN AND THE HIDDEN WORLD OF PHNOM PENH POLITICS

1. Minutes 14, Council of Ministers, Feb. 8, 1985 (*Doc. 12–57*).

2. For Chey Saphon's background and role within the PRK, see Minutes 14, Council of Ministers, Feb. 8, 1985 (*Doc. 12–57*); Minutes, Party Ministerial Committee, Aug. 31, 1982 (*Doc. 5–53*); "Some Documents About the Situation in Cambodia," [Vietnamese] Expert Group, Political Committee, 1984 (*Doc. 3KN*). Jennar, *Les clés du Cambodge*, p. 193.

3. Minutes 14, Council of Ministers, Feb. 8, 1985, pp. 2–3 (*Doc. 12–57*).

4. For the role of the Ministry of Foreign Affairs, see Circular 10, KPRC, Mar. 2, 1981 (*Doc. 6–24*); Minutes 04, Cabinet, Council of Ministers, Jan. 19, 1984, p. 3 (*Doc. 7–116*); Minutes, Council of State, Jan. 30–31, 1984, p. 3 (*Doc. 6–53*). For Heng Samrin's comments, see Minutes 04, Party Ministerial Committee, April 1982, p. 9 (*Doc. 5–49*).

5. Minutes 13, Cabinet, Council of Ministers, Mar. 23, 1982, pp. 2–3 (*Doc. 10–115*). Former

Ministry of Foreign Affairs cadres now in the cabinet include Cham Prasith (Commerce), Hor Namhong (Foreign Affairs), and Sok An (Council of Ministers).

6. For a description of an interview with Hun Sen, see Bekaert, *Cambodia Diary*, p. 22. For Ngo Dien's role in training Hun Sen, see Interview, Bui Tin, Paris, May 2, 1999; Interview, former Ministry of Foreign Affairs official, Phnom Penh, May 19, 1999.

7. Minutes 78, Cabinet, Council of Ministers, Aug. 30, 1991, p. 6 (*Doc. 7–35*). Regarding the border dispute between Democratic Kampuchea and Vietnam, see Kiernan, *Pol Pot Regime*, pp. 111–25; Chanda, *Brother Enemy*, pp. 32–33, 97–98.

8. Minutes 72, Cabinet, Council of Ministers, July 3, 1986 (*Doc. 8–20*). Agreement, July 7, 1979 (*Doc. 10–18*). Decree 8, Council of State, July 31, 1982, p. 2 (*Doc. 10–20*). For Vietnamese fishing, see Letter 5, Vietnamese Volunteer Army, 979, 1983 (*Doc. 10–105*).

9. Agreement, Aug. 6, 1983 (*Doc. 10–27*). Minutes 38, Joint Commission Determining the Cambodian-Vietnamese Border, Mar. 24, 1984 (*Doc. 7–112*). "Tun" was likely Pham Tun. Interview, Kong Korm, Phnom Penh, May 6, 1999. Regarding the Council of Ministers meeting at which Hun Sen explained the commission's progress, see Draft Agenda, May 25–26, 1984 (*Doc. 10–118*). (Plans for the meeting include Vietnamese notes.) For the complaints of members of the commission, see Minutes 39, Joint Commission to Determine the Cambodian-Vietnamese Border, June 26, 1984 (*Doc. 7–111*).

10. Minutes, Council of State, Jan. 30–31, 1986, p. 7 (*Doc. 4–12*). For Hun Sen's consolidation of border issues, see Report, Cabinet, Council of Ministers, November 1988, pp. 2, 11 (*Doc. 5–17*). For the agreement, see Report, Council of State, 1986 (*Doc. 5–71*).

11. Minutes 98, Cabinet, Council of Ministers, July 13, 1983, p. 2 (*Doc. 11–106*). Minutes 13, Cabinet, Council of Ministers, Mar. 23, 1982, p. 3 (*Doc. 10–115*). Minutes 25, Cabinet, Council of Ministers, Feb. 11, 1983, p. 2 (*Doc. 11–127*).

12. For numbers of Party members, see "Report on the Situation in Cambodia," [Vietnamese] Expert Group, Political Committee, 1985 p. 2 (*Doc. PP*).

13. For changes in the Party leadership, see "Some Documents About the Situation in Cambodia," [Vietnamese] Expert Group, Political Committee, 1984 (*Doc. 3KN*); Peter Schier, "Kampuchea in 1985: Between Crocodiles and Tigers," *Southeast Asian Affairs*, 1986, p. 154; Vickery, *Kampuchea: Politics*, p. 81; Interview, Central Party official, Phnom Penh, May 17, 1999.

14. "Some Documents About the Situation in Cambodia," [Vietnamese] Expert Group, Political Committee, 1984 (*Doc. 3KN*). Interview, former Hanoi-trained Party leader, Phnom Penh, May 1999.

15. "Some Documents About the Situation in Cambodia," [Vietnamese] Expert Group, Political Committee, 1984 (*Doc. 3KN*). Interview, Central Party official, Phnom Penh, May 19, 1999. Vickery, *Kampuchea: Politics*, pp. 77, 81.

16. Minutes, Council of State, Nov. 28, 1985, pp. 4–5 (*Doc. 5–58*). Bou Thang's replacement as minister of defense, Koy Buntha, was a pre-1975 Khmer Rouge soldier and the Party secretary of Battambang.

17. Minutes 42, Cabinet, Council of Ministers, Apr. 4, 1987, p. 3 (*Doc. 13–37*). For the growth of the Council of Ministers, see Report, Cabinet, Council of Ministers, November 1988, p. 2 (*Doc. 5–17*).

18. Decision 19, Cabinet, Council of Ministers, April 1987 (*Doc. 4–55*). For the role of the Ministry of Justice, see Circular 31, Council of Ministers, July 11, 1981 (*Doc. 13–68*); Minutes 04, Party Ministerial Committee, April 1982, p. 6 (*Doc. 5–49*). For the discussion on the Ministry of Justice's role, see Minutes 108, Cabinet, Council of Ministers, July 5, 1986, p. 2 (*Doc. 5–6*).

19. Minutes, Legislation Commission, Aug. 2–6, 1982, p. 12 (*Doc. 10–28*).

20. Minutes, Council of State, Jan. 30–31, 1986, p. 4 (*Doc. 4–12*). Interview, Bui Tin, Paris, May 2, 1999.

21. Minutes, Council of State, Aug. 29, 1986, p. 3 (*Doc. 4–73*). For more on the supplemental elections, see Minutes, Council of State, Apr. 23, 1987, p. 3 (*Doc. 5–83*); Minutes, Council of State, Feb. 27, 1987, p. 10 (*Doc. 4–64*); Minutes, Council of State, July 1, 1987, pp. 6–7 (*Doc. 4–13*); Minutes, Council of State, Aug. 29, 1986, p. 3 (*Doc. 4–73*).

22. For the views of Nou Peng and Men Chhan, see Minutes, Council of State, Jan. 20, 1990, pp. 3, 4 *(Doc. 4–14);* Minutes, Council of State, June 27–29, 1988, pp. 5, 9 (*Doc. 4–15*).

23. Minutes, Council of State, Jan. 30–31, 1984, p. 2 (*Doc. 6–53*). For Chan Ven's period of "study" in Hanoi, see Minutes, Cabinet, Council of State, Sept. 10, 1982 (*Doc. 11–31*).

24. Interview, Vandy Ka-on, Paris, Aug. 12, 1997. For the bypassing of the commission, see Minutes, Council of State, Oct. 26, 1984 (*Doc. 9–119*); Minutes, Council of State, Aug. 10–11, p. 7 (*Doc. 5–54*).

25. Khing Hoc Dy, "Khmer Literature Since 1975," in May M. Ebihara and Judy Ledgerwood, eds., *Cambodian Culture Since 1975: Homeland and Exile,* Ithaca, N.Y.: Cornell University Press, 1994, pp. 30–32. For restrictions on music, see Minutes 8, Phnom Penh Security Committee, Sept. 9, 1981, pp. 5–6 (*Doc. 10–156*).

26. Radio Phnom Penh, Aug. 17, 1983, FBIS, Aug. 18, 1983. Luciolli, *Le mur de bambou,* pp. 138–40.

27. For a description of the anti-Sihanouk dance performances, see Bekaert, *Cambodia Diary,* pp. 23–34.

28. Interview, Vandy Ka-on, Paris, Aug. 12, 1997. Interviews, Thun Saray, Phnom Penh, Dec. 9 and 18, 1996. For rumors of Ka-on's defection, see Minutes 06, Party Branch 2, Aug. 1, 1981, pp. 3–4 (*Doc. 10–70*).

29. Interview, Ang Eng Thong, Phnom Penh, May 27, 1999. For the Party's policy on intellectuals, see Letter 544, National Front Council, Mar. 25, 1986 (*Doc. 4–3*); Directive Circular 49, Party Central Committee, Sept. 2, 1987 (*Doc. 4–44*); Policy on Intellectuals, Party Central Committee, July 16, 1986 (*Doc. 4–45*).

30. Report 166, Ministry of the Interior, Office of the Phnom Penh Police, Feb. 12, 1986, p. 2 (*Doc. 9–76*).

31. Interview, Thun Saray, Phnom Penh, Dec. 9, 1996.

32. Institute of Sociology, *Scientific Research,* nos. 2 and 4, 1987.

33. Minutes, Council of State, Feb. 27, 1987, pp. 12–13 (*Doc. 4–64*). Minutes, Council of State, Apr. 5, 1985, pp. 7–8 (*Doc. 4–65*). For the PRK education system, see Minutes, Council of State, Jan. 30–31, pp. 14–15 (*Doc. 4–12*); Minutes 04, Cabinet, Council of Ministers, Jan. 19, 1984, p. 3 (*Doc. 7–116*).

CHAPTER TEN. WARTIME: CONSCRIPTION, PROFITEERING, AND K5

1. Timothy Carney, "Heng Samrin's Armed Forces and a Military Balance in Cambodia," in Ablin and Hood, *Cambodian Agony,* pp. 180–81. Michael Eiland, "Kampuchea in 1984: Yet Further from Peace," *Asian Survey* 25, no. 1 (1985), pp. 106–7.

2. Peter Schier, "Kampuchea in 1985: Between Crocodiles and Tigers," *Southeast Asian Affairs,* 1986, pp. 140–41. The resistance, which is not addressed in depth in this book, has been described in a series of articles published in *Southeast Asian Affairs* and *Asian Survey.* For the Khmer Rouge, see Christophe Peschoux, *Enquête sur les "nouveaux" Khmers rouges (1979–1991)—Reconstruction du mouvement et reconquête des villages: Essai d'éclaircissement,* Paris: L'Harmattan, 1992. For a description of conditions in the refugee camps, see Lawyers Committee for Human Rights, *Seeking Shelter: Cambodian Refugees in Thailand,* New York, 1987.

3. See Raszelenberg and Schier, *Cambodia Conflict,* pp. 84–88; *New York Times,* Mar. 12, 1985; Eiland, "Kampuchea in 1984," pp. 107–8, 120; Schier, "Kampuchea in 1985," pp. 142–43; Becker, *When the War Was Over,* p. 460.

4. Tim Huxley, "Cambodia in 1986: The PRK's Eighth Year," *Southeast Asian Studies,* 1987, p. 170. Raszelenberg and Schier, *Cambodia Conflict,* pp. 88, 92–93.

5. Minutes, Council of State, July 11–13, 1985, p. 8 (*Doc. 6–20*). For statistics on infiltration, see Minutes 2, Cabinet, Council of Ministers, Jan. 9, 1988 (*Doc. 12–64*).

6. Minutes 108, Cabinet, Council of Ministers, July 17, 1984, p. 2 (*Doc. 12–14*). Circular 227, Party Central Committee, July 10, 1984 (*Doc. 6–60*). Minutes 2, Cabinet, Council of Ministers, Jan. 9, 1988, pp. 2–3 (*Doc. 12–64*). Minutes, Council of State, July 11–13, p. 6 (*Doc. 6–20*). Circular 4, Council of Ministers, Mar. 19, 1984 (*Doc. 6–64*). See also Margaret Slocomb, "The K5 Gamble: National Defence and Nation Building Under the People's Republic of Kampuchea," *Journal of Southeast Asian Studies* 32, no. 2 (2001), pp. 204–6.

7. Minutes, Council of State, July 11–13, 1985, pp. 6–7 (*Doc. 6–20*).

8. Ibid.

9. Minutes, Council of State, Sept. 1, 1988, p. 4 (*Doc. 1–32*). For statistics on defections of officers, see "Report on the Situation in Cambodia," [Vietnamese] Expert Group, Political Committee, 1985, p. 4 (*Doc. PP*).

10. Minutes, Phnom Penh Command, Nov. 10, 1982 (*Doc. 8–64*). Resolution 2, Party Central Committee, July 17, 1979, p. 1 (*Doc. 8–81*). Secret Telegram 44, Steung Treng (*Doc. 9–50*).

11. Draft Agreement, Ministry of Defense, June 1981 (*Doc. 9–99*). Draft Agreement, Ministry of Defense, June 1981 (*Doc. 9–100*). Timothy Carney, "Kampuchea in 1981: Fragile Stalemate," *Asian Survey* 22, no. 1 (1982), p. 80. Carney, "Armed Forces," p. 169. For the incorporation of the operation teams into the military, see Circular, Party Central Committee, September 1980 (*Doc. 11–8*); Resolution 2, Party Central Committee, July 17, 1979, pp. 20–21 (*Doc. 8–81*); Carney, "Armed Forces," p. 160. For the numbers of Cambodian soldiers, see "Report on the Situation in Cambodia," [Vietnamese] Expert Group, Political Committee, 1985, p. 3 (*Doc. PP*).

12. Document 362, Army, General Ministry of Politics and the Military, undated (*Doc. 8–*

42). For "volunteerism," see Minutes, Council of State, Aug. 5, 1985, p. 4 (*Doc. 6–55*); Document 362, Army, General Ministry of Politics and the Military (*Doc. 8–42*).

13. "Characteristics of the Intellectual Class in Cambodia," Department of Propaganda and Education, Central Political School, 1980, pp. 1–2 (*Doc. MMM*).

14. Michael Eiland, "Cambodia in 1985; From Stalemate to Ambiguity," *Asian Survey* 26, no. 1 (1986), pp. 120–21. For figures on the Cambodian military, see "Report on the Situation in Cambodia," [Vietnamese] Expert Group, Political Committee, 1985, pp. 3–4 (*Doc. PP*). For 1982 conscription policy, see Determination 7, Council of Ministers, Feb. 4, 1982 (*Doc. 14–13*).

15. For debates on conscription, see Minutes 68, Cabinet, Council of Ministers, May 18, 1985, pp. 2–3 (*Doc. 10–13*); Letter 40, Council of Ministers, May 25, 1985 (*Doc. 10–14*); Minutes 10, Cabinet, Council of Ministers, Feb. 7, 1985, pp. 1–2 (*Doc. 12–59*); Minutes, Council of State, Aug. 5, 1985, pp. 3–5 (*Doc. 6–55*); Report 27, Cabinet, Council of State, July 8, 1985 (*Doc. 10–17*); Letter 40, Council of Ministers, May 25, 1985 (*Doc. 11–165*); Letter 38, Council of Ministers, May 17, 1985 (*Doc. 11–166*); Directive Circular 2, Council of Ministers, July 27, 1986 (*Doc. 11–148*).

16. Minutes, Council of State, Aug. 5, 1985, p. 5 (*Doc. 6–55*).

17. Minutes 10, Cabinet, Council of Ministers, Feb. 7, 1985, p. 2 (*Doc. 12–59*).

18. Letter 40, Council of Ministers, May 25, 1985, pp. 2–3 (*Doc. 10–14*).

19. Minutes, Council of State, Aug. 5, 1985, p. 4 (*Doc. 6–55*).

20. Interview, Central Party official, Phnom Penh, June 1, 1999. Interview, Battambang Party official, Battambang, May 26, 1999. Porter, *Politics of Bureaucratic Socialism,* p. 83. Subdecree 25, Council of Ministers, Nov. 20, 1985 (*Doc. 11–181*).

21. Circular, Council of Ministers, 1981 (*Doc. 13–64*). Circular 48, Council of Ministers, Nov. 9, 1981 (*Doc. 13–65*). Minutes, Council of State, Mar. 20, 1982, p. 4 (*Doc. 6–47*). Interview, Battambang Party official, Battambang, May 26, 1999. "Report on the Situation in Cambodia," [Vietnamese] Expert Group, Political Committee, 1985, p. 3 (*Doc. PP*). For Hun Sen's comments, see Minutes, Cabinet, Council of Ministers, undated (est. 1987), p. 32 (*Doc. 13–36*).

22. For military fishing, see Report, Ministry of Agriculture, undated (est. 1982), p. 5 (*Doc. 10–142*); Minutes 27, Cabinet, Council of Ministers, Mar. 22, 1984, p. 2 (*Doc. 7–113*). For Ung Phan's comments, see Minutes, Council of State, Aug. 5, 1985, pp. 5–6 (*Doc. 6–55*). Regarding military fishing techniques, see Minutes 19, Cabinet, Council of Ministers, Jan. 31, 1990, p. 6 (*Doc. 3–93*).

23. For Koy Buntha's comments, see Minutes, Cabinet, Council of Ministers, undated (est. 1987), p. 35 (*Doc. 13–36*). For complaints regarding military logging, see Letter 8128, Ministry of Agriculture, Oct. 26, 1983 (*Doc. 9–35*); Letter 7033, Ministry of Agriculture, Sept. 8, 1983 (*Doc. 9–37*); Letter 1264, Ministry of Agriculture, Timber Department, Oct. 11, 1983 (*Doc. 11–33*). For Ung Phan's comments, see Minutes 118, Cabinet, Council of Ministers, Sept. 7, 1985, p. 2 (*Doc. 12–38*); Minutes, Council of State, Aug. 5, 1985, p. 6 (*Doc. 6–55*).

24. Minutes, Council of State, July 6–7, 1987, pp. 8–9 (*Doc. 5–88*).

25. Ibid.

26. Minutes 2, Cabinet, Council of Ministers, Apr. 26, 1986, p. 1 (*Doc. 7–48*). Minutes 53, Cabinet, Council of Ministers, Apr. 29, 1985, pp. 1–5 (*Doc. 12–51*). Report 52, K5 Committee, July 4, 1985, pp. 3–4 (*Doc. 11–41*). "Report on the Situation in Cambodia," [Vietnamese] Expert Group, Political Committee, 1985, p. 3 (*Doc. PP*). Rich Arant helped with the translation of Khmer-language K5 documents.

27. Minutes 37, Cabinet, Council of Ministers, Dec. 25, 1985, p. 7 (*Doc. 12–61*). Minutes 53, Cabinet, Council of Ministers, Apr. 29, 1985, p. 3 (*Doc. 12–51*). Interviews, former Ministry of Planning official, Phnom Penh, May 24 and June 2, 1999. Interview, Ministry of Finance official, May 25, 1999. For Hun Sen's comments, see Minutes 2, Cabinet, Council of Ministers, Apr. 26, 1986, p. 1 (*Doc. 7–48*).

28. Decision 155, Council of Ministers, Sept. 28, 1984 (*Doc. 6–87*). Minutes 2, Cabinet, Council of Ministers, Apr. 26, 1986, p. 1 (*Doc. 7–48*). Decision 188, Council of Ministers, Dec. 22, 1986 (*Doc. 8–15*).

29. Nheum Vanda, Personal history (*Doc. 5–44*), translation by Rich Arant. Interview, former Ministry of Planning official, Phnom Penh, June 2, 1999.

30. Interview, former Ministry of Planning official, Phnom Penh, June 2, 1999. Decision 188, Council of Ministers, Dec. 22, 1986 (*Doc. 8–15*). Minutes, Council of State, Apr. 6, 1988, p. 8 (*Doc. 1–30*). Letter 143, Ministry of Justice, Feb. 2, 1980 (*Doc. 8–69*).

31. Decision 155, Council of Ministers, Sept. 28, 1984 (*Doc. 6–87*). Minutes 53, Cabinet, Council of Ministers, Apr. 29, 1985, pp. 2–3 (*Doc. 12–51*). Minutes 37, Cabinet, Council of Ministers, Dec. 25, 1985, pp. 5–7 (*Doc. 12–61*). Minutes, Council of State, June 27–29, 1988, pp. 5–6 (*Doc. 4–15*). Minutes 127, Cabinet, Council of Ministers, Oct. 12, 1988, p. 2 (*Doc. 13–24*). Decision 132, Council of Ministers, 1986, pp. 4–5 (*Doc. 8–14*). Report 52, Central K5 Committee, July 4, 1985 (*Doc. 11–41*).

32. Minutes 127, Cabinet, Council of State, Oct. 12, 1988, p. 2 (*Doc. 13–24*).

33. Esméralda Luciolli, a medical professional working in Cambodia for Médicins Sans Frontières, interviewed returning K5 workers. Luciolli, *Le mur de bambou,* pp. 113–18.

34. For corruption and losses in K5, see Report 52, Central K5 Committee, July 4, 1985, p. 9 (*Doc. 11–41*); Minutes 53, Cabinet, Council of Ministers, Apr. 29, 1985, p. 5 (*Doc. 12–53*); Minutes 37, Cabinet, Council of Ministers, Dec. 25, 1985, pp. 5–7 (*Doc. 12–61*). For Ros Chhun's report, see Minutes 37, Cabinet, Council of Ministers, Dec. 25, 1985, p. 5 (*Doc. 12–61*). For interviews, see Luciolli, *Le mur de bambou,* pp. 113, 115. My translation from the French.

35. Report 52, K5 Committee, July 4, 1985, pp. 9–10 (*Doc. 11–41*).

36. Minutes 53, Cabinet, Council of Ministers, Apr. 29, 1985, pp. 4–5 (*Doc. 12–53*). Minutes 37, Cabinet, Council of Ministers, Dec. 25, 1985, p. 2–5 (*Doc. 12–61*).

37. Luciolli, *Le mur de bambou,* pp. 122–27.

38. "Dan Eung" is a transliteration from the Khmer. Minutes 37, Cabinet, Council of Ministers, Dec. 25, 1985, p. 6 (*Doc. 12–61*).

39. Minutes 37, Cabinet, Council of Ministers, Dec. 25, 1985, pp. 4–5 (*Doc. 12–61*). Minutes 53, Cabinet, Council of Ministers, Apr. 29, 1985, p. 5 (*Doc. 12–51*). Minutes, Council of State, Dec. 20, 1985, p. 6 (*Doc. 6–18*).

40. Minutes 37, Cabinet, Council of Ministers, Dec. 25, 1985, p. 5 (*Doc. 12–61*). Minutes, Council of State, Dec. 20, 1985, p. 6 (*Doc. 6–18*).

41. Luciolli, *Le mur de bambou,* p. 128.

42. Ibid., pp. 119–20.

43. Report 52, Central K5 Committee, July 4, 1985, p. 7, table (*Doc. 11–41*). Margaret Slocomb, who has documented the human cost and unpopularity of K5, describes the project as successful in sealing off the border. Slocomb, "K5 Gamble," p. 209.

44. Interview, Vandy Ka-on, Paris, Aug. 12, 1997. Interview, Uk Bunchheuan, Phnom Penh, May 31, 1999.

CHAPTER ELEVEN. LAW, HUMAN RIGHTS, AND THE CASE OF THE YENS

1. Minutes 113, Council of Ministers, Sept. 15, 1988, p. 27 (*Doc. 5–43*).

2. Interview, Uk Bunchheuan, Phnom Penh, May 31, 1999. The allegations against Uk Bunchheuan were made by one of the returning Hanoi veterans, Hem Samin, separately to Ben Kiernan and Stephen Heder. Kiernan, "Wild Chickens," p. 159.

3. Report, Council of Ministers, undated (est. 1985–86) (*Doc. 9–77*).

4. Kiernan, "Wild Chickens," pp. 175–98.

5. Minutes, Council of State, Sept. 1, 1988, p. 4 (*Doc. 1–32*).

6. Determination 218, KPRC (*Doc. 10–67.1*).

7. Minutes, Party, Feb. 26, 1981, p. 7 (*Doc. 5–48*). Letter 242, Ministry of Justice, Sept. 13, 1980 (*Doc. 8–30*). Letter 114, Ministry of Justice, July 30, 1980 (*Doc. 8–51*). Interview, Uk Bunchheuan, Phnom Penh, May 31, 1999.

8. Report 973, Ministry of Justice, Oct. 19, 1981 (*Doc. 5–23*). Minutes, Party, Feb. 26, 1981, p. 7 (*Doc. 5–48*).

9. Report, Ministry of Justice, Mar. 19, 1982, pp. 9–10 (*Doc. 8–80*). Report 436, Ministry of Justice, May 1982 (*Doc. 9–136*). Report 387, Ministry of Justice, May 7, 1982 (*Doc. 9–125*). Report 205, Ministry of Justice, Feb. 1982, p. 4 (*Doc. 9–127*). For the attitudes of Chan Sok and other ministry personnel, see Report 1060, Ministry of Justice, Oct. 31, 1981, pp. 3–5 (*Doc. 5–55*).

10. Minutes, Party, Feb. 26, 1981, p. 8 (*Doc. 5–48*). For Bunchheuan's failure to communicate with other ministers, see Report 973, Ministry of Justice, Oct. 19, 1981, p. 5 (*Doc. 5–23*).

11. Report, Ministry of Justice, Oct. 19, 1981, p. 4 (*Doc. 5–23*). Minutes, Party, Feb. 26, 1981, p. 8 (*Doc. 5–48*).

12. Interview, Uk Bunchheuan, Phnom Penh, May 31, 1999. Interview, Heng Chi, Phnom Penh, Dec. 19, 1996. Interview, Uk Sokun, Phnom Penh, May 24, 1999. *Hoc Tap* no. 6, June 1972, referred to in *Who's Who in North Vietnam,* p. 63. Work Summary 333, Ministry of Justice, Oct. 10, 1980 (*Doc. 8–63*).

13. Interview, Uk Sokun, Phnom Penh, May 24, 1999. Interviews, Ministry of Justice staff, Phnom Penh, May 20 and 24, 1999. Interview, Uk Bunchheuan, Phnom Penh, May 31, 1999. For one such meeting, see Minutes 71, Ministry of Justice, Aug. 22, 1983 (*Doc. 9–112*).

14. Interview, Lueng Chhai, Phnom Penh, Feb. 17, 1997. Interview, Uk Bunchheuan, Phnom Penh, May 31, 1999. Minutes, Cabinet, Council of State, Sept. 10, 1982 (*Doc. 11–31*). Report 62, Ministry of Justice, July 5, 1980, pp. 3–4 (*Doc. 8–53*). Letter 478, Ministry of

Justice, School of Administration, Nov. 2, 1982 (*Doc. 9–122*). Minutes 115, Ministry of Justice, School of Administration, June 3, 1982 (*Doc. 9–148*). Report 415, Ministry of Justice, School of Administration, Sept. 15, 1982 (*Doc. 9–124*). Report 356, Ministry of Justice, School of Administration, June 9, 1982 (*Doc. 9–144*).

15. Minutes, Council of State, Jan. 30–31, 1986, p. 18 (*Doc. 4–12*). Minutes, Council of State, Feb. 27, 1978, p. 8 (*Doc. 4–64*). Minutes 6, Cabinet, Council of Ministers, Feb. 14, 1989, p. 3 (*Doc. 6–92*). Report 1176, Ministry of Justice, Dec. 11, 1982, pp. 3, 13 (*Doc. 9–129*). Report 890, Ministry of Justice, Sept. 26, 1981 (*Doc. 8–89*). Minutes, Legislation Commission, Aug. 2–6, 1982, p. 15 (*Doc. 10–28*). Letter 551, Ministry of Justice, June 8, 1982 (*Doc. 11–32*). Minutes 4, Party Branch 2, Mar. 1983, p. 4 (*Doc. 10–124*). Minutes 126, Cabinet, Council of Ministers, Aug. 25, 1989, p. 2 (*Doc. 7–20*).

16. For the lack of functioning courts, see Report, Council of State, Feb. 5, 1983 (*Doc. 6–38*). For ministry plans, see Draft Document, Ministry of Justice, undated (*Doc. 8–56*). For Ung Phan's comments, see Proceedings, Second National Assembly Session, Feb. 5–10, 1982, p. 22 (*Doc. 9–87*). For the Phnom Penh court and the show trials, see Report, Cabinet, KPRC, April 1981 (*Doc. 11–82*); Report 28, Cabinet, Council of Ministers, May 6, 1982 (*Doc. 13–18*); Report 36, Cabinet, Council of Ministers, May 28, 1982 (*Doc. 13–20*); Amnesty International, *Kampuchea: Political Imprisonment and Torture,* London, 1987, pp. 65–69; Phnom Penh Domestic Service, Oct. 22, 1981, FBIS, Oct. 23, 1981.

17. For the appointment of judges, see Minutes 04, Party Ministerial Committee, April 1982, p. 7 (*Doc. 5–49*); Report 277, Ministry of Justice, 1982, p. 8 (*Doc. 9–126*). For Uk Bunchheuan's comments, see Minutes, Council of State, Mar. 20, 1982, p. 3 (*Doc. 6–47*). The Cambodian justice system also re-created the Vietnamese tradition of "People's Assessors," who were in theory chosen by the court to represent defendants. Selected from the local mass organizations and unpaid, the People's Assessors were also vetted by the Central Party. Circular 396, KPRC, Nov. 12, 1980 (*Doc. 6–34*). Porter, *Politics of Bureaucratic Socialism,* p. 172n.

18. Letter 31, Ministry of Justice, Dec. 22, 1981 (*Doc. 8–73*). Letter 90, Ministry of Justice, Jan. 30, 1981 (*Doc. 8–76*). Letter 122, Ministry of Justice, Mar. 16, 1981 (*Doc. 8–77*). Letter 24, Ministry of Justice, Nov. 17, 1981 (*Doc. 8–78*).

19. Report 277, Ministry of Justice, 1982 (*Doc. 9–126*).

20. Document, Legislation Commission, 1982, pp. 8–9 (*Doc. 10–119*). Report, Ministry of Justice, Dec. 1981 (*Doc. 10–26*).

21. Minutes 35, Cabinet, Council of Ministers, Feb. 26, 1983 (*Doc. 11–125*). For previous references to human rights organizations, see Report, Ministry of Justice, Mar. 19, 1982, p. 3 (*Doc. 8–80*). The leadership's concerns may have had to do with early attempts at dialogue made by Amnesty International. Personal communication, Stephen Heder. Chem Snguon was a cautious and laconic former diplomat who spent the Khmer Rouge period in a special labor camp for politically suspect loyalists of the FUNK. After the establishment of the PRK, he was sent to "study" in Vietnam and returned with an acceptable understanding of communist principles. Usually supportive of the ministry's legal agenda, he was also willing to promote some of the Party leadership's more ideologically rigid inclinations. One example was his approach to the reestablishment of population centers, which, he told the leadership, would "entice the entire production workforce to come

trade in the markets, which would result in the reemergence of a capitalist regime." For positions taken by Chem Snguon, see Minutes, Council of State, Jan. 30–31, 1984, p. 8 (*Doc. 6–53*); Minutes 8, Party Branch 2, Sept. 9, 1983 (*Doc. 10–117*).

22. Minutes, Party Ministerial Committee, Apr. 2, 1983, pp. 4–5 (*Doc. 10–124*).

23. Minutes 59, Cabinet, Council of Ministers, Apr. 27, 1983, p. 6 (*Doc. 11–120*). Proceedings, Second National Assembly Session, Feb. 5–10, 1982, p. 14 (*Doc. 9–87*)

24. Minutes 69, Cabinet, Council of Ministers, May 21, 1985, p. 4 (*Doc. 12–46*). The Ministry of Justice began the drafting process in 1982. Letter 220, Ministry of Justice, Mar. 24, 1982 (*Doc. 9–143*)

25. Minutes 84, Cabinet, Council of Ministers, June 6, 1985, p. 4 (*Doc. 12–42*).

26. Ibid. For references to meetings of Vietnamese advisors, see Minutes 69, Cabinet, Council of Ministers, May 21, 1985, pp. 1, 4 (*Doc. 12–46*).

27. Minutes 84, Cabinet, Council of Ministers, June 6, 1985, p. 3 (*Doc. 12–42*).

28. Ibid. See also Minutes 69, Cabinet, Council of Ministers, May 21, 1985, p. 5 (*Doc. 12–46*).

29. Minutes 84, Cabinet, Council of Ministers, June 6, 1985, p. 4 (*Doc. 12–42*).

30. Minutes 112, Cabinet, Council of Ministers, Aug. 19, 1985, p. 7 (*Doc. 12–39*). Minutes 69, Cabinet, Council of Ministers, May 21, 1985, pp. 2–3 (*Doc. 12–46*). Report 4, Council of Ministers, Aug. 19, 1985, p. 2 (*Doc. 11–172*). The final version of Decree-Law 27 was translated by Michael Vickery and included in Vickery's "Criminal Law in the People's Republic of Kampuchea," *Journal of Contemporary Asia* 17, no. 4 (1987), pp. 508–18.

31. Minutes 112, Cabinet, Council of Ministers, Aug. 19, 1985, pp. 2–3 (*Doc. 12–39*).

32. Minutes, Council of State, Oct. 30, 1985, pp. 5–6 (*Doc. 6–19*).

33. Minutes 112, Cabinet, Council of Ministers, Aug. 19, 1985, p. 5 (*Doc. 12–39*). Minutes, Council of State, Oct. 30, 1985, p. 4 (*Doc. 6–19*).

34. Say Phouthang also supported citizen searches, citing Vietnamese precedent. Minutes, Council of State, Oct. 30, 1985, pp. 4–5 (*Doc. 6–19*). See Decree-Law 27, article 20, permitting citizens' searches. For Uk Bunchheuan's position, see Minutes 112, Cabinet, Council of Ministers, Aug. 19, 1985, p. 5 (*Doc. 12–39*). For Chay Sang Yaun's statement, see Minutes, Phnom Penh Command Committee, Nov. 10, 1982, p. 2 (*Doc. 8–64*).

35. Minutes 112, Cabinet, Council of Ministers, Aug. 19, 1985, p. 6 (*Doc. 12–39*).

36. Minutes, Council of State, Oct. 30, 1985, pp. 6–7 (*Doc. 6–19*). Letter 90, Council of Ministers, Sept. 11, 1985 (*Doc. 11–38*).

37. Report 54, Legislation Commission, Oct. 11, 1985, pp. 3–4 (*Doc. 9–70*). See Lawyers Committee for Human Rights, *Kampuchea, After the Worst,* New York, 1985.

38. Minutes, Council of State, Oct. 30, 1985, p. 7 (*Doc. 6–19*).

39. Ibid., pp. 6–7. Report 42, Cabinet, Council of State, Oct. 26, 1985, p. 2 (*Doc. 9–69*). For Khang Sarin's earlier position, see Minutes 112, Cabinet, Council of Ministers, Aug. 19, 1985, p. 5 (*Doc. 12–39*).

40. Letter 737, Cabinet, Council of State, Nov. 13, 1985 (*Doc. 9–68*).

41. Letter 5603, Party Central Committee, Dec. 26, 1985 (*Doc. 9–67*).

42. Minutes 69, Cabinet, Council of Ministers, Aug. 21, 1985, pp. 2–3 (*Doc. 12–46*).

43. Minutes 10, Cabinet, Council of Ministers, Jan. 22, 1986, pp. 2–3 (*Doc. 7–103*).

44. Minutes, Council of State, Sept. 1, 1988, p. 4 (*Doc. 1–32*).

45. Subdecree 23, Council of Ministers, Aug. 19, 1987 (*Doc. 11–59*). Porter, *Politics of Bureaucratic Socialism,* p. 176.

46. Minutes, Council of State, June 23, 1992, p. 5 (*Doc. 6–8*). Minutes, Council of State, Sept. 1, 1988, pp. 4–5 (*Doc. 1–32*). Minutes, Council of State, Nov. 20, 1987, p. 3–5 (*Doc. 5–85*). Minutes, Council of State, Jan. 28–29, 1988, p. 12 (*Doc. 1–29*). Minutes, Council of State, June 27–29, 1988, p. 11 (*Doc. 4–15*). Minutes, Council of State, Jan. 20, 1990, p. 5 (*Doc. 4–13*). Minutes, Council of State, Oct. 30, 1985, p. 13 (*Doc. 6–19*). Minutes, Council of State, Aug. 28, 1987, p. 9 (*Doc. 5–87*).

47. Minutes 174, Cabinet, Council of Ministers, Dec. 27, 1987, p. 5 (*Doc. 13–35*). Report, Ministry of the Interior, Office of the Phnom Penh Police, Feb. 14, 1986 (*Doc. 9–76*). Report, Council of State, June 18, 1986, p. 2 (*Doc. 5–40*). Minutes, Council of State, Feb. 27, 1987, p. 7 (*Doc. 4–64*).

48. Report, General Procurator of the People's Supreme Court, June 19, 1988, p. 5 (*Doc. 4–16*).

49. Minutes 113, Council of Ministers, Sept. 15, 1988, p. 27 (*Doc. 5–43*).

50. Minutes, Council of State, Aug. 28, 1987, pp. 9–10 (*Doc. 5–87*). Amnesty International, *Kampuchea: Political Imprisonment and Torture;* Amnesty International, *Kampuchea: Officially Reported Political Arrests and Allegations of Torture and Arbitrary Detention,* London, 1988, p. 2.

51. Minutes, Council of State, Aug. 28, 1987, p. 10 (*Doc. 5–87*).

52. Minutes, Cabinet, Council of Ministers, Sept. 15, 1988, p. 35 (*Doc. 5–43*). For Khang Sarin's comments, see Minutes, Council of State, Jan. 28–29, 1988, p. 12 (*Doc. 1–29*).

53. The story of the Yens is told in Report 48, Cabinet, Council of State, Oct. 8, 1986 (*Doc. 10–44*); Letter 31, Cabinet, Council of State, Sept. 12, 1986 (*Doc. 10–45*); Letter 149, Party Central Committee, Sept. 9, 1986 (*Doc. 10–46*); Report 37, Cabinet, Council of State, Aug. 20, 1986 (*Doc. 10–47*); Report 24, Ministry of Justice, June 30, 1986 (*Doc. 10–48*); Letter 09, Phnom Penh People's Court, 1986 (*Doc. 10–49*); Minutes, Phnom Penh People's Court, June 4, 1986 (*Doc. 10–50*); Minutes, Council of State, Apr. 23, 1986, p. 2 (*Doc. 10–51*); Report 13, Cabinet, Council of State, Apr. 18, 1986 (*Doc. 10–52*); Report 8, Ministry of Justice, Feb. 25, 1986 (*Doc. 10–53*); Minutes, Council of State, Aug. 29, 1986, pp. 4–10 (*Doc. 4–73*); Minutes, Council of State, Oct. 29, 1986, pp. 13–14 (*Doc. 5–79*).

54. Minutes, Council of State, Aug. 29, 1986, p. 4 (*Doc. 4–73*). For police statistics, see Report 166, Ministry of the Interior, Office of the Phnom Penh Police, Feb. 14, 1986, p. 6 (*Doc. 9–76*).

55. Report 13, Cabinet, Council of State, Apr. 18, 1986, p. 2 (*Doc. 10–52*).

56. "Nguyen Hoc" is a transliteration from the Khmer. Minutes, Phnom Penh People's Court, June 4, 1986, p. 2 (*Doc. 10–50*).

57. Minutes, Council of State, Aug. 29, 1986 (*Doc. 4–73*).

58. Minutes, Council of State, Oct. 29, 1986, pp. 13–14 (*Doc. 5–79*). For Heng Samrin's previous complaints, see Minutes, Council of State, July 11–13, 1985, p. 9 (*Doc. 6–20*).

59. Minutes, Council of State, Oct. 29, 1986, pp. 13–14 (*Doc. 5–79*).

60. Minutes, Council of State, July 1, 1987, p. 4 (*Doc. 4–13*). Minutes, Council of State, Oct. 13, 1983, pp. 2–3 (*Doc. 6–51*). Minutes, Council of State, Nov. 20, 1987, pp. 3–4 (*Doc. 5–85*). Minutes, Council of State, June 3, 1987, p. 3 (*Doc. 5–84*), Minutes, Council of State, Feb. 22, 1985, p. 6 (*Doc. 9–121*).

61. Minutes, Council of State, Feb. 22, 1985, pp. 6–7 (*Doc. 9–121*).
62. Ibid.
63. Minutes, Council of State, June 3, 1987, pp. 2–5 (*Doc. 5–84*).
64. Minutes, Council of State, July 1, 1987, p. 4 (*Doc. 4–13*).
65. Minutes, Council of State, Dec. 31, 1986, pp. 4–6 (*Doc. 5–81*).
66. Minutes 113, Cabinet, Council of Ministers, July 18, 1986, p. 2 (*Doc. 8–16*). Decree-Law (*Doc. 6–29*). Minutes, Legislation Commission, Aug. 2–6, 1982 (*Doc. 10–28*).
67. Minutes 111, Cabinet, Council of Ministers, July 18, 1986, pp. 2–3 (*Doc. 8–17*).
68. Minutes 155, Cabinet, Council of Ministers, Dec. 19, 1985, p. 3 (*Doc. 12–62*). Minutes, Council of State, Sept. 29, 1988, p. 9 (*Doc. 1–33*). Draft text, Legislation Commission, p. 3 (*Doc. 3–79*).
69. Report, General Procurator of the People's Supreme Court, May 31, 1990 (*Doc. 5–61*). For problems related to the establishment of the Supreme Court, see Report 17, Cabinet, Council of State, Apr. 21, 1989, p. 4 (*Doc. 1–1*); Minutes, Council of State, Apr. 4, 1988, pp. 4–5 (*Doc. 1–30*); Minutes, Council of State, July 1, 1987, pp. 8–9 (*Doc. 4–13*); Minutes, Council of State, Jan. 28–29, 1988, pp. 10–11 (*Doc. 1–29*); Report, People's Supreme Court, June 16, 1988 (*Doc. 4–18*); Minutes, Council of State, Sept. 1, 1988, p. 10 (*Doc. 1–32*).
70. Minutes, Council of State, May 24–25, 1985 (*Doc. 4–11*). Resolution 2, Party Central Committee, July 17, 1979, pp. 7–8, 24 (*Doc. 8–81*). Minutes, Council of State, Mar. 15, 1989, pp. 8–11 (*Doc. 1–36*). Report 166, Ministry of the Interior, Office of the Phnom Penh Police, Feb. 14, 1986, p. 9 (*Doc. 9–76*).
71. Minutes, Council of State, Nov. 20, 1987, pp. 5–6 (*Doc. 5–85*). Regulation 1, Council of Ministers, Jan. 12, 1984 (*Doc. 6–69*). See Porter, *Politics of Bureaucratic Socialism,* pp. 175–76.
72. Minutes, Council of State, Nov. 20, 1987, pp. 5–8 (*Doc. 5–85*). Letter 207, Council of Ministers, Dec. 5, 1988 (*Doc. 13–3*). Letter 219, Council of Ministers, Dec. 14, 1988 (*Doc. 13–4*). Minutes 174, Cabinet, Council of Ministers, Dec. 27, 1987, p. 4 (*Doc. 13–35*). Minutes, Council of State, Dec. 30, 1988, p. 10 (*Doc. 1–35*). Minutes, Council of State, May 21, 1988, pp. 8–9 (*Doc. 1–31*). Draft Decree, Council of State, 1988 (*Doc. 2–45*).
73. Minutes, Council of State, Sept. 1, 1988, pp. 4–7 (*Doc. 1–32*). Decision 175, Council of Ministers, Dec. 21, 1987 (*Doc. 11–64*). Minutes, Council of State, Apr. 27, 1990, p. 4 (*Doc. 10–101*). Minutes, Council of State, Nov. 20, 1987, p. 6 (*Doc. 5–85*).

CHAPTER TWELVE. THE POLITICS OF ECONOMIC REFORM

1. Minutes, Council of State, June 27–29, 1988, p. 5 (*Doc. 4–15*).
2. Minutes, Council of State, Jan. 30–31, 1984, pp. 6–7 (*Doc. 6–53*). Viviane Frings analyzes the reasons for the disintegration of the various types of collectives, including the lack of inputs and competent cadres. Frings, *Failure of Agricultural Collectivization,* pp. 17–20, 51–54.
3. Instructions, Council of Ministers, 1984, p. 3 (*Doc. 5–11*). Minutes 98, Cabinet, Council of Ministers, July 13, 1983, p. 2 (*Doc. 11–106*). For Mat Ly's comments, see Minutes 120, Cabinet, Council of Ministers, Oct. 1, 1983, p. 4 (*Doc. 11–111*).

4. Views of Discussion Group 1, p. 6, Proceedings, Fifteenth National Assembly Session, July 7–11, 1988.

5. Minutes, Cabinet, Council of Ministers, Dec. 3, 1987, p. 2 (*Doc. 13–34*).

6. Minutes 56, Cabinet, Council of Ministers, May 12, 1988 (*Doc. 13–1*).

7. Minutes 113, Cabinet, Council of Ministers, June 24, 1988, p. 4 (*Doc. 5–43*).

8. Ibid., pp. 8, 16–17, 23. Regarding lack of leadership support for collectivization, see Frings, *Failure of Agricultural Collectivization,* pp. 55–61.

9. Minutes, Council of State, June 27–29, 1988, p. 5 (*Doc. 4–15*).

10. Proceedings, Fifteenth National Assembly Session, July 7–11, 1988.

11. Minutes, Council of State, Dec. 30, 1988, p. 3 (*Doc. 1–35*).

12. Ibid.

13. Law Concerning the Amendment of Articles 15, 16, and 17 of the Constitution of the PRK (*Doc. 4–22*). Minutes 23, Cabinet, Council of Ministers, Mar. 21, 1991, pp. 1–2 (*Doc. 7–70*). Implementing Circular 3, Council of Ministers, June 3, 1989 (*Doc. 7–47*). Bulletin 111, Ministry of Agriculture, Oct. 31, 1989 (*Doc. 12–30*). Frings, *Failure of Agricultural Collectivization,* pp. 40–43. Viviane Frings, "Cambodia After Decollectivization (1989–1992)," *Journal of Contemporary Asia* 24, no. 1 (1994), pp. 49–66.

14. Interview, former Ministry of Planning official, Phnom Penh, May 24, 1999. Minutes 162, Cabinet, Council of Ministers, Dec. 21, 1987, p. 4 (*Doc. 13–34*).

15. Stern, *Conflict and Transition.* Porter, *Politics of Bureaucratic Socialism.*

16. Raszelenberg and Schier, *Cambodia Conflict,* pp. 99, 102.

17. Radio Phnom Penh, Mar. 11, 1987; Vietnam News Agency, Mar. 15, 1987; Agence France Press, Mar. 17, 1987, FBIS, Mar. 18, 1987—all in Raszelenberg and Schier, *Cambodia Conflict,* pp. 113–16. See also Becker, *When the War Was Over,* p. 467; Friedemann Bartu, "Kampuchea: The Search for a Political Solution Gathers Momentum," *Southeast Asian Studies,* 1989, p. 177.

18. Minutes 107, Cabinet, Council of Ministers, July 15, 1989, p. 2 (*Doc. 7–14*). Raszelenberg and Schier, *Cambodia Conflict,* p. 133. *Bangkok Post,* Jan. 9, 1988.

19. Raszelenberg and Schier, *Cambodia Conflict,* pp. 143–145. Nayan Chanda, "Cambodia in 1987: Sihanouk at Center Stage," *Asian Survey* 28, no. 1 (1989), pp. 111–12. Becker, *When the War Was Over,* pp. 473–74, 560.

20. Minutes 131, Cabinet, Council of Ministers, Sept. 30, 1988, p. 9 (*Doc. 13–25*).

21. Minutes 113, Cabinet, Council of Ministers, June 23–24, 1988, pp. 3, 28 (*Doc. 5–43*). Letter 110, Cabinet, Council of Ministers, Feb. 4, 1988 (*Doc. 1–13*).

22. Minutes 113, Cabinet, Council of Ministers, June 23–24, 1988, pp. 19–20 (*Doc. 5–43*).

23. Ibid.

24. Minutes 131, Cabinet, Council of Ministers, Sept. 14, 1988, pp. 4–5, 9–10 (*Doc. 13–25*).

25. Minutes 128, Cabinet, Council of Ministers, Sept. 22, 1988, p. 6 (*Doc. 13–23*).

26. Minutes 124, Cabinet, Council of Ministers, Oct. 1, 1988, p. 1 (*Doc. 13–26*).

27. Interview, Central Party official, Phnom Penh, May 17, 1999.

28. Decision 107, Council of Ministers, Sept. 4, 1987 (*Doc. 11–61*). Minutes, Cabinet, Council of State, Nov. 13, 1986 (*Doc. 3–89*). Luciolli, *Le mur de bambou,* pp. 65–68.

29. Minutes, Council of State, Aug. 12, 1987, p. 3 (*Doc. 3–88*).

30. Minutes, Council of State, July 6–7, 1987, p. 11 (*Doc. 5–88*). For political vetting of students, see Report 1305, Ministry of the Interior, Sept. 22, 1984 (*Doc. 5–34*).

31. Minutes 139, Cabinet, Council of Ministers, Sept. 19, 1989 (*Doc. 6–71*).

32. Minutes 91, Cabinet, Council of Ministers, June 19, 1989, pp. 4–5 (*Doc. 6–100*).

33. Minutes 113, Cabinet, Council of Ministers, June 23–34, 1988, p. 9 (*Doc. 5–43*).

34. Ibid.

35. Amnesty International, "State of Cambodia: Human Rights Developments, 1 October 1991 to 31 January 1992," London, p. 37.

36. Circular 11, Council of Ministers, Sept. 26, 1985 (*Doc. 12–50*). Directive Circular 15, Council of Ministers, Sept. 7, 1985 (*Doc. 11–175*). For Cha Reang's comments, see Minutes 149, Cabinet, Council of Ministers, Oct. 23, 1989, p. 3 (*Doc. 6–74*).

37. Minutes 113, Cabinet, Council of Ministers, June 23–34, 1988, pp. 13, 22, 27–28 (*Doc. 5–43*). Report, Council of Ministers (*Doc. 4–2*).

38. Minutes 115, Cabinet, Council of Ministers, Aug. 10, 1990, p. 15 (*Doc. 8–3*). Minutes 149, Cabinet, Council of Ministers, Oct. 23, 1989 (*Doc. 6–74*). Minutes 145, Cabinet, Council of Ministers, Oct. 17, 1989 (*Doc. 6–72*). Minutes 166, Cabinet, Council of Ministers, Nov. 18, 1989 (*Doc. 6–77*). Minutes, Council of State, Dec. 30, 1988, pp. 3–4 (*Doc. 1–35*). Minutes 6, Cabinet, Council of Ministers, Feb. 14, 1989 (*Doc. 6–92*).

39. Raszelenberg and Schier, *Cambodia Conflict,* p. 133.

40. Chhang Song, who returned to live under the PRK, served as an advisor to Chea Sim. Minutes 115, Cabinet, Council of Ministers, Aug. 3, 1989, p. 4 (*Doc. 7–18*).

41. Minutes 149, Cabinet, Council of Ministers, Oct. 23, 1989, pp. 2–3 (*Doc. 6–74*). Jennar, *Les clés du Cambodge,* p. 247.

42. Minutes 149, Cabinet, Council of Ministers, Oct. 23, 1989, pp. 2–3 (*Doc. 6–74*). Minutes 71, Cabinet, Council of Ministers, Aug. 7, 1991, p. 6 (*Doc. 1–42*). Minutes 145, Cabinet, Council of Ministers, Oct. 17, 1989 (*Doc. 6–72*). Minutes 6, Cabinet, Council of Ministers, Feb. 14, 1989 (*Doc. 6–92*).

43. Minutes 19, Cabinet, Council of Ministers, Dec. 21–22, 1989, p. 44 (*Doc. 3–93*). Minutes 91, Cabinet, Council of Ministers, June 19, 1989, p. 3 (*Doc. 6–100*). Minutes, Council of State, May 15, 1989, p. 3 (*Doc. 1–25*). Minutes, Council of State, Feb. 27, 1987, p. 3 (*Doc. 4–64*). Minutes 15, Cabinet, Council of Ministers, Jan. 22, 1990, p. 4 (*Doc. 8–22*). Minutes 149, Cabinet, Council of Ministers, Oct. 23, 1989, p. 3 (*Doc. 6–74*).

44. Minutes 20, Cabinet, Council of Ministers, Jan. 31, 1990, p. 10 (*Doc. 3–92*). Minutes 19, Cabinet, Council of Ministers, Dec. 21–22, 1989, p. 25 (*Doc. 3–93*). Minutes 149, Cabinet, Council of Ministers, Oct. 23, 1989, p. 3 (*Doc. 6–74*). Minutes 21, Cabinet, Council of Ministers, Mar. 31, 1989, p. 2 (*Doc. 6–95*). Minutes 23, Cabinet, Council of Ministers, Feb. 7, 1990, p. 2 (*Doc. 8–27*). Interview, Ouk Rabun, Phnom Penh, Jan. 15, 1997.

45. Minutes 113, Cabinet, Council of Ministers, June 23–24, 1988, pp. 12–13 (*Doc. 5–43*). Minutes 116, Cabinet, Council of Ministers, Sept. 23, 1988, p. 2 (*Doc. 13–22*).

46. Kiernan, *Pol Pot Regime,* pp. 69–76.

47. Minutes, Council of State, Aug. 11–12, p. 3 (*Doc. 10–136*). Minutes 64, Cabinet, Council of Ministers, May 12, 1984, p. 2 (*Doc. 7–109*). Minutes 40, Cabinet, Council of Ministers, June 4, 1982, pp. 3–4 (*Doc. 13–52*). Minutes 156, Cabinet, Council of Ministers,

Oct. 18, 1984, p. 4 (*Doc. 11–26*). Interview, former Ministry of Planning official, Phnom Penh, June 2, 1999.

48. Minutes 115, Cabinet, Council of Ministers, Aug. 10, 1990, pp. 2–3 (*Doc. 8–3*). Minutes 61, Cabinet, Council of Ministers, May 19, 1988, p. 2 (*Doc. 13–2*). Minutes 113, Cabinet, Council of Ministers, June 23–34, 1988, p. 14 (*Doc. 5–43*).

49. Minutes 113, Cabinet, Council of Ministers, June 23–24, 1988, pp. 3–4 (*Doc. 5–43*). Minutes 59, Cabinet, Council of Ministers, Apr. 28, 1983, p. 3 (*Doc. 11–120*).

50. Minutes 19, Cabinet, Council of Ministers, Dec. 21–22, 1989, p. 22 (*Doc. 3–93*). Directive 24, Ministry of Commerce, May 31, 1989 (*Doc. 4–47*). Minutes 113, Cabinet, Council of Ministers, June 23–34, 1988, p. 3 (*Doc. 5–43*). Circular 14, Council of Ministers, Oct. 14, 1988 (*Doc. 4–58*). Minutes 19, Cabinet, Council of Ministers, Mar. 29, 1989, p. 2 (*Doc. 6–94*). For Hun Sen's remarks, see Minutes 142, Cabinet, Council of Ministers, Oct. 8, 1988, p. 2 (*Doc. 13–26*).

51. Minutes 61, Cabinet, Council of Ministers, May 19, 1988, pp. 2–3 (*Doc. 13–2*). See also Minutes 124, Cabinet, Council of Ministers, Oct. 8, 1988, pp. 4–5 (*Doc. 13–26*); Minutes 113, Cabinet, Council of Ministers, June 23–24, 1988, p. 3 (*Doc. 5–43*).

52. Minutes 113, Cabinet, Council of Ministers, June 23–34, 1988, p. 12 (*Doc. 5–43*). Minutes, Council of State, Jan. 28–29, 1988, p. 7 (*Doc. 1–29*). Minutes 6, Cabinet, Council of Ministers, Feb. 14, 1989, p. 2 (*Doc. 6–92*). Decision 181, Council of Ministers, Sept. 24, 1988 (*Doc. 11–96*). For Chum Hol's analysis, see Minutes 61, Cabinet, Council of Ministers, May 19, 1988, pp. 2–3 (*Doc. 13–2*).

53. Raszelenberg and Schier, *Cambodia Conflict,* pp. 205–6. Minutes 108, Cabinet, Council of Ministers, July 20, 1989, p. 2 (*Doc. 7–15*).

54. "Some Documents About the Situation in Cambodia," [Vietnamese] Expert Group, p. 2 (*Doc. 3KN*). Interview, Pen Sovan, Takeo, May 17, 1999. Kiernan, *Pol Pot Regime,* pp. 69–76.

55. Minutes 48, Cabinet, Council of Ministers, Apr. 23, 1987 (*Doc. 13–38*). For Say Phouthang's comments, see Minutes, Council of State, Feb. 22, 1985, p. 3 (*Doc. 9–121*).

56. Minutes, Cabinet, Council of Ministers, 1987, p. 35 (*Doc. 13–36*). Minutes 15, Cabinet, Council of Ministers, Jan. 22, 1990, p. 4 (*Doc. 8–22*). Minutes 124, Cabinet, Council of Ministers, Oct. 8, 1988, p. 13 (*Doc. 13–26*). Minutes 131, Cabinet, Council of Ministers, Sept. 30, 1988, p. 5 (*Doc. 13–25*). Minutes 103, Cabinet, Council of Ministers, July 11, 1989, p. 4 (*Doc. 7–57*). For Tea Banh's comments, see Minutes 108, Cabinet, Council of Ministers, July 20, 1989, p. 2 (*Doc. 7–15*).

57. Minutes 108, Cabinet, Council of Ministers, July 20, 1989, p. 1 (*Doc. 7–15*).

58. Interview, Cham Prasith, Phnom Penh, Feb. 10, 1997.

59. Ibid.

60. Minutes 166, Cabinet, Council of Ministers, Nov. 18, 1989, pp. 2, 5 (*Doc. 6–77*). Minutes 149, Cabinet, Council of Ministers, Oct. 23, 1989, p. 3 (*Doc. 6–74*). Minutes 108, Cabinet, Council of Ministers, July 20, 1989, p. 3 (*Doc. 7–15*).

61. Minutes 126, Cabinet, Council of Ministers, Oct. 12, 1987 (*Doc. 13–16*). Minutes, Cabinet, Council of Ministers, 1987, pp. 37–38 (*Doc. 13–36*).

62. Minutes 126, Cabinet, Council of Ministers, Oct. 12, 1987, p. 2 (*Doc. 13–16*). Minutes 3,

Cabinet, Council of Ministers, Feb. 6, 1989, pp. 2–3 (*Doc. 6–91*). Minutes 118, Cabinet, Council of Ministers, Sept. 7, 1985, p. 4 (*Doc. 12–38*). Minutes 113, Cabinet, Council of Ministers, Sept. 15, 1988, p. 7 (*Doc. 5–43*).

63. Minutes 03, Cabinet, Council of Ministers, Feb. 6, 1989, pp. 7–8 (*Doc. 6–91*).

64. Minutes 19, Cabinet, Council of Ministers, Dec. 21–22, 1989, p. 5 (*Doc. 3–93*).

65. Minutes 118, Cabinet, Council of Ministers, Sept. 7, 1985, p. 4 (*Doc. 12–38*). Decision 274, Council of Ministers, Dec. 2, 1988 (*Doc. 1–16*). Minutes 108, Cabinet, Council of Ministers, July 20, 1989, pp. 2, 5 (*Doc. 7–15*). Decision 77, Council of Ministers, May 25, 1990 (*Doc. 3–77*).

66. Minutes 108, Cabinet, Council of Ministers, July 20, 1989, p. 2 (*Doc. 7–15*).

67. Ibid. Minutes 3, Cabinet, Council of Ministers, Feb. 6, 1989 (*Doc. 6–91*).

68. Minutes 108, Cabinet, Council of Ministers, July 20, 1989, p. 8 (*Doc. 7–15*).

69. Minutes 103, Cabinet, Council of Ministers, July 11, 1989, pp. 2–3 (*Doc. 7–57*). Minutes 108, Cabinet, Council of Ministers, July 20, 1989, p. 3 (*Doc. 7–15*). Minutes 127, Cabinet, Council of Ministers, Oct. 12, 1988, p. 8 (*Doc. 13–24*).

70. Minutes 103, Cabinet, Council of Ministers, July 11, 1989, pp. 2–4 (*Doc. 7–57*). Minutes 108, Cabinet, Council of Ministers, July 20, 1989, p. 9 (*Doc. 7–15*).

71. Minutes 103, Cabinet, Council of Ministers, July 11, 1989, pp. 1, 4 (*Doc. 7–57*).

72. Ibid., p. 5.

73. Directive Circular 462, Interministerial Committee, Ministries of Defense and Finance, Mar. 30, 1982 (*Doc. 9–52*). Interview, Battambang Party official, Battambang, May 26, 1999. Interview, Central Party official, Phnom Penh, May 17, 1999. Interview, former Ministry of Planning official, Phnom Penh, June 2, 1999.

74. Minutes 107, Cabinet, Council of Ministers, Sept. 9, 1987 (*Doc. 13–15*). Minutes 78, Cabinet, Council of Ministers, Aug. 6, 1982, p. 3 (*Doc. 13–88*). Minutes 67, Cabinet, Council of Ministers, May 25, 1988 (*Doc. 12–36*). Decision 106, Council of Ministers, July 2, 1988 (*Doc. 1–14*).

75. Decision 183, Council of Ministers, Sept. 24, 1988 (*Doc. 1–15*). Minutes 6, Cabinet, Council of Ministers, Feb. 14, 1989, pp. 5–7 (*Doc. 6–92*).

76. Minutes 3, Cabinet, Council of Ministers, Feb. 6, 1989, p. 5 (*Doc. 6–91*). Minutes 6, Cabinet, Council of Ministers, Feb. 14, 1989, pp. 5–7 (*Doc. 6–92*). Minutes 114, Cabinet, Council of Ministers, Aug. 2, 1989, p. 8 (*Doc. 7–17*). Minutes 103, Cabinet, Council of Ministers, July 11, 1989, pp. 5–6 (*Doc. 7–57*). Minutes 108, Cabinet, Council of Ministers, July 20, 1989, p. 8 (*Doc. 7–15*). Slocomb, "K5 Gamble," pp. 207–8.

77. Minutes 103, Cabinet, Council of Ministers, July 11, 1989, p. 5 (*Doc. 7–57*).

78. Minutes 26, Cabinet, Council of Ministers, Apr. 1, 1991 (*Doc. 7–69*). For Hun Sen's comments, see Minutes 115, Cabinet, Council of Ministers, Aug. 10, 1990, pp. 12, 16 (*Doc. 8–3*).

79. Minutes 115, Cabinet, Council of Ministers, Aug. 10, 1990, pp. 5–6 (*Doc. 8–3*). Interview, Battambang Party official, Battambang, May 26, 1999.

80. Minutes 26, Cabinet, Council of Ministers, Apr. 1, 1991, p. 4 (*Doc. 7–69*). Minutes 115, Cabinet, Council of Ministers, Aug. 10, 1990, pp. 21–22 (*Doc. 8–3*).

81. Minutes 115, Cabinet, Council of Ministers, Aug. 10, 1990, pp. 21–22 (*Doc. 8–3*).

82. Ibid.

CHAPTER THIRTEEN. THE END OF THE OCCUPATION

1. Radio Phnom Penh, Apr. 29, 1989, FBIS, May 1, 1989.

2. Radio Phnom Penh, Feb. 17, 1989, FBIS, Feb. 21, 1989. Réponses de Norodom Sihanouk du Cambodge aux Question de Mr. Guy Dinmore, Reuters, Beijing, Feb. 17, 1989, in *Bulletin mensuel de documentation du Secrétariat Privé de S.A.R. le Prince Norodom Sihanouk du Cambodge,* Beijing, January–March 1989, in Raszelenberg and Schier, *Cambodia Conflict,* pp. 213–14.

3. Raszelenberg and Schier, *Cambodia Conflict,* pp. 200–201, 208–10. *The Nation* (Bangkok), Feb. 28, 1989, in ibid., p. 218.

4. Radio Hanoi, Apr. 26, 27, and 28, 1989, in British Broadcasting Corporation, ed., *Summary of World Broadcasts,* Part 3: *Asia-Pacific,* Reading, U.K., May 6, 1989 (Special Supplement), in Raszelenberg and Schier, *Cambodia Conflict,* pp. 220–21.

5. Radio Phnom Penh, Mar. 25, 1989, FBIS, Mar. 27, 1989.

6. Report, Cabinet, Council of State, Mar. 23, 1989 (*Doc. 4–21*). Jennar, *Les clés du Cambodge,* pp. 209, 247.

7. Minutes, Council of State, Apr. 28, 1989, p. 7 (*Doc. 1–24*).

8. Circular 5, Council of Ministers, May 19, 1989 (*Doc. 12–26*). Minutes, Council of State, Apr. 28, 1989 (*Doc. 1–24*). Raszelenberg and Schier, *Cambodia Conflict,* pp. 227–29. Jennar, *Les clés du cambodge,* p. 99.

9. Minutes, Cabinet, Council of Ministers, Aug. 25, 1989, p. 2 (*Doc. 7–20*).

10. Ibid. Minutes, Council of State, Mar. 15, 1989, pp. 8–11 (*Doc. 1–36*). Minutes 23, Cabinet, Council of Ministers, Feb. 7, 1990, p. 1 (*Doc. 8–27*).

11. Draft Text, Legislation Commission, National Assembly, p. 4 (*Doc. 3–79*). For Vandy Ka-on's association of filmmakers, see Report 92, Cabinet, Council of Ministers, Sept. 11, 1989 (*Doc. 6–80*); Minutes, Council of State, July 12, 1990, p. 5 (*Doc. 6–4*).

12. Speech, Legislation Commission, National Assembly, 1989, p. 8 (*Doc. 10–103*).

13. National Assembly Session, July 1989, pp. 62–63. Interview, Vandy Ka-on, Paris, Aug. 12, 1997. Minutes, Council of State, July 12, 1990, pp. 5–6 (*Doc. 6–4*).

14. *Economics,* no. 1, Phnom Penh, 1990.

15. Raszelenberg and Schier, *Cambodia Conflict,* p. 226.

16. Minutes, Council of State, Apr. 28, 1989, p. 6 (*Doc. 1–24*). "Minority parties" in Vietnam include the Vietnam Democratic Party and the Vietnam Socialist Party. Directorate of Central Intelligence, *Directory of Officials of Vietnam.*

17. Seventeenth National Assembly Session, July 1989, p. 18.

18. Remarques, Suggestions et Souhaits formulés par Norodom Sihanouk en égard au Project de Constitution qui est l'oeuvre du Parti Révolutionnaire du Peuple Kampuchéen, May 23, 1989, in Raszelenberg and Schier, *Cambodia Conflict,* pp. 237–38. Minutes, Council of State, Apr. 28, 1989, p. 6 (*Doc. 1–24*).

19. Minutes 107, Cabinet, Council of Ministers, July 10, 1989, p. 2 (*Doc. 7–14*). Minutes 114, Cabinet, Council of Ministers, Aug. 2, 1989, pp. 4–5 (*Doc. 7–17*).

20. Minutes 107, Cabinet, Council of Ministers, July 10, 1989, p. 3 (*Doc. 7–14*). Raszelenberg and Schier, *Cambodia Conflict,* pp. 244–56. Becker, *When the War Was Over,* pp. 490–91.

21. Minutes 114, Cabinet, Council of Ministers, Aug. 2, 1989, pp. 7–8 (*Doc. 7–17*). For Heng Samrin's views on the peace process, see Minutes, Council of State, Nov. 13, 1991, p. 2 (*Doc. 5–68*).

22. Minutes 114, Cabinet, Council of Ministers, Aug. 2, 1989, p. 6 (*Doc. 7–17*).

23. Minutes 29, Cabinet, Council of Ministers, Dec. 24, 1989, pp. 1–2 (*Doc. 8–26*).

24. Report 253, Ministry of the Interior, Sept. 24, 1990, p. 5 (*Doc. 7–83*). Decision 69, Council of Ministers, May 7, 1991 (*Doc. 7–1*). Raszelenberg and Schier, *Cambodia Conflict,* pp. 260–62.

25. Minutes 57, Cabinet, Council of Ministers, June 27, 1982, p. 9 (*Doc. 13–91*). Minutes 06, Cabinet, Council of Ministers, Jan. 14, 1987, p. 3 (*Doc. 13–39*). Minutes, Council of State, Feb. 27, 1987, p. 10 (*Doc. 5–82*). Minutes 08, Cabinet, Council of Ministers, Mar. 19, 1988, p. 1 (*Doc. 11–72*).

26. Minutes, Council of State, Feb. 27, 1987, p. 10 (*Doc. 5–82*). Minutes 06, Cabinet, Council of Ministers, Jan. 14, 1987, pp. 3–4 (*Doc. 13–39*). Research Document, Cabinet, Council of Ministers, Dec. 16, 1985, pp. 2–3 (*Doc. 5–20*).

27. Minutes 08, Cabinet, Council of Ministers, Mar. 19, 1988, p. 2 (*Doc. 11–72*).

28. Minutes, Council of State, Mar. 23, 1988, p. 2 (*Doc. 9–4*).

29. Ibid., pp. 2–3.

30. The last of the Soviet, Eastern European, Cuban, and Lao advisors were also leaving Cambodia. Minutes 73, Cabinet, Council of Ministers, May 24, 1990, pp. 1–2 (*Doc. 8–33*). See also Minutes 135, Council of Ministers, Sept. 15, 1989, p. 4 (*Doc. 6–70*).

31. Minutes 05, Cabinet, Council of Ministers, Jan. 17, 1991, p. 3 (*Doc. 7–56*). Minutes 91, Cabinet, Council of Ministers, Jan. 19, 1989, p. 2 (*Doc. 6–100*). Minutes 150, Cabinet, Council of Ministers, Nov. 21, 1990, p. 2 (*Doc. 8–9*).

32. "Nguyen Cuc Binh" is a transliteration from the Khmer. Minutes 91, Cabinet, Council of Ministers, May 7, 1988 (*Doc. 13–10*).

33. Minutes 113, Cabinet, Council of Ministers, June 23–24, p. 7 (*Doc. 5–43*). Minutes 19, Cabinet, Council of Ministers, Dec. 21–22, 1989, p. 8 (*Doc. 3–93*). Minutes, Council of State, July 12, 1990, p. 4 (*Doc. 6–4*). Minutes 150, Cabinet, Council of Ministers, Nov. 21, 1990, pp. 2–3 (*Doc. 8–9*). Minutes 127, Cabinet, Council of Ministers, Nov. 30, 1992, p. 26 (*Doc. 3–55*). Minutes 6, Cabinet, Council of Ministers, Mar. 9, 1993, p. 72 (*Doc. 3–80*). Report 115, Cabinet, Council of Ministers, Aug. 21, 1990, p. 3 (*Doc. 7–74*). Minutes 61, Cabinet, Council of Ministers, July 3, 1991, p. 2 (*Doc. 7–32*).

34. Minutes 150, Cabinet, Council of Ministers, Nov. 21, 1990 (*Doc. 8–9*).

35. Minutes 112, Cabinet, Council of Ministers, Aug. 4, 1990, p. 3 (*Doc. 8–2*).

36. Minutes 114, Cabinet, Council of Ministers, Aug. 2, 1989 (*Doc. 7–17*). Minutes 74, Cabinet Council of Ministers, Aug. 17, 1991 (*Doc. 7–34*). Minutes 50, Cabinet, Council of Ministers, June 18, 1991 (*Doc. 7–40*). Minutes 5, Cabinet, Council of Ministers, Jan. 17, 1991 (*Doc. 7–56*). Minutes 112, Cabinet, Council of Ministers, Aug. 4, 1990 (*Doc. 8–2*). Minutes 15, Cabinet, Council of Ministers, Jan. 22, 1990, p. 14 (*Doc. 8–22*). Minutes 74, Cabinet, Council of Ministers, May 1989 (*Doc. 6–98*). Decision 99, Council of Ministers, June 21, 1989 (*Doc. 4–50*).

37. Minutes 61, Cabinet, Council of Ministers, July 3, 1991 (*Doc. 7–32*). For Bou Thang's views, see Minutes 112, Cabinet, Council of Ministers, Aug. 4, 1990, p. 3 (*Doc. 8–2*).

CHAPTER FOURTEEN. BUYING POWER: PRIVATIZATION, CORRUPTION, AND PATRONAGE

1. Minutes 91, Cabinet, Council of Ministers, June 19, 1989, p. 4 (*Doc. 6–100*). Minutes 6, Cabinet, Council of Ministers, Mar. 9, 1993, p. 5 (*Doc. 3–80*). Minutes 20, Cabinet, Council of Ministers, Jan. 31, 1990 (*Doc. 3–92*). Interview, Ministry of Finance official, Phnom Penh, May 21, 1999.

2. Minutes 6, Cabinet, Council of Ministers, Mar. 9, 1993, p. 5 (*Doc. 3–80*). Minutes 19, Cabinet, Council of Ministers, Dec. 21–22, pp. 3–6, 18 (*Doc. 3–93*). Minutes 20, Cabinet, Council of Ministers, Jan. 31, 1990, pp. 2, 5, 22 (*Doc. 3–92*). Minutes 55, Cabinet, Council of Ministers, June 24, 1991, pp. 1–2 (*Doc. 7–38*). Minutes 145, Cabinet, Council of Ministers, Nov. 7, 1990, p. 5 (*Doc. 8–10*). Minutes 23, Cabinet, Council of Ministers, Feb. 7, 1990, p. 1 (*Doc. 8–27*).

3. Minutes 19, Cabinet, Council of Ministers, Dec. 21–22, 1989, pp. 3–4 (*Doc. 3–93*).

4. Minutes 166, Cabinet, Council of Ministers, Nov. 18, 1989, p. 5 (*Doc. 6–77*). Bulletin, Cabinet, Council of Ministers, July 12, 1990, p. 11 (*Doc. 1–38*). Minutes 6, Cabinet, Council of Ministers, Mar. 9, 1993, pp. 8, 17 (*Doc. 3–80*). Minutes 113, Cabinet, Council of Ministers, June 23–24, 1988, p. 4 (*Doc. 5– 43*). Interview, former Ministry of Planning official, Phnom Penh, June 2, 1999. Interview, Ministry of Finance official, Phnom Penh, May 25, 1999.

5. Minutes 150, Cabinet, Council of Ministers, Nov. 21, 1990, p. 3 (*Doc. 8–9*).

6. Joint Declaration 0060, Ministries of Agriculture and Finance, Aug. 7, 1989 (*Doc. 7–60*). Minutes 3, Cabinet, Council of Ministers, Jan. 4, 1990 (*Doc. 8–23*). Subdecree 8, Council of Ministers, May 20, 1991 (*Doc. 2–1*). Subdecree 09, Council of Ministers, May 20, 1991 (*Doc. 7–6*). Subdecree 20, Council of Ministers, Sept. 12, 1991 (*Doc. 7–3*). Subdecree 240, Council of Ministers, Dec. 24, 1991 (*Doc. 2–17*). Minutes, Council of Ministers, Aug. 3, 1991, pp. 1–2 (*Doc. 1–52*). Decision 129, Council of Ministers, Sept. 14, 1990 (*Doc. 7–84*).

7. Minutes 91, Cabinet, Council of Ministers, June 19, 1989, p. 5 (*Doc. 6–100*).

8. Minutes 46, Cabinet, Council of Ministers, Mar. 28, 1990 (*Doc. 8–28*). Minutes 19, Cabinet, Council of Ministers, Dec. 21–22, 1989, p. 16 (*Doc. 3–93*). Minutes 20, Cabinet, Council of Ministers, Jan. 31, 1990, pp. 4–6 (*Doc. 3–92*).

9. Minutes 12, Cabinet, Council of Ministers, Dec. 19–20, 1991, p. 35 (*Doc. 4–77*). For Chea Chantho's comments, see Minutes 31, Cabinet, Council of Ministers, Apr. 26, 1991, p. 3 (*Doc. 7–46*).

10. Minutes 12, Cabinet, Council of Ministers, Dec. 19–20, 1991, p. 36 (*Doc. 4–77*). For the Party takeover of factory management, see Minutes 19, Cabinet, Council of Ministers, Dec. 21–22, 1989, p. 15 (*Doc. 3–93*).

11. Minutes 114, Cabinet, Council of Ministers, Aug. 2, 1989, pp. 9–10 (*Doc. 7–17*). Minutes 20, Cabinet, Council of Ministers, Jan. 31, 1990, p. 7 (*Doc. 3–92*). Minutes 113, Cabinet, Council of Ministers, June 23–24, 1988, p. 7 (*Doc. 5–43*).

12. Minutes 127, Cabinet, Council of Ministers, Oct. 17, 1992, pp. 17, 20 (*Doc. 3–55*). Minutes 19, Cabinet, Council of Ministers, Jan. 31, 1990, p. 9 (*Doc. 3–93*). Minutes 46, Cabinet, Council of Ministers, Mar. 28, 1990, p. 2 (*Doc. 8–28*).

13. Minutes, Council of State, Jan. 20, 1990, pp. 2–3 (*Doc. 4–14*). Minutes 91, Cabinet,

Council of Ministers, June 19, 1989, p. 5 (*Doc. 6–100*). Minutes 29, Cabinet, Council of Ministers, Feb. 15, 1990, p. 2 (*Doc. 8–26*). Minutes 19, Cabinet, Council of Ministers, Dec. 21–22, 1989, p. 40 (*Doc. 3–93*).

14. Joint Bulletin 354 (Ministry of Agriculture) and 012 (Ministry of Finance), Oct. 18, 1990 (*Doc. 2–29*). Joint Declaration 0060, Ministries of Agriculture and Finance, Aug. 7, 1989 (*Doc. 7–60*). Report, Council of State, July 1990, p. 3 (*Doc. 6–40*). Minutes, Council of State, Jan. 20, 1990, pp. 2–3 (*Doc. 4–14*). Frings, *Cambodia After Collectivization,* pp. 55–57.

15. Minutes, Council of State, July 12, 1990, pp. 2–3 (*Doc. 6–4*). Minutes, Council of State, Jan. 20, 1990, pp. 2–3 (*Doc. 4–14*). Minutes 103, Cabinet, Council of Ministers, July 11, 1989, pp. 4–6 (*Doc. 7– 57*). Circular 01, Council of Ministers, Jan. 18, 1990 (*Doc. 7–93*). For Uk Bunchheuan's comments, see Minutes 113, Cabinet, Council of Ministers, June 23–24, 1988, pp. 21, 25, 27 (*Doc. 5–43*).

16. Minutes 120, Cabinet, Council of Ministers, Sept. 1, 1990, p. 2 (*Doc. 8–4*).

17. Minutes, Legislation Commission, National Assembly, Aug. 2–6, 1982, p. 11 (*Doc. 10–28*).

18. Speech, Legislation Commission, 1989, p. 5 (*Doc. 10–103*). Minutes, Council of State, June 27– 29, 1988, p. 13 (*Doc. 4–15*). Minutes 111, Cabinet, Council of Ministers, July 17, 1986, pp. 5–6 (*Doc. 8– 17*). Minutes 120, Cabinet, Council of Ministers, Sept. 1, 1990, p. 3 (*Doc. 8–4*).

19. Report, Council of State, July 1990, p. 2 (*Doc. 6–40*). Minutes 19, Cabinet, Council of Ministers, Dec. 21–22, 1989, p. 15 (*Doc. 3–93*).

20. Minutes 15, Cabinet, Council of Ministers, Jan. 22, 1990, pp. 10, 13–14 (*Doc. 8–22*). Minutes 23, Cabinet, Council of Ministers, Mar. 21, 1991, p. 2 (*Doc. 7–70*). Minutes 19, Cabinet, Council of Ministers, Dec. 21–22, 1989, p. 30 (*Doc. 3–93*).

21. Subdecree 8, Council of Ministers, May 20, 1991 (*Doc. 2–1*). Minutes, Council of State, June 10, 1988, p. 10 (*Doc. 1–28*). Minutes 72, Cabinet, Council of Ministers, Aug. 10, 1991, p. 3 (*Doc. 7–33*).

22. Minutes 57, Cabinet, Council of Ministers, June 19, 1991, pp. 2–3 (*Doc. 7–30*). For the 1981 policy, see Minutes 9, Phnom Penh Security Committee, Sept. 16, 1981, p. 2 (*Doc. 10–157*).

23. The Um Bunna case is described in Special Regulations, Council of Ministers, Oct. 19, 1982 (*Doc. 14–28*); Minutes, Council of State, May 5, 1985, pp. 3–4 (*Doc. 4–65*).

24. Minutes, Council of State, May 5, 1985, p. 5 (*Doc. 4–65*).

25. The case of Um Bunna established a precedent, for the regime and for the Ministry of Industry. Five years later, in 1990, when another scandal erupted at the ministry, the Party's response was almost identical. Two deputy ministers received "warnings," a third experienced "censure," Meas Samnang was forced to "retire to avoid discipline," and the new minister, Ho Non, escaped punishment altogether. Minutes, Council of State, Jan. 20, 1990, p. 4 (*Doc. 4–14*).

26. Subdecree 86, Council of Ministers, June 28, 1989 (*Doc. 7–64*). Subdecree 85, Council of Ministers, June 28, 1989 (*Doc. 7–65*). Minutes 120, Cabinet, Council of Ministers, Sept. 1, 1990, p. 3 (*Doc. 8– 4*). Report, Council of State, 1988 (*Doc. 4–17*). Minutes, Council of State, June 27–29, 1988, p. 12 (*Doc. 4– 15*). Report, Council of State, 1988 (*Doc. 11– 91*). Report, Council of State, July 1, 1988 (*Doc. 10–95*).

27. Minutes, Council of State, June 15, 1989, pp. 13–14 (*Doc. 1–36*).

28. Ibid.

29. Minutes, Council of State, June 15, 1989, p. 14 (*Doc. 1–36*). Letter, Inspection Committee, Party Central Committee, Sept. 1988 (*Doc. 4–19*). Report 9, Cabinet, Council of State (*Doc. 4–20*).

30. Minutes, Council of State, July 12, 1990, p. 3 (*Doc. 6–4*).

31. Minutes 120, Cabinet, Council of Ministers, Sept. 1, 1990 (*Doc. 8–4*). Minutes 124, Cabinet, Council of Ministers, Sept. 11, 1990 (*Doc. 8–5*). For the SOC's public anticorruption campaign, see SPK, Sept. 28, 1990, in British Broadcasting Corporation, ed., *Summary of World Broadcasts*, Part 3: *Asia-Pacific*, Reading, U.K., May 6, 1989 (Special Supplement), Oct. 1, 1990, in Raszelenberg and Schier, *Cambodia Conflict*, pp. 403–4.

32. Minutes 107, Cabinet, Council of Ministers, Aug. 31, 1983, p. 4 (*Doc. 11–109*). Minutes 8, Party Branch 2, Sept. 9, 1983, p. 4 (*Doc. 10–117*). Minutes 04, Cabinet, Council of Ministers, Jan. 19, 1984, p. 6 (*Doc. 7–116*). Minutes, Council of State, July 6–7, 1987, p. 6 (*Doc. 5–88*). Minutes, Council of State, Jan. 29, 1988, pp. 5–6 (*Doc. 1–29*). Letter 207, Council of Ministers, Dec. 5, 1988 (*Doc. 13–3*).

33. Circular 27, KPRC, June 8, 1981 (*Doc. 6–36*). Circular 11, Ministry of the Interior, Dec. 22, 1981, pp. 1–2 (*Doc. 9–43*). Directive Circular 462, Interministerial Committee, Ministries of Defense and Finance, Mar. 30, 1982, p. 1 (*Doc. 9–52*). Minutes 04, Cabinet, Council of Ministers, Jan. 19, 1984, pp. 5–6 (*Doc. 7–116*). Report, Council of Ministers, 1985, p. 2 (*Doc. 9–77*).

34. Circular 1, Council of Ministers, Jan. 22, 1985 (*Doc. 11–180*). Minutes, Council of State, Jan. 30–31, 1986, p. 14 (*Doc. 4–12*).

35. Minutes 19, Cabinet, Council of Ministers, Dec. 21–22, 1989, pp. 23, 36 (*Doc. 3–93*). Minutes, Council of State, Dec. 20, 1985, p. 6 (*Doc. 6–18*).

36. Decision 33, Council of Ministers, Mar. 11, 1989 (*Doc. 7–11*). Minutes 15, Cabinet, Council of Ministers, Dec. 28, 1989, p. 8 (*Doc. 8–22*).

37. Decision 33, Council of Ministers, Mar. 11, 1989, p. 2 (*Doc. 7–11*). Minutes 145, Cabinet, Council of Ministers, Nov. 7, 1990, pp. 2–5 (*Doc. 8–10*).

38. Decision 100, Council of Ministers, Aug. 21, 1987 (*Doc. 11–60*). Minutes 7, Cabinet, Council of Ministers, Mar. 12, 1988, p. 4 (*Doc. 12–65*). Minutes 148, Cabinet, Council of State, Nov. 16, 1987 (*Doc. 13–33*).

39. Minutes 7, Cabinet, Council of Ministers, Mar. 12, 1988, pp. 3–5, 10 (*Doc. 12–65*). Minutes 48, Cabinet, Council of Ministers, Nov. 16, 1987, p. 2 (*Doc. 13–33*).

40. Minutes 91, Cabinet, Council of Ministers, Apr. 19, 1989, p. 5 (*Doc. 6–100*).

41. Report, Council of State, Jan. 15, 1991, p. 7 (*Doc. 6–44*). Minutes, Council of State, July 11, 1991, p. 3 (*Doc. 6–11*).

42. Minutes 157, Cabinet, Council of Ministers, Dec. 7, 1988, p. 2 (*Doc. 13–29*).

43. Report, Council of State, Jan. 20, 1987 (*Doc. 10–98*). Minutes 7, Cabinet, Council of Ministers, Mar. 12, 1988, p. 9 (*Doc. 12–65*). Decision 121, Council of Ministers, Aug. 30, 1990 (*Doc. 7–85*). Minutes 62, Cabinet, Council of Ministers, May 21, 1988, pp. 6, 13 (*Doc. 12–35*). For militias, see "Report on the Situation in Cambodia," [Vietnamese] Expert Group, Political Committee, 1985, p. 3 (*Doc. PP*).

44. Minutes 127, Cabinet, Council of Ministers, Aug. 31, 1988, p. 8 (*Doc. 13–24*).

45. Minutes 128, Cabinet, Council of Ministers, Aug. 29, 1989, p. 4 (*Doc. 7–21*). Regarding the A-Teams, see Minutes 115, Cabinet, Council of Ministers, Aug. 10, 1990, pp. 17–18, 21, (*Doc. 8–3*); Report 253, Ministry of the Interior, Sept. 24, 1990, p. 6 (*Doc. 7–83*); Minutes 127, Cabinet, Council of Ministers, Oct. 12, 1988, pp. 8–10 (*Doc. 13–24*); Sub-decree 5, Council of Ministers, Feb. 8, 1990 (*Doc. 9–13*); Decree 27, Council of Ministers, July 11, 1989 (*Doc. 7–62*).

46. Secret Telegram 01, Council of Ministers, Jan. 20, 1990 (*Doc. 7–95*). For Ke Kim Yan's comments, see Minutes 128, Cabinet, Council of Ministers, Aug. 29, 1989, pp. 2–3 (*Doc. 7–21*).

47. Minutes 127, Cabinet, Council of Ministers, Oct. 12, 1988, p. 14 (*Doc. 13–24*).

48. Ibid., pp. 13–14. Minutes 128, Cabinet, Council of Ministers, Aug. 29, 1989, p. 5 (*Doc. 7–21*). Interview, Battambang Party official, Battambang, May 26, 1999.

49. Minutes, Council of State, Nov. 17, 1982, p. 7 (*Doc. 6–9*). Minutes 115, Cabinet, Council of Ministers, Aug. 10, 1990, p. 13 (*Doc. 8–3*).

50. Minutes 13, Office, Council of Ministers, Mar. 23, 1982, p. 1 (*Doc. 10–115*).

51. Minutes 124, Cabinet, Council of Ministers, Oct. 8, 1988 (*Doc. 13–26*). Minutes 19, Cabinet, Council of Ministers, Jan. 31, 1990, p. 35 (*Doc. 3–93*). Minutes 127, Cabinet, Council of Ministers, Nov. 30, 1992, pp. 12–20 (*Doc. 3–55*). Interview, former Kampong Cham official, Phnom Penh, May 1999.

52. Minutes 19, Cabinet, Council of Ministers, Dec. 21–22, 1989, pp. 30–31 (*Doc. 3–93*). Interview, Central Party official, Phnom Penh, May 17, 1999. Interview, Kong Korm, Phnom Penh, May 6, 1999.

53. Minutes, Council of State, July 11, 1991, pp. 10–14 (*Doc. 6–11*). Minutes 30, Cabinet, Council of Ministers, Apr. 10, 1991, p. 2 (*Doc. 7–67*). For Chantho's statements, see Minutes 145, Cabinet, Council of Ministers, Nov. 7, 1990, p. 4 (*Doc. 8–10*).

CHAPTER FIFTEEN. THE THROES OF PEACE

1. Summaries of the peace process are taken from Raszelenberg and Schier, *Cambodia Conflict.*

2. Tokyo Kyodo, May 6, 1990, FBIS, May 7, 1990. Raszelenberg and Schier, *Cambodia Conflict,* p. 323.

3. Porter, *Politics of Bureaucratic Socialism,* p. 100n. Louis Stern, *Renovating the Vietnamese Communist Party: Nguyen Van Linh and the Programme for Organizational Reform, 1987–1991,* New York: St. Martin's Press, 1993, p. 102.

4. Minutes 29, Cabinet, Council of Ministers, Dec. 29, 1989 (*Doc. 8–26*).

5. Minutes 67, Cabinet, Council of Ministers, May 25, 1988, pp. 16–17 (*Doc. 12–36*). Minutes 47, Cabinet, Council of Ministers, May 28, 1982, pp. 5–6 (*Doc. 13–94*). Minutes 19, Cabinet, Council of Ministers, Dec. 21–22, 1989, p. 26 (*Doc. 3–93*). Minutes 3, Cabinet, Council of Ministers, Jan. 13, 1986, pp. 3–4 (*Doc. 7–99*).

6. Interview, Nou Saing Khan, Phnom Penh, May 18, 1999.

7. Interview, Thun Saray, Phnom Penh, Dec. 18, 1996.

8. Interview, Nou Saing Khan, Phnom Penh, May 18, 1999.

9. "Cambodia: Arrest and Detention of Government Officials," Amnesty International In-

dex ASA 23/02/90. "Cambodia: Recent Human Rights Developments," Amnesty International Index ASA 23/07/90. *The Nation* (Bangkok), June 20, 1990, in Raszelenberg and Schier, *Cambodia Conflict,* p. 330.

10. Minutes 85, Cabinet, Council of Ministers, May 25, 1990 (*Doc. 8–35*).

11. "Voice of the People of Cambodia," Aug. 15, 1990, in British Broadcasting Corporation, ed., *Summary of World Broadcasts* [Daily Report], part 3: Asia Pacific, Reading, Berkshire, Aug. 24, 1990, in Raszelenberg and Schier, *Cambodia Conflict,* p. 363. Jennar, *Les clés du Cambodge,* pp. 216, 252–53.

12. Raszelenberg and Schier, *Cambodia Conflict,* pp. 327–36.

13. Ibid., pp. 349–52.

14. For the Beijing meeting, see ibid., pp. 365–66. For the "framework" agreement, see ibid., pp. 370–77. For the Chengdu meeting, see ibid., pp. 385–87.

15. Ibid., pp. 392–98, 420–21. ·

16. Ibid., pp. 433–68.

17. Ibid., pp. 509, 523–30.

18. For a summary of the events and speeches in Paris, see ibid., pp. 567–70.

19. United Nations, Department of Public Information, *Agreement on a Comprehensive Political Settlement of the Cambodia Conflict: Paris, 22 October 1991* (DPI/1180–92077–January 1992–IOM).

20. Interview, Nou Saing Khan, Phnom Penh, May 18, 1999. Interview, Thun Saray, Phnom Penh, Dec. 18, 1996.

21. Raszelenberg and Schier, *Cambodia Conflict,* p. 565. Becker, *When the War Was Over,* p. 511.

22. Amnesty International, *State of Cambodia—Human Rights Developments: 1 October 1991 to 31 January 1992,* London, 1992, p. 36.

23. Ibid.

24. Minutes, Council of Ministers, Dec. 19–20, 1991, pp. 23–24 (*Doc. 4–77*).

25. Amnesty International, *State of Cambodia,* p. 38.

26. Ibid., pp. 38–48.

27. Ibid., pp. 48, 52–53.

28. Ibid., p. 54. Interview, Thun Saray, Phnom Penh, Dec. 18, 1996.

29. Amnesty International, *State of Cambodia,* p. 6–23, 55–58.

30. Interview, Nou Saing Khan, Phnom Penh, May 18, 1999. Interview, Thun Saray, Phnom Penh, Dec. 18, 1996. Amnesty International, *State of Cambodia,* pp. 59–60. Letter 164, Council of Ministers, Jan. 28, 1992. Nate Thayer, "Leading Cambodian Dissident Wounded," Associated Press, Jan. 28, 1992.

31. Minutes, Council of Ministers, Dec. 19–20, 1991, p. 25 (*Doc. 4–77*).

EPILOGUE

1. For descriptions of the UNTAC period, see Heder and Ledgerwood, *Propaganda, Politics, and Violence in Cambodia;* William Shawcross, *Cambodia's New Deal,* Washington, D.C.: Carnegie Endowment for International Peace, 1994; Michael Doyle, *UN Peacekeeping in Cambodia: UNTAC's Civil Mandate,* Boulder, Colo.: Lynne Rienner, 1995;

Trevor Findlay, *Cambodia: The Legacy and Lessons of UNTAC*, New York: Oxford University Press, 1995.

2. These and subsequent events are covered in the pages of the *Phnom Penh Post* (which began publishing during the UNTAC period) and the *Cambodia Daily*. For summaries and analyses, see Frederick Z. Brown and David G. Timberman, eds., *Cambodia and the International Community: The Quest for Peace, Development, and Democracy*, New York: Asia Society, 1998.

3. The eventual failure of the coalition government is discussed in David Ashley, "The Failure of Conflict Resolution in Cambodia: Causes and Lessons," in ibid., pp. 49–78.

4. Reports written by the nongovernmental organization Global Witness have highlighted timber problems in Cambodia. See also Kirk Talbott, "Logging in Cambodia: Politics and Plunder," in ibid., pp. 149–68.

Index

17957490R20278

Made in the USA
San Bernardino, CA
22 December 2014